DOMESDAY BOOK STUDIES

DOMESDAY BOOK

STUDIES

ALECTO HISTORICAL EDITIONS
LONDON
1987

ISBN 0 948459 51 4

Printed in England. Second impression

ALECTO HISTORICAL EDITIONS
46 Kelso Place, London W8 5QG, England

CONTENTS

FOREWORD

THIS volume follows upon the publication in 1986 of the facsimile of Great Domesday Book by Alecto Historical Editions. As a collection of studies it stands on its own, but it is designed as a companion piece to the individual volumes which comprise the County Edition of Great Domesday. It is proposed to continue with the three counties of Little Domesday at a later date.

The name of Domesday Book reflects the awe with which it was regarded. The survey was ordered by William I at a council in Gloucester at Christmas 1085, and executed with the written report cast in the form in which we now have it, in the astonishingly short time of a year and nine months. Less than a century later a treatise on the management of the royal Exchequer—the *Dialogus de Scaccario*—says that Domesday was so called by the populace because its record was, like the sentences of the Almighty on the Day of Judgment, beyond appeal. It seems certain that the sentiment recalls the making of the survey as much as it acknowledges the awesome authority of the text, and that the enterprise was known by that name from the beginning.

Something of awe has attached to the work ever since. For several centuries Domesday was kept close to the heart of the royal administration, carried about in the wake of the king and his judges, and consulted on matters of administrative practice and legal title. Even before the end of the Middle Ages exemplifications of the text made for formal purposes were written out in a hand that imitated the script of the original. From the sixteenth century, antiquarian curiosity about the text grew as its practical uses declined, and extracts from Domesday Book, laboriously and expensively copied, passed from generation to generation of antiquaries and local historians. In the eighteenth century the desirability of publishing the whole text was long and earnestly discussed, and in 1783 there appeared the remarkable edition transcribed by Abraham Farley, one of its official custodians, and printed in a type specially cut for the purpose.

The object of that edition, which was first printed for Parliament by John Nichols and then reissued with supplementary volumes in 1817 by the Record Commissioners, was to make Domesday Book available for study in a form that reproduced both the number and the arrangement of the lines of text on each page, and even many of the details of the original handwriting. It was a remarkable achievement in itself, a climax of more than a century of antiquarian publishing, and an ingenious resolution of the problem of replicating a manuscript source without the distortions and exorbitant costs that hand-engraved plates would entail.

From 1817 Domesday Book and its principal related texts were available for general study, but the academic world was scarcely ready to use them. As historical techniques advanced in the middle of the nineteenth century, another striking endeavour produced a photographic version of both Great and Little Domesday. The Ordnance Survey photographed the entire text folio by folio at Southampton between 1861 and 1863, and printed a two-colour facsimile from zinc plates. The results compel admiration even today, although the plates were incised in places by hand to improve the impression, which is therefore not an invariably reliable image. The enterprise, approved by Sir Francis Palgrave in one of his last acts as Deputy Keeper, shows the Victorians at their most boldly innovative.

As the volumes had to be dismantled to be photographed, they were subsequently rebound in 1869 by Robert Rivière in the silver-mounted black morocco in which they remained until 1952. In that form they were displayed to the public in 1886, when the eight hundredth anniversary of the survey was marked by an exhibition in the Public Record Office. The same year saw the publication of two volumes of commemorative essays by the Royal Historical Society, and the beginning of an intense scholarly interest in the text of Domesday Book which has continued to the present day.

At the end of the nineteenth century the publishers of the *Victoria History of the Counties of England* began to commission authoritative translations of and commentaries on the county texts of Domesday for general study. The genealogical researches of J. H. Round and others elucidated the history of Norman families and their estates, and the remarkable density of eleventh-century settlement allowed most local histories to begin with or draw upon the riches of the Domesday text. The making and purpose of the survey remained enigmatic, however, in the face of Round's conclusion that it rested upon the assessment of the geld; a dogma that did little to explain what Domesday actually recorded.

The issue was resolved by V. H. Galbraith's hypothesis that Exon Domesday and Little Domesday were the last survivors of a series of regional returns compiled in accordance with a carefully prepared plan, in which the material from the counties was first digested circuit by circuit, and then returned to a central point, presumably at Winchester, for final editing into what we call Great Domesday. The theory received powerful support from an analysis of Domesday Book undertaken at the Public Record Office in 1952–3, when both volumes were rebound and their physical structure examined in detail for the first time. It became clear from the arrangement of the text that it had been written, with controlled haste, to a plan in which the individual counties were treated discretely but in as uniform a manner as the material allowed.

The assimilation of Galbraith's work was accompanied by a remarkable new version of the Domesday survey by Professor H. C. Darby, whose *Domesday Geography* (1952–77) reconstituted the geographical setting of eleventh-century English society in a series of regional volumes. There again, as in most previous studies, the constituent units are the counties of which the landscape and settlement can be inferred from the returns of the fiefs and manors which the commissioners had found.

Over the last century, therefore, Domesday Book has sustained a remarkable weight of scholarly attention, and the development of computer-assisted studies now offers a new means of exploring its intricately detailed text. It was clear as its nonagenary year approached that it would be scrutinized more closely than ever. It was also remarkable and anomalous that no complete photographic record of the text had been made since the Ordnance Survey's pioneering edition. In preparation for the anniversary in 1986 the two volumes were again dismantled in 1984 and their sheets carefully conserved and photographed before they were rebound. The complete Alecto Facsimile was then published in the summer of 1986, during the commemorative exhibition held at the Public Record Office in Chancery Lane.

The present county volumes with their associated facsimiles, apparatus, and maps are therefore the latest and also the fullest exposition of the text of Domesday Book. They commemorate not only the making of the original survey and its many uses over the centuries, but also the pattern of local government which the Normans found in England and which they and their successors vigorously exploited. Here are the shires of Anglo-Saxon and Norman England, with their articulate communities, and their strong-points and meeting-places in the boroughs carefully distinguished from the feudal estates in the final returns. They provided the means by which the king managed a rich and well-ordered kingdom, and they have remained the mainstay of local administration ever since. It is entirely fitting that they should be invoked to present to its latest investigators the substance of the oldest, and arguably the most richly rewarding of the public records.

G. H. Martin, *Keeper of Public Records*
April 1987

ACKNOWLEDGEMENTS

THE publication of the facsimile of Great Domesday was timed to coincide with its nine hundredth anniversary in 1986. In anticipation of this occasion, the Public Record Office, under the direction of the Keeper of Public Records, Dr G. H. Martin, took the decision to unbind the manuscripts of Great and Little Domesday for conservation and rebinding, as well as to facilitate photography for complete facsimile reproductions. Accordingly, on 27 September 1984, the parchment sheets of Great Domesday were separated in a specially constructed laboratory set up within the Conservation Department at Kew, where repairs were then carried out.

In January 1984 the Keeper had invited the publishers to undertake the accomplishment of the facsimile, and they immediately began a series of experiments to establish the most faithful method of reproducing the text. The technique adopted was continuous-tone offset lithography ('contone'). By this method a high degree of definition can be maintained as all photography of the original is carried out at full size, whilst features of the script are printed screenless in solid colours so that they retain their integrity even under magnification.

The publishers appointed Westerham Press Ltd, Westerham, Kent, as the printers of the facsimile since J. A. Parfitt, the master printer there, had spent some fifteen years improving the potential qualities of contone printing. Starting in early January 1985, the repaired sheets of Great Domesday were photographed at Kew, and completed eight months later on 16 September. After a trial run of the Northamptonshire folios carried out in August 1985, Mr Parfitt began the printing of 2,000 complete sets of the facsimile in September 1985 at the Westerham Press, and finished in early March 1986. Of the 2,000 sets, 250 were retained for the specially bound 'Penny' Edition, 750 for the Library Edition, and the rest were allocated to the county volumes.

The present 'Studies' volume is common to all sets of the County edition. It is also issued as an optional supplementary volume to the complete Library Edition of Great Domesday Book, of which the main purpose has been to provide scholars with a practical apparatus for study in the foreseeable future and which should therefore, so far as is possible, avoid involvement with the controversies of the present day. 'Domesday Book Studies', by contrast, has been conceived as a convenient compendium of introductory articles on topics relating to Domesday Book which inevitably and frankly express the individual opinions of their authors. As such, it could perhaps be looked upon as a commemorative *Festschrift* and bear the sub-title 'Essays presented to Domesday Book on the occasion of its ninth centenary', for beside Professor Loyn's extensive Introduction, essays they all are; some being up-to-date summaries of matter already well-covered in print, and others breaking new ground altogether.

Editorial policy has been established with the guidance of an Editorial Board consisting of R. H. C. Davis, E. M. Hallam, J. C. Holt (chairman), H. R. Loyn, and G. H. Martin. At Alecto Historical Editions, Elaine Shaughnessy has been responsible for marshalling and copy-editing text, while Sally Liddell has organized the illustrations. Editorial assistance has also been given by Suzanne Bosworth, and the proof-reading, copy-preparation and indexing of this volume have been undertaken by L. G. Swash. George Tulloch was responsible for copy-preparation at Oxford University Press.

All aspects of production have been co-ordinated by Basil Harley acting as consultant to the publishers in collaboration with L. E. Hoffman for the firm, again with the assistance of Elaine Shaughnessy and Sally Liddell. The General Introduction and the Special Studies have been typeset by Oxford University Press, and the rest of the volume by Westerham Press, Westerham, Kent. Rowland Phototypesetting and St Edmundsbury Press of Bury St Edmunds, Suffolk, have been responsible for make-up and printing. The various volumes and folders that make up each of the individual sets of the County Edition have been bound by Smith Settle of Otley in Yorkshire. The facsimile folios have been assembled at the craft bindery of A. W. Lumsden, Loanhead, Edinburgh. The accompanying maps have been prepared and printed by Cook, Hammond & Kell, Mitcham, Surrey.

The typography has been designed by Ian Mortimer of I. M. Imprimit, London, assisted by Lucy Roberts. The type-face is Monophoto Garamond 156. All details of the folios of Great and Little Domesday reproduced in Special Studies XIII–XVI have been taken from a complete set of Fujichrome transparencies photographed for Alecto by Miki Slingsby in 1985, during the period when both manuscripts were available at Kew in their unbound state.

The examples of script and the marginal signs found in Domesday Book that illustrate Special Studies XIV–XVI, and also Appendices I and II, have been inscribed by Michael Gullick. The coins in Special Study X, Fig. 1, are taken from the steel-engravings published in E. Hawkins, *The Silver Coins of England* (London, 1887), Pls. XVIII and XIX. Otherwise all maps, plans and line-illustrations have been redrawn or adjusted by John Laing from various more recent publications, and Alecto Historical Editions wish here to record their gratitude to the following for permission to use their origination for the illustrations listed below.

Special Study I: Fig. 1, Cambridge University Press, for maps in H. C. Darby, *The Domesday Geography of Eastern England*, 3rd edn., H. C. Darby and E. M. J. Campbell (eds.), 1971; Fig. 2, idem, *The Domesday Geography of South-East England*, 1962; and Figs. 3–15, idem, *Domesday England*, 1977.

Special Study IV: Fig. 1, the Municipalité de Bayeux; Figs. 2–6, the Trustees of the British Library.

Special Study V: Figs. 1–3, Methuen and Co. for drawings in J. G. Hurst, 'The Pottery', *The Archaeology of Anglo-Saxon England*, ed. D. M. Wilson, 1976; Fig. 4, Croom Helm for a plan in D. N. Hall, 'The Origins of Open Field Agriculture, The Archaeological Fieldwork Evidence', *The Origins of Open Field Agriculture*, ed. T. Rowley, 1981; Figs. 5–7, Oxford University Department for External Studies for plans in G. Cadman and G. Foard, 'Raunds: Manorial and Village Origins', *Studies in Late Anglo-Saxon Settlement*, ed. M. L. Faull, 1984.

Special Study VIII: Figs. 1 and 2, Surrey Archaeological Society for plans in J. Blair, *Landholding, Church and Settlement in Early Medieval Surrey*, forthcoming; Fig. 3, Cambridge University Press for architectural elevations in H. M. Taylor and J. Taylor, *Anglo-Saxon Architecture*, iii, 1978.

Special Study IX: Figs. 1 and 4, the Municipalité de Bayeux; Fig. 2, HMSO for a plan in R. Allen Brown, *Tower of London*, 1984; Figs. 3 and 5, the Committee for Aerial Photography, Cambridge University.

Special Study XIV: Fig. 10, the University of Exeter.

Appendix III: the diagram of gatherings is based on that printed in *Domesday Re-bound*, published by the Public Record Office, HMSO, 1954.

Ann Williams, *Editor-in-chief*

R. W. H. Erskine, *General Editor*

The following is a list of abbreviations which are used throughout this edition

AntJ	*Antiquaries Journal*
ArchJ	*Archaeological Journal*
ASE	*Anglo-Saxon England*
BAR	British Archaeological Reports
BL	British Library
CA	*Current Archaeology*
DB	Domesday Book
EconHR	*Economic History Review*
EETS	Early English Text Society
EHR	*English Historical Review*
EPNS	English Place-Name Society
Exon	Exeter Domesday Book
GDB	Great Domesday Book
HMSO	Her Majesty's Stationery Office
JBAA	*Journal of the British Archaeological Association*
JMH	*Journal of Medieval History*
LDB	Little Domesday Book
MA	*Medieval Archaeology*
MS, MSS	Manuscript(s)
MS	*Mediaeval Studies*
NGR	National Grid Reference
N&Q	*Notes and Queries*
PBA	*Proceedings of the British Academy*
PRO	Public Record Office
TRHS	*Transactions of the Royal Historical Society*
VCH	*The Victoria Histories of the Counties of England*

A GENERAL INTRODUCTION TO
DOMESDAY BOOK

H. R. LOYN

A GENERAL INTRODUCTION TO DOMESDAY BOOK

H. R. LOYN

Domesday Book

The chronicler who wrote the sole surviving version of the Anglo-Saxon Chronicle for the later years of the reign of King William I gave a frank and at times quite brilliant summary of the king's achievements and faults, the equivalent of a modern obituary notice, under the year 1087. He tells us, among many other things, that William ruled over England and that by his acumen (*geapscip*, which may also mean 'cunning') 'it was so investigated that there was not one hide of land in England that he did not know who owned it, and what it was worth, and then set it down in his record [*gewrit*]'.[1] The Chronicle is deeply reflective at this stage, elegiac and religious, and the annals from 1083 onwards take on the attributes of short annual histories in their own right. The chronicler was a good witness who had once lived at the royal court and he leaves the clear impression that the record in some sort of usable form was ready before William died, that is before September 1087. He knew a lot, too, about the preparations that had been made for the creation of Domesday Book. His description of the way in which the survey was initiated is justly famous, possibly the best known of all the documentary evidence relating to Domesday Book. Under the year 1085 the chronicler wrote:

> Then at Christmas the king was at Gloucester with his council and held his court there for five days, and then the archbishop and clerics had a synod for three days. There Maurice was elected Bishop of London, and William for Norfolk, and Robert for Cheshire: they were all clerics of the king. After this the king had much thought and very deep discussion [*mycel geðeaht and swiðe deope spæce*] with his council about this country—how it was occupied and with what sort of people. Then he sent his men over all England into every shire and had them find out how many hundred hides there were in the shire or what land and cattle the king had himself in the country, or what dues he ought to have in twelve months from the shire. Also he had a record made of how much land the archbishops had, and his bishops and his abbots and his earls—and though I relate it at too great length—what or how much everybody had who was occupying land in England, in land and cattle and how much money it was worth. So very narrowly did he have it investigated, that there was no single hide nor virgate of land, nor indeed (it is a shame to relate though it seemed to him no shame to do) one ox nor one cow nor one pig which was there left out, and not put down in his record [*on his gewrite*]; and all these records were brought to him afterwards.[2]

There is no mistaking the importance of the discussion nor the effort needed to implement the decision. The chronicler, writing with obvious hindsight, knew that the venture was successful and that the records were indeed brought to the king. The full weight of royal, baronial, and ecclesiastical authority was thrown into the survey; and the finished product, ultimately given the title Domesday Book, stands as a permanent memorial to the intensity of the effort and the magnitude of the achievement.

In one respect, however, the achievement appears to have been incomplete. Domesday Book is the name that we give not to one but to two manuscripts now in the Public Record Office. This was not the original intention. A Worcester annalist, writing in the second quarter of the twelfth century,

[1] D. Whitelock *et al.* (eds.), *The Anglo-Saxon Chronicle: A Revised Translation* (London, 1961), 164; C. Clark (ed.), *The Peterborough Chronicle, 1070–1154* (2nd edn., Oxford, 1970) provides a good modern text in the original language.

[2] Whitelock *et al.* (eds.), *Anglo-Saxon Chronicle*, 161–2.

translated the Chronicle's account of the making of the record and added the further information that all should be written in one volume and that this volume should be placed in the Treasury at Winchester and kept there.[1] For reasons that are still not completely clear the three eastern counties of Essex, Suffolk, and Norfolk were treated differently from the rest of England and their surveys remain separately inscribed in the very much smaller manuscript that we presently refer to as Little Domesday. The difference between the two documents is not merely one of size but also of substance and arrangement. As we shall see later they represent different stages in the creation of the record. The larger volume, usually called 'Great Domesday' and sometimes referred to as the Exchequer Domesday, is a large folio 'fairly written on 382 double pages of parchment in a small but plain character and in double columns on each page'.[2] It deals with thirty-two English counties (including Lancashire and Rutland which are special cases). Little Domesday, although it deals with only three counties, consists of over 450 double pages of parchment in single columns in a variety of hands, well written and substantially clear though not of the excellent disciplined standard of the main volume.[3] The name itself, 'Domesday Book', is a product of the twelfth century. Early references to it describe the record as a *descriptio* or a survey, or the Book of the Treasury, or in due course of the Exchequer.[4] It was kept from the earliest days, as far as we can judge, with the king's seal and was treated, among other things, as an important financial record. The powerful tract, the 'Dialogue of the Exchequer', written in the late 1170s, is the first to give the popular name and goes to considerable lengths to explain how it had come about. The writer, who may well have been Richard fitzNigel, the Treasurer himself, saw the purpose of the survey as primarily legal, to ensure that each man, being content with his own rights, would not with impunity usurp the rights of another. He explained that the book (one book, be it noted, and not two) was called by the English 'Doomsday', that is by metaphor the day of judgement. In a fine rhetorical passage he then goes on to say: 'For just as the sentence of that strict and terrible Last Judgement cannot be evaded by art or subterfuge so, when a dispute arises in this realm concerning facts which are there written down and an appeal is made to the book itself the evidence it gives cannot be set at naught or evaded with impunity.'[5] The book, in other words, was called 'Doomsday' not because it passed judgement (dooms) but because it was no more possible to contradict its decisions than those of the Last Judgement. Modern usage with its insistence on the spelling 'Domesday', a close approximation to the Anglo-Saxon *Domesdæg*, serves to highlight this distinction already firmly made in the twelfth century.

Speculation about the name brings out strongly the feelings of the twelfth century that here was an achievement in the art of government of maximum importance. It also involves some reflections on the purpose and substance of the survey. William and his councillors were busy men and a project which clearly threw the whole administration of the country into a ferment of activity and confusion cannot have been undertaken lightly. We shall consider some of the deeper motives later but there is an immediate historical and political background that demands initial exploration. An easy answer to questions of motive sees them as functions of conquest; and there is an undeniable element of truth in such a solution. The Norman Conquest and resulting settlement brought about some of the most profound social changes ever experienced in these islands. William claimed to be the lawful successor of his kinsman, Edward the Confessor, but he was also a conqueror and it was natural for him to want to know how much land he held and what it was worth. He also wanted to have an up-to-date account of the revenues he might expect from the shires and from the towns. There was also a pressing need to know what geld, good honest land-tax, could be exacted, and the relationship of that tax to the value of the holdings of the tenants-in-chief. The tenants-in-chief, the vast majority of whom were new men, were glad themselves to have a reliable statement of their own wealth and rights. For the

[1] F. Liebermann, *Ungedruckte Anglo-Normannische Geschichtsquellen* (Strassburg, 1879), 21; D. C. Douglas and G. W. Greenaway (eds.), *English Historical Documents, 1042–1189* (abbr. *EHD*), ii (repr. London, 1961), no. 202.

[2] P. C. Webb, *A Short Account of Some Particulars concerning Domes-Day Book, with a view to promote its being published*, Society of Antiquaries (London, 1756); V. H. Galbraith, *The Making of Domesday Book* (Oxford, 1961), 4.

[3] Ibid. 4–5: 'in every way inferior to vol. i, though no less accurately and carefully compiled.' Its folios measure some 11 by 8 inches, substantially smaller than the 15 by 11 inches of Great Domesday.

[4] Ibid. 208–9; J. H. Round, *Feudal England* (London, 1895), 143 ff.

[5] Douglas and Greenaway (eds.), *EHD* ii. no. 70, ch. xvi; C. Johnson *et al.* (eds.), *Dialogus de Scaccario* (London, 1950), 60–4.

lesser men, too, Frenchmen and English alike, it was useful to have an authoritative ruling on tenure, wealth, and taxable capacity. Domesday Book must not be read as an odious tax-book, an ugly, prying symbol of bureaucratic mastery. It was truly as much a function of settlement as of conquest and the speed of its production is a fair reflection of the co-operative nature of the enterprise.

The immediate political background to the production of Domesday Book was troubled enough to make the expenditure of administrative effort fully intelligible. The last years of the Conqueror's reign were uneasy on many fronts. The northern part of England had flared into rebellion in 1080 with the murder of Walcher, Bishop of Durham, and the rebellion harshly repressed by Odo, Bishop of Bayeux, left the frontier with the Scots even more restive. York itself, with the heavy marks of its treatment during the early reign of William still on it, remained a substantial Anglo-Scandinavian city and the threat of renewed attack from Denmark was not taken lightly. The Anglo-Saxon chronicler tells that William himself returned from Normandy to England in 1085 with a larger force of mounted men and foot-soldiers 'than had ever come to this country'[1] precisely because of this fear of Danish invasions, and leaves us in no doubt that difficulties over provisioning this army, dispersed as it was among his vassals all over the country, provided the direct background to the Domesday survey. There are also hints at difficulties over the succession. William was still in rude health in his late fifties but he had quarrelled violently with his eldest son, Robert; and the quarrel cast shadows over the question of inheritance. Representatives of the old legitimate West Saxon dynasty, the three children of Edward Ætheling and grandchildren of Edmund Ironside, found it expedient to move out of William's direct orbit in 1086. Edgar Ætheling went from England, probably to Apulia, because he had received no honour from the king (the chronicler adds the pious hope that God may grant him honour in the future), and his sister, Cristina, took the veil at the Abbey of Romsey.[2] The third sibling, and the most powerful of the three, was Margaret, queen of Scotland, the wife of Malcolm Canmore, and the strong English presence in the Scottish court must have served as a further spur to William to make sure of his control of the southern kingdom. The Domesday survey represented in the administrative and financial fields important steps towards such consolidation. William I was no idle king. Guided by able advisers, bishops and magnates, he took the ambitious and successful decision to initiate a full-scale detailed and businesslike survey of the whole kingdom of England.

The Making of Domesday Book

Careful investigation of Domesday Book itself and of other documents related to the survey has brought about reasonable certainty of the mechanics by which the inquisition was carried out and the written evidence assembled and shaped into final form.[3] After the 'deep discussion' at Gloucester commissioners were appointed and groups of shires allotted to them within which they could make their inquiry. Internal evidence from the completed book, peculiarities in terminology and arrangement, make it likely that there were seven of these groups or 'circuits', though it is just possible, as some nineteenth-century scholars used to think, that there were further subdivisions in one or two of the larger groups.

Southern England was divided into two great circuits, Kent, Sussex, Surrey, Hampshire, and Berkshire to the south-east, and Wiltshire, Dorset, Somerset, Devon, and Cornwall to the south-west. There were three circuits for the Midlands. Middlesex, Hertford, Buckingham, Cambridge, and Bedford made up one group, radiating out from London; Oxford, Northampton, Leicester, and Warwick constituted the second with its principal base possibly at Oxford; and Gloucester, Worcester, Hereford, Stafford, Shropshire, and Cheshire made up the third, the West Midland group, covering the border shires with Wales with some significant entries relating to Wales itself in the Gloucestershire,

[1] Whitelock *et al.* (eds.), *Anglo-Saxon Chronicle*, 161: 'mid swa mycclan here ridendra manna ond gangendra of Francrice ond of Brytlande'.

[2] Ibid. 162 (1086).

[3] Galbraith, *Making of Domesday Book*, and *Domesday Book: its Place in Administrative History* (Oxford, 1974). The initial breakthrough came in his remarkable article, also entitled 'The Making of Domesday Book', *EHR* 57 (1942), 161–77; A. Ballard, *The Domesday Inquest* (London, 1906), 12–13, proposed the division into seven circuits described below.

Herefordshire, and Cheshire folios. The lands between the Ribble and the Mersey, the heart of historic Lancashire, were also surveyed under the Cheshire folios. For the northern Danelaw and the North generally there seems to have been one great circuit that embraced Huntingdon, Derby, Nottingham, Rutland, York, and Lincoln. Some entries in the Yorkshire folios refer to lands in Cumbria and northern Lancashire but Northumberland and Durham were untouched by the survey. Last of the seven circuits, and in some degree the most complicated, are the eastern shires of Essex, Norfolk, and Suffolk which still remain in the relatively unfinished state of Little Domesday. There are oddities about the arrangements—the sheer size of the sixth circuit, which included both Yorkshire and Lincolnshire, the separation of Leicestershire from the other constituent parts of the 'Five Boroughs', the long straggle along the Welsh border which brought Gloucestershire and Cheshire into the same circuit—but by and large the division was sensible and practical. The commissioners themselves were men of the highest rank and authority, charged with judicial powers direct from the royal court; and they appear to have been sent to areas where they themselves did not hold extensive lands or rights. Bishop Remigius of Lincoln (accompanied by a clerk and two monks), Henry de Ferrers, Walter Giffard, and Adam fitzHubert (the brother of Odo the Steward) acted on the Worcester circuit while Bishop William of Durham was one of the commissioners for the South-West.[1] Terms of reference were drawn up and we are fortunate enough to possess a copy preserved in the archives of the Abbey of Ely where the whole enterprise is described as 'an inquiry [*inquisitio*] made by the king's barons according to the oath of the sheriff of the shire and of all the barons and their Frenchmen and of the

[1] T. Hearne (ed.), *Heming's Cartulary*, i (London, 1723), 288, provides the names of the Worcester commissioners; R. Welldon Finn, *Domesday Studies: the Liber Exoniensis* (London, 1964), 101, notes that Bishop William of Durham, who is associated with geld inquiries in the South-West, was probably a commissioner.

whole hundred court, the priest, reeve and six villans from each village'.[1] With a little effort of the historical imagination the practical procedures can be reconstructed from this description. Much preliminary work must have been done by routine methods in the traditional courts of the shire and its constituent hundreds. The commissioners, the king's barons, in all their dignity and with all their authority sat in judgement in the shire court, listening to the oaths sworn or receiving adequate testimony as to the oaths sworn relating to the written testimony delivered by the sheriff, by the great feudal lords whose interests lay in the shire (or their trusted representatives), and by representatives of each of the hundred courts. We are further told the detail of what was required from the survey:

> They inquired what the manor was called; who held it at the time of King Edward; who holds it now; how many hides there are; how many ploughs in demesne and how many belonging to the men; how many villans; how many cottars; how many slaves; how many freemen; how many sokemen; how much woodland; how much meadow; how much pasture; how many mills; how many fisheries; how much had been added to or taken away from the estate; what it used to be worth altogether; what it is worth now; and how much each freeman and sokeman had and has. All this was to be recorded thrice, namely as it was in the time of King Edward, as it was when King William gave it and as it is now. And it was also to be noted whether more could be taken than is now being taken.[2]

These are indeed exact terms of reference and it is an astonishing tribute to the whole venture that we find time and time again a close correlation between these questions posed in the Ely document (the Inquisitio Eliensis) and the answers given in the final, polished form of Domesday Book. Whoever wrote the Ely document either knew the final version well or had a powerful hand in its construction; and the immediacy of the evidence speaks in favour of the latter proposition. Even the names of the jurors are preserved and we learn, for example, that in the hundred of Staine in the county of Cambridge the following men gave sworn evidence: 'Aleran; Roger, the man of Walter Giffard; Richard the reeve [*prefectus*] of the hundred; Farman; Huscarl of Swaffham; Leofwine; Harold, the man of Hardwin de Scales; Ælfric of Wilbraham; and all the other Frenchmen and Englishmen of this hundred.'[3]

The whole country must have been thrown into considerable turmoil over the enterprise, involving as it did so many of the great men of the realm and virtually all of the literate administration. It followed a general tightening-up of the taxation system and a series of inquiries that are commonly termed 'geld inquests'. The Domesday survey provided an attempt to sort order out of chaos in many different directions; and it may have been confusion between the regular efforts to sort out the geld and the extraordinary nature of the commissioners' activities in 1086 that prompted the well-informed and able Bishop of Hereford, Robert de Losinga, to make his somewhat gnomic comment, still not completely explained, when he wrote of the inquiry that 'other investigators followed the first; and men were sent into provinces which they did not know, and where they were themselves unknown, in order that they might be given the opportunity of checking the first survey and, if necessary, of denouncing its authors as guilty to the king'.[4] A bishop, particularly as intelligent a bishop as Robert, would know what was going on in the shire court and his 'other investigators' were clearly important people, presumably the commissioners themselves. It may well be, however, that Robert of Hereford is telling us no more than that the preliminary sorting-out and massing of evidence, much of it written, demanded initial meetings of some length and complexity at the shire court before the commissioners arrived; and that from the standpoint of the local men the function of the commissioners was indeed to ensure that the sheriff and the shire court had done their work properly and accurately.

The one certainty is that knowledge of the basic material needed by the commissioners, along the lines of the Ely terms of reference, must have been available at the county court well in advance of the

[1] H. Ellis (ed.), *Inquisitio Eliensis* (*the Ely Inquest*), in vol. iv of the Record Commission's magnificent edition of *Domesday Book* (London, 1816), 497–528; N. E. S. A. Hamilton gives the standard modern edition in the *Inquisitio Comitatus Cantabrigiensis* (London, 1876), 97–195; Douglas and Greenaway (eds.), *EHD* ii. no. 215, 946–50.

[2] Ibid. 946.

[3] Ibid. 947.

[4] W. H. Stevenson, 'A Contemporary Description of the Domesday Survey', *EHR* 22 (1907), 74.

hearing at which the commissioners were present. From the local administrator's point of view the task set was difficult but not impossible. The sheriff and his officers would have written information available relating to the hundreds, whether or not in private hands, and to the manorial structure of the shire. Geld records would give him the names of the landowners and their obligations. The Church also possessed lists relating to the payment of Church dues, such as Peter's Pence. It has been shown conclusively for Kent that the framework into which the detailed information could be fed was available as a matter of routine, inherited by the Normans from the relatively sophisticated Anglo-Saxon administrative system.[1] Geld lists prepared before the Domesday inquiry anticipate the characteristic shape of Domesday Book by recording obligations in feudal form according to the names of the principal tenants within the shire structure. Statistics could not have been provided both in 1066 and 'when King William gave the estate' (their provision is, in fact, patchy and varies from shire to shire) without the existence of written records. Manorial details about the type and status of the peasantry, the arable capacity and potential, the detailed wealth and value of the estates, the number of livestock, were quite another matter. Reeves of estates and men looking after their lords' interests were prominent among the jurors; and this is what one would expect. They and they alone would be able to testify to the factual information needed, particularly to the detail concerning livestock (omitted from the Ely record and from Great Domesday). It is unthinkable that the barons and bishops would have sat still and listened to the haggling over detailed returns. Even so, and making full allowance for the quick and efficient performance of the preparatory work, the supervision of sworn oaths and validation of sworn testimony must have taken several days at each of the shire courts under the commissioners' care. If time spent hearing pleas and recording decisions where decisions were possible is taken into account many of William's chief men, appointed as commissioners, must have spent many weeks of their active lives on business directly connected with the production of Domesday Book.

After the validation of the evidence at the shire court the work of the commissioners was done and it was left to the administrators to take the next steps. Practice may have varied from circuit to circuit in detail but the overall pattern seems to have been standard throughout the country, indeed must have been so if the urgency of the royal master was to be met. Material, the authenticity of which had been vouched for on a territorial basis hundred by hundred, was assembled at each shire court in feudal form, that is to say in accordance with the holdings of the tenants-in-chief. There would normally be separate quires (collections of leaves) for all the principal tenants, but the smaller holdings would be grouped, again feudally according to the holding of tenants-in-chief, into integral quires. In this form the evidence could be retained at the regional headquarters, and indeed by good chance it appears that one such assemblage has survived at Exeter. The so-called Liber Exoniensis, usually abbreviated as Exon, still among the prized possessions of the cathedral at Exeter, was bound together with extra material relating largely to the geld later in the Middle Ages, but initially it represented such a collection of quires put into feudal shape on a regional basis.[2] From such collections fair copies were made, if necessary, and sent to headquarters at Winchester where they were abstracted and compressed into the format of Great Domesday by the master administrator. The eastern counties did not receive this treatment and it is probable that our existing second volume, Little Domesday, represents one such regional return. There have been many attempts to explain why the East should have proved so anomalous. The most likely explanation is connected with the complexity of the tenurial position in East Anglia and Essex where there were so many relatively small holdings. The difficulty of reducing them all to standard Domesday form demanded more time than was available. The king had given his orders and expected quick results. It is possible that had William lived until Christmas 1087 the eastern counties would also have conformed to the format used for the rest of England. As it is, the second volume remains as a precious clue to the processes by which Domesday Book was created. It gives us a precise date when it states in a colophon at the end of the folios that

[1] S. P. J. Harvey, 'Domesday Book and its Predecessors', *EHR* 86 (1971), 753–73.

[2] Welldon Finn, *Liber Exoniensis*, 1–7, gives a clear description of the manuscript as it now survives. The Record Commission text in *Domesday Book*, vol. iv, is good but a modern edition is much to be desired.

'In the year 1086 from the incarnation of the Lord, the twentieth of the reign of William, this survey [*descriptio*] was made not only through these three counties but through the whole of England'.[1]

It is sometimes asked how such a record could have been made so quickly, and how England could have produced such a body of literate clerks. It must be confessed that some of the exact work needed before a full answer can be given to such questions has not been done. There is, for example, a splendid uniformity about much of the script in the first volume and many good critics hold that it is substantially the work of one scribe.[2] The palaeographical investigation needed to confirm or reject this view is in its early stages and we still have to fall back on inference and impression. Some scholars believe that while there was one master-mind directing the whole enterprise it is quite likely that several scribes, well trained in the same style of penmanship, contributed to the volume. Welldon Finn was the modern scholar most interested in the speed of production and his considered and judicious conclusion was that the initial returns from the circuits could have been constructed in the summer of 1086, possibly by 1 August when a great assembly was held at Salisbury, attended by all landholders of any account, at which the lesser landholders, the principal tenants of the great feudal magnates, swore a special oath of fealty to their overlord, King William, before he departed for Normandy.[3] Preparation of the regional returns, submitted in the form of quires, would have been completed easily in the time-span with perhaps eight or ten clerks busy at work at each section. The final production of Domesday Book as we know it could then have been set in train in the winter months. It has been estimated that the copying and construction of the first volume would have occupied something in the region of 240 days' work by one well-trained scribe. It is a distinct possibility that the book reached its present stage by the September of 1087 with the eastern counties in reserve ready to be abstracted in the autumn months. On 9 September the death of William, the mainspring of the enterprise, brought the work to a halt; and Domesday Book remains now as it was then, a composite two-volume work, the eastern counties left in their rough penultimate state.

Contents

Domesday Book is a remarkable record, but even so one must not expect too much from it. The standard of accuracy and consistency is high but there are mistakes, omissions, misunderstandings, and variations in procedure that compel the careful reader to be cautious in his use of its evidence. For example, it is not strictly true to describe the Domesday survey as a survey of all England. Its construction depended on the administrative system inherited from Anglo-Saxon England, and the basic division of England into administrative units known as shires provided the framework for the investigation. For most of England the shires remained recognizable and identifiable throughout the medieval and modern period, with only relatively minor boundary changes, up to 1974: but the shiring process was still incomplete in 1086. The northern boundary with the kingdom of the Scots was fluid and uncertain. Durham and Northumberland were untouched by the survey, and entries for Cumberland, Westmorland, and north Lancashire were confined to royal lands and the fiefs of Hugh fitzBaldric and Roger de Poitou. Holdings in those districts (140 in north Lancashire, 27 in Westmorland, and 5 in Cumberland) contained a very high proportion of waste and were entered in the Yorkshire folios.[4] In south Lancashire, the district 'between the Ribble and the Mersey' as it is called in Domesday Book, entries are limited to the six great holdings, centred on hundredal manors formerly in the hands of Roger de Poitou and now held by the king. They are described under the Cheshire folios in a separate section at the end of the county record which goes into some detail over

[1] Record Commission, *Domesday Book*, ii. 450. Vol. i of the manuscript is henceforth referred to as GDB, vol. ii as LDB.

[2] Galbraith, *Domesday Book: its Place in Administrative History*, 51, where he notes in the course of a discussion of the possible role of Samson, a royal chaplain who became Bishop of Worcester (1096–1112), as compiler and possible scribe of Great Domesday Book, that 'I am now entirely convinced that the whole volume was written by a single scribe'; see also M. Gullick, 'The Great and Little Domesday Manuscripts', Special Study XIV, pp. 98–102 below.

[3] R. Welldon Finn, *An Introduction to Domesday Book* (London, 1963), 92–4.

[4] H. C. Darby and I. S. Maxwell (eds.), *The Domesday Geography of Northern England* (Cambridge, 1962), 1 and 392–418 (by I. B. Terrett); *VCH Yorkshire*, ii (1906), 133–4, where the territories of Amounderness, Lonsdale, Kendal, Cartmel, Furness, and part of Copeland are described as colonial regions.

the special customs of this area, the hundreds of West Derby, Newton, Wallington, Blackburn, Salford, and Leyland, all of which appear to have borne many of the characteristics of marcher military rule dependent on the strength of newly built castles.[1] Elsewhere in England, Rutland, as so often, provides something of an anomaly. In late Anglo-Saxon times its southern half had often been taken as an integral part of Northamptonshire while the north of the shire had been treated as a great liberty used as a dower for Anglo-Saxon queens. In Domesday Book the two wapentakes nearest to Nottinghamshire were surveyed in a separate section at the end of the Nottinghamshire folios, where we are told that Rutland rendered £150 of silver to the king.[2] Other Rutland entries appear under Lincolnshire and Northamptonshire. For the most part, however, the shires are in familiar form, thirty of them in all from Kent at the beginning of Great Domesday to Yorkshire at the end, with the further three eastern shires of Essex, Norfolk, and Suffolk in the smaller volume.

Within the shires two features appear so regularly that we may consider them to have been part of an ordered programme. It is often the custom to start the record with an account of the chief town in the shire and it is normal to be given a list of the chief landholders in the shire, headed by the king—a working index, as it were. Variations in the practice of dealing with the towns will be discussed later. Some of the largest towns are omitted and in some shires, such as Dorset and Wiltshire, there are multiple entries; but over large tracts of country and in several circuits the pattern is regular, and indeed north of the Thames in Great Domesday it is virtually unbroken, apart from Middlesex (no entry for London); Gloucester and Lincoln (multiple entries, though on a modest scale—Winchcombe and Chepstow with Gloucester; and Stamford and Torksey with Lincoln); and a curious joint entry for Derby and Nottingham.[3] Lists of the chief tenants are given for all the shires, even for Rutland, though a compressed entry for Cheshire merely states, after a detailed survey of Chester itself, that the bishop holds from the king all that pertains to his see in Chester and that Earl Hugh holds the rest of the shire with his men from the king.[4] Roger de Poitou's fief, now held by the king, also receives a special mention and the surveyors clearly have observed their brief, though in very compressed form.[5] There are occasional omissions and errors in the lists but for the most part they are accurate and provide an efficient index to the feudal holdings within each shire. The normal order was for the royal lands to be surveyed first, followed by the lands of the ecclesiastical tenants-in-chief in order of rank, and then in turn by the lay tenants-in-chief. The number of entries could vary greatly. In areas where one or other of the great feudal lords was dominant there could be very few. So, for example, there were only six apart from the king in Cornwall, where Robert de Mortain, the king's half-brother, held far and away the biggest fief; only nine in Shropshire, where Roger of Montgomery dominated the border with Wales; and only Hugh Lupus as Earl of Chester, together with a brief reference to the bishop's urban rights, in Cheshire itself. At the other extreme more than fifty tenants appear by name in Hampshire (with more for the Isle of Wight and the New Forest), Berkshire, Wiltshire, Dorset, Devonshire, Buckinghamshire, Oxfordshire, Gloucestershire, Bedfordshire, Northamptonshire, and Lincolnshire in Great Domesday; and more than sixty in Norfolk, seventy-five in Suffolk, and close on ninety (including the *liberi homines regis*) in Essex.[6]

Hertfordshire provides a standard example and the lands surveyed in that shire are divided into forty-five sections relating to the holdings of tenants-in-chief. The list at the head of the county survey (the index list, as we may call it) gives only forty-four names, omitting the Abbot of Ramsey, who held the manor of Therfield.[7] There is, however, a further check on the numbering of the fiefs, a series of numbers placed in the margin of the text of the survey by the side of the first holding in each of the fiefs; and sure enough the abbot's holding is numbered XII accurately and in its proper form in the

[1] *VCH Lancashire*, i (1906), 270; GDB 269v–270; J. Tait, *The Domesday Survey of Cheshire*, Chetham Society, 75 (Manchester, 1916), 6.

[2] *VCH Rutland*, i (1908), 120–42. The wapentakes of Alstoe and Martinsley were annexed for fiscal purposes to the shrievalty of Nottingham. Eight of the twelve estates described under Alstoe are duplicated in the Lincs. folios (GDB 293v).

[3] J. Tait, *The Medieval English Borough* (Manchester, 1936), 43–66, provides a survey of the Domesday evidence that has permanent value. Nottingham and Derby are described separately at the beginning of the Notts. folios (GDB 280), immediately before a statement of the customs of the joint shires.

[4] GDB 262v.

[5] Ibid., and 269v–270.

[6] H. Ellis, *A General Introduction to Domesday Book*, 2 vols. (London, 1833; repr. 1971) still provides the essential statistical base for Domesday studies; see also W. J. Corbett, 'The Development of the Duchy of Normandy and the Norman Conquest of England', *Cambridge Medieval History*, eds. J. R. Tanner *et al.*, v (Cambridge, 1926), ch. xv, 503–13, for a remarkable analysis of the baronial statistics.

[7] GDB 132.

main text. The result of the omission is that the index list is one behind the marginal numeration right through the Hertfordshire folios to the forty-second fief, when the marginal annotator in turn blundered, listing both the land of the king's thegns and the land of the wife of Richard fitzGilbert as number 42. Both the index list and the marginal numbers are therefore one out in their final calculations. The royal lands are, as always, described first (19 entries), followed by those of the Archbishop of Canterbury (5) and of five other bishops—Winchester (1), London (25), Odo, Bishop of Bayeux, the king's half-brother (26), Lisieux (1), and Chester (1). The ecclesiastical element was completed with the lands of four abbots and an abbess (Ely (3), Winchester (10), St Albans (20), Ramsey (1), and the Abbess of Chatteris (1)); and the holdings of the Canons of London at St Paul's (5) and the Canons of Waltham (2). The lay fiefs in Hertfordshire are then described with some attempt at a logical presentation in order of rank. Four men with the title of *comes* (count or earl) are given precedence: Robert de Mortain (the king's other half-brother, with 13 entries, including the fine manor of Berkhamsted with its borough, mills, and vineyard), Alan of Richmond (12 entries), Eustace de Boulogne (15), and Roger de Montgomery (1 only in Hertfordshire, a patch of land in Broadfield worth 5*s*.). The succeeding nineteen tenants included some of the most powerful men in England, among whom Geoffrey de Mandeville (20 entries), Geoffrey de Bec (25), Peter de Valognes (19), and Hardwin de Scales (23) owed a substantial proportion of their total wealth to their possessions in the county. The survey is completed by a succession of small fiefs, two properties held by Edgar the Ætheling, single parcels of land held by Mainou the Breton and Gilbert fitzSolomon, two estates of Sigar de Chocques, the land of the king's thegns (fifteen properties divided among a miscellaneous group of English, newcomers, and priests), and finally—a special feature of the Hertfordshire entries—three fiefs held in their own right by great ladies: a substantial manor at Standon, worth £33, held by Rohais, the wife of Richard fitzGilbert, and two solid holdings at Broxbourne by Adelaide, the wife of Hugh de Grandmesnil, and at Hunsdon by the daughter of Ralph Taillebois.[1]

The lands of Odo of Bayeux are often recorded as if he were still an active tenant-in-chief even though he had been in prison since 1082.[2] Similar incongruities occur elsewhere, not only with his fief but with others whose owners had died or been disgraced—a possible reminder of the tendency to fossilize the territorial position in this generation immediately following the Conquest. Within the larger fiefs there were lands drawn from several hundreds in the county and there is a general tendency, shown also in the Hertfordshire folios, for the hundredal entries to follow a systematic order. Professor Sawyer, who has examined this problem in depth, has pointed out that more than half the counties of Domesday Book show clear traces of a consistent hundredal order, a further indication of the way in which the administrative arrangements, necessarily dependent on existing territorial structures, were adapted to a feudal use.[3] Most of the shires follow a similar pattern, though there are exceptions. In Nottinghamshire the three *comites*, Alan of Richmond (the Breton), Hugh Lupus, and Robert de Mortain, precede the ecclesiastics, even Odo of Bayeux, but in Norfolk Odo comes first, to be followed by the lay tenants-in-chief, headed by the *comites* Robert de Mortain, Alan, Eustace de Boulogne, and Hugh.[4] Terminology relating to the minor landholders, some of them Englishmen, varies greatly and they appear at times as *taini* (thegns) and at others as *servientes* or simply as *homines* or *liberi homines regis*.

The strategy of the survey, planned to show who were the landowners, how much land they owned, and how much tax they were responsible for, was sound but the special strength of Domesday Book lies in the high degree of consistency it achieved over a wide area. The basic unit recorded was not the vill but the manor, and to whatever part of England we turn, no matter how diverse the basic social patterns, we find substantially the same type of information about geld, the agrarian capacity

[1] J. Morris (ed.), *Domesday Book: Hertfordshire* (Chichester, 1976).

[2] It was noted by David Bates in an unpublished doctoral thesis (Exeter University, 1970) that in seventeen of the twenty-two counties in which Odo held as tenant-in-chief at the time of his imprisonment in 1082, his estates are recorded with his name in the rubric but that in the other five (Sussex, Hants, Berks., Cambs., and Glos.) they are listed as part of the royal demesne or under the estates of the *de facto* tenant.

[3] P. H. Sawyer, 'The "Original Returns" and Domesday Book', *EHR* 70 (1955), 177–97, esp. 181–2.

[4] GDB 280v; LDB 109.

of the land, the peasantry, the ancillary attributes—pasture, mills, woodland, fisheries—and the value, often together with some comment on the historic value in 1066 and when the new lords took over. Two examples from the great fief of Roger de Montgomery help to illustrate the point. His two prime holdings were in Sussex and in Shropshire but he held land in many other shires as well. In Middlesex the following description is given of his fine manor of Harlington:

> Harlington defends itself [i.e. pays geld] for 10 hides. Alvred and Olaf hold it from Earl Roger. There is land there for 6 ploughs. In demesne there are now 2 ploughs; the villans have 3 ploughs and there could be a fourth. A priest holds half a hide and there are 12 villans, each holding a virgate. 4 villans hold half a virgate each. 2 bordars have 11 acres and there are 8 cottars and a slave. There is meadow for 2 ploughs. In total value it is worth 100*s*., when acquired the same, TRE £8. Vigot held this manor and 1 sokeman held 2 hides of the land: he could not sell it without permission.[1]

It is not too difficult to reconstruct a picture of this large manor with its prosperous farmers and sound arable capacity and potential from this entry.

Earl Roger also held land in Staffordshire, at Alveley in Seisdon Hundred, and the entry for this manor, though simpler, betrays the same curiosity about the same things:

> The earl holds Alveley. Earl Ælfgar held it. There is 1 hide. There is land for 9 ploughs. There are 2 in demesne and 8 villans with a priest and 4 bordars with 6 ploughs. There is 6 acres of meadow and woodland 2 leagues long and half a league in breadth. TRE it was worth £6, now 100*s*.[2]

The same systematic intent is in evidence in Little Domesday. Allowance has to be made for differences in the technique of assessment of the geld and collection of tax, and for the inclusion of more detailed figures relating to livestock, but the main pattern of inquiry is identical to that of the larger volume. Hugh de Montfort, for example, held some eighteen properties in Norfolk and his estate in the Hundred of South Greenhoe is described as follows:

> The lands of Hugh de Montfort. Bondi held Bodney. Then there were 8 villans, later 4, and now 7 bordars. Then there were 6 slaves, now 3. Then 3 ploughs in demesne, later 2, now 1. Then 3 ploughs between the men, now ½. There is woodland for 100 pigs, 5 acres of meadow, 1 mill and ¼ of another. When he acquired it 1 rouncie [cob], now 2, then 13 head of cattle, now 3, then 41 pigs, now 9, then 51 sheep, now 11, then 16 goats, now 5. It has 1 league less 2 furlongs in length and 4 furlongs in breadth and pays 8*d*. in geld with those who hold in it. It was valued then at 100*s*., now 60*s*.[3]

On lands held by the king, by his greatest tenants-in-chief, by great ecclesiastical princes, or by humble men and women holding small parcels of land the type of information collected is identical. The standardization of information is our best evidence for the sophistication of surveying techniques.

It is also generally recognized that special value attaches to the information contained in Domesday Book because of its systematic organization on a national basis. What then is that information? The main categories are much in line with the terms of reference suggested by the Ely record. To begin with there is the straightforward presentation of the names of the manors and their owners, a superb framework to the tenurial structure of early Anglo-Norman England. Then there is the more complex matter of taxable capacity. Over much of England this was based on the unit known as a hide, which had in the remote past been related to the arable needed to support one *familia* (the *terra unius familiae* of the early records), 120 acres in parts of the country and as little as 48 or 40 acres in others, such as fertile Wiltshire. In Kent the equivalent basic unit was the double hide or *sulung* and over much of the Danelaw the *carucate* or ploughland. East Anglia enjoyed a special tax system

[1] GDB129. [2] GDB248. [3] LDB237.

where villages paid so many pence to every portion of a pound due from a territorial unit known as a leet.[1]

It has been estimated that England as a whole contained something of the order of 70,000 hides or their equivalents, though not all of them were in fact liable to taxation.[2] There were many royal manors that did not pay and much Church land was exempt. The demesne of the tenants-in-chief was exempt and no geld was taken from land in the royal forests. Domesday Book is careful in its record of this obligation to geld and gives plentiful evidence of the flexibility of the system. Reduction in hidation had sometimes taken place because of war or political devastation. Northamptonshire had suffered severely in the troubles of 1065–6 and its total hidage reduced to only about a half of what it had been before the Conquest.[3] Other disasters could account for reductions, as at Fareham in Hampshire where the amount due was decreased by a third owing to the encroachments of the Vikings, because it was on the sea.[4] Beneficial hidation could be dramatic and sustained, as at the great manor of Chilcombe, also in Hampshire, where the hidage had been reduced from 100 hides to a mere token one hide in favour of its owner, the Old Minster at Winchester.[5] The normal geld was levied at the rate of 2*s.* a hide, and the geld imposed near the time of the Domesday survey at the rate of 6*s.* a hide was regarded by contemporaries as excessively heavy.[6] Only very rarely is there a hint of the actual mechanics of payment. In Berkshire, for example, we are told that it was the pre-Conquest custom for two equal instalments of geld to be paid from each hide, 3½*d.* before Christmas and 3½*d.* at Pentecost.[7]

Hidage refers to tax assessment but information is also given about the arable wealth capable of meeting the tax bill in terms of land for so many ploughs and of plough-teams. The coverage is not universal and in some shires, notably in the South-East, the information is given rather spasmodically. At times the scribe has written 'Land for . . .', only to leave the space blank and the number of ploughs unstated.[8] As we have already seen, however, a normal entry would declare that there was land for, say, eight ploughs, that there were two on the lord's demesne and that the peasantry owned the other six (or it might be more or less). Discrepancies between the amount of land available and the number of teams at work give us precious clues to the prosperity of individual manors and indeed at times to the prosperity of shires or parts of shires. They also remind us that the commissioners took seriously their terms of reference, by which they were instructed to find out what the land was worth and how much more it could yield.

We shall discuss the nature of the peasantry later when we turn to consider the value of Domesday Book, but it is well to remind ourselves of the mass of factual material provided about the inhabitants of rural England. Most fall systematically into the categories employed by the surveyors: villans, bordars and cottars, freemen, sokemen, and finally, slaves. References to other categories are relatively scarce, sometimes attributable to regional peculiarities and sometimes to function in society. For example, there were many thousand priests in England and it was expected that a priest would be available together with a reeve and six men to give evidence on oath for each vill, but only some 900 or so are referred to specifically in Domesday Book. In similar fashion only 56 reeves, 71 smiths, 10 shepherds, 2 carpenters, and half a dozen millers are mentioned as such.[9] Occasionally the surveyors have found it impossible to force larger groups into their basic categories and the presence of numbers of *radmen* or *radknights* in the shires bordering Wales (i.e. men with special mobile

[1] F. M. Stenton, *Anglo-Saxon England* (3rd edn., Oxford, 1971), 645. The leets were grouped so that each of them paid an equal sum (40*d.*, for example, in the Suffolk hundred of Thedwestry) towards each and every pound exacted from the hundred in which they were placed.

[2] R. Welldon Finn, *Domesday Book: a Guide* (London and Chichester, 1973), 27.

[3] *VCH Northamptonshire*, i (1902), 257–356. J. H. Round edited the Domesday Book section in this volume and showed that the evidence suggests a vast reduction of the assessment previous to the compilation of Domesday Book (p. 260).

[4] GDB 40v: King Edward had reduced the obligation of Fareham to 20 hides, although there were 30 hides there, 'causa Wickingarum quia super mare est'.

[5] GDB 41: There was land for sixty-eight ploughs and the value had increased from £73. 10*s.* in 1066 and later to £104, £80 of which was ascribed to the monks' land and £24 to that of the men.

[6] S. P. J. Harvey reminds us that this geld, levied in 1084 at the rate of 6*s.* on the hide, entailed an imposition amounting to almost one-third of the annual return from land, which averaged roughly £1 a hide: 'Domesday Book and Anglo-Norman Governance', *TRHS* 5th ser., 25 (1975), 181.

[7] GDB 56v. A good discussion of the mechanics of collection is given by Welldon Finn, *Liber Exoniensis*, 100–8.

[8] In Kent, for example, on the great fief of Odo of Bayeux, there are some sixty gaps of this nature and other discrepancies too, relating notably to the number of ploughs on the demesne.

[9] Ellis, *General Introduction*, i (1833), 91–4. Convenient summaries are offered in Welldon Finn, *Domesday Book: a Guide*.

duties as 'riding-men'), or of *drengs* in the North or *coliberti* (freedmen), indicates oddities in social organization that the surveyors found hard to explain. The relatively unusual but important mention of *milites* as such also illustrates a difficulty experienced by those who drew up this massive survey where status and function were inevitably on occasion hard to separate.[1]

The main concentration of Domesday Book lies on the resources that come from exploitation of arable farming but the ploughlands, the teams of oxen, and the peasantry that coped with the arable could not be treated in isolation. Meadow was needed for hay, and pasture, though irregularly recorded, was also a matter for general concern. Food for plough-beasts and for sheep was needed on most manors and once, at least, there was reference to pasture for horses, said to have been used (though the jurors did not quite know how) by Godric the sheriff at the royal manor of Kintbury in Berkshire.[2] Meadow is normally assessed in acres though a rubric is adopted in the East Midlands which relates the amount of meadow to the number of plough-teams it is capable of feeding. Access to woodland was also essential for the health of the rural community and in some parts of the country it was customary to assess the quantity of woodland according to the amount of swine-pasturage, that is to say according to the number of pigs it was reckoned to be able to accommodate. In other parts woodland was measured according to linear measurements, so many leagues in length and breadth, while elsewhere assessments in hides and acres or in pannage (that is, rent) were the custom. Differentiation in methods of calculating the extent of woodland provides one of the clues to variation of procedures from circuit to circuit.[3]

Many other aspects of rural life came into the orbit of the Domesday surveyors, sometimes generally, sometimes for specific regional reasons. Something like 6,000 mills are mentioned, mostly water-mills, and the concern of the surveyors was often to establish the mill-rent in terms of cash or, on occasion, the number of eels provided for the lord of the mill. Mill-ponds no doubt would prove quite productive but the horrendous number of eels expected from some mills would suggest something of the nature of a subsidiary fishing industry as a side-product of the activity.[4] Farm animals are recorded, especially in Little Domesday, and nearly all on demesne land apart from plough-beasts. Large numbers of sheep are entered in the eastern counties and in the South-West, and there is one reference, at Stallingborough in Lincolnshire, to a shearing-shed.[5] Horses, unbroken mares, pigs, she-goats, hawks, and falcons appear in the record, but the statistics, apart from those relating to sheep and pigs, are too spasmodic to offer more than a glimpse of the agrarian wealth concealed under the standardized forms of the record. There are occasional indications of concentration of specialist effort that demand attention. At Battersea in Surrey the seven mills provided a render of more than £42 on a royal manor valued in all at £75.[6] Fisheries were recorded at places where there must have been a significant local industry. At Southease in Sussex the villans provided 38,500 herrings a year for Hyde Abbey in Winchester and paid £4 for their catches of porpoises.[7] The ancillary activity involved in such a render by way of providing salt for preservation and transport is a reminder of the relative complexity of the economic base beneath the superstructure described in Domesday Book. Fishing was an important organized industry along many coastal reaches from Suffolk to Dorset and references to salmon fisheries at Tidenham in Gloucestershire, where the Wye meets the Severn, and in Cheshire indicate the importance of that natural resource in the western rivers.[8] Salt was at times associated with fisheries but was also an important industry in its own right. Salt-pans are mentioned throughout the survey, notably in coastal areas where salt could be obtained by evaporation from sea-water. No fewer than 100 salt-pans were recorded, for example, at 'Rameslie' in Sussex.[9] The most interesting and important entries, however, are undoubtedly those dealing with

[1] S. P. J. Harvey, 'The Knight and the Knight's Fee in England', *Past and Present*, 49 (1970), 3–43: some 500 examples have been noted and the normal knightly holding shown to be about 1½ hides (pp. 15 ff.).

[2] GDB 57: *sed nesciunt quomodo*. The king also held Lambourn, a hint that the traditions of stabling on the Berkshire Downs may run deep.

[3] H. C. Darby, *Domesday England* (Cambridge, 1977), 171–207, and 'Domesday Woodland', *EconHR* 2nd ser., 3 (Cambridge, 1950–1), 21–43.

[4] R. Lennard, *Rural England 1086–1135* (Oxford, 1959), 278–87, the best modern introduction to the problems associated with the mills of Domesday Book.

[5] GDB 340: a *lanina*.

[6] GDB 32: £42. 9*s*. 8*d*. 'aut frumentum ejusdem precii'.

[7] GDB 17v.

[8] GDB 192 (Wisbech), 155 (Dorchester), 263v (Eaton by Chester), and 164 (Tidenham); H. R. Loyn, *Anglo-Saxon England and the Norman Conquest* (London, 1962), 359–61.

[9] GDB 17: 'Rameslie', situated on the coast near Fairlight, was substantially lost to the sea by erosion, and its urban function passed to Rye.

the inland salt-producing areas of Cheshire and Worcestershire.[1] At Droitwich we have a description of what appears to have been the principal salt industrial centre in the country, and in Cheshire the three 'wiches' of Northwich, Middlewich, and Nantwich were separately surveyed with a valuable reference to their brine-pits and boilings. The influence of such centres was widespread. Many places in the West Midlands owned salt-pans at Droitwich or recorded their rights to a specific number of loads or measures. Other extractive industries receive only an occasional reference, lead-mining in Derbyshire, iron at Corby and Gretton and the Forest of Dean, or rare mention of quarrying and work with stone.[2] Forests were legally a Norman innovation, and with one great exception do not appear to have been a prime object of inquiry. The exception is to be found in the New Forest itself, which was separately surveyed within the Hampshire folios.[3] Incidental notices appear in places such as Gravelinges in Wiltshire, Wimborne in Dorset, Windsor in Berkshire, and Wychwood in Oxfordshire.[4] References to parks and to hunting practices, the setting up of deer-hedges and *stabilitiones* (places for stalling the deer), serve to remind us of the importance of hunting in the social life of the day. Vineyards, very much the innovations of the new Norman lords, normally measured in arpents, were well scattered over southern England though only in one instance, that of Rayleigh in Essex, is there specific reference to yield that might be expected from such a possession: we are told that Swein, the lord of Rayleigh, might expect a return of twenty modios in a good season.[5] The assessment of waste, so often recorded in Domesday Book, is a matter of some complexity. Some estates described as waste nevertheless were held to possess value. Close on 1,000 of the 1,300 or so places said to be waste occur in Lincolnshire and the shires that lay further north, a clear indication of the devastation caused by the 'harrying of the North' (1069–70) and later political disturbance.[6] Other land is described as waste because of the destruction by the king's army, or because of the king's forest, or because of the encroachment of the sea; and the term 'waste' is clearly often applied not to deserted land, to waste land in the modern sense, but to land which for one reason or another had ceased to be profitable to the lord.

There remain two general institutions that receive substantial notice in Domesday Book and which demand notice in any description of its contents: the churches and the towns. The custom of the Domesday surveyors varied greatly in relation to the churches.[7] In Suffolk and in Huntingdonshire and to a considerable extent in Norfolk they are meticulous in their record of village churches. It has been shown that a high percentage of named places in these shires were stated to possess a church (some 345 out of 369 in Suffolk, which was also rich in its references to the parson's glebe lands, and 53 out of 83 in Huntingdonshire).[8] Norfolk was rather different. A large number of churches were mentioned (217, or 30 per cent of the named places) but some were inserted almost as an afterthought as an interlinear addition and there is a long section, from LDB 119v to 131, with no reference to a church at all.[9] Kent had many more churches, as we know from other contemporary sources, than are referred to in Domesday Book. Elsewhere there are large tracts of country with only scanty and spasmodic references to priests or to churches, though it is fair to assume that mention of a church implied the presence of a resident priest. Of those that are mentioned some are well endowed and others are poor. Their arable holdings represent, of course, only part of their endowment but variation in the glebe lands was great, ranging from several hides in exceptional cases to only a few acres.[10] The Domesday surveyors seem to have looked at them primarily as sources of income and

[1] Tait, *Domesday Survey of Cheshire*, 39 ff., gives a good introduction to the salt industry of Cheshire: GDB 268. At Droitwich the sheriff was rendering £65 and two measures of salt for the farm, but in 1066 the king and the earl had received £76, £52 to the king and £24 to the earl.

[2] Welldon Finn, *Domesday Book: a Guide*, 59.

[3] GDB 37v, 51, 51v: nine holdings, including those of Ranulf Flambard and of 'Hugo and Odo and many others', are surveyed 'circa Novam Forestam et intra ipsam'.

[4] GDB 74, the royal foresters held 1½ hides in the forest of Gravelinges; 78v, Horton Abbey held in the forest of Wimborne; 56v, the forest of Windsor; 154v, Rainald paid £10 a year to the king for all appertaining to the forest in 'Scotone', 'Stauuorde', 'Wodestock', 'Corneberie', and 'Hucheuuode' in Oxon.

[5] LDB 43v.

[6] Darby and Maxwell (eds.), *Geography of Northern England*, 445, 448; W. E. Kapelle, *The Norman Conquest of the North* (London, 1979), 60–74, reinforces traditional views concerning the severity of the Norman impact.

[7] Lennard, *Rural England*, 288–338, notably 291–3.

[8] H. C. Darby, *The Domesday Geography of Eastern England* (3rd edn., Cambridge, 1971), 190–2 (Suffolk), 346 (Hunts.).

[9] Lennard, *Rural England*, 293; Darby, *Geography of Eastern England*, 138–9.

[10] Lennard, *Rural England*, 306–17, gives examples of churches owning as much as 5 hides (Shrivenham in Wilts.: GDB 57v).

revenue, rather like the mill. Fat livings tended to be in the hands of absentees or pluralists, sometimes religious houses overseas; and the village priest himself was very much a member of the peasant community.[1]

Towns present a special problem, so much so that it has been seriously suggested that the original intention was not to include them in the survey.[2] There is no mention of them in the Ely terms of reference and the variation in approach to recording them is great, in marked contrast to the tight discipline imposed on the manorial entries. London and Winchester are not recorded at all, and indeed it is difficult to see how anything more than a condensed statement of the principal customs of such complex communities could have been incorporated within the Domesday Book format. Nevertheless, more than a hundred boroughs or places with burgesses were recorded, though some other obvious urban centres, such as Bristol and Tamworth (both boroughs that lay on the borders of shires), were omitted. In some respects the surveyors and the scribes showed themselves well able to cope with urban complexity. The most elaborate of the towns that were recorded were noted with their administrative subdivisions, York with its seven 'shires', Stamford with its six wards, one of which (the later Stamford Baron) lay in Northamptonshire, Cambridge with its ten wards, and Huntingdon with four quarters. Care was taken to give the laws and customs of some towns (notably those on the Welsh border, Chester, Shrewsbury, and Hereford, and some of the shire towns such as York or Norwich) in a reasonably full manner with detailed information about many characteristics. These might include the number of burgesses, the legal customs, the number of tenements, the houses destroyed or waste because of the building of castles, the names of the owners of houses, some details about the churches, the customs of the Frenchmen, and a range of miscellaneous facts from the value of the borough to the king and the earl to the nature of the renders paid: martens' pelts from Chester, horseshoes and hunting duties from Hereford, a bear and hunting dogs from Norwich.[3] Great insight into the social life of the towns is provided by Domesday Book but not on a fully systematic basis. This is true even of their major characteristics. There are four institutional features that we expect to find in a developed eleventh-century borough—rights of jurisdiction, internal tenurial complexity, a market, and a mint. We hear something of all four, though rarely in connection with any one single borough. There was no attempt at completeness: for example, mints were not always recorded. Anglo-Saxon legal evidence tells us that each borough was to have at least one mint, and numismatic evidence confirms that even as late as 1086 there was no marked tendency to consolidate minting rights in fewer boroughs, and many places struck coins though there was no mention of their minting rights in Domesday Book. When reference *was* made it is often exceedingly helpful. Some mints were very profitable. The sum of £75 was taken annually from the moneyers of Lincoln.[4] At Hereford there were seven moneyers, one of whom belonged to the bishop; and we are told of them that 'when the coinage was renewed, each of them gave 18*s*. for the dies, and within one month after the day on which they returned (from the die-cutting centre at London) each of them gave 20*s*. to the king and the bishop likewise had 20*s*. from his moneyer. When the king came to the city the moneyers made him as many pence as he wished from the king's silver.'[5] The moneyers were men of substance, enjoying the rights of jurisdiction at Hereford. In spite of the inevitable feeling that the treatment of Domesday boroughs is something of a rag-bag we are left in the end with a composite picture of developing institutions. Information about markets, dues, and tenures reminds us of the complexities. The boroughs were predominantly royal in nature, heavily dependent on the king and his officers, the earls who in favoured areas still enjoyed the right to the 'third penny' from the borough revenues, and the sheriffs.[6] They were also acquiring a corporate set of rights of their own; and the Domesday evidence bears direct witness to this immensely important phenomenon.

[1] Lennard, *Rural England*, 329.

[2] Galbraith, *Domesday Book: its Place in Administrative History*, 151–3: the absence of towns from the Ely terms of reference is interpreted as a reminder of the overwhelming importance of landowning and agrarian wealth to Domesday England.

[3] Tait, *The Medieval English Borough*, has assembled the basic material: Chester, GDB 262v; Hereford, GDB 179; Norwich, LDB 116–18.

[4] GDB 336v: Lincoln itself is said to have rendered £100 to the king in 1086 compared to £20 in 1066 with an additional £10 to the earl.

[5] GDB 179.

[6] Tait, *The Medieval English Borough*, 140–54, marks the essential contrast between the situation in 1066 and 1086, by which date most of the earl's 'third pennies' had escheated to the Crown.

The Purpose of Domesday Book

Domesday Book was, as we have already suggested, a direct product of the Norman Conquest and even more so of the Norman settlement of England. It provided the new ruling group, king, baron, and churchman alike, with information vital for them to know if government were to be carried out efficiently. Can we go further than that? There is a lot to be said for giving a simple answer to what is essentially a simple question; and Sir Frank Stenton did precisely that when he reminded us not to forget the obvious. Royal curiosity was the prime motive force behind the survey, the driving force without which the whole project would never have been initiated and certainly would never have been carried through.[1] William wanted to know. Where we may have added something positive to Stenton's comment in a later generation is in our insistence that the great barons also wanted to know. They were for the most part fully co-operative, not tax-resistant. It was in their interest so to be.

Such simplicity is praiseworthy and helpful but cannot, of course, supply the complete picture. The knowledge required in 1086 was both complex and selective and now that we accept the unity of the survey and the end-product it is all the more important to consider carefully possible motives and to sense the bearing of those motives on the various stages of construction. Domesday Book itself was the prime objective of the exercise and the by-no-means accidental result of the survey. Stenton's common-sense view of the importance of sheer royal curiosity demands deeper analysis and the posing of further and more refined questions relating to timing and nature.

Politics provides a partial answer. The threat from Scandinavia, the summons of fighting men from France, unease over succession demanded knowledge of resources. Domestic politics associated with the feudal settlement also provided a link with the wider scene. V. H. Galbraith consistently and accurately emphasized the feudal motives behind the construction of the book as well as the feudal elements within it. He broke with much received opinion by insisting that it was in many respects a feudal book, a record of the introduction of feudal law into England.[2] For decades no serious historian had dared to say that. How could Domesday Book be called feudal when it said virtually nothing of feudal service, of the military service paid by tenant to lord, the heart of the complex of rights and duties that we call feudal? Galbraith's case was nevertheless strong and in line with the views held by an earlier generation of historians and antiquarians. Martin Wright, for example, the eighteenth-century legal historian, in his introduction to what became a standard and influential work on the laws of tenure, insisted that William's object in creating Domesday Book was to discover 'the quality of every man's fee and to fix his homage'.[3] The basic arrangement of the book tells us much of a feudal purpose. Administrators had to rely on existing structures and the folios are naturally assembled into the units which constitute the primary territorial divisions of the realm into shires; but within each and every shire the information is put together according to feudal divisions, that is to say according to the fiefs or honours held from the king by the tenants-in-chief. Within the fiefs again one can recognize clearly in many shires a further territorial grouping of information according to the hundred or wapentake, arranged in systematic order. From the user's point of view there is one clear line that can be drawn from Domesday Book: he can find out easily and quickly who held what in each shire and *a fortiori* can relatively easily reconstruct the great fiefs into which England had been apportioned. Domesday Book provides a splendid example of the success of the Norman dynamic at work, vitally concerned with land and vassals. The knight service that was due from the tenements so faithfully recorded was truly incidental. It seems perfectly just therefore to say that the analysis of feudal wealth embodied in Domesday Book was an important element that provides a clue to the motives behind its construction.

Is it possible to go further helpfully? Some scholars, notably D. C. Douglas, have done so along a

[1] Stenton, *Anglo-Saxon England*, 657.

[2] Galbraith, *Making of Domesday Book*, 160: 'the formal written record of the introduction of feudal tenure, and therefore of feudal law into England.'

[3] M. Wright, *An Introduction to the Law of Tenures* (London, 1729), 56–7, associating the survey with 'consent to tenures and the oath at Salisbury and arguing that no better reason could be assigned why it should be taken at this time or indeed why it should be taken at all'.

somewhat neglected track by emphasizing the legal attributes of Domesday Book.[1] The commissioners on their circuits were great men, exercising some of the legal authority associated in a later age with royal justices on eyre. They held pleas, they recorded disputes over the ownership of land in terse legal language, heard evidence relating to title, referred some matters to the royal court, and even, on occasion, when they had time and the cause was relatively clear-cut, settled disputes themselves. The accounts of Yorkshire, Lincolnshire, and Huntingdonshire list the legal claims (*clamores*) which came before the commissioners as they made their inquiries. In Huntingdonshire alone, by no means a large or notoriously litigious shire, they listened to plaints concerning the great Church of St Mary in the borough, and much land that concerned the Abbey of Ramsey, the former holdings of King Edward, Earl Harold, Earl Tostig, Earl Waltheof, sheriffs past and present, the church of Peterborough, and the Bishopric of Lincoln.[2] The great men of the shire or their representatives caught the ear of the commissioners and had their claims recorded. Evidence of similar activities elsewhere, notably in the South-West, indicates that the judicial attributes of the so-called survey were formidable. Thirty-one folios of the Liber Exoniensis are taken up with items referred to as *terrae occupatae*, more than 400 instances in all of grievances over the occupation of land analogous to the *clamores* of the northern shires.[3] At the end of the accounts in the three eastern shires in Little Domesday appear similar lists of *invasiones*, or illegal occupation of estates.[4] Odd references throughout the whole of Domesday Book tell of the active concern shown by the commissioners in all circuits to determine the legal title to land, to hear testimony concerning charters, or the 'writ and seal of the king', to hear what the jurors had to say. Sometimes the jurors themselves confessed their ignorance—or stated that they did not know how to tell the truth of it. The rare examples of direct decision illustrate the potential authority they held. In Buckland in Devonshire and in some Lincolnshire estates the dispute was such that the commissioners referred the matter to the royal court.[5] They dispossessed the Abbey of Tavistock of the manor of Warrington because the gift had been made after 1066 by Gytha, the widow of Earl Godwine (and the mother of King Harold), without the permission of King William.[6] The Domesday survey in its legal dimension needs to be read in proper sequence from William's immediate insistence from the earliest days of his reign that all land belonged ultimately to the king through the series of great pleas over land which characterized the middle years of his reign. There is a neat and absolute link between the feudal settlement and legal stability. Men wished to know where they were over rights to land. To go further and to read judicial concern as the prime motive behind the making of Domesday Book would, however, be to confuse central and important peripheral interests. The commissioners for the most part had neither time nor, one might guess, inclination to realize the full potential of their legal powers.

Finally we come to what used to be taken automatically as the main theme in any discussion of the motives that led to the making of Domesday Book, and that is the financial element. Domesday Book became a Winchester record, attached to the Treasury and then to the Exchequer, and wherever you look in it you find money and concern over finance. How much to tax, how many hides, what assessment, how much is the manor worth now, when the new lords took over in 1066, how much more can be got out of it? No wonder that our greatest legal historian, F. W. Maitland, was so taken with this aspect that he described Domesday Book as 'a geld-book', no more, no less.[7] Even Homer nods, and the one sure conclusion to come from modern investigation is that this is not so. Domesday Book would drive the poor tax-collector to despair. For the taxman on the ground it was useless. This is not to say, of course, that the principal finance officers at Winchester or the royal court would not

[1] D. C. Douglas, 'Odo, Lanfranc, and the Domesday Survey', *Historical Essays in Honour of James Tait*, eds. J. G. Edwards, V. H. Galbraith, and E. F. Jacob (Manchester, 1933), 47–57, and 'The Domesday Survey', *History*, 21 (1937), 249–57.

[2] *VCH Huntingdonshire*, i (1926), 345–55: F. M. Stenton in his introduction to the section on Domesday Book commented (p. 315) that the inquest fulfilled some of the functions of a judicial institution.

[3] Welldon Finn, *Liber Exoniensis*, 55–96, refers to the *terrae occupatae* as 'a record of illegalities, for to the Domesday scribe *occupare* always conveys a suggestion of malpractice' (p. 55).

[4] R. Welldon Finn, *Domesday Studies: the Eastern Counties* (London, 1967), 42–5.

[5] GDB 58v: 'unde judicium non dixerunt sed ante regem ut judicet dimiserunt'. The Lincs. estates are referred to in GDB 377v: 'dimittunt in iudicio regis'.

[6] GDB 101; R. Welldon Finn, *Liber Exoniensis*, 60, with reference to Exon 178v where it is stated that the English testified that Werrington did not belong to the abbey at Tavistock on the day on which King Edward was alive and dead.

[7] F. W. Maitland, *Domesday Book and Beyond* (Cambridge, 1897; repr. London, 1960), 27–8.

be glad of it. Domesday Book provided as accurate and authoritative an account as was possible of landed wealth, an immediate work of reference for all royal officers, sheriffs, royal reeves, and men of business looking after the affairs of tenants-in-chief, lay and ecclesiastical; and further it gave an immediate source to check on their own work. It also gave a record of the answerability of estates to the geld, still useful in the later twelfth century. Quite as important to the king and to all landowners in the country was the statement of annual values, sometimes given at three separate points, bearing a degree of correlation to the intrinsic agrarian or pastoral wealth of many estates. This could be useful and was indeed used for calculating feudal incidents, notably reliefs, and for estimating returns from vacant bishoprics. There was also a strong element of fiscal reassessment about the whole enterprise, and in this respect it has been pointed out that the use of ploughlands as a vehicle of assessment may have amounted in parts of the country at least to a recalculation of the rateable units on which taxation was levied.[1] A further element, sometimes neglected in modern investigation but clear enough to all financial administrators in the eleventh and twelfth centuries, should also be taken into account. Domesday Book gives a superb reminder of the great simplification that was going on behind the scenes in early Norman England and which was to make the creation of an efficient Exchequer possible. The organization of multiple estates and the resulting greater financial coherence in the localities needed some such authoritative statement as Domesday Book which facilitated the future enterprise of the new Norman masters bent on exploiting their legal rights on their new estates.[2]

It is reasonable, therefore, to conclude that a mixture of political, feudal, judicial, and financial motives prompted the creation of Domesday Book and that it was royal curiosity and the royal will, coinciding happily with the interests of the tenants-in-chief, that made the enterprise practicable. The energy released in preparing for the survey and in carrying the project through to a successful conclusion accelerated in turn the production of a new bureaucratic framework for effective written administration both at the centre and in the localities. Domesday Book legitimized new agglomerations of territory brought about by the Norman settlement. Multiple estates, composite estates, collections of sokelands and berewicks linked with a manorial headquarters were given permanent institutional life by the strong executive government and firm administrative structures of the Anglo-Norman kings. The Exchequer of Henry I could move more resolutely with the authority of Domesday Book attached to it. We are right to concentrate on the big national concepts when we reflect on the motives that underlay the production of Domesday Book. Its making and purpose need to be thought of as matters for central government. We should not, however, ignore the elements of consolidation and ultimate relative efficiency involved deep in the heart of landed society by the process of clarification of tenure which reached a significantly crucial point in 1086. Domesday Book helped, by its prestige as a permanent record, to freeze the composite, multiple estates of 30 hides, 20 hides, $7\frac{1}{2}$ hides into their financial units. Reeves and stewards and financial officers flourished mightily; and ultimately, as always, the peasants paid up. Administrative and financial efficiency are not always welcome at base level: but at worst they offered a legal statement of what estates were worth and what could be extracted from them, a theoretical safeguard against gross exploitation. There is much to be said for the view that respect for written evidence gives hope for protection against tyranny; and Galbraith was surely right when he interpreted the Domesday inquest as a first great step 'towards a *jus scriptum* and a bureaucratic society which did its business on a documentary basis'.[3]

The Value of Domesday Book

Domesday statistics, as has been well said by Welldon Finn, one of the most patient of modern investigators, do indeed 'formidably display their frequent eccentricities'.[4] Even so, critically handled,

[1] Harvey, 'Domesday Book and Anglo-Norman Governance', 186–9.

[2] D. Hooke, 'Pre-Conquest Estates in the West Midlands: Preliminary Thoughts', *Jnl of Hist. Geography*, 8 (1982), 227–44, indicates elements of continuous development in the emergence of these coherent fiscal units back into the Anglo-Saxon past.

[3] Galbraith, *Making of Domesday Book*, 151.

[4] R. Welldon Finn, *The Norman Conquest and its Effect on the Economy* (London, 1971), 18.

they can provide more material for a proper understanding of the workings of English society than is available for any other European community until the advanced Italian cities began to keep and preserve comprehensive records in the fourteenth century. Finn himself was able to make advance, by a systematic study of variation in Domesday values, 1066 compared with 1086, to our understanding of the progress of the Norman armies in the first flush of conquest and, much more significantly, of the impact of Norman settlement and mastery on the whole economy.[1] Yet we must not expect too much. The first important lesson to be learned in dealing with Domesday evidence is not to force the material into moulds for which it is ill equipped. Domesday Book, for example, was not a census. Elaborate attempts have been made to show that the population of England in 1086 can be worked out from the number of people mentioned in the book, but the results are bound to be approximate and tentative and must be recognized as such.[2] There are too many uncertainties, omissions, variations in procedure, and assumptions, especially over the multipliers needed to transform the number of recorded population into an acceptable figure for the total population. Even on matters concerning the legal and social status of the inhabitants of the kingdom Domesday evidence has to be handled with care. The very success of the survey is enough to warn us of the degree of standardization involved in the surveying techniques. We can tease some social certainties out of the method itself. The peasantry is normally described under five headings: *villani* (rendered 'villans' to distinguish them from the later medieval villeins), bordars or cottars, slaves, freemen, and sokemen. The order, as laid down in the Ely terms of reference, is in itself significant. The first three groups represent the dependent manorial peasantry whose financial obligations to the geld would be paid for them. Freemen and sokemen were a freer and more responsible element in the community who would pay their tax directly.[3] The raw numbers, as recorded in Domesday Book, for all their imperfections, betray some aspects of truth about the social structure. There were about 200,000 dependent peasants (108,000 or so villans, over 82,000 bordars, nearly 7,000 cottars), some 12,000 freemen, and 23,000 sokemen. All these men were free in a strict legal sense, though their degree of social dependence could make a mockery of such a status. Against them were some 25,000 or so recorded as slaves and over 600 *ancillae* or female slaves.[4] It is certain that there were many more slaves than those who were recorded, but the rough proportion of free peasant to unfree remains a fact of historical value. Even more significant is the geographical distribution of the various groups. The heavy preponderance of the proportion of freer peasants in parts of the Danelaw, notably Lincolnshire, Leicestershire, and East Anglia, remains a phenomenon that demands full explanation. In similar fashion the distribution of the recorded slave population, many male, few female, exhibits peculiarities that the social historian has to take into account: a tendency to heavy grouping on the larger manors and on some ecclesiastical estates, and the marked drop apparent, for example, in the Essex folios between 1066 and 1086, in which function as ploughmen seemed to be ousting the older crude division into free and unfree as a mark of status.[5] In some areas the intrusion of specialist terms such as *radknight* or *radman* or *dreng* hints at complexities that would otherwise escape us, and varying convention in including priests or millers or smiths *eo nomine* adds further spice to the terminological brew. In the last resort the precious detailed information about peasant status, valuable though it is, must be read as a guide to understanding, not as an absolute and complete set of figures such as one would be entitled to expect from a modern social survey. On some matters, however, we can be more positive and unqualified. Allowing for occasional blunders and omissions we can still say that Domesday Book provides an astonishingly complete picture of the landholding situation in the top ranks of society. The names of all the tenants-in-chief are given in its pages and an authoritative assessment made of their wealth and of the distribution of their lands. The result is the record of a social revolution of the first order. The king retained close on a seventh of all the landed wealth of England in his own hands. The Church, substantially under new Norman

[1] Welldon Finn, *The Norman Conquest*, 19–23, for a discussion of the movements of the Norman army in the months after Hastings. There is much of permanent value in the careful collection of evidence assembled elsewhere in the book.

[2] Darby, *Domesday England*, 87–91: there is an acute comment on the distribution of population, pp. 92–4.

[3] Maitland, *Domesday Book and Beyond*, 48–9 (24–5 in the 1897 edition), clarified this distinction.

[4] Ellis, *General Introduction*, ii (1833), 511–14.

[5] Maitland, *Domesday Book and Beyond*, 24–6, 60–1 (35–6 in the 1897 edition).

leadership as bishops and abbots were replaced in King William's reign, held more than a quarter. There were some 1,400 tenants-in-chief all told, lay and ecclesiastical, and of these only about eighty or so, the overwhelming majority of whom were new men—Frenchmen, Bretons, and above all Normans—enjoyed effective wealth, land which brought them £100 a year or more, the sum later considered desirable in a man of baronial rank. Within that group there was a still smaller group again, ten or twelve great magnates who between them held a quarter of the landed wealth of the whole kingdom.[1] These men were tremendously wealthy on a European scale. Odo, Bishop of Bayeux and Earl of Kent, half-brother of the Conqueror, was a tenant-in-chief in no fewer than twenty-two counties at the time of his imprisonment in 1082 and the value of his holdings has been estimated to be over £3,000 per annum, derived from 439 manors. The Domesday surveyors enter his estates under a normal rubric (in spite of his imprisonment) in seventeen of the shires, though elsewhere his holdings, still identified as Odo's lands, are listed under the name of the king or of the *de facto* tenant.[2] His brother, Robert de Mortain, was not so wealthy but still had land worth over £2,000 per annum in twenty counties, more than 1,000 manors in all.[3] The distribution of the lands of these two half-brothers to the king has special interest. Whereas Odo's wealth and possessions were concentrated for the most part heavily in the East, notably in Kent, Robert's lay elsewhere: in the western shires, Cornwall (where he had virtually an earl's authority), Devon, Somerset, and Dorset; north-west of London around his castle at Berkhamsted in Hertfordshire and Buckinghamshire; in Sussex; and in Yorkshire. Analysis of the fiefs of other great tenants suggests a strong element of political and military strategy in the distribution of lands. Indeed if we are intent on isolating the special value of Domesday Book we must recognize that the two most clear-cut conclusions that can be drawn from its statistics both treat of the position of the tenants-in-chief. Concentration of wealth is the first of these conclusions, a concentration which helps to explain the dynamic elements in the Norman settlement, the upsurge in the building of castles, cathedrals, abbeys, and lesser churches that followed the Norman triumphs. The second is the shape of the fiefs, which also gives cause to ponder. Most of the great men, the barons, held estates in many shires, though often with one or two central concentrations that reflect military or governmental responsibility in specific areas. Without Domesday Book we would know from narrative sources and ancillary evidence alone that men of the stamp of Hugh Lupus at Chester, Roger de Montgomery at Shrewsbury, or (to the time of his death in 1071) William fitzOsbern at Hereford were the great men of the borderlands with Wales but we might easily miss the subtlety of the arrangements which provided them also with land and wealth elsewhere in England. Geoffrey de Coutances and Richard fitzGilbert would be known to us as prominent figures at court and in the administration but we would miss (if it were not for the Domesday record) the significance of their special interests, Geoffrey's in Somerset and Gloucestershire with the defence of the Severn estuary in mind, Richard's in Surrey, Essex, and Suffolk. The strategic importance of Sussex both in the initial stages of the Conquest and as a constant route for supply and reinforcement would be evident on common-sense grounds, but Domesday evidence enables us to grasp the importance of the powerful new lordships established in the Rapes of Sussex by Robert de Mortain at Pevensey, William de Warenne at Lewes, Robert de Eu at Hastings, Roger de Montgomery at Arundel with Chichester, and William de Braose at Bramber.[4] The relative completeness of the Domesday record helps us also to recognize still the importance of the scattered nature of the holdings within the great fiefs, not anti-baronial in any sense but the fruit of the pace of the settlement and of the co-operative nature of the settlement; and we recognize too the importance for the future of English institutions of the balance of forces built up in nearly all the shires of England at the county courts.[5] Changes occurred, radical changes. The fitzOsbern family fell into disgrace after the rebellion of William

[1] Ellis, *General Introduction*, ii (1833), 511; Corbett, 'Development of the Duchy of Normandy', 505–13.

[2] Corbett, ibid. 508, estimates that the fiefs of the two half-brothers of the Conqueror, Odo and Robert, were between them worth some £5,050 per annum; also D. Bates, 'Odo of Bayeux', unpublished thesis (Exeter University, 1970).

[3] I. Soulsby, 'The Fiefs in England of the Counts of Mortain, 1066–1106', unpublished thesis (University College, Cardiff, 1973).

[4] J. F. A. Mason, *William the First and the Sussex Rapes* (Historical Association, London, 1966).

[5] Lennard, *Rural England*, 34–5, notes that dispersed estates helped to whittle down the diversities of manorial custom. Balance within the shires and breadth of interests on the part of the great men and their officers contributed significantly to the unification of the country.

fitzOsbern's son and successor in 1076. Odo of Bayeux was imprisoned, as we have seen, in 1082. But Domesday Book, in its hesitations in handling the fiefs of men such as Odo or fitzOsbern or Roger de Poitou, sometimes helped to perpetuate the shape and traditions of the great fiefs of the initial settlement.[1] Better knowledge in detail of the inner structure of those fiefs is yielding a clearer picture of the way in which the new aristocracy was planted in England and its potential realized, some of the subtenants siring families that were to rise to baronial rank themselves, others set on the path that was going to produce a characteristic twelfth-century country gentry pattern, anticipating the later influence and power of the knights of the shire. The Anglo-Saxon ruling groups had by 1086 disappeared from positions of authority. Domesday Book is the prime and supreme source for the study of the new aristocracy.

At other levels also Domesday Book provides vital information for understanding English society. Ecclesiastical tenants-in-chief, bishops and abbots for the most part, were dealt with as thoroughly as the lay magnates, and their interest in the legality of their tenure, as representatives of undying corporations, probably did more than anything else to perpetuate the myth as well as the reality of Domesday Book. We have already discussed the insights given to the urban situation. Domesday Book brings home the immediacy of the position when it shows how initially destruction of town houses to make room for the new castles could lead to elements of local decline and oppression. Castles are mentioned comparatively rarely outside the towns but from time to time useful reference is given. Swein, sometime sheriff of Essex, the son of Robert fitzWimarc, for example, raised his great mound and motte at Rayleigh and we hear of his vineyard and can trace the settlement of his trusted retainers, his knights, on tenements near the castle which was to prove the nucleus of his fief.[2] Items already mentioned among the contents of the book, such as details of the livestock or mills or fisheries, yield a rich harvest to the economic historian. Mints are described only occasionally, but the information given about their workings is invaluable to the numismatist. To the topographer Domesday Book evidence is of vital importance, sometimes of especial value, as in references to forest-land and parks, and as often infuriating. Local detail that would be so helpful is lost under the mask of general description and tax return. For the place-name expert and the scholar interested in personal names the wealth of material is unique, accurately dated, and of prime importance for detailed technical investigation of onomastic forms and language development. Without Domesday Book our knowledge of eleventh-century England would be vastly poorer. With it we can approach with some confidence a better understanding of one of the most successful conquests in recorded European history.

To this point emphasis has been laid on the value of Domesday Book to the modern historian anxious to interpret English society at a moment of great crisis. There is a danger in such emphasis and in the past it has led to the charge that Domesday Book is no more than a source-book for the historian, a piece of antiquarianism on the part of the compilers, even a vast administrative mistake.[3] The fact that it has been preserved in such good condition through the centuries has curiously been held against it, as an indication of how little used it had been; but all are now agreed that its good condition is to be taken as a proof of the care devoted to it, not as an indication of neglect.[4] Men of business, royal officers, sheriffs, feudal tenants concerned for the security of their lands and rights,

[1] D. C. Douglas (ed.), *The Domesday Monachorum of Christ Church, Canterbury* (London, 1944), 27–33, for a discussion of the fief of Odo of Bayeux; *VCH Oxfordshire*, i (1939), 388: F. M. Stenton notes that the fitzOsbern lands are still recorded under a separate rubric in Oxfordshire though elsewhere they are incorporated in royal demesne or let out to other tenants-in-chief; Galbraith, *Making of Domesday Book*, 187–8: uncertainty over the status of Roger de Poitou's lands (taken into the king's hands, apparently late in 1086) is used by Galbraith as a firm pointer to the conclusion that the two volumes of Domesday Book and the Exeter Domesday were completed in the reign of William I. Roger rose to such prominence in the reign of William II that uncertainty of that nature would have been unthinkable.

[2] LDB 43v; *VCH Essex*, i (1903), 484: J. H. Round remarked in relation to the four Frenchmen who held 2 hides of Swein in Rayleigh that it was customary, in the case of a manor on which the tenant-in-chief resided, to find his under-tenants by knight-service holding small estates there.

[3] H. G. Richardson and G. O. Sayles, *Governance of Mediaeval England* (Edinburgh, 1963), 28.

[4] M. M. Condon and E. M. Hallam, 'Government Printing of the Public Records in the Eighteenth Century', *Jnl of the Soc. of Archivists*, 7 (1982–5), no. 6 (1984), 348–88, where evidence is given of the great care taken over the preservation of Domesday Book in more modern days. Before the 1740s it was kept in a record room by the Tally Court under no fewer than three locks and the jealous custodianship first of the deputy chamberlains and then of the keeper of records in the Chapter House, Westminster (p. 373). A fee of 6*s.* 8*d.* was exacted to consult it, 4*d.* a line for transcripts, and 6*d.* a sheet for stamped paper on which transcripts were made; see also E. M. Hallam, 'Annotations in Domesday Book since 1100', Special Study XVI, pp. 136–50 below.

found it expedient at a very early stage to make their own abstractions from the Domesday records, either from the book itself or from the detritus of the survey assembled in the localities, at great abbeys or administrative centres. Early twelfth-century documents, for example, relating to the lands of the monks of Christchurch in Kent and to the ecclesiastical estates of the bishopric of Worcester preserve early copies made directly and accurately from the folios of Great Domesday.[1] The Worcester evidence has a special importance because it may well have been assembled during the episcopate of Samson, Bishop of Worcester (1096–1112), who as a royal chaplain was active in the production of Domesday Book and who may even have been the principal agent in its production.[2] References in cartularies and elsewhere, culminating in the adoption of the name 'Domesday' Book, suggest an extensive use both at national and at local level. It would seem likely indeed that most large landowners would expect to have available transcripts of Domesday entries relating to their property. In the 1160s Thomas Brown, a key administrator at the Exchequer, appears to have been responsible for ordering the so-called 'Hereford Domesday' to be made, a fine transcript of the Domesday entries relating to the shire—Brown benefited at the rate of 5*d.* a day from the farm of Herefordshire—and the attempt made in the manuscript to bring the information up to date proves that Domesday Book was still a living document in the eyes of the royal administrators during the reign of Henry II.[3] Indeed, its prestige increased rather than diminished with the passage of time as the need for legal proof of tenure grew more precise and sophisticated. Surviving full-scale thirteenth-century abbreviations (the *Abbreviatio* at the Public Record Office and two late thirteenth-century copies, both curiously connected with South Wales monasteries) indicate the value placed on the record in the central Middle Ages.[4] The *Abbreviatio*, handsomely written and illuminated, is in fine condition and probably represents a fair copy made for a special occasion of what may well have been a standard abbreviated text in use at the Exchequer from the very earliest years.[5] An administration bent on creating an authoritative record, i.e. Domesday Book itself, would not spare the resources to create effective working copies. Quotations in legal records continued to proliferate. Evidence from Domesday Book, throughout the later Middle Ages and even when imperfectly understood, was regularly adduced in matters relating to royal lands, to ancient demesne, to the status of villeins on ancient demesne, to forest-land, and especially as the fourteenth century progressed to matters concerning the lands of the Church and urban rights. Disputes over monastic boroughs such as St Albans or Abingdon or over royal rights to tallage in towns were resolved in the light of the evidence of Domesday Book. Professor Galbraith, who did more than any other twentieth-century scholar to place Domesday Book in proper perspective, referred to it as 'the oldest and greatest book of precedents known to the royal bureaucracy'.[6] Zealously safeguarded in the Exchequer, increasingly authoritative as a statement of legality in tenure and exercise of rights, Domesday Book, the final and purposeful product of the inquest, stood in the eyes of lawyers and administrators as an acknowledged source of sound judgement. Seen in that light, its value to the whole sweep of English legal and constitutional history is incontestable.

[1] BL MS Cotton Vitellius C. VIII; Hearne (ed.), *Heming's Cartulary*.

[2] Galbraith, *Domesday Book: its Place in Administrative History*, 110–11.

[3] V. H. Galbraith and J. Tait (eds.), *Herefordshire Domesday circa 1160–1170*, Pipe Roll Soc., 63, ns 25 (London, 1950).

[4] PRO Misc. Books (TR), 284; the copies are to be found in BL MS Arundel 153, and in PRO Misc. Books 1.

[5] Galbraith, *Domesday Book: its Place in Administrative History*, 110–11.

[6] Ibid. 114.

SPECIAL STUDIES

I. THE GEOGRAPHY OF DOMESDAY ENGLAND

H. C. DARBY

DOMESDAY BOOK has long been regarded as a unique source of information about economic, social, and legal matters. But it is also a remarkable assemblage of geographical facts from which we can reconstruct some of the main features of the face of England in the eleventh century. Generally speaking, the entries in the book follow the same plan, and they comprise two groups of information. In the first place, there are six basic items that appear in almost every entry: place-names; hides (or carucates in the Danish districts), which were units of taxation; population and its various categories; ploughlands; plough-teams at work; annual values for 1066 and 1086, and sometimes for an intermediate date. The most revealing of these basic items for a geographer are place-names, population, and plough-teams. The second group consists of those items that appear as and when relevant, and they include wood, meadow, pasture, and a variety of other geographical features.

The first group enables us to obtain a general view of the human geography of the time. Against this background we can set the items of the second group, and so identify those local characteristics that marked the economy of this or that region.

PLACE-NAMES, POPULATION, AND PLOUGH-TEAMS

PLACE-NAMES

The basis of the geographical study of Domesday Book is the exact identification of place-names, and some 13,400 names are recorded in its folios. Not all survive as the names of modern settlements; their villages have become extinct at various times and for a variety of reasons. Some are represented today by the names of farms and houses or of topographical features such as fields, hills, and localities. Others have vanished from the ground as well as from the map, but a number of these can be approximately located. Finally, some 3 per cent of the total remain completely unidentified. An idea of the changes may be gained from the figures for Bedfordshire; here, 32 out of a total of 145 Domesday names (i.e. 22 per cent) are not names of parishes; conversely, 19 of the 133 parishes of the modern county (i.e. 14 per cent) do not appear in Domesday Book.[1]

Some changes were the result not of human but of natural causes. Along the coast of the East Riding, Domesday vills have disappeared under the sea, although the names of some of these places have been preserved on the nearby remaining land. To the south, along the Humber estuary, Tharlesthorpe was inundated and abandoned in 1393. There are no lost villages along the Lincolnshire coast, but one ploughland at Wrangle was waste in 1086 on account of the sea ('Wastum est propter fluxum maris'). Portions of some settlements in East Anglia have also vanished, but only two have completely disappeared: Newton to the north of Lowestoft, and Dunwich where the sea had already carried away ('abstulit') some of its land.

There is a further complication. A number of settlements not named in Domesday Book must certainly have existed in 1086 because their names appear in pre-Domesday, and again in post-Domesday, documents. The components of some large manors are entered as so many un-named berewicks or members or *appendicii*. Thus among the Shropshire entries we read of fourteen such berewicks at Ford and thirteen at Worthen, and we cannot tell whether these were at places named on other folios for the county. Some entries do not even give the number of such dependencies but merely refer to their existence, as in the consecutive entries for Wolstanton and Penkhall in Staffordshire.

Another difficulty arises because some Domesday names are represented in later times by two or more adjoining places distinguished from one another by such words as Great and Little or East and West; and we cannot tell whether the separation had already taken place by 1086, and whether, say, 'Fontel' in Wiltshire covered two settlements in 1086 as it certainly did by the fourteenth century—Fonthill Bishop and Fonthill Gifford.

Yet other non-Domesday names appear in sources contemporary or near-contemporary with Domesday Book. The Exeter Domesday Book itself reveals the absence of thirteen place-names from the Great Domesday Book. The Lindsey Survey (*c.*1118) adds another twelve new names. The Kentish documents closely related to the Domesday returns add many more. Or, again, chance evidence for Herefordshire provides the names of ten places described in anonymous holdings in the Domesday text for the county.

There is a further constraint on any study of settlement in 1086 in that Domesday place-names cover very different types of settlement, ranging from nucleated villages on the one hand to dispersed hamlets and isolated farmsteads on the other hand. We cannot with any certainty indicate the relative distribution of these various types in the eleventh century. The south-west peninsula, that part to the west of the river Parret, is

[1] H. C. Darby, *Domesday England* (2nd edn., Cambridge, 1979), 49–50. No further detailed references to the Domesday text are given because they appear in the above volume.

today very largely a land of dispersed settlement. It may also have been so in 1086. The Domesday place-names of Devonshire amount to 980, but the number of separate settlements has been placed at many times that total, by apportioning the details of many manors among the isolated farmsteads of modern parishes.[1]

These limitations in the nature of the evidence mean that maps of Domesday place-names enable us to gauge the intensity of settlement over the face of the country only in a very general way. Certain broad features stand out—the emptiness of much of the Fenland and of the Breckland and other areas of light infertile soils. But as we think of such areas we must remember that the lack of Domesday names in the Weald, for example, does less than justice to its scattered pioneer communities (see p. 31 below).

Our estimate may come near to the truth, however, for those areas over 800 ft. above sea-level, where the absence of names almost certainly implies an absence of inhabited sites. The Pennines and the North Yorkshire Moors stand out as empty areas, but it is interesting to note the few vills on the very margins of continuous occupation. Here on the Carboniferous Limestone of the Derbyshire Pennines were vills that took advantage of the water supply yielded by the junction of the limestone itself with the various igneous rocks intruded into it. Moreover, the district was the scene of lead-mining from metalliferous ores within the limestone. Records of lead are entered for the royal manors of Ashford, Bakewell, and Hope with their total of twenty-seven named berewicks, many above the 800-ft. contour.

In the South, the large granite mass of Dartmoor lies well over 1,000 ft., and so above the limit of continuous occupation, but there were a few western settlements, e.g. Willsworthy at about 900 ft., where 4 slaves had 1 plough-team. The eastern margin of Dartmoor, on the other hand, is broken by the valleys of the Dart, the Bovey, and the Teign, and a few settlements were to be found up to and even beyond the 1,200-ft. contour, such as Natsworthy at about 1,200 ft. with a recorded population of 5, with 2 teams, and with even a little wood and meadow. Considerable tracts of the grit and shale of Exmoor are also above 1,000 ft. Its peaty soil provided little inducement to settlement, but there were some vills in the valleys that break its surface. At about 1,200 ft. in Devonshire was Radworthy with 4 recorded people and $1\frac{1}{4}$ teams together with some wood, meadow, and pasture; and at about the same height was Lank Combe with a solitary villan who had no team yet who rendered 3*s*., but for what we are not told. Among the smaller areas over 800 ft. in the South-West are Bodmin Moor, the Quantock Hills, and the Blackdown Hills, all without recorded names. This was also true of the upland areas along the Welsh border.

Population

The inhabitants of the Domesday vills were largely engaged in agriculture, and the details of the peasantry range from freemen and sokemen to slaves, with intermediate categories of villans, bordars, cottars, and others. The total number of people thus recorded amounts to some 270,000. But these were heads of households and we must multiply the total by some factor in order to obtain the actual population. The factor frequently used is 5, which gives a total of about $1\frac{1}{2}$ million. To this we must add the clergy of abbeys and cathedrals, the tenants-in-chief, the under-tenants, and also the likely population of towns and boroughs. These might bring the total up to, say, $1\frac{3}{4}$ million. But some scholars have said that 5 is too great a factor.[2] If we adopt a lower figure, say 4, we might end up with a total of $1\frac{1}{2}$ million. Both figures are far from being precise and can only indicate an order of magnitude.

There are yet other uncertainties. Slaves amount to about 10 per cent of the recorded population, and they raise two difficulties. In the first place, very few slaves are entered for the eastern counties, and none for those of Yorkshire, Lincolnshire, Huntingdonshire, and 'Roteland'. But a summary in the Inquisitio Eliensis records the presence of slaves on a few holdings of the Abbot of Ely in Huntingdonshire, and thus raises the possibility of slaves on the Huntingdonshire fiefs. The suspicion is strengthened by the fact that the 24 slaves recorded for Nottinghamshire are restricted to 3 of its 30 or so fiefs, and that of the 20 slaves recorded for Derbyshire, 13 are entered for a single fief out of 17 or so. Can we be sure that there were no slaves elsewhere, even in Lincolnshire and Yorkshire? The other difficulty about the record for slaves springs from the fact that they may have been entered as individuals, not as heads of households, but we must hasten to add that the general pattern of the distribution would not be greatly affected.[3] In any case Domesday Book shows us that slavery was disappearing. There is only one reference to trade in men (at Lewes in Sussex), and a number of entries record a reduction in slaves between 1066 and 1086. One entry for Hailes in Gloucestershire refers specifically to the freeing of slaves. Not included in the preceding calculations were female slaves. They sometimes appear in combined entries such as 'inter servos et ancillas', and most of them are recorded in the folios for Gloucestershire, Herefordshire, Worcestershire, and Shropshire.

There are also other references to women, sometimes as landholders, or as dairymaids, female cottars, nuns, and widows. They sometimes break the repetitive uniformity of entry after entry in curious and unexpected ways. At Oakley in Buckinghamshire in the time of King Edward, Godric the Sheriff had given Alwid the maid half a hide, to hold as long as he was sheriff, on condition that she taught his daughter embroidery. And at Barfreston in Kent there was one poor woman ('una paupercula mulier') who rendered $3\frac{1}{2}$*d.* annually, and who has thus gained immortality.

[1] W. G. Hoskins, *Provincial England* (London, 1963), 15–52.

[2] J. C. Russell, *British Medieval Population* (Albuquerque, 1948), 52; J. Krause, 'The Medieval Household: Large or Small?', *EconHR* 2nd ser., 9 (1956–7), 420–32.

[3] P. Vinogradoff, *English Society in the Eleventh Century* (Oxford, 1908), 463–4; F. W. Maitland, *Domesday Book and Beyond* (Cambridge, 1897), 17, 34.

Included in the total recorded population of 270,000 is a variety of miscellaneous people described mainly in terms of their occupation. But can we believe that there were only 92 fishermen or 64 smiths or 6 millers or a solitary carpenter in the whole realm? We can only suppose that these were so entered by chance, and that their respective fellow workers are included in one of the general categories, e.g. that of villans.

Whatever the multiplier used to convert recorded into actual population, the result enables comparison to be made between one district and another. The way in which the information may be plotted, village by village, can be seen from the example of Cambridgeshire. There was a marked contrast between the north and the south of the county. The north was largely undrained fen with no villages except on the islands in the marsh, and it stood in distinct contrast to the well-occupied upland to the south (Fig. 1).

Plough-Teams

However many the complications affecting any estimate of population, it is clear that the majority of the population worked with their plough-teams in the arable fields. From hints in late Anglo-Saxon documents we may suppose that some of this arable was arranged in open-field strips. There is, however, only one Domesday entry that seems to refer to scattered strips—that for Garsington in Oxfordshire. For possible variations in field arrangements in the eleventh century, we can only speculate from later evidence. But although Domesday Book gives us no information about these matters, it does enable us, in a broad way, to perceive the relative distribution of arable.

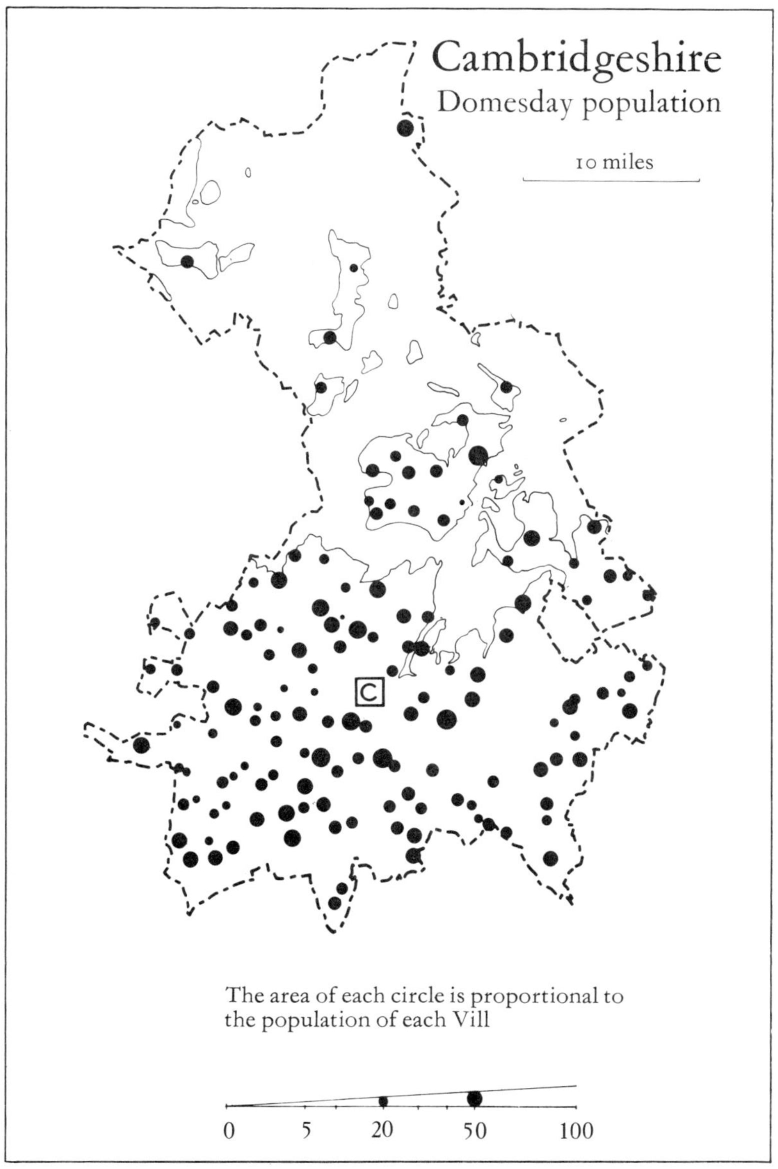

Fig. 1

C indicates the Domesday borough of Cambridge. The outlines of the upland and of the islands are shown.

Entry after entry states (*a*) the amount of land for which there were teams (*terra carucis*); and (*b*) the number of teams (*carucae*) actually at work. The first statement sounds very straightforward, and may well be so for some counties, but it has provoked considerable discussion. The formula varies in detail and is absent from some counties; the number of teams sometimes exceeds that of ploughlands; and for yet other counties (e.g. Lincoln and Nottingham) the figures are such as to suggest that they are artificial or conventional and that they may refer to some earlier and obsolete assessment. We are therefore thrown back on the second statement, from which, it is reasonable to suppose, we are told of land that was in cultivation. Although the teams at work may have varied in size, a comparison of different entries suggests that, for the purpose of computation, eight oxen made a Domesday team. It is true that this view has been challenged for the South-West, but the balance of evidence seems in favour of a standard eight-oxen team.[1] An example of the way in which this information can be plotted is provided by Hertfordshire, where there was a contrast between the north-east and the south-west. The latter had fewer settlements and fewer plough-teams because it was fairly heavily wooded at the time of the survey (Fig. 2).

The total number of plough-teams in Domesday England amounted to just over 81,000. A number of attempts have been made to estimate what acreage this implies, and have come to the conclusion that the amount of arable in 1086 was not so very different from that in the closing years of the nineteenth century.[2] Such calculations must be accepted only with caution. Whether or not the arable of 1086 was near in extent to that of 1900, its distribution was very different. By 1900 or so the land available for cultivation had been greatly reduced by the spread of towns and industry; moreover, the arable of this later period included large areas of rotation grass. Furthermore, it lay very largely in districts where great enterprises of improvement had taken place since 1600 as a result of the draining of marshes and the reclamation of light soils. But, however hypothetical the estimates, they open up an interesting vista of speculation, and leave us in no doubt that the extent of arable of 1086 was very considerable.

When the distributions of population and plough-teams are compared over the country as a whole, a number of broad features emerge. On Figs. 3 and 4 the

[1] H. G. Richardson, 'The Medieval Ploughteam', *History*, 26 (1942), 287–96; R. Lennard, 'Domesday Plough-Teams: the South-Western Evidence', *EHR* 60 (1945), 217–33; H. P. R. Finberg, 'The Domesday Plough-Team', *EHR* 66 (1951), 67–71; R. Lennard, 'The Composition of the Domesday *Caruca*', *EHR* 81 (1966), 770–5.

[2] Maitland, *Domesday Book and Beyond*, 435; R. Lennard, *Rural England 1086–1135* (Oxford, 1959), 393; J. Z. Titow, *English Rural Society, 1200–1350* (London, 1969), 71–2.

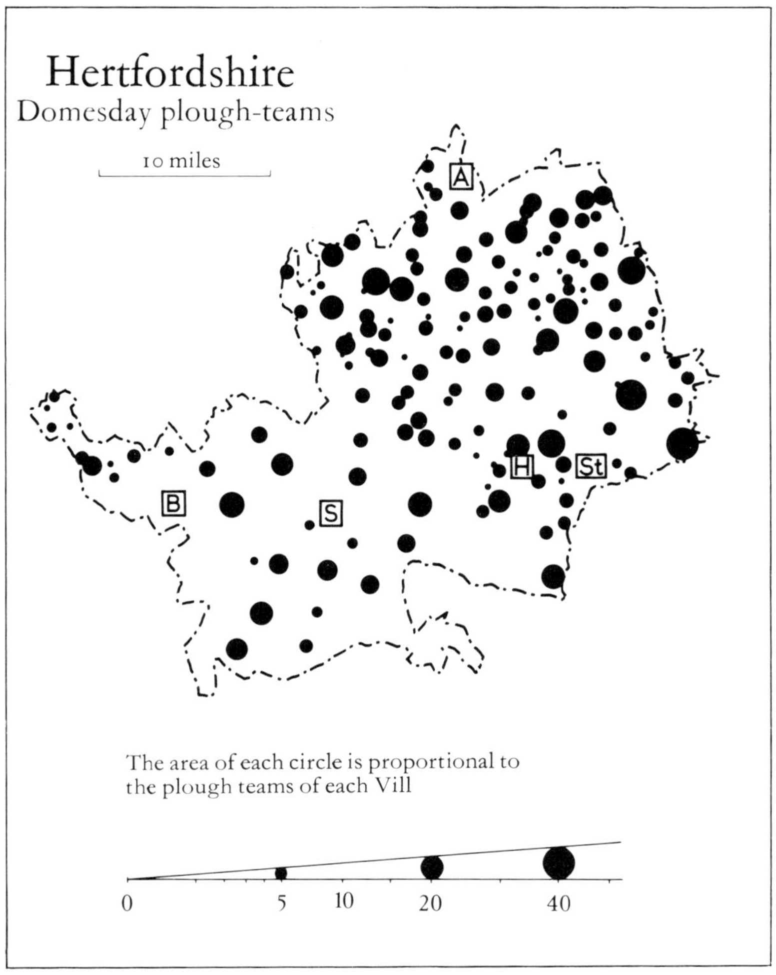

FIG. 2

Domesday boroughs are indicated by initials: A, Ashwell; B, Berkhamsted; H, Hertford; S, St Albans; St, Stanstead Abbots.

information has been calculated in densities per square mile. Both distributions show a general contrast between the North and West, where population was often sparse and teams relatively few, as compared with the high densities in parts of the South and East. This is not surprising, in view of the inhospitable uplands of parts of the North and West together with effects of raiding and of the havoc wrought by the harrying of 1069–70 (see p. 33 below). Even in the more prosperous South-East, low figures for population and teams were also to

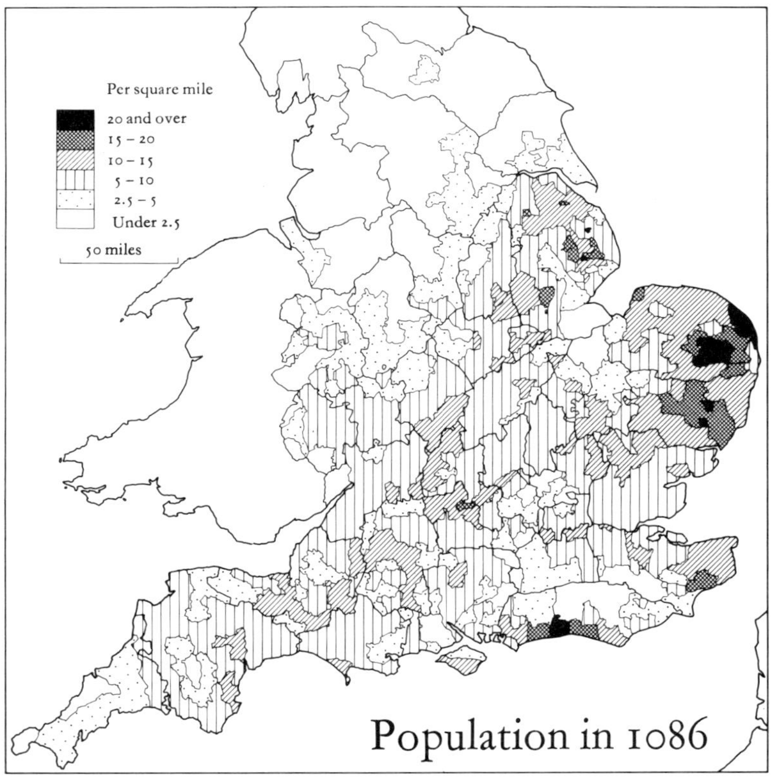

FIG. 3

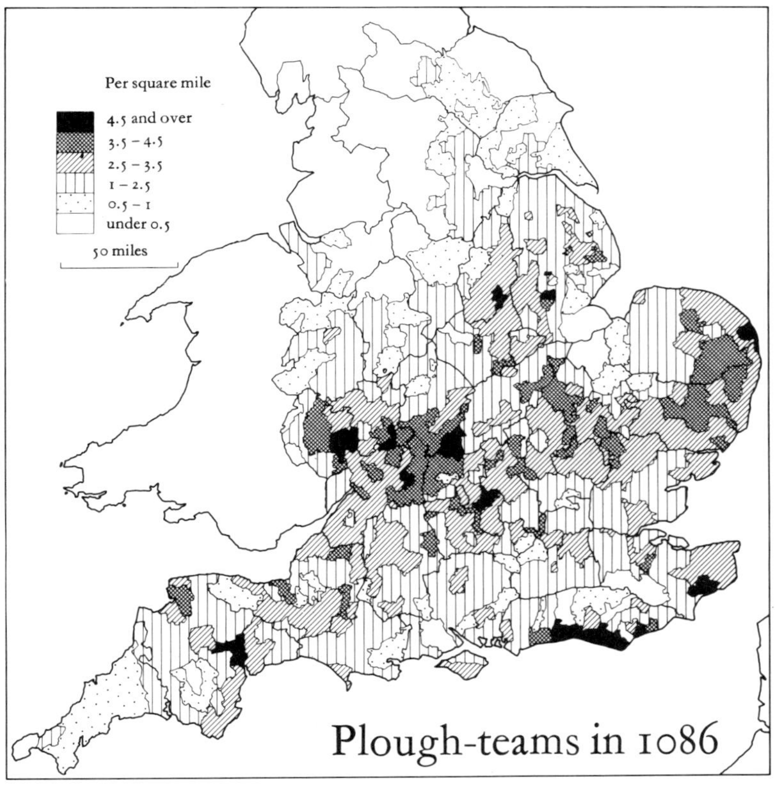

FIG. 4

be found in many areas: the Fenland and the Somerset marshes; the light soils of Breckland; the Dorset heathlands and the infertile sands of Surrey and neighbouring counties; the Weald; and such barren areas as Charnwood Forest in Leicestershire and Sherwood Forest in Nottinghamshire; and also in remote and rocky Cornwall.

There is, however, one striking fact about the relation between population and teams that may come as a surprise. While the number of recorded people per team for Domesday England as a whole is almost exactly 3.3, there are marked regional differences in this ratio. At one extreme, holdings in Norfolk and Lincolnshire (especially in Lindsey) were small, that is the number of men per team was as high as 5 and over; so it was in Suffolk.[1] At the other extreme, holdings in Gloucestershire, Herefordshire, and Worcestershire were large, that is there were under 2 men per team (Fig. 5). Could Lincolnshire and Norfolk have been over-populated so that many of their inhabitants (even if they were freemen or sokemen) were poor owing to the small size of their holdings? Were their resources barely adequate for subsistence? Or were they helping to maintain themselves by other activities such as sheep farming? And what of the fairly large numbers of teams in other counties? Were they dependent, or not, upon activities other than tillage for a livelihood? On these, as on so many other matters, Domesday Book does not enlighten us.

Reginald Lennard encountered the problem in a different way.[2] He was concerned not with broad geographical generalizations but with the relative economic position of villans, sokemen, bordars, and cottars as measured by 'the number of ploughing oxen that each

[1] F. M. Stenton, *Anglo-Saxon England* (Oxford, 1943), 510.

[2] R. Lennard, 'The Economic Position of the Domesday *villani*', *Economic Jnl* 56 (1946), 244–64; 'The Economic Position of the Domesday Sokemen', *Economic Jnl* 57 (1947), 179–95; 'The Economic Position of the Bordars and Cottars of Domesday Book', *Economic Jnl* 61 (1951), 342–71, and *Rural England*, 356.

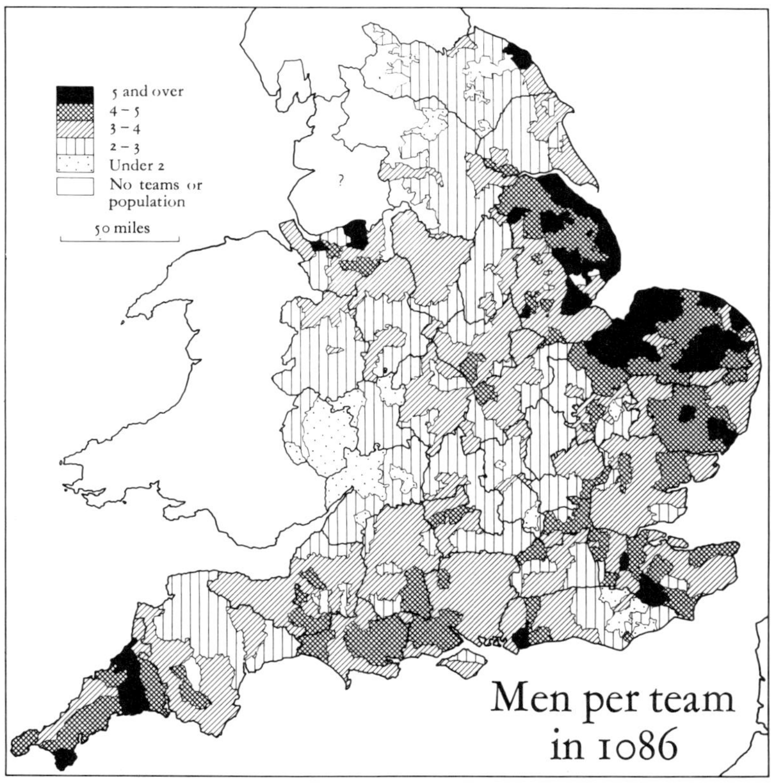

Fig. 5

man possessed'. His evidence points to the conclusion that in each category there was 'a remarkable regional difference' between the very small holdings in the counties on the east coast south of the Humber and the especially large holdings in Herefordshire, Gloucestershire, and Worcestershire. Thus for different categories of peasantry as well as for the total population, differences in the size of holdings were a marked feature of the agrarian geography of Domesday England.

REGIONAL ECONOMIES

Generally speaking, arable formed the basic element in the land utilization of the country as a whole; but there were other activities that gave a distinctive character to some areas. The Domesday entries for these reveal local economies associated with meadow, pasture, woodland, vineyards, fisheries, and water-mills. In addition, there was the special character of land that had been placed in the king's 'forest', or that had been devastated. Although industry was not important in the eleventh century, we might have expected to hear more of it than we do. There are, it is true, a few references to lead-working in the Peak District, and to iron-working and quarrying in other places, but only for the salt industry are we told much. Finally, there were towns and boroughs, about which we hear far less than about the countryside.

Meadow

'Meadow' denoted land bordering streams liable to flood and producing hay, important in an age without root crops and the so-called artificial grasses. Its extent was indicated in a variety of ways. For most counties it was measured in acres, but we do not know what was implied by such an 'acre'; for the five counties of the circuit that included Cambridgeshire it was entered in terms of the oxen which its hay could support; and occasionally its size was expressed in terms of money renders or in some other way (see p. 35 below). One thing is clear. The distribution of meadow was uneven (Fig. 6). A notable feature was its abundance in the plain that stretches north-eastward below the chalk escarpment from Wiltshire to the Fenland. Throughout the belt a close network of streams and tributaries crossed the clay, and almost every village had an appreciable amount of meadow. In the southern portion of the belt was the Vale of White Horse, drained by the Ock, a tributary of the Thames; and for three places in the Vale we hear of dairy farms and renders of cheese—at Buckland, Shellingford, and Sparsholt. Here we see the emergence of the well-watered Vale as an important dairying district of the later Middle Ages. Downstream, meadow was also abundant along the Thames itself and along its tributaries, the Kennet and the Lea.

In the West, meadow was also widely distributed throughout lowland Somerset, especially in the Lias Clay plain. In the North, substantial amounts are entered for villages along the Trent in Derbyshire and Nottinghamshire. A surprising feature is the relative scarcity of meadow along the Severn as compared with the Thames and the Trent. More puzzling are the large amounts entered for Lincolnshire villages as compared with those of, say, Norfolk and Suffolk. It is difficult to see why this should be so. Can we suppose that the term 'meadow' was used in a very extended sense in Lincolnshire? No meadow is entered for two counties: its absence from the Lancashire folios is understandable in view of the abbreviated description of Lancashire; its absence from the Shropshire folios is more difficult to understand. Could this be due to some eccentricity in the returns for the county?

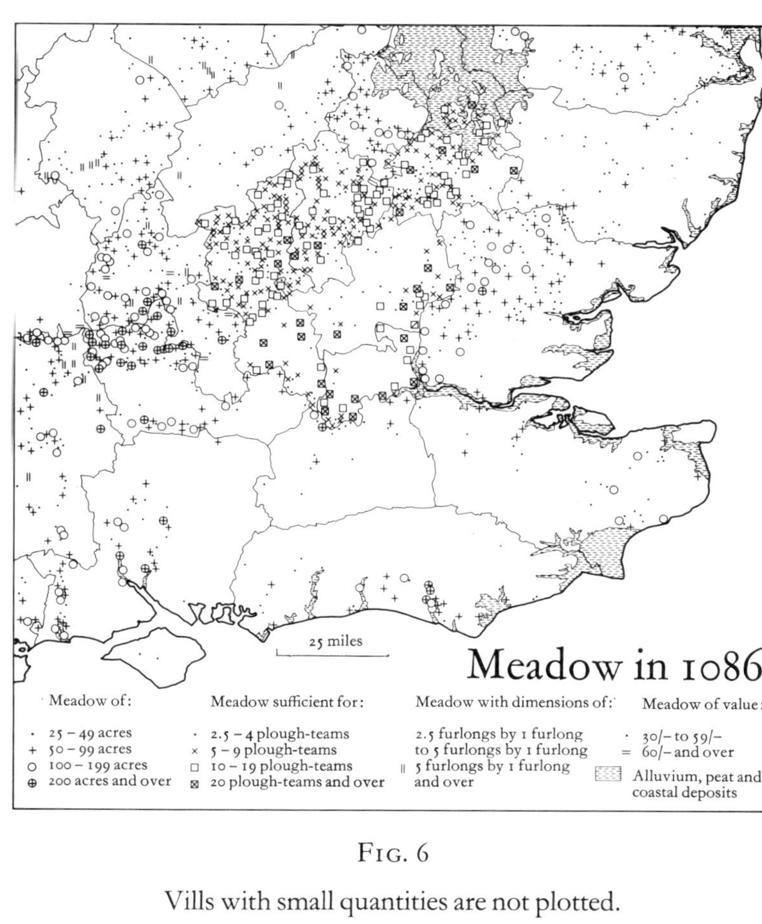

Fig. 6

Vills with small quantities are not plotted.

Pasture

Pasture was very unevenly entered, not only as between one circuit and another, but as between counties within the same circuit and as between places within the same county. There is no record for pasture at all for some counties and only an infrequent record for others. It is most usually entered for the counties of the south-west circuit, especially Cornwall. For three counties, all in the same circuit, the phrase used is 'pasture for the cattle of the village'—for those of Cambridge, Hertford, and Middlesex. Taking the three counties together it appears for some 63 per cent of their villages. Are we then to assume that the remaining villages in these counties had no pasture beyond the arable field that was taking its turn as fallow? This is unlikely. It is reasonable to regard the complete or almost complete lack of pasture entries as the result of some idiosyncrasy in the making or editing of the returns, the kind of idiosyncrasy in which Domesday Book abounds. There are occasional glimpses of the arrangements under which the pasture was used. Scattered entries for Devonshire and Somerset refer to common pasture. So do the entries for the boroughs of Oxford and Cambridge. Then again there is the famous reference to the pasture of the Suffolk hundred of Colneis which was 'common to all the men of the hundred'.

We might perhaps connect the many pasture entries of the South-West with the chalklands of Dorset and Wiltshire, with the uplands of Devonshire and Somerset, and with the bare surfaces of Cornwall. Supporting evidence comes from the Exeter Domesday Book, which records large flocks of sheep, e.g. the Cranborne flock of 1,037 and the Ashmore flock of 826. These and other large flocks were closely associated with the chalk downlands of Dorset; and large flocks were to be found elsewhere in the South-West. The Little Domesday Book also reveals large flocks on the light sandy soils of western Norfolk and Suffolk, especially in the district later known as Breckland (Fig. 7). As many as 1,029 sheep were entered for Mildenhall, and there were flocks of 750 and over at a number of places near by. The Inquisitio Comitatus Cantabrigiensis extends the evidence into southern Cambridgeshire, where there were 767 sheep at West Wratting and 765 at Weston Colville. They may have grazed on the open chalk belt between Royston and Newmarket. On the silt of the northern Fenland between King's Lynn and Wisbech, as many as 2,100 sheep were entered for West Walton and 515 for Terrington. Such details enable us to perceive something of the pastoral economy of this or that district. But there were other districts of which we know nothing. There must have been sheep-walks in, for example, the Cotswolds; but only when we read, in an early twelfth-century survey, of flocks of 1,012 at Avening and 467 at Minchinhampton, do we realize what Domesday Book does not tell us.[1]

Amidst this unpromising material there is one group of entries that provides interesting evidence of a distinc-

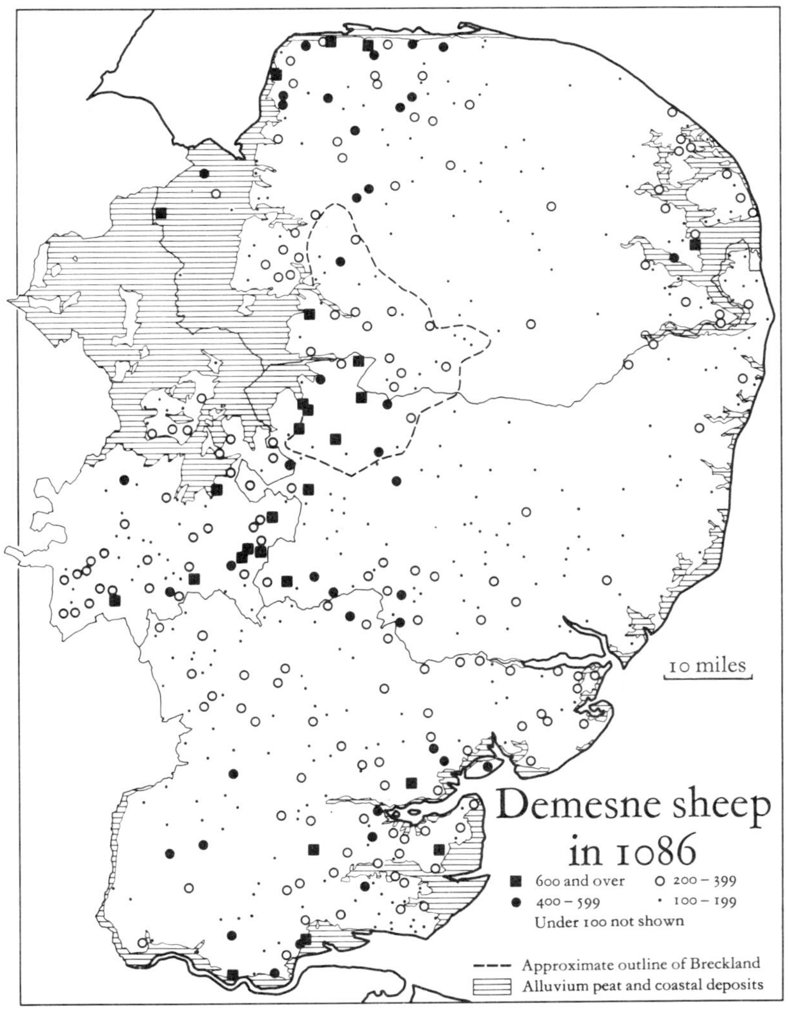

Fig. 7

The distribution in eastern England. Vills with less than 100 demesne sheep are not plotted.

tive economy in part of Essex. Here, as well as a few of the more usual pasture entries, we hear of 'pasture for sheep' at 114 places. These lay in a belt along the coast, some on the coast itself, others a little way inland (Fig. 8). Both groups had the right of pasturing their sheep on the marshes of the coastal alluvium. It is clear that the Domesday pasture coincided with the Essex marshes famous in later times for the making of cheese from ewes' milk.[2]

Vineyards

An exotic element in the cultivated landscape of the eleventh century was the vineyard. The vine had been introduced into England in Roman times, if not before; and we occasionally hear of vineyards throughout the Anglo-Saxon period.[3] Domesday Book records them for forty-five places, usually on estates held directly by tenants-in-chief (Fig. 9). Most were measured by the foreign unit of the arpent (roughly equal to an acre), and a number are said to have been but recently planted. They were to be found mostly in southern England and the most northerly was at Ely. One unusual entry is that for Wilcot, held by no less a person than Edward of Salisbury, the Sheriff of Wiltshire: here was 'a new church, an excellent house, and a good vineyard'.

[1] Lennard, *Rural England*, 264.

[2] *VCH Essex*, i (1903), 368–74.

[3] G. Ordish, *Wine Growing in England* (London, 1953), 20–1; S. Appelbaum, 'Roman Britain', H. P. R. Finberg (ed.), *The Agrarian History of England and Wales* (Cambridge, 1972), 103–4, 117–18, 516.

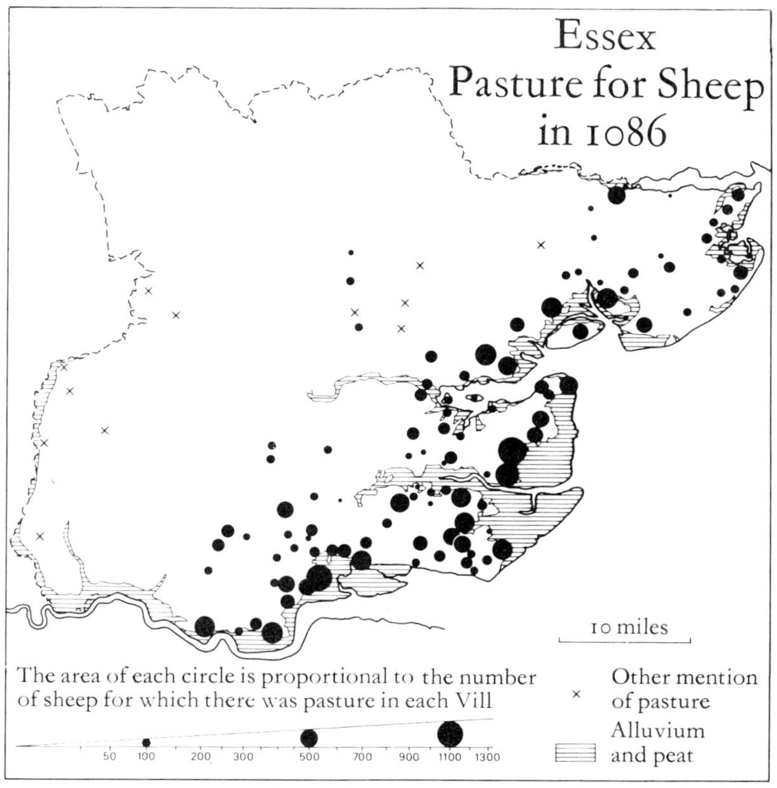

FIG. 8

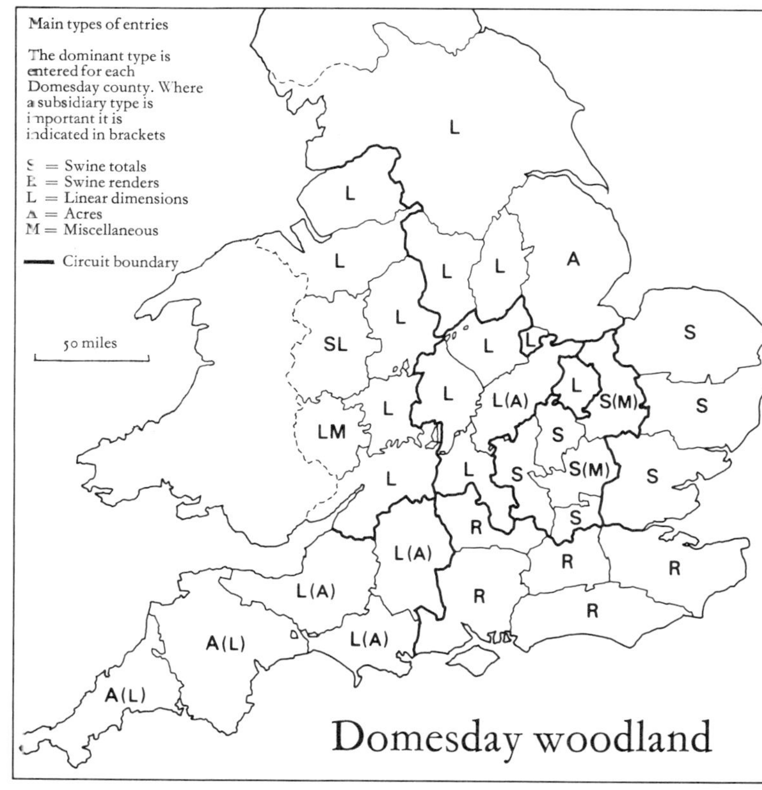

FIG. 10

WOOD

One of the questions asked by the Domesday commissioners was 'How much wood?' Broadly speaking, the answers fell into one of five categories (Fig. 10). Some said that there was enough wood to support a given number of swine, who fed upon acorns and beechmast; but we cannot be sure what acreages such figures implied. A variant of this was a statement not of total swine but of annual renders in return for pannage. A third type of answer gave the length and breadth of a wood in terms of leagues, furlongs, and perches, but whether the information referred to mean diameters or to some other notion we cannot say. A fourth type of entry stated the size of a wood in terms of acres, but we can hardly assume that these were the equivalent of our modern statute acres. The fifth category of answers was a miscellaneous one which included a variety of phrasing, e.g. wood for fuel or for repairing the fences. Normally each county was characterized by one main type of entry with a few other entries of a different style.

Apart from the difficulties presented by each type of entry there is one fundamental general problem. It is impossible satisfactorily to equate swine, swine renders, linear dimensions, and acres in any conclusive way and so reduce them to a common denominator. We cannot therefore be sure that a map of Domesday woodland (as indeed one of meadow) covering a number of counties conveys a correct visual impression as between one wooded area and another. We can, of course, try to secure equivalence by making assumptions, but the result can only be subjective. Then, again, other difficulties arise from the fact that some woodland may not have been recorded. Yet, in spite of these limitations, much can be gained from such a map (Fig. 11). With all its problems, it leaves us in no doubt about the wooded nature of large tracts of countryside in 1086. It can, moreover, be discussed in connection with other evidence, thus forming an important clue in the reconstruction of past countrysides and economies.

One surprising feature is the apparent absence of wood from the Weald. The reason lay in the peculiar economy of the region. Pre-Domesday documents show that many villages around had come to possess their own particular swine pastures or 'denes' in the Weald; and the woodland of such denes was entered under the names of their parent villages.[1] Over fifty such denes are recorded but they can have been only a fraction of the total, because wood often appears in an entry without any specific mention of its dene. Some of these denes were already developing into agricultural settlements by 1086 but were still without separate names. A third stage was reached by a few settlements which had grown into 'adult' villages with their own names. Such was Benenden (the dene of Bionna's people) or Newenden (the new dene) with twenty-nine households, five teams, and even a market. Others were to follow in later

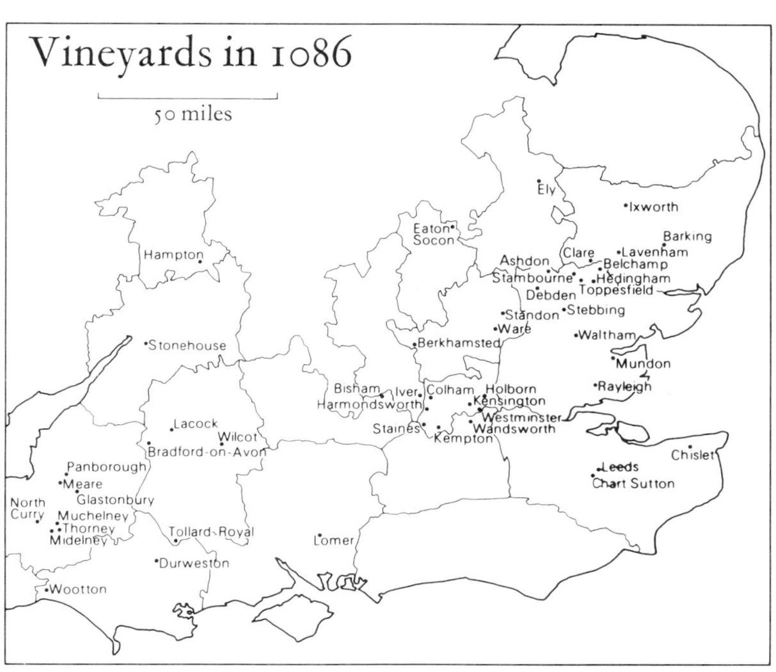

FIG. 9

[1] N. Neilson, *The Cartulary and Terrier of the Priory of Bilsington, Kent* (British Academy, London, 1928), 1–12.

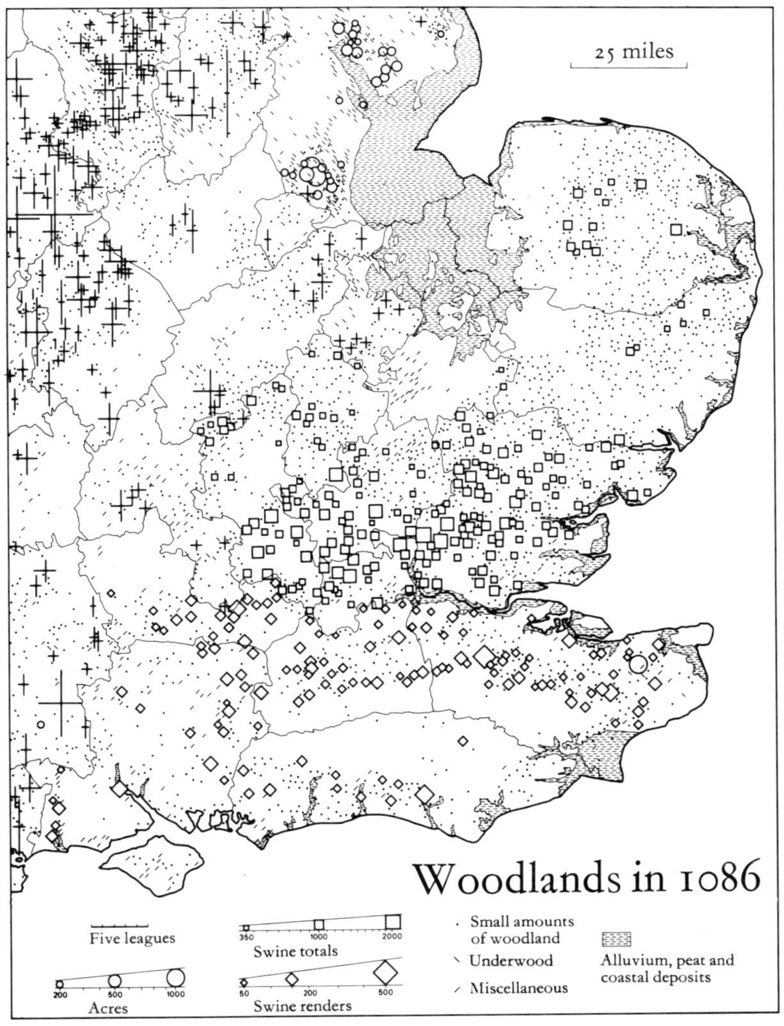

FIG. 11

The distribution in east and south-east England. 'Small amounts of woodland' include quantities under one league by one league, below 200 acres, less than 350 swine, and less than 50 swine renders.

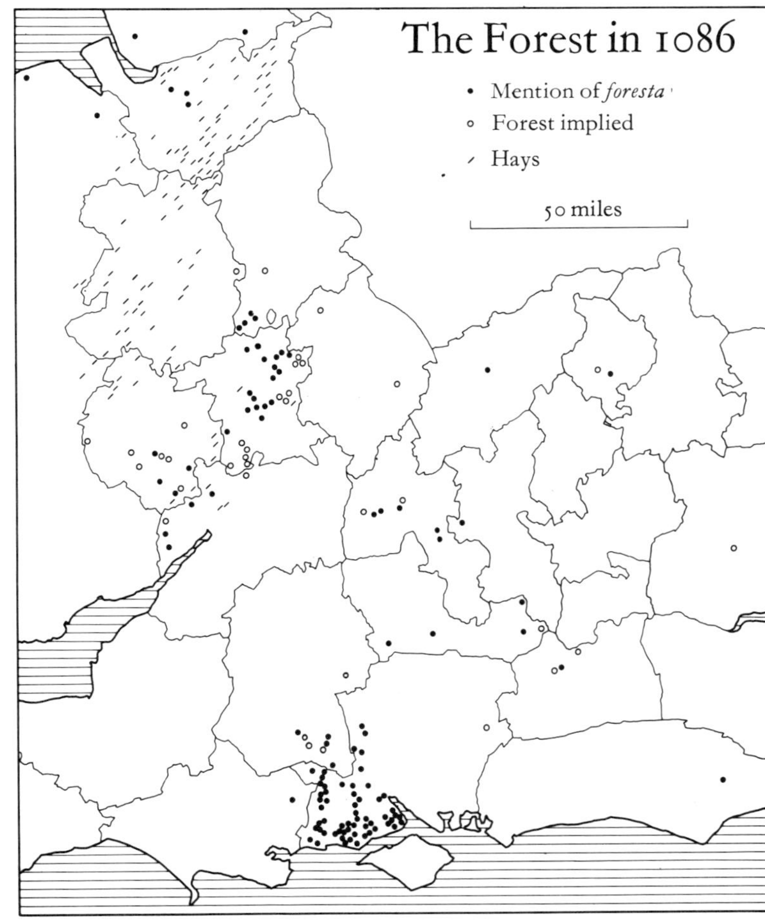

FIG. 12

For places with both forests and hays, only the former are plotted.

centuries. Clearly, many pioneer communities were spread across the Weald despite the scarcity of Domesday place-names there. The result of these peculiar arrangements is that the symbols for wood in 1086 must be 'spread out' by eye over the adjoining Weald. Even so we are still left with the impression that they cannot represent all the wood in existence in 1086.

FORESTS

Anglo-Saxon kings had enjoyed hunting, but with the Conquest such royal activities greatly increased. The Norman kings had a passionate love of the chase and, as the Anglo-Saxon chronicler wrote under the year 1087, King William 'made large forests for deer'. The word 'forest' in this context is neither a botanical nor a geographical term but a legal one. Forests usually included woodland but they frequently also comprised open land. They were essentially game preserves and, as such, they are rarely specifically described in Domesday Book. We are merely told that a holding had been placed 'in the forest' or 'in the king's forest'. Only a few forests are mentioned by name: Dean (Glos.), Grovely (Wilts.), Wimborne (Dorset), Windsor (Berks.); and the Oxfordshire folios provide the names of 'five demesne forests of the king' in Shotover and Stowood to the east of Oxford, and in Cornbury, Woodstock, and Wychwood to the west (Fig. 12).

The king's subjects also hunted, and we hear of their activities along the marches of Wales (see p. 33 below). That they hunted elsewhere in the West, we may assume from the frequent reference to hays (*haiae*) or hedged enclosures, usually in woodland, constructed to control the driving and capture of animals; they were particularly frequent in the thinly populated border counties of Shropshire and Cheshire. We also hear of deer parks, particularly in the south and east of the realm. Falconry was another favourite sport, again along the Welsh border and especially in Cheshire.

There is one forest for which Domesday Book gives much detail.[1] This is the New Forest, and its description forms a special section of the Hampshire folios. Chroniclers of the twelfth century said that the king had reduced a flourishing district to a waste by the wholesale destruction of villages. On the other hand, the poor sands and gravels of the area can never have supported a very flourishing agriculture. Even so, over thirty villages were placed wholly 'in the forest', and it is significant that only sixteen of these can be identified today. Portions of another thirty or so were also included. The subsequent history of the Forest has been entangled in all kinds of legal complications. Its limits have shrunk, but there has grown up a movement to preserve it in the interests of amenity. It still covers 92,000 acres, and remains a unique memorial of Norman England.

WASTE

The Domesday term 'waste' seems to imply not the natural waste of mountain, heath, and marsh, but land that had gone out of cultivation, mainly as the result

[1] F. H. Baring, 'The Making of the New Forest', *EHR* 16 (1901), 427–38; reprinted as 'The Evidence of Domesday as to the New Forest', *Domesday Tables* (London, 1909), 194–205.

of deliberate devastation and also, perhaps, because of some local event unknown to us. To a large extent such devastation by raiders and armies must have been the reason for the low densities of plough-teams and population in the West and more particularly in the North of England (Fig. 13).

Some of the wasted villages in Cheshire, Shropshire, and Herefordshire were the result of Welsh raids even before the Conquest, but many were due to the crushing of rebellion by the king's armies during the years 1068–70. Much of the wasting was still evident in 1086, and something of the character of this frontier region is conveyed by two Herefordshire entries which tell of thirteen villages lying waste 'on the marches of Wales'; one of the entries says that 'on these waste lands there have grown up woods in which Osbern (fitzRichard) hunts, and he has there whatever he can seize'. But in general there had been much recovery here by 1086; and, moreover, a series of Norman castles now protected the border.

It was in northern England that William inflicted the greatest damage. Here, there had been repeated unrest, and, towards the end of 1069, he went north to Yorkshire, not for the first time. By Easter 1070 the campaign was over. The entry under 1069 in the Anglo-Saxon Chronicle merely says that the king 'laid waste all the shire', but other accounts tell of the ferocity with which the harrying had been carried out. The chronicler of Evesham Abbey in Worcestershire describes how the destruction extended southward over Cheshire, Derbyshire, and Staffordshire, and he tells how fugitives from William's devastation crowded into the town, and how

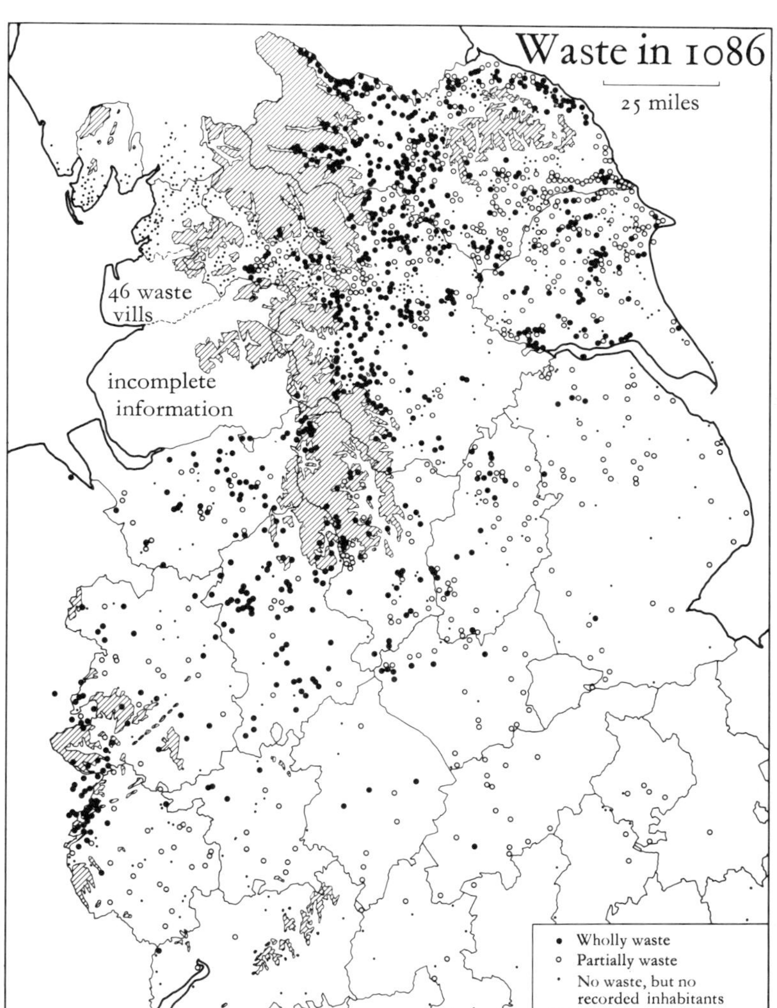

FIG. 13

many died of hunger.[1] To the damage by the king's armies must be added that inflicted on other occasions by the Scots and the Danes.

The general statements of the chronicles are borne out in a vivid manner by the evidence of Domesday Book, and it is summarized in Table 1 below. Seventeen years had not sufficed to repair the damage, and entry after entry on folio after folio reads, 'It is waste'.

TABLE 1. Percentages of Waste Vills in Five Northern Counties

	Wholly waste	Partly waste	Total
Yorkshire	27	18	45
Cheshire	16	6	22
Derbyshire	13	8	21
Staffordshire	18	2	20
Nottinghamshire	6	12	18

It is possible that even these figures do not give a complete picture of the empty countryside in the North. A number of vills not specifically described as waste have no recorded population (and usually no plough-teams) entered for them.

Some scholars, however, have found it difficult to accept the Domesday evidence at its face value.[2] They have tried to interpret the statement about 'waste' in various ways, e.g. by postulating migration from the uplands to the lowlands, or by suggesting that a waste holding was merely one that was administratively worthless. The various hypotheses have many elements of uncertainty. Moreover, one may find it difficult to believe that, for example, almost the whole of what is now north Lancashire was uninhabited in 1086, but that is what the account of the area around Preston (surveyed in the Yorkshire folios) implies when it says that sixteen vills were inhabited by a few people but that it was not known how many the inhabitants were, and that the remaining forty-six vills were waste.

SALT-WORKING

Salt was especially important in the Middle Ages for the preservation of fish and meat. It was obtained by evaporation from sea-water or from inland brine springs; and salt-works are recorded for places along the coasts of every maritime county from Lincolnshire to Cornwall. The number in an entry varied from one or two up to forty. Occasionally, there is reference to the salt-workers themselves. Along the Dorset coast, for example, there were 27 at Lyme, 16 at Charmouth, and 13 at Ower; those at Ower were the only recorded inhabitants in the settlement.

[1] W. D. Macray (ed.), *Chronicon Abbatiae de Evesham*, Rolls Ser. 29 (London, 1863), 90–1; R. R. Darlington, 'Aethelwig, Abbot of Evesham', *EHR* 48 (1933), 177.

[2] T. A. M. Bishop, 'The Norman Settlement of Yorkshire', *Studies in Medieval History Presented to Frederick Maurice Powicke*, eds. R. W. Hunt *et al.* (Oxford, 1948), 1–14; A. Raistrick, *West Riding of Yorkshire* (London, 1970), 40–1; W. E. Wightman, 'The Significance of "Waste" in the Yorkshire Domesday', *Northern Hist.* 10 (Leeds, 1975), 55–71; W. E. Kapelle, *The Norman Conquest of the North* (London, 1979), 158–90.

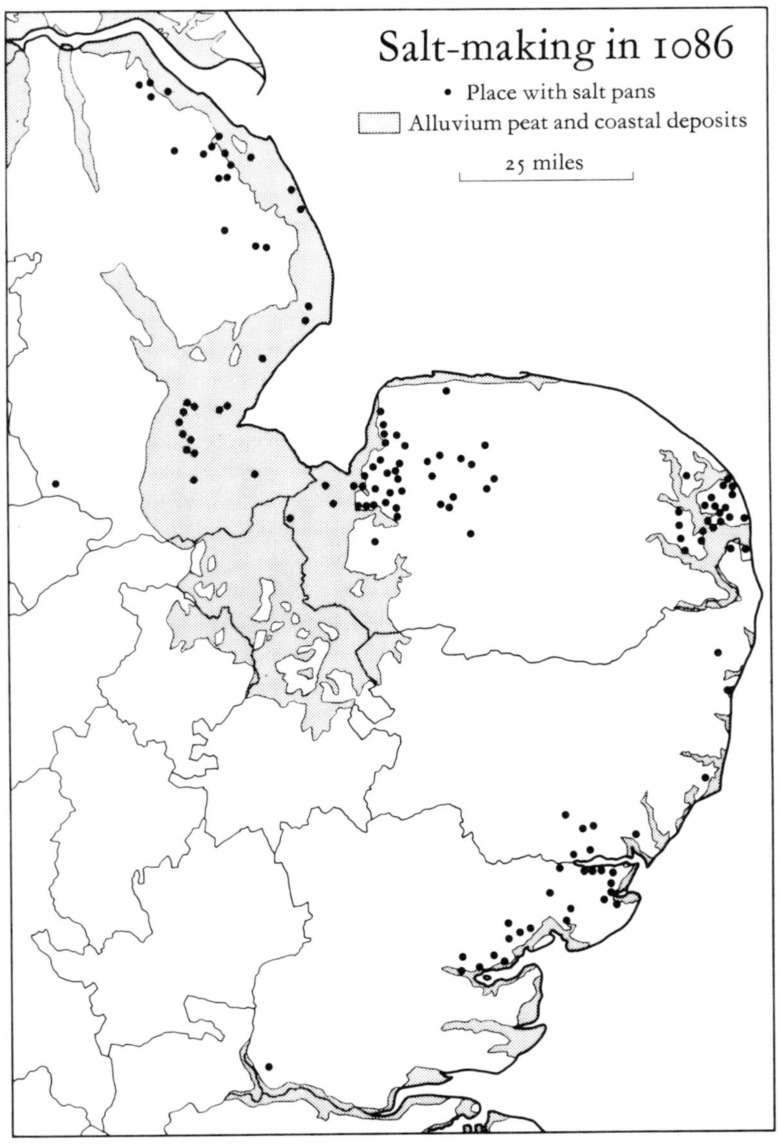

FIG. 14

The distribution in eastern England.

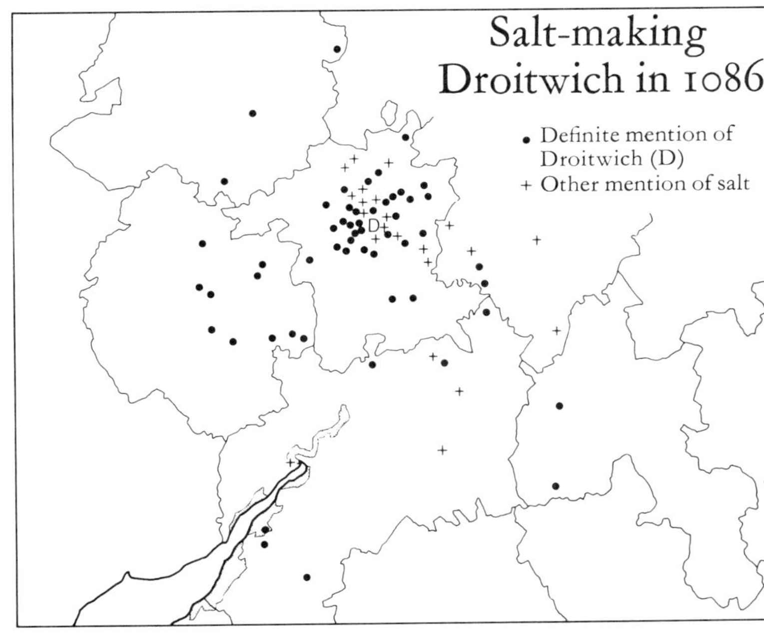

FIG. 15

A striking feature is the great cluster of works in western Norfolk (Fig. 14). Some of these could not possibly have been at the inland villages for which they are recorded, and they must have been on the coast some distance away. There are other conspicuous clusters of salt villages in Norfolk Broadland and along the estuaries of Suffolk and Essex. Yet others are to be found near the alluvial areas of Kent, Romney Marsh, and elsewhere along the estuaries of the south coast. We cannot tell how complete is the record of coastal works, but we may well suppose that the Domesday record does not give a full picture. The entry for Salcombe Regis in Devonshire, for example, makes no reference to salt-pans, although the name means 'salt valley' and is mentioned in a charter from the years just before 1086.[1] Likewise, in Essex no salt-pan is entered for the Domesday village of 'Salcota' (now called Virley) on a creek of the Blackwater estuary.

The inland brine springs were derived from the Keuper marls in Cheshire and Worcestershire. The Cheshire industry was centred at the 'wiches' of Northwich, Middlewich, and Nantwich. All three places had suffered from the disturbances of 1070 (see p. 33 above), and they had far from recovered by 1086. We hear nothing of the population of these centres, but there are a few allusions to the processes of manufacture, and we are told of 'boilings' and of a 'brine pit' at Nantwich for making salt. A large part of the account is occupied with details of the tolls levied on those who transported salt away, whether on foot or on horseback or by ox-cart. The tolls paid on salt increased with the distance from which a purchase was made, whether from the same hundred, or from another hundred, or from another county.

The industry in Worcestershire was centred at the borough of Droitwich, and salt-works are entered both for the borough itself and for a number of villages around (Fig. 15). As for Cheshire, there is but little reference to the processes of manufacture, but we do hear of leaden vats and of furnaces, and a few entries refer to the fuel that sustained the industry; thus the entry for Martin Hussingtree mentions an annual render of '100 cart-loads of wood for the salt-works of Droitwich'. The ramifications of the industry were considerable. Some thirty or so villages outside Worcestershire owned, or had rights in, the Droitwich salt-works. The most remote village was Princes Risborough about 70 miles away in Buckinghamshire, and it had a salt-worker in Droitwich who rendered an unspecified number of loads of salt. Names such as Saltway, Salter's Corner, and Salford, mentioned in pre-Domesday charters, appear on our Ordnance Survey maps today; and they reveal a network of salt-ways radiating from Droitwich. Like that for Cheshire, the evidence suggests some interesting reflections on the internal commerce of eleventh-century England.[2]

FISHERIES: INLAND AND COASTAL

Fish played an important part in the life of the Middle Ages, and fisheries are mentioned in many Domesday entries. Sometimes we are merely told the number of fisheries, but more usually their annual render is also given in money or fish or both. Fractions are frequent but it is not always possible to assemble them together

[1] J. E. B. Gover, *The Place-Names of Devon*, EPNS 9, pt. 2 (Cambridge, 1932), 595.

[2] F. T. S. Houghton, 'Salt-Ways', *Trans. and Proc. of the Birmingham Archaeol. Soc.* 54 (1929–30), 1–17; W. B. Crump, 'Saltways from the Cheshire Wiches', *Trans. of the Lancs. and Cheshire Ant. Soc.* 54 (1939), 84–142.

in any comprehensible fashion. Where, for example, along the Trent was the missing portion of the $3\frac{1}{2}$ fisheries at Rampton in Nottinghamshire? The species normally mentioned is that of eels, and these often appear as renders from mills, but salmon were also recorded for places along the Severn, the Dee, and along the Avon and the Dart in Devonshire. It is likely that the record of a fishery implied some kind of fixed structure. A number of entries speak not of fisheries (*piscariae*) but of weirs (*gurgites*), and occasionally we hear of fisheries being made or built.

The fisheries were located along the main rivers, such as the Thames, the Severn, the Trent, the Wye, and their tributaries. It is clear that fishing gave a distinctive character to the economies of a number of localities. At Eaton on the Dee above Chester, six fishermen (out of a total recorded population of ten people) rendered 1,000 salmon annually; and at Tidenham on the northern shore of the Severn estuary there were as many as sixty-five fisheries, mostly along the Severn itself but some also along the Wye. There were other groups of fisheries in the Somerset Levels and in the Isle of Axholme. But the most important fishing area was the Fenland. The description of Whittlesey Mere refers to fishermen and their boats; that of Soham Mere refers to fishermen and their nets. Large renders of eels came from many places in the Fenland; some were said to come 'from the fisheries', others 'from the marsh'. As many as 33,260 eels were rendered annually from Wisbech, 27,150 from Doddington, 24,000 from Stuntney, and 17,000 from Littleport. It is not surprising that Ely, 'the eel district', had obtained its name from its most characteristic product. The only Domesday reference to other products of the Fenland is the solitary mention of 16*d.* 'from the rushes' at Wilburton on the island of Ely. In this, as for other matters, the Domesday evidence is incomplete. No fisheries are recorded for Leicestershire, yet it is difficult to believe that there were not some along the Soar and the Wreak. Or again, can we believe that there were none at all in, say, Wiltshire?

Sea fisheries are only occasionally mentioned. There were, for example, herring renders from a number of villages along the Suffolk coast; there was a 'sea weir' (*heie maris*) belonging to Blythburgh; and the twenty-four fishermen at Yarmouth are likely to have been seamen. Renders of herring also appear for London and Southwark and for a number of places along the coasts of Kent and Sussex; we even hear of renders of porpoises at Southease in Sussex and at Stone in Kent. But just as for inland fisheries, we can only conclude that the evidence is incomplete. It is difficult to believe that there was no fishing off the coasts of, say, Cornwall. The references to sea fisheries are but stray indications of what must have been considerable activity along the shores of the realm.

Water-Mills

The earliest reference to a water-mill in England is in a document of 762 relating to Chart in Kent. Such references became relatively frequent in the centuries that followed. The earliest mention of a windmill, on the other hand, is as late as 1191, and appears in a document relating to the abbey of Bury St Edmunds. It is reasonable to suppose, therefore, that the mills of Domesday Book were water-mills. Their spread over the country in the 300 years or so before 1086 was a remarkable achievement. Domesday Book sometimes merely records the number of mills on a holding, but frequently we are told of their renders in money, ranging from a few pence to a substantial number of pounds; there are also renders in kind, e.g. in grain and especially in eels from mill-ponds and mill-streams. Occasionally there is reference to a 'winter mill', which reflects the seasonal nature of its stream.

It is impossible to be precise about the total number of recorded mills because of fractions—that is, because mills were sometimes held jointly by two or more people, or shared by neighbouring villages. Fractions range downwards to an eighth of a mill, as at Tasburgh on the river Tas to the south of Norwich; but here, as often elsewhere, we are given no clue to the remaining fraction. Taking the numbers of recorded mills at their face value, the total comes to just over 6,000 at 3,550 places, that is to say for about only one-quarter of the places named in Domesday England.

The mills were situated along the rivers of the countryside, but if we consider their distribution more generally over the face of, say, a county, marked contrasts appear. For Domesday England as a whole there were 25 mills for every 1,000 recorded households. Cornwall, however, had only one per 1,000, and the corresponding figure for Devonshire was seven as compared with 34 for Somerset, 43 for Dorset, and 50 for Wiltshire. Could the record for the south-western circuit be especially defective for Cornwall and Devonshire? In any case, the differences in the ratios between other counties are also striking—between, say, Suffolk with 13 mills per 1,000 households, Oxfordshire with 34 mills, and, as we have seen, Wiltshire with 50 mills. The corresponding ratios between mills and plough-teams are likewise very unequal as between one county and another.

We might fall back on the view that much grinding of corn was done by hand, and that the rivers of some counties were more suitable for mills than those of other counties. Or again, we might suppose that some mills served settlements in addition to their own, that, for example, the seven mills at Battersea in Surrey which rendered £42. 9*s.* 8*d.* 'or corn of like value' ground corn from other places and sent the product to other places; this is not surprising when we remember that no mills were entered for about three-quarters of the recorded Domesday settlements. Or must we suppose that the Domesday record was unreliable as between one hundred or one county and another? Or, yet again, that all these possibilities affected the final result?

Towns and Commerce

However great the difficulties of interpretation, the information for rural England is remarkably detailed and is systematically presented. When we turn to the towns and boroughs all is different. The information is as incomplete as it is unsystematic. We sometimes hear much of legal matters and of administrative arrangements. Some towns had markets or mints or were centres of overseas trade. Others had castles or monasteries that needed to be maintained. A number were centres of a sea-fishing industry—Yarmouth, Beccles, and Dunwich in East Anglia, and Sandwich in Kent. Droitwich is unique in that we are told much of its salt industry. But it is usually impossible to form any clear idea of the size of a town or of the economic and other activities that sustained it.

Altogether some 112 places seem to have been boroughs. By far the most important must have been London, and we know from other sources something of its importance and of its trading connections, wide in the context of the time.[1] It is therefore particularly unfortunate that folio 126, where London should have been described, is almost completely blank. There is also a great blank space on folio 37 where the account of Winchester should have appeared. Of the other boroughs we may conjecture that the following had at least 4,000 inhabitants each: York, Lincoln, Norwich, and, possibly, Thetford. Then came the county towns such as Leicester and Nottingham with, say, 2,000 or more. At the lower end of the scale were small boroughs with populations to be reckoned not in thousands but in hundreds; such were Calne and Malmesbury in Wiltshire. The Anglo-Saxon word *burh* ('borough') signified a fortified centre, and the test of burghal status was neither size nor general prosperity.

The immediate effect of the Conquest on many boroughs was the destruction of houses for the building of castles, like those at York, Lincoln, Cambridge, and elsewhere. Besides these, there were also waste houses at other boroughs, sometimes the result of fire, but usually we are not told why. As well as these temporary setbacks, there had begun to operate forces which were to give the English borough its most lasting characteristic—that of a trading centre. Many Domesday entries reveal a continued expansion of commerce. One indication is the establishment of new boroughs alongside the old at Norwich, Northampton, Nottingham, and other places. Groups of French burgesses had also settled at, for example, Shrewsbury, St Albans, and Wallingford. The burgesses at Hereford and Rhuddlan were granted many of the laws and customs of the Norman town of Breteuil; and at Southampton we are specifically told that a French colony had settled 'after King William came to England'. But for only one place does something of the bustle of a town show through the Domesday text, and this was for a place not specifically called a borough. The town of Bury St Edmunds in Suffolk had been a substantial community in 1066, but the next twenty years were to see another 342 houses cover land which had been under the plough. We hear not of burgesses but of clergy and of 'bakers, ale-brewers, tailors, washerwomen, shoemakers, robemakers, cooks, porters, and stewards', who waited daily 'upon the Saint, the abbot, and the brethren'. These fragments of evidence point to the new age that the Conquest had inaugurated.

[1] Stenton, *Anglo-Saxon England*, 531–3.

II. HOW LAND WAS HELD BEFORE AND AFTER THE NORMAN CONQUEST

ANN WILLIAMS

WILLIAM I acquired the kingdom of the English by right of conquest. His victory on 14 October 1066 vindicated his claim to be the legitimate heir of Edward the Confessor and all who opposed him were rebels and their lands forfeit. All the land in England belonged to the king and all who held land held it as his tenants, whether they were Normans and other Frenchmen who had received estates by his gift, or Englishmen who had redeemed their possessions by submitting to him.[1] The terms on which land was held varied. Most tenants, including the bishops and abbots of the older Benedictine houses, held by military service; in the new, feudal, vocabulary, their lands were fiefs (also called honours or baronies). Some ecclesiastical land was held *in elemosina*, what came to be called free alms, that is, by the service of prayer. For at least twenty years after the Conquest, some Englishmen continued to hold as king's thegns, thus preserving the English system. Much of the land held by such men was later held by sergeanty (*per seriantiam*), that is, for the performance of some specific service (as a cook or a huntsman, for instance); and in 1086 some men (mainly Frenchmen) are described as sergeants, though their service is rarely stated. Such tenures were, however, a small part of the whole; the characteristic tenure of 1086 was feudal, military service.

Domesday Book is rarely explicit about the nature of tenures in 1086. It can be assumed, however, that those men under whose names the estates within each shire are listed were, unless otherwise stated, holders of feudal honours; modern commentators refer to them as tenants-in-chief. Though Domesday does not say so, they owed in return for their lands a fixed quota of fully armed and equipped knights (the *servitium debitum*). Such men sub-enfeoffed others, called by modern historians mesne-tenants or under-tenants, men holding of a lord other than the king. It was possible for a man to hold some land as a tenant-in-chief and some as a mesne-tenant, and indeed many mesne-tenants were rich and powerful lords. The quota imposed on the tenants-in-chief could be fulfilled in various ways. The tenant-in-chief could maintain knights in his own household (most great lords would have a household retinue) or he could grant to some or all of them fiefs and lands on which they could support themselves. The two methods are not mutually exclusive; some knights could be supported partly by stipends paid by their lords, and partly by the rents from small parcels of land. Many of the *milites*, named or unnamed, who appear in Domesday with tiny pieces of land probably fall into this category.

The endowment of Normans meant the dispossession of Englishmen. William intended, however, that his Norman followers should inherit the responsibilities as well as the rights of their English predecessors, and it is therefore usual, though not invariable, for Domesday Book to record the name of the pre-Conquest tenant, as well as that of the holder of the estate in 1086. This information is sometimes accompanied by a description of the terms on which land was held, often brief and uninformative, such as that the land was held *libere* ('freely'). Even where greater detail is given, its import is not always clear. For this the lapse in time must be in part responsible (as Maitland justly remarked, 'we cannot expect that men will be very accurate in stating the legal relationships that existed twenty years ago'[2]), and at first sight the terminology used by Domesday to describe pre-Conquest tenures is bewildering in its variety. Closer inspection shows, however, that this variety is largely illusory. It is clear that usages differed from circuit to circuit and that what appear to be descriptions of different types of tenure may in fact be two ways of describing the same thing. The use of the term *in allodium* ('as an alod') and its associated *allodiarius* ('the holder of an alod') is virtually confined to the shires of the south-eastern circuit (Kent, Surrey, Sussex, Hants, and Berks.). While the meaning of the word *allodium* is uncertain, it is possible that in this context it implies no more than free tenure and may be the south-eastern equivalent of the more generally used *libere* ('freely').[3] The same may be true of the phrase *dare vel vendere potuit* ('he could give or sell') and its variants, used of some landholders in the shires of the third circuit (Middx., Herts., Beds., Cambs., and Bucks.). Similar language is used in Little Domesday (Essex, Norfolk, and Suffolk), but is rare elsewhere. It is likely that all these usages relate to the best-documented tenure in pre-Conquest England, that of bookland. Bookland was land the title to which was possession of a royal diploma or land-book, the effect of which was to confer perpetual ownership of the estate, with free right of disposition; the land was also freed from all secular service except for those specifically reserved in the diploma (usually the military obligations of bridge-building, repair and building of fortified *burhs*, and service in the *fyrd* or host).[4] Recipients of bookland included both ecclesiastical bodies and individual king's thegns; in-

[1] H. R. Loyn, *The Governance of Anglo-Saxon England, 500–1087* (London, 1984), 180.

[2] Maitland, *Domesday Book and Beyond*, 63.

[3] For the meaning of *allodium* (a word imported from Continental usage) see D. Bates, *Normandy before 1066* (London, 1982), 122–6.

[4] It should be emphasized that the diploma itself was evidentiary and that the actual conveyance of the land was effected by means of a public oral ceremony, of which the diploma was the record. Since only

deed it seems likely that possession of bookland was one of the distinguishing marks of a king's thegn. Since free disposition of the land was one of the characteristics of bookland, it is difficult to believe that anything else can be meant by the Domesday phrase *dare vel vendere potuit*, but the geographical distribution of surviving royal diplomas is far wider than the shires to which the use of this phrase in Domesday is restricted. The shire for which royal diplomas survive in the greatest number is in fact Kent, one of those where the terms *allodium*, *allodiarius* occur.[1] No definite conclusions can be drawn, however, without a full investigation of the whole question of pre-Conquest English land tenure.

Holders of bookland could make temporary grants of land for limited periods, with reversion to the grantor; land so given was called loanland. A large number of leases of this kind have been preserved, largely from the archive of the Church of Worcester. The terms of these grants varied; the most common are leases for the lifetime of the grantee only, and for his life and those of two heirs (the latter are known as three-life leases). Domesday records both kinds, and indeed its descriptions of such leases are perhaps the most unambiguous of all its references to pre-Conquest tenures.[2] Leases should be distinguished from grants in reversion to religious houses, which are occasionally mentioned in Domesday. In such cases, the donor made a grant of land to a church to take effect on his death (or that of one of his heirs), thus preserving a life-interest in the estate. Though loanland is found mostly in connection with ecclesiastical estates, it was not restricted to the church and loans made by laymen are occasionally recorded.[3] When Domesday states that one layman held *de* ('of') or *sub* ('under') another, the possibility that the land was loanland cannot be excluded. Rather similar to the loan is the farm (*firma*), in which the grantor rented land to a tenant (the *firmarius* or farmer) either for a fixed annual sum or a lump payment, in return for which the farmer received the dues from the estate.

The question of pre-Conquest dependent tenures is complicated by the fluidity of English commendation. Commendation is the English equivalent of the Continental vassalage, whereby one freeman (the vassal or *homo*) places himself under the protection of another (the lord or *dominus*) to whom he owes fidelity and service. The commendation might be purely personal, or the vassal might receive land from his lord, or commend his own land (or part of it) along with himself. It was also quite possible for a man to be commended to more than one lord. Domesday does sometimes distinguish between men who have no lord but the king, and men who have commended themselves to someone else; phrases like *ire quo volebat* ('he could go where he would') imply the former, whereas *non se vertere potuit* ('he could not withdraw') imply the latter. Statements to the effect that commendation had or had not taken place do not, in themselves, tell very much about the tenure of the land which the man held.[4]

While some of the distinctions implied by the usage of Domesday may be apparent rather than real, others are based on genuine divergency of custom. It is clear that the estates of what is loosely called the Danelaw (the northern and eastern shires) differed in structure from those of the South and West (the old kingdom of Wessex and western Mercia). The common pattern in the North and East seems to have been one of a central estate (which alone is called a manor by Domesday) and its dependent settlements (berewicks), to which were attached other portions of land (sokeland), the ownership of which did not necessarily lie with the holder of the central manor. The term 'territorial soke' has been applied to such estates by modern historians, but the use of the alternative and descriptive term 'multiple estate' is gradually replacing it. It was once thought that the appearance of such estates in England was a consequence of the Danish settlement in the ninth century, but it is now believed that such estates were once much more widespread than their distribution in 1086 would indicate.[5] The rights of the lord over such an estate are expressed by the use of the words *soca* ('soke') and *saca et soca* ('sake and soke'), both of which are frequently employed in Domesday, especially but not exclusively in relation to the northern and eastern shires. In origin 'soke' meant the obligation to attend the court of the sokeman's lord ('suit of court'), and 'sake' the case heard in the court to which suit was owed, but by the eleventh century, possession of sake and soke implied more than merely jurisdictional powers, and covered the right to a number of dues and services, in money and in kind, from the tenants on the land over which sake and soke was exercised.[6] Holders of sake and soke, like holders of bookland (with whom they may be synonymous), could grant parts of their property to tenants, and the distinction drawn by Domesday between rights of sake and soke and rights of soke alone may indicate that holders of the latter had only the jurisdictional powers.

SELECT BIBLIOGRAPHY

R. Allen Brown, *The Normans and The Norman Conquest* (London, 1969)

H. R. Loyn, *Anglo-Saxon England and the Norman Conquest* (London, 1962)

F. W. Maitland, *Domesday Book and Beyond* (Cambridge, 1897)

F. M. Stenton, *Anglo-Saxon England* (3rd edn., Oxford, 1971)

the king could grant exemptions of the public burdens on land, the issue of diplomas was a royal monopoly in pre-Conquest England.

[1] D. Hill, *An Atlas of Anglo-Saxon England* (Oxford, 1981), 23.

[2] Holders of loanland were required to perform service to the lord who granted the lease. Domesday sometimes mentions that service was due, but rarely specifies what it was.

[3] R. E. Lennard, *Rural England 1086–1135* (Oxford, 1959), 166 n. 1.

[4] For some illustration of the relationships which could be deduced from Domesday's references to commendation, see A. Williams, 'Land and Power in the Eleventh Century: the Estates of Harold Godwineson', *Proc. of the Battle Conference 1980*, iii (1981), 178 ff.

[5] P. H. Sawyer, *From Roman Britain to Norman England* (London, 1978), 175–8.

[6] F. E. Harmer, *Anglo-Saxon Writs* (Manchester, 1952), 73–82. Though the surviving grants of sake and soke are to ecclesiastical persons and bodies, Domesday is itself evidence that such rights could be held by laymen.

III. THE LIFE OF THE MANOR

BARBARA F. HARVEY

HISTORIANS have long concerned themselves with the manor, and, following Maitland, they have tried to elicit the meaning which the word (Lat. *manerium*) had for contemporaries. As a rule, however, they have distilled its meaning from the characteristic features, as they see them, of the societies where manors either existed by name or—and we must remember here that the word is not actually used before the second half of the eleventh century—where they may be said to have been in process of formation. To this significantly different approach we owe an idea not found in medieval sources, namely that there was such a thing as a manorial system or, as it is often called, manorialism. In medieval sources 'manor' normally seems to denote a unit of lordship or unit of estate management (in Domesday Book the former), and in each case we have a genus with many species. Manorialism has a more specialized meaning, relating to a certain kind of economic organization in the countryside. This has the bizarre consequence that one may ask of an entity explicitly described in contemporary sources as a manor whether or not the manorial system developed there, and the degree to which it developed. Yet the historians' model of the manorial system—for model it is—provides a useful starting-point for consideration of the social realities underlying Domesday manors.

The manor, on this view, had a characteristic, if not essential, feature, and the degree of development of this is a measure of the development of manorialism in the individual case. This was a demesne, or home farm, cultivated by the labour of tenants holding lands and dwellings of the lord. Labour services were of two kinds. Week-work, as its name implies, was due on a certain number of days per week throughout the year; but there were also occasional services, such as ploughing, mowing, or reaping, which were due only in the appropriate seasons. Week-work had derogatory implications for those who performed it: they were indubitably of servile status, and this meant that they were not free to leave the manor even if they wished to do so. A free tenant, however, might bring his plough to the lord's demesne or assist at harvest boons without jeopardizing his freedom, which included freedom to move. In a heavily manorialized system, much of the labour used on the demesne was provided by the lord's tenants, and among their services the derogatory kind was prominent. In a lightly manorialized system, derogatory services were little used, and services of all kinds were less used than wage labour: indeed, the extensive use of wage labour signifies the decline of the manor or its failure to develop at all. If, on the other hand, the demesne was cultivated by the labour of slaves living as menials in the lord's court, the estate was still in its pre-manorial phase. Whatever rights the lord claimed over the inhabitants of the manor, at regular intervals he held a court where they could be enforced.

Relatively few parts of England can ever be described as highly manorialized in the sense outlined above. In every century from the seventh to the fourteenth there were peasants whose lives were deeply affected by involvement in domanial husbandry, and from the eleventh century their numbers were, to our knowledge, large. But even in the Midlands and South, where the manor struck its earliest and deepest roots, we never seem to encounter tenant dues lacking a component of money rents (and as a rule a large component), or demesnes that did not rely to a considerable extent on various forms of wage labour. In the North and East manorialism was patchy and for the most part superficial; over much of this vast area seigneurial demesnes, the *sine qua non* of strong manorialism, may not have existed. For all this, several reasons can be suggested: the precocious development of a cash economy; the vitality of the public courts in England and the correspondingly restricted sphere of private jurisdiction; Scandinavian settlement, perhaps arresting in half a dozen counties a pre-existing trend towards the debasement of the peasantry; the predominantly pastoral economy of the North. The most important factor may have been a change in the pattern of land ownership. Manorialism always flourished best on large estates and where the manor itself was large. Probably from the eighth century onwards, the large, multiple estates which had been features of early Anglo-Saxon society were fragmented by royal and seigneurial grants to retainers.[1] Out of the pieces, some new large estates were formed, but many more small ones. After the momentary interruption of the Norman Conquest, the process of fragmentation was carried much further, in a different but analogous form, as tenants-in-chief made grants to the honorial baronage, and the latter to their lesser knights. In these ways, a great deal of land passed into the hands of small owners who lacked the resources to perfect manorial institutions.

When Domesday Book was made, the factors mentioned above were already combining to set limits to the development of manorialism in England. Considered on its own, however, the second half of the eleventh

[1] G. R. J. Jones, 'Multiple Estates and Early Settlement', *Medieval Settlement: Continuity and Change*, ed. P. H. Sawyer (London, 1976), 15–40; P. Stafford, *The East Midlands in the Early Middle Ages* (Leicester, 1985), 29 ff.

century, and especially the generation following the Norman Conquest, must be regarded as a period when manorial institutions acquired a new efficiency and vitality. The decision taken in 1086 to use the manor, the unit of lordship, in preference to village and hamlet, the units of settlement, for the ordering of the survey at the local level both gave expression to this trend and helped it on. We have to see the Domesday manors in this dual setting of short-term and long-term change. Amid great variety, three or four main types can be distinguished. Some manors were conterminous with a single village or—where the lordship of the village was divided—contained within it. Some were discrete estates, consisting of a chief settlement with outlying dependencies known as berewicks. Although we can assume that in these cases the lord of the manor exercised a jurisdiction over his tenants, his rights over the land were, in Stenton's phrase, proprietary: in the qualified sense which any reference to ownership must bear in an early medieval context, he owned most of it.[1] In the remaining cases to be considered, rights of jurisdiction assume greater prominence. These were the manors associated with so-called sokes. A lord did not own his sokeland: he received rents from its inhabitants, and they acknowledged his jurisdiction. Sokes differed widely in extent and were of diverse origin. Many seem to have perpetuated ancient administrative divisions, known in the North as 'shires', which had been used for the collection of royal and seigneurial dues.[2] The discrete manor, only now receiving the attention which it deserves, was probably a relic of the multiple estate which suffered a degree of fragmentation in the late Anglo-Saxon period. Since the Domesday clerks often omitted berewicks dependent on a chief settlement, such manors must be seriously under-recorded in the survey.

It will be clear that Domesday Book is principally concerned with one facet of manorial life, the degree to which the inhabitants of each manor depended on a lord. In pursuit of this, other no less vital relationships are ignored. Thus, as Maitland pointed out, when Domesday notes of a freeman TRE that he could sell his land, it means only that no lord could prevent the transaction: we are not to infer that the man could disregard the interests of his family.[3] Not only did the typical inhabitant of a Domesday manor have a family; if he lived in a village or hamlet, and not in an isolated farmstead, he was a member of a community that was, quite possibly, older than the manorial organization now enveloping it. Wherever he lived, his presence was occasionally required at public courts meeting elsewhere. If he lived near a town, he may have been in the habit of selling his small surpluses there. Although his life was greatly influenced by its manorial context, this was far from being the only important influence.

Domesday normally employs the fivefold classification of manorial society that we encounter in the preamble to the Ely Inquest, or some variant of this.[4] In the order in which they appear in the latter source, the classes were: villans, cottars, slaves, freemen, and sokemen. Near-contemporary sources sometimes employ different categories, and many additional ones—*coliberti*, for example, and radmen—are occasionally employed in Domesday itself. (*Coliberti* were small tenants of an extremely dependent status, but freer than the slaves; by contrast, radmen, sometimes called radknights, were superior people whose distinctive function was riding on the lord's errands.) In fact, manorial society was not as neatly ordered as Domesday would have us believe.

The fivefold classification had regard to legal status and economic condition, two attributes of peasant existence that can never usefully be considered the one apart from the other in this period. Status is most helpfully envisaged as a continuum, unbroken by any great divide of the kind that, a century later, would separate the freeman who could sue in the king's court from the villein who could not.[5] In Domesday England everyone who was not a slave had standing in the courts, and not even the slave was rightless: for example, he probably had a modest place in the system of wergilds. (A wergild was the compensation payable to the kin of a slain man by the slayer or his kin; officially the amount varied according to the status of the slain man, but in practice negotiated settlement is often to be envisaged.) A man's precise position along the line of legal status was mainly determined by the nature of his relationship to a lord, for lordship pervaded eleventh-century society, and no one escaped its embrace. Lordship, however, had this degree of influence partly because in a great many cases it determined how much land a man held: legal and economic status were inextricably intertwined.

Freemen and sokemen represent 14 per cent of the enumerated population in 1086, and it is clear that the Domesday clerks often found it impossible to distinguish between them. We know from the survey and other sources that many in each category owed renders in cash and kind to the lord of the manor with which they were associated, and sometimes a variety of services, including agricultural services too. Freemen may have been justiciable in the lord's court, as sokemen certainly were; and in the late eleventh century men of each class voluntarily commended themselves to a lord, a common formal stage in the creation of a seigneurial nexus of relationships. More often than sokemen, however, freemen may have retained the capacity to alienate their land and, with this, a greater freedom of movement. In 1086 both classes were more carefully enumerated in eastern England, where the smallest among them paid his taxes direct to the royal officers, than in some other parts of the country, where the lords of manors had in practice assumed responsibility for collection, and the exact number and liability of the free peasantry were, accordingly, matters of indifference to the king. The

[1] Stenton, *Types of Manorial Structure in the Northern Danelaw*, 61.

[2] G. W. S. Barrow, *The Kingdom of the Scots: Government, Church and Society from the Eleventh to the Fourteenth Century* (London, 1973), 22–8, 56–64.

[3] Maitland, *Domesday Book and Beyond*, 144.

[4] Record Commission, *Domesday Book*, iv (PRO, London, 1816), 497.

[5] Hence the distinction in spelling, now commonly observed by historians, between Domesday vill*ans* and later vill*eins*.

most highly manorialized regions of England were freer than the survey may suggest. But it may still be true that freemen and sokemen were most commonly found in six counties: Norfolk, Suffolk, Lincolnshire, Nottinghamshire, Leicestershire, and Northamptonshire.

To an extent that was probably nowhere true of freemen or sokemen, villans (41 per cent of the enumerated population) were drawn into the domanial economy. Domesday Book is reticent about the size of the villan's holding. Where this information is given, notably in Middlesex, a standard unit, usually a virgate or half-virgate, is the norm, and early manorial surveys point to the same conclusion. It has been suggested that such a holding is not yet to be envisaged as a bundle of strips in the fields which had been permanently allocated to the tenant in question, but as a standard share in the village's resources, made up of different strips each year.[1] Whatever view we take of this matter, the fact that a manor's villans so often had equal holdings invites explanation. It points to strong lordship, restricting alienation and the fragmentation of holdings among family heirs beyond a certain point. In this sense the land of the villans was dedicated to the service of the demesne. Moreover, although week-work is scarcely mentioned in Domesday Book, the early surveys show that villans normally owed such service. But they also show that it varied in amount from manor to manor and was not infrequently commuted into a money rent. How much did the difference in status between villan and freeman matter in daily life? In many cases, perhaps little enough. After all, it was often the villan who had the larger holding; in village meetings his voice may have carried as well as that of the freeman; and on days when the lord's reeve called for ploughing services or reapers, villan and freeman often worked together. If the freeman's farm was situated in the chief settlement of the manor or in a berewick, and not in an isolated soke, they must habitually have worked side by side in the fields. For much of his existence, in fact, the villan was just a peasant farmer. Both freeman and villan lived dangerously, in a condition of extreme dependence on nature.

With the cottars we must consider the bordars. The latter are often enumerated alongside the former, and sometimes only bordars are mentioned. Together they make up 32 per cent of the enumerated population. Evidently, the Domesday clerks found it hard and at times impossible to distinguish the one from the other. In Middlesex, where each class is enumerated separately, some bordar holdings may have been as large as 10 or 15 acres; but in the majority of cases where this item is recorded—unfortunately a small proportion of the whole number—the holding was of 5 acres. Cottars in this county normally held considerably less. Characteristically, both cottars and bordars were smallholders. In Robert of Hereford's much quoted description of the Domesday inquest, 'those dwelling in cottages' are actually distinguished from those possessing houses and arable holdings.[2] With so little land of their own to look after, how did cottars and bordars spend their time?

It has been suggested that these classes were particularly active in colonization in Domesday England, and, secondly, that they may often have been under-tenants of the villans, freemen, and sokemen, who used them as their work-force when necessary.[3] Bordars, in particular, seem often to be associated with forest and pasture. These explanations nicely fit the geographical distribution of the cottars and bordars, who form a conspicuous element in the recorded population in 1086 in such counties as Norfolk and Suffolk, which were heavily populated, and Hampshire, Worcestershire, and Cornwall, where forest and pasture were indeed extensive. Moreover, they help us to understand how it was that in 1086 England was already a fully settled country, having a vast extent of land under the plough. Assarting was always a risky and expensive venture, to be undertaken on a large scale only by those with considerable resources of capital and manpower. If the contribution of the free peasant was often heroic, we may suspect that the role of lords in the great conquests from the waste had been indispensable; in the cottars and bordars of Domesday we glimpse their agents. If so, we have part of the answer to the question, 'how did these smallholders spend their time?' They are to be imagined putting the axe to the tree, rooting up stumps, making a ditch round the new field, cutting the first sods, and guiding the plough along the first furrows. And no doubt they occasionally worked for hire on the farms of the villans and freemen.

Some bordars and cottars were also intimately involved in the cultivation of the demesnes, so much so that they can be regarded as the forerunners of the permanent or semi-permanent labourers known as *famuli* who provided the very core of domanial labour forces in a later period.[4] Here their role shades off into that of the slaves, and it is only sensible to consider all three classes together. As many as 28,000 slaves and nearly 500 *ancillae* (female slaves) are enumerated—10 per cent of the entire recorded population, and almost certainly many were omitted from the survey. A few, perhaps, were menials living in the lord's court and eating at a common table. The rest are to be imagined with dwellings of their own and, very likely, tiny holdings. If legally they remained severely disadvantaged, economically they were now often hard to distinguish from other smallholders engaged in the routine domanial tasks: ploughing and carting, looking after the cows and the dairy, the pigs and the beehives. The domanial servants with specialized tasks who are enumerated separately in some manors—smiths, for example, and *bovarii* (ploughmen)—must in others be subsumed under the categories of bordar, cottar, or slave. It is even possible

[1] P. D. A. Harvey (ed.), *The Peasant Land Market in Medieval England* (Oxford, 1984), 9–13.

[2] Lennard, *Rural England*, 339 n., and 'The Economic Position of the Bordars and Cottars of Domesday Book', *Economic Jnl* 61 (1951), 342–71.

[3] S. P. J. Harvey, 'Evidence for Settlement Study: Domesday Book', *Medieval Settlement*, ed. Sawyer, 195–9.

[4] M. M. Postan, *The Famulus* (*Econ HR* Supplement no. 2, 1954), 5 ff.

that in a number of manors the miller, whom Domesday occasionally associates very closely with the lord's hall, belonged to one or other of these categories. But the little evidence we have makes it seem more likely that this important official, destined to enjoy so many opportunities of personal gain and incur so much obloquy in the process, was a more substantial figure in 1086—a peasant occupying a virgate or half-virgate holding which he worked in addition to the mill. In general, under the headings of bordars, cottars, and slaves, Domesday brings to our attention those familiar participants in English agrarian life down the ages: farm labourers living in tied cottages.

SELECT BIBLIOGRAPHY

M. Bloch, 'The Rise of Dependent Cultivation and Seignorial Institutions', *Cambridge Economic History of Europe*, i (2nd edn., Cambridge, 1966), 235–90

R. H. C. Davis, 'East Anglia and the Danelaw', *TRHS* 5th ser., 5 (1955), 23–39

R. Lennard, *Rural England 1086–1135* (Oxford, 1959)

F. W. Maitland, *Domesday Book and Beyond* (Cambridge, 1897)

F. M. Stenton, *Types of Manorial Structure in the Northern Danelaw* (Oxford, 1910)

P. Vinogradoff, *English Society in the Eleventh Century* (Oxford, 1908)

IV. AGRICULTURE IN LATE ANGLO-SAXON ENGLAND

HELEN CLARKE

EVEN though England at the time of Domesday was highly urbanized in comparison with many other countries of north-west Europe the backbone of its economy was still rural, and was to remain so for many centuries to come. The wealth of the nation depended on raising crops, breeding animals, and utilizing the products of the land.

And yet our knowledge of agricultural practices before the Norman Conquest remains woefully incomplete. Domesday Book itself, with its constant reiteration of 'ploughs', 'ploughlands', and 'plough-teams', underlines the importance, if not pre-eminence, of arable as opposed to pastoral farming in Anglo-Saxon and early Norman England, but it gives us little information about the physical aspects of farming and organization. Domesday Book remains virtually silent on pastoral farming, which must have been part of the rural economy in all parts of the country, and its mainstay in some areas.

The information that we do have about Anglo-Saxon agriculture, although slight, comes from a wide range of sources. There are illuminated manuscripts of the tenth and eleventh centuries which illustrate the characteristic occupations of each month and various rustic activities and crafts; there is an invaluable early eleventh-century treatise on estate management and the duties of a reeve (*Rectitudines Singularum Personarum* and *Gerefa*); there are occasional illustrations in the Bayeux Tapestry; and, finally, there is archaeological evidence, mainly obtained through recent excavations on rural settlement sites. The archaeological evidence has increased in quantity over the past few years and, although still fairly limited in extent, it has the most potential for expanding our knowledge in the future as more excavations take place. A few recent publications have used the above evidence as the basis for surveys of Anglo-Saxon agriculture, either concentrating almost entirely on documentary sources[1] or combining these with archaeological material;[2] they remain the best modern introductions to the subject although recent archaeological excavations have modified some of their conclusions.

The varied nature of England's geology and climate makes it difficult to generalize about agricultural practices at any period, let alone when the evidence is so scanty. Nevertheless, the evidence that is available to us suggests that the main arable crops grown in the Anglo-Saxon fields of southern and eastern England were wheat, barley, oats, rye, and legumes,[3] even though excavations in Gloucester have shown spelt still to be a significant element in the cereal crops of the Severn valley in the tenth and eleventh centuries, long after it had fallen out of favour further south and east. Moreover, barley, common elsewhere, was virtually unknown in the West.[4] The diet of the English, so far as cereals are concerned, must, therefore, have varied from area to area, according to the soil type and the climate.

We are only gradually coming to understand what the fields in which these crops were grown looked like at the time of Domesday. On their arrival in England in the fifth century the Anglo-Saxons probably took over and farmed the already existing Romano-British system of square or rectangular fields, 'Celtic fields', but during the subsequent centuries of Anglo-Saxon occupation the English fields must have evolved towards the elongated ridge-and-furrow form well known from the medieval Midlands and dependent on the use of the mould-board plough. This field-type has long been thought to be a post-Conquest development but its origin has now been firmly dated to the Anglo-Saxon period through the archaeological discovery of ridge-and-furrow fields in secure pre-Conquest contexts: under blown sand at Gwithian, Cornwall,[5] and beneath the banks of castle baileys at Hen Domen, Montgomery,[6] and Sandal, Yorkshire.[7]

Thus, at some date before the Norman Conquest, at least some farmers in these three widely separated areas of the country used the type of plough capable of turning a furrow and of building up ridges. This must have been the mould-board plough, which would also have had a coulter for cutting through heavy soils. It is interesting to note that at Hen Domen the ridge-and-furrow immediately overlay simple plough-marks, that is, mere scratchings of the ground surface made by a simpler and lighter plough incapable of turning the soil. A share from such a plough, unique in England, is known from a hoard of Anglo-Saxon artefacts found at Naze-

[1] H. P. R. Finberg (ed.), *The Agrarian History of England and Wales*, Vol. I, pt. ii: *A.D. 43–1042* (Cambridge, 1972).

[2] P. V. Addyman, 'Archaeology and Anglo-Saxon Society', *Problems in Social and Economic Archaeology*, ed. G. de G. Sieveking (London, 1976), 309–22; P. J. Fowler, 'Farming in the Anglo-Saxon Landscape: An Archaeologist's Review', *ASE* 9 (1981), 263–80; D. M. Wilson, 'Anglo-Saxon Rural Economy: a survey of the archaeological evidence and a suggestion', *Agricultural Hist. Rev.* 10, pt. 2 (1962), 65–79.

[3] Fowler, 'Farming in the Anglo-Saxon Landscape', 278.

[4] C. M. Heighway *et al.*, 'Excavations at 1 Westgate Street, Gloucester, 1975', *MA* 23 (1979), 189.

[5] P. J. Fowler and A. C. Thomas, 'Arable Fields of the Pre-Norman Period at Gwithian', *Cornish Archaeol.* 1 (1962), 61–84.

[6] P. A. Barker and J. Lawson, 'A Pre-Norman Field System at Hen Domen, Montgomery', *MA* 15 (1971), 58–72.

[7] P. Mayes and L. Butler, *Sandal Castle Excavations 1964–1973* (Wakefield, 1983), 70.

FIG. 1

ing, Essex, and probably deposited in the early eleventh century.[1]

Archaeological evidence for Anglo-Saxon ploughs is sparse, for most of the parts of a plough were made of wood which will have long since rotted away. Only the ploughshare and the coulter were of iron, and a few Anglo-Saxon examples have been preserved, for instance shares from St Neots, Hunts.,[2] and Thetford, Norfolk,[3] and both share and coulter from Westley Waterless, Cambs.[4] All three shares were of heavy iron, triangular in shape and with a socket at one end for attachment. Their equivalents can be seen on the seven illustrations of ploughs in pre-Conquest illuminated manuscripts and on the Bayeux Tapestry, all of which also show other agricultural activities.

Although executed in different styles, two manuscripts, the astronomical treatise BL MS Tiberius B. V (Fig. 2), and BL MS Julius A. VI, show identical scenes of a ploughman steering a wheeled plough which has a mould-board and a coulter held in place by a peg and rope. Two pairs of oxen pull the plough, encouraged by a man brandishing a goad. Neither illustration shows how the oxen were harnessed to the plough; this can be seen more clearly in the Cædmon manuscript, Bodleian Library MS Julius 11,[5] where two scenes show a similar wheeled plough being pulled by two oxen yoked together. In all these examples the ground surface is indicated by a jagged line, which could perhaps be taken as a schematic representation of ridge-and-furrow. The Bayeux Tapestry also depicts a similar plough (Fig. 1) but with a donkey-like creature as draught animal. The next scene shows a horse-drawn harrow: a square wooden frame surrounding rows of nail-like spikes. This is the only representation of a harrow in Anglo-Saxon art and it is interesting to see that it is indisputably pulled by a horse harnessed by a horse-collar. Draught animals in both Anglo-Saxon and medieval times were generally oxen so this representation of a horse may indicate that speed rather than strength was required for harrowing the ground after ploughing.

Between the plough and the harrow on the Tapestry walks a man broadcasting seed from a basket, the traditional method of sowing seed. Scenes of harvesting are not recorded on the Tapestry but are faithfully shown in both MS Julius A. VI and MS Tiberius B. V, where haymaking in June (Fig. 3) and harvesting in August (Fig. 4) are shown. In June the labourers cut the hay with sickles and toss the bundles on to a cart with pitchforks. Neither sickles nor pitchforks have yet been found in archaeological excavations, but many long-handled scythes similar to those in the August scene of both manuscripts are known, the best examples being from the Hurbuck hoard, Co. Durham,[6] where one of the four scythe-blades is complete down to its upturned tang, which would have been hammered into the wood of the scythe-shaft. The scythes in the manuscript illuminations are held by handholds protruding from their shafts at right angles, just as in a modern scythe, and it is interesting to see how little the agricultural tools of the Anglo-Saxons differ from those still in use up to recent years. Even such a simple implement as a whetstone is recognizable; in the August scene a man on the left is honing his scythe-blade with a whetstone which he probably dipped into the bucket standing at his feet. Hinged flails used in threshing in the December scene of the same manuscript and the riddle employed in sieving the grain have their modern equivalents (Fig. 5), as do billhooks and pruning knives. We are warned by some

[1] C. A. Morris, 'A Late Saxon Hoard of Iron and Copper-Alloy Artefacts from Nazeing, Essex', *MA* 27 (1983), 32, fig. 2.

[2] T. C. Lethbridge and C. F. Tebbutt, 'Huts of the Anglo-Saxon Period', *Proc. of the Cambridge Ant. Soc.* 33 (1933), 145–6.

[3] A. Rogerson and C. Dallas, 'Excavations in Thetford 1948–59 and 1973–80', *East Anglian Archaeol.* 22 (1984), 81.

[4] C. Fox, *The Archaeology of the Cambridge Region* (Cambridge, 1933), 300.

[5] I. Gollancz, *The Cædmon Manuscript of Anglo-Saxon Biblical Poetry*, i (Oxford, 1927), 54, 77.

[6] D. M. Wilson, *The Anglo-Saxons* (Harmondsworth, 1971), 78, fig. 11.

FIG. 2
January: Ploughing, f. 3.

FIG. 3
June: Haymaking, f. 5v.

FIG. 4
August: Harvesting, f. 6v.

The seasons from BL MS Cotton Tiberius B.V.

FIG. 5

December: Threshing and Winnowing, f. 8v.

authorities[1] not to place absolute reliance on manuscript illustrations, which may be representations of illustrations in other manuscripts rather than of the objects themselves, but the basic simplicity of the tools and their similarity to modern examples make it reasonable to accept their authenticity.

Spades, however, which appear in manuscripts and the Bayeux Tapestry, did differ from the modern spade in that they were entirely of wood, apart from a rim or shoe of iron on the cutting edge. They could also be asymmetrical, as in the scene in the Bayeux Tapestry showing the building of Hastings Castle (Fig. 1, Special Study IX, p. 70 below), with most of the blade being to the left or to the right of the shaft.

The final activity associated with cereal growing was grinding the grain into flour. This was done either on hand querns or in water-mills, many hundreds of which are mentioned in Domesday Book and two of which have been excavated. The late Anglo-Saxon royal mill at Old Windsor, Berks.,[2] was an elaborate structure with three vertical water-wheels fed by water from a leat about three-quarters of a mile long and cut across a loop of the Thames. At Tamworth, War., a somewhat earlier water-mill with a horizontal wheel has been excavated more recently.[3] Both mills ground their grain with circular millstones of Niedermendig lava imported from the Rhineland, and the same type of stone has been found on virtually every middle and late Anglo-Saxon settlement site in the form of querns, or hand-mills, used by many householders in preference to the lord's mechanized mill.

Although the number of agricultural tools found through excavations is small, it is increasing as more excavations take place and more ironwork is analysed scientifically. The quantities found, however, will probably never be very great as the majority of tools used by the Anglo-Saxons would have been reforged to make new implements when the old were broken or worn out; few would have been lost or thrown away for later retrieval by archaeologists. The eleventh-century *Gerefa* lists the tools necessary for the efficient running of an Anglo-Saxon estate; some, such as those mentioned above, have been discovered by excavation but others are unknown and likely to remain so.[4]

There should, however, be little limitation on the quantities of animal bones retrieved from excavated sites and, always bearing in mind that the animal bones from settlements represent what was eaten rather than what was bred, study of such bones can tell us a great deal about pastoral farming in Anglo-Saxon times.

Recent publications of the animal bones from a number of settlement sites occupied from the eighth to the eleventh centuries have vastly increased our understanding of Anglo-Saxon pastoral economy. Cattle were the most common domestic animal throughout the period. There is evidence for their cross-breeding and comparatively large size at North Elmham, Norfolk,[5] and for a high standard of husbandry with rigorous culling of sickly animals and good-quality winter feeding at Portchester.[6] At Portchester also, one-third of the cattle were female and two-thirds were castrates, probably reflecting the use of oxen for traction. Use as traction animals is also likely at North Elmham, where the age of slaughter of cattle suggests that a high proportion were kept for some purpose other than food production, and that they were only eaten after a long and useful life.

Sheep grew in numbers, and therefore in importance, during the tenth and eleventh centuries at both above-mentioned sites. At North Elmham their size, the standard of feeding, and also the proportion of castrated rams all increased over time, and it seems certain that

1 Wilson, 'Anglo-Saxon Rural Economy', 77.

2 D. M. Wilson and J. G. Hurst, 'Medieval Britain in 1957', *MA* 2 (1958), 184.

3 P. A. Rahtz, 'The Archaeology of West Mercian Towns', *Mercian Studies*, ed. A. Dornier (Leicester, 1976), 123, figs. 24, 25.

4 Addyman, 'Archaeology and Anglo-Saxon Society', 319–21.

5 P. Wade-Martins, 'Excavations in North Elmham Park 1967–1972', *East Anglian Archaeol.* 9 (1980), 385, 396.

6 B. Cunliffe, *Excavations at Portchester Castle II*, Soc. of Antiquaries Research Report (1976), 286.

FIG. 6

September: Swine feeding in woodland, f. 7.

sheep were being kept primarily for their wool, the fleeces of castrates growing more luxuriantly than those of other sheep. The increasing importance of textile production in Anglo-Saxon England has been a commonplace assertion among historians, and it gains support from the study of animal bones, as it does from the textile-working implements such as spindle-whorls, thread-pickers, and heckle teeth found on settlement sites. At Goltho, Lincs., for example, a weaving shed was discovered as part of an Anglo-Saxon manorial complex.[1]

The domestic pig seems still in the Anglo-Saxon period to have been closely related to wild swine, being dark, hairy, and long-legged. These animals can be seen in the woodland illustration in MS Tiberius B. V (Fig. 6). In some areas pigs may have been kept as only partially domesticated animals throughout the Anglo-Saxon period, although at Ramsbury, Wilts., pigs from the eighth- and ninth-century settlement were very small and showed no signs of cross-breeding with wild swine.[2]

The other animals and birds on Anglo-Saxon settlement sites are less well represented in the excavated bones: horses are relatively rare, cats and dogs are present, and the birds are mostly domestic fowl. The paucity of horse bones may well reflect the absence of horse flesh from the normal diet rather than an absence of horses themselves. Horses were probably kept for riding or for traction.

The use of traction animals presupposes the existence of vehicles. We have already seen the ploughs pulled by oxen and the harrow drawn by a horse. There is also evidence for carts which may have been pulled by either. There are no archaeological remains of carts, but the illustrations in MS Tiberius B. V for June (Fig. 3) and July show the loading of hay and timber on to wagons, and in the Bayeux Tapestry a cart loaded with a huge barrel of wine and other military equipment is shown being conveyed to the Norman fleet.[3] Strangely, however, none of these vehicles is shown being pulled by animals and that on the Tapestry has one or two men harnessed for traction. Can it be that human power rather than animal power was used to pull carts? Did the hay-wain of the *Gerefa* rely on men as traction? Did the system of communications discussed elsewhere in this publication rely on pack-animals and human legs alone? It is difficult to believe that this was so, but as yet there is neither illustrative nor archaeological evidence to the contrary.

[1] G. Beresford, 'Goltho Manor, Lincolnshire: The Buildings and their Surrounding Defences *c.*850–1150', *Proc. of the Battle Conference 1981*, iv (1982), 15–36.

[2] J. Haslam *et al.*, 'A Middle Saxon Iron Smelting Site at Ramsbury, Wiltshire', *MA* 24 (1980), 47.

[3] F. M. Stenton *et al.* (eds.), *The Bayeux Tapestry* (London, 1957), pl. 12.

V. THE ARCHAEOLOGY OF THE DOMESDAY VILL

DAVID AUSTIN

DOMESDAY BOOK is a snare for any unwary student who believes that it records the physical reality of the eleventh century. Yet historians can still be trapped into believing that the text everywhere records a landscape in 1086 of villages and open fields much as it emerges into the full light of manorial documentation in the thirteenth century. In their discussion of statistics, status, and institutions, some still carry with them an image of a countryside probably more familiar to Piers Plowman than to the commissioners, local officials, and peasant farmers who compiled the information needed so hurriedly by the Conqueror. Lennard, for example, in 1959 was keen to assert the teeming life in the old densely farmed landscape of 1086:

> And of England as a whole . . . the unassailable evidence of Domesday Book enables one to assert without hesitation that the great majority of Englishmen lived in villages

but he added as a parenthesis:

> or hamlets that were probably associated to form village-townships for administrative purposes . . . To those familiar with the English countryside today and inclined to take its layout for granted, this may seem a trite conclusion.[1]

It does and it is, but this was not the fault of that great scholar. He was writing before historical geographers and archaeologists began to question seriously whether the information contained in the folios of Domesday Book could only be viewed with this kind of landscape in mind. Consistently the answer has begun to come back that the people recorded in 1086 could and did live in a great variety of settlement forms, from single, isolated, and seasonal shepherd's cots to great trading towns, and that these were intermingled in a bewildering network across the face of the landscape in a manner only dimly discernible to those of us who try to visualize them today. The closer we look and the more we gather and assess contemporary evidence the more we understand how little we really know. For it is also clear now that Domesday Book records not a landscape caught in a stable equilibrium created centuries before, as Lennard believed, but one in the process of changes perhaps more fundamental than anything seen since the later Bronze Age. Domesday England was indeed 'an old country', but the ancient and fundamental pattern was one of dispersed farms and hamlets, enclosed arable fields, and common permanent pastures. The new agriculture, only a couple of centuries old in the East Midlands and still being introduced in parts of the North, the West Midlands, and the South, was the village and the open arable field with its pasture created by fallow rotation. In some parts of England this was still being introduced in the late eleventh, twelfth, and thirteenth centuries and fitfully even later. In some parts 'village England' never happened, and in some, perhaps the largest, the old and the new were mixed together with nucleated villages existing alongside ancient farms and hamlets in the same and neighbouring vills. Indeed, it may be said that the widespread abandonment of the village form and the open field in the later Middle Ages and the modern period was merely a reversion to the basic, ancient pattern of the English landscape. Potentially, therefore, the places named in the leaves of Domesday Book—vills, manors, berewicks, and others—may have had almost any type of layout and the population may have lived almost anywhere within the bounds of the place designated.[2] The realization of this has been slow to dawn, but historians are themselves contributing to the undermining of our former certainty and the message is clear:

> There is no need to emphasise the inadequacy of Domesday Book as a source for the study of settlement . . . Just as one name could be used to describe a large estate with many settlements in it, so too what appear to be 'village' names may well refer not to nucleations but to dispersed settlements . . . I will do no more than underline the danger of assuming that the places named in Domesday Book were nucleated settlements. Neither demesne farming nor co-aration necessarily implies the existence of nucleated settlements.[3]

So we must talk of the archaeology not of the Domesday village, but of the vill or township—that unit of social and economic organization many believe to be the basic building block of the British landscape.[4]

In recent years archaeologists have worked closely with historical geographers, particularly in the field of settlement morphology and retrogressive analysis. In other words the plans, particularly of villages, have been studied to define and classify their principal elements,[5] and documents, including Domesday Book, have been used to explore the antiquity of these forms.[6] Maps and plans, however, are largely post-medieval, and England as a whole is not effectively covered until the nineteenth century. Nevertheless it is certain that, even so late, the

[1] R. Lennard, *Rural England 1086–1135* (Oxford, 1959), 20.

[2] For some of these challenging ideas see the work of C. C. Taylor, particularly *Village and Farmstead* (London, 1983).

[3] P. H. Sawyer, 'The Anglo-Norman Village', *Medieval Villages, a Review of Current Work*, ed. D. Hooke (Oxford, 1985), 5.

[4] e.g. D. H. Michelmore, 'The Reconstruction of the Early Tenurial and Territorial Divisions of the Landscape of Northern England', *Landscape Hist.* 1 (1979), 1–9.

[5] B. K. Roberts, 'The Anatomy of the Village: Observation and Extrapolation', *Landscape Hist.* 4 (1982), 11–20.

[6] e.g. M. A. Aston, 'Rural Settlement in Somerset: Some Preliminary Thoughts', *Medieval Villages*, ed. Hooke, 80–100.

plans of settlements, if read carefully, carry indications and evidence of their own origins. In part, medieval and later documents can help the student to isolate those elements which are earlier and eliminate those which are later. These have their limitations, however, and for periods earlier than the thirteenth century there is an increasing need to justify claims for the date of particular settlement forms and changes by recourse to archaeology, principally to field-work and excavation; that is, walking across ploughed fields to recover artefacts on sites of former habitation and digging scientific holes to reveal evidence of past ways of life and behaviour.

Yet even here we find limitations, if we want to discover what any Domesday vill actually looked like. One problem, for example, is dating. Very largely archaeologists have to rely on pottery fragments to provide some indication of when their sites were functioning, although metalwork, architectural features, and physical methods (especially carbon-14) can be used in the right circumstances. Yet even for relatively recent periods date-brackets of less than fifty years' duration are almost impossible to assign. The eleventh century falls towards the end of the ceramic phase known as the Saxo-Norman (*c*.850–1150), a period when production was centred in the growing and prospering towns of England, such as Stamford, Thetford, Norwich, Nottingham, York, Winchester, and Stafford. The ability of specialists to subdivide this phase into smaller units varies from centre to centre, and on sites, especially rural ones, with long periods of occupation early material will be mixed with late so that it may be possible to tell only approximately when any given area was in use. Some centres of production, particularly those of eastern England, seem also to have been efficient enough for their wares to swamp and destroy the rural craft of pottery-making in their hinterlands and in some instances penetrate beyond their immediate market catchments. Elsewhere, in the South, West, and North of England, the vills did not receive products in the same quantities, and in some areas, such as Devonshire and Cornwall, the marches of Wales, and Northumbria, the rural areas seem not to have used pottery until the twelfth century. In these circumstances field-walkers and excavators alike have found it difficult to record the settlement patterns and forms of the Norman period and earlier. The patchy distribution of the pottery belies the very fine quality of Saxo-Norman wares, which were almost universally made on a fast wheel. The fabric of the vessels is usually hard and well fired, but with the use of glazes restricted to only a few centres such as Stamford, Nottingham, and Winchester. Their forms, illustrated in Figs. 1–3, are dominated by tall jars, spouted pitchers, and bowls.[1]

Saxo-Norman pottery, despite its archaeological limitations, does serve to underline the regional nature of Domesday England, and four examples from different areas will serve to illustrate this and show what we can and cannot say about the places mentioned so fleetingly in the survey. In recent years a series of impor-

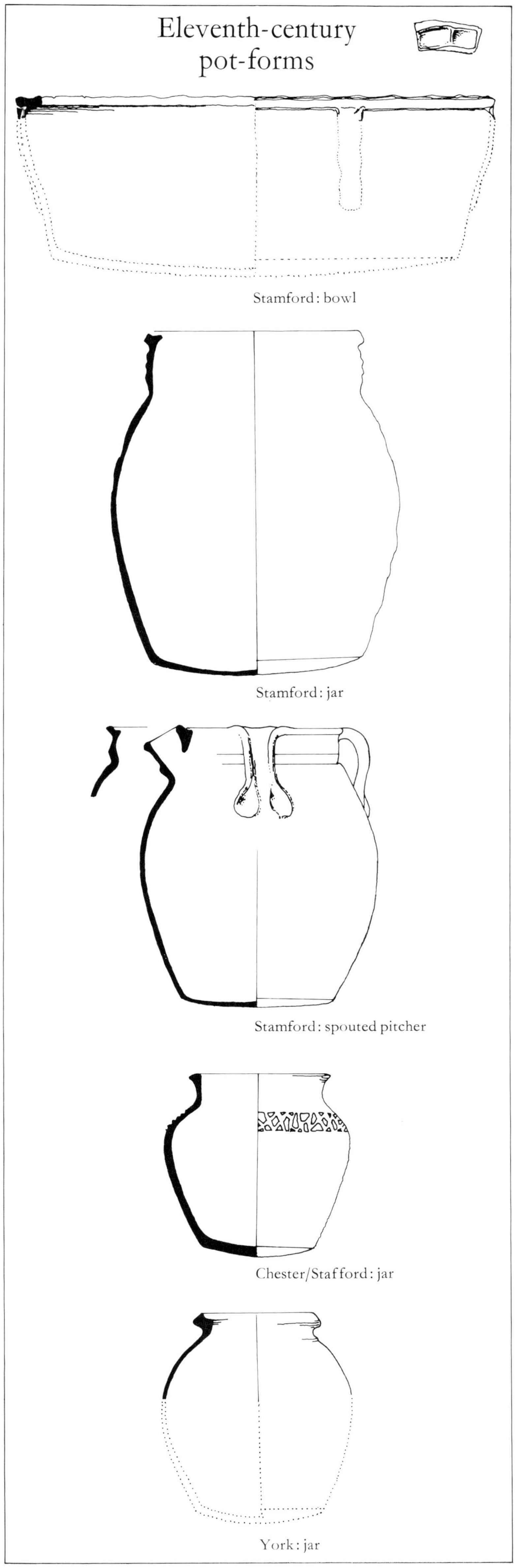

FIG. 1

[1] J. G. Hurst, 'The Pottery', *The Archaeology of Anglo-Saxon England*, ed. D. M. Wilson (London, 1976), 314–48.

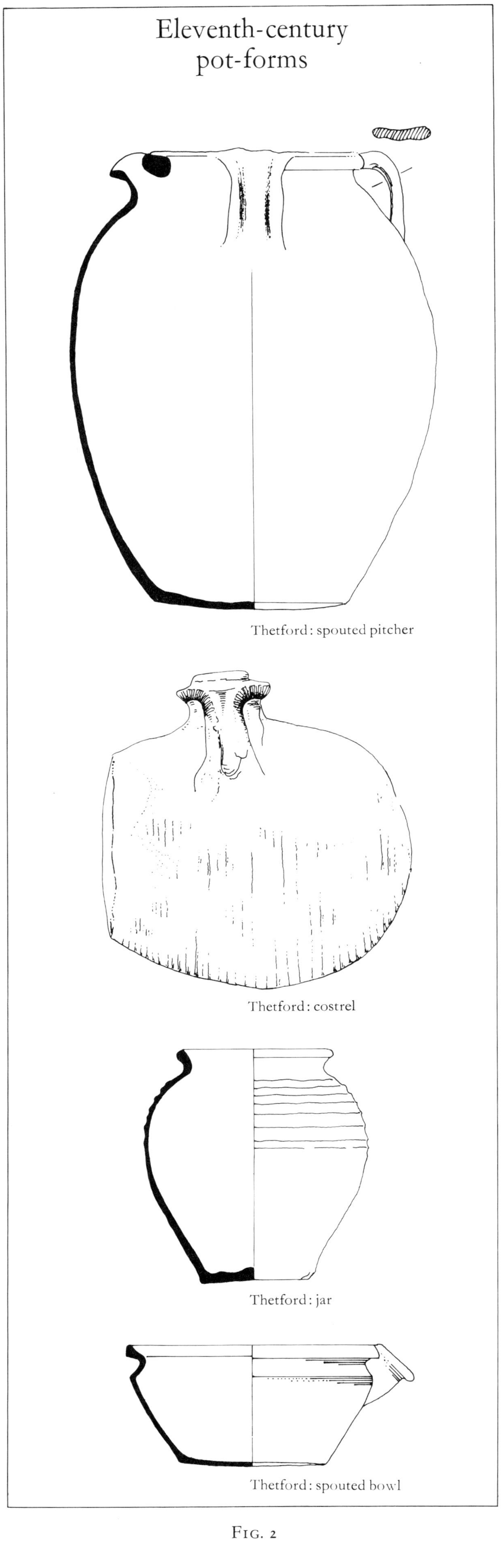

FIG. 2

tant parish studies has been conducted by David Hall in the Northamptonshire landscape and neighbouring counties.[1] Working with post-medieval surveys and terriers of open fields which survived into the eighteenth and nineteenth centuries, Hall has demonstrated that the complex arrangements of furlongs at this late date, so typical of the developed Midland system as defined by Gray,[2] have an underlying simplicity based on long strips, or lands, laid out in a small number of large blocks allotted to tenants in regular cycles (Fig. 4). Indications in later medieval documents suggest that these arrangements were in place before 1300, but prior to that the written evidence becomes much more tenuous. Domesday Book, as Sawyer warned, does not itself describe field organization; but like many before him, Hall argues that similarities between hidation ploughland assessments in 1086 and acreages and assessments in the later texts are strong indications for the existence of open field in the eleventh century and before. Unsupported, this would be taking the evidence too far, since the assessments are primarily indicators for tenure and the distribution of wealth in various communities and say nothing directly about the physical partition of the landscape. It could just as easily be argued that the organization of wealth and tenure would stay the same despite radical alterations in the physical layout of the landscape; a good analogy might be the enclosure movement. As an archaeologist, however, Hall's most persuasive evidence comes from the fields themselves. The ridge-and-furrow and the headland dykes, which correspond to the strips and furlong boundaries of the later plans, have been ploughed down in many parishes in Northamptonshire, and field-walking has revealed that they were laid out over earlier occupation sites whose presence is betrayed by scatters of pottery. Consistently, in parishes such as Wellingborough and Brixworth, the sequence of sites, stretching back to the prehistoric, ends in the Middle Saxon period about AD 800, and the extent of the pottery-scatters further suggests that these are the remnants of small, dispersed hamlets or farms. Hall has concluded, therefore, that there was a widespread reorganization of the landscape at this time, involving the layout of new field systems and the relocation of rural populations in nucleated settlements or villages. In the simple regularity of the systems Hall sees the hand of strong lordship, which alone, he contends, would have had the authority to carry out such large-scale alterations.

By 1086, on this argument, the new agriculture was firmly in place. But there are problems: how many of the pot-scatters, for example, really are traces of small settlements and what form did they take? What is the evidence for simultaneous nucleation in the villages? What can be said about the numerous farm and hamlet complexes which existed in the Northamptonshire landscape in the later Middle Ages and which are rarely mentioned in Domesday Book: were they new creations

[1] D. N. Hall, 'The Origins of Open Field Agriculture—the Archaeological Fieldwork Evidence', *The Origins of Open Field Agriculture*, ed. T. Rowley (London, 1981), 22–38.

[2] H. L. Gray, *English Field Systems* (Cambridge, Mass., 1915).

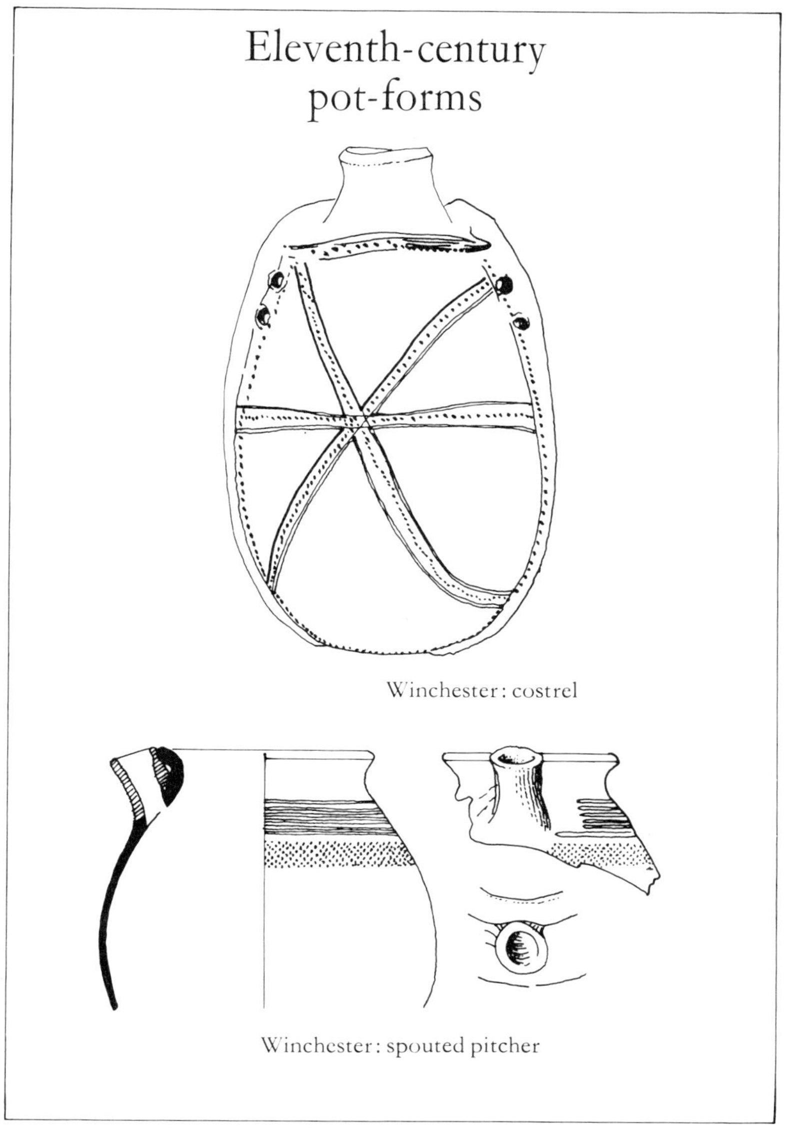

FIG. 3

of the twelfth or thirteenth centuries or were they survivors of the old system which failed to be separately recorded in 1086 because they were subsumed under the main vill-heading and name? Analysis by Christopher Taylor of village plans in this region suggests that they may be fusions of neighbouring, but dispersed, elements which in many cases may have been lordship tenements later manifesting themselves as manor-houses or even castles.[1] This is, however, only one of the processes involved, and evidence of date and of whether these are sudden or planned events is hard to find. Answers to these questions can only be achieved by excavations, but these need to be on a scale large enough to provide the right kind of information, since we need to know not just the size and nature of any given village at any time in its life, but also the location and form of any contemporary settlements within the vill. This requires long-term projects, and one such has begun at Raunds in Northamptonshire (Figs. 4–7), where excavations have taken place within the principal village and a dependent hamlet called West Cotton. It is early days here yet, writing in 1985, but it is already clear that the structure of the village plan is very complex and surprisingly fluid, with at least two manorial enclosures and two churches at Domesday, a fact for which the survey itself does not directly prepare us. There is no space here to discuss the detail of the excavations, but it is to be hoped that as this project continues it will add significantly to our knowledge of rural England in the eleventh century.[2]

Further north similar research has been conducted by various scholars on the settlements of Holderness, the Yorkshire Wolds, and the Vale of York. Mary Harvey in her analyses of open-field systems has found even clearer evidence for regularity and furlong simplicity,[3] and June Sheppard has shown how certain village plans appear to be laid out to standard measurements with such remarkable order in the morphology that some single act of planning, probably seigneurial, is responsible.[4] Like Brian Roberts with his work on settlement plans in County Durham,[5] Sheppard and Harvey have pointed to William's 'harrying of the North' in 1069–70 as a time when the devastation of the rural communities was so complete that the new Norman lords could impose a reformed, planned landscape at will. Domesday Book does, indeed, seem to show that much of the North of England was still waste in 1086, but it is arguable to what extent the greatly reduced values to be found in the Yorkshire entries do actually represent derelict vills and unfarmed lands. Indeed Harvey, taking account of this dispute and influenced by the evidence produced by Hall in Northamptonshire, has suggested that the circumstances of the Danish settlement in the late ninth century might have provided an even better opportunity for the creation of these planned landscapes.[6] Again, a major archaeological project in the region is providing some evidence for dating and understanding some of the developments taking place. At Wharram Percy on the north-western scarp of the Wolds a remarkable sequence of settlement has been uncovered, again involving origins in a dispersed pattern of farms. Current thinking suggests that a regularly planned three-row village was laid out with its fields by the Conquest, incorporating two manor-houses, a church, a central green, and two mills.[7]

The descriptions of settlement in the North of England as presented here might suggest that a simple pattern of village creation is being established by recent work, but this would be to mask the true state of affairs. Vills with irregular villages and complex fields, those with no nucleations at all, those with extensive systems of closes and commons, and those with multiple nucleations all exist and need to be fitted into the picture at some time in the future. Turning to the South of England, we have an immediate contrast: much less morphological study has been done, with a few notable

[1] C. C. Taylor, 'Polyfocal Settlement and the English Village', *MA* 21 (1977), 189–93.

[2] G. Cadman and G. Foard, 'Raunds: Manorial and Village Origins', *Studies in Late Anglo-Saxon Settlement*, ed. M. L. Faull (Oxford, 1984), 81–100.

[3] M. Harvey, 'Regular Field and Tenurial Arrangements in Holderness, Yorkshire', *Jnl of Hist. Geography*, 6 (1980), 3–16.

[4] J. Sheppard, 'Metrological Analysis of Regular Village Plans in Yorkshire', *Agricultural Hist. Rev.* 22 (1974), 118–35.

[5] B. K. Roberts, 'Village Plans in County Durham: A Preliminary Statement', *MA* 16 (1972), 33–56.

[6] M. Harvey, 'Open Field Structure and Landholding Arrangements in Eastern Yorkshire', *Trans. of the Inst. of Brit. Geographers*, ns 9 (1984), 60–74.

[7] J. G. Hurst, 'The Wharram Research Project: Results to 1983', *MA* 28 (1984), 77–111.

FIG. 4

The plan shows the extent of the village as it was in 1798 (see Fig. 5) and the blocks (furlongs) and directions of strips as reconstructed by David Hall from fieldwalking, aerial photography, and late terriers. Note in particular the large furlongs with long strips and the great extent of land under rotated arable production.

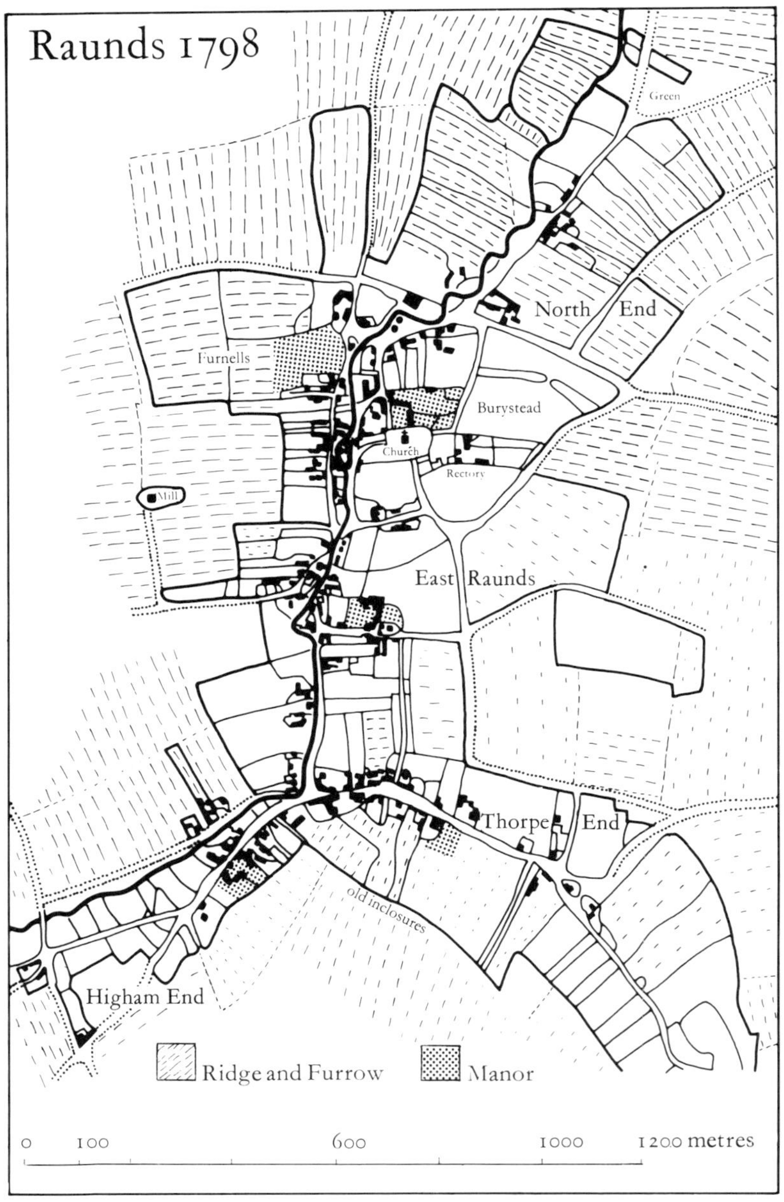

FIG. 5

This, the earliest extant survey, shows the apparently random structure of the village along a north-south axis aligned on a stream. It is uncertain how all elements in this plan were in existence by 1086, but evidence from Furnells suggests much may have been there by that date. Note the characteristic strips of property (crofts) which lie behind the buildings and yards (tofts) which front onto the streets.

exceptions, and the analysis of field systems has not been integrated with archaeological work on settlements in quite such a comprehensive way. The problems of pottery distribution are part of the reason for this, but the diversity of agrarian systems and settlement patterns can be bewildering and daunting, as James Bond has recently shown for Oxfordshire, where 617 nucleations must be classified and examined, without even beginning to consider the dispersed forms.[1] From excavation rather more is known about earlier Anglo-Saxon sites than later, with some important major work at places like Chalton Church Down, Hants,[2] Cowdery's Down, Hants,[3] and Bishopstone, Sussex,[4] which give us considerable information on early and middle Saxon farms and minor nucleations. Yet examination of a range of excavations on later village and manorial sites, as well as those of an earlier date, by Michael Hughes in Hampshire has shown a great variety of settlement changes in the years leading up to the Norman Conquest.[5] Of twenty-three sites with 'reasonable' evidence, three were abandoned in the seventh century, having begun in the fifth, six began in the seventh or early eighth and continued into the later Middle Ages, two started in the later Saxon period and failed before the twelfth, and two started in the later eighth century and ten in the tenth or eleventh centuries and survived as later settlements. This does not take into account the number of sites which have produced evidence of post-Conquest occupation, but none of Anglo-Saxon. Simple counts such as this graphically illustrate the nature of the archaeological problems, but only detailed studies can begin to demonstrate some of the processes involved. In the parish of Chalton, Hants, for example, considerable field-work and excavation by a number of people have produced evidence for site abandonment and village creation in the eighth and ninth centuries, and by Domesday Book a complex network of both nucleated and dispersed settlement had emerged, not, however, to remain static.[6]

[1] C. J. Bond, 'Medieval Oxfordshire Villages and their Topography', *Medieval Villages*, ed. Hooke, 101–23.

[2] T. Champion, 'Chalton', *CA* 59 (1977), 364–9.

[3] M. Millett with S. James, 'Excavations at Cowdery's Down, Basingstoke, Hampshire', *ArchJ* 140 (1983), 151–279.

[4] M. G. Bell, 'Excavations at Bishopstone', *Sussex Archaeol. Collections*, 115 (1977), 1–299.

[5] M. Hughes, 'Rural Settlement and Landscape in Late Saxon Hampshire', *Studies in Late Anglo-Saxon Settlement*, ed. Faull, 65–79.

[6] Ibid. 72–8 for a recent discussion of this important project.

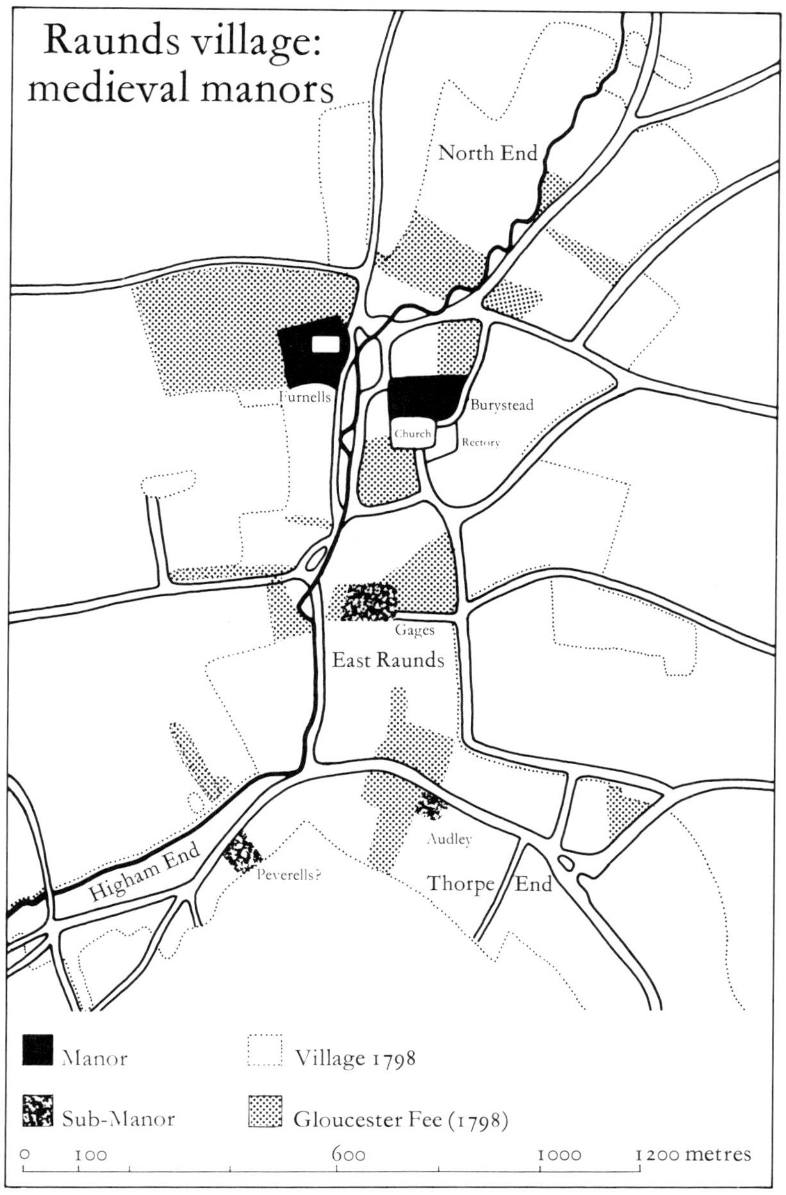

FIG. 6

Analysis of the documents and village plan by Glenn Foard show, in fact, that the apparently random pattern consists of an interlocking set of individual elements which can be identified with five separate manors known to be in Domesday Book. This agglomerated nucleation of elements in separate ownership has been called 'poly-focal' by Christopher Taylor.

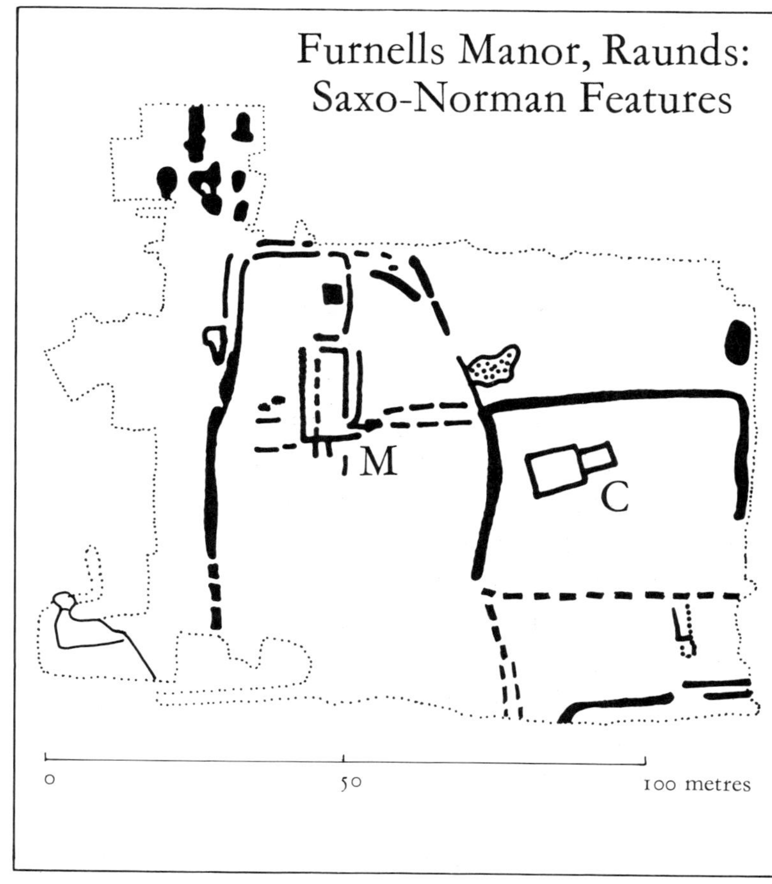

FIG. 7

This plan of the eleventh-century phase (4.i.) shows clearly the manorial enclosure and principal buildings (M) which developed in the later Anglo-Saxon period and the church with its cemetery enclosure (C) which are appended to the manor complex.

Finally, if we turn our attention to the South-West and to Devonshire in particular, the nature of the archaeological evidence changes again. In a region virtually without pottery, there is little conclusive evidence for the forms and patterns of settlement before the twelfth century, and Domesday Book with its account of manors and vills obscures the fine detail of a landscape consisting essentially of farms and small hamlets. Okehampton, for example, held by Baldwin in 1086, is a single entry, but the assessments almost certainly cover a number of unnamed places which only appear for the first time in the Book of Fees for *c.*1270.[1] Excavations in the parish in recent years underline the opportunities offered to, and the approaches taken by, archaeologists in this kind of landscape. By and large, the sites of the medieval holdings in the valley and lowland parts of the parish are still occupied by flourishing pastoral farms and as such are unavailable for field-walking or excavation. Attention has switched, therefore, to sites of abandoned medieval farms and fields on the northern flanks of Dartmoor. In Okehampton expansion of demesne farming in the twelfth century seems to be the cause of the extension on to the upland, but the date of origin, being determined by the pottery, may have been slightly earlier. Elsewhere on Dartmoor[2] an Anglo-Saxon date has been argued for the beginnings of such activity, with roots in transhumant pastoralism, a form of agriculture not apparent in the Devonshire Domesday although clearly flourishing at the time and mentioned in other parts of the country, such as the Weald and the Arden.[3] The truth is, however, that archaeologists will not understand the Domesday landscape of these western parts of England until there is a coherent project to work on the lowland areas as well as the upland.

This has all, perhaps, been more an account of how far archaeologists have still to travel before the potential of their contribution to Domesday studies is even partially realized. With so much of the landscape to understand we have an almost limitless resource, although one that is under constant threat of piecemeal destruction. Yet even the little which has been achieved so far is enough to show how diverse and dynamic was the countryside farmed by the men and women so dimly seen in 1086. If there is one message which an archaeologist can give on the nine hundredth anniversary of

[1] D. Austin, R. H. Daggett, and M. J. C. Walker, 'Farms and Fields in Okehampton Park, Devon: The Problems of Studying Medieval Landscape', *Landscape Hist.* 2 (1980), 39–57.

[2] G. Beresford, 'Three Deserted Medieval Settlements on Dartmoor', *MA* 23 (1979), 98–158; D. Austin, 'Dartmoor and the Upland Village of the South-West of England', *Medieval Villages*, ed. Hooke, 71–9.

[3] For the Weald see K. P. Witney, *The Jutish Forest: a Study in the Weald of Kent from A.D. 450 to 1380* (London, 1976). For the Arden, T. R. Slater and P. J. Jarvis, *Field and Forest, an Historical Geography of Warwickshire and Worcestershire* (Norwich, 1982).

this great survey, it is that the next nine hundred years must see us more methodically examining the physical remains of the landscape and on a larger scale than we have before. It would be useful to be able to describe on a regional basis the typical settlement of the eleventh century from the firm grounding of excavations of entire farms, hamlets, and villages of the period. As it is, I can offer at the end only a glimpse 'as through a glass, darkly' of what some of the elements might have looked like in some imaginary settlement somewhere approximately in the middle of England. These elements must be gleaned from a number of excavations.

At the spiritual heart of the community was the church, by this time in the throes of being converted from its earlier organization of royal minsters and proprietorial churches into the parochial system familiar today and only finally in place by the twelfth century.[1] Characteristically the church is located next to the principal freehold or manor-house in the vill, and as Raunds demonstrates, vills with multiple manors may originally have had multiple churches sited quite close to each other. Many churches were already built in stone at this time and an unknown proportion of the original total has survived in present-day structures. Many, however, were still built of timber, but of whatever material they were constructed their small size and simple one- or two-cell plans looked back to the proprietorial origins rather than forward to the more communal aspects of the parish. There were, however, some larger parochial churches in place by the mid century, and the flux of settlement at the time is well reflected in the physical state of the church as shown at such places as Rivenhall, Essex, Wharram Percy, North Yorks., and Raunds, Northants.[2] To add to the complexity of the picture it must also be said that in more dispersed areas and parishes of multiple vills there was also the phenomenon of the field or common church placed on its own centrally among the various constituent elements of its territory. An aerial photograph of one such site near Malmesbury in Wiltshire has recently been published.[3] Most churches, however, lay within their own enclosures, where burial was the regular and accepted custom.

Moving into the secular part of the community we pass into even greater uncertainty. There is in particular only occasional evidence at this date from nucleated sites for the structure of boundaries defining discrete property blocks or tofts so characteristic of the earthworks of later deserted medieval villages[4] and so essential in the morphological discussion of settlement origins. This is fundamental because without a discernible framework of boundaries we cannot define the individual units which might be related to the various elements of the social and agrarian hierarchy as they appear in Domesday Book and other texts. Thus we have as yet little idea what the domestic and working layout may be for the farms of a villan, bordar, cottar, sokeman, or whatever status of peasant Domesday may categorize, because it is virtually impossible to separate one building or one group of buildings from another. One reason for this may be that the scale of excavation on the later settlements has been too small, often restricted to single toft areas. Another explanation may be that the demarcation of properties by ditches and banks or fences may be a largely post-Conquest phenomenon and part of a process of manorialization and estate adjustment suggested for at least certain parts of the country in the eleventh and twelfth centuries. Important exceptions to this general rule, however, are the ditches and fences around principal tenements or manor-houses of late Saxon and Norman date, something which can be traced back to the early Anglo-Saxon period and earlier. Such enclosures have been found at places like Raunds (seventh to thirteenth centuries), Sulgrave (tenth to twelfth centuries), and Goltho (ninth to twelfth centuries),[5] this latter earthwork semi-defensive in character and ending as a small castle. These enclosures contain major timber buildings interpreted as halls, the *geburas* or chambers of the Anglo-Saxon documents, and domestic and farm buildings such as weaving sheds and barns (see Fig. 7 for the plan of Raunds).

Further down the agrarian hierarchy, it is impossible to differentiate the farm buildings of individual landholding and dependent classes. Large timber buildings are surprisingly common outside the principal enclosures as well as smaller structures, but rarely can their function be assigned.[6] They may be halls of freemen or villans whose domestic groups may include extended or stem families and servants, but they might just as easily house nuclear families and slaves. Rarely can buildings designed specifically for housing cattle be clearly identified, and the classic stone-built longhouse which serves this and domestic purposes does not appear in the lowlands of England until the twelfth or thirteenth centuries. Sites such as Ribblehead, West Yorks., and Simy Fold, Co. Durham, in the Pennines, and Mawgan Porth in Cornwall[7] show, however, that some vernacular stone buildings had already appeared by late Saxon times in upland pastoral contexts.

Most rural communities were self-sufficient both in

[1] R. K. Morris, 'The Church in the Countryside: Two Lines of Inquiry', *Medieval Villages*, ed. Hooke, 46–60.

[2] For these and others see W. Rodwell, *The Archaeology of the English Church* (London, 1981).

[3] J. Hampton, 'The Evidence of Air Photography: Elementary Comparative Studies Applied to Sites at Mount Down, Hampshire, and near Malmesbury, Wiltshire', *AntJ* 61 (1981), 316–21.

[4] e.g. G. Beresford, *The Medieval Clayland Village: Excavations at Goltho and Barton Blount* (London, 1975), 13.

[5] Cadman and Foard, 'Raunds'; B. K. Davison, 'Excavations at Sulgrave, Northamptonshire', *ArchJ* 125 (1968), 305–7; G. Beresford, 'Goltho Manor, Lincolnshire: The Buildings and their Surrounding Defences *c*.850–1150', *Proc. of the Battle Conference 1981*, iv (1982), 13–36.

[6] P. A. Rahtz, 'Buildings and Rural Settlement', *The Archaeology of Anglo-Saxon England*, ed. Wilson, 49–98. For an example of the possibilities and problems of reconstructing Anglo-Saxon timber buildings from excavated evidence see Millett with James, 'Cowdery's Down'.

[7] A. King, 'Gauber High Pasture, Ribblehead: An Interim Report', *Viking Age York and the North*, ed. R. A. Hall (London, 1978), 21–5; D. Coggins, K. J. Fairless, and C. E. Batey, 'Simy Folds: An Earlier Medieval Settlement Site in Upper Teesdale, Co. Durham', *MA* 27 (1983), 1–26; R. L. S. Bruce-Mitford, 'A Dark Age Settlement at Mawgan Porth, Cornwall', *Recent Archaeological Excavations in Britain*, ed. R. L. S. Bruce-Mitford (London, 1956), 167–96.

food and in many of the basic skills required for agriculture and building, but some considerable degree of industrial specialization had already occurred in the late Anglo-Saxon towns. Carpenters capable of constructing the timber-framed buildings almost universal at this date would therefore be found in most major, and probably not a few of the minor, settlements. Examples of their tool-kit survive and these in large part must have been supplied by smiths who were probably to be seen almost as commonly as the carpenters. Although tools are found on archaeological sites, neither group of craftsmen seems to have had specialist structures of its own except for the occasional shaft-furnace for the production of iron. This raises the question of whether these skills were employed by full-time craftsmen or part-time agriculturists and landholders, and Domesday Book mentions them only very infrequently. By contrast, the survey records 5,624 mills on 3,463 manors, all, we must assume, for the grinding of corn, some of which was dried in kilns. Water must have been the principal source of power, since windmills do not appear to have been introduced until the twelfth century, but we should not discount the possible use of animal or human energy and hand-mills are a common feature. Those very few mills that have been excavated show that the wheels could be mounted either horizontally or vertically, and water channelled to them by fairly sophisticated leat and pond systems. Of other rural crafts mention should finally be made of weaving, because loom-weights for vertical frames are a common feature on excavated sites. Yet cloth from urban centres and imports must have been forcing the decline of this craft in rural areas, as it had already done for leather-working and pottery.[1]

[1] D. M. Wilson, 'Craft and Industry', *The Archaeology of Anglo-Saxon England*, ed. Wilson, 253–81.

VI. THE DOMESDAY BOROUGHS

G. H. MARTIN

By the time the Normans came to England, towns were a well-established feature of the kingdom.[1] They contained approximately one in ten of the population, a proportion that may seem small to us, used to an almost precisely opposite imbalance, but one that reflects a comparatively advanced economy and society. Those are not words which medieval men would themselves have used to assess towns, nor were the ideas that lie behind them of much conscious interest at the time. Nevertheless there were towns in England, with a distinctive economic and a complex social function, and the compilers of Domesday Book observed and recorded them.

In discussing what they wrote, we have to face a problem of nomenclature. We see and usually think of towns as centres of trade and industry, but we also expect their consequence to be marked by a formal civil status. The historic name for a settlement so distinguished is 'borough', a word which both in Old English (*burh*) and Norman French (*bourg*) originally meant a fortified place, but which in the late eleventh century was also coming to mean what we might call an urban community. The transition, however, was by no means complete, and various other terms were in use just as they were in later times. Whilst Domesday refers to most of the principal towns as boroughs (*burgi*), some places, including Canterbury[2] and Gloucester,[3] were dignified with the name of *civitas*, or city, though it is not easy to see how they were distinguished.

The English called a place with a market a *port*, and on occasions probably also called it a *tun*, which meant simply a place where people lived. The Normans called a *tun* a vill, or *villa* in Latin, and that word is sometimes used in Domesday of a place which from other indications might be called a borough. To simplify the issue, the term 'borough' is used here as though it were used uniformly in Domesday Book. It may have to be glossed on occasions, but rather less than any other single word that might suggest itself.

There is a reason for choosing to speak of boroughs which brings us close to the heart of Domesday Book and the society that it describes. The compilers of Domesday were often more concerned with the status of individuals than with the existence or condition of institutions, and burgesses (*burgenses*, dwellers in a *burgus* or *bourg*) are noted more systematically than boroughs. Even where they were in a minority, their concern with trade, crafts, and perhaps manufacture gave them the character, and with it the status, of the inhabitants of an urban community. In some instances, therefore, such as St Albans[4] or Louth,[5] we have come to regard what is described in Domesday as a vill as being truly a borough, because its inhabitants are said to include burgesses. We ought not on such indications alone to suppose that such a vill or manor had anything more than an urban aspiration about it, but with that precaution we can weigh a distinction that appears in the text of Domesday Book, and that evidently held some significance for its compilers.

That some boroughs occupied a special place in the kingdom is clear from even a brief examination of the pages of Domesday. Almost everywhere north of the Thames and in several other instances the entries for each county are preceded by an account of the principal borough, the place in which the shire court met, and sometimes of one or more others. The exceptions hardly weaken the significance of the arrangement, as there are blank spaces at the beginning of Middlesex and Hampshire which were evidently intended for descriptions of London[6] and Winchester,[7] and whilst the description of Derby comes at the end of the account of Derbyshire, it is associated there with that of Nottingham,[8] with which it shared a sheriff. There is also an echo of the arrangement in Sussex, where a blank on the first page was apparently reserved for Hastings,[9] and the boroughs of Chichester and Arundel,[10] Lewes,[11] and Pevensey[12] are all distinguished in the rapes in which they lie. If we turn to the eastern counties in Little Domesday we find Colchester,[13] Norwich,[14] Great Yarmouth,[15] Thetford,[16] and Ipswich[17] each distinctively treated, and presented in a manner which would have allowed them to be picked out in a final draft in the same fashion as the eponymous boroughs of the Midland counties.

The places thus distinguished are, in the main, the

[1] H. R. Loyn, *The Governance of Anglo-Saxon England, 500–1087* (London, 1984), 148–54. For a recent general survey of work on the subject, see G. H. Martin, 'Domesday Book and the Boroughs', *Domesday Book: A Reassessment*, ed. P. H. Sawyer (London, 1985), 143–63. The standard account is still J. Tait, *The Medieval English Borough* (Manchester, 1936), but there is much valuable discussion in S. Reynolds, *English Medieval Towns* (Oxford, 1977). M. Biddle (ed.), *Winchester in the Early Middle Ages: an Edition and Discussion of the Winton Domesday*, Winchester Studies, i (Oxford, 1976), is a magisterial study of both documentary and archaeological evidence. For detailed references to the literature, especially on guilds, see G. H. Martin and S. C. McIntyre (eds.), *A Bibliography of British and Irish Municipal History*, Vol. I: *General Works* (Leicester, 1972).

[2] GDB 2.

[3] GDB 162.

[4] GDB 135v.

[5] GDB 345.

[6] GDB 126–126v.

[7] GDB 37–37v.

[8] GDB 280.

[9] GDB 16.

[10] GDB 23.

[11] GDB 26.

[12] GDB 20v.

[13] LDB 104–107v.

[14] LDB 116–118.

[15] LDB 118–118v.

[16] LDB 118v–119.

[17] LDB 290–290v.

most developed of the boroughs that Domesday Book records. Altogether, however, there are references to 112 boroughs of all kinds in the survey, a number probably though not demonstrably greater than the number that existed in 1066.[1] Norman lords, including the king himself, had been exploiting their estates, and although in many places their actions bore heavily on their tenants there were instances in which they sought to encourage trade, an activity that demanded some measure of freedom for those who practised it. They accordingly sheltered privileged tenants, the burgesses, outside or even inside their castles, as at Ewyas Harold,[2] or enfranchised some of the tenants on a manor, like the fifty-two burgesses of the Count of Mortain at Berkhamsted.[3] The process was not an irreversible one—there are examples in later centuries of lords repining of their enterprise and withdrawing commercial privileges—but it was one with important economic consequences and with some political and social potential. Domesday portrays it in an interesting phase.

The boroughs appear in Domesday Book in what might be regarded as the fourth stage of their historic development. For the first three centuries of the Anglo-Saxon period urban life was thin and precarious. There were tribal centres on the sites of Roman towns such as Canterbury and Lincoln,[4] some of which also became the seats of bishoprics, but the nexus of markets and administrative functions which characterized the Roman Empire had passed away. The culture of the Germanic tribes, although it was familiar with trade, coinage, and degrees of political authority, did not depend on maintaining substantial groups of population to sustain them. However, the survival of London, and the early growth of commercial settlements on sites such as 'Hamwih' (Southampton) and Ipswich, which had no substantial Roman precursors, show that not all long-distance trade was seasonal and rootless. Ipswich, in the seventh century, even manufactured a distinctive pottery which was widely distributed.[5]

The second phase began with the Scandinavian raids in the eighth century, and lasted through the wars which ended with the emergence of the West Saxon kings as kings of the English. Marauding raids led to invasions and to long-term campaigns in which both sides used fortified camps and raised or repaired defences around existing settlements. A charter of the late ninth century shows a Mercian lord and his wife, who was Alfred's daughter, arranging for the fortification of Worcester,[6] and reserving taxes from the market and the properties gathered round the cathedral to pay for the walls.[7] Some of the campaigning quarters were abandoned again, but in many other places the wars, despite the damage that they inflicted, proved a stimulus to economic growth. The victorious West Saxons imposed upon their new lands a system of government which derived from their own institutions, but also absorbed the customs and energies of the Scandinavian settlers.

The former territories of Mercia and Northumbria were divided into shires, a name taken from a smaller West Saxon unit, each with shire-reeve or sheriff to represent the king, and with a principal borough in which the shire court assembled. Leicestershire, looking to Leicester,[8] Yorkshire, drawn round York,[9] are respectively neat and sprawling examples of the new administrative pattern. In the East Midlands, where five Danish armies had settled at Derby, Leicester, Lincoln, Nottingham, and Stamford,[10] four of their five boroughs became the capitals of shires, and Stamford, the fifth, might also have enjoyed that status for a time if the superior weight of Lincoln had not told against it.[11] The new shire boroughs and some others gradually became the seats of special courts, distinct from the shire courts, and housed markets and mints.

That major reorganization marked a third and deeply significant phase in the life of the English town. In the course of the tenth century a remarkably uniform system of local administration developed, with the shires subdivided into districts called hundreds, another ancient name for a new or revised institution. The boroughs both supported and stood apart from the scheme. Their courts seem sometimes to have been equated with hundred courts, and sometimes to have originated separately, but there are indications in them of local customs appropriate to mercantile communities.[12] More important is the regularity of the system: it speaks of settled habits that depend upon economic security. The sheriffs administered the law, and collected the king's income. The surplus from the royal estates came to the markets in the boroughs and was turned into money that was minted in the boroughs to a uniform design. The money paid for the business of administration and in resolute times for the levies of war. In less vigorous or inadequately reflective days it went into the Danegeld with which Æthelred the Redeless sought to buy off the new waves of Scandinavian invaders. Whatever the merits of funded appeasement, the economy, fed by surpluses of grain, and wool, and woollen cloth, and in later years by a growing population, grew in strength until the prize beckoned irresistibly to Duke William and his recently Latinized Norsemen.

In their West Saxon beginnings the boroughs had military functions, and it may be that when they were first spread over the liberated territories it was as citadels as well as administrative centres. There are some echoes of such a phase in Domesday Book, but even by 1066 it was probably only a memory.[13] The citizens of London discussed resistance, but turned to negotiate with William. Exeter defied him in 1068, and there were probably

[1] See the list and discussion in H. C. Darby, *Domesday England* (Cambridge, 1977), 289–320, 364–8.
[2] GDB 185.
[3] GDB 136v.
[4] GDB 36–36v.
[5] R. Hodges, *Dark-Age Economics: The Origins of Towns and Trade, A.D. 600–1000* (London, 1982), 47–86.
[6] GDB 172.
[7] Tait, *Medieval English Borough*, 19–21.

[8] GDB 230.
[9] GDB 298–298v.
[10] GDB 236v.
[11] A. Rogers (ed.), *The Making of Stamford* (Leicester, 1965), 27–31. For the reconstruction of local administration under the West Saxon kings, see Loyn, *Governance of Anglo-Saxon England*, 131–48.
[12] G. H. Martin, 'The Registration of Deeds of Title in the Medieval Borough', *The Study of Medieval Records: Essays in Honour of Kathleen Major*, eds. D. A. Bullough and R. L. Storey (Oxford, 1971), 155.
[13] Martin, 'Domesday Book and the Boroughs', 147–8.

unrecorded gestures elsewhere, but boroughs had other uses for both English and Normans. They were, however, regularly chosen as the sites of castles, both for their command of routes and especially of river crossings, and for their political potential as centres of wealth and population. The entries for Oxford[1] and Norwich show that houses were destroyed in some numbers to accommodate the castles, and there are references, as at Cambridge,[2] Lincoln, and Shrewsbury,[3] to the misfortunes that the townsmen had suffered from the rapacity of their Norman governors. At the best their dues had been raised, and they claimed often that their means to pay had been diminished. At the same time there had been new foundations, as in the French quarters of Norwich and Nottingham, and at Tutbury[4] and Windsor[5] we can see burgesses gathered at the castle gates.

It is therefore clear in Domesday Book that the Normans were not indifferent to the boroughs, but regarded them at least as places to watch, control, and exploit, and on occasions in which to invest. It is also clear, however, both from Domesday itself and from what we know of the way in which it was made, that the boroughs had no prominent place in the minds of the king and his ministers when the survey was planned. The evidence is partly negative. The questions preserved in the text known as the Inquisitio Eliensis, which the contents of Domesday Book show to have been the basis of the inquest, made no reference to boroughs, burgesses, or the resources of towns.[6] Of the boroughs placed at the head of their shires, only Buckingham[7] is described in what might be called straightforwardly manorial terms, and even Buckingham has, as we shall see, one unconformable feature in the presence of properties attached to rural manors.[8] More important, the other major boroughs are apparently described to no set formulae at all. Some accounts give their hidage for the assessment of the geld, as at Bedford,[9] Chester,[10] and Hertford,[11] others do not. Some speak of inhabitants: of men at Hereford,[12] or of burgesses at Northampton;[13] whilst others refer to properties, to houses at Dorchester,[14] to haws, or enclosed plots, at Wallingford,[15] and to inhabited *mansiones* at Lincoln and at York. Some entries reckon such resources in men and in tenements indifferently. Nor is there a recognizable order in which the information is presented.

The difference would be less remarkable if the final text had paid no particular attention to the boroughs, but had treated them as casual anomalies. As it is, some sense of their special status can be seen in the earlier drafts of the returns represented by the Exeter Domesday and Little Domesday.[16] It remained for the designer of Great Domesday's folios to raise some to the prominence that they command in the text. The unconformity of the king's apparent unconcern and the commissioners' sense of the boroughs' importance is less strange than it might seem. Like manors, the royal boroughs were a source of income, but unlike manors they were communities, and they were deeply embedded in the administrative system upon which the collection and management of the king's revenue depended. Before and after the Conquest, down to the date of Domesday Book, the king maintained control of the shire boroughs, as he did of most of the smaller boroughs in Wessex which the reconquest of the Danelaw had left behind both geographically and politically. It was only in the next century that Leicester and Warwick were allowed to pass into the hands of their earls, and that a few seigneurial enterprises, like Bishop's Lynn, became comparable with royal boroughs.

In Wessex the king and the local earl had shared the revenue from the boroughs, in a proportion of two-thirds to one-third.[17] The arrangement had spread into, or was standardized in, the Midlands, and to William at least the product of the two-thirds was not different from the rent and tolls which the Bishop of Lincoln drew from his commercial tenants, the eighty burgesses of Louth. To the commissioners, however, as they travelled through the shires, the shire boroughs proved to be something more than the settings of the shire courts. Their men gave fluent, sometimes bewildering, accounts of their obligations, laced with references to their rights. In some places, of which Colchester seems to be an example, they may even have produced documents.[18] They owed dues to the king, and they had few remedies against the sheriff's importunities, but they were not all directly the king's tenants. It must have seemed best to the commissioners to record what they were told, which seems to have been on occasions more than they were asked, and to indicate in doing so that the king's advisers could make what they would of it.

The entries in Domesday suggest that it was decided at Winchester to reproduce the record substantially as it came to hand. The treatment of the boroughs described in Exon Domesday shows some stylistic changes, but substantially less editing than was visited upon the manorial returns. At the same time, the royal boroughs were given an eminent place in the general scheme. The contrast between their visual presentation and the disparate information that the entries yield has been something of a disappointment to those who study the history of towns, and who have expected so purposeful an array to be supported by an equally purposeful store of material.[19] Yet, properly considered, both the style and the substance are significant.

Domesday Book does, in fact, offer a good deal of information about the boroughs. It generally speaks of their settlement, whether in terms of inhabitants, or

[1] GDB 154. [2] GDB 189. [3] GDB 252.
[4] GDB 248v. [5] GDB 56v.
[6] V. H. Galbraith, *The Making of Domesday Book* (Oxford, 1961), 36–9. [7] GDB 143.
[8] Martin, 'Domesday Book and the Boroughs', 147–8.
[9] GDB 259. [10] GDB 262v. [11] GDB 132.
[12] GDB 179. [13] GDB 219. [14] GDB 75.
[15] GDB 56.
[16] Martin, 'Domesday Book and the Boroughs', 155–6.

[17] Tait, *Medieval English Borough*, 141–8.
[18] Martin, 'Domesday Book and the Boroughs', 157 and n.; see also p. 60 n. 7 below.
[19] See, for example, the comments in H. C. Darby and R. Welldon Finn (eds.), *The Domesday Geography of South-West England* (Cambridge, 1967), 117, 196, 279–80.

properties, or both, and so tells us something of their size. In doing so it often uses the Old English word *haga*, cognate with the name of The Hague in the Netherlands, which originally meant an enclosure but seems to have become a technical term for an urban plot, like the post-Conquest word 'burgage'. In a number of places, as at Colchester and Chester, it refers to the defensive walls, and at Oxford a reference to *mansiones murales* reveals a system of charging individual tenements with the costs of maintaining the fortifications. There are many references to churches, including eight in York and fifteen in Norwich, which show that their multiplicity was a feature of the eleventh-century, as well as of the twelfth-century and later English borough. Bridges appear at Chester and Cambridge, and the king's special protection over the approaches by land and water to Nottingham and York is an explicit testimony to the importance of trade and the collection of tolls. Tolls are mentioned widely, and are set out in some detail at Chester again, and at Lewes in Sussex, where the tolls on livestock included a levy on slaves, a trade which was a staple of the Old English economy and the suppression of which was one of the few humanitarian acts, if such was indeed its motivation, to which the Normans might lay claim.

The evident importance of tolls makes the lack of explicit reference to markets one of the more surprising weaknesses in the general picture. Of the sixty markets named in Domesday Book, only nineteen are in places described as boroughs.[1] The previous history of the boroughs and the references to tolls in Domesday make it certain that there were markets there, but also point to the fact that the commissioners' brief did not include the question 'Is there a market?' On the other hand, the absence of references to burgesses or any other urban feature in many instances prevents us from assuming that all the places with markets were also boroughs, though if their markets were legitimized by the acknowledged collection of tolls then it is likely that in some sense they were. What distinguishes many of them is that they were the manors of individual lords, and that their markets were public institutions which, if they were noted, were unlikely to be edited out of the record. Those in the towns were rather taken for granted. There is an interesting illustration of the process at York,[2] where there is no general reference to a market. The Count of Mortain had two stalls *in macello*, the shambles, which the accompanying reference to the Church of Holy Cross enables us to identify with the famous street running northward from The Pavement. It is impossible to believe that York had only a market for meat: we can rather suppose from that rare reference to an identifiable locality that the other quarters of specialized trades, like Coppergate, were also already to be distinguished, but did not come to the commissioners' notice.

In the same way, there are only scattered references to the internal organization and government of the towns. At York, Stamford, Huntingdon, and Cambridge the borough is said to have been divided into wards or other units—shires or shares at York, where the king's shire and the archbishop's are distinguished. The distribution of those references leaves us uncertain as to whether or not the arrangement was one peculiar to areas of Scandinavian settlement. The same is true of the privileged class of lawmen who appear at Cambridge, Lincoln, and Stamford, whose numbers suggest comparison with the twelve judges of Chester, another borough open to Viking influences. That the burgesses met for judicial and administrative purposes is, like their concern with trade, certain, but it made only occasional impressions on the survey. The guildhall of Dover is mentioned, but probably because its value had been lost to the burgesses, and therefore to the king. A similar concern with what had been taken from the common stock, by one means or another, misappropriation or physical damage, and so withdrawn from the available fiscal resources, may account in part for the often negative and depressed picture that has been drawn of the Domesday borough.[3]

Certainly the customs of the boroughs are presented largely in terms of what is owed, which was the matter of most concern to the king. There are many instances of military dues, such as the services owed to the royal host at Leicester and Hereford, and of renders in kind, ranging from corn at Derby and honey at Leicester to 360 iron rods for horseshoes at Gloucester. Agricultural produce and services are commonplace, for even the largest boroughs were in some measure farming communities, but the burgesses of Cambridge complained of the sheriff's excessive demands for the use of their ploughs, and his exaction of unwarranted carrying services. The duties of escorting and riding for the king which were owed at Shrewsbury and Wallingford were of another kind, as were the ferrying services of the burgesses of Torksey.[4] Carting and carrying, however, led to markets as well as to manors, and the concentration of traffic and trade in the boroughs is well evidenced, although explicit references to commodities, such as the Irish marten pelts at Chester, are comparatively rare. Ironically enough, the fullest account of the internal business of a town occurs under Bury St Edmunds,[5] with its brewers, tailors, laundresses, porters, and general dealers, which is not explicitly described as a borough. It is interesting to note that another varied and lively description, of Canterbury, occurs in one of the satellite texts, the Inquisition of St Augustine's Abbey, and was reduced in the later recensions of the survey.[6] Like St Edmund's, St Augustine's monks gave the commissioners a more extended account of their estates than the occasion demanded: the object was to survey the king's rights and other men's resources as they affected the king, not to depict the life of boroughs or of any other institutions.

Nevertheless, the characteristics of the boroughs

[1] Darby, *Domesday England*, 318–19, 369–70; G. H. Martin, 'Eleventh-Century Communications', Special Study VII, pp. 61–4 below.

[2] GDB 298.

[3] Martin, 'Domesday Book and the Boroughs', 156–60.

[4] GDB 337.

[5] LDB 372.

[6] A. Ballard, *An Eleventh-Century Inquisition of St. Augustine's, Canterbury* (London, 1920), viii, 7–9.

emerge piecemeal, and the variety and even the imperfections of the account testify in an instructive way to the difficulties that the commissioners faced and overcame. One of the most striking features of the royal boroughs is the presence in them of inhabitants and properties said to belong to rural manors, usually but not invariably in the same county, and often at a considerable distance. Malmesbury[1] had some forty-five burgesses, houses, and plots attached to thirteen neighbouring manors; Hythe[2] had more than 200 related to two estates of the Archbishop of Canterbury. Such properties are variously noted under the borough itself, as at Buckingham and Hertford,[3] under the seigneurial manors themselves, as at Barnstaple,[4] or under both, as at Guildford,[5] Stafford,[6] and many other places. A number of boroughs, including Hastings, London, and Winchester, appear only through the manorial entries that make reference to them.[7]

The matter is tantalizing, as our estimates of the total population of the boroughs are marred by uncertainty as to whether or not the various entries exclude or repeat each other, but it shows at least that the burgesses were men of mixed allegiance. Maitland made what he called the 'tenurial heterogeneity' of the boroughs the mainstay of his garrison theory, a hypothesis that the boroughs owed their origins and their distinct administrative status to a role as communal fortresses, first manned by professional fighting-men and maintained by the community of the shire by a systematic allocation of resources. Ballard elaborated the theory, and called the rural properties with such tenants in the boroughs 'contributory properties', believing that they represented a coherent administrative system.[8]

The weakness of both expositions, though Maitland was a man of unsurpassed learning and perception, was that they sought to marshal exceptionally untidy evidence into a single rational and uniform scheme. The imperfections of the Domesday record are probably themselves close enough to the truth. There were many reasons why manorial lords both before and after the Conquest should hold property in boroughs, including privileged access to markets, an additional stake in the community, and the simple convenience of accommodation near the shire court. What matters most is firstly the commissioners' sense that the boroughs needed special treatment, and secondly the fact that although the boroughs were seen and treated as communities, they had not yet the power, as they had in the following centuries, to assimilate entirely to themselves those who lived in them and accepted communal responsibilities in them.

That subsequent change may have owed something to the finished form of Domesday Book. The boroughs had evidently obtruded themselves upon the survey: if they were not uppermost in the king's mind in 1085 they could hardly be absent from his ministers' minds when they consulted Domesday, as they frequently did, in the years that followed. In the course of the twelfth century the king, although disavowing none of his rights, took increasingly to bargaining with the boroughs, and to granting them privileges to receive in return what he could once simply demand. In the process the burgesses' tentative aspirations became firm and confident, and their boroughs eventually became corporations, personalities in law with the rights and powers of individuals. That was a condition still remote when the text of Domesday Book was assembled in 1086, but it was insensibly advanced when the clerks placed the boroughs above the list of the tenants-in-chief.

[1] GDB 64v. [2] GDB 4, 4v. [3] GDB 132.
[4] GDB 100. [5] GDB 30, 35v.
[6] GDB 246, 247v, 248, 248v.
[7] It is particularly interesting that the order in which the manorial properties are listed is always at variance with the list of landholders in the county. The implication is that the extracts were not made from the final array of the returns, and there is at least a strong possibility that some of the information was provided by the boroughs themselves.

[8] Martin, 'Domesday Book and the Boroughs', 147–8.

VII. ELEVENTH-CENTURY COMMUNICATIONS

G. H. MARTIN

THE most striking testimony to the quality of communications in eleventh-century England is in the existence of Domesday Book itself. It records a country able to take stock of its resources in minute particulars. We know from the survival of Anglo-Saxon writs that the pre-Conquest kingdom was governed by the written word, in the sense that the king's instructions were regularly conveyed to the sheriffs, his representatives in the shires, in letters authenticated by his seal, and effected in a network of local courts.[1] From those survivals alone we might hardly have seemed justified in supposing the system as complete and efficient as the text of Domesday Book shows it to have been. The survey covered the entire country, as Durham was a marcher land and the ground north of the Tyne and the middle Eden was occupied by, or in contention with, the Scots. The king's commissioners obtained comprehensive answers to their questions everywhere, and sent in their digests, probably to Winchester, within a year. The major recension of Great Domesday was then completed in a matter of months, excluding only Little Domesday. The Conqueror was a self-willed and violent man, but violence does not of itself produce written texts, or assemble and collate them. Both the local apparatus of government and the internal communications of the kingdom must have been in competent working order.[2]

Such a system implies both men to run it and very many more to pay for it. Payment demands both a surplus above mere subsistence and the means of realizing its value. The Old English state had achieved both the surplus and the means; the Normans made many additional demands upon the kingdom's resources, especially in building and garrisoning castles, and found the system equal to them. When we reflect upon Domesday Book and what it tells us we can to some extent take the economy for granted, but the communications are a challenge, partly because the evidence is fragmentary, and partly because it has too often been discounted. The difficulties of travel before the age of mechanical transport were real, but Domesday Book reminds us on every page that in practice they were not overwhelming.[3]

As the occupant of half the island of Britain, England looked in large part to the sea. Indeed in the time of Cnut and his sons it had been a member of the Scandinavian world, tied in with Iceland, the Northern Isles, and Scandinavia by the wide-ranging longships of the Vikings. The kingdom was practically self-sufficient in foodstuffs and raw materials, but there was a well-established trade with parts of Western Europe, in wine and some finished goods, and indirectly with the international entrepôts of the Middle East in fine wares and spices.[4] The Norman Conquest and settlement further stimulated traffic across the Channel. The Church imported aromatics for incense and spices for condiments and medicines. There was a growing general market for spices, which may have brought the Jews to England for the first time in the Normans' wake. In return for what they imported the English had long exported wool and woollen cloths, corn, and slaves. Ships were not then distinguished by their functions as warships or merchantmen, and the substance both of naval power and of the carrying trade lay in the fisheries. The naval duties of the coastal towns later known as the Cinque Ports, which can be seen in their early stages in the accounts of Dover[5] and Sandwich[6] in Domesday Book, were based on their fishing fleet, the seasonal visits of which to the North Sea also established the herring fair at Great Yarmouth.[7] References in Domesday to tolls in the Sussex ports[8] and at Dover, where a new mill had impaired the entrance to a busy harbour, are only incidental to the survey, but reflect the importance of shipping in the Channel and the narrow seas.

The major rivers extended the range of shipping far into the country, and many streams that would now be thought unnavigable led to landing-places in the Middle Ages.[9] Water transport was convenient for many bulky and heavy cargoes. In particular, building stone, usually native but sometimes imported from Normandy, was a commodity better so moved, though its uses were more extensive in the twelfth century and later than in the eleventh. With all the major towns sited on rivers many of the tolls referred to in Domesday Book may have been levied on water-borne goods, but it is only rarely, as on the Trent at Nottingham,[10] or in the reference to the special king's peace that protected the approaches to York both by land and by water,[11] that we have specific reference to such traffic.

With the overwhelming growth of overland travel, especially since the nineteenth century, we are now apt

[1] On the general significance of the writ, see F. E. Harmer, *Anglo-Saxon Writs* (Manchester, 1952), 3–6.

[2] F. Barlow, *William I and the Conquest of England* (London, 1965), 54, 118–35; J. Campbell, 'Observations on English Government from the Tenth to the Twelfth Century', *TRHS* 5th ser., 25 (1975), 39–43.

[3] G. H. Martin, 'Road Travel in the Middle Ages: Some Journeys by the Warden and Fellows of Merton College, 1315–1470', *Jnl of Transport Hist.*, ns 5 (1976), 159–61.

[4] R. Hodges, *Dark-Age Economics: The Origins of Towns and Trade, AD 600–1000* (London, 1982), 104–29.

[5] GDB 1.

[6] GDB 2.

[7] K. M. E. Murray, *The Constitutional History of the Cinque Ports* (Manchester, 1935), 23–7.

[8] GDB 20v, 26.

[9] W. G. Hoskins, *Field-work in Local History* (London, 1957), 59–64.

[10] GDB 280.

[11] GDB 298v.

to regard rivers and watercourses as barriers to be crossed rather than as routes to be followed, and it is true that on the administrative map they frequently mark boundaries. In earlier times, however, they had both qualities, and were freely used as highways. The burgesses of Wallingford[1] owed carrying services to the king, either by land with horses or upstream and downstream on the Thames between Benson and Reading. The accounts in Little Domesday of two neighbouring lordships at Bures[2] and Nayland,[3] both now parishes in Suffolk but then straddling the Stour well into Essex, provide one instance of the river as a focal, rather than a dividing line. The nearby presence in Ipswich, Suffolk, of a burgage connected with the manor of Moze, in Essex, across the estuaries of the Orwell and Stour and deep in the Walton backwaters, says much the same of communications along the coast.[4]

Eventually, however, ships come to shore, and their passengers and cargoes must move by land. Few aspects of medieval society have been more widely misunderstood and underrated than roads and their traffic. The confusion begins with the Roman roads. They were technically very accomplished, but they were laid out to meet the needs of the Roman settlement.[5] The fact that they later fell largely though not entirely into decay tells us less than we sometimes suppose about the Anglo-Saxons and their requirements. In particular the question of whether the remaining Roman roads were in better or worse repair in the Middle Ages than when archaeologists and historians subsequently became interested in them is largely irrelevant.[6] Substantial parts of the main Roman trunk roads such as Watling Street and the Fosse Way remained useful and therefore stayed in use. So probably did many minor roads which have not been identified precisely because they lie under later accretions. The parts of the system which fell into decay were some stretches of the main routes which attract our attention now because we are impatient of diversions, and roads which served vanished settlements and have since been recovered by observation and excavation. That the truncated system should simply have served the medieval economy *faute de mieux* is an impossibility: the medieval road system is that which we see today, overlaid by applications of concrete and tar macadam, and short-circuited since the eighteenth century by turnpikes, by arterial roads and bypasses, and most recently by motorways. Its medieval foundations are intricate and often indistinct, for the highway in common law was rather a right of passage than a physical entity, but we can be sure that they tied every settlement in the kingdom into a web of moots and markets.

Domesday Book is concerned with agrarian resources, to a limited extent with levies on trade, and hardly at all with the substance and means of trade. It therefore has little to say about commodities, and even less about transport and roads. There are, however, a number of specific and many inferential references to carriage overland, and their presence, given the nature of the survey, may seem on reflection even more surprising than what is omitted.

The common ground between the two kinds of reference is, appropriately, the market-place, though markets themselves are most sparingly noted in Domesday.[7] Of the mere sixty that do appear, fewer than twenty occur in descriptions of boroughs, though we can reasonably suppose all the other boroughs to have housed and to have depended on markets. The rest are in places without other distinguishable urban characteristics. No doubt they served there to distribute more widely the commodities of external trade, but they also represent the continuous process by which food was gathered in from the farms both to feed the towns and to supply baronial households, the Church, and above all the king. Something of the kind probably shows, for example, in the references in Hertfordshire to carrying services concentrated on Hitchin.[8] Amongst the renders due to the king from every shire was the ancient food-rent known as a 'night's farm', a sum representing what the royal household would have consumed *per noctem* if it had sojourned on a particular estate. By the eleventh century the renders had long been translated into sums of money for which the sheriff accounted and which Domesday notes in many places, as at Wimborne in Dorset.[9] The king still travelled with his voracious court, for royal government remained personal and peripatetic for some centuries, but it was possible and therefore convenient to turn into cash those supplies which could not be readily consumed on the spot. The carrying and escorting services noticed at Wallingford, above, or at Shrewsbury,[10] where the burgesses had a duty to provide the king with twenty-four horses to take him to his nearest manor in Staffordshire, may still have served their turn, but even they could be rendered into money, and for most of the time money in hand was worth many sumpter horses in the outback.

We can, therefore, occasionally see manorial dead- and live-stock, as well as the royal household itself, on the move, and must remember constantly that much that seems static, fixed by Domesday in its localities, was necessarily mobile, and that produce was transported and exchanged as commonly as it was consumed. A good deal of the produce moved on its own hooves. Our technical term for personal property, 'chattels', derives from 'cattle', and is a reminder that the Anglo-Saxon saw worldly wealth as horned and four-legged. The roads and market-places of the eleventh century and long after had more in common with the American Wild West than with the Brent Cross Shopping Centre or the Burlington Arcade.[11] The details of their trade are more difficult to recover, as tolls are usually referred to in general terms, and the explicit tariffs at Lewes,[12] which

[1] GDB 56. [2] LDB 84v, 360, 392. [3] LDB 401v.
[4] LDB 411v.
[5] On Roman roads in general, see I. D. Margery, *Roman Roads in Britain* (3rd rev. edn., London, 1973).
[6] Martin, 'Road Travel in the Middle Ages', 160 and nn.

[7] H. C. Darby, *Domesday England* (Cambridge, 1977), 369–70; G. H. Martin, 'The Domesday Boroughs', Special Study VI, pp. 56–60 above.
[8] GDB 132v. [9] GDB 75. [10] GDB 252.
[11] On market-places, see G. H. Martin, 'The Town as Palimpsest', *The Study of Urban History*, ed. H. J. Dyos (London, 1968), 163–5.
[12] GDB 26.

include charges for horses and oxen, or those at Chester,[1] are exceptional. There are, however, many examples of renders of fish, from both inland and coastal fisheries, and those we can relate particularly to the trade in salt, which is unusually well represented both for its intrinsic importance and because it obtruded itself upon the general pattern of manorial occupations. Coastal salt-pans are represented by extensive but probably incomplete references throughout Great and Little Domesday. The more interesting entries are those that relate to the brine workings at Droitwich in Worcestershire, which impinged upon the economy not only of the immediate neighbourhood of the borough but also of places in adjoining and more distant counties. Many manors had properties and shares in the works in Droitwich. Wood to fuel the salt-boilers was drawn from parts of Herefordshire (Cleeve, Leominster, and Much Marcle[2]), and a number of manors in Gloucestershire, such as Sodbury[3] and the two Guitings,[4] included renders of salt from Droitwich among their assets. There is a reference to lead-works at Northwich[5] which probably made the lead vats for the brine referred to under Bromsgrove[6] and elsewhere. The routes known later as saltways can be traced through the Cotswolds to places such as Bampton[7] in Oxfordshire and further afield as far as Risborough in Buckinghamshire[8] and also north-eastwards to Binton[9] and Hillborough[10] in Warwickshire.[11]

The name of the saltways invokes one trade and implies others. Firewood is mentioned in the Herefordshire and Worcestershire references, but not all salt was paid for in wood, and other commodities must have flowed in return from many parts of southern and midland England. For the most part journeys were probably short, but localized supplies such as salt, tin from Cornwall, and lead from Derbyshire travelled as far as the demand for them extended. There is an explicit reference in the Peak District to measured cart-loads of lead from Ashford, Bakewell, and Hope,[12] which can be set against any assumption that dense loads were moved only by water or by pack-horse. Cart-loads of salt appear at Middlewich, Cheshire,[13] where there were differential tolls for hundred- and shire-dwellers, as distinct from off-comers, and a special rate for dealers. The tolls that are noticed spasmodically in Domesday Book, on salt at Chedworth, Gloucestershire,[14] in general at Aylesbury in Buckinghamshire[15] and elsewhere, were raised on cart-loads as well as on pack-horse teams.

The roads which bore the traffic are hardly noted at all. There is a rare reference at Bramshall in Staffordshire[16] to a *via* as a boundary marking off the king's share of a simple virgate. There it is probably a survivor of many such local details, common enough in pre-Conquest charters but superfluous to the needs of the Domesday survey.[17] Entries in Nottinghamshire[18] and Yorkshire[19] refer to the king's peace on major roads, and at Nottingham the road to York is specified, and protected against encroachment by ploughing or ditching. There are references at Chester[20] to the bridge both as a landmark and as a public structure maintained on the same terms as the city wall, but the bridge over the Welland at Stamford[21] is named only to distinguish the ward that lay beyond it. A similar reference to Bridge Ward at Cambridge is preserved in the Inquisitio Eliensis[22] but has been excised in Domesday Book, a further reminder that, whilst we must be grateful for what we have, it is dangerous to judge the familiarity of things from their incidence in single texts.

The concentration of river and road traffic in towns encouraged the building and rebuilding of bridges, and especially the replacement of fords, as at Oxford, to allow both unhindered navigation and easy crossings. There were also ferries, especially on the larger rivers. Domesday records three in Nottinghamshire: Fiskerton[23] and Gunthorp,[24] where ferry and a boat were worth 30*s.* 8*d.*, are both on the Trent, and the ferry attributed to Southwell[25] is more likely to have been on the Trent than on the Greet. There was another at Weston-on-Trent in Derbyshire,[26] and five in Lincolnshire, including one at Grimsby[27] which may have plied over the Humber to Ravenser Od in Holderness, and another at Barton[28] which survived to the recent building of the Humber suspension bridge.

In some places rivers can be seen to have supplemented roads rather than interrupted them. The men of Torksey, Lincolnshire,[29] had a duty to assist the king's messengers on their way to York with their ships and sailing gear, whilst the sheriff paid for the keep of both the messengers and the sailors during their journey. The king's messengers also appear in Kent, where Canterbury provided a field for their horses to graze.[30] At Dover they paid different rates, twopence and threepence, for their passage in summer and winter, and the town provided a crew for their crossing. There we see provision, probably archaic in 1086, when it is described as the practice in King Edward's day, for the regular travels of the king's couriers, men whose journeys, with or without such services to support them, would have set a pattern for others to follow. Their particular work had its counterpart in every baronial household, for the wide distribution of baronial estates, seen once as an example of the Conqueror's guile, but shown in Domesday Book to reflect an Old English practice, rested on a regular system of communications just as the structure of government and society depended on a constant exchange of skills and resources.[31]

1 GDB 262v. 2 GDB 179–180. 3 GDB 163v.
4 GDB 167, 167v. 5 GDB 173v. 6 GDB 172.
7 GDB 154v. 8 GDB 143v. 9 GDB 243.
10 GDB 243v.
11 H. C. Darby and I. B. Terrett, *The Domesday Geography of Midland England* (2nd edn., Cambridge, 1971), 39–40.
12 GDB 272v–273. 13 GDB 268 14 GDB 164.
15 GDB 143. 16 GDB 249.

17 See, for example, H. P. R. Finberg, *The Early Charters of the West Midlands* (Leicester, 1972), 32, 141–2. 18 GDB 280.
19 GDB 298v. 20 GDB 262v. 21 GDB 336v.
22 Record Commission, *Domesday Book*, iv: *Inquisitio Eliensis* (*The Ely Inquest*), ed. H. Ellis (London, 1816), 507. 23 GDB 283.
24 GDB 285v. 25 GDB 283. 26 GDB 273.
27 GDB 343, 363. 28 GDB 354v. 29 GDB 337.
30 GDB 2.
31 For a discussion of carrying services in a complex of estates, see E. Miller, *The Abbey and Bishopric of Ely* (Cambridge, 1951), 78–9, 83–7; Martin, 'Boroughs', pp. 56–60 above.

Our evidence of the speed of movement comes from particular and uncharacteristic occasions, such as the transit of the English army from Stamford Bridge on the Humber to Hastings in a fortnight, including several days' stay in London. The pace of much ordinary travel and transport may have been more leisurely, but a horseman in a hurry could sustain 40 or 50 miles a day on long journeys. However, most journeys would be short and diurnal, made to and from courts and fairs and markets. At Eye in Suffolk Little Domesday refers[1] to the establishment by William Malet of a Saturday market which had forced the Bishop of Norwich to hold his neighbouring market at Hoxne on Fridays, to what he believed to be his loss. Hoxne is within an hour's walk of Eye, and the competition and benefits of the new market were probably also felt rather further afield. Jurors in other places may have told even more dramatic stories, but the process impinges on us only in the one entry. At least it allows us to register the presence of a spirit of curiosity, perhaps even a sense of good cheap, abroad in Hartismere Hundred when William Malet began to improve his estate at Eye.

What Domesday Book has to tell us has always to be read against what it implies. It depicts the Conqueror's realm as it was twenty years after Hastings, county by county and manor by manor, with the value of every lord's dues and resources. The results of the survey were rich in detail, and in their earlier stages extensively annotated, but they could only be usefully presented in an abbreviated and static form. In the final editing they were standardized with extraordinary skill, with their anomalies minimized, and what was uniform and familiar duly stressed. We know from the Domesday satellites that behind that orderly account there lies a mass of still more minute detail, abundant disputes and counterclaims, uncounted hours of discussion, and many miles of travel. In the same way the systematic recital of the stock and values of each manor implies not only the constant round of the farming year but also the business of marketing and some of the skills of accountancy. Behind the whole text there is a world of restless movement, and a constant exchange of ideas as well as of commodities.

[1] LDB 379.

A final word on the internal coherence of Norman England might come from its other monuments, the physical structures such as Durham Cathedral or Colchester Castle, that like Domesday Book survive to challenge our imagination. The great churches, every one supported by a nexus of estates, were symbols of a faith that transcended physical boundaries and the divisions that men imposed upon each other. Amid many local variations in usage, the liturgical and administrative uniformity of the Church, like the homogeneity of its architectural styles, expressed the unity at least of Western Christendom. At another extreme of human preoccupation and endeavour the castles speak of a social order which rested not on immobility but on the control of movement. Each one was sited with a view to tactical advantage and the command of ground; each one depended, in an age when battles were fought hand to hand, not upon its intrinsic security but upon the presence of a mobile garrison. It was the garrison, not the castle, that controlled the district in which the castle was placed, and that control lay in darting forays to inhibit or secure communications along routes that were determined by the lie of the land and known from daily usage. The warfare for which Norman society was organized was a war of movement. England was the Normans' great prize of war, but the effort of maintaining what they had won led them into civil exertions of an unfamiliar but highly successful kind. Their castles have had a long life in desuetude; the communities that they were raised to overawe and secure, like the routes between them, are with us still.

VIII. PARISH CHURCHES IN THE ELEVENTH CENTURY

JOHN BLAIR

By the 1180s England had a two-tier parochial system: dioceses with cathedrals, and parishes served by parish churches. The position in the 1080s was very different. On the one hand the framework of local parishes had yet to crystallize, though the parish churches of the future were springing up thick and fast in the countryside. On the other hand there remained a third category of church, fast declining yet still important, interposed between the other two: the 'minster' of secular priests. If local churches were the dynamic element, their growth must still be seen in the much older context of minster parishes.

Minsters had been the basis of local church organization in the seventh, eighth, and ninth centuries.[1] They were staffed by communities of priests, who served big parishes (covering perhaps five to fifteen later ones) and provided the first Christian teaching for rural communities. But gradually the churches of private lords, served by single priests, encroached on the minsters and assumed their pastoral functions.

By 1086 this encroachment had deprived the minsters of much of their original *raison d'être*. Yet in Domesday Book they are still, in different guises, much in evidence. Any church entry which goes beyond the standard formulaic phrases is, in fact, a strong sign of a former or still-functioning minster. Various features recur:[2] direct references to groups of priests, clerks, or canons; endowments of at least one hide or carucate; separate tenure of the church by a royal clerk or other named ecclesiastic; separate valuations and surveys; and miscellaneous marks of status, including named dedications, geld-exemptions, and (very occasionally) references to church-scot or mother-church rights.

Over 300 such churches appear in Domesday Book, and it seems that a high proportion of them (with many others that the survey ignores) still had teams of priests. On the other hand, many royal minsters had been appropriated to support the king's clerks, with the great Regenbald holding the lion's share. A typical entry is for Cookham, Berks.: 'Of these twenty hides Regenbald the priest has of the king 1½ hides in alms, and the church of that manor with 8 cottars and 1 plough and 15 acres of meadow; it is worth 50*s*.'[3] What Domesday Book hardly ever mentions are the rights of minsters over 'daughter' churches in their parishes, but later evidence shows that these could be extensive. Many church-founding lords in Domesday England still had to reckon with their local minsters.

Numerically, it is not the minsters which dominate Domesday Book but the thousands of little manorial churches. Why this should be so is most clearly stated in an early eleventh-century treatise which explains how a successful peasant could better his status: 'If a *ceorl* thrived so that he had fully 5 hides of land of his own, a church and a kitchen, a bell and a fortress-gate, a seat and special office in the king's hall, he was worthy thereafter to be called a thegn.' The thegn's 'basic' portion, thus defined, is in fact the most typical of Domesday manors: 5 hides in extent, with a manor-house (kitchen, bell-cote, and presumed hall within a gated enclosure) and a church. These things are singled out not for their significance to a village community, but for what they say about their owner. The church, no less than the others, is a piece of property and a normal mark of status; something that any thegn might be expected to have.

How long this had been the case is still controversial. Some historians argue that private churches were already numerous by the eighth century. That some existed is beyond doubt: Bede describes Bishop John of Hexham (687–705) dedicating a church on a nobleman's manor. But there are good reasons for doubting if the era of rapid growth, the critical shift from minsters to 'one-priest' churches, began before the tenth century.[4] Alfred's laws (*c*.885–99) still seem to assume that priests will live in communities, and it is Edgar's second code (960–2) which first proposes a legal *modus vivendi* between minsters and private founders: all tithe is to go 'to the old minster to which the obedience pertains', but a thegn whose church has a graveyard may endow it with one-third of his demesne tithes. Archaeology tells the same story, for parish-church excavations are consistently finding an initial building phase in the tenth or eleventh century. This is, indeed, exactly what the general economic context should make us expect. At this time the old 'multiple estates' seem to have been fragmenting into self-contained local manors, the land-base of what may have been a greatly enlarged class of minor thegns. It was into their world that most of our medieval parish churches were born.

It would be wrong, however, to attribute all foundations to laymen. From the 960s onwards, pastoral care would have prompted the reformed abbeys to build churches on their own manors, and many such appear in Domesday Book. Even unreformed minsters might devolve some of their priests to chapels founded from the centre, or co-operate with lay founders. In *c*.1090 a Hampshire landowner who wanted to build a church on

[1] For minsters see Blair, 'Secular Minster Churches'; Brooke, 'Rural Ecclesiastical Institutions'; Lennard, *Rural England*, 396–404.

[2] Blair, 'Secular Minster Churches', 106; Barlow, *English Church 1000–1066*, 187–92.

[3] GDB 56v.

[4] Blair, 'Secular Minster Churches', 117–18; 'Minster to Parish Church'; and *Early Medieval Surrey*, chs. 4–5.

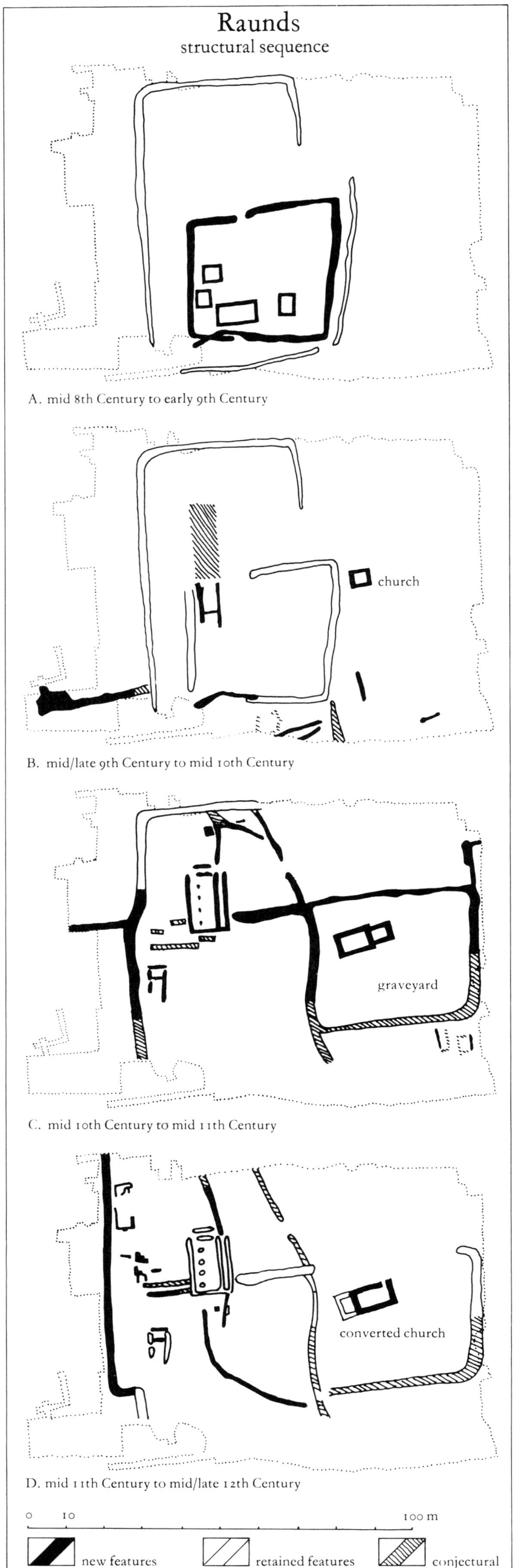

FIG. 1

his manor consulted the dean of Christchurch minster, who sent one of his own minster-priests to serve it.[1] We should not underrate the continuing role of minsters, even in the great age of private churches.

Domesday Book provides no pre-Conquest data for manorial churches, so it is impossible to say how many were new since 1066. If anything, the Norman settlement is likely to have quickened the pace of church-building. The proprietary church was as much a status symbol in Norman as in Anglo-Saxon society, and the granting of land to subtenants created new proprietary interests. It seems possible that there is a distinct class of very small churches on very small manors, built by relatively humble and hitherto landless knights of the first post-Conquest generation.[2]

Given their origins, the status of most churches in 1086 can hardly have been other than informal. To judge from the few counties where Domesday Book gives glebe acreages, the normal endowment of a local church was the standard peasant smallholding of the region.[3] Its priest would probably be unlearned, reckoned a member of the peasant community, and appointed by the lord, who was to all practical purposes the 'owner' of the church. Its parish was the manor, and there is little reason to think that the bounds of manorial (as against minster) parishes had at this date any other formal identity. So chaotic a scene—some manors with churches, some without, and residual areas still served from minsters—can scarcely be called a 'parochial system'. When, in the twelfth century, order came it was imposed from above, as canon law developed to embody new ideals of clerical rights and lay obligations, and reforming bishops put them into practice.[4] As the framework hardened, it preserved many reminders of its lordship-based origins (which is why the boundary clauses of late Anglo-Saxon charters so often correspond with modern parish boundaries). What we cannot know is how many anomalies were ironed out: it is conceivable that some churches which were purely proprietary, and which had nothing to offer on rational pastoral grounds, were simply swept away (Fig. 1).

The Domesday data for local churches are, with some exceptions, confined to a very large number of bare references, usually (depending on circuit) in the form 'there is a church', 'there is a priest', or 'there is a church with a priest'. The completeness of these entries is, of course, a crucial problem. Recording of churches certainly varied greatly between circuits, and even seems to have varied within them. The Leicestershire, Northamptonshire, Oxfordshire, and Warwickshire circuit

[1] Blair, 'Secular Minster Churches', 142.
[2] Blair, *Early Medieval Surrey*, ch. 5.
[3] Lennard, *Rural England*, 306–16, 327–33.
[4] Blair, *Early Medieval Surrey*, ch. 6.

Fig. 1 Raunds, Northamptonshire: the birth and death of a private manorial church. An ordinary mid-Saxon settlement site *(a)* was overlain in the tenth century by a timber hall set alongside a tiny church *(b)*. Towards the end of the Anglo-Saxon period, the church was rebuilt on a larger scale and a graveyard grew up around it *(c)*. Exceptionally, it fell into disuse during the twelfth century, and was converted into a secular building *(d)*.

ignored most churches; other circuits (notably the south-western) only record minsters. The Domesday Monachorum shows that only about half the Kentish churches standing in 1086 appear in Exchequer Domesday;[1] yet Surrey, in the same circuit, may have a near-complete coverage.[2] The silence of Domesday Book must never be taken as conclusive evidence that a manor had no church in 1086, and for some counties it is wholly useless as a guide to the incidence of churches.

Occasional lapses in Domesday Book's staccato style provide glimpses of local church life.[3] In the manorially fragmented eastern counties, churches were often divided between lords (notably the two at Threekingham, Lincs., held in tiny fractions).[4] At Thorney, Suffolk, four free brothers had built a chapel near the mother-church 'because it could not accommodate the whole parish'.[5] Old Byland, Yorks., had a 'wooden church'; Wilcot, Wilts., had a 'new church'; while at Netheravon nearby the church was 'abandoned and unroofed so that it is almost ruinous'.[6] The joint entry for Offenham, Littleton, and Bretforton, Worcs., evokes what must have been a familiar sight in Domesday England: 'there are oxen for one plough, but they are hauling stones to the church'.[7]

The view that Domesday Book catches in full spate an unprecedented 'boom' in minor church-building is well supported by the churches themselves. It has become clear that between 1050 and 1100 they were built in enormous numbers, some replacing stone or timber predecessors (Fig. 1) and others on new sites. Most 'Anglo-Saxon' buildings must be very late in the period; indeed, it has recently been claimed that over half belong to a 'school of minor churches, inhabiting the hundred years from the second quarter of the eleventh century to the second quarter of the twelfth, which is neither simply "Saxon" nor simply "Norman"'.[8] While there is a clear difference between English and Norman styles and techniques, it must be recognized both that all English builders did not die at Hastings, and that the influence of Norman Romanesque may already have been felt before the Conquest.

Most eleventh-century church buildings of minster status seem to have followed a pattern set by reformed monasteries in the late tenth: a central tower, an aisleless nave, a chancel, and north and south porches. This plan, or a more sophisticated Romanesque version of it, was often reproduced after the Conquest when greater-than-average churches were rebuilt.[9] A simpler tripartite plan—nave, axial tower, and chancel—became stan-

[1] Lennard, *Rural England*, 293–4.
[2] Blair, 'Minster to Parish Church', and *Early Medieval Surrey*, ch. 5.
[3] For this paragraph see Darby, *Domesday England*, 52–6.
[4] GDB 341v, 365v, 370.
[5] LDB 281v.
[6] GDB 320v, 69, 65.
[7] GDB 175v.
[8] Fernie, *Architecture of the Anglo-Saxons*, 171. For the 'overlap' see also Gem, 'Parish Church in 11th and 12th Centuries'.
[9] Blair, 'Secular Minster Churches', 121–2.

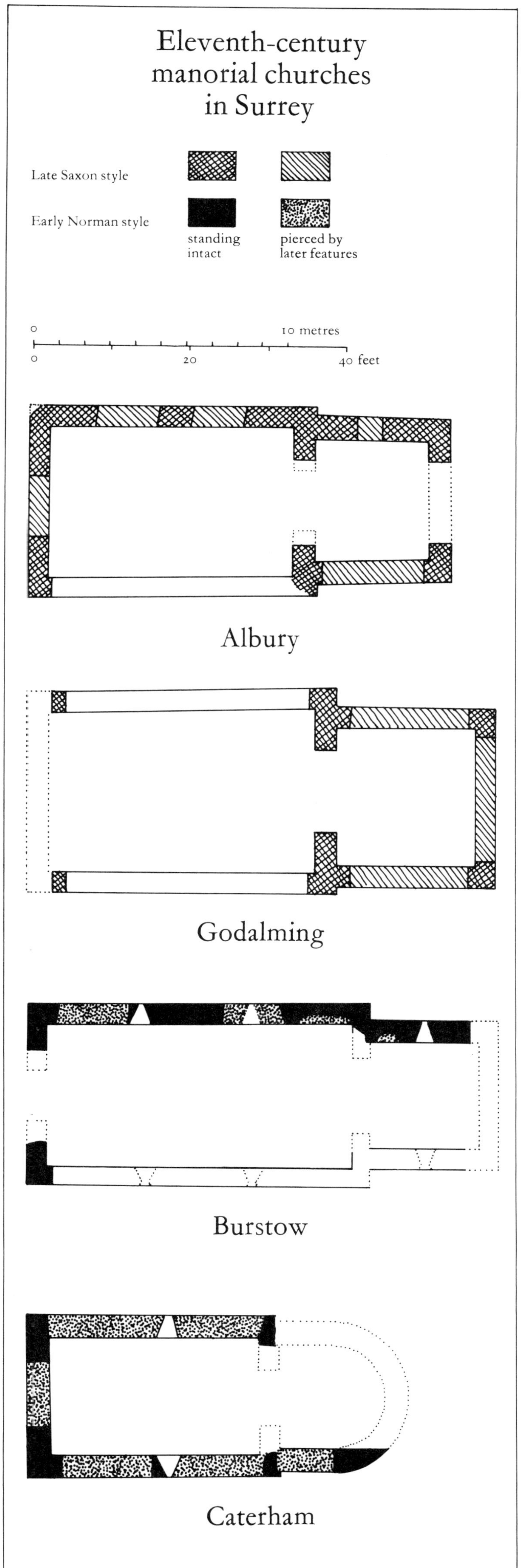

FIG. 2

FIG. 2 The first phases of these four Surrey churches show how, despite changes in style and building practice, the last Anglo-Saxon founders and the first Anglo-Norman ones used the same basic, simple ground-plan for their churches. The churches at Albury and Godalming are mentioned in Great Domesday Book ff. 35v, 30v.

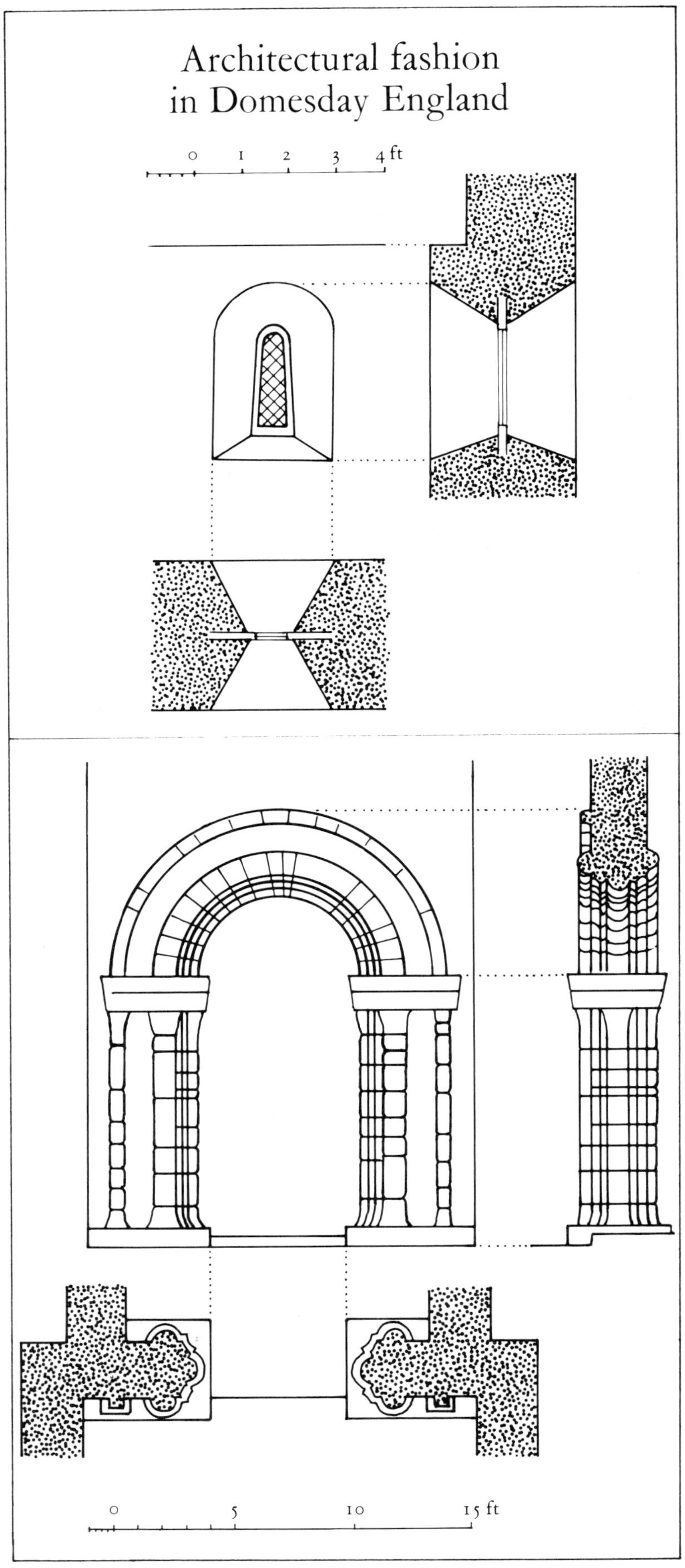

FIG. 3

Above: The double-splayed window is the most characteristic late-Saxon detail, though this example (at Thursley, Surrey) may be as late as the 1080s or 1090s. *Below*: This chancel arch (at Wittering, Northamptonshire) is unmistakably Anglo-Saxon in character, but its round mouldings show the influence of Norman Romanesque; it cannot have been built earlier than the 1050s, and probably dates from the Domesday generation.

dard for demesne churches of wealthy lords throughout the Anglo-Norman period.

The ground-plans of most ordinary churches have a simple uniformity which makes comparison with great buildings unhelpful.[1] The two most popular forms were a rectangular nave with a slightly narrower square chancel to the east (Fig. 2), and a plain rectangle (the 'chancel' space perhaps separated from the nave by a timber screen). On manorial churches west towers are only common in the eastern counties (where they are sometimes round); few are likely to pre-date the 1050s, and most are post-Conquest. Chancels are generally square-ended until *c.*1080, when the sudden popularity of the apse reflects Norman influence.

The main structural features of minor late Anglo-Saxon buildings are: tall, narrow proportions; walls less than 3 ft. thick; 'double-splayed' windows (tapering inwards from both the inner and outer faces of the wall to a central frame, as in Fig. 3 *above*); shallow strip-work decoration; 'long-and-short' quoins (tall, narrow stones alternating with flat, thin ones); and a preference for very large, often irregular, blocks. Norman masons built thicker walls, windows tapering in one direction only, and fine-jointed, regular stonework using relatively small blocks.[2] In some 'overlap' buildings these contrasting techniques are intermixed, but often we can reasonably deduce that one church was supervised by an English and another by a Norman master-mason.

The spectacular growth of Romanesque architecture in Normandy after 1000 produced new decorative forms and mouldings. How much, and how soon, England saw similar advances remains a matter for debate.[3] Edward the Confessor's rebuilding of Westminster Abbey in the Norman fashion, perhaps from the early 1050s, may have been influential, and a few minor churches with Romanesque detail (notably Kirkdale, Yorks., dated to 1055–65) are shortly pre-Conquest. 'Overlap' works of *c.*1050–1100 (such as Wittering, Fig. 3 *below*) combine the massive strength of Anglo-Saxon masonry with the round mouldings and shafts of Norman Romanesque. This is our main architectural legacy from the great age of minor church-building, the age of Domesday Book.

SELECT BIBLIOGRAPHY

F. Barlow, *The English Church 1000–1066* (2nd edn., London, 1979)

J. Blair, 'Secular Minster Churches in Domesday Book', *Domesday Book: A Reassessment*, ed. P. H. Sawyer (London, 1985)

—— 'Introduction: from Minster to Parish Church', *Minsters and Parish Churches: The Local Church in Transition 950–1200*, ed. J. Blair (Oxford, forthcoming)

—— *Landholding, Church and Settlement in Early Medieval Surrey* (Surrey Archaeol. Soc., forthcoming)

C. N. L. Brooke, 'Rural Ecclesiastical Institutions in England: the Search for their Origins', *Settimane di Studio del Centro Italiano di Studi sull' Alto Medioevo*, 28 (2) (1982), 685–711

H. C. Darby, *Domesday England* (Cambridge, 1977)

E. Fernie, *The Architecture of the Anglo-Saxons* (London, 1983)

R. D. H. Gem, 'A Recession in English Architecture during the Early Eleventh Century', *JBAA* 3rd ser., 38 (1975), 28–49

—— 'The English Parish Church in the 11th and 12th Centuries: a Great Rebuilding?', *Minsters and Parish Churches*, ed. Blair

R. Lennard, *Rural England 1086–1135* (Oxford, 1959)

H. M. and J. Taylor, *Anglo-Saxon Architecture*, i–iii (Cambridge, 1965–78)

[1] Taylor and Taylor, *Anglo-Saxon Architecture*, iii. 974–94.

[2] For a full analysis of these features see Taylor and Taylor, *Anglo-Saxon Architecture*, iii; Gem, 'Parish Church in 11th and 12th Centuries'.

[3] See the contrasting views of Gem, 'Recession in English Architecture'; Fernie, *Architecture of the Anglo-Saxons*, 112–73.

IX. THE CASTLES OF THE CONQUEST

R. ALLEN BROWN

THE Domesday survey makes casual mention of some fifty castles (normally *castellum*, *castrum*) in England and Wales. Mrs Armitage in her fundamental work, *Early Norman Castles of the British Isles*, by a careful search of contemporary charters and chronicles as well as Domesday Book, also found reference to eighty-four castles in England alone by the year 1100.[1] Formidable though these numbers may seem, they are certainly only a fraction of the unknown totals of castles already in the realm respectively by the death of the Conqueror and the death of Rufus his son. Any list for the eleventh century compiled from contemporary written sources is bound to be very incomplete. Even one drawn from the comparatively abundant records of the period 1154–1216—giving a total of 350 active castles in England and Wales about the year 1200—may well be incomplete by at least 12 per cent.[2] That Domesday is casual in its reference to castles (as to churches) is well known, and may be illustrated by the case of Eye in Suffolk, a castle then of the first rank, founded by William Malet as the *caput* or headquarters of his new honour of Eye in East Anglia and elsewhere. It finds no mention in the detailed survey of Eye itself, but is referred to by chance under neighbouring Hoxne in the context of the damage it had done to the bishop's market there.[3] Similarly, another great castle of another of the Conqueror's companions and major vassals, William de Warenne, at Lewes in Sussex, is not mentioned there but only under the Warenne lordship of Castle Acre in far-off Norfolk.[4] If we seek some notion of the number of castles raised in the first generation of the Norman Conquest we would do well to remember, even if we do not wholly believe, the chronicler Robert of Torigny's curiously precise figure of 1,115 'adulterine' or unlicensed castles destroyed by Henry II in 1154 at the end of the civil war of Stephen's reign.[5] A recent survey based primarily upon field archaeology produced an overall total of 1,580 visible castle sites of all periods in England and Wales[6]—and while that figure includes a number of later fortresses which are not properly castles it necessarily omits castles which have left no physical trace.

What is clear is that the great majority of castles in England and Wales have an early foundation, i.e. soon after 1066, and because a substantial number of such early castles were subsequently abandoned, and because new castles on new sites were comparatively rare after, say, 1154, there were never more castles in the realm (perhaps even reaching four figures) than in the first century after the Norman Conquest, and as the direct result thereof. Castles were the very means whereby the Norman Conquest, and more particularly the Norman settlement, were carried out and rendered permanent. Immediately on landing at Pevensey on 28 September 1066 the Conqueror raised a castle there, and soon after moved on to Hastings where he raised another (Fig. 1), as shown on the Bayeux Tapestry.[7] After his victory at Hastings on 14 October, the duke marched on Dover and placed a castle within the existing Old English *burh* and Iron Age fortress.[8] According to William of Poitiers, before his entry into London William sent lieutenants ahead to raise a fortress (*munitionem*) in the city, and after his coronation at Westminster on Christmas Day 1066 the new king withdrew to Barking while fortifications (*firmamenta*) were completed 'against the inconstancy of the huge and savage population'.[9] In these notices we may perhaps see the foundation not only of the future Tower of London (Fig. 2) but also of the two other castles within the city, Baynard's and Montfichet. After 1066 the take-over and settlement of England and the concurrent penetration of Wales and Scotland by the Norman king and his vassals are marked by the castles which were raised as the centres of their new lordship. William of Poitiers relates how from Barking the king pursued his march into divers parts of the kingdom, everywhere making dispositions as he pleased, and that 'he placed capable castellans with ample forces of horse and foot in his castles (*castella*), men brought over from France in whose loyalty no less than competence he could trust. He gave them rich fiefs (*opulentia beneficia*) in return for which they willingly endured hardship and danger.'[10] The Anglo-Saxon Chronicle, giving now the worm's-eye view of events, states that when the king-duke made his triumphal return to Normandy in the spring of 1067 he left Odo, Bishop of Bayeux, and William fitzOsbern behind to

[1] Armitage, *Early Norman Castles*, 94–5. This remarkable work was published in 1912 and has never yet been superseded.

[2] R. Allen Brown, 'A List of Castles, 1154–1216', *EHR* 74 (1959), and cf. *English Castles*, 215.

[3] LDB 319v–320, 379.

[4] LDB 163; cf. 157, 172.

[5] R. Howlett (ed.), *Chronicles of the Reigns of Stephen, Henry II and Richard I*, Rolls Ser. 82, iv (London, 1889), 177.

[6] King and Alcock, 'Ringworks of England and Wales', 124–5; cf. D. J. C. King, *Castellarium Anglicanum*, 2 vols (London, New York, Nendeln, 1983).

[7] J. Marx (ed.), *Guillaume de Jumièges, Gesta Normannorum Ducum*, Société de l'histoire de Normandie (Rouen, Paris, 1914), 134; William of Poitiers, *Histoire de Guillaume le Conquérant*, ed. R. Foreville (Paris, 1962), 168; D. Whitelock *et al.* (eds.), *The Anglo-Saxon Chronicle: A Revised Translation* (London, 1961), 143; F. M. Stenton *et al.* (eds.), *The Bayeux Tapestry* (2nd edn., London, 1965), pl. 51.

[8] For the matter of Dover, see esp. Allen Brown, 'The Norman Conquest and the Genesis of English Castles', 10–11, and 'An Historian's Approach to the Origins of the Castle in England', 144–5.

[9] Poitiers, *Histoire de Guillaume le Conquérant*, ed. Foreville, 218, 236.

[10] Ibid. 236–8.

FIG. 1

The construction of the castle at Hastings in October 1066 from the Bayeux Tapestry. The raising of the motte is shown (in a series of rammed down layers) with a timber palisade about its summit.

govern in his absence, and that 'they built castles [*castellas*] far and wide throughout the country, and distressed the wretched folk, and always after that it grew much worse. May the end be good when God wills!'[1] Orderic Vitalis (following William of Poitiers) notes the foundation of Exeter castle (*castellum*) in the South-West in 1068 after the defiance of the Conqueror by that city, and in writing of William's first northern expedition in the same year describes how he 'rode to all the remote parts of his kingdom and fortified strategic sites against enemy attacks', and specifically refers to the raising of castles (*castra*) at Warwick, Nottingham, York, Lincoln, Huntingdon, and Cambridge.[2] Throughout subsequent years the pattern is continued, and the castle-building programme in England and the marches of Wales in the first generation of the Norman settlement must have been without parallel in scale and concentration, the only possible analogies—with the Normans in Italy and the Normans and other Franks in Outremer—being (certainly in the case of the first) more piecemeal and prolonged, and (probably in the case of both) lacking the same immediate access to abundant resources.

The distribution of these castles is comprehensive throughout the length and breadth of the land. To some extent they are necessarily concentrated on the borders of the kingdom, in the marches of Wales and the North into Scotland, though in both cases as much for penetration as for defence. In the South-East the rapes were set up very early for the defence of the invasion coast, each an unusually compact lordship or *castellaria* with a castle as its centre.[3] Yet also they are thick on the ground everywhere and there is no English county without numerous early castle sites.[4] The explanation lies in the castle's role and function. It is only partly military, and that part at least as offensive as defensive, by means of the knights and mounted men based upon it. The castle thus controlled the surrounding countryside and its range was the range of the horse. It was the perfect instrument of conquest, colonization, and settlement by a small, alien, and military ruling class, which is the sociological pattern of the Norman Conquest. But also the castle was the residence of the great, and for this reason and by reason of its visible strength it was the conscious symbol of the new feudal lordship as well as the centre of local government and administration. The contemporary word applied to its architecturally dominant feature, whether motte, great tower, or inner en-

[1] Whitelock *et al.* (eds.), *Anglo-Saxon Chronicle*, MS D *s.a.* 1066 (translation p. 145).

[2] M. Chibnall (ed.), *The Ecclesiastical History of Orderic Vitalis*, 6 vols, Oxford Medieval Texts (Oxford, 1969–80), ii (1969), 218.

[3] *VCH Sussex*, i (1905), esp. 354; J. F. A. Mason, 'The Rapes of Sussex and the Norman Conquest', *Sussex Archaeol. Collections*, 102 (1964), 68–93; E. Searle, 'The Abbey of the Conquerors: Defensive Enfeoffment and Economic Development in Anglo-Norman England', *Proc. of the Battle Conference 1979*, ii (1980), 157.

[4] King and Alcock, 'Ringworks of England and Wales', 124–5.

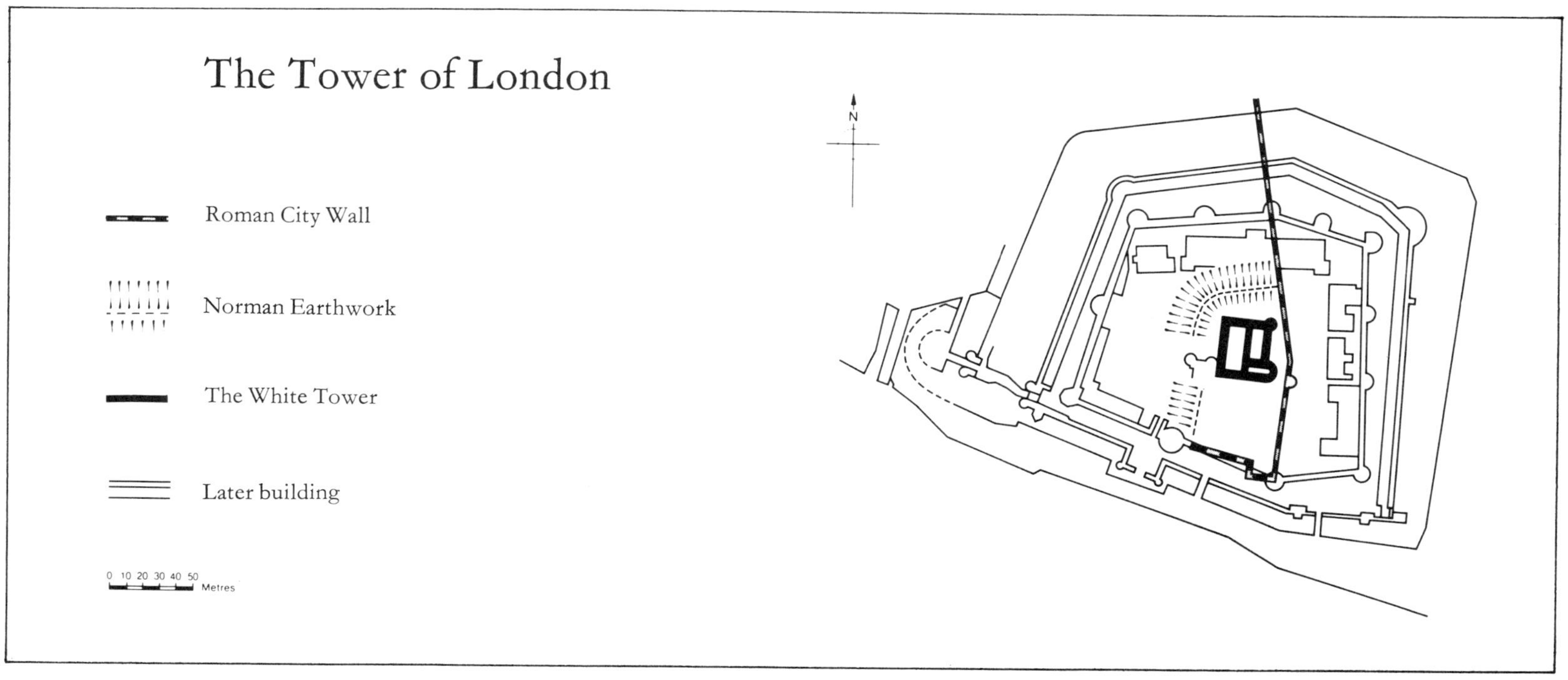

FIG. 2

The Tower of London *c.*1100, showing the Conqueror's ditch and White Tower within the south-east angle of the Roman city wall. All else is later development and expansion, principally of the twelfth and thirteenth centuries, breaking through the city wall in the latter period.

closure, the ultimate strong-point and inner sanctum of lordly residence, was *donjon*, which is derived from the Latin *dominium* meaning 'lordship'.[1]

The castle, if it is to be properly defined, is the fortified residence of a lord—any lord, not necessarily the king or prince. It is significant that Domesday itself can evidently refer to Roger of Montgomery's new castle at Quatford in Shropshire as *nova domus* ('new house')[2]—and in so doing distinguish it from the *burh* (*burgus*)—and certainly refers to *domus defensabiles* (in Herefordshire),[3] i.e. 'strong houses', of the type which English archaeologists call 'fortified manors' and the French call *maisons fortes*, as opposed to the more heavily fortified castles. In France the word *château* is retained for the great country house, its fortifications dropped away. The castle, thus, as the fortified residence of a lord, is clearly different from Old English (and Scandinavian) fortifications, and from the *burhs* of Alfred and his successors, which were communal fortresses, public and royal, by 1066 surviving as fortified towns and cities. Though some early castles on the Continent might be very large as the fortified descendants of Carolingian palaces,[4] the usual difference in scale and concept from the *burh* is often visible to the naked eye, as the Normans placed castles within the *burhs* of Winchester, Dover, Pevensey, Hastings, Wallingford, and many other towns and cities, as, for example, London (three) and York (two).[5] That castles were absent from pre-Conquest England is characteristic of a surviving Carolingian-type monarchy, and contrasts significantly with the situation in France or West Frankia, where they began to appear in the tenth century as great lords of necessity took over the sovereign right of fortification in the decline of late Carolingian royal authority. The earliest surviving castle site in France is Doué-la-Fontaine (Maine-et-Loire), dating from *c.*950. That castles were a Norman importation into England and Britain, the means and the result of the Norman Conquest and settlement, is proved above all by the overwhelming evidence of the widespread castle-building following 1066, and not least those entries in Domesday which note the number of houses and messuages destroyed in towns and cities to make way for the new castle—166 at Lincoln, 113 at Norwich.[6] Obviously the planting of castles on this scale would not have been necessary had castles existed in pre-Conquest England as the centres of Old English estates and lordships now taken over by the Normans and their allies. Orderic Vitalis gave the lack of castles in England as one reason for its defeat: 'the fortifications [*munitiones*] called castles [*castella*] by the Normans were scarcely known in the English provinces, and so the English—in spite of their courage and love of fighting—could put up only a weak resistance to their enemies'.[7] In spite of the revived interest on both sides of the Channel in the study of the origins of the castle during the last two or three decades, and the archaeological research which has resulted, the facts are still as Mrs Armitage noted, that the only

[1] The native English word *keep* only appears in the sixteenth century (*OED*).

[2] GDB 254; cf. Chibnall (ed.), *Ecclesiastical History*, v (1975), 224–5 and n. 3. See Armitage, *Early Norman Castles*, 191; Renn, *Norman Castles in Britain*, 289; J. F. A. Mason and P. A. Barker, 'The Norman Castle at Quatford', *Trans. of the Shropshire Archaeol. Soc.* 57 (1961–4), 37–46.

[3] GDB 184v, 187.

[4] In Normandy, e.g. Fécamp and Caen. Cf. P. Héliot, 'Sur les résidences princières bâties en France du xe au xiie siècle', *Le Moyen Âge*, 61 (1955). For the Old English *burh*, see esp. C. A. Ralegh Radford, 'The Later Pre-Conquest Boroughs and their Defences', *MA* 14 (1970), 83–103.

[5] For Winchester, see esp. M. Biddle (ed.), *Winchester in the Early Middle Ages: an Edition and Discussion of the Winton Domesday*, Winchester Studies, i (Oxford, 1976), 302 ff., 449 ff. For Pevensey and Hastings, see A. J. Taylor, 'Evidence for a Pre-Conquest Origin for the Chapels in Hastings and Pevensey Castles', *Château-Gaillard*, iii. 144–51.

[6] GDB 336v; LDB 116v.

[7] Chibnall (ed.), *Ecclesiastical History*, ii. 218.

FIG. 3

The classic Norman 'motte-and-bailey' site at Pleshey in Essex. The castle and fortified vill or township which went with it were raised in open country as the centre or *caput* of the new Mandeville lordship after the Conquest.

known castles in pre-Conquest England are those very few raised in the reign of Edward the Confessor by the king's Norman and French friends already here as the precursors of the Conquest—Richard's Castle, Ewyas Harold, Hereford itself and one or more others in Herefordshire, together probably with Clavering in Essex.[1]

The fact that the origins of the castle in England lie in the Norman Conquest and its antecedents is of deep significance for the nature of late Old English society and the origins of English feudalism. For the castle, the fortified residence of a lord, and often enough the *caput* of his honour, first certainly appearing in northern France in the tenth century with the development of feudal society itself, is a fundamentally feudal institution. French feudalists, of course, are entirely aware of the fact and Mrs Armitage established it in England more than seventy years ago, but it would be well if it were more widely and consistently remembered in the interminable insular argument about the origins of English feudalism.[2]

In raising their castles in England and Wales (and southern Scotland) the Normans and their allies of the first generation used and exploited those methods and techniques of fortification with which they were familiar in Normandy and elsewhere in France. Far and away the commonest type of early castle on this side of the Channel was the 'motte and bailey', where the ditched and banked enclosure of the bailey is dominated by the motte (a contemporary word), usually to one side and with its own ditch about it (Fig. 3). Variants are two baileys, one on either side of the motte (Windsor, Arundel), and, rarely, the motte within the bailey (Bramber), or two mottes (Lewes, Lincoln), or double ditches (e.g. Berkhamsted). The banks of the bailey and the summit of the motte were further defended by a timber stockade or palisade, and the bailey contained all those buildings, presumably of timber in the first generation, for which there was no room upon the flat top and confined fighting space of the motte. The motte was joined to the bailey by a bridge and bore a timber tower, which could be elaborate (as shown by the representation of Bayeux on the Bayeux Tapestry,[3] by the well-known description by Lambert of Ardres of 'the great and lofty house [*domus*]' on the motte at Ardres

[1] See esp. Allen Brown, 'The Norman Conquest and the Genesis of English Castles', and 'An Historian's Approach to the Origins of the Castle in England'. For the recent research project of the Royal Archaeological Institute into the origins of the castle in England, see *ArchJ* 134 (1977).

[2] P. Guilhiermoz, *Essai sur l'origine de la noblesse en France au Moyen Âge* (Paris, 1902), 143–65; M. Bloch, *Feudal Society*, trans. L. A. Manyon (London, 1961), 300, 400; Armitage, *Early Norman Castles*, e.g. 63–4, 76–8, 79; R. Allen Brown, *Origins of English Feudalism* (London, 1973), esp. 30–1, 72–82.

[3] Stenton *et al.* (eds.), *Bayeux Tapestry*, pl. 28.

FIG. 4

In the Bayeux Tapestry, the castle of Dinan is represented by its motte or donjon, which clearly bears a timber palisade and tower.

in 1117,[1] and by excavation some years ago at South Mimms[2]) and at least often contained some of the best residential accommodation for the lord of the castle (as it certainly did at Ardres and South Mimms). Like the contemporary great tower of stone-built castles, the motte was thus the donjon, the dominant feature, the ultimate strong-point, the inner sanctum of lordship and its symbol (Fig. 4). As late as 1789 in parts of France lingering feudal dues were rendered 'à cause de la motte'[3] and it is significant that the Bayeux Tapestry represents all its castles simply by the motte—save probably in one instance where the castle of Rouen is represented by its great tower.[4]

Sometimes the place of the motte is taken by an inner enclosure (the so-called 'ring-motte') fulfilling the same function, as, for example, at the recently excavated Castle Acre in Norfolk. Sometimes the castle may consist simply of the one enclosure of ditch, bank, and palisade (the so-called 'ring-work') sheltering the residential buildings disposed within, though it is hard to believe that in such cases there was not some inner sanctum and some dominant architectural feature, i.e. a donjon. Pevensey and Rochester were thus in the beginning simply enclosure castles, before the addition of their great tower keeps in the twelfth century, and there were many others. Though it may seem primitive, the type persists throughout the Middle Ages to include some of the grandest and most sophisticated castles in the realm, as witness Caernarvon and Conway or their concentric (a double enclosure, inner and outer) rivals in strength, Beaumaris, Harlech, and Caerphilly. Indeed, it is a mistake sharply to distinguish between 'earthwork and timber castles' and 'stone castles', as archaeologists are prone to do, for the principles of fortification are the same in both and there is much overlap between the two. Many stone castles make as much use of ditches and banks, i.e. earthworks, as do castles of earthwork and timber; each may have constituent parts of either timber or masonry; both exploit the same defensive devices irrespective of the building material used, e.g. tower, wall-walks and crenellation, projecting timber hoarding or stone machicolation. It is also, of course, a fact that those many castles thought to have consisted exclusively of earthwork and timber in their early origin, if they survived into later periods, were refortified and rebuilt in stone—thus producing, to cite one detailed example, the so-called shell keep (Windsor, Arundel, Lewes, and many more) which is simply a wall of masonry instead of a timber palisade about the summit of the motte (Fig. 5). Classic instances of early post-Conquest sites subsequently developed in masonry abound, and include Windsor, Arundel, Warwick and Rochester, Warkworth, Barnard Castle and Pickering, Raglan, and even Caernarvon itself.

Finally it is to be noted that, just as stone fortification and building occurs in Continental castles from the tenth century and from the beginning, so it does in England as soon as possible after 1066 if not before. Richmond and Ludlow display towered curtain walls

[1] V. Mortet, *Recueil des textes relatifs à l'histoire de l'architecture . . . en France*, ii (Paris, 1911), 183.

[2] No proper report on the excavations at South Mimms has yet been published: see J. P. C. Kent, 'Excavations at the Motte and Bailey Castle of South Mimms, Herts, 1960–1967', *Barnet and District Local Hist. Soc. Bull.* 15 (1968).

[3] Ph. Siguret, 'Trois mottes de la région de Bellême (Orne)', *Château-Gaillard, Etudes de Castellologie Européenne*, i (Caen, 1964), 135 n. 4.

[4] Stenton *et al.* (eds.), *Bayeux Tapestry*, pl. 14, p. 81.

FIG. 5

Aerial view of Windsor Castle from the east by north-east, showing the Conqueror's original layout of a motte and two baileys beneath the accumulated masonry of later ages. The shell keep on the motte (much heightened in the modern period) was probably constructed under Henry I. The date of the last medieval building, St George's Chapel, is 1477–1528.

of the eleventh century, and the hall of the former is of the same date. So is the gate tower at Exeter (*c.*1068?), which resembles the gate tower at Le Plessis-Grimoult in Normandy (pre-1047). Amongst these masonry works of early castles the great tower, in English parlance tower keep, the donjon *par excellence*, is also there from the beginning on both sides of the Channel. In northern France the keeps of Doué-la-Fontaine and Rouen itself date from the mid tenth century, Langeais, Montbazon, and Nogent-le-Rotrou from the late tenth and early eleventh. In Norman England the White Tower (*the* 'Tower of London') and Colchester pre-eminently date from the Conqueror's reign. Indeed one cannot get closer to the spirit of the Conqueror than in the Chapel of St John within the White Tower at London, and if one adds to that great building those of Colchester and the huge Anglo-Norman churches, Durham above all, which the Conquest brought about, one gets very close indeed to that dominant spirit of *Normanitas* which also conceived and carried through the Domesday survey.

SELECT BIBLIOGRAPHY

E. S. Armitage, *The Early Norman Castles of the British Isles* (London, 1912)

R. Allen Brown, 'The Norman Conquest and the Genesis of English Castles', *Château-Gaillard, European Castle Studies*, iii (Chichester, 1969 for 1966)

—— 'An Historian's Approach to the Origins of the Castle in England', *ArchJ* 126 (1970 for 1969)

—— *English Castles* (3rd edn., London, 1976)

—— *The Architecture of Castles: a Visual Guide* (London, 1984)

B. K. Davison, 'The Origins of the Castle in England', *ArchJ* 124 (1967)

D. J. C. King and L. Alcock, 'Ringworks of England and Wales', *Château-Gaillard*, iii (Chichester, 1969 for 1966)

D. F. Renn, *Norman Castles in Britain* (Chatham, 1968)

X. THE MONETARY SYSTEM UNDER WILLIAM I

PHILIP GRIERSON

Denominations

The coinage unit in Domesday Book is the *denarius* (Fr. *denier*), or penny in English. Since it was the only coin then struck in England, it was occasionally simply called a *nummus*.[1] *Oboli*, i.e. halfpennies, which are mentioned occasionally, were not separate coins but were made by cutting pennies into halves. Farthings (*ferdingi*) occur only in the Norfolk and Suffolk returns in Little Domesday,[2] similar figures elsewhere having presumably been rounded off to the nearest penny, but they may be coins designated as *minuta* in a list of small payments at Chester.[3] Such cut halfpennies and farthings occur occasionally, but only in small numbers, in coin hoards of the period. Foreign coins did not normally circulate, but the renders of two manors in Devonshire belonging to St Mary's of Rouen are recorded as £70 *rodomensium*,[4] i.e. £70 of the much lighter and baser Norman deniers of Rouen (*roumois*) worth only a third of their English counterparts. They would probably be paid, however, in English coin.

The higher units, also not struck as distinct coins, were the *solidus* (Fr. *sou*) or shilling of 12*d.* and the *libra* (Fr. *livre*) or pound of 20*s.*, the latter usually expressed as *xxs* in order to avoid confusion with the unit of weight. These accounting units had been the same in both England and France before the Conquest, though local reckonings of 4*d.* or 5*d.* to the shilling had existed in Mercia and Wessex respectively. These, like another accounting unit, the Anglo-Saxon *mancus* of 30*d.*, do not appear in Domesday Book, but over most of England we find reckonings in terms of an *ora* of either 16*d.* or 20*d.* and a *mark* of 8 oras. These terms were Scandinavian in origin (cf. mod. Danish *øre*) and referred to units of weight. The lighter ora corresponded to the Danish 'ounce' of *c.*25 g. with a mark of *c.*200 g., a figure a little lower than the Danish mark in the later Middle Ages of *c.*210–15 g. but very close to the *c.*196 g. of lead weights of the Viking period discovered at Hedeby. It has been argued that the 20*d.* unit, expressed in such phrases as *de xx in ora* and *ad numerum de xx in ora*, implied payments by tale in contrast to 16*d.* ones of blanched silver by weight, but an allowance of 4*d.* for loss of weight in circulation would have been quite excessive and it is more likely to have been an Anglo-Saxon ounce of 20 pennyweights, with a mark of 13*s.* 4*d.* Such payments were much more widespread than specific references to the 20*d.* ora indicate, for they lie behind sums such as 3*s.* 4*d.*, 5*s.*, or 8*s.* 4*d.*, which are multiples of 20*d.* The few cases of sums expressed in gold, usually ceremonial in character and supplementary to payments in silver, are by weight (marks and ounces). Since there was little gold actually available these would normally have been settled in silver, probably at the conventional figures, well documented in the twelfth century and independent of small fluctuations in the ratio between the precious metals, of 15*s.* for an ounce and £6 for a mark.

The penny was a silver coin some 20 mm in diameter, about the size of the modern bronze penny but much thinner and lighter. By 1086 its weight had been stabilized at a theoretical $22\frac{1}{2}$ grains (1.46 g.)—the modern bronze penny weighs 3.56 g.—the difference between $22\frac{1}{2}$ grains and the 24-grain 'pennyweight' of the weight system helping to defray the cost of minting. The designs were on the obverse the king's head either facing or profile, with no attempt at portraiture, and on the reverse some type of cross, but the details were changed at frequent intervals, probably of three years, as a result of the practice introduced a century earlier of regular *renovationes* (or *mutationes*) *monetae*, though initially the intervals between such recoinages were nearer six years than three. The coins are undated, but the order of issue of each type can be established by the overlapping contents of coin hoards and the occasional muling of an obverse of one type with the reverse of another, or the over-striking of a penny of one type on a penny of an earlier one. At the date of Domesday the pennies in circulation were apparently those of William's eighth coinage, that called by numismatists the *Paxs* type from the ringed letters **PAXS** in the quarters of the cross on the reverse (see Class VIII in Fig. 1), which is usually dated *c.*1086–8. The king's head was on all types surrounded by his name and title, preceded by a small cross, while the reverse legend had the moneyer's name and that of the mint, also preceded by a cross.

Payments were effected in various ways which are only casually referred to in Domesday Book but are more precisely defined in the twelfth-century *Dialogus de Scaccario*. In ordinary day-to-day transactions coins would change hands at their face value by simply counting them (by tale, *numero*, *ad numerum*), though recipients could no doubt reject coins that seemed to them counterfeits or were damaged or unduly light. But, as in most societies before the coming of paper money, large transactions would have taken place by weight (*ad pensum*), or by tale with the addition of a few pence in the pound to compensate for loss of weight through wear and the tendency of users to hoard such heavier ones as came their way. The fineness of the coins would sometimes be checked, for returns in Domesday Book

[1] GDB 164.
[2] LDB 135, 360.
[3] GDB 268.
[4] GDB 104.

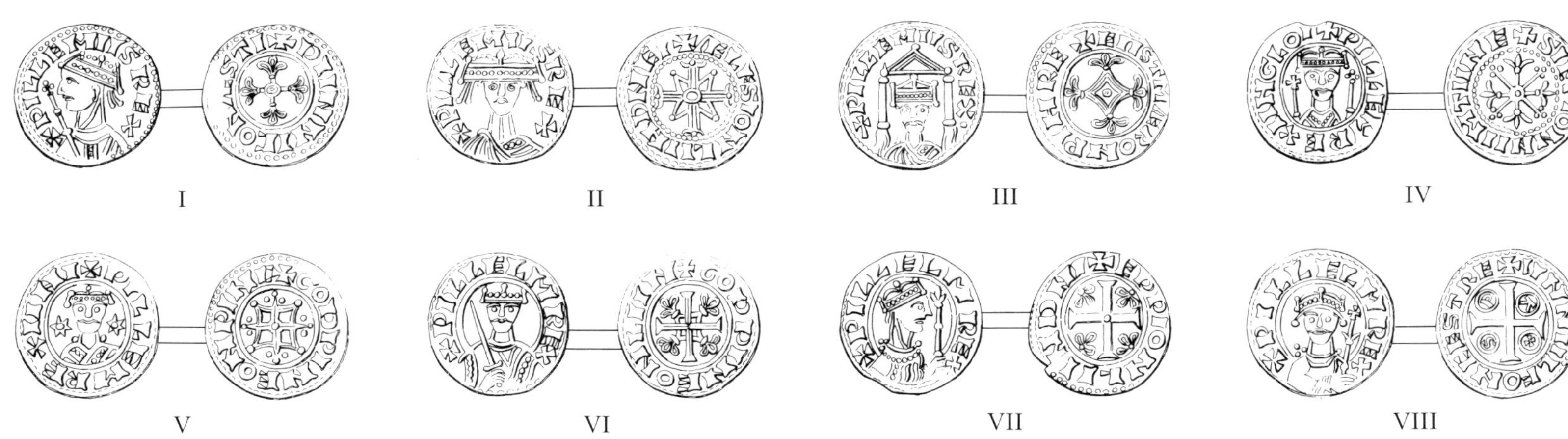

FIG. 1

The eight successive classes of silver penny of William I, in the order in which they were issued. The last (Class VIII), bearing the letters P A X S in the angles of the cross on the reverse, is generally believed to be the coin struck during the period of the Domesday survey.

frequently present a contrast between payments in (*librae*) *arsae et pensatae*, pounds 'burnt' (i.e. assayed) and weighed, and those 'in white pennies' (*de albis denariis*) or in 'pennies of white silver' (*denarii de albo argento*), the latter often in substitution for payments in kind that had earlier been customary. Sums *arsi et pensati* may sometimes have been paid in ingot form, but one suspects that it was generally just a legal formula. Those in 'white pennies' would certainly be in actual coin, but whether with an allowance to compensate for loss of weight or possible deficiencies in fineness, as the term 'blanched' later implied, we do not know. The late Anglo-Saxon penalty of amputation of the hand for convicted counterfeiters, and for moneyers found issuing light or base coin, will have contributed to keeping the coinage in good condition.

Mints and Moneyers

The coins were struck at local mints, of which there was at least one in each county, though the dies were supplied centrally by the Exchequer, the office of die-cutter (*cuneator*) becoming hereditary under the Normans in the fitzOtho family. The term 'mint' is something of a misnomer—Stenton preferred to employ the expression 'minting-place'—for to the modern ear it implies a level of permanence and organization that must often have been absent. Sixty-eight mints are known from the coin legends to have existed at one time or another during William's reign, though only sixty-four took part in the *Paxs* coinage (see Fig. 2 and Table below). They varied greatly in size, with only one moneyer at such small mints as Cricklade and Pevensey and up to seven or more at London and Canterbury, but the numbers were not fixed and in a few cases, most notably at York, changed substantially during the reign. There must have been about two hundred moneyers in the country, but one cannot give a precise figure because the *Paxs* class is the only one of the reign for which comprehensive hoard evidence is available and some of the moneyers who took part in its issue will have been minting in succession and not simultaneously. Also, because it was possible for a moneyer to work in more than one locality, one cannot always be sure whether the same name on coins of several mints represents one or more persons.

Of the sixty-four mints active when the Domesday material was being collected only twenty are mentioned, either directly or indirectly, in Domesday Book (underlined in Fig. 2), and only thirteen of the equally numerous mints that had existed before the Conquest (TRE). The localities that did provide returns varied greatly in what was thought worth mentioning, but this is only one aspect of the general irregularity of information regarding the boroughs, which were evidently questioned in a much less systematic fashion than were communities in rural areas. Hence the anomaly of the entries for some boroughs putting TRE practices on record but omitting to state that the same places were still active in 1086, as we know from the coins to have been the case, while others record payments in 1086 but make no mention of what was done TRE. Only five boroughs admit to minting both before as well as after 1066.

William's Reform

A comparison of TRE and TRW entries does indeed show that William had carried out a major change in mint organization for which Domesday Book is our only evidence. TRE payments were made by the moneyers, normally £1 each annually for the privilege of minting—the sum is often stated as 1 mark, presumably by omission of one-third of the total retained by the earl—and an extra £1 *quando moneta vertebatur*, effectively every three years when the coinage was changed. This has sometimes been regarded as the payment for the new dies that would then be needed, but the Hereford entry makes it clear that the two were distinct and the dies were paid for separately. There is no reference to any payments by the boroughs, or indeed to any further payments by the moneyers, presumably because the moneyers were either the king's men—*tres monetarios habebat ibi rex* is the specific formula at Shrewsbury[1]—or those of some ecclesiastical institution—e.g. one of the seven moneyers at Hereford who worked for the bishop[2]—to whom the king had conceded part of the

[1] GDB 252.

[2] GDB 179, 181v.

profits of minting. The division of these profits would be arranged between the king and the moneyers, but how exactly they were assessed, and what they amounted to, we have no idea. They must have varied greatly from one year to another, being substantial in the first months of each recoinage and, at least in normal circumstances, much smaller thereafter.

This system had two drawbacks. The king had little idea in advance of how much to expect, and the public was faced with the possibility of changes in the weight of the penny, which should not in theory have influenced its domestic purchasing power but would certainly affect its value outside the country. This was an important consideration for merchants and indeed for the king and the greater magnates who had need of money abroad. The remedy in England, as in some other countries, was the introduction of a general tax known as *monetagium* in return for the prince's renunciation of *renovationes*, or at least of those involving changes in weight or fineness. It is this system that first appears in the post-Conquest entries in Domesday Book.

These are quite different in form and content from the TRE entries, for the payments are made by the burgesses, not the moneyers, and take the form of substantial annual sums, not quite small ones of a token character. The annual payment of £1 per moneyer has disappeared: it was in fact subsumed into the general geld paid by the borough, for twelfth-century Pipe Rolls sometimes include allowances *per defalta monetariorum*, at the rate of £1 per head for a year, to boroughs which have allowed their minting to lapse. The triennial payments *quando moneta vertebatur* have likewise disappeared and the phrase is in fact never used again, for though triennial changes in coin types persist, the weights of the coins remain unaltered. The big change is in the annual payments, usually described as *de moneta* but in the Leicester entry as *de monetariis*,[1] in the Huntingdon one[2] as *geldum monete*, and in the Lincoln one as *geldum regis de monedagio*.[3] The payment for Pevensey, given as only £1,[4] is so small that it is probably a misdescribed TRE payment, though a special concession is conceivable. The others, apart from a perhaps erroneous £5. 12*s*. at Lewes, are all multiples or fractions of £5, the usual figure being £20 (Colchester *cum* Maldon, Gloucester, Ipswich, Leicester, Oxford) but rising above this to £30 (Huntingdon), £40 (Thetford), and even £75 (Lincoln), and elsewhere £10 (Nottingham), £5 (Bath, Malmesbury), and £2. 10*s*. (Taunton). The Colchester–Maldon figure was in dispute, for the burgesses claimed that the king had reduced it to £10 but that the Bishop of Winchester, Walkelin, who apparently had it in farm and for whose avarice there is other evidence, was contesting this and claiming £40 of arrears.

The implication of this different pattern of payments is that control over the moneyers had been transferred to the burgesses, and it was up to the borough authorities to find the sums due to the king, either from the moneyers or by setting some local rate. A hearth tax is indeed suggested by the Lincoln entry regarding three tofts held by a certain Turold 'in quibus habet omnes consuetudines praeter geldum regis de monedagio', and this was later the practice with *monetagium* in Normandy, for this had the alternative name of *focagium* or *fouage* (from *foca*, 'feu'). The sums could easily fall into arrears, as happened at Ipswich.[5] At Ipswich and Leicester, and perhaps very generally, the earl retained a third of the sum collected, though favoured magnates might be allowed a half, as were William de Warenne at Lewes and Robert of Rhuddlan at Rhuddlan. At Ipswich the sum is stated to have been paid by the moneyers, not the borough, and it has been suggested that in some cases the geld may have been farmed collectively by the local moneyers, but the Ipswich wording has resulted from the phrase being continued from one describing the payments TRE and the scribe having forgotten the subject of the sentence.

The only light that Domesday Book throws on the date at which the new minting arrangements were introduced is provided by the allusions to the payments at Ipswich having fallen £53 in arrears over the previous four years and to the new system having been introduced at Colchester in the time of Waleram. The last piece of information does not help directly, for although Waleram figures several times in Domesday as a former landowner and possibly sheriff, he was dead by 1086 and we do not know the exact date. The Ipswich entry, however, implies a date for the introduction of the new system earlier than 1082 and Walkelin's claim at Colchester indicates the same, for £40 would correspond to an alleged underpayment of £10 a year for four years. *Monetagium* as a general term meant a tax compensating a ruler for the profits he might otherwise have made by changing the weight and fineness of his coins. In an English setting only changes in weight can have been involved, and in fact the coins of William's Class VI were raised from 21 or $21\frac{1}{2}$ grains to $22\frac{1}{2}$ grains, a figure at which the penny was to remain stable for over two centuries and which provides the most probable explanation of the term 'sterling' applied to the English penny (*steor*, 'firm'). The introduction of Class VI is usually dated to 1080, when the king returned to England after a three-year absence in Normandy, and it therefore seems likely that William's long-forgotten minting reform should be placed in 1080 or 1081.

[1] GDB 230.
[2] GDB 203.
[3] GDB 336v.
[4] GDB 20v.
[5] LDB 290v.

Table of Mints and Moneyers

The mints are known mainly from the coins, fewer than a third of them being mentioned either directly or indirectly in Domesday Book as existing under William. In the table below, the probable number of moneyers in each place during William's later years is given and also the number of moneyers per mint attested on the coins for his Class VIII. The occasional differences between these two figures can be due to the movement of moneyers from mint to mint. The references to mints in GDB, LDB, and Exon Domesday are divided into those stated as existing before the Conquest and those active under William I.

Four of the mints in the table (and on the map, Fig. 2) did not take part in the issue of Class VIII and so were inactive when Domesday Book was being compiled. They were Bedwyn (active TRE and participated in William's Class I but subsequently replaced by Marlborough), Bury St Edmunds (abbatial mint inactive during most of William's reign), Christchurch (Twynham) in Hampshire, which was briefly active in Class VII, presumably during an emergency at some nearby mint, and Peterborough, whose moneyer at Stamford had during the issue of Class II momentarily transferred his activities to Peterborough itself. Bridport, Cardiff, and St Davids are known only for Class VIII, the coins of Cardiff and St Davids being virtually obsidional issues, and the coinage of Durham only started with this class.

	Probable number of moneyers striking *c.*1075–87	Number of moneyers' names recorded on coins of Class VIII	References to pre-Conquest mints	References to post-Conquest mints
Barnstaple	1	1		
Bath	2	3		GDB 87, Exon 114v
Bedford	2	1		
Bedwyn	1			
Bridport	1	2	GDB 75, Exon 12	
Bristol	3	5		
Bury St Edmunds	1			
Cambridge	1	1		
Canterbury	7	8		
Cardiff	1	3?		
Chester	3	4/5	GDB 262v	
Chichester	2	2		
Christchurch (Twynham)	1			
Colchester	4	4	LDB 107	LDB 107v
Cricklade	2	1		
Derby	2	2		
Dorchester	2	2	GDB 75	
Dover	3	5		
Durham	1	1		
Exeter	3	3		
Gloucester	4	4		GDB 162
Guildford	1	1		
Hastings	3	2		
Hereford	4	4	GDB 179, 181v	
Hertford	2	2		
Huntingdon	1	1	GDB 203	GDB 203
Hythe	1	1		
Ilchester	2	1		
Ipswich	4	6	LDB 290v	LDB 290v
Launceston	1	1		
Leicester	2	1		GDB 230
Lewes	3	3	GDB 26	GDB 26
Lincoln	5	2		GDB 336v
London	9	8		
Maldon	2	3		LDB 107v
Malmesbury	1	2		GDB 64v
Marlborough	1	1		
Northampton	3	3		
Norwich	4	8?		LDB 117v
Nottingham	2	2	GDB 280	GDB 280
Oxford	6	3		GDB 154, 154v
Peterborough	1			
Pevensey	1	1		GDB 20v
Rhuddlan	1	1		GDB 269
Rochester	2	2		
Romney	3	2		
St Davids	1	1		
Salisbury	3	2		
Sandwich	2	3		
Shaftesbury	3	3	GDB 75, Exon 11	
Shrewsbury	3	3	GDB 252	
Southwark	3	4		
Stafford	2	2		
Stamford	3	3		
Steyning	1	1		
Sudbury	1	1		LDB 286v
Tamworth	2	2		
Taunton	1	1		GDB 87v
Thetford	6	6		LDB 119
Wallingford	3	2		GDB 56
Wareham	3	4	GDB 75, Exon 12v	
Warwick	3	4		
Watchet	1	1		
Wilton	3	3		
Winchcombe	1	1		
Winchester	6	8		
Worcester	4	4	GDB 172	
York	4	4		GDB 298

Table 1

FIG. 2

Mints mentioned directly or indirectly in Domesday Book are underlined.

XI. WEIGHTS AND MEASURES

PHILIP GRIERSON

MOST traditional measures go back ultimately to parts of the human body or to simple human activities, but they have been artificially brought into relationship with each other by convenient decimal or duodecimal multiples. Generalized through a mixture of imitation and authority, they were finally made uniform by the distribution of standards and the enforcement of their use. Legislation in the late Anglo-Saxon period frequently prescribed uniformity, and the code known as III Edgar had tried to impose the standards of London and Winchester. Subsequent legislation shows local standards being held by borough authorities, and by parish priests in the countryside, but there is no evidence for any general distribution of specially prepared standards by the central government before Richard I's Assize of Measures in 1196. The earliest surviving ones are from subsequent distributions in the fourteenth and fifteenth centuries which probably reproduce quite accurately the standards of 1196. Anglo-Saxon ones may have been slightly different, for the length of the foot and the inch had been redefined earlier in the twelfth century as $\frac{1}{3}$ and $\frac{1}{36}$ respectively of the newly introduced (cloth-)yard of 3 feet (91.44 cm.). In interpreting Domesday figures one is sometimes uncertain as to whether any particular figure is using the 'normal' hundred of ten times ten or the 'long' hundred of 120 (sixscore), called in the Lincoln record in Domesday the hundred 'by English reckoning' ('Hic numerus anglice computatur, 1 centum pro centum viginti', and again on the same folio in the next column '200 anglico numero 240').[1]

MEASURES OF LENGTH AND AREA

The basic small units of length were the inch (OE. *ynce*, Lat. *uncia*), originally the breadth of the thumb-nail (*unguis*), the foot (OE. *fot*, Lat. *pes*), and the ell (*ulna*), though there were a few others—the palm, the hand, the shaftment (i.e. the distance covered by the width of the hand and the extended thumb), the span—that were occasionally used for measurements of specific kinds. The inch and foot may have been slightly shorter than the modern units (inch = 2.54 cm., foot = 30.48 cm.), though the differences cannot have been great. The ell was notionally the length of the forearm (whence 'elbow') but seems in fact to have been equated with 2 feet. The inch and the ell do not appear in Domesday Book and the foot only rarely. It is used in the definition of a very precise road distance around Canterbury,[2] in the measurement of some house frontages at York,[3] and in a few Norfolk returns pedantically giving the sizes of estates or fields to the nearest foot.[4] The three fell far short of the land measures that were its compilers' main concern, the rod or perch and the furlong on which the notional acre was based.

The perch took its name from the Latin *pertica*, but was also known as a rod (Lat. *virga*), or pole or yard (OE. *gyrd*), both having the primary meaning of 'rod' or 'stick'. The term 'yard' was only later transferred to the familiar 3-foot unit introduced under Henry I.

The larger measures of length were the furlong (40 perches), the mile (8 furlongs), and the league (12 furlongs). Those of area were the virgate (square perch, later called the 'rood'), the acre (160 virgates), and the hide (notionally 120 acres), though in the former Danelaw the hide was replaced by the carucate (120 acres) divided into bovates, and in Kent by the sulung (240 acres) divided into juga. Confusion is caused by the fact that the term 'carucate' sometimes meant a much smaller unit, and by the 'acre' being sometimes used as a measure of length and 'league' as one of area, with considerable uncertainty in the last case as to exactly what was meant by the term.

The length of the Roman *pertica* had been 10 Roman feet (2.96 m.), but the standard English 'field' perch, from the later Middle Ages onwards, was the much longer and apparently quite irrational figure of $16\frac{1}{2}$ feet (5.03 m.). This length was in widespread use at a very early date—there was a structure in the seventh-century palace at Yeavering exactly $16\frac{1}{2}$ feet square—but its origin is uncertain, the best suggestion being that its 198 inches correspond to that of a pole exactly 20 'natural' feet of 10 inches stepped out on the ground. But while the $16\frac{1}{2}$-foot perch was ultimately adopted as the national standard it was in the later Middle Ages only one of many variants ranging from about 14 to 18 feet. These were often physically represented by local standards embedded in church or cemetery walls or other public places to prevent disputes arising over their exact length, but no early standards have survived and how far the later variants reproduced pre-Conquest patterns we do not know. The $16\frac{1}{2}$-foot perch was in any case a field measure. The perch used for defining uncultivated land was larger, the standard 'forest' perch being generally taken as 25 feet but varying locally between about 20 feet and 28 feet. Whether these longer perches were in use by 1086 is doubtful. The sizes of woodland are often stated in Domesday Book in terms of leagues,

[1] GDB 336. [2] GDB 2. [3] GDB 298. [4] e.g. LDB 160v.

furlongs, and perches, but where furlongs and perches were involved such external measurements would have been most easily determined in relation to the cultivated areas on which the 'forests' abutted, in which case they would have been those normally used for arable measures.

The furlong, as its name implies, was the length of a furrow, or notionally the distance that a team of oxen could easily plough before stopping to rest and turn. It was conventionally taken as 40 perches, as the term *quarentena* (cf. Fr. *quarante*) used throughout Domesday Book implies. The acre took its name from the Latin *ager*, meaning a field, and was notionally defined as 4 × 40 perches, i.e. 160 square perches (*virgatae*) or roods. The width of 4 perches, the 'acre's breadth' of 66 feet (which has survived as the length of the cricket pitch), was itself treated as a linear measure. The lengths of town walls in the document known as the Burghal Hidage are defined in acre's breadths, and it is this distance that is meant in Domesday Book when fields are sometimes defined as *x* furlongs long and *y* acres wide. This figure was based on the assumption that acres were ten times as long as they were broad, but in practice the shape of fields must often have been quite irregular, depending on the lie of the land and any natural features involved. In any case, while the Domesday acre had always an area of 160 square perches, its precise size in any particular instance would depend on the local length of the perch, and this we usually do not know. At the conventional figure of $16\frac{1}{2}$ feet the acre would have been the same as the modern one, 4,840 sq. yds. (43,560 sq. ft.) or 0.405 hectares.

Side by side with the acre as an agrarian measure of comparable size is the arpent (*arpenz*, *aripenna*), a French term used over thirty times in Domesday Book as a measure for vineyards, which were largely if not entirely novelties (e.g. 'vinea novella;'[1] 'nuperrime plantata'[2]) and were usually in Norman hands. There are a few cases of the word being applied to meadows and woodland,[3] as there are of vineyards being measured in acres.[4] The word was one of Gaulish origin which in Roman times had been absorbed into the technical vocabulary of official surveyors and equated with a *semijugerum*, about half an acre, but in medieval France it was taken as 100 square perches, thus becoming something between a third and a half of a modern hectare (between five-sixths of an acre and $1\frac{1}{4}$ acres) according to the length of the local perch.

The larger agrarian measures form two groups, those of the hide and the carucate, with the sulung exclusive to Kent in addition. There is some confusion in terminology between the hide and the carucate systems, though the concepts behind them, and to a large extent the units themselves, were basically the same. The higher units were in any case only 'measures' in a somewhat secondary sense.

The hide (OE. *híd*) was notionally the extent of land that would support a household—the *híd* of the Old English translation of Bede was *familia* in the original Latin—and was widely thought of as involving 120 acres of arable, though the inclusion of land for grazing and other purposes has made it possible for scholars to work it out at a variety of figures, usually much larger ones. Further confusion has resulted from the many charitable concessions which allowed original numbers of hides to be reckoned, for taxation purposes, at much smaller and quite nominal figures. The hide was normally divided into four quarters, fractions of 30 acres where the hide was 120 acres, and by analogy with the smaller virgate that was a quarter of an acre these were called virgates as well. Further confusion arises from the division of hides in some parts of England into carucates—e.g. 6 carucates in Lancashire between the Mersey and the Ribble,[5] for this term was used in the Danelaw for a unit roughly equivalent to the hide.

Behind the carucate lay the notion of the size of farm that could be ploughed in a year by a team of eight oxen, the Latin term for a plough (*carruca*) providing its Latin name and its natural division being an eighth or bovate (from *bos*, 'ox'). The use of both terms, which were familiar in Normandy, is characteristic of the former Danelaw—Yorkshire, Lincolnshire, Nottinghamshire, Leicestershire, Rutland, Norfolk, and Suffolk—where they were presumably used to translate vernacular words having the same implications, probably 'ploughgang' and 'oxgang', though the native forms are not known for certain. Carucates are also used in Shropshire and some other counties for waste land, presumably when the local juries could not provide any figures for hides and the commissioners resorted to rough estimates in terms of French agrarian measures with which they were familiar. The size of the carucate is generally taken to have been about the same as that of the hide, though the actual areas were probably equally variable.

The equivalent in Kent of the carucate was the sulung (Lat. *solin*, and in Domesday Book indeclinable; also *aratra*, 'plough'), the word deriving from OE. *sulh*, 'plough'. But the Kentish fields had Celtic and Roman traditions behind them, so that the sulung was divided into four 'yokes' or *juga* (OE. *ioclet*), the fraction being deducible from a number of sources, including Domesday Book ('pro uno solin se defendit. Tria juga sunt intra divisionem Hugonis, et quartum jugum est extra').[6] The size of the sulung has been much discussed, and it is clear that it became in course of time somewhat uncertain, but it seems to have been originally 2 hides or 240 acres and to have remained in many localities at this figure. The equation with 2 hides ('duos manentes') is made in a charter of 814, and the thirteenth-century Black Book of St Augustine's notes for Chistelet that 'quelibet sulunga habet 200 acras', i.e. 240 acres reckoned by the sixscore English hundred.

The two itinerary measures of the eleventh century are the mile and the league, though the latter was not normally used in a strictly 'itinerary' sense. The first took its name from the Roman mile of 1,000 paces (*mille passuum*), the equivalent of 1,619 modern yards (1,480

[1] GDB 175v. [2] GDB 138v. [3] e.g. GDB 73, 74v.
[4] GDB 69, 83.

[5] GDB 269v. [6] GDB 13.

m.), but since English measures did not include the pace as a standard unit the mile came to be redefined in terms that would give an approximation to it, the result being the slightly longer modern 'statute' mile of 8 furlongs or 1,760 yards (1,609 m.). Several Anglo-Saxon texts show that this redefinition had come about before 1086, but the varying lengths of the furlong means that the 'mile' cannot have been uniform throughout the country. As for the league (*leuga*, *leuuva*), this was an old Gaulish measure which the Romans had treated as the equivalent of $1\frac{1}{2}$ of their miles, though we do not know precisely how many paces or other smaller units it was taken by the Gauls to represent, or consequently how close the correspondence may have been. The term occurs in England in only a few pre-Conquest documents, but from 1066 onwards it is common, being taken as 12 furlongs or $1\frac{1}{2}$ English miles (2,414 m.).

Although the two measures should have been distinct, they were often confused in practice, 'league' being used where 'mile' was intended and vice versa. The 'mile' measured in each direction ('mile gemet ælce healfe') around Ripon which Athelstan granted to the Archbishop of York is the 'leuga S. Wilfridi' in Yorks. 303v, and the forms of the returns from Norfolk, the only county in which the term *mille* occurs, show that distances longer than 8 furlongs are in each case intended. Narford, for example, is described[1] as having '1 mille in longitudine et 8 quarentenas in late', a formula that would have been impossible if the *mille* were also 8 furlongs. Similarly, the description of Hildeburgh[2] as half a mile and 2 furlongs in length and 7 furlongs in breadth implies that the first distance exceeds 7 furlongs, which would be the case for half a league of 12 furlongs but not for half a mile of only 8. Probably 'mile' was thought of as essentially a road measure, but Domesday Book, though referring occasionally to the 'king's highway' (*via regis*), classed localities under their owners and not as contiguous estates and was unconcerned with the distances between them. The league, on the other hand, was something to be estimated roughly and was thus suited for measuring areas of uncultivated land, usually woodland, but in Lincoln and East Anglia it is used to define entire estates.

Leagues were in fact the normal measure used for woodland in the northern counties and those of the West Midlands, while the returns from East Anglia and the South-East preferred figures based on the number of swine it would support, and there is a sprinkling of acre measurements in Lincoln and the West Country. The meaning of the term 'league' in such contexts has been much discussed, the figures being often so improbably large that Round was at one time inclined to believe that it represented a measure of 4 furlongs instead of 12. The sizes of woodlands and pasture are in fact usually rounded off to the nearest league or half-league, and can be taken as outside estimates of the length and breadth of the areas in question at their widest point without implying that the breadth was uniform or that total area can be ascertained by multiplying one figure by the other. It has been argued that the *leuga* as a measure of breadth meant only a furlong, just as the 'acre' as a linear measure meant the breadth of the notional acre and only 4 perches, but since the *leuga* was initially a linear and not a superficial measure this would have created an ambiguity that renders it unlikely. Where dimensions are given in terms of leagues and smaller units—furlongs commonly, perches rarely, and feet very rarely—one must assume that some precise measurement is intended, perhaps taken from a written grant or determined in the course of litigation, though whether they were accurate is another matter. Certainly some of those recorded in Domesday Book must be either exaggerated or copyist's errors, for they imply areas larger than the total size of the subsequent parishes.

A complication arises out of the occasional use of *leuga* to define an area, despite the existence of a derivative term *leugata* that had this meaning. *Leugata*, which gave rise to the obsolete English word *lowy*, probably meant basically a square league, though it was also used in the vaguer sense of a large property, like that of the lowy of Richard of Tonbridge to which so many scattered estates in Kent are said to belong[3] and which Richard had received in exchange for his lowy of Brionne in Normandy. *Leuga* as a measure of area, however, is probably a measure comparable to the linear acre and implying a league as only one of its measurements, the other being a furlong, though sometimes square leagues are implied. This at least seems to fit the facts better than any other hypothesis. The 'furlong' used for woodland in Domesday Book is, it should be said, probably one based on the normal perch of about 16 feet and not the much longer 'forest' perch of between about 20 and 28 feet. This seems to have come into existence in post-Conquest times by increasing the figure for the local perch by a half in order to make the furlong : league and furlong : mile ratios both 1 : 8.

Measures of Capacity

The basic measures of capacity in England, from the later Middle Ages onwards, have been the pint (for liquids) and the bushel (dry measure) of 8 gallons or 64 pints. However, the bushel is shown by its name (from Lat. *bussellus*, 'basket', by way of Fr. *boisseau*) to be post-Conquest and the large measures of capacity used in Domesday Book were the sester and amber, both used in Anglo-Saxon times and ultimately of Roman origin, and the modius, which was French but also went back to Rome. The pint itself, though occurring in Anglo-Saxon texts, is nowhere mentioned, no doubt because it was small, and the same is true of the amber of 48 sesters as a liquid measure, in this case because it was large, though the figures recorded for renders in honey are often precise fractions of it (e.g. 6, 12, or 24 sesters). How closely the Anglo-Saxon pint corresponded to the modern one of 0.57 litres is not known.

The sester is the measure used to express renders of honey in almost every part of England. It took its name

[1] LDB 144v. [2] LDB 167v. [3] e.g. GDB 3,4.

from a Roman measure (*sextarius*), so called from its being a sixth of a *congius* ('bucket'), about three-quarters of the modern gallon. The sester was defined as 2 (Roman) lb., i.e. 24 oz. or 0.68 kilos, a definition ('two silver pounds') reproduced in a late Anglo-Saxon medical text, though a mid-eleventh-century grant of a sester of honey to St Albans prescribed the use of a 32-oz. sester, one-third as large again, and it seems to have been assumed that there was no generally accepted standard. At Gloucester the burgesses are recorded as having paid 12 sesters of honey 'ad mensuram ejusdem burgi'[1] before 1066, while at Deerhurst in the same county a payment of 8 sesters of honey is 'ad mensuram regis'[2] and at Warwick one of 24 sesters is 'cum majori mensura'.[3] Such differences may be in part the explanation of variations in the pecuniary commutations of honey renders—12*d.* a sester in Wiltshire,[4] 13*d.* at Colchester,[5] 15*d.* at Warwick.[6] In some counties, notably in Essex and East Anglia, it is frequently noted how many hives (*vasa apiorum*) there were on a manor, but nowhere is there an estimate of how much a hive was expected to produce.

In Domesday Book the sester is also used for wine,[7] though rarely, and Anglo-Saxon documents show it used for beer, vinegar, and soap. The Domesday scribes, or at least some of them, preferred the imported terms *cupa* for beer or ale and *modius* for wine. The first of these, a Latin word meaning a tub or cask without implying any specific measure, became *coupe* in French as a liquid measure varying between 4 and 8 litres, far larger than our own 'cup'. Its only occurrences in Domesday are on the Celtic borderlands, one at St Germans in Cornwall ('una cupa cervisae')[8] and the other in Cheshire ('una cuva plena cervisia'),[9] where it was presumably used to represent some unfamiliar Cornish or Welsh measure and we cannot expect to know its precise content. The *modius* had been a Roman measure usually taken as equivalent to 8.75 litres, but its French derivative the *muid* was extraordinarily variable and its Domesday dimension is unknown.

The sester, amber, and modius were also dry measures of capacity, but with meanings different from those they had as liquid measures. The sester enters into a few rents involving grain, sometimes milled, and the figures are too small—'3 sextarii frumenti et ordei',[10] '8 sextarii siliginis'[11]—for the measures to be either the 2-pint measure used for liquids or the sixteenth of a modius that it had been in the Roman system. Probably it was something equivalent to the 12-bushel sester occasionally found in later centuries, the transfer of name having resulted from the 6-bushel measure known as a 'boll' being treated as the unit. As for the amber as dry measure, Domesday Book shows it used in Sussex as a measure for salt, but as a quite small one valued at only 1*d.* ('5 salinae de 110 ambris salis aut 9 solidos et 2 denarios').[12] This must have been something quite different from what it became later, for fourteenth-century records define it as half a quarter (i.e. 4 bushels) 'by the London standard'. The modius could also be a corn measure,[13] but this is exceptional.

Loads could be transported by porters, by pack-horses, or by carts. The carrying capacity of the individual is once referred to, but it is unlikely that the 'onus hominis' in Cheshire[14] indicated any precise weight. Cart-loads (*caretedae*) of faggots or of mast for feeding pigs are referred to occasionally (e.g. Melchet Forest: '80 caretedes lignorum'[15]), and sheets of lead from the Derbyshire mines were transported in similar fashion by wagons: '5 plaustratae plumbi de 50 tabulis',[16] but the state of the roads limited the normal use of carts to transport within the boundaries of a manor or between related or contiguous manors, and here again it is unlikely that the cart-load represented a precise measure. Effective transport was by pack-horse, and this gave rise to the now forgotten measure of the 'seam'.

The seam (*summa*, whence 'sumpter') took its name ultimately from the Greek word for a pack-saddle (*sagma*) and was a measure widely used throughout Western Europe in the Middle Ages and early modern times. In Domesday Book it was identical with a 'measure' (*mensura* or *mitta*), since what from the point of view of the distributor and recipient was a horse-load would naturally become a standard 'measure' for the producer. *Mensura* and *mitta* are terms used indifferently (e.g. 'mensura salis';[17] 'mitta salis'[18]), and a thirteenth-century entry in the register of Worcester Priory shows the *mitta* as a horse-load ('Quilibet equus portabit unam mittam'). A Devonshire entry shows '2 saginas salis' in the Exeter Domesday[19] changed to '2 summas salis' in the main text.[20]

In Domesday Book the seam appears mainly as a measure for salt, but it is sometimes used for such commodities as corn or malt,[21] peas,[22] and fish.[23] In later times it was given precise values according to the commodities involved, such as 8 bushels of grain or 100 lb. of glass, but these varied from one locality to another. It could be worked into the hundredweight system by making it a unit of 2 cwt., i.e. 240 lb., which is in fact the figure accepted for the seam of salt in Devon in the fourteenth century. It was a measure, however, that lent itself to abuse: the Cheshire salt regulations preserved in Domesday Book are anxious to prevent it being made so heavy that a horse was over-burdened, or so light that a distributor could stretch it into becoming two ('qui de una summa salis faciebant duas').[24] One passage defines it as 15 'boilings' ('bulliones de quibus 15 faciebant unam summam salis'),[25] notionally the salt produced by the evaporation of a single pan of brine in a day and apparently about 16 lb., but the word does not seem to recur later in the relatively well-documented records of the Cheshire salt industry. Nor can we say what the Domesday seam was for other commodities.

1 GDB 162.
2 GDB 166.
3 GDB 238.
4 GDB 69.
5 LDB 107.
6 GDB 238.
7 e.g. GDB 43, 43v.
8 GDB 120v.
9 GDB 269.
10 GDB 179v.
11 GDB 257v.
12 GDB 28.
13 GDB 23, 69, 183, 260, 269.
14 GDB 268.
15 GDB 68.
16 GDB 273.
17 GDB 166.
18 GDB 177.
19 Exon 218.
20 GDB 105v.
21 GDB 143v, 146.
22 GDB 17v.
23 GDB 115v.
24 GDB 268.
25 GDB 268.

Special Measures

In contrast to these large measures of a general character there were two of a more specific application, the wey (*pensa*), used only for cheese, and the ingot (*massa*) or 'bloom' (*bloma*), used only for iron.

The *pensa* (OE. *wæge*) occurs in Domesday Book mainly in describing the cheese renders from several localities in a famous dairying region, the Vale of White Horse in Domesday Berkshire, where one passage shows it valued at the high figure of 40*d*.[1] Thirteenth-century figures for the wey of cheese show it to have varied between 175 lb. and 196 lb., the exact weights depending on the 'stone' customary in each locality but seeming to imply one and a half times the 'long' hundredweight of 120 lb. A smaller and probably local measure for dairy produce was the *rusca*, used for butter in Cheshire.[2] The word was of Celtic origin and meant a containing vessel of straw or bark (OIr. *rusc*, Gaelic *rusg*); it is the same root as the French word for a beehive (*ruche*). It did not survive in England as the name of a measure, but was still used in Normandy and Picardy in the eighteenth century as a measure for salt and grain of about 50 lb. *poids de marc*, i.e. the equivalent of about a bushel.

Renders in iron, mainly from the counties of Somerset and Gloucester (the Wye valley, the Forest of Dean), are stated in terms of 'blooms' (*blomae*), 'leads' (*plumbei*), ingots (*massae*), and 'dickers' (*dicra*). The last of these, however, is not a measure but a multiple of ten (see below), and the *plumbei*, usually explained as large lead dishes for holding ore, more likely represent the word *blomae* misheard and misinterpreted at some stage in the compilation of the record. *Massae* and 'blooms' were probably the same thing, for the sense of the words is the same, the bloom being the name applied to an iron ingot either in its first, unworked state as the metal solidified at the bottom of the smelters or to such an ingot after it had received its first hammering. The word still survives in the iron industry both alone and in such combinations as bloom-tongs and blooming-mill. In the later Middle Ages the bloom was standardized at different figures varying from place to place, being some 90 lb. in Sussex and 200 lb. in Durham. It probably varied in a similar fashion in 1086.

Numerical Units

There are, finally, four obsolete numerical units, in addition to the 'long hundred' referred to already, that require explanation. The first is the 'stick' or 'stitch' (*sticha*), a multiple of 25 applied to eels and referred to in entries from every part of the country. It was in this form that the hundreds of eels or other small fish that sometimes made up renders were most easily counted and transported, the name being taken from their being held together in twenty-fives either by a stick passed through their gills—this is the usual explanation—or more probably from their being 'stitched' together on a loop of cord. Exceptionally, however, eels were reckoned by the score, as the form of some Sussex entries shows.[3] The second obsolete unit is the 'dicker', from Latin *decarius* and meaning a bundle of ten units. It was the aggregate regularly used in the later Middle Ages for leather and skins, and derivatively for pairs of gloves and, by analogy, sets of horseshoes. The 36 dickers of iron ('dicras ferri') paid by Gloucester annually to the king[4] is probably not 360 iron bars of some conventional length, as is usually assumed, but thirty-six sets of four horseshoes. The third obsolete unit is the 'timber', used only once to record a render of 3 timbers of marten skins ('3 timbres pellium martrinium') at Chester.[5] The term, of which this is the earliest known record, was one widely used in the fur trade in north Germany and the Baltic region in the later Middle Ages, the meaning being a bundle of 40 skins. It occurs also in French, but exactly how and where it originated is unknown. The final numerical unit, which still survives in Scotland and the North of England, is the 'thrave', a multiple of 2 shocks of 12 sheaves each. Its only occurrence in Domesday Book is in recording the obligation of the burgesses of Derby to pay the king '12 trabes annonae', of which the Abbot of Barton has 40 *garbas* ('sheaves').[6]

Conclusion

To the reader unfamiliar with Domesday Book it must seem surprising to discover how rarely the linear measures and those of area, weight, and capacity so meticulously recorded in its folios can be expressed in terms of precise modern equivalents. Also, having come unquestionably to accept the need for national and even multinational systems of mensuration, he must find it difficult to comprehend how so many methods of reckoning could function together and why common terms for measurement should represent such widely differing quantities within a single, unified realm.

Since few of the measures were Norman imports the explanation must lie very largely in the way that the kingdom of England had come into existence. Some inconsistencies reflect its previous separation into English and Danish areas. Others were the result of political and ethnographical divisions which had evolved earlier still, whether under the Heptarchy or at the formative period of the Anglo-Saxon settlement. In Kent, and in Cornwall and on the Welsh borderland, Domesday gives evidence of usages which had survived into the eleventh century from Roman times or even before. Long-established local measures in the field, on the trackway, or in the market-place would inevitably be resistant to change in a setting where travel was limited and in a society where there was no comprehensive medium of public communication to influence the introduction of standard systems of measurement.

It is true that Anglo-Saxon legislation had occasion-

[1] GDB 58v, amending 32*s*. to 33*s*. in the text.
[2] GDB 269.
[3] GDB 23v: '180' first written as '9'; other totals divisible by 20 but not by 25.
[4] GDB 162.
[5] GDB 262v.
[6] GDB 280.

ally provided for the standardizing of weights and measures, but the confusion that existed in later centuries shows that little was done to make such provisions effective. The reason was very largely that no need for uniformity was generally perceived. It was only the requirements of the developing wool trade that in the twelfth century resulted in the creation of the yard of 3 feet and the distribution of metal standards intended to make possible the enforcement of its use. Local measures continued to exist for other purposes long after this, and it was not till the nineteenth century that most of them were eliminated, though a few special trade measures survive even today.

The king's commissioners in 1086 would thus have found little uniformity in the course of their enquiries, and had no obligation to attempt a policy of standardization themselves. Their primary duty was to record all that contributed to the king's revenues, and the main element in this was the number of taxable hides or carucates in each holding. Neither the geographical extent of each property nor the precise distribution of its parts (as on a map) would interest the Exchequer, though the presence of assets such as pasture or woodland was worth setting down as a guide to their potential economic yield. Mills and fisheries were included for the same reason, with the emphasis on profitability rather than on their physical nature. Equally, with products such as honey, salt, or metal, it was always the render that was of prime concern for Domesday's fiscal purposes, whether recorded in money or in kind, and not the relative bulk or weight of the substance in question. Like the estate that provided the commodity, it mattered less to the central authority what it looked like than what it was worth.

This means that although Domesday Book conscientiously records values in a currency accepted as standard throughout the kingdom, the weights and measures from which those values were originally computed could still be expressed in their diverse regional guises. A study of these must consequently be limited to describing the variety and sources of mensuration encountered by the Norman commissioners of the Conqueror's survey, and cannot hope to provide modern equivalents for them in anything but the most approximate fashion.

XII. THE ECONOMICS OF DOMESDAY ENGLAND

JOHN McDONALD and G. D. SNOOKS

OVER the last few centuries Domesday Book has attracted the attention of a large number of distinguished historians and geographers, yet surprisingly it has been ignored by economists. While much is known about the social, political, legal, and spatial aspects of Domesday England, our knowledge of its underlying economic relationships and processes is very limited despite the wealth of available economic data. In an attempt to redress the balance a summary is provided here of the results that are currently emerging from a large-scale study of the Domesday economy at the Flinders University of South Australia, Adelaide. This account portrays the Anglo-Norman economy in its normal (or non-devastated) aspect.[1]

DOMESDAY BOOK AS A SOURCE OF ECONOMIC DATA

Domesday Book is, as H. C. Darby has claimed, 'the most remarkable statistical document in the history of Europe'.[2] In this sense, not only was it unique in its own time, it is also without peer even today. No publicly available statistical source in modern England provides such comprehensive data concerning the performance of individual production units (i.e. farms). It is important, therefore, to understand why the Conqueror undertook such an ambitious survey. Although this has been a matter of dispute in the past, it is now generally accepted that William's purpose was both fiscal and feudal.[3] It would appear that the survey was intended to provide a comprehensive basis for revising the taxation system, to define the new feudal structure in order to rationalize the collection of feudal dues, to solve disputes over ownership of land, and to make possible a more rational redistribution of estates. Yet William's legacy was greater than he could have anticipated, because in the process he collected a body of data which can be used to reconstruct the Domesday economy.

The rapidity with which Domesday Book was compiled (January 1086 to September 1087) is thought to have been facilitated by the use of existing hidage (or tax) lists, which appear to have their origins in the early Anglo-Saxon period. To conduct the survey the counties of England were grouped into seven circuits, each of which was visited by a different team of commissioners. The commissioners were responsible for circulating a questionnaire to landholders, for subjecting the responses to verification in the county courts, and for supervising the compilation of county and circuit returns. Of particular interest is the manner in which an attempt was made to ensure the accuracy of the data: questionnaire responses were scrutinized in the county courts by juries consisting of French and English tenants from each village. There is every reason to believe that the juries were able to evaluate effectively the information presented to them in court, because, in addition to possessing local knowledge, they were under oath and risked severe penalties for perjury. Even the commissioners were overseen by other agents of the king. The collection of economic data in 1086, therefore, was a public rather than a private event (in contrast to similar surveys today) with little prospect of significant falsification going undetected.

The uniqueness of the Domesday survey can be highlighted by contrasting it with official data of a similar nature collected today. An appropriate comparison can be made with *Agricultural Statistics for England*, an official publication which provides for each county a breakdown of data on agricultural output and input quantities as well as prices. Although this rural survey has broadly similar features to Domesday Book, there are important differences. The purpose of this modern survey, for example, is to provide data on rural activities at an industry or commodity level rather than at the individual farm level of Domesday Book. But the major difference centres upon the methods employed in the two surveys. The current survey relies entirely upon the postal service for both the delivery of questionnaires to farmers and their return to the collecting office, a method which leads to major delays and some non-compliance. More importantly, as respondents are completely responsible for the information supplied and as the returns are subject to strict confidentiality rules, detection of falsification is difficult. Only the most blatant discrepancies are, and indeed can be, checked by telephone or post. In the collection of modern agricultural statistics, therefore, it is not possible to evaluate systematically the accuracy of individual responses as was done in 1086. Accordingly, as a source of economic data, Domesday Book can bear even greater scrutiny than comparable modern survey data.[4]

[1] The first volume of this study, McDonald and Snooks, *Domesday Economy: A New Approach to Anglo-Norman History*, focuses upon macro-economic relationships in a sample of counties (Essex and Wilts.) which reflect the normal operations of the economy. Later volumes will be concerned with the micro-economic relationships of Domesday together with Domesday economy in crisis.

[2] H. C. Darby, *Domesday England* (2nd edn., Cambridge, 1979), 12.

[3] Harvey, 'Domesday Book and its Predecessors', 769–71.

[4] This is discussed in more detail in McDonald and Snooks, 'Statistical Analysis of Domesday Book (1086)'.

ECONOMIC RELATIONSHIPS

Reconstruction of the Domesday economy requires the use of modern economic theory, statistical technique, and electronic technology. While much remains to be done, the broad outlines of the Norman economy are emerging from the economic and statistical analysis already completed. Using the lay and ecclesiastical data for the counties of Essex and Wiltshire in 1066 and 1086, we have examined the economic relationships between tax assessments for geld and (separately) the economic resources and annual values of manors, between annual values and resources of manors, and between manorial production and economic resources.[1] This analysis has produced revealing results which provide not only a new interpretation of key economic relationships, and thereby the building blocks needed for the reconstruction of the Domesday economy, but also considerable confidence in the reliability of Domesday Book data.

TAXATION AND EQUITY

The assessment for geld (i.e. the hidage system) was an important part of the data collected in 1086 because this non-feudal tax was both an important source of royal revenue and a considerable burden on landholders (absorbing 16 per cent of revenue for the average Essex lay manor in 1086). In Domesday literature the central issues concerning geld assessments are their relation to the economic base (or capacity to pay) of manors, and the way in which they were applied. The prevailing interpretations of these issues, which have their origins in the work of J. H. Round, are that the assessments were 'artificial' in the sense that they were not related to the economic capacity of manors to pay this tax, and that they were imposed initially on the hundreds from above rather than being built up from the manorial level. Round's view was based largely upon his study of Inquisitio Comitatus Cantabrigiensis, in which he produced evidence for his famous five-hide pattern. On the basis of limited evidence for the recording of hides in multiples of five at the level of the vill, Round postulated: 'Assessment was not objective, but subjective, it was not fixed relatively to area or to value, but to the five-hide unit. The aim of assessors was clearly to arrange the assessment in sums of five hides, ten hides etc.'[2] This interpretation remained accepted down to the present time in the works of F. W. Maitland (1897), P. Vinogradoff (1908), F. M. Stenton (1943), and H. C. Darby (1952–77), and was not challenged until the work of J. McDonald and G. D. Snooks.[3]

Despite the longevity of this interpretation, there are compelling *a priori* reasons for doubting its validity. In the face of inevitable and widespread opposition to an arbitrary taxation system and the costs involved in suppressing discontent, it is difficult to understand how such a tax could survive. The geld, however, was levied for almost two centuries.

Further, the technique employed by Round to test whether there was a relationship between assessments and the capacity of manors to pay this impost is far from conclusive, as it is an indirect test of this hypothesis and it involves a high degree of subjectivity. His test is highly subjective for two reasons. First, it involves aggregating vills into clusters of varying size whenever the predetermined pattern is not evident at the level of the individual vill, which could result in making covert allowance for the different resources of vills. Secondly, it enables selective use of data by focusing attention upon those observations which exhibit the desired pattern while ignoring the rest. Also, as Round's method is indirect it does not exhaust all competing explanations of an observed pattern. It seems better, therefore, to use regression analysis to test directly the relationship between assessment and capacity of manors to pay, thereby eliminating unnecessary subjectivity and alternative explanations. This direct method has been employed in our work.

Capacity to pay can be measured either by the total resources of the manor or by the annual values (income). Both relationships have been tested in the case of all lay and ecclesiastical manors for Essex and Wiltshire (treated separately) in 1066 and 1086, using the latest statistical techniques. These techniques allow the data to select the appropriate functional form (which defines the nature of the relationship) rather than the often-used alternative of imposing a predetermined, and possibly arbitrary, functional form on the data (e.g. either linear or log-linear). The results of this analysis for 1066 and 1086 are most revealing.[4] First, contrary to the prevailing view, our results demonstrate a strong and positive relationship between assessment and capacity to pay, irrespective of whether the latter is measured by annual values or total resources. Accordingly, geld assessments cannot be regarded as 'artificial' or arbitrary. In addition, these results cast considerable doubt upon the plausibility of Round's related hypothesis that hides were imposed initially on the hundreds from above rather than being built up from the manorial level. This is not inconsistent, however, with the further claim that the hundred was the administrative unit for the geld. Secondly, whatever its origin the geld in 1066 and 1086 can no longer be thought of as a tax solely on arable land, which suggests that the king's agents were attempting to take account of the growing sophistication of rural settlement when framing their non-feudal taxes. By this time the geld was either an income tax or a total resources tax. Thirdly, the geld was a regressive tax, in the sense that its marginal rate declined as the revenue of the manor increased. This may have reflected the Conqueror's need to placate his powerful barons, without whose support he could not have come to power in

[1] The statistical data employed in this analysis of Essex and Wilts. have been taken from the *Victoria County History* (and checked against the Farley edition) and transferred to computer tapes by the authors at the Flinders University of South Australia.

[2] Round, *Feudal England* (2nd edn., 1964), 48–9.

[3] McDonald and Snooks, 'Were the Tax Assessments of Domesday England Artificial? The Case of Essex'.

[4] The statistical methods and results are discussed in detail in McDonald and Snooks, 'Were the Tax Assessments of Domesday England Artificial?' More comprehensive results can be found in McDonald and Snooks, *Domesday Economy*.

1066. Finally, there is some evidence that a tax deduction may have been granted on meadow-land in order to encourage the extension of this critically important resource, which was required for the maintenance of plough-beasts and war-horses.

Annual Values and Manorial Resources

In many respects the key item in Domesday Book is the manorial annual value (or income). It is, at face value, a summary of the economic performance of the Anglo-Norman manor, and as such can be employed in conjunction with the resource data to throw light upon the process of manorial production. Curiously, the long-standing view in the literature is that no systematic relationship exists between manorial values and resources. Beginning with Round and Maitland this view can be traced down to the work of H. C. Darby, who repeatedly claimed: 'It is clear that the values were not directly related to the number of working teams or to the recorded population. Nor does a consideration of other resources help us to understand the figures.'[1] Although some doubt has been expressed about this conclusion by P. H. Sawyer,[2] no attempt was made to test it before the work of McDonald and Snooks.[3] This omission is difficult to understand because, if it is assumed that the Normans were not completely incompetent in running their estates, it implies that the data in Domesday Book are meaningless.

A statistical model similar to that employed for the tax analysis was adopted to test the relationship between annual value and resources for the lay and ecclesiastical estates of Wiltshire and Essex in 1066 and 1086. The annual value, which is the income received by the lord of the manor, consists of either rents or demesne profits or some combination of both, while the resources include land (arable, pasture, meadow, and woodland), labour (principally freemen, sokemen, villans, bordars, and slaves), and capital (mainly plough-teams, livestock, and mills). Once again the results of our statistical analysis provide the basis for a radically different interpretation. Most importantly it was discovered that there is a very strong and positive relationship between manorial values and resources (stronger indeed than that between tax assessment and resources) which contradicts the prevailing view. What this tells us is that, on average, an increase in resources will lead to an increase in annual value at the manorial level. As this is what can be expected of any viable economic system, it is reasonable to conclude that the data in Domesday Book are meaningful and that it is possible to penetrate the bewildering detail to the underlying reality of Anglo-Norman England.

This statistical analysis also helps to clarify a number of debates in the literature concerning the nature and importance of certain economic resources in Domesday Book. In the first place it has been shown in the case of Essex (contained in Little Domesday) that the omission of livestock from the relationship between value and resources makes little difference to our results. This is important because it means that the livestock variable is not critical to this relationship (as has been suggested by Sawyer[4]) and consequently that our model can be applied validly to the thirty-one counties contained in Great Domesday for which livestock are not recorded. Secondly, this analysis enables clarification of the important issue of whether mill renders were included in the annual values. While Darby assumes they were included, our results are consistent with the hypothesis that they were not. Finally, this analysis supports the suggestion in the literature that, in the main, horses were not an economic resource in Domesday England, but rather a resource devoted to leisure and war.

The System of Manorial Production

Having established the existence of a strong relationship between value and resources, it is possible to proceed further by drawing out the implications of these results for the system of manorial production in Domesday England. For this purpose it is necessary first to develop a model that characterizes manorial production in 1086—a model of production that could have reasonably generated the data recorded in Domesday Book—and secondly to reconsider our former results by viewing them in terms of a more general, and hence less restrictive, production function framework than that employed above.[5]

Our model assumes that the landholder maximized manorial income subject to feudal institutional constraints which chiefly involved fixed input levels in the short run. This model provides a more satisfactory basis for interpreting our statistical results than the type usually employed by economists in which a profit-maximizing firm (or farm) in a perfectly competitive environment is able to vary its input levels in the short run. It must be emphasized, however, that an economic model is not a precise description of reality but rather an abstract characterization of the way in which an economic system works: a characterization that captures the essence of that system. Briefly, our Domesday model of manorial production is as follows:

1. The peasants (villans and bordars) worked on the lord's demesne in return for 'protection' and the use of land to grow their own crops, while the slaves received only 'protection', food, and shelter. Not only was the

[1] H. C. Darby and I. S. Maxwell (eds.), *The Domesday Geography of Northern England* (Cambridge, 1962), 43, 125, 199, 302–3, 352, etc.

[2] P. H. Sawyer's review of H. C. Darby in *EconHR* 2nd ser., 16 (1963–4), 155–7.

[3] McDonald and Snooks, 'The Determinants of Manorial Income in Domesday England: Evidence from Essex'. It should be noted that Harvey in 'The Extent and Profitability of Demesne Agriculture in England in the Later Eleventh Century', *assumes* that values can be used as an index of profitability (which *implies* that the values are not arbitrary) but does not attempt to test this assumption or even draw attention to the conflict (as Sawyer did) with Darby, whose work she quotes with approval.

[4] Sawyer, *EconHR* 16, 155.

[5] A detailed theoretical and statistical analysis can be found in McDonald and Snooks, *Manorial Production Functions for Domesday England: A Study of Essex in 1086*.

estate worked by a resident rather than an outside workforce, but the standard contract between peasants and lord, which involved a given amount of week- and boon-work, was essentially fixed in the short run. Similarly, the various types of land and capital were relatively fixed in the short run. As a first approximation, therefore, the Domesday manor can be characterized as operating with a fixed set of resources and with fixed payments being made to labour.

2. All goods produced on the manor can be regarded as tradable (although, of course, they were not all traded). These goods included cereals, vegetables, cheese, meat, wool, honey, fish, and salt. Our analysis focuses on the dominating activities of arable and livestock farming.

3. It is assumed that the same rural technology was *available* to all estates within a single county (which is not to say that all estates employed exactly the same technology). This assumption is plausible because arable farming was largely based upon the use of the large Anglo-Saxon plough-team in conjunction with a broadly similar system of cropping and field rotation and similar methods of animal husbandry (at least within regions as small as a county).

4. The annual value was the income accruing to the lord from working the demesne or leasing out the manor in part or in whole. It is reasonable to suppose that rents received by the lord reflected the income-generating capacity of manors. Manorial values can be interpreted, therefore, as value added in the production process: that is, the gross value of production less intermediate goods (such as grain seed) and goods produced on the manor to maintain resources (such as feed and rough shelter for livestock and slaves, and the subsistence-food output on peasants' plots). Accordingly, the relationship between annual value and resources can be interpreted as a production function relating net output to a set of productive inputs.

5. Finally, it is assumed that the lord of the manor attempted to organize production in a technically efficient manner and to choose outputs in order to maximize the net value of goods produced.

With this model it is possible to explain why manors were operated with widely different resource ratios (e.g. the ratio of peasants to plough-teams) and at different production levels (e.g. manorial size)—a puzzle for those who have the perfectly competitive model in mind, which predicts a tendency for manors to achieve a single optimum size with a given combination of resources. The reason is simply that the initial conditions—the history, geography, and natural processes (such as population growth) of a particular region—determined the size and resources of the estate, and the feudal system fixed the level of input use. Also it is possible to view the estimated relationship between annual value and resources as a production function which traces out the average relationship between net output and productive inputs.

By interpreting the estimated relationship for Essex in 1086 as a production function, a number of significant conclusions can be reached concerning the economics of the manorial system. First, in the matter of production relationships it was discovered that manorial production increased as resources increased (in economic jargon, marginal products were positive); that the *increments* to production diminished as one resource, say peasant labour, was substituted for another resource, say plough-teams (diminishing marginal rates of substitution); that a given manorial output could be achieved with a wide range of resource combinations (a high degree of substitutability of inputs); and a proportional increase in inputs resulted, approximately, in the same proportional increase in net output (near-constant returns to scale). Secondly, our results confirm the dominance of arable farming (as the percentage increase in output resulting from a given percentage increase in input for arable land was 2.6 times that of pastoral resources), and suggest that demesne plough-teams made a larger contribution (approximately twice as much) to production than peasants' plough-teams. Finally, it was also discovered that the contribution to demesne production of villans was greater (by about 40 per cent) than that of bordars, the contribution of slaves was only half that of villans, and that of freemen and sokemen was quite minor.

SELECT BIBLIOGRAPHY

H. C. Darby *et al.*, *The Domesday Geography of England*, 6 vols (Cambridge, 1952–77)

S. P. J. Harvey, 'Domesday Book and its Predecessors', *EHR* 86 (1971)

—— 'The Extent and Profitability of Demesne Agriculture in England in the Later Eleventh Century', *Social Relations and Ideas: Essays in Honour of* R. H. *Hilton*, eds. T. H. Aston *et al.* (Cambridge, 1983)

J. McDonald and G. D. Snooks, *Flinders Domesday File: A Computerised Data Base for the Domesday Book Counties of Cambridgeshire, Essex and Wiltshire* (Adelaide, 1984)

—— —— 'The Determinants of Manorial Income in Domesday England: Evidence from Essex', *Jnl of Economic Hist.* 45 (1985)

—— —— 'Were the Tax Assessments of Domesday England Artificial? The Case of Essex', *EconHR* 2nd ser., 38 (1985)

—— —— 'Statistical Analysis of Domesday Book (1086)', *Jnl of the* R. *Statistical Soc.* ser. A, 148 (1985)

—— —— *Manorial Production Functions for Domesday England: A Study of Essex in 1086*, Working Papers in Economic History, Flinders University, no. 8 (1985)

—— —— *Domesday Economy: A New Approach to Anglo-Norman History*, i (Oxford, 1986)

F. W. Maitland, *Domesday Book and Beyond* (Cambridge, 1897; repr. London, 1960)

J. H. Round, *Feudal England* (London, 1895; 2nd edn., 1964)

F. M. Stenton, *Anglo-Saxon England* (Oxford, 1943)

XIII. APPARENT REPETITIONS IN DOMESDAY BOOK

ANN WILLIAMS

It is not uncommon in Domesday Book to find the same piece of land entered twice, or even three times, in different places. These double entries occur in the surviving circuit returns (Exon and Little Domesday) as well as in the Great Domesday itself.[1] They are not duplicates and even the comparatively small number which appear to be mere repetitions are not identical. Sometimes the second entry has been noticed and marked for deletion, as has happened in the case of Hinxton, Cambs. (Figs. 1 and 2). In the following quotation from the Latin text,[2] the variant readings are italicized:

Cambs. 189v	Cambs. 190 (marked for deletion)
In Histetone iacet wara de *i hida* et dimidia de *manerio Cestreforde* et est *in Exsesse appreciata. Hanc terram tenuit Algar comes.* (Fig. 1)	In Histetone iacet wara de *hida* et dimidia de *Cestrefordes manerio* et est *appreciata in Exexe. Algar comes tenuit.* (Fig. 2)

Even though these two entries are clearly based on the same original, and are identical in content, they show, as Round remarked, that the scribe (or scribes) of Domesday was no mere copyist.[3] The Domesday entries are composed from the sources, not transcribed. The fact that the second entry is cancelled rather than erased is also of interest. Richard fitzNigel, treasurer to Henry II, in describing the compilation of the Pipe Rolls (the records of the annual account of the twelfth-century Exchequer), tells us that 'if from carelessness, or from some other accident, he [the scribe] makes a clerical error . . . he must not venture to make an erasure, but must cancel by drawing a fine line underneath . . .'. He goes on to explain that the Exchequer records, like charters and other formal documents, should not contain erasures 'and this is why it has been provided that the "pipes" [the rolls] should be made on sheepskin, on which it is difficult to make an erasure without its showing plainly'.[4] Domesday, like the later Pipe Rolls, is a parchment (sheepskin) manuscript and it seems as if the same prohibition on erasure may have been applied.[5]

In the case of the Hinxton entries, the only difference is that of phrasing, but elsewhere additional or even contradictory information is included. The manor of Blackmanston, Dorset, is entered twice, but whereas the value is omitted in the first version, it is recorded in the second.[6] It is hard to see, in this case, why the second entry was made, since there is enough space in the first entry for the missing value to have been added.[7] The whole fief of Robert *hostiarius*, consisting of four manors, is entered twice in the Leicestershire folios.[8] The first version is entered under Robert's name in the correct sequence as indicated by the list of landowners at the beginning of the county. The second follows immediately upon the account of the fief of Earl Hugh of Chester (itself misplaced), without space or separate heading; indeed were it not for the fact that in the entry relating to his first manor Robert is said to hold of the king, we should assume that he was Earl Hugh's tenant. Although the substance of the two versions is the same, there are differences in the arrangement and phrasing, and the second gives us the names of Robert's father and of the pre-Conquest holders of the land, which are omitted in the first. The third and fourth entries, both relating to the vill of Long Clawson, which are separate in the first version, have been amalgamated in the second, and in the process the second entry records four bordars there, as opposed to three in the first version.

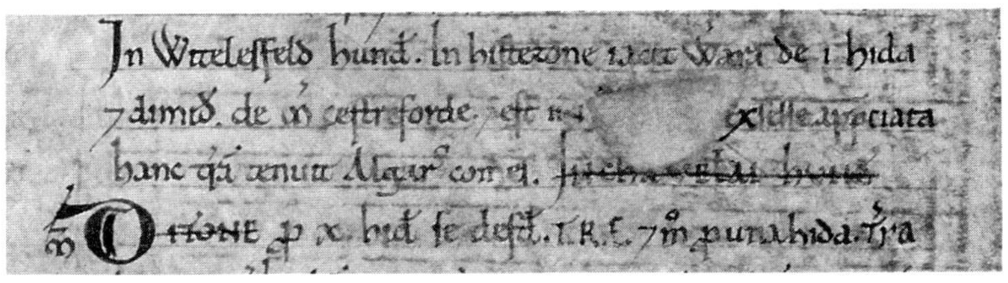

Fig. 1

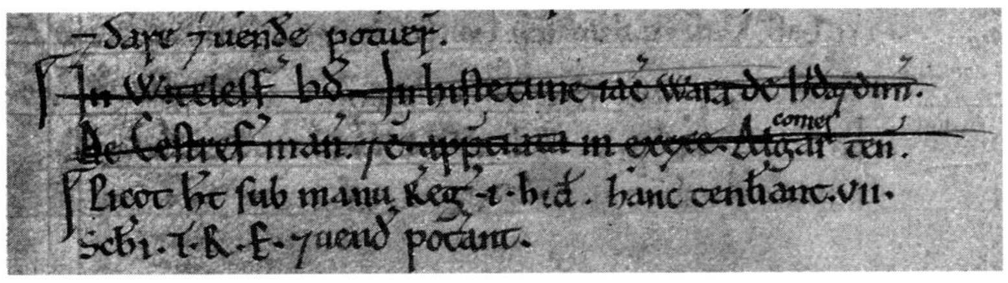

Fig. 2

[1] For the double entries of Exon, see R. Welldon Finn, *Domesday Studies: the Liber Exoniensis* (London, 1964), 78–81; for Little Domesday, see Galbraith, *Making of Domesday Book*, 162–5; R. Welldon Finn, *Domesday Studies: the Eastern Counties* (London, 1967), 49–51; *VCH Essex*, i (1903), 410–11.

[2] 'In Hinxton lies the geld obligation of (1) hide and a half of the manor of Chesterford (of Chesterford manor) and it is valued in Essex. Earl Ælfgar held (this land).'

[3] Round, *Feudal England*, 27. For the question of whether more than one scribe was involved in the writing of Great Domesday, see M. Gullick, 'The Great and Little Domesday Manuscripts', Special Study XIV, pp. 98–105 below.

[4] C. Johnson *et al.* (eds.), *Dialogus de Scaccario* (London, 1950), 31.

[5] Gullick, 'Great and Little Domesday Manuscripts', pp. 93, 109, below.

[6] GDB 84v. In *VCH Dorset*, iii (1968), 8, it is stated that the hidage is omitted from the second entry, but this is not so.

[7] Galbraith used some similar examples from the account of Essex in Little Domesday to show that they were not 'mere accidental repetitions drawn from a single source' but represent a second meeting of the hundred jury which corrected the errors of the first. Since the south-western circuit largely ignores the hundred, this is unlikely to be the explanation of the Blackmanston entries (Galbraith, *Making of Domesday Book*, 162–4).

[8] GDB 235, 237.

As in the case of Blackmanston, it is difficult to see why the second version was included, but it must be related to the displacement of the fief of Earl Hugh, and to that of the land of the Count of Meulan's men, which follows upon it, instead of being included under the count's fee, earlier in the text.[1]

All three examples discussed were clearly based upon common originals, and entered in error, though only in the case of Hinxton was this noticed. Though such mistakes are rare, they are of great importance for what they reveal about the compilation of Domesday Book. The variation in expression and the occasional inclusion of matter omitted elsewhere (the name of Robert *hostiarius*'s father, for instance) show that no pre-set formulae were rigidly applied. Round's comment on the use of 'synonym and paraphrase' should be kept in mind in any examination of the vocabulary of Domesday Book.[2]

Just as the general agreement seen in the above examples argues a common source, so the wide discrepancies found elsewhere show that the entries were based on different and divergent material. The case of Preston, Som., an appendage of the royal manor of Brompton Regis, illustrates this point. It is entered under the *Terra Regis* (the land of the king) and under the fief of the Count of Mortain, to whom it belonged in 1086:

Som. 86v (*Terra Regis*)	Som. 92 (the Count of Mortain)
The king holds Brompton '*Brunetone*'. Gytha held it . . . Of this manor the Count of Mortain holds 1 hide in Preston '*Prestetune*' which belonged to the demesne farm TRE. There is land for 4 ploughs. There are 2 ploughs. It was and is worth 40*s*.	Robert holds of the count 1 hide in Preston '*Prestitone*'. Earl Harold held this. There is land for 4 ploughs. In demesne is half a plough with 1 slave and 6 villans and 2 bordars with 2 ploughs. There is a mill rendering 12*d*. and 5 acres of meadow and 3 acres of pasture and 11 acres of woodland. It was and is worth 30*s*. This land lay in Brompton '*Burnetone*', a manor of the king, with the farm.

Though both these entries clearly relate to the same estate, the variation here goes far beyond matters of phrasing and organization. Not only is the second version much fuller than the first, it also conflicts with it, particularly over the value of Preston, reckoned at 40*s*. in the first entry and 30*s*. in the second. Though the other differences are explicable (the forms of the place-names fall within the usual range of variation and Gytha was Earl Harold's mother) this conflict is irreconcilable. The difference already existed in the source from which the account of Somerset was compiled, that is, in Exon Domesday, the circuit return for the south-western shires. Indeed the Exon text reveals yet another irreconcilable difference. It gives the name of the count's tenant as Hugh de Vautourt in the first entry and Robert fitzIvo (the Robert of Domesday Book) in the second. It is obvious that these two versions cannot be based on a common original. Round argued that 'the entry found under the count's fief is derived from the general return, while the entry under the *Terra Regis* is derived from a special and separate return . . . made for the king's land'.[3] Galbraith, while agreeing that 'two separate and varying accounts given to the king's commissioners' underlay these passages, offered a different explanation.[4] He suggested that in this and similar cases, the shorter account 'preserves the basic facts recorded at the formal sessions of the Inquest', while the fuller version 'includes further manorial detail supplied out of court to the commissioners by the actual tenant of each estate'.[5] Whatever the procedure involved, the reason for the two entries is clear. Preston was a berewick of Brompton, which had been given to, or perhaps taken by, the king's half-brother Robert, Count of Mortain, and not only occurs as part of his fief, but is also still listed as one of the appurtenances of the royal manor to which it had belonged.

Such berewicks are quite often the subjects of double entries, especially where they had been detached from their manors, or when the berewick concerned lay in a different shire. Thus the land at Hinxton appears not only in Cambridgeshire (twice) but also in Essex, where the manor of Chesterford, to which it was appurtenant, lay. It is interesting that in this and other cases the appurtenance was valued (*appreciata*) as part of the central manor, but paid its geld (*wara*) in the shire in which it was actually situated.[6] The entry for Hinxton in Essex[7] is not significantly different from those in Cambridgeshire, but this was not always the case. Shelford was also in Cambridgeshire, but like Hinxton appurtenant to an Essex manor, in this case Newport.[8] It therefore appears twice, but there is considerable contradiction between the two entries, summarized in the following table:

	Cambridgeshire	*Essex*
Hidage	3 hides	3 hides and 46 acres
Population	5 villans 6 bordars	8 villans 5 bordars
Meadow	enough for 4 ploughs	15 acres
'Render'	£4 assayed and weighed 20*s*. by tale	£25. 16*s*.

These contradictory statements must in part be due to the different usages of the commissioners for Circuit III, which included Cambridgeshire, and Circuit VII, in which Essex lay; also, since the Essex version comes from Little Domesday, whose material was never worked over by the scribe of Great Domesday, we are not comparing like with like. Even when these allowances are made, however, the extraordinary difference in the value is inexplicable.

[1] GDB 237, 237v. In the list of landowners, Earl Hugh is listed in thirteenth place, but his fief is omitted and entered in forty-third place, after the lands of the king's sergeants. He therefore has another entry (in forty-third position) in the list of landowners. The demesne manors of the Count of Meulan are entered in ninth place, but those of his men follow those of Earl Hugh, and the last entry on the list of landholders is 'the men of the Count of Meulan'. The second version of Robert's fief is between these two, but is unnumbered in the text and has no entry in the list of landowners.

[2] Round, *Feudal England*, 26.

[3] *VCH Somerset*, i (1906), 427.

[4] Galbraith, *Making of Domesday Book*, 228.

[5] Ibid. 119–20.

[6] Round, *Feudal England*, 115–17; Welldon Finn, *Introduction to Domesday Book*, 259.

[7] LDB 3v.

[8] LDB 7, GDB 19.

Another reason for double entries is disputed ownership. Where land had been illegally occupied, or where two men claimed the same manor, it often happens that the manor is entered under the names of both claimants (though this is not always the case).[1] Two examples of particular interest concern Bushley (now in Gloucestershire, but lying in Worcestershire in 1086) and Barston, War. Bushley appears among the manors of the Bishop of Worcester in Worcestershire, but is also entered among the king's lands in Herefordshire. These two counties were in the same circuit, but the variations between the entries are considerable:

Worcs. 173	Herefs. 180v
The bishop holds Bredon . . . Beorhtric son of Ælfgar held 1 hide of this manor from the bishop at Bushley '*Biselege*'. He paid rent to the same bishop every year and moreover rendered to the bishop's soke whatever he owed to the king's service. Now it is in King William's hand. It was and is worth 40*s*. There are 20 acres of meadow and woodland half a league long and 3 furlongs wide.	The king holds Bushley '*Biselie*'. Beorhtric held it and bought it from Lyfing, Bishop of Worcester, for 3 gold marks . . . and held it so freely that he did no service for it to any man. In this manor [is] 1 hide and in demesne are 2 ploughs and 4 villans and 8 bordars and a reeve and a beadle. Between them all they have 4 ploughs. There are 8 slaves, male and female, and a cowman and a dairymaid. There is a forester, who holds half a virgate of land. In Pull there are 3 virgates of land which lay in Longdon, a manor of Earl Odda's. Earl William put this land in Bushley . . .

At first sight these entries resemble those for Preston, Som., discussed above. The king has acquired a member of the Bishop of Worcester's manor of Bredon, and it therefore appears under the *Terra Regis*, with its manorial details, and, more briefly, under the bishop's name. The conflict over the tenure of the pre-Conquest holder, however, is much more revealing. The two descriptions must represent the conflicting claims of the Bishop of Worcester, Wulfstan, and those who actually held the estate, that is, Beorhtric, succeeded by Earl William, succeeded by the king. The two entries allow us to reconstruct the history of the estate. It was leased by Lyfing, Wulfstan's predecessor as bishop, to Beorhtric son of Ælfgar, whom we know from other sources to have been lord of Tewkesbury, Glos., and one of the richest men in the West. Either Beorhtric, or his successor Earl William, had claimed to hold the land, not as a lease from the bishop, but absolutely, by outright sale. Earl William was William fitzOsbern, Earl of Hereford (1067–71). It must have been he who removed Bushley from the bishop's manor of Bredon and attached it to his comital manors in Herefordshire, and when his son Roger rebelled against King William in 1075, Bushley escheated along with his other lands, and passed into the king's hand, hence its appearance among the royal estates in Herefordshire. Bishop Wulfstan, however, did not abandon his claim, which is recorded by including his account of the tenure of Beorhtric at Bushley in the description of his lands in Worcestershire. The commissioners have thus received two conflicting accounts of the land at Bushley, and, being unable to decide the dispute, have included both.

The second example, Barston, is a similar case. It occurs in the fief of the English tenant-in-chief, Thorkil of Warwick, and in that of the Norman Robert Despenser. The variants in the two entries are italicized in the following quotations:

War. 241 (Thorkil)	War. 242v (Robert Despenser)
Robert d'Oilly holds Barston *in pledge*. There are *9* hides. There is land for *11* ploughs. *In demesne is 1 plough* and 6 freemen *with* 9 villans and 4 bordars have 10 ploughs. There is a mill rendering 4*s*. [There is] woodland half a league long and 3 furlongs wide. It was and is worth 100*s*. Almær held it and sold it with *the king's* permission to Æthelwine the sheriff, *Thorkil's father*.	*Robert Despenser* holds *10* hides in Barston. There is land for *10* ploughs. There are 6 freemen *and* 9 villans and 4 bordars with 10 ploughs. There is a mill rendering 4*s*. [There is] woodland half a league long and 3 furlongs wide. It was and is worth 100*s*. Almær held it *freely* and sold it with *King William's* permission to Æthelwine the sheriff.

There is considerable similarity between the two entries and at first glance one would assume that they were based upon a common original, but the difference between the hidage and ploughland assessments militates against this, though the latter may be due to the omission of the demesne in the second version. It is obvious that there is a continuing dispute over the ownership of Barston between Robert Despenser on the one hand and Robert d'Oilly and Thorkil of Warwick on the other. Both have stated their case and the commissioners have included both versions. If we could assume that each tenant-in-chief submitted a written return for his land, the discrepancies between the manorial details might be explained, but such an assumption has not been universally accepted.[2] Like the entries for Bushley, those for Barston show how double entries can provide additional information which would be otherwise unavailable. The second entry reveals that Almær's sale of the land to Æthelwine the sheriff took place in King William's reign, and thus that these two Englishmen continued in occupation of their land for some time after the Conquest. The double entries of Domesday are valuable for the light they throw not only on the compilation of the final manuscript, but also on the particular estates to which they refer.

SELECT BIBLIOGRAPHY

V. H. Galbraith, *The Making of Domesday Book* (Oxford, 1961)
J. H. Round, *Feudal England* (London, 1895)
R. Welldon Finn, *An Introduction to Domesday Book* (London, 1963)

[1] Welldon Finn, *Liber Exoniensis*, 80.

[2] See the discussion in Galbraith, *Making of Domesday Book*, 81–2, and *Domesday Book: its Place in Administrative History* (Oxford, 1974), 72.

XIV. THE GREAT AND LITTLE DOMESDAY MANUSCRIPTS

MICHAEL GULLICK

DESPITE the enormous importance of the Domesday survey to English history and scholarship, it may be found curious that the original manuscripts have received relatively little attention. The fine pioneer study by Jenkinson appeared in 1954 and it has been the basis of all serious discussion ever since.[1] Jenkinson worked after almost a lifetime of handling medieval documents and at a time when a great deal was known about the survey, for since the late eighteenth century the texts of the Great and Little Domesday manuscripts had been available in print and had become objects of close attention for many of our greatest medieval historians. An earlier study of the manuscripts might well have been unfruitful or, even worse, confusing.

Jenkinson was able to examine the manuscripts in minute detail when they were disbound for repair in 1952, and while the need for a re-examination in the light of recent scholarship has been felt (partly prompted by Jenkinson's work itself), the size of the task and the limited access quite properly allowed to the original volumes has so far inhibited that undertaking. In the last thirty-odd years considerably more has become known about the survey and very much more is understood about medieval manuscript production. More recently, the disbinding of the manuscripts in 1985 both for repair and for the making of the present facsimile has provided the opportunity for some further investigation into the physical evidence, and has led to a re-evaluation of a number of Jenkinson's conclusions with all the advantages that only an examination of the individual, unbound sheets can provide. The present account is the result of that fresh examination of the two volumes which was made at the invitation of the Public Record Office in 1985, and while it is not the exhaustive study that is needed, it does offer an advance on some of the conclusions arrived at in 1954 and it also presents a few new and important observations.

What follows is a description, in more or less chronological order, of the procedures followed in making the Domesday manuscripts; procedures that were common to the production of all medieval books with variations from century to century and from place to place. In this regard Great and Little Domesday are no less children of their time than are their cousins made in monastic scriptoria. Since both Domesday manuscripts present very different features, Great Domesday is here dealt with first and is then followed by an account of Little Domesday.[2]

GREAT DOMESDAY BOOK

PARCHMENT MANUFACTURE AND PREPARATION

Most medieval manuscripts were written on parchment manufactured from animal pelts. A skin taken from an animal slaughtered by stunning and bleeding was subjected to a process of washing in water, immersion in a liquor of lime (to ease the removal of hair and fat), dehairing, further immersion in lime, and further washing. It was then stretched on a wooden frame (or herse) and allowed to dry out under tension. While on the herse the skins may have been scraped with a sharp, crescent-shaped blade and possibly treated in several further ways to extract more fat.

The quality and character of parchment depends not only on the age, sex, and diet of the animals used (sheep, calf, and goat were the most common) but also on the skills of the parchmenter, in particular in the control of the drying process. The manufacture of a skin may have taken three or four weeks and when it was cut from the herse the skin, now properly parchment, was more or less ready for the scribe.[3]

The parchment of Great Domesday was manufactured from sheep skins and rather fewer than 200 animals were needed. There are nearly 200 sheets (400 leaves) in Great Domesday but some skins provided two sheets and others one, as shown in Fig. 1. The parchment is homogeneous, supple, thinnish for the size of the page (much is thinner than the pages of this book), and of moderate to good quality. The flesh sides are whitish and the hair sides vary from a yellowy-white to a darkish, yellow-brown colour: the difference between the two sides is clearly visible in the facsimile. All the parchment is generally free from surface blemishes and holes and it is clear that the sheets were carefully selected.

The parchment was almost certainly made by a professional craftsman, for by the late eleventh century it is probable that all important urban centres would have had parchmenters and leather-workers working in them. In Winchester, where Great Domesday is thought to have been written, there was a street of tanners (*Tænnerestret*) in 990 and Ainulf, the earliest English

[1] PRO, *Domesday Re-bound.* I am deeply indebted to the firm foundations of this pioneer publication without which the present work could not have been accomplished.

[2] A convenient summary is in Rumble, 'Palaeography of the Domesday Manuscripts', 28–49.

[3] R. Reed, *Ancient Skins, Parchments and Leathers* (London, New York, 1972), 127–73. Briefer accounts are in D. V. Thompson, *The Materials and Techniques of Medieval Painting* (London, 1936; repr. Dover, New York, 1956), 24–6; L. C. Hector, *The Handwriting of English Documents* (London, 1958), 15–16. I have also been able to consult an unpublished report on the parchment of the Domesday manuscripts made for the Public Record Office by Dr R. Reed in 1985.

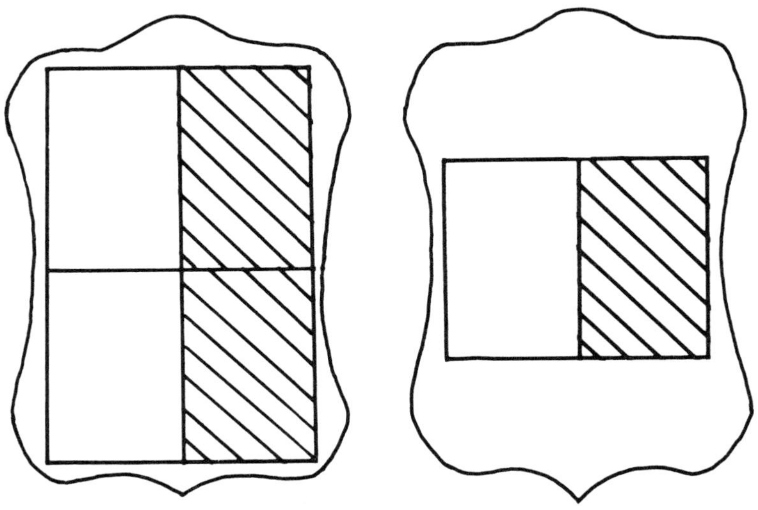

FIG. 1

The method of cutting one or two parchment sheets for Great Domesday Book out of a sheep skin (neck uppermost); the fold was always aligned along the spine of the animal. The area of a single folio is shaded.

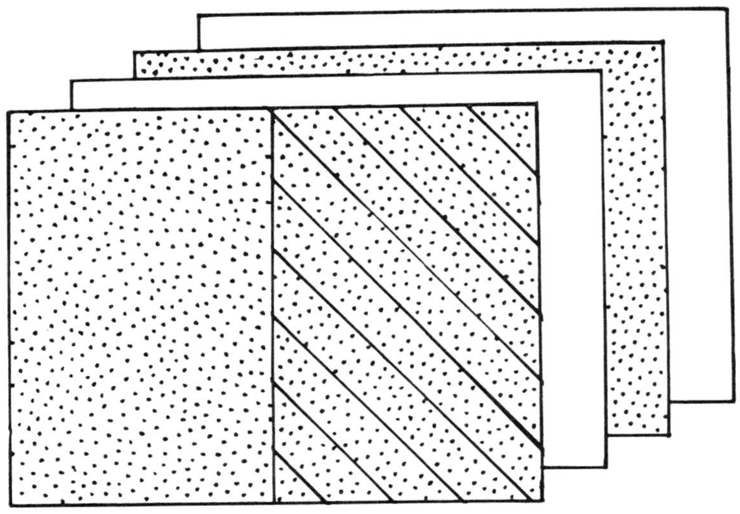

FIG. 2

Four sheets ready for folding and assembly into a quire. The hair sides are stippled, and what will become the first page of the quire is shaded.

parchmenter known by name, had property in the city in the middle of the twelfth century.[1]

Before or after the sheets were cut to size, the surface of the parchment was probably prepared on both sides and the flesh side, being fattier, may have needed different treatment from the hair side. The presence of broad, sweeping marks that have slightly abraded the surface of a few leaves suggests that at least some of the sheets were rubbed with pumice; an abrasive as well as a fat absorbent. Other substances such as chalk and sandarac might have been used, either separately or in combination. It is also possible, though perhaps doubtful, that the surface of the parchment was scraped with a sharp knife. The purpose of all this preparation was to reduce the greasy nature of the surface to make it easier to write upon with a water-based ink.[2]

SCRIBAL PRELIMINARIES

The sheets would next have been arranged into quires, the basic working units of the scribe. A quire comprises a number of sheets folded down the centre and inserted into one another (as in a modern newspaper), and a scribe usually delivered his completed work to a binder in quires rather than as single sheets.

A pile of four sheets was made with hair sides facing hair sides and flesh facing flesh, so that eventually facing pages would be of similar colour and texture. The pile was arranged so that a hair side was on the outside of the quire, as in Fig. 2. The number of sheets, four, as well as their arrangement is quite usual for this eleventh-century date, although some Great Domesday quires have five sheets, and a few have three; an irregularity contrived to provide separate quires for each county. The general intention to contain one county in one or several quires was not completely realized for there are three quires containing folios for more than one county. This may be clearly seen in the Gatherings Charts in Appendix III, pp. 164–5 below.

The shorter edges of the sheets in the pile were aligned together and, with the aid of a template, a regular series of holes was pricked at the fore-edge with an awl (or similar tool) through all the leaves of the quire. The pricking was usually made from what would become the first leaf of the quire to the last. Another series of holes was pricked in the head and tail margins with the aid of some prior guide marks, though probably without a template (Fig. 3). At least three different templates were used in Great Domesday for the fore-edge pricking as there is a common pattern of holes discernible in certain groups of quires, as shown in Fig. 4. There is no apparent regularity in the position of the holes pricked in the head and tail margins from one quire to another. The sheets were opened flat when the pricking had been completed and the quires disassembled.

The pricked holes were used as guides for the ruling of vertical and horizontal lines to assist the scribes when writing. Every quire has all or some of its guide holes in the head and tail margins, but in many quires the guide holes at the fore-edge have been trimmed off by a binder (the surviving holes show as dark dots in the facsimile). The tool used for ruling the lines was a hard point, and the ruling was done on the hair side of each of the sheets with enough pressure to incise furrows on the hair side with corresponding ridges on the flesh side (Fig. 5). Because of the arrangement of the sheets in the quires, facing pages would have either furrows or ridges but not both. The ruled lines are often visible in the facsimile.[3] The leaves of the quires in Great Domesday were usually pricked together, but it is probable that some quires were assembled from sheets pricked and ruled at different times. The half-sheets inserted into some quires were also probably pricked and ruled at a

[1] M. Biddle (ed.), *Winchester in the Early Middle Ages: an Edition and Discussion of the Winton Domesday*, Winchester Studies, i (Oxford, 1976), 235, 427 and 118, 147. The parchment of Great Domesday is not very much like any of the parchment used in late eleventh-century Winchester monastic manuscripts that I have seen.

[2] For some medieval evidence, see M. Gullick, *Extracts from the Precentors' Accounts concerning Books and Bookmaking of Ely Cathedral Priory* (Hitchin, 1985), 2–3; for an account by a modern scribe, S. Somerville, 'Parchment and Vellum', *The Calligrapher's Handbook*, ed. H. Child (London, 1985), 59–83.

[3] See also N. R. Ker, *English Manuscripts in the Century after the Norman Conquest* (Oxford, 1960), 40, 42–3.

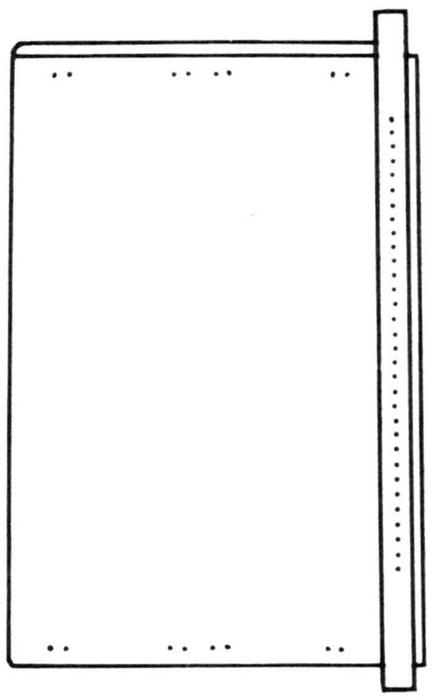

FIG. 3

The assembled quire ready for pricking, with a template pierced with guide holes in position over the fore-edge.

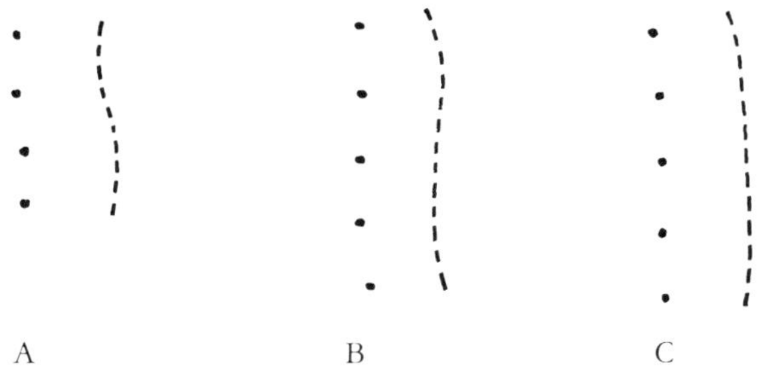

FIG. 4

The profiles of the three different templates A–C used for the fore-edge pricking of the quires of Great Domesday Book. To the left the upper four or five holes are shown at actual size, while the dotted lines to the right have been added to emphasize the slight curves of their configuration.

different time from the quires in which they were placed. When the ruling was completed the sheets were once again assembled into their quires.

The arrangement and number of ruled lines on a page is called a 'ruling pattern'. In most well-made manuscripts the ruling pattern is more or less uniform, but in Great Domesday it varies considerably and this is probably the result of different pricking and ruling programmes. It appears that only enough quires for immediate needs were pricked and ruled at any one time. The importance of the different ruling patterns lies in the possibility of placing them in chronological order. It appears that forty-four horizontal lines per page were allowed at first, and, as the writing proceeded, more horizontal lines were ruled per page until eventually they were dispensed with altogether. This may be one of the clearest indications that the writing of Great Domesday began before most of the material that was to be included in it was available. The broad spacing of the ruling and writing in what may be the earliest quires to be written was quickly realized to be too generous, having resulted in Yorkshire and Lincolnshire being spread over four and a half quires each. It must soon have been decided that if the manuscript was not going to become too unwieldy, more material would have to be written per page. The several changes of ruling pattern led to more and more material being incorporated in each folio, and enabled the later counties to be

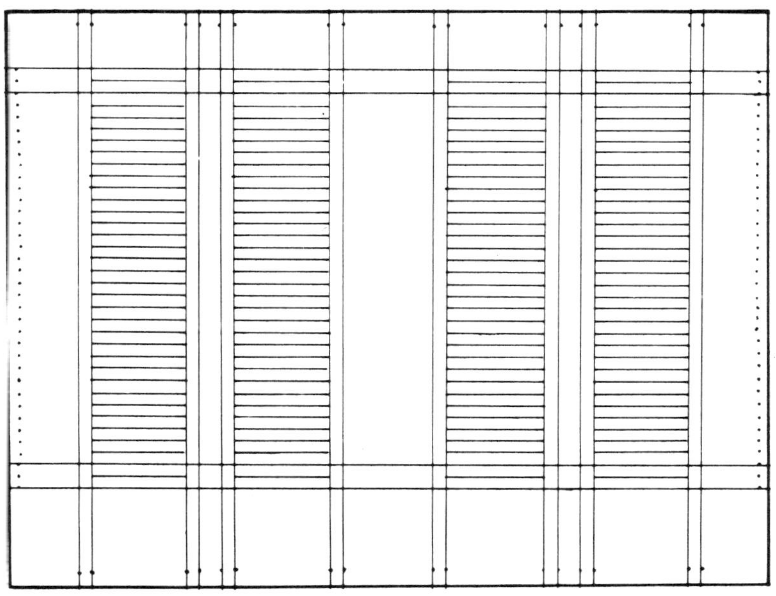

FIG. 5

A fully-ruled sheet. The extension to the edge of the ultimate and antepenultimate lines at the head and foot was a common practice.

contained in one or two quires, with the two exceptions of Hampshire which occupies three, and of Devonshire which occupies two and a half.

There are four main ruling patterns in Great Domesday and within each there is a good deal of minor variation. The widths of the columns and the gaps between them are not always constant from quire to quire, and in some ruling patterns there are occasional variations in the number of horizontal lines. The final pattern has no horizontal lines at all apart from one each at the head and foot, an arrangement that is called a 'frame ruled' pattern.

It is especially striking to note how the different ruling patterns correspond to the proposed circuits into which England was divided for the purposes of the survey.[1] Thus the testimony of the ruling patterns not only helps to provide a chronology for the writing of the manuscript, but can also help to confirm the geographical distribution of these circuits. Several details of evidence derived from the pricking and ruling of the folios do suggest what has long been suspected: that Yorkshire and Lincolnshire may have formed a separate circuit. The conjectured chronological order of the ruling patterns is shown in Fig. 6. A knowledge of the proposed circuits combined with the evidence of the writing should eventually make it possible not only to establish which of the circuit returns were available first, but also to elucidate which parts of which circuits were entered at the same time into Great Domesday.

There is nothing in the character and execution of the pricking and ruling to contradict the strong impression that it was all executed by one hand. This has some support from an idiosyncratic feature found in all the ruling patterns, for the central space between the two ruled writing spaces is not, as might be expected, parallel, but is often narrower at the head than at the foot, as shown in Fig. 7.

[1] A correspondence between the ruling patterns and the circuits of the commissioners was first noted in 1954: PRO, *Domesday Re-bound*, 25. For the circuits, see Galbraith, *Making of Domesday Book*, 7–9, 59–66; H. R. Loyn, 'A General Introduction to Domesday Book', pp. 3–7 above, with map.

Ruling pattern 1*a*

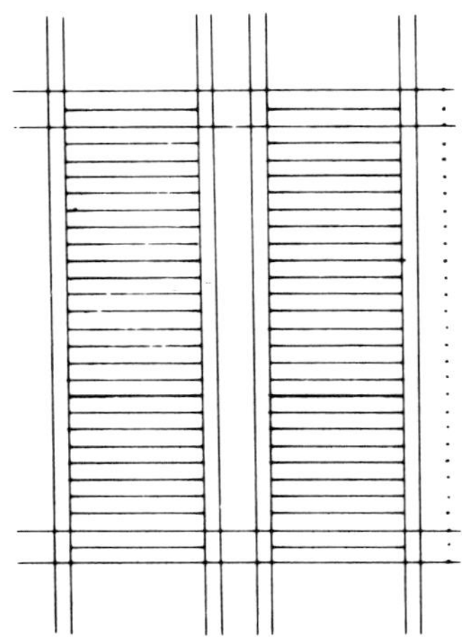

Quire No.	County	Lines per page	Template
CIRCUIT III			
17	Middx.	44	B
19	Bucks.	44	B
24	Cambs. 1	44	B
25	Cambs. 2	44	B
27	Beds.	44	B
CIRCUIT VI			
26	Hunts.	44	B
35	Derbys.	44	B
36	Notts. 1	44	B
37	Notts. 2 & Rut.	44	B

Ruling pattern 1*b*

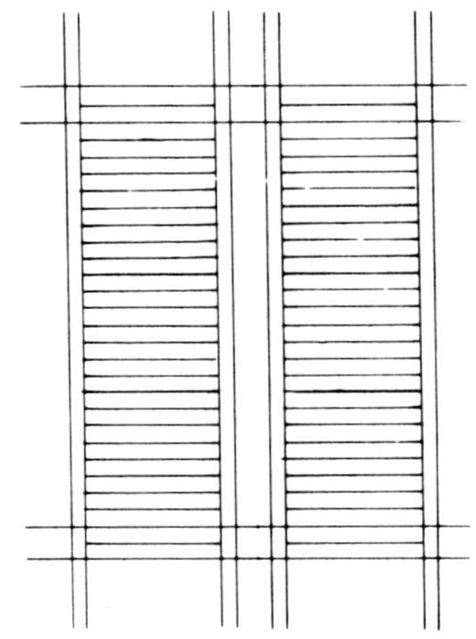

Quire No.	County	Lines per page	Template
CIRCUIT I			
2	Kent 2	44	–
Re-ruled with 51 or 52 lines			
CIRCUIT III			
18	Herts.	44	–
CIRCUIT VI			
38	Yorks. 1	47 or 49	–
40	Yorks. 3	44	–
41	Yorks. 4	44	some C
42	Yorks. 5 & Lincs. 1	44	–
43	Lincs. 2	44	–
44	Lincs. 3	44	–
45	Lincs. 4	44	–
46	Lincs. 5	44	–

Ruling pattern 2

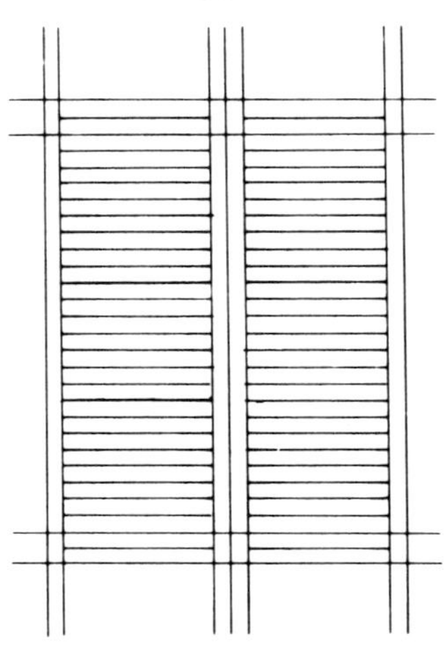

Quire No.	County	Lines per page	Template
CIRCUIT I			
1	Kent 1	50	–
3	Sussex 1	50	A
4	Sussex 2	50	–
5	Surrey	50	A
6	Hants 1	50	A
7	Hants 2	50	A
8	Hants 3	50	A
9	Berks.	50	A
CIRCUIT IV			
29	Leics.	50	A
Only one sheet. The other sheets have ruling pattern 3.			
CIRCUIT V			
21	Glos.	–	–
The first ten lines of the first *recto* were ruled.			
CIRCUIT VI			
39	Yorks. 2	38, 40 or 43	–
47	*Clamores*	52	–

Ruling pattern 3

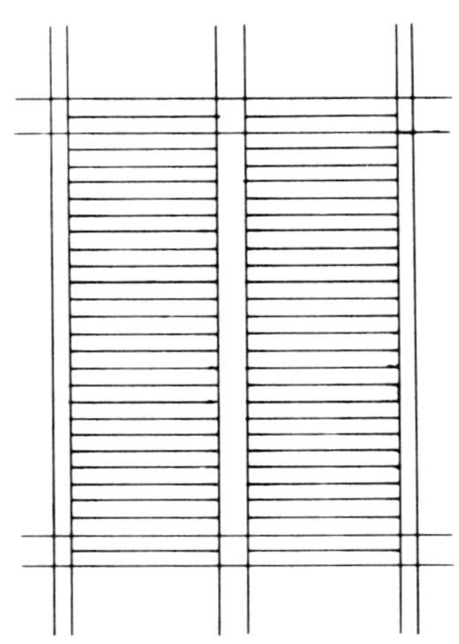

Quire No.	County	Lines per page	Template
CIRCUIT II			
10	Wilts.	53	–
11	Dorset	53	–
CIRCUIT IV			
29	Leics.	51, 52 or 54	–
Largely ruled by *leaf* and not by *sheet*. A fourth sheet has ruling pattern 2.			

Ruling pattern 4

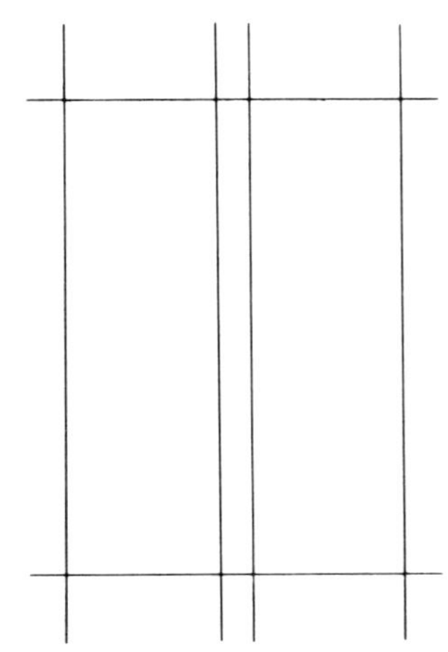

Quire No.	County	Template
CIRCUIT II		
12	Som. 1	–
13	Som. 2	–
14	Devon. 1	–
15	Devon. 2	–
16	Devon. 3 & Corn.	–
CIRCUIT IV		
20	Oxon.	–
28	Northants	–
30	War.	–
CIRCUIT V		
22	Glos. & Worcs.	–
23	Herefs.	–
31	Staffs.	–
32	Shrops. 1	–
33	Shrops. 2 & Ches. 1	–
34	Ches. 2 & Lancs.	–

FIG. 6

The four basic ruling patterns in Great Domesday Book. No. 1 is divided into 1*a* and 1*b*, the difference being that the former employed the pricking-template B. The circuits are listed below the ruling patterns used for them; the lines ruled per page is not always the same as lines written. For a concordance of quires (gatherings) and counties, see the gatherings chart in Appendix III below, pp. 164–5.

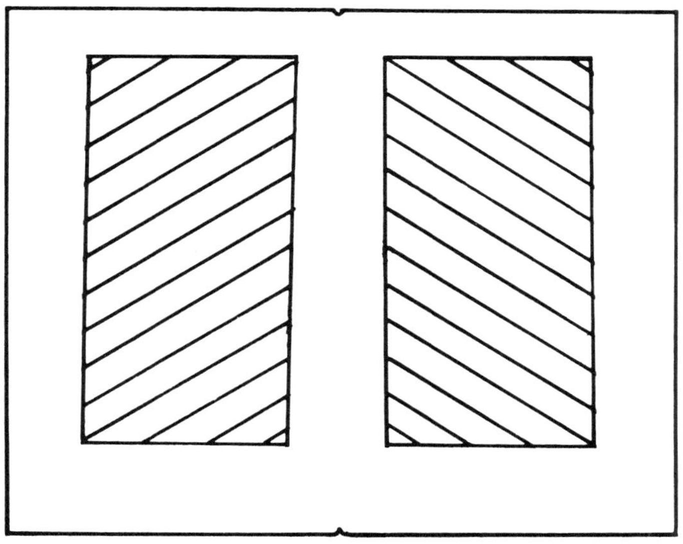

FIG. 7

The space between the two ruled areas (here shown shaded) is often narrower at the head of the page than at the foot. Occasionally this relationship is reversed, while in a few sheets the spacing is the same.

SIZE, LAYOUT, AND FORMAT

The scale and format of Great Domesday, with a page size of 365 mm. × 255 mm. (not including some small loss from later bindings), and with the text arranged in two columns, is the same as some of the largest monastic books made in the late eleventh and early twelfth centuries. The two-column format, rare in England before the Conquest, came to be adopted for certain long texts in the programme of bookmaking instituted by Norman abbots and priors in a number of English houses. The use of two columns in Great Domesday is an early example of the format in England and is certainly due to Continental influence. The ruled space in Great Domesday (that is, the area of the page ruled for writing) is perhaps a little larger than its cousins (280–300 mm. × *c.*200 mm., as opposed to 260–300 mm. × 170–190 mm.), and the extra size probably represents an allowance made for the amount of material expected for inclusion. The height of the minims of the letters (about 2 mm.) and the interlinear space (about 4 mm.), giving a ratio of roughly 1 : 2, is also a relationship similar to that followed by monastic scribes.[1] It must be emphasized, however, that this was the format allowed at the beginning of the writing of Great Domesday, for much of the manuscript was subsequently written ignoring the ruling, and, as has already been described, the horizontal guide-lines for writing were eventually dispensed with entirely.

The layout of the text was clearly made to a plan that was largely maintained. Large red initials (some modestly decorative) were drawn at the beginning of the counties, the largest of which opens the description of the first county, Kent. Within the text there are several diminishing sizes of initials, indicating principal divisions and subdivisions, which are touched with red and are slightly set out into the margins. The principal headings were written in red capital letters (called Rustic capitals), and the secondary headings in smaller Rustic capitals, almost invariably emphasized with red horizontal lines drawn through them. All this, as well as the numbered lists of the principal landholders and the corresponding numbers in the text (although in fact these numbers often do not correspond), makes Great Domesday easy to understand and use.

An original feature is the use of running titles at the heads of the leaves. The county names were written in red Rustic capitals in this position, and this obvious aid for the reader is rarely found in monastic manuscripts until the second quarter of the twelfth century. There is no doubt that the rubrication—the initials, headings, and underlining—in Great Domesday is all the work of one hand.[2]

INK AND VERMILION

The ink for Great Domesday was made from a mixture of galls (or possibly bark), gum arabic, and iron salts (ferrous sulphate). The galls would have been crushed and soaked in water, boiled, and strained, the gum and iron salts added, and possibly wine or beer as well. The gallic and tannic acid in the galls would react with the iron salts, and although the resulting solution would have been almost colourless (some colouring may have been added), on exposure to the air the ink would have turned black.[3]

The drawback to such ferrogallotannate ink is its tendency to turn brown over the centuries, and this is indeed what has happened in Great Domesday. The colour of the ink now varies widely, from near black to a pale brown, and from this evidence it may eventually be possible to establish which parts of the manuscript were written at the same time.

The pens were quills made from the primary feathers of birds, and since the writing in Great Domesday is rather small it may have been written with small feathers.[4] The rubrication was also written entirely with quills, and the large initials, if not written, were drawn with quills.

The red for the initials, titles, and underlining is vermilion made from mercury and sulphur (mercuric sulphide). Vermilion occurs naturally as cinnabar but in the eleventh century the secret of its manufacture by

[1] Ker, *English Manuscripts*, 40–5.

[2] For reader's aids, see M. B. Parkes, 'The Influence of the Concepts of *Ordinatio* and *Compilatio* on the Development of the Book', *Medieval Learning and Literature: Essays Presented to Richard William Hunt*, eds. J. J. G. Alexander and M. T. Gibson (Oxford, 1976), 116–41; R. H. and M. A. Rouse, '*Statim invenire*: Schools, Preachers, and New Attitudes to the Page', *Renaissance and Renewal in the Twelfth Century*, eds. R. L. Benson and G. Constable (Oxford, 1982), 201–25. Two curious features of the rubrication noticed in PRO, *Domesday Re-bound*, 34, are the frequent upward extension of some of the *i*s in numerals when there were three or more minims (i.e. *ili* for *iii*), and the vertical stacking of one or two *i*s above two others (i.e. *ii* with the third *i* above the other two instead of *iii*). Neither of these features regularly occur in the body of the text.

[3] Thompson, *Materials and Techniques*, 81–3; J. Watrous, *The Craft of Old Master Drawings* (Madison, 1957), 69–74; Hector, *Handwriting of English Documents*, 19–20. For two detailed medieval recipes see M. P. Merrifield, *Original Treatises on the Arts of Painting*, i (London, 1849; repr. Dover, New York, 1967), 288–93.

[4] I am unaware of any medieval evidence concerning the preparation of quills. For an account by a modern scribe see D. Jackson, 'Preparation of Quills and Reeds', *Calligrapher's Handbook*, ed. Child, 15–36.

chemical means had long been known. It is a beautiful pigment with good covering power and in Great Domesday its appearance varies from 'lean' (thinnish and a little transparent) to 'fat' (dense and glossy). The gloss was produced by the addition of a drop or two of yolk of egg to the pigment, usually bound with glair (the beaten whites of eggs).[1] It is clear that the vermilion was applied in different programmes of rubrication and eventually it might be possible to establish their incidence from the surface qualities of the pigment.

The scribe would have sat at a sloping desk bearing either a single sheet of ruled and prepared parchment, or a whole quire which may have been temporarily sewn together. With a quill in one hand and a knife in the other to hold the parchment securely to the surface of the desk, and with ink at hand in a pot or a horn, the scribe would have begun to write.

The Scribes of Great Domesday

Earlier historians tended to assume that a number of scribes were employed on Great Domesday and it was not until 1954 that the proposal was put forward that the whole manuscript was written by one hand.[2] Among modern historians, Finn preferred the old view[3] but Galbraith, and most recently Rumble, have stated their support for the latter opinion.[4] It now seems certain that neither view is entirely correct. The ascription of Great Domesday to many scribes stemmed from an inability to distinguish superficial variations in an individual hand, for it is now clear to the present writer that by far the greatest part of the manuscript was indeed the work of a single person, henceforth designated here as the 'main' scribe; and that there was a second scribe also, to be discussed below, who made a small but significant number of contributions.

The old view gained its greatest support from the belief among students of Domesday that it was not possible for one man to do so considerable an amount of work in such a short period of time. But this argument would assume the assembly and training of a team of scribes to write virtually identical hands and to adopt common orthographical practices within an even shorter period of time. It does not now seem possible that such a team existed in any late eleventh-century English or Norman scriptorium, however well disciplined, and it did not exist for Domesday. Speed of execution, visible on nearly every page of the manuscript, is a condition that would not lead a team of scribes to write identical, self-effacing hands, but would rather tend towards diversity in individual writing and clearly visible distinctions between the work of one scribe and another.

It is the letters themselves which resolve the problem, for although at first sight the irregularities of the script may seem symptomatic of several scribes, there is an underlying uniformity and consistency in many of the details of the letter-forms, and in the manner of their execution, that can only be explained as the work of one hand. It is necessary to see beyond the varied surface details of the writing to the fundamental forms of the letters, and from these it is impossible, on close analysis, not to ascribe the writing of nearly the entire manuscript to one man.

The Main Scribe

The main scribe of Great Domesday wrote a hand that is clear, distinctive, and suggests a powerful personality. Once seen it is not forgotten. It is a book hand with some informal elements for in the eleventh century most writing was in the same script, a version of a script that was used, with local variations, all over north-western Europe. It was a direct descendant of the 'Caroline minuscule' script developed in the first half of the ninth century in France, named after Charlemagne, and it is this script which is also the ancestor of the letters printed in this book.

The late eleventh century was one of the more unstable periods in the history of writing in England.[5] The purity of Anglo-Caroline had been in decline since early in the century and the Norman newcomers brought with them Continental forms of Caroline. Some centres in England continued to write clearly recognizable English hands until the early twelfth century, while others adopted, soon after the Conquest, a script obviously dependent on Norman models. Many English scribes continued to write English hands, often alongside their Norman counterparts,[6] but whilst it is perhaps unlikely that Normans ever wrote hands of English type, it is possible that English scribes could have modified and altered their hands to conform more with Continental examples. It has probably never been difficult for even moderate scribes to write more than one type of script.

It is against this background that the hand of the main scribe of Great Domesday must be seen and it appears to be a striking reflection of the unstable elements of late eleventh-century writing. It is a hand that has both particular and elusive qualities with features that depend on both English and Continental models, and while some details are curious, others are very idiosyncratic.

Some aspects of his hand suggest that he was originally English-trained and a study of one orthographical aspect of his work suggests that he was a native Englishman.[7] All the features deserve a closer examination than they have yet received, especially as more is

[1] Thompson, *Materials and Techniques*, 103–8 and 50–2, 55–7. For vermilion see further R. J. Gettens and G. L. Stout, *Painting Materials, a Short Encyclopaedia* (New York, 1942; repr. Dover, New York, 1966), 170–3.

[2] PRO, *Domesday Re-bound*, 34–5.

[3] R. Welldon Finn, *The Domesday Inquest* (London, 1961), 179–80; *Domesday Studies: the Liber Exoniensis* (London, 1964), 147–53; and *Domesday Book: a Guide* (London, Chichester, 1973), 18–21.

[4] V. H. Galbraith, *Domesday Book: its Place in Administrative History* (Oxford, 1974), 48; Rumble, 'Palaeography of the Domesday Manuscripts', 45.

[5] T. A. M. Bishop and P. Chaplais, *Facsimiles of English Royal Writs to A.D. 1100 Presented to Vivian Hunter Galbraith* (Oxford, 1957), pp. xvii–xviii.

[6] For the distinction between English and Norman hands, see Ker, *English Manuscripts*, 22–3; for English hands, T. A. M. Bishop, *English Caroline Minuscule* (Oxford, 1971).

[7] P. H. Sawyer, 'The Place-Names of the Domesday Manuscripts', *Bull. of the John Rylands Lib.* 38 (Manchester, 1955–6), 483–506.

now known about eleventh-century script and book production than thirty years ago. Examples of the main scribe's hand are illustrated in Fig. 8 and are taken from folios which exemplify the variety of letter-size and spacing found in the manuscript. Also illustrated are two of his most important individual characteristics. The first of these is the use of the horned *e*; that is, an *e* with a distinct entry stroke at the upper left. This letter is a pronounced version of the form used in the writing of Anglo-Saxon and which is also occasionally found in late eleventh-century Latin script. It appears only to have been used by English scribes.[1] The second feature is a very unusual form of an abbreviation used for final *-us* after *b*, which begins almost on the baseline of the lettering, and is made like an undulating line in which the form of the normal abbreviation is almost, but not quite, lost. A special significance of this final *-us* form will be returned to below.

All the features of the main scribe's hand will have to wait for a future, more intense, scrutiny. But one judgement of the character of the hand which has been made by several historians must be refuted, for there is not the least evidence to support the belief that the hand is 'curial'. The hand is a book hand and appears to have no features that might be identified as characteristic of the precocious Anglo-Norman Chancery.[2]

The main scribe often writes with deliberation and care at the beginnings of counties, but many of the additions, which often spill into the margins, are sometimes written more informally. Some of the marginal notes are almost cursive in execution. The pages of Great Domesday have a distinct appearance, the letters having tall ascenders, while the capital letters, and the extension below the baseline of letters such as *r* and long *s* (*ſ*), combine to give a vertical emphasis to the page. Some characters are very prominent, in particular the *7* (the sign for *et*, 'and').[3] Another striking feature is the consistently heavy abbreviation of the text, and the omission of letters or groups of letters from words, indicated with special signs and marks. Medieval scribes usually abbreviated what they wrote,[4] but the particular need for compression in this manuscript and the technical nature of the text led to more abbreviations than is usual for this date. All the significant abbreviations in Great Domesday are listed in the chart compiled by A. R. Rumble in Appendix II, pp. 162–3 below.

a. Left: The horned *e* frequently used by the main scribe. *Right:* His consistent and highly idiosyncratic form of *-us* after *b* extending far below the base-line, with the rare initial oblique entry stroke at the top.

b. The final *-us* after *b* appears in *aliq(ui)bus* at the end of the middle line, where also the horned *e* is used for both occurrencies of *e(st)*. In the last line the *g* is carefully formed, while the ampersand and *7* are both used for *et*. (Yorks. 299, *slightly reduced*)

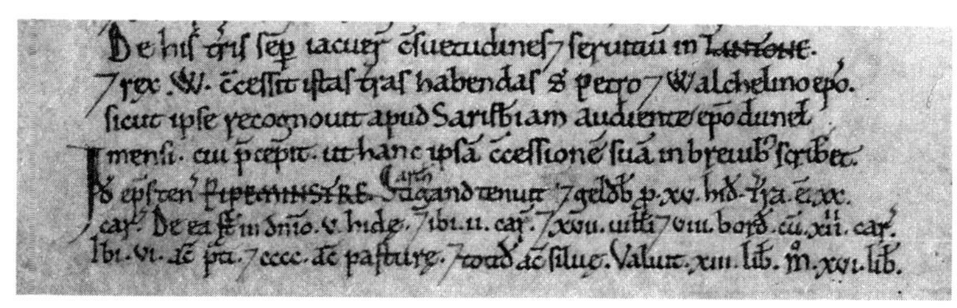

c. Long *r* occurs in *rex, t(er)ras* and *Petro* in line 2, and in *pastur(a)e* (bottom line) in which the long *s* is also employed. There is no hyphen for the word break at the end of line 3, *dunel|mensi*. (Som. 87v, *slightly reduced*)

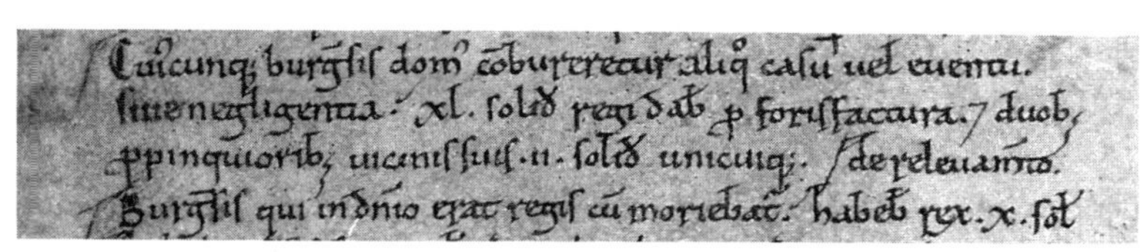

d. On the bottom line the round *d* in *d(omi)nio* is finished with an oblique stroke at the top. The form of the *g* is less complex in this example, but the final *-us* is evident in *duobus*, at the end of line 2, and *p(ro)pinquioribus*, at the beginning of line 3. (Shrops. 252, *slightly reduced*)

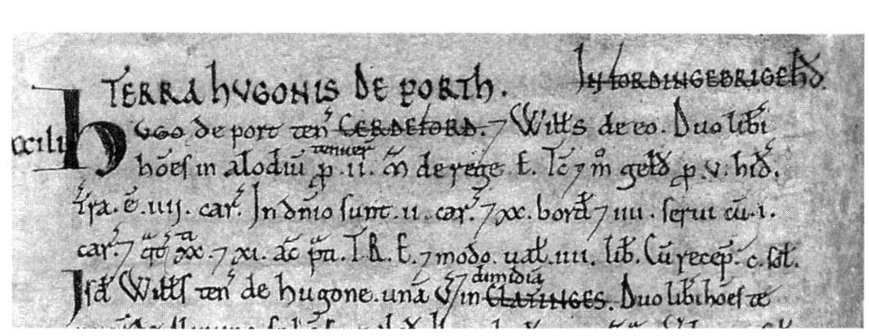

e. Suprascript additions by the main scribe using the long *r* in *tenuer(ant)*, and the serifed round *d* in *7 dimidia(m)*. (Hants 44v, *slightly reduced*)

FIG. 8

Typical features of the main scribe's hand.

[1] N. R. Ker, *Catalogue of Manuscripts Containing Anglo-Saxon* (Oxford, 1957), pp. xxix. For English scribes using horned *e* in Latin script, see Ker, *English Manuscripts*, pls. 1*b*, 11.

[2] Both Welldon Finn and Galbraith habitually describe the script of Great Domesday as 'curial' as opposed to more recently Rumble, 'Palaeography of the Domesday Manuscripts', 45.

[3] It is instructive to compare the hand of the main scribe with the hand of the scribe who wrote most of the Wiltshire Geld Accounts B and C (now bound with Exon Domesday) in or about 1086, and who also wrote books at Salisbury. He may have been a professional; see N. R. Ker, 'The Beginnings of Salisbury Cathedral Library', *Books, Collectors and Libraries: Studies in the Medieval Heritage*, ed. A. G. Watson (London, 1985), 143, 154–9, and pls. 20*a*, *b*. The writing in the accounts is informal and that in the books formal.

[4] There are extensive discussions of medieval abbreviations in print. For a useful summary, see Hector, *Handwriting of English Documents*, 28–34.

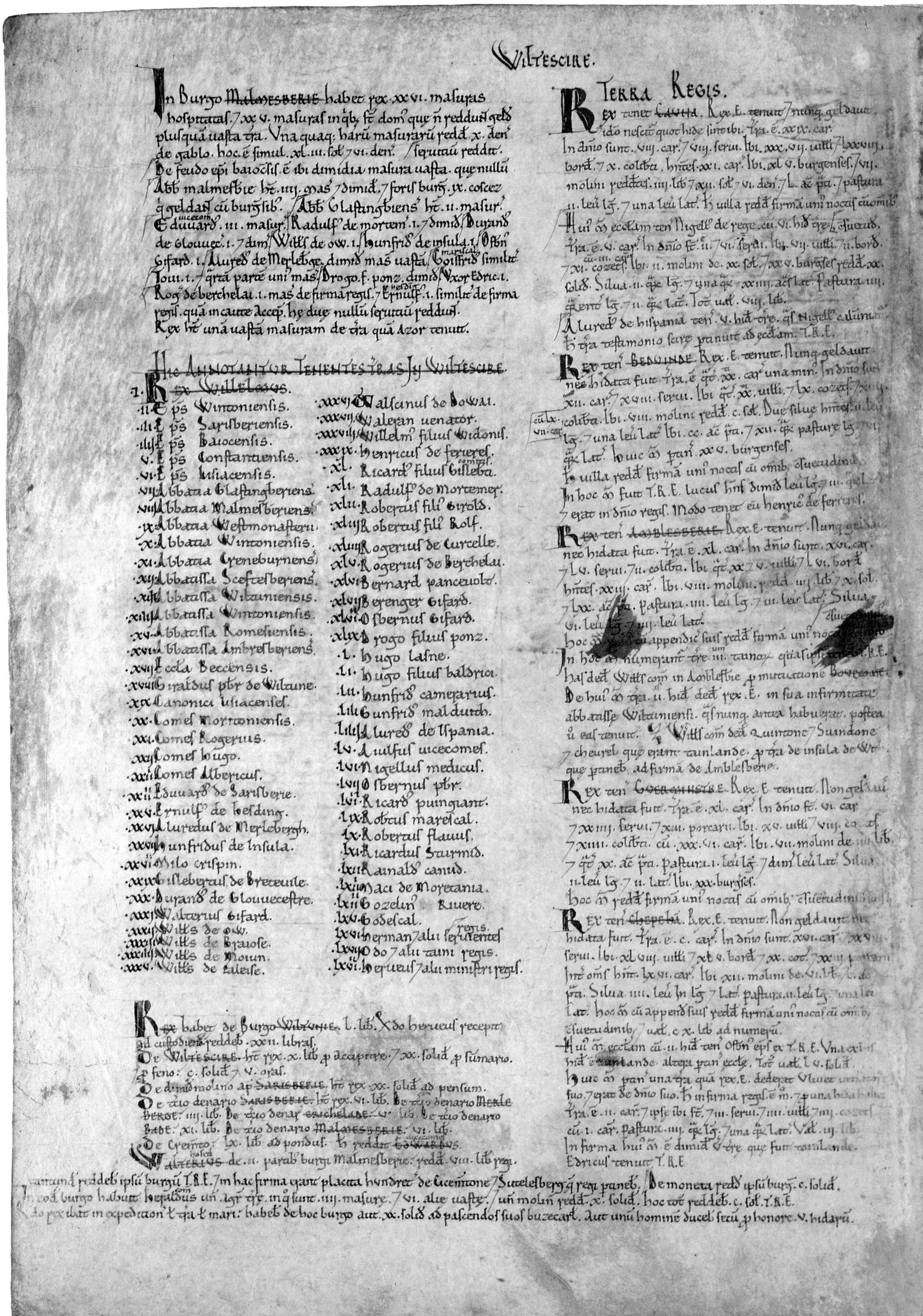

FIG. 9

Three passages on one folio written at different times. The list of landholders in the middle section of the left column is written in a larger script than the short section above and below it as well as the *Terra Regis* section in the right column. It is not clear which of these was entered first, but the divided section on the left, listing payments due from the Wiltshire boroughs, was clearly written last of all, as the scribe had left insufficient space and had to complete the passage in three lines right across the foot margin.

(Wilts. 64v, *slightly reduced*)

The order of the entries of the counties must have been previously planned, with the principal town usually first, followed by the holdings of the king, the ecclesiastics, and finally the laymen, the last two in descending order of importance. This was clearly understood by the scribe but what is not clear today is the exact process by which he copied from his exemplar on to the pages of Great Domesday. It seems most likely that he edited and composed the entries from the longer summaries of the circuit returns,[1] of which only two have survived; Little Domesday from the East Anglian Circuit and Exon Domesday from the South-Western. As he worked he left blank what he did not understand or what was missing or uncertain, so that he could return to it later.[2] There is no doubt that Great Domesday was not written from beginning to end in one programme in the order in which the quires are now bound. However, it is likely that it was originally planned to be bound up in that order, because there is a certain logic in the sequence of the counties that is unrelated to the conformations of the original circuits.[3]

The problem of unravelling the order in which the counties were entered into the manuscript, as well as the order of writing the contents of the individual counties, is exceedingly complex. There appears to be no simple progression in the changing character of the hand of the main scribe, for some early entries appear to have been rapidly written while some later writing appears to have been executed with care and deliberation. Yet there is also no doubt that some later work was also written very rapidly and with little care. One example will demonstrate the difficulty.

The opening page of Wiltshire (64v, Fig. 9) is made up of three constituents: the account of the boroughs, the list of landholders, and, in the column on the right, the opening lines of the king's holdings. Each of these three passages appears to have been written at different times, and the last to be inscribed was the section on the boroughs. However, the space left for it at the top of column 1 was insufficient, and the scribe had to continue the entry below the list, and even finish it right across the foot margin. Yet it is obvious that the character of the hand that describes Malmesbury is deliberate and formal and was presumably written at leisure. This example also typifies the awkward visual articulation of the openings of other counties, for it is clear that the borough information entered at the heads of many of

Stage 1: Early	Stage 2: Middle	Stage 3: Middle	Stage 4: Late
CIRCUIT III	CIRCUIT I	CIRCUIT IV	CIRCUIT II
Middlesex	Kent	Oxfordshire	Wiltshire
Hertfordshire	Sussex	Northamptonshire	Dorset
Buckinghamshire	Surrey	Leicestershire	Somerset
Cambridgeshire	Hampshire	Warwickshire	Devon
Bedfordshire	Berkshire		Cornwall
CIRCUIT VI	CIRCUIT V		
Yorkshire	Staffordshire	Gloucestershire	
Lincolnshire	Shropshire	Worcestershire	
Huntingdonshire	Cheshire	Herefordshire	
Derbyshire	Lancashire		
Nottinghamshire			
Rutland			

Table showing a relative chronology for the compilation of Great Domesday Book tentatively divided into four stages. Under each circuit the counties are listed in the order in which they appear in the manuscript, though they were not necessarily written in that order. Circuit VII is contained in Little Domesday Book.

Galbraith, *Making of Domesday Book* pp. 189–204 proposed that the earliest counties to be written lacked the words *Hic annotatur* in the headings for their lists of landholders. This is also true of Yorkshire and Lincolnshire (not mentioned by Galbraith) in which the lists were particularly large and well-written. None of the counties in Circuit III have this phrase except Middlesex, suggesting that it was the last county of that group to be inscribed.

them was written after the matter that followed on the page.

The variations in the hand of the scribe taken with the variety of the colour of the ink and of the ruling patterns make it possible to suggest a tentative chronology for the writing of the counties, which is shown in the Table. The order of production has been set out in four stages, but it must be understood that the counties were not necessarily written in the order in which they appear within those stages, and that all counties required additions of one kind or another at other times.

The scribe checked what he had written against his exemplar, and then corrected mistakes over erasures made by scraping the surface of the parchment with a knife and preparing it again for writing.[4] The rewriting varies in length from a few words to several lines, although the longer passages may represent amendments rather than corrections. He returned to some of the spaces that he had left for the insertion of missing or uncertain material and filled them in, although many still remain blank and were never filled at all. Additional or new information was added or inserted in the margins and in four places written on narrow strips of parchment which were later bound into the manuscript.[5] One county, Dorset, was never completed and breaks off in mid sentence,[6] while the writing-up of the East Anglian Circuit was never begun: it survives only as Little Domesday. There are other major omissions for which space had been allowed, such as the cities of London and Winchester; while, most curiously of all, there is no

[1] There must have been extensive written material of one kind or another behind the final compilation of Great Domesday: see S. P. J. Harvey, 'Domesday Book and its Predecessors', *EHR* 86 (1971), 753–73; H. B. Clarke, 'The Domesday Satellites', *Domesday Book: A Reassessment*, ed. Sawyer, 50–70. A reference to one written record is in Great Domesday itself: 'in brevi scriptas' ('written in the records'), Hunts. 203.

[2] Galbraith, *Making of Domesday Book*, 189–92; Loyn, 'Introduction', pp. 6–7 above. One view is that there was a fair copy made of what is now Exon Domesday and this (lost) exemplar was used by the main scribe. This notion is challenged in C. and F. Thorn (eds.), *Domesday Book: Devon* (Chichester, 1985), pt. 2, 'Exon. Introduction: Relationship between Exon. and Exchequer DB'. The authors suggest that the intervening fair copy never existed; see also C. Thorn, 'Marginal Notes and Signs in Domesday Book', Special Study XV, p. 118, n. 3.

[3] Galbraith, *Making of Domesday Book*, 201.

[4] Ker, *English Manuscripts*, 50–3.

[5] The ruling on three of these slips (Hants 42, Dorset 76 and 81) does not correspond to any of the ruling patterns of Great Domesday so that it appears that they were not cut from rejected leaves intended for Great Domesday itself.

[6] Dorset 85.

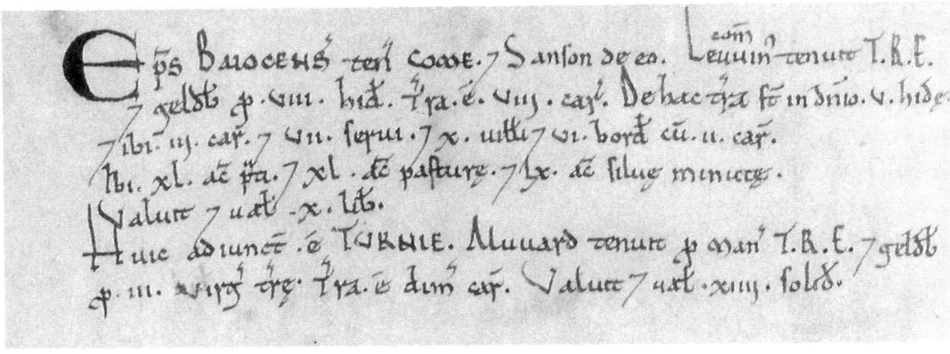

FIG. 10

A passage written by the main scribe in Exon Domesday. The entry concerned Samson, a royal chaplain. (Exon 153v, *slightly reduced*)

record that large parts of the North were ever surveyed at all, including the whole of the newly settled counties of Northumberland and Durham.[1]

Some of the mechanics of the writing procedure may be observed in the notes left by the scribe in the margins, mostly reminders and instructions to himself to check passages where further information was needed.[2] Occasionally these are written in red. One marginal note on Surrey 32 records a change in the geld assessment of a manor held by Westminster Abbey, and the original grant of William I concerning the change has survived. It is dated 'post descriptionem totius Angliae' ('after the survey of all England'), and this is one of the earliest references to the Domesday survey.[3] Another marginal note on Hampshire 48 states that the king had restored the manor of *Icene* (Itchen Abbas) to St Mary's, Winchester. In the adjacent text the manor was stated to have been held by Hugh fitzBaldric and there is a note at the end stating that the Abbess of St Mary's was claiming it; clearly her claim was upheld.[4] Both these notes written by the main scribe reveal that even as Great Domesday was being written the text was being worked over with the intention of keeping it as up-to-date as possible.

A glance at the pages of Great Domesday can do nothing but create feelings of admiration for the industry and drive of the main scribe. Not only does it appear that he edited the text as he worked, but he also had to correct, amend, add, annotate, and to bear ever in his mind the whole purpose and realization of the survey. Moreover, it seems likely that he was also responsible for the pricking and the ruling of the parchment, whilst it is certain that it was he who rubricated the red initials and headings. Although like many medieval cathedrals the manuscript was never to be finished, the achievement of the main scribe of Great Domesday Book is truly astonishing.

The hand of this scribe also appears elsewhere. He wrote three entries in Exon Domesday concerning the holdings in Somerset of Samson, a royal chaplain, and Robert fitzGerald (Fig. 10). The hand, the letter-forms, and the formulae are unmistakable. Although there has been some reticence among scholars in accepting that the hand in Exon is the same as that in Great Domesday, there can be little doubt that both belong to the same scribe.[5]

If the three entries in Exon Domesday have long been suspected as the work of the scribe of Great Domesday, the occurrence of his hand in three other manuscripts is an entirely new discovery. It is known that one of these certainly belonged to the Old Minster at Winchester in the sixteenth century; another may also have come from a Winchester house; and the third is of uncertain provenance. The origins of all three manuscripts are at present unknown but it is important that they are all certainly monastic books.[6]

The Correcting Scribe

The presence within the original text of Great Domesday of a second hand has not been recognized before, and its author is hereafter called the 'correcting' scribe. He wrote only a few extensive passages, but he did make a considerable number of additions to the main scribe's work by supplying omissions and corrections (usually by insertion, occasionally over erasure), as well as some marginal notes. He appears to have worked throughout the manuscript, although some counties have many more examples of his hand than others: in particular he added a good deal of material to the counties of the South-Western Circuit. The extent and importance of his activity has yet to be assessed properly, but it appears that he may have supervised the main scribe. The role

[1] Galbraith, *Making of Domesday Book*, 4, 53, 196; PRO, *Domesday Re-bound*, 5; Loyn, 'Introduction', pp. 7–8 above.

[2] For all marginalia, see Thorn, 'Marginal Notes', pp. 113–35.

[3] H. W. C. Davis (ed.), *Regesta Regum Anglo-Normannorum*, i: 1066–1100 (Oxford, 1913), no. 236; Bishop and Chaplais, *Facsimiles of English Royal Writs*, no. 26 and pl. xxiv.

[4] *VCH Hampshire*, i (1900), 436–7.

[5] Exeter Cathedral MS 3500. The character of these entries written on the versos of two otherwise blank leaves at the end of quires, ff. 153v and 436v, was first noticed by H. Ellis (ed.), *Libri Censualis vocati Domesday Book, Additamenta*... (London, 1816), p. ix n. 1, and published by R. Welldon Finn, 'The Evolution of Successive Versions of Domesday Book', *EHR* 66 (1951), 561–4. The entries have since been discussed by Welldon Finn, *Liber Exoniensis*, 130–1; Galbraith, *Making of Domesday Book*, 109–12; Rumble, 'Palaeography of the Domesday Manuscripts', 47–8 and pl. 3.5.

[6] They are: (1) a sermon of Augustine, ff. 89v–91 in Oxford, Trinity College MS 28, with a sixteenth-century ex-libris of the Old Minster, Winchester; (2) a life of St Catherine, ff. 140–143v in London, British Library, Harley MS 12; and (3) Hereford Cathedral MS P.I.10, the scribe having written the contents list on the upper pastedown. The principal scribe of Harley 12 may have worked a little earlier than the main scribe of Great Domesday; the scribes of the two other manuscripts are his contemporaries.

of the two men, scribe and corrector, is paralleled in monastic manuscripts where, albeit in rather different circumstances, texts were often corrected by persons other than those who wrote them.[1]

The correcting scribe wrote a book hand that is distinctly Norman[2] and it is very probable that he was a Norman. It is an easy hand to distinguish from that of the main scribe because of the characteristics illustrated in Fig. 11*a*. Fortunately the few longer passages written by the correcting scribe are of sufficient extent to enable his many smaller contributions to be recognized.

One of the longest passages is the antepenultimate entry in Berkshire 63v for Robert fitzRolf (Fig. 11*b*). The text repeats, almost exactly, an earlier entry on 62, the crucial difference being the name of the landholder, Robert fitzGerald. These two entries are one of a number of pairs of duplicate entries in Great Domesday, but the unique importance of this particular pair lies in the fact that the second is followed by other entries written by the main scribe. It therefore appears incontrovertible that the correcting scribe worked with the main scribe rather than after him. This entry in the hand of the correcting scribe is not rubricated, neither are others of his contributions that could have been rubricated, nor are the entries that follow, which were written by the main scribe.

Another pair of duplicate entries represents a further example of the correcting scribe's work. In Cambridgeshire 190 there are two entries written at the foot of a column, of which the first is the duplicate (Fig. 2, Special Study XIII, p. 90 above). It presents certain textual differences that are significant because they appear to show that the two scribes edited the exemplar independently as they composed the entries.[3]

The following table lists the fourteen longer passages written by the correcting scribe at full size and which contain six or more words each. Two are illustrated in Fig. 11*b* and *c*.

	Folio	*Column*	*Lines*	*Fig.*
Berkshire	63v	right	42–5	11*b*
Devonshire	117v	right	49	
Gloucestershire	166	right	24	
Herefordshire	180	right	2	
Cambridgeshire	190	left	42–5	
Cambridgeshire	191	right	23	
Cambridgeshire	191v	left	1–2	11*c*
Nottinghamshire	281v	left	3 and 46	
Nottinghamshire	283	right	13	
Nottinghamshire	286	right	18	
Nottinghamshire	287	right	38	
Nottinghamshire	288	left	16	
Lincolnshire	367	left	2	

Besides the above there are at least as many as 400 smaller additions, some consisting of a few characters

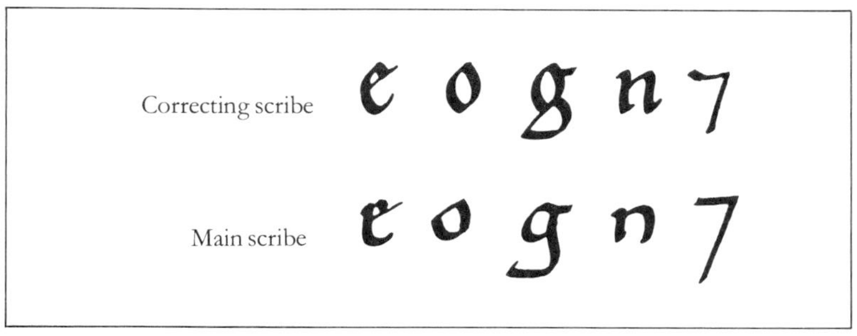

a. The comparison of certain letters shows how the correcting scribe wrote a rather more pointed hand than the main scribe, and finished his minims with upward flicks.

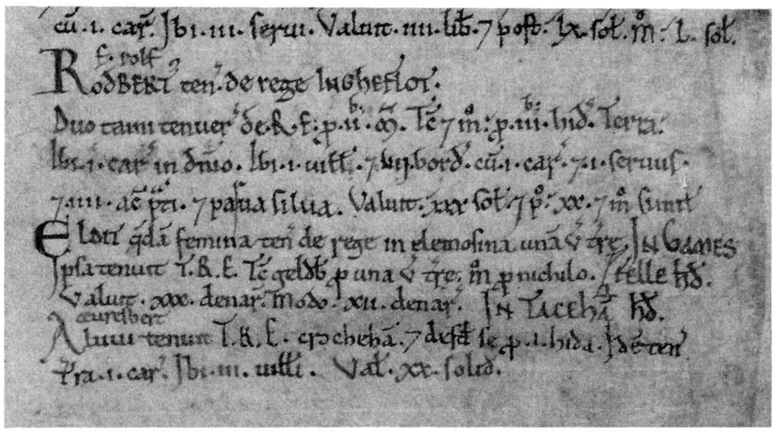

b. Proof on the final page of Berkshire that both scribes were working simultaneously. The correcting scribe wrote the entry for Robert fitzRolf (here lines 2–5), which was then followed by two entries written by the main scribe. None are rubricated.

(Berks. 63v, *slightly reduced*)

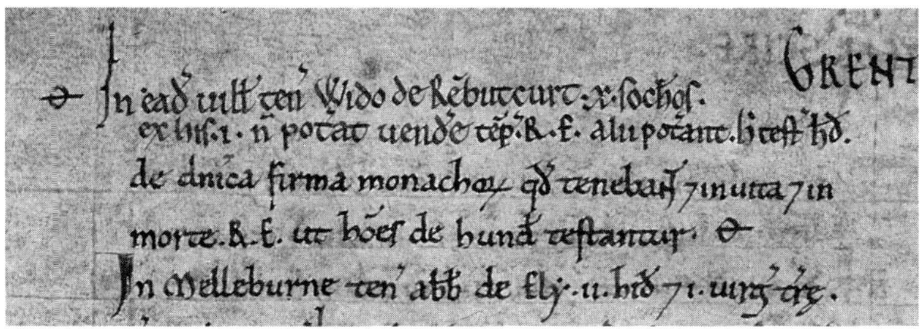

c. The two top lines were added by the correcting scribe, who began the initial *I* in the wrong place and restarted a little lower. The hand has a generally pointed, compressed character. The *s* hardly descends below the base-line at all, and the punctuation points fall at mid-minim height, noticeably higher than those of the main scribe.

(Cambs. 191v, *slightly reduced*)

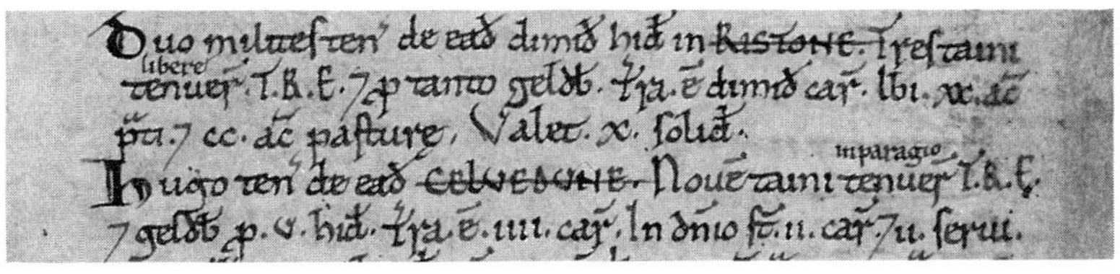

d. Two suprascript additions by the correcting scribe, *libere* and *in paragio*. His compressed, pointed manner is evident even at this small scale.

(Dorset 83v, *slightly reduced*)

Fig. 11

Typical features of the correcting scribe's hand.

[1] For the correction of texts at Salisbury by a scribe who may be Osmund, Bishop of Salisbury 1078–99, see Ker, 'The Beginnings of Salisbury Cathedral Library', 143–73. Lanfranc, Archbishop of Canterbury 1070–89, also corrected and amended texts when at Bec: M. T. Gibson, *Lanfranc of Bec* (Oxford, 1978), 39–40.

[2] Cf. p. 98 n. 6 above.

[3] A. Williams, 'Apparent Repetitions in Domesday Book', Special Study XIII, pp. 90–1 above, where these two entries are discussed.

only, e.g. Fig. 11*d*. The hand varies much as does the hand of the main scribe; some passages are written deliberately and carefully while others were evidently written with less of an eye for effect. How much the work of the correcting scribe can reveal about the making of the manuscript will only be appreciated when a full list of his contributions has been compiled and analysed.

It appears that the relationship of the two scribes is a microcosm of the procedure adopted for the survey itself, for in a famous near-contemporary text, Robert, Bishop of Hereford, describes how the initial inquiries were made and then checked by independent investigators, no doubt to ensure accuracy.[1] A similar process of checking was evidently followed in the making of the manuscript itself.

Later Scribes

Additions by four later scribes will be noticed here, of whom two made only single amendments to the main text. One hand wrote a series of letters under the outer column of the last versos of the final ten quires (Fig. 19, Special Study XV, p. 133 below). These letters, or quire signatures, run backwards (which is unusual) from *a* followed by one dot, *b* followed by two, *c* followed by three, *d* followed by four, and then *e–k*. The letters are probably closely contemporary with the writing of Great Domesday but differ from the hands of both the text scribes. The hand looks English and the letters may have been written just before binding. It is probably significant that these ten quires contain Yorkshire and Lincolnshire, which were, with the exception of Hampshire in three quires and Devonshire in two and a half, the only counties in Great Domesday to run to more than two quires. Their proper order may therefore not have been immediately clear to a binder and perhaps this scribe marked the quires to avoid the chance of their being bound up in the wrong order.

A second hand wrote the greater part of three names over erasures in the list of tenants in Hampshire 37v, and a third hand (having first carefully erased something) added a detail not found in Exon Domesday on Cornwall 121. Neither of these passages can be attributed to either the main or the correcting scribes, although both are probably of late eleventh-century date.[2]

The final later scribe wrote the only extensive addition made to the manuscript in medieval times. This was the survey of the lands of Robert de Bruis added to the manuscript on the previously blank Yorkshire folios 332v–333, between about 1120 and 1129 (Fig. 12). The 'Bruis' scribe wrote a sprawling, unattractive hand, displaying many informal elements, which stands out in distinct contrast to the neat execution of the rest of

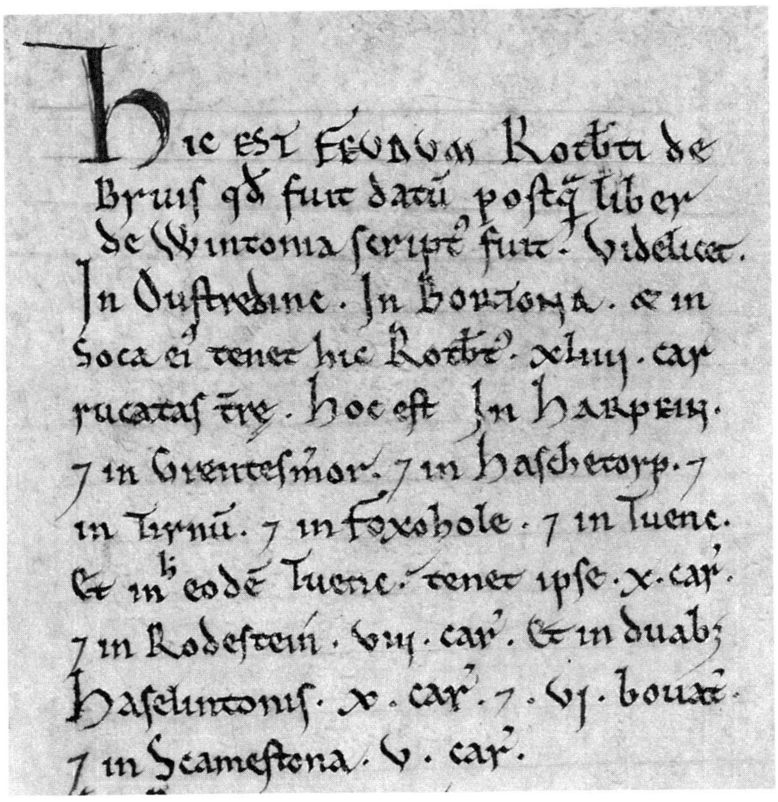

Fig. 12

The 'Bruis' scribe also employed the unusual form of the final *-us* after *b* characteristic of the main scribe, as in *duabus* at the end of the third line from the bottom. (Yorks. 332v, *slightly reduced*)

Great Domesday Book.[3] It is notable that the scribe employed the unusual form of the final *-us* sign following *b* that is such an important feature of the hand of the main scribe.

The Identity of the Scribes and their Location

There is no evidence to show that the royal household possessed an established writing office until the twelfth century.[4] Only one royal scribe, almost certainly a Norman, seems to have been employed during the reign of William I, and it was not until the last years of his successor that there were two.[5]

It is curious also that virtually the whole of the task of writing Great Domesday devolved upon only one scribe, especially when a characteristic of the survey was its urgency. It could be argued that this was a reflection of the limited personnel available in the royal household and the small extent of whatever writing office then existed. But as the hand of the main scribe has not been found in any royal documents (from a period from which a handful have survived), while it has now been found in three manuscripts of definitely monastic origin (from a period from which about 250 have survived),[6] the probability is that the main scribe was not himself a

[1] Galbraith, *Making of Domesday Book*, 52; E. M. Hallam, *Domesday Book through Nine Centuries* (London, 1986), 20; Loyn, 'Introduction', p. 5 above.

[2] Great Domesday 37v, nos. 54–6; 121, left column, line 22. For the Hampshire entries, probably by an English hand, see J. Munby (ed.), *Domesday Book: Hampshire* (Chichester, 1982), notes; for the Cornish entry, C. and F. Thorn (eds.), *Domesday Book: Cornwall* (Chichester, 1979), notes.

[3] G. F. Jensen, 'The Domesday Book Account of the Bruce Fief', *EPNS Jnl* 2 (1969–70), 8–17.

[4] T. A. M. Bishop, *Scriptores Regis* (Oxford, 1961), 23–6.

[5] Bishop and Chaplais, *Facsimiles of English Royal Writs*, pp. xviii and nos. 10, 27, pls. ix, xxv*a*; P. Chaplais, 'Une charte originale de Guillaume le Conquérant pour l'abbaye de Fécamp: la donation de Steyning et de Bury (1085)', in his *Essays in Medieval Diplomacy and Administration* (London, 1981), 93–104.

[6] The figure of about 250 is calculated from the convenient list by H. Gneuss, 'A Preliminary List of Manuscripts Written or Owned in England up to 1100', *ASE* 9 (1981), 1–60.

permanent member of the royal household. This would contradict the commonly held assumption to the effect that the manuscript was written, probably at Winchester, by royal clerks.[1]

To elucidate this matter further, it will be necessary to locate the scriptorium at which the main scribe originally worked before his association with Domesday Book. Such an identification will depend on the discovery of the place or places of origin of the three monastic manuscripts in which his hand has now been recognized (see p. 102 above). At present all that may safely be said is that it seems to have been a monastic institution under strong Norman influence and that Winchester is therefore unlikely to provide a candidate. The crucial pointer may lie in the unusual feature of the main scribe's hand discussed and illustrated above in Fig. 8: the *-us* abbreviation like a *ȝ* following a *b*. So far this form of the abbreviation has only been found in manuscripts from two places, Exeter and Durham, both centres that do exhibit obvious Norman characteristics in the late eleventh century.[2]

However, even if the scriptorium in which the main scribe worked should ever be identified for certain, his relationship with the making of Great Domesday will still have to be defined. Also, wherever his original scriptorium may have been, it does not follow that Great Domesday was written there for it was always possible for the scribe to be transferred to Winchester to carry out the work. Certainly Winchester was the Anglo-Norman capital in the late eleventh century; it has always been assumed that Winchester was the focus for the direction of the survey, and there can be little doubt that Great Domesday was produced for the fledgeling royal administration at Winchester.[3]

The ascription of the writing of Great Domesday to two scribes and the discovery of the main scribe's work in other manuscripts only points more sharply to the greatest void in Domesday studies today: we do not know who was responsible for the central direction of the survey, let alone the production of Great Domesday itself. If ever this were to be established it might become clear why almost the entire manuscript was written out by one scribe, probably a native Englishman, in a distinctive hand that betrays strong Norman influence.

At different times attempts have been made to associate the making of Great Domesday with one of two royal chaplains, Samson and Ranulph Flambard, but the case for either of them being responsible for directing the survey is weak. Galbraith pointed to the exceptional insertion by the main scribe of Samson's Somerset holding into Exon Domesday as one factor linking Samson with Great Domesday (Fig. 10), on the grounds that the Exon entry may perhaps have been prompted by his personal direction.[4] Also cited is the fact that Samson received the see of Worcester in 1096 as a reward for some undisclosed service to the Crown, but there is nothing to suggest that that service comprised or included the management of the Domesday survey.

The evidence concerning Ranulph Flambard, the second royal chaplain to have been considered, is even slighter.[5] This man, who was to become infamous as the ruthless servant of William II, was also rewarded with a bishopric—that of Durham in 1099. In Ranulph's case the nature and extent of his services are very much better known than Samson's and again there is nothing to connect him with the events of 1086–7. Nor is there any perceptible link between either of these two royal servants and the main scribe of Great Domesday: any further proposals for a candidate will have to establish such a link, whether he comes from within or without the royal household.

The Period of Writing

In 1954 the distinguished scribe Alfred Fairbank considered that the whole of Great Domesday could have been written at the rate of about six columns a day, and thus taken about 240 days in all. Finn considered this pace leisurely, but this author's own practical experiments have confirmed Fairbank's estimate.[6] It seems hardly possible that Great Domesday could have been started much before the middle of 1086, and if its production was abandoned at William I's death in September 1087, that would allow a little over a year for the work. As it appears that the main scribe probably had to edit, correct, and amend the text as well as to write it out, this seems a much more likely timetable than the period proposed in 1954, which ends with the departure of William for France in the late summer of 1086. The writings that were brought to William, as described in the Anglo-Saxon Chronicle, seem much more likely to have been versions of the circuit returns rather than all or part of Great Domesday itself.[7]

It also seems unlikely that the main scribe did manage regularly to write anything like six columns every day (between 280 and 300 lines). This is a speed of writing that exceeds the fastest known rate achieved in the Middle Ages. One late eighth-century manuscript was written at the rate of about 200 lines per day, and an early ninth-century one at about 150. These manuscripts were both written in minuscule and are similar to Great

[1] But see P. Chaplais, 'The Anglo-Saxon Chancery: from the Diploma to the Writ', *Prisca Munimenta: Studies in Archival and Administrative History presented to Dr A. E. J. Hollaender*, ed. F. Ranger (London, 1973), 43–62.

[2] This rare form of the abbreviation also occurs in Hereford Cathedral MS P.I. 10. See also A. C. de la Mare, 'A Probable Addition to the Bodleian's Holdings of Exeter Cathedral Manuscripts', *Bodleian Lib. Record*, 11 (1983), 79–88 and fig. 1; R. A. B. Mynors, *Durham Cathedral Manuscripts to the End of the Twelfth Century* (Oxford, 1939), pl. 25; E. Temple, 'A Note on the University College Life of St. Cuthbert', *Bodleian Lib. Record*, 9 (1978), 320–2 and pl. 24*a*. Whether all the late eleventh-century manuscripts of Norman style owned by the two places were actually made at them, has not yet been established.

[3] Biddle (ed.), *Winchester in the Early Middle Ages*, i. 292–305, 470–88. For government and local officials, see J. H. Round, 'Bernard, the King's Scribe', *EHR* 14 (1899), 417–30.

[4] V. H. Galbraith, 'Notes on the Career of Samson, Bishop of Worcester (1096–1112)', *EHR* 82 (1967), 86–101, and *Domesday Book: its Place in Administrative History*, 50–1. Against this see F. Barlow, *The Norman Conquest and Beyond* (London, 1983), 239.

[5] S. P. J. Harvey, 'Domesday Book and Anglo-Norman Governance', *TRHS* 5th ser., 25 (1975), 173–93.

[6] PRO, *Domesday Re-bound*, 34; Weldon Finn, *Liber Exoniensis*, 149.

[7] The passage is quoted by Loyn, 'Introduction', p. 1 above.

Domesday, if somewhat better executed. Both are examples of straight copying, but it should be borne in mind that the circumstances of the production of most early medieval manuscripts is uncertain. A later fifteenth-century scribe who wrote a humanistic minuscule (similar to Caroline) proudly described himself as a fast writer and stated in one manuscript that he could manage about thirty-four lines an hour (270 lines in an eight-hour day).[1]

There is evidence from the character of the writing that may point to the last entries to be written into Great Domesday. At the end of Staffordshire 250 there are two entries that are clearly late additions (Fig. 13). They come at the end of the second column; they are written rather formally in black ink; and they are unrubricated.[2] The first describes a holding in Sibford in Oxfordshire owned by William fitzCorbucion, and the second another holding in Drayton, also in Oxfordshire, belonging to one Turstin. This latter passage is one of a pair of double entries, its duplicate being entered in the Oxfordshire folio 160v. The one main difference between these two almost identical entries for Drayton is that the Oxfordshire entry lists Thorkill, and not Turstin, as the landholder.[3] Turstin cannot be identified, but Thorkill of Arden is a well-known figure because he was one of the very few prominent Englishmen who is recorded as still retaining his lands at the time of the survey in 1086. However, two years later in 1088 his property was finally forfeit and was given over to the newly created Earl of Warwick.[4] Such lands as Thorkill and his Arden descendants were to possess subsequently were held as tenants of the earls of Warwick, in the same way as Ardens also held Drayton from the earls of Warwick in the thirteenth century. It seems unlikely to be due only to coincidence that again in 1088 the lands of the other person who figures in these entries, William fitzCorbucion, appear similarly to have been taken and made over to the same nobleman,[5] for in the early thirteenth century this Sibford property was held by a descendant of William under a tenancy to the then Earl of Warwick. Might it be that both these entries for places in Oxfordshire, only a few miles apart, were inserted into Great Domesday as a result of the troubles of 1088? If so, their presence implies that the manuscript was still being worked upon during the year following the death of William I in September 1087.

Further support for this view may be found in a familiar Domesday conundrum: that of the possessions of Roger de Poitou. It is clear from the descriptions of his holdings in both Great and Little Domesday that

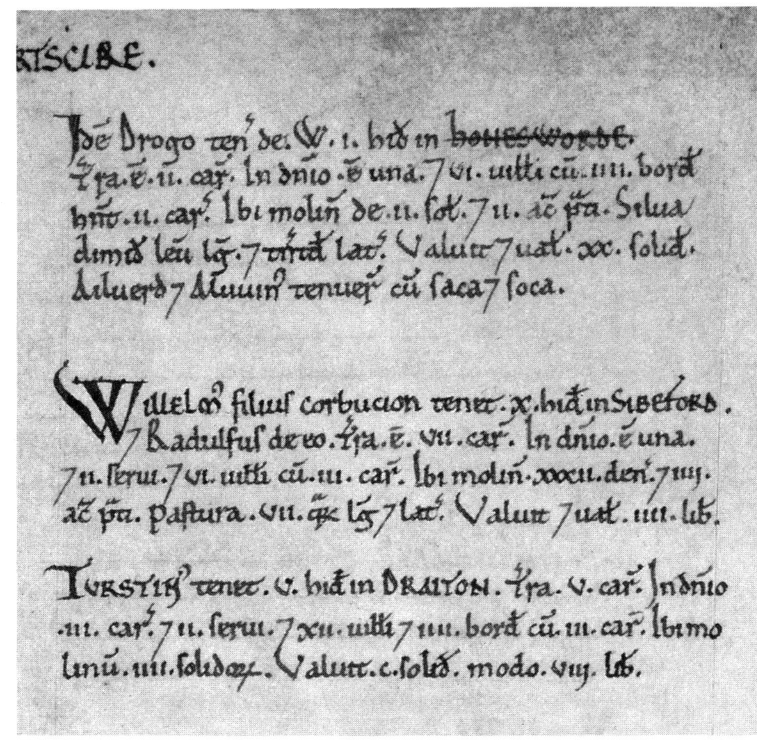

FIG. 13

Internal evidence suggests that the last two entries may have been written in 1088. (Staffs. 250, *slightly reduced*)

while the survey was in progress in 1086 William I was taking Roger's lands back into his own hands. Most of these estates were listed normally, except that his properties in Yorkshire were entered at the end of the county folios and his name does not appear among the list of tenants at the beginning. Another discrepancy occurs in both the Derbyshire and the Norfolk folios, where his lands are listed in the normal way, but carry a concluding statement that they were then in the hands of the king. However, in direct opposition to the latter, a holding of Roger's in Hampshire is entered in the margin of 39v among the king's possessions (Fig. 14), and is followed by a comment which states that Roger de Poitou holds the land *modo*, 'now'. This addition to Hampshire is clearly late as it is indeed in the margin; it is not rubricated; and it is carefully written, as are other, but not all, additions to the text. The circumstances were that Roger had gone abroad and did not come back to England until early in 1088 when his lands were eventually restored to him. The apparent confusion in the state of his holdings in Domesday Book therefore becomes perfectly clear if it can be accepted that this marginal entry in Hampshire was written into Great Domesday after his return in 1088.[6]

Not only the change of monarch in 1087, but also the confiscations made by William Rufus in 1088[7] would have rendered much of the information in Domesday Book out of date. So also would the process of selling off lands that began under the Conqueror and was continued by his son and successor.[8] Nevertheless, the

[1] E. A. Lowe (ed.), *Codices Latini Antiquiores*, Supplement (Oxford, 1971), no. 1773; W. M. Lindsay, *Palaeographia Latina*, ii (Oxford, 1923), 22; J. Kirchner, *Scriptura Latina Libraria* (Munich, 1955), no. 40*a* and pl.; T. de Marinis, *La Biblioteca Napoletana del Re d'Aragona*, i (Milan, 1952), 50.

[2] The writing of the two entries may be compared with that of the Hunts. *Clamores*, 208–208v, also partly unrubricated.

[3] For the Sibfords, see *VCH Oxfordshire*, x (1972), 234–5; for Drayton, ibid. ix (1969), 104.

[4] Previously Henry de Beaumont: G. E. Cokayne *et al.*, *The Complete Peerage*, 13 vols (London, 1910–59), 12, pt. 2 (1959), 358.

[5] *VCH Warwickshire*, i (1904), 278.

[6] Galbraith, *Making of Domesday Book*, 187–8; J. F. A. Mason, 'Roger de Montgomery and his Sons (1067–1102)', *TRHS* 5th ser., 13 (1963), 1–28; F. Barlow, *William Rufus* (Berkeley, 1983), 79, 84, 91.

[7] F. M. Stenton, *Anglo-Saxon England* (3rd edn., Oxford, 1971), 655–6 and 655 n. 1.

[8] D. Whitelock *et al.* (eds.), *The Anglo-Saxon Chronicle: A Revised Translation* (London, 1961), 163; Hallam, *Domesday Book through Nine Centuries*, 147.

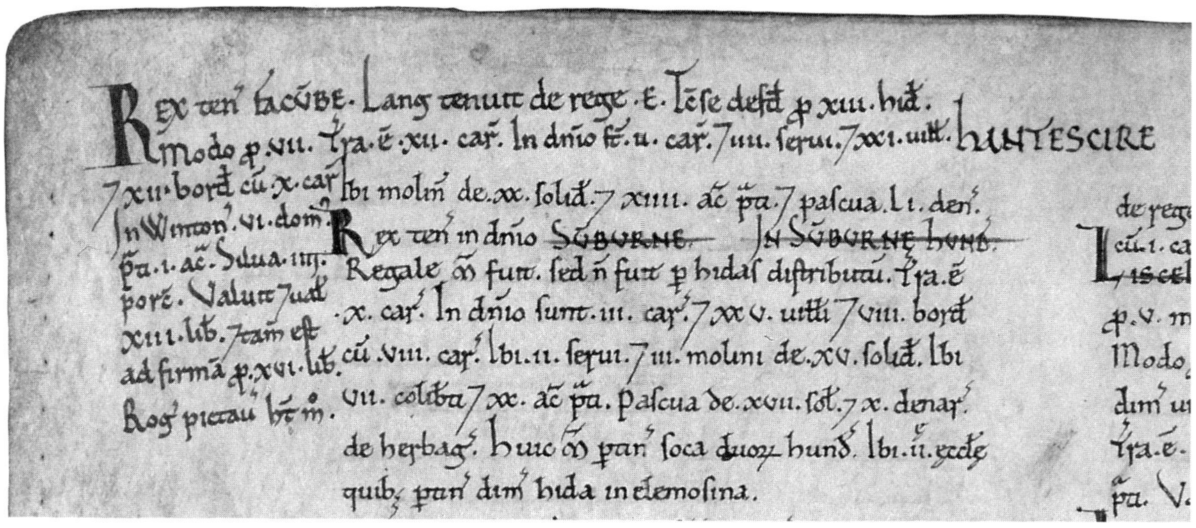

FIG. 14

Another late addition to Great Domesday. Among the holdings of the king in Hampshire, the entry for Faccombe had been omitted, and was subsequently written in the margin. The last line reads *Rog(er) Pictav(ensis) h(abe)t m(od)o*, 'Roger de Poitou has it now'.

(Hants 39v, *actual size*)

possibility that Great Domesday was still being worked over in 1088 is not a new suggestion, though clarification is most likely to follow upon a re-examination of the character of the writing, especially that of the obvious additions to the text.

BINDING

When, ultimately, work ceased on the manuscript, it may have been handed over to a binder immediately, although it is also possible that it remained in unbound quires for some time. Nevertheless there are some physical signs which point to an early date for the first binding, besides the erratic description of Great Domesday as *liber* 'a book' from about 1100.[1] It seems likely that the earliest binding is of eleventh-century date.

The principal evidence consists of the perforations in the spine-folds of the sheets, and the actual boards that were taken off in the nineteenth century and preserved. The perforations (known as sewing-stations) occur where the primary thread passed from the centres of the quires to the spine exterior and around the sewing supports. These supports, passing horizontally across the spine, would be attached to boards probably covered with skin.

Each of the several bindings of Great Domesday (there are at least six) used new sewing-stations. However, the first binder made a series of tiny holes (showing as dark dots in the facsimile) about 5 mm. from the spine-folds to mark up the position of the five primary sewing-stations.[2] The holes appear in every quire and seem to have been made from the recto of the first leaf of the folded quire to the verso of the last leaf, as shown in Fig. 15*a*. The number of sewing-stations and their configuration make it virtually certain that they are incidental products of the earliest binding.

The marking-up of the position of the primary sewing-stations did not include the end-band stations at the head and tail, but fortunately some of the end-band threads have left stains on the leaves in the centre of a number of quires which are just visible (Fig. 15*b*). This thread was blue but it is likely that the original end-bands alternated between blue and plain thread, the latter leaving no stain. The internal sewing pattern is shown in Fig. 15*c*, where the gap between the kettle stations and the two inner end-band stations is notable. It is a pattern that is neither rare nor common, but its recovery is important for it is different from that of Little Domesday.

The boards of the first binding would almost certainly have been of oak and covered with alum-tawed skin.[3] If Great Domesday was written in the royal household it seems unlikely that the binding was made there too. At a time when the private ownership of books was very limited there were probably no binders to be found outside monastic houses. It may be that Great Domesday was first bound in a monastic scriptorium, near to wherever the manuscript was written. It is notable that the distinctive internal sewing pattern has not been found in any eleventh-century Winchester manuscript, of which almost all have now been examined. Possibly the scribe who wrote the quire signatures on the last ten quires of Great Domesday was the first binder of the manuscript.[4]

The subsequent bindings may be dealt with briefly. The original binding survived up to about 1500, when

[1] Galbraith, *Domesday Book: its Place in Administrative History*, 103–4; Hallam, *Domesday Book through Nine Centuries*, 35.

[2] This manner of marking up has rarely been noticed in print. Examples were cited by R. Powell, 'The Lichfield St Chad's Gospels: Repair and Rebinding 1961–1962', *The Library*, 5th ser., 20 (London, 1965), 259–65, on p. 262. I have seen a number of examples, and two Continental examples are noticed in L. Gilissen, *La Reliure Occidentale antérieure à 1400* (Brepols-Turnhout, 1983), 91, 137 and pls. xli, lix.

[3] English boards are almost invariably made from oak and in the eleventh and twelfth centuries covered with alum-tawed skin.

[4] For binding structures, see G. Pollard's pioneer papers, 'The Construction of English Twelfth-Century Bindings', *The Library*, 5th ser., 17 (London, 1962), 1–22; 'Some Anglo-Saxon Bindings', *The Book Collector*, 24 (London, 1975), 130–59, and 'Describing Medieval Bookbindings', *Medieval Learning and Literature*, eds. Alexander and Gibson, 130–59. For post-medieval binding, see B. Middleton, *A History of English Craft Bookbinding Techniques* (2nd edn., London, 1977).

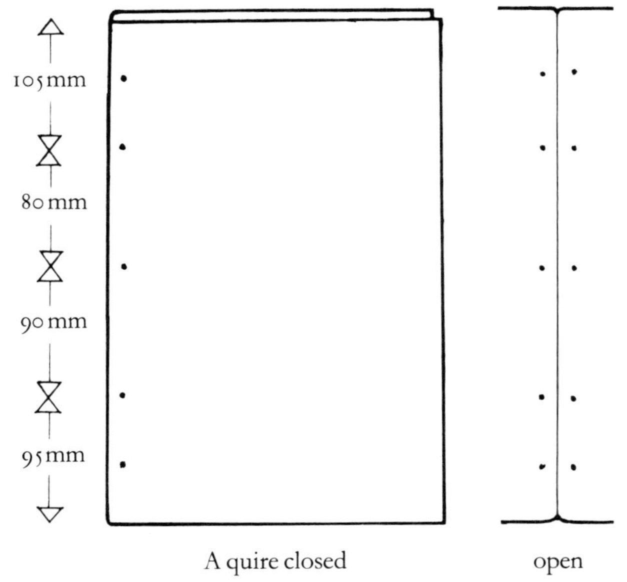

a. The primary sewing-stations. Five guide holes were pricked through all quires of Great Domesday to establish the position of the primary sewing-stations. The holes at the top and bottom marked the kettle sewing-stations through which the primary sewing thread was to be passed from one quire to the next. The remaining three holes marked the position of the spine-bands which divided the height of the book into four roughly equal parts.

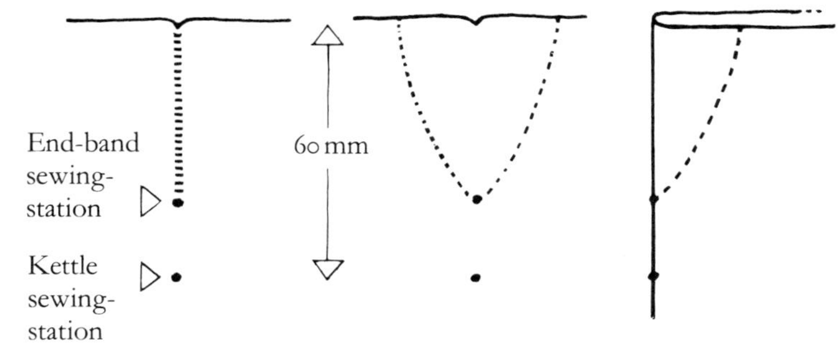

b. The end-band sewing-stations. Two additional sewing-stations were positioned outside the two kettle stations at the head and tail. The end-band threads were either looped round the edges of the sheets, or possibly were passed through further sewing-stations pierced near the edges which are now lost, having been trimmed off in the course of a subsequent binding. Some end-band threads frayed and broke loose so that they were only attached at the inner end-band stations, and stand away from the spine-fold. Several such threads were caught between the pages of the book when closed and have left V-shaped stains on the centre sheets of certain quires, notably 11 (Dorset), 12 (Som. 1), 14 (Devon. 1), 27 (Beds.), 32 (Shrops.), and 34 (Ches. 2).

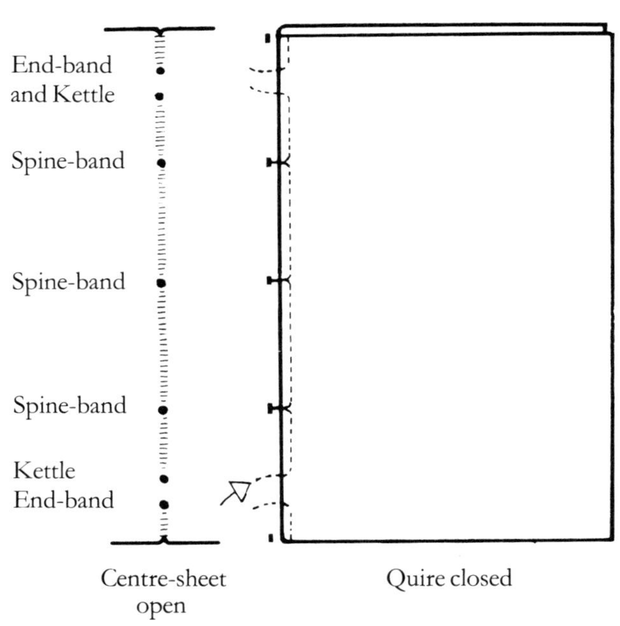

c. Entering the quire from the outside, the primary thread was passed through the lower kettle station and then pulled up inside the fold to emerge through the lowermost spine-band station. Here it was passed round a sewing support, returned inside again and drawn up to the next spine-band station, and so on upwards until it was finally pulled out at the upper kettle station and passed into the next quire. The end-band threads were passed round two end-band cores in a similar fashion to the primary thread and spine-bands.

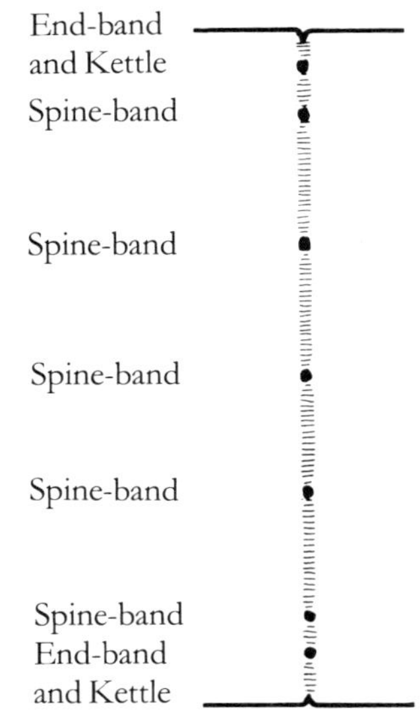

d. The internal sewing pattern of the 'Tudor' binding (*c.*1500.) In this five spine-bands were employed instead of three, and the two kettle sewing-stations were combined with the end-band stations.

FIG. 15

a, b, c. The first binding of Great Domesday Book (probably eleventh century). *d.* The 'Tudor' binding (*c.* 1500).

the manuscript was resewn and rebound with boards of beech (unusual in English bindings) which were covered with tanned leather. The primary sewing of this binding has left clear stains in the spine-folds of the centre sheets of the quires (Fig. 15*d*). Toward the end of the sixteenth century, or early in the seventeenth, some metal furniture was applied to the exterior of the boards (corner-pieces and a central piece on both boards) and the spine covering was repaired with new skin, probably doe-skin. This all survived until the early nineteenth century. In 1819 the manuscript was resewn and rebound, and following the making of the nineteenth-century facsimile, bound again in 1869 by Rivière of London. In the twentieth century the manuscript was repaired, resewn, and rebound in 1952 by the Public Record Office, and most recently in 1985 by the same agency, when Great Domesday was divided into two volumes.[1]

LITTLE DOMESDAY BOOK

General and Physical Observations

Little Domesday is not at all like Great Domesday in size, layout, script, or content. Its formulae and orthography are quite different from those of the larger volume and it is better compared with Exon Domesday in its scope and purpose. Both Little Domesday and Exon represent the writing-up of local circuit returns for delivery to a central bureau. Little Domesday is generally agreed to be the final circuit return for the eastern counties of Norfolk, Suffolk, and Essex, and since its contents were never entered into Great Domesday, it was retained intact to complete the coverage of the survey as an independent companion volume to the main text. Exon Domesday, on the other hand, has been thought to comprise an early version of the returns from the South-Western Circuit from which a fair copy was made, and that it was this lost recension from which Great Domesday was compiled. However, work of more recent date has suggested that the putative fair copy in fact never existed and common sense would confirm this view.[2]

The parchment of Little Domesday was made from sheep and is of poorer quality than that of Great Domesday. Its colour varies from white to greyish, and its thickness also lacks consistency. The thicker sheets were often put on the outsides of quires. Occasionally there are 'bites' missing from the edges of the sheets; irregularities present in the edges of the skins. The quires are arranged in a regular manner with the hair sides on the outsides and they usually consist of four sheets only, as in Fig. 2 above.

The sheets were pricked and ruled in the same way as Great Domesday and most of the pricking survives. There are four ruling patterns, which usually have twenty-four or twenty-five lines per page, but occasionally there are more or fewer, ranging between twenty-three and twenty-seven lines (Fig. 16). The ferrogallotannate ink of the script is generally black and the red is red lead, occasionally tending towards orange.[3]

There is a list of contents at the beginning of each of the three counties and the arrangement of the entries is similar to that of Great Domesday, though occasionally somewhat muddled. There is no reason to suppose that

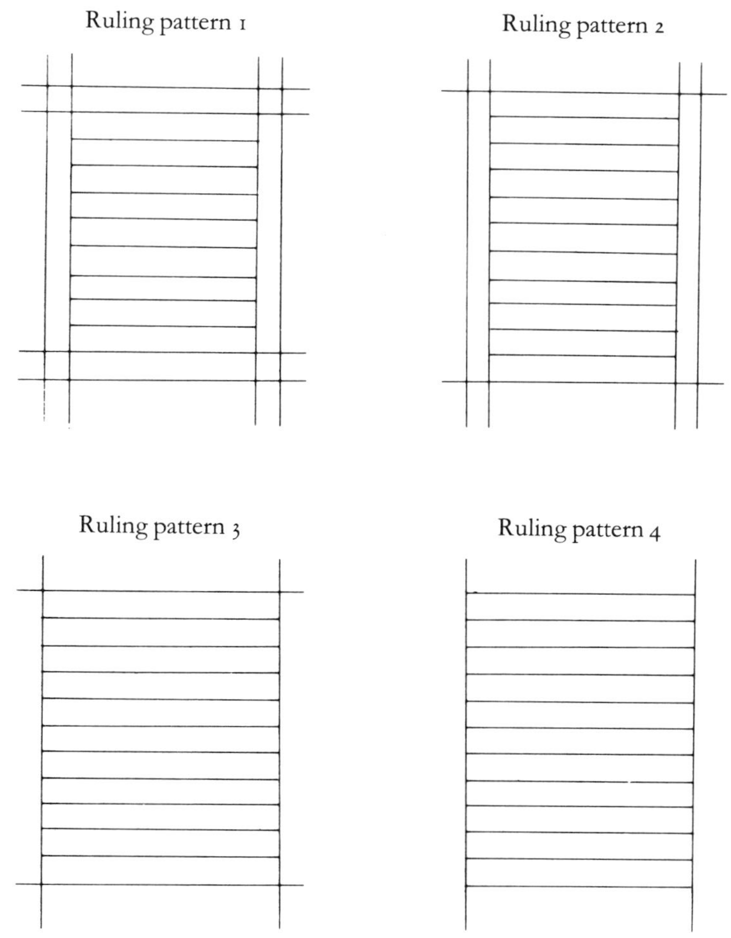

Fig. 16

The ruling patterns of Little Domesday Book. No. 1 is usual for the last part of Suffolk and no. 2 for the first part of Essex. Nos. 3 and 4 are most frequent in the last part of Essex, in Norfolk, and in the first part of Suffolk. There is considerable variation within each pattern.

the manuscript was written in the order in which the quires are now bound.[4]

The Scribes and their Location

It appears that seven scribes worked on the manuscript of Little Domesday; none are comparable to the two scribes of Great Domesday. One wrote an undistinguished hand of English type and the rest equally undistinguished hands of Norman type. The greater part of Little Domesday was written by only three scribes and each of them seems to have been responsible for correcting his own stints, either by erasure or by insertion. The first principal scribe wrote most of Essex (1 *verso*–103v, Fig. 17*a*);[5] the second the first part of Norfolk (109v–156) and most of the first part of Suffolk (281v–356, interrupted on 289–290v, Fig. 17*b* and *c*).[6] The third wrote the last part of Suffolk (356v–449v, Fig. 17*d*). The scribe responsible for the next largest contribution wrote part of Norfolk (222v–273v to line 6),[7] and the rest made occasional contributions throughout. The scribe with the English hand wrote

[1] For the post-1500 bindings, except for the last, see PRO, *Domesday Re-bound*, 17–20. The date of the first nineteenth-century binding has only recently been established: see Hallam, *Domesday Book through Nine Centuries*, 150–1. Also ibid. 29, 159–161, 172, and pls. 10, 68, 78, 79 for the bindings, including the last.

[2] For Little Domesday and Exon Domesday, see Galbraith, *Domesday Book: its Place in Administrative History*, 56–72; Thorn and Thorn (eds.), *Domesday Book: Devon*. For all the Domesday satellite manuscripts, see Clarke, 'The Domesday Satellites', 50–70.

[3] Gettens and Stout, *Painting Materials, a Short Encyclopaedia*, 152–4; Thompson, *Materials and Techniques*, 100–2.

[4] R. Welldon Finn, *Domesday Studies: the Eastern Counties* (London, 1967), 64–78; Galbraith, *Making of Domesday Book*, 32.

[5] PRO, *Domesday Re-bound*, pl. v, 1 and 3. The titles at the beginning of Essex 1 are probably by this scribe.

[6] PRO, *Domesday Re-bound*, pl. v, 4 and pl. vi, 9. The cancelled titles in Essex 9 and 17, the title at the head of Essex 49, the titles at the beginning of Norfolk 109 and Suffolk 281, the titles in Suffolk 292, and the cancelled ones on Suffolk 372 are all by this scribe.

[7] Rumble, 'Palaeography of the Domesday Manuscripts', pl. 3.3.

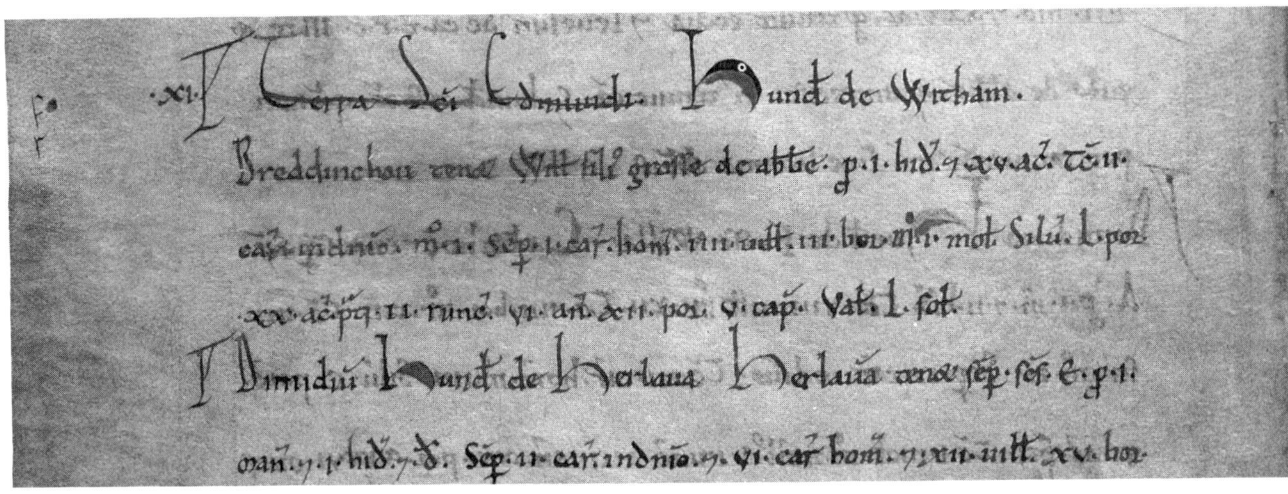

a. The scribe for most of Essex. Note the footed form of his *paragraphos* sign. The sign for *7 (et)* has a wavy upperstroke and, as in the bottom line, its downward stroke usually descends below the base-line. The *c*- shaped addition to *p (pro)* in line 2 is very low down on the descending stroke.

(Essex 19v, *actual size*)

b. The scribe of the first part of Norfolk, formal title-page. The upward finishing strokes to the *m* and the pointed *o* and *e* in the left column strongly suggest that the scribe was a Norman. The *g* in *bigot*, line 1, is particularly well formed, and the *f* is usually long as in *dapifer*, line 4, and *fili(us)*, line 3.

(Norfolk 109, *actual size*)

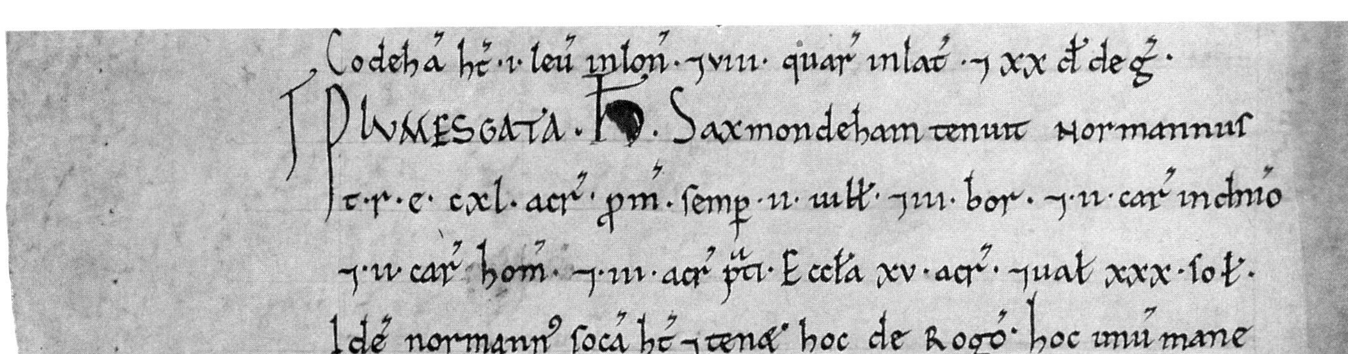

c. The scribe of the first part of Norfolk, normal text. His is a very plain *paragraphos* sign and his *7* for *et* has a long, vertical descender. The *g* is less carefully formed than in *(b)* above but is clearly by the same hand. This is the best hand of the three scribes.

(Suffolk 338v, *actual size*)

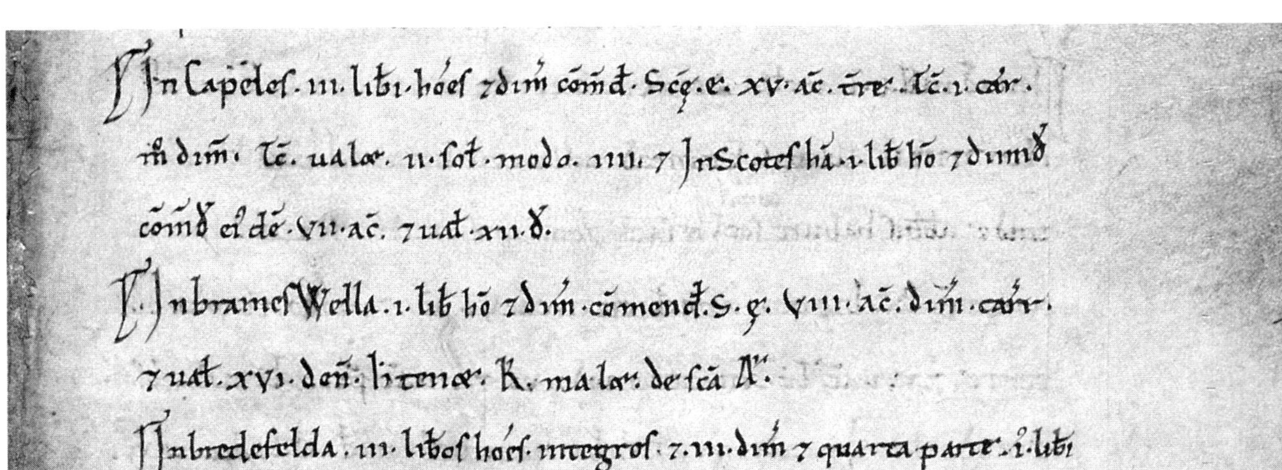

d. The scribe of the last part of Suffolk. He uses a more florid *paragraphos*, and his *7* for *et* has a distinct foot resting on the base-line, as does also the long *s* and *f* on the bottom line.

(Suffolk 387, *actual size*)

Fig. 17

The three principal scribes of Little Domesday Book.

FIG. 18

The dated colophon of Little Domesday, written in red, on Suffolk 450: 'In the one thousand and eighty-sixth year from the Incarnation of Our Lord, and in the twentieth [year] of the reign of William there was made this survey, not only through these three counties, but also through others.' *(actual size)*

the last few leaves of Essex (104–107v),[1] and a few leaves in Norfolk (157–159v). The first of the three principal scribes wrote in all three counties and the second in the last two.

Two further scribes who had not worked on the text wrote the running titles. The position of the titles so close to the head of the text suggests that they may not have been part of the original plan, but were added after Little Domesday was completed and possibly even after it was bound. The second of these two scribes probably also wrote the dated colophon on Suffolk 450 at the end of the book (Fig. 18). The evidence of this important inscription is that this manuscript was written in 1086, and that it was therefore completed before Great Domesday.[2]

While Little Domesday is largely the work of the three principal scribes, two principal scribes were responsible for Exon Domesday.[3] The organization of labour is quite different in each book, for in Little Domesday long stints were the rule, whereas in Exon they were very short. This may well reflect the different working habits in the centres that produced these two documents, of which Little Domesday was certainly the more carefully planned. Both manuscripts were presumably written in important centres either within, or very close to, the counties and circuits they describe, but while there is some evidence to suggest that Exon was produced at Salisbury[4] there is none that points to the location of the Little Domesday scriptorium. What makes both manuscripts so especially rewarding is the wealth of detail they contain, their closeness to the original circuit returns, and in the case of Exon, the manner in which it was edited and shortened in the writing of Great Domesday.

BINDING

Little Domesday was marked up in the same manner as Great Domesday, with small holes a few millimetres from the spine-folds for the four primary sewing-stations. However, the internal sewing pattern is different from that of Great Domesday. It seems probable that Little Domesday was also first bound in the eleventh century, perhaps in the county where it was written, before it was sent away. However, the binding did not last long and the manuscript was resewn and recovered in or soon after 1200 (and probably before about 1225) to four sewing supports and possibly without end-bands, as shown in Fig. 19. The configuration of the sewing supports is unusual.[5] They were made of alum-tawed skin of which parts may still be seen in the oak boards used in this binding, which are still extant. The boards were re-used (and probably reshaped) in 1320 when Little Domesday was resewn again and covered once more with alum-tawed skin, stained pink on the exterior faces of the boards. It is recorded that William the bookbinder of London was paid 3*s*. 4*d*. for the work.[6]

The subsequent bindings parallel those of Great Domesday except that the binding of *c.* 1500 did not use new boards, but merely covered the earlier alum-tawed skin with tanned leather. Metal furniture was added to the boards and the spine covering repaired. Two

[1] PRO, *Domesday Re-bound*, pl. v, 2 and pl. vi, 5.

[2] The significance of the inscription is discussed in Galbraith, *Making of Domesday Book*, 180–5.

[3] R. Welldon Finn, 'The Exeter Domesday and its Construction', *Bull. of the John Rylands Lib.* 51 (Manchester, 1958), 360–87, where the figure of about a dozen scribes is given; Welldon Finn, *Liber Exoniensis*, 27–32. My brief examination of the manuscript confirms Finn's analysis of many changes of hand. For a reproduction of a page of Exon Domesday, see H. C. Darby and R. Welldon Finn, *The Domesday Geography of South-West England* (Cambridge, 1967), frontis.

[4] See p. 99 n. 3 above.

[5] I know only one similar example, an early thirteenth-century English manuscript: Oxford, Jesus College MS 94.

[6] The pink staining was almost certainly made from kermes, one of the oldest dyes known to man: see Gettens and Stout, *Painting Materials, a Short Encyclopaedia*, 123. For William the bookbinder, see PRO, *Domesday Re-bound*, 38, and for the boards, ibid. pl. viii. An examination by the carbon 14 method to determine the age of the boards has suggested that they are somewhat older than the date of the binding. For the results of the scientific analysis of all the constituents of the medieval and post-medieval bindings of Great and Little Domesday, see H. Forde, *Domesday Preserved* (HMSO, London, 1986). I am grateful to Dr Helen Forde for telling me of the initial results of the various tests prior to this publication.

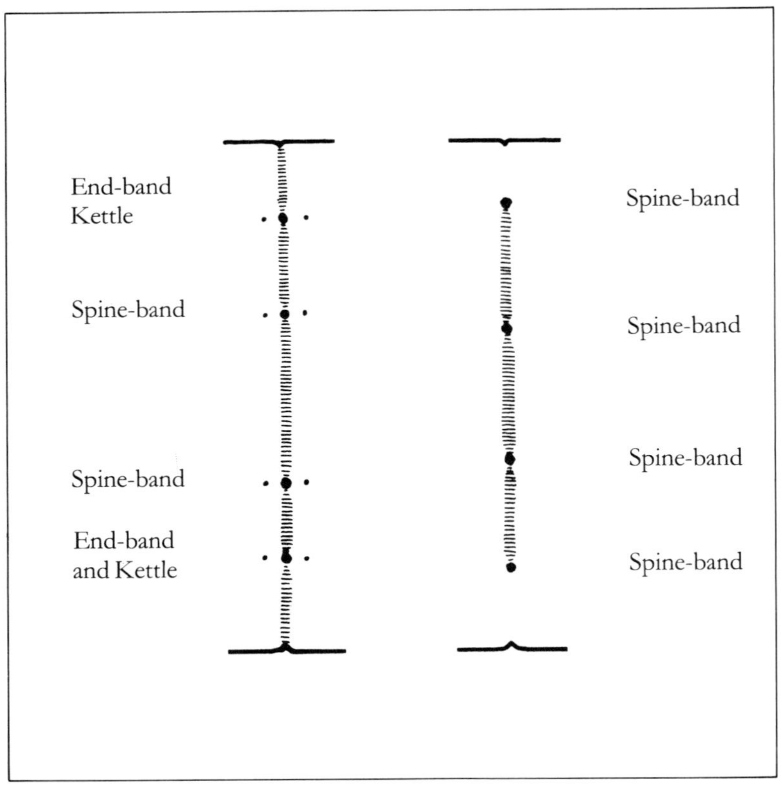

FIG. 19

The internal sewing patterns of Little Domesday Book. In the earliest binding, *left* (probably late 11th century) pricked guide holes established the position of each of the primary sewing-stations. The two spine-bands divided the height of the manuscript into three roughly equal parts. In the later binding, *right* (probably early 13th century), the outermost spine-bands were situated close to the edges of the leaves and it is uncertain whether end-bands were used at all.

nineteenth- and two twentieth-century rebindings followed, and in 1985 the manuscript was separated into three volumes, each containing one county.

The Domesday manuscripts are the physical remains of one of the greatest medieval enterprises. The energy of the Norman conquerors, allied to the system of administration developed by the English, speaks directly from every page. But it must be remembered that the manuscripts are also monuments to a handful of long-dead craftsmen. Many of their secrets, and the secrets of the whole survey, remain to be discovered. A modern historian has remarked that records will 'only speak when they are spoken to, and they will not talk to strangers'.[1] By the publication of the present facsimile it will be possible to look at and hear from the past, and if we are humble and curious, the manuscripts will speak to us all.

[1] C. R. Cheney, *Medieval Texts and Studies* (Oxford, 1973), 8.

AUTHOR'S NOTE

I am grateful to the Keeper of Public Records, Dr G. H. Martin, for inviting me to examine the manuscripts of Great and Little Domesday and to report on them in connection with the Domesday exhibition of 1986.

In preparing this study I am especially grateful, for their help and encouragement, to Mrs Caroline Thorn and Dr Elizabeth Hallam. For their help in making the Domesday manuscripts available to me I am grateful to Dr Helen Forde, Mrs Jane Cox, Mr Don Gubbins, Mr Frank Haynes, and Mr John Abbott of the Public Record Office.

For allowing me to see books and manuscripts in their care I am especially grateful to Mrs Audrey Erskine, Archivist, Exeter Cathedral Library; Miss P. E. Morgan, Honorary Librarian, Hereford Cathedral Library; Mrs B. Carpenter Turner, Librarian, Winchester Cathedral Library; and Dr P. D. Partner, Fellows Librarian, Winchester College; as well as to the librarians and staff at the British Library, the Bodleian Library, Cambridge University Library, and the Library of the University of London.

I owe my knowledge of the Hereford manuscript (Hereford Cathedral P.I. 10) to Mrs Tessa Webber, to whom I am grateful not only for allowing me to publish her discovery but also for discussing the hand of the main scribe with me.

When most of this Special Study was in typescript I discovered that Dr Pierre Chaplais had long been working on the problem of the person responsible for the management of the survey and the location of the scriptorium where the main scribe worked. At the time of writing, Dr Chaplais's views are more developed and advanced than my own views and are soon to be published. I am deeply grateful to him for his kindness and generosity in our exchanges of views and material.

M. GULLICK

SELECT BIBLIOGRAPHY

M. T. Clanchy, *From Memory to Written Record: England 1066–1307* (London, 1979)

H. Forde, *Domesday Preserved* (HMSO, London, 1986)

V. H. Galbraith, *The Making of Domesday Book* (Oxford, 1961)

D. Jackson, *The Story of Writing* (London, New York, 1981)

Public Record Office (abbr. PRO), *Domesday Re-bound* (HMSO, London, 1954)

A. R. Rumble, 'The Palaeography of the Domesday Manuscripts', *Domesday Book: A Reassessment*, ed. P. H. Sawyer (London, 1985), 28–49.

G. Zarnecki *et al.* (eds.), *English Romanesque Art 1066–1200* (Arts Council, London, 1984)

XV. MARGINAL NOTES AND SIGNS IN DOMESDAY BOOK

CAROLINE THORN

THE content of Great and Little Domesday Book has been much studied in the last century or so, but until recently very little has been written about the manuscripts themselves,[1] their layout, the method of their inscription, and the use to which these important volumes have been put throughout the past nine hundred years.[2] More especially, the marginalia of both manuscripts have been almost totally neglected; and although there are some fleeting references to certain letters and signs in a handful of general books and articles, no systematic attempt has been made to explore the significance of the whole. Yet some of these marginalia can tell us much about the manner in which the scribes went about their work, how they checked their text and accommodated information not available or omitted at the time of writing. Other marginalia reveal how the manuscripts were used in the succeeding centuries, both when Domesday Book was still a working record and also later, when it came to be regarded as an historical monument, an object of antiquarian research.

This tendency to ignore the study of Domesday as a manuscript was reinforced by the publication of Abraham Farley's excellent transcription in 1783. Before that time antiquarians wishing to consult Domesday Book either had to obtain permission to view the volumes themselves, or had to rely upon transcripts especially made for them or for their predecessors. Furthermore, the Ordnance Survey photozincographic facsimile of 1861–3, published in county volumes at a relatively moderate price, meant that the majority of historians and scholars no longer felt the need to consult the manuscripts at all. But these two admirable publications have the serious drawback for the Domesday student that material was omitted from both. Farley was inclined to eliminate anything which he believed to be later than the main text, although he was not always consistent in this,[3] and it is far from clear in his edition what was actually written in the margins. Moreover, the photozincographic process employed for the Ordnance Survey facsimile did not reproduce many of the fainter marginalia, and distorted the outlines of many of the rest. Also, although more annotations were included than in Farley, a decision was taken to mask out most of those dating from the sixteenth and seventeenth centuries. In the present facsimile, however, nothing has been deliberately omitted and for the first time the reader can appreciate the variety of the marginalia and begin to understand their function.

A marginalium is easy to define, owing to the presence of clear scorings made with a hard point on the folios of both manuscripts in order to delimit the text. In Great Domesday this framework consisted of horizontal rulings at the top and bottom of the page, and four, seven, or eight vertical lines which marked out the two columns.[4] In a little over half the counties further horizontal lines were ruled as a guide for the writing, varying in number per column. Little Domesday has either two or four vertical rulings, defining the single columns on each page,[5] and is scored with an average of twenty-five lines. The scribes of both volumes[6] for the most part wrote within this frame, so that whatever is written outside can be classed as a marginalium, except where the scribe of the main text inadvertently overran these limits to complete a word or phrase.

The incidence of marginalia varies from county to county,[7] but as a whole the Domesday manuscripts have more written outside the rulings than other contemporary documents.[8] The reason for this is threefold, the first and most important being the nature of the Domesday survey and the manner in which it was carried out. The Anglo-Saxon machinery for the collection of geld must already have existed with lists of tenants, their manors and the hundred in which they lay, besides their assessment and obligations, and these were undoubtedly used as a starting-point by those conducting the Conqueror's

[1] The main work is that of the Public Record Office (abbr. PRO), *Domesday Re-bound* (HMSO, London, 1954), supplemented by H. Forde, *Domesday Preserved* (HMSO, London, 1986).

[2] But see E. M. Hallam, *Domesday Book through Nine Centuries* (London, 1986).

[3] For example, he printed a few, but by no means all, of the marginal *fs* (on which see section 2(*a*), p. 129 below).

[4] See the examples illustrated in M. Gullick, 'The Great and Little Domesday Manuscripts', Special Study XIV, p. 96, Fig. 6, above.

[5] However, the Landholders' Lists are ruled for four columns (Essex) and three columns (Norfolk and Suffolk). For the ruling patterns see Gullick, 'Great and Little Domesday Manuscripts', p. 109, Fig. 16, above.

[6] There was only one scribe for virtually all the main text of Great Domesday, but probably seven for Little Domesday; see Gullick, 'Great and Little Domesday Manuscripts', pp. 98–104, 109–11 above.

[7] Cornwall has very little in the margins, whereas Lincs., Yorks., Notts., Northants, Glos., Hants, and the three counties forming Little Domesday have a great many marginal additions and signs, both contemporary with, and later than, Domesday Book.

[8] Later abbreviations of Domesday Book often had many annotations, added both at the time of writing or soon after, and later by those who came to possess them (and for whom they may have been made). The Exchequer *Abbreviatio*, made in the first half of the thirteenth century, in particular has several marginalia of a similar nature to those in Domesday Book; see Hallam, *Domesday Book through Nine Centuries*, 42 ff. However, no systematic attempt was made to 'update' Domesday Book with the names of later tenants or further to identify holdings, as was the case with the twelfth-century copy of Domesday for Herefordshire; see V. H. Galbraith and J. Tait (eds.), *Herefordshire Domesday circa 1160–1170*, Pipe Roll Soc. 63, ns. 25 (London, 1950).

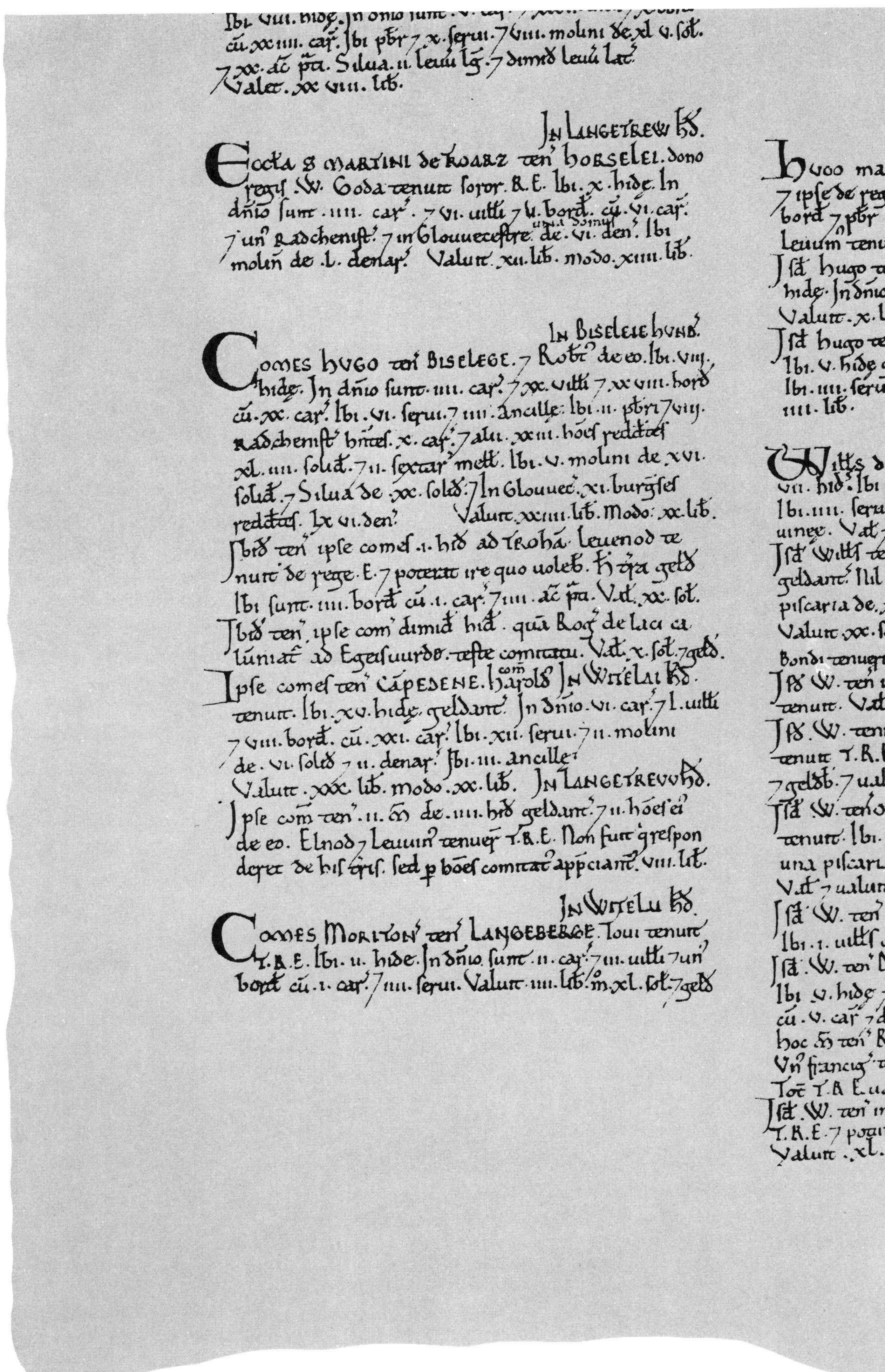

FIG. 1

The order of writing and of annotating a complex part of Glos. 166v: stage 1 (*actual size*).

The main scribe completed the chapters of ecclesiastical land with the single-entry chapter for the Church of Troarn. Then, after erasing a line of text, he continued in the normal way with the holdings of the principal laymen beginning with Earl Hugh of Chester and Robert Count of Mortain.

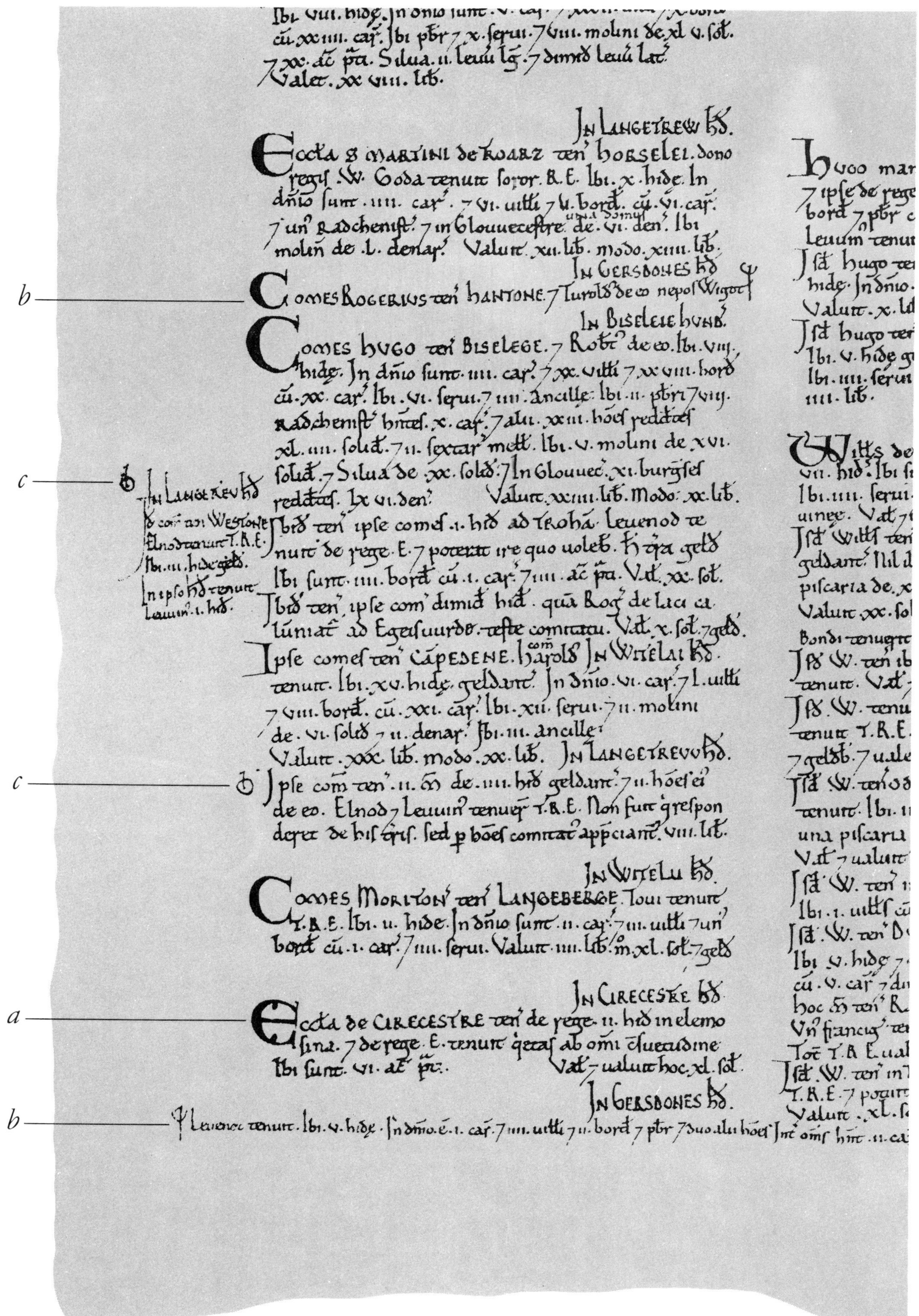

FIG. 2

The order of writing and of annotating a complex part of Glos. 166v: stage 2 (*actual size*).

a. The main scribe then discovered that there were two more ecclesiastical tenants to include: the Church of Cirencester and Regenbald the priest. The former he added at the end of the column, after the Count of Mortain's single entry, and, apart from the hundred heading, the latter at the top of the next column. He would clarify the order when he rubricated the Gloucestershire folios later on.

b. He also discovered that Earl Roger of Shrewsbury had land that he had so far omitted, for which there was now insufficient room. His only course was to crowd in as much text as possible in the space caused by the erasure between the Church of Troarn's land and that of Earl Hugh, and to continue the entry along the bottom line across the page. He then connected the two separate elements of the entry with the transposition sign ⚲.

c. Perhaps at about this time additional information concerning the last of Earl Hugh's holdings came to hand. The scribe had to write the extra matter in the margin, and used another transposition sign ♁ to relate it to its entry within the column.

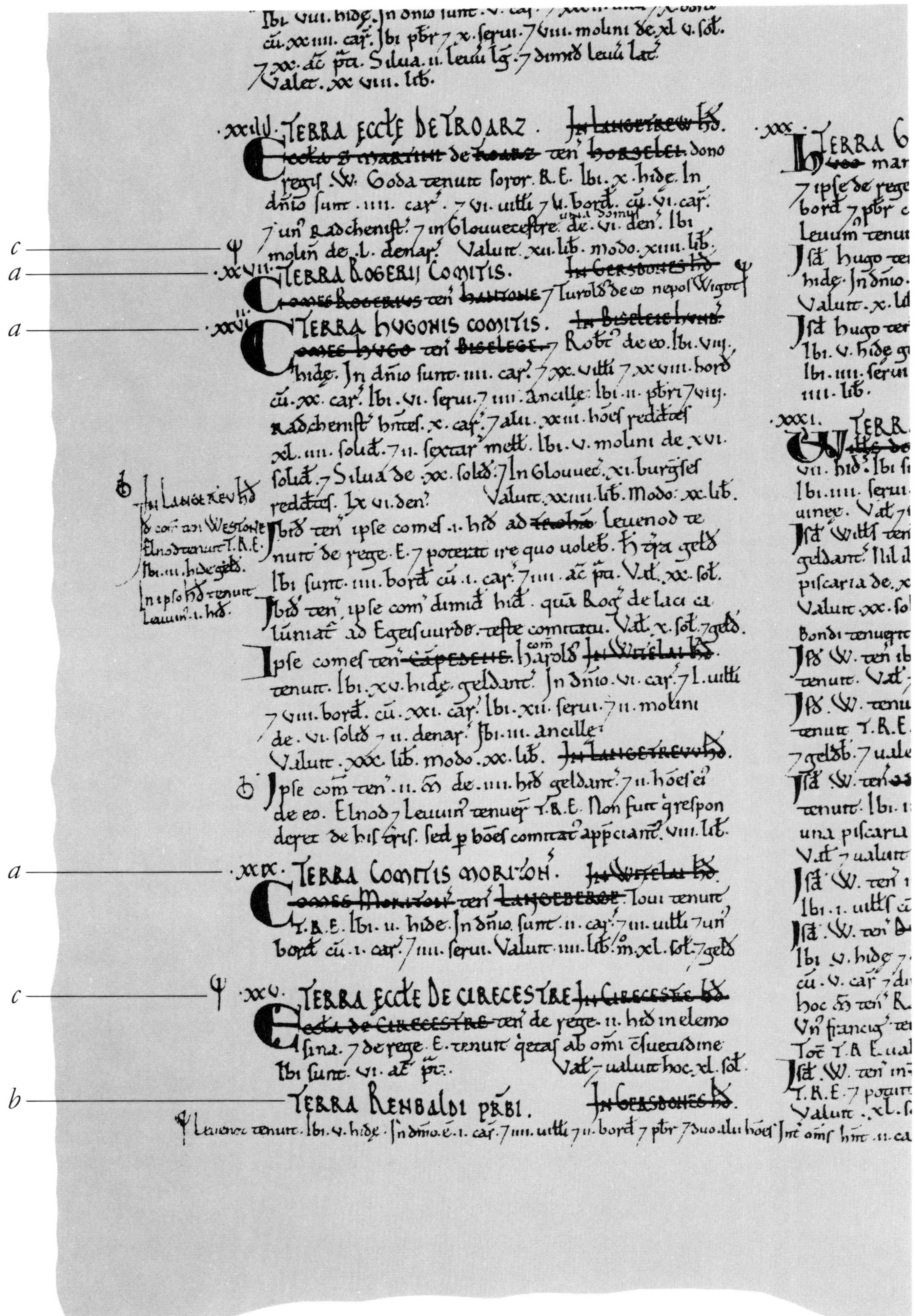

FIG. 3

The order of writing and of annotating a complex part of Glos. 166v: stage 3 (*actual size*).

When this folio came to be rubricated, also by the main scribe, he filled in the chapter headings in rustic capitals and allotted a running number to each.

a. He began by numbering Earl Roger's fief XXV, Earl Hugh's XXVI, and the Count of Mortain's XXVII. However, on reaching the land of the Church of Cirencester at the bottom of the column he realized his mistake. He then added II to both XXV and XXVI to make them XXVII and XXVIII, and erased the VII of XXVII to alter it to XXIX.

b. He had already written 'In Garsdon Hundred' at the bottom of this column, presumably before he realised that the lands of Regenbald the priest formed a separate fief from those of his Church of Cirencester. Accordingly he wrote the chapter heading *TERRA RENBALDI PR(ES)B(ITER)I* at the bottom of this column also, but put its correct number, XXVI, up at the top of the next column (not illustrated here), where the entries for Regenbald's holdings actually begin.

c. For additional clarity he inscribed the transposition sign ⚲, also in red, beside the misplaced Chapter XXV, and also beside XXVI at the top of the next column (not here illustrated). He then drew the matching ⚲ at the end of Chapter XXIIII, further up, to show that both should rightly be positioned after that point among the other ecclesiastical holdings.

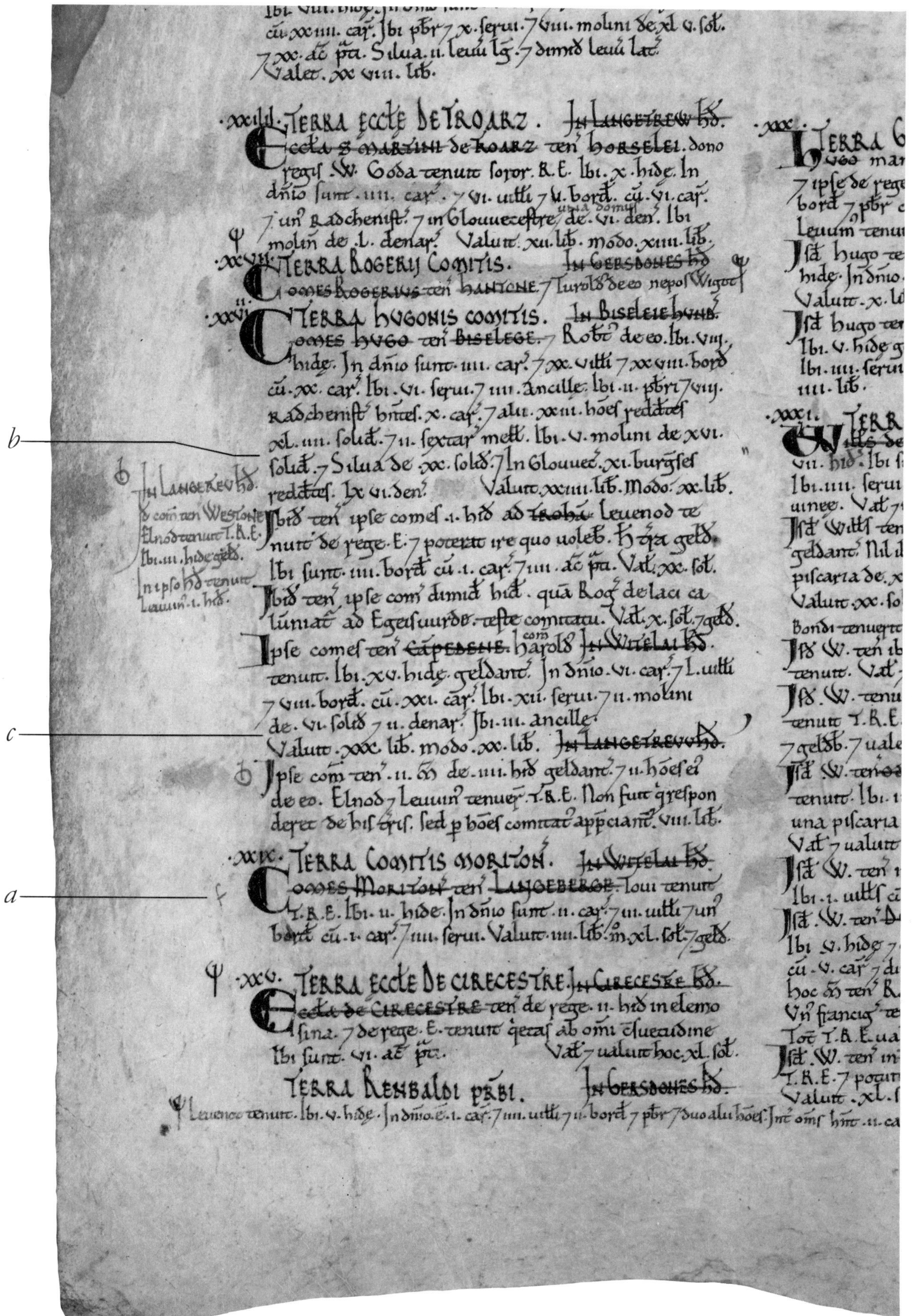

FIG. 4

The order of writing and of annotating a complex part of Glos. 166v: stage 4 (*actual size*).

The final appearance of the folio. Probably later in the Middle Ages, and perhaps at different times, clerks using the manuscript have inscribed their various annotations and checking marks in the margins.

a. The small ʄ beside the Count of Mortain's land at Longborough possibly indicates that the Count had made a return for it himself, or that it had become a knight's fee in later times. However, the ʄ may be contemporary with Domesday Book.

b. The unobtrusive ɲ in the centre margin may notify the fact that the entry beside it on the right did not make a return.

c. The comma-shaped sign ɔ further down, which also refers to the right column, is a checking mark possibly written as late as the fourteenth century, and is found only against entries containing land taken into the king's forest.

survey.[1] Nevertheless, no one had ever before attempted to gather together such an immense mass of statistics on the inhabitants and resources of the thousands of manors, nor had anyone previously been given the task of combining oral and written testimony of diverse provenance and then packing such dense matter into a working document that would not prove impossibly unwieldy in use.[2] Although it seems not unlikely that a number of 'circuit volumes' were compiled first, of which the Liber Exoniensis (Exon)[3] certainly, and Little Domesday possibly, are the only surviving examples,[4] whoever was responsible for the compilation of Great Domesday was still left with the problems of condensing their content even further.[5] Moreover, it appears that not all the information was immediately available,[6] for even a cursory study of the manuscript shows that the scribe was in a hurry to begin work on his material (Figs. 1–4). Secondly, for many centuries after its inscription Domesday Book was consulted for precedent on legal and fiscal matters as it recorded royal and lay tenure and ancient rights; several of the marginal marks, signs, and even words may have been added during the process of these later searches.[7] Thirdly, the reign of Elizabeth I saw the beginning of antiquarian and archival work done by the deputy chamberlains who had charge of Domesday Book. Of these, Arthur Agarde initiated the practice of noting items of scholarly interest in the margins of the manuscripts and on loose pieces of parchment, which over the centuries have become inseparable from Domesday Book and are all now bound up with it.[8]

[1] H. R. Loyn, 'A General Introduction to Domesday Book', pp. 5–6 above. According to S. P. J. Harvey, 'Domesday Book and Anglo-Norman Governance', *TRHS* 5th ser., 25 (1975), 178 ff., records of the fixed charges, farms, and miscellaneous dues from boroughs and royal estates also existed at Winchester and formed the basis of the description of these parts of the survey.

[2] Domesday Book was always intended as a working document. Almost a century after it was compiled, the *Dialogus de Scaccario*, written by Henry II's treasurer Richard fitzNigel, describes it as one of 'several things in the vaults of the Treasury which are taken about the country . . . which are needed for daily use while the Exchequer is sitting', C. Johnson *et al.* (eds.) (2nd edn., Oxford, 1983), 62.

[3] This contains the returns for all of Som. and Corn., most of Devon., less than half of Dorset, and for only one Wilts. fief, the remainder having not survived. A close study of the Exon and Exchequer manuscripts has proved to me, beyond a reasonable doubt, that the Exchequer scribe copied directly from Exon as we have it now, not from a copy of it, as had been thought by V. H. Galbraith and R. Welldon Finn among others. For a brief summary of my evidence with especial reference to Devon., see C. and F. Thorn (eds.), *Domesday Book: Devon* (Chichester, 1985), pt. 2, 'Exon. Introduction: Relationship between Exon. and Exchequer DB'.

[4] Little Domesday is thought to be the fair copy of the 'circuit volume' for the East Anglian counties, but see p. 130, n. 3 below.

[5] In abbreviating Exon, for example, he omitted details of the livestock on the individual holdings, fuller versions of many of the holders' names, more precise dating of the values of manors and how they were held, the names and holdings of various tenants before 1066, the amount of land held by the villans as well as in demesne, etc.

[6] There are several spaces in Exon, most of them reproduced in the Exchequer volume, but never filled.

[7] See Hallam, *Domesday Book through Nine Centuries*, *passim*, on the uses to which Domesday Book was put from its inscription to the seventeenth century.

[8] See E. M. Hallam, 'Annotations in Domesday Book since 1100', Special Study XVI, pp. 140–9 below.

The marginalia fall into four broad, but reasonably distinct, categories: (1) those marginalia, by far the largest number, that were definitely added while work on Domesday was still in progress and certainly before the death of King William in 1087; (2) those that may or may not be contemporary with Domesday Book; (3) those that are certainly later; and (4) those that were added by the keepers of the two manuscripts from 1570 up to the eighteenth century.

1. The Annotations of the Original Scribes at the Time of Writing the Manuscripts during 1086–1087

It has been shown in Special Study XIV above that Great Domesday was almost completely written by one scribe, possibly working in Winchester, and he also inscribed the majority of the additions to the main text. A second scribe, a Norman, has also been shown to have been responsible for many corrections and additions, especially those in the margins. He is here known as the 'correcting' scribe. Seven scribes have so far been identified in Little Domesday, although none of these is the same as either of the scribes of Great Domesday. This first and largest category of marginalia can be further subdivided into seven headings, here designated by the letters (*a*)–(*g*).

(*a*) *Additions to the Text*

Because of the speed necessary to complete Great Domesday Book, the main scribe had to start writing up his material before it was all available, and in several counties it is evident that he began before he had made a definitive plan for dealing with what he had to hand.[9] He left many spaces in the text, and some were later filled with details which often overran into the margin because he had left insufficient room. But the requisite information to complete a great number was never forthcoming and they remained blank.[10] More frequently, however, the scribe left no spaces at all, or simply forgot to include certain manorial details, so that these had to be added in the margin when discovered, often by the other, correcting, scribe. Such additions include almost every aspect of a typical entry from the hidage to details of woodland and the values of countless holdings in Yorkshire (Fig. 12*a*);[11] selected examples are illustrated in Fig. 5. They appear in every county in Great Domesday and are particularly numerous in Lincolnshire, Yorkshire, Nottinghamshire, and Devonshire. At the end of many chapters the scribe left spaces for the later inclusion of further entries, should they transpire; he did this particularly in the case of the king's lands.[12] These were sometimes filled, though

[9] For example, in Lincs., one of the first counties to be written up, the scribe tried out several methods of dealing with the details of the sokelands of large manors in Ch. 1.

[10] For example, the plough-team estimates in Kent.

[11] For example, Worcs. 175, 176; Yorks. 300, 300v, 301, 301v, 331v.

[12] In Notts. one-fifth of a column and a side of one whole folio was left blank at the end of the king's fief and similarly almost a whole column in Yorks. Lincs. is also fairly unusual in having large spaces left after seven other of its sixty-eight chapters and smaller ones after

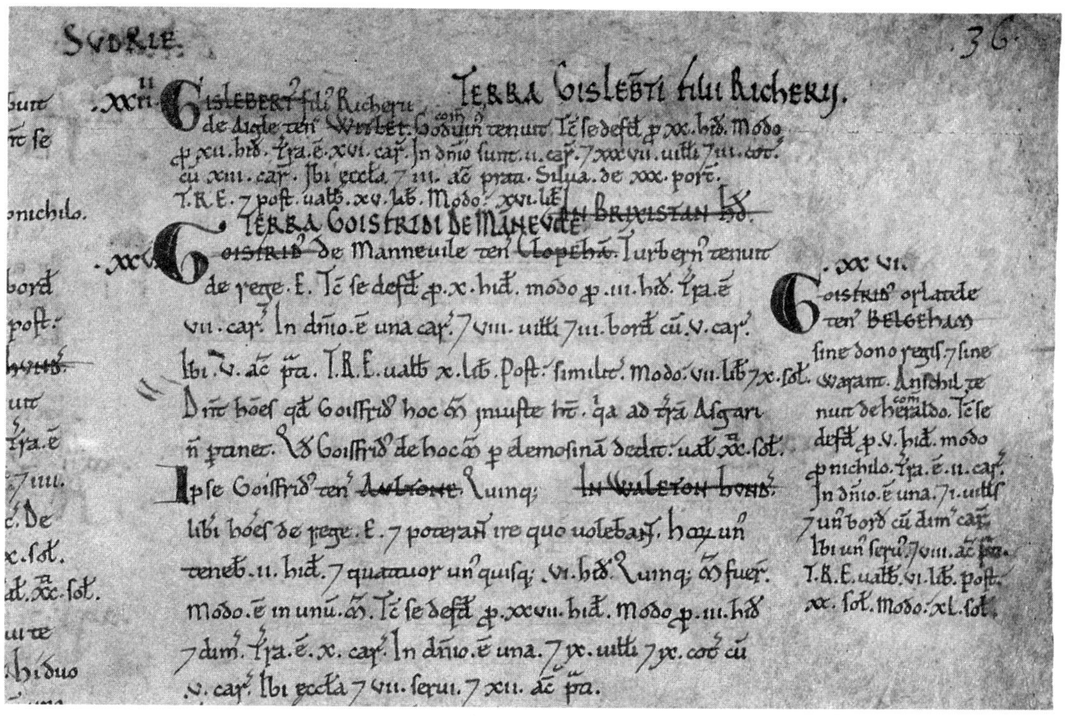

a. Two substantial additions to Surrey 36. An entry at the top of the column had been erased and the main scribe was able to squeeze Chapter XXIIII into this space. But there was no room at all within the column for Chapter XXVI, the land of Geoffrey Orlateile, so that it had to be entered in the margin.

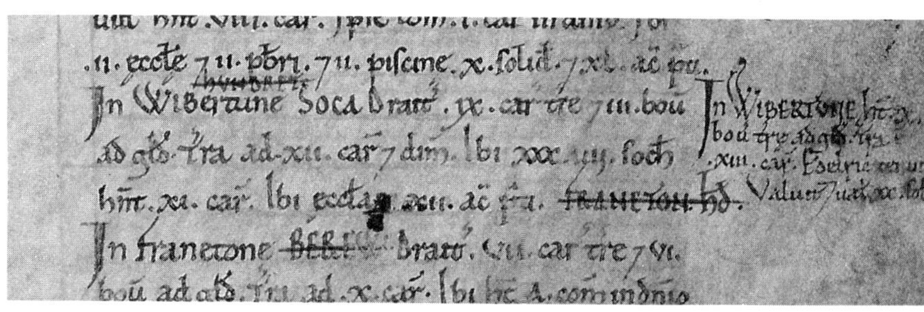

b. A missing entry inscribed in the right margin of Lincs. 348.

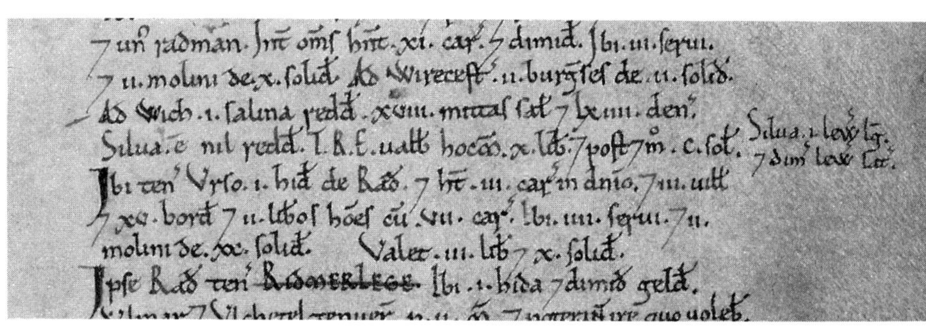

c. Details of woodland added in the right margin of Worcs. 176.

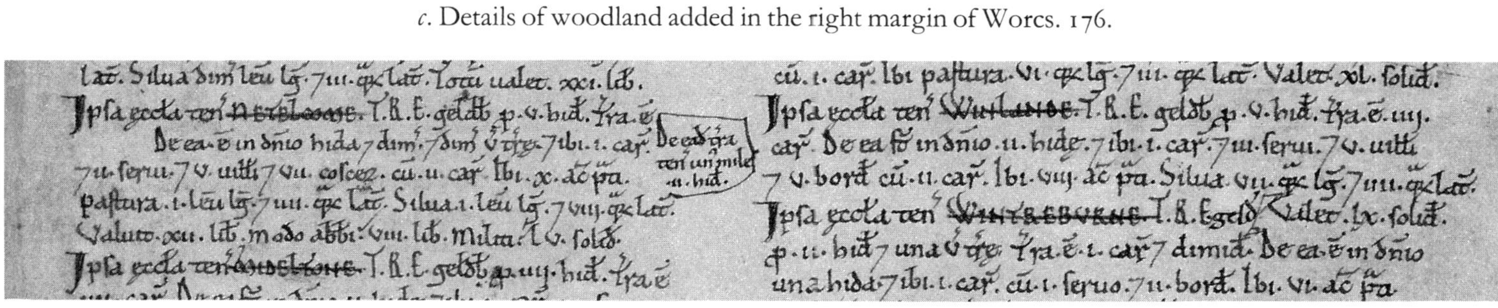

d. 'Of the same land a knight holds 2 hides' added in the centre margin of Dorset 78 and referring to an entry in the column on the left.

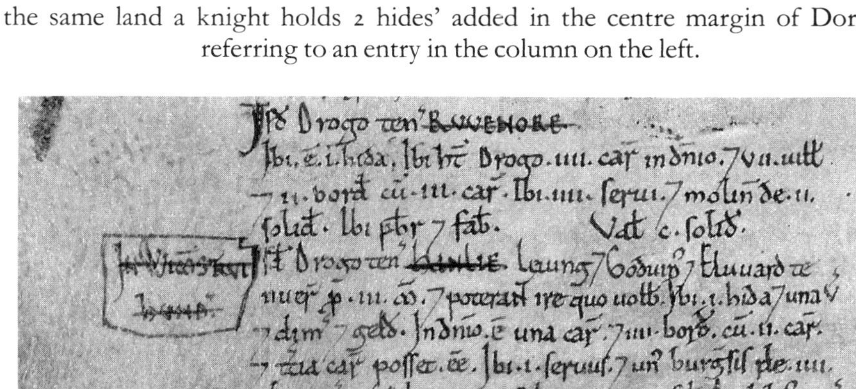

e. 'In Winstree Hundred' omitted from Herefs. 186v and added in the left margin.

FIG. 5

Additions to the text of Great Domesday (*slightly reduced*).

more often left blank; but in the case of Dorset the scribe failed to leave sufficient space after Chapter 1 and had to squeeze in one entry and then add another one on a small, separate piece of parchment.[1] Likewise space was regularly left at the beginning of a county for the later insertion of the sections on the borough(s) and this sometimes proved too small, resulting in marginal additions, such as that in Wiltshire 64v (Fig. 9, Special Study XIV, p. 100 above).[2] In several counties the scribe had to add complete entries, both in the side and in the bottom margins. Such are the entries for the Church of St Werburgh's manor of Clifton in Cheshire 263 and for Roger de Lacy's manor of Mathon in Herefordshire 184v.[3] Lincolnshire leads the way in the number of additional entries: the fiefs of the Bishop of Bayeux and of Count Alan have no fewer than three marginal additions each.[4]

We can only guess at the reasons for the initial omission of many of these entries, but we can be fairly certain in the case of Fulcher's manor of Huish and the holding of Nicholas at Northleigh which are added in the bottom and side margins of Devonshire 117v. Here, when the holdings of three crossbowmen and of Almerg d'Arques were abstracted from the composite section of Exon to form four separate chapters, these ones were accidentally missed. When Exchequer Domesday was subsequently checked against Exon (as much evidence suggests that it was), the omissions became apparent and were made good.[5]

Even whole chapters had to be inserted in the margins of Great Domesday, such as the fiefs of Hugh fitz-Baldric in Wiltshire 73, of Geoffrey Orlateile in Surrey 36 (Fig. 5*a*), and of Hascoit Musard in Oxfordshire 159v and 160.[6] Most of these were rubricated and given numbers corresponding to the list of landholders near the beginning of the county, so were presumably either the scribe's inadvertent omissions which he rectified at an early date, or the information for them arrived before the county in question was rubricated.

fifteen of the rest. It would appear that those counties which were written up first have more spaces left in them than those written towards the end, where the scribe abandoned horizontal ruling and the degree of compression of the text is greater.

[1] Dorset 75v, 76. The additional sheet of parchment, which was bound and later foliated with the others, was one of four similar ones (see also Dorset 81, Surrey 33, Hants 42) cut off from the side of a presumably spoiled sheet which had already been ruled out; it was then turned round and written crosswise, so that the original horizontal rulings appear as vertical scores.

[2] In Berks. 56v the scribe managed to squeeze the section on Wallingford into the space he had left. But in the case of Hants this space, one and a half sides of a folio, was never used, probably because Winchester proved too complex a borough to describe. Nor were the spaces left at the beginnings of Sussex and Som. ever filled.

[3] As many as three marginal entries were added on Staffs. 282v.

[4] Lincs. 342, 342v, 343; 347v, 348. The fief of Kolsveinn (Lincs. 356v–357v) also has three misplaced entries, but the scribe discovered the omission of these while still writing the chapter and incorporated them in the columns.

[5] These entries are written in very much paler ink than the main text at that point and are not rubricated, the latter fact definitely suggesting addition after the main text for the county was complete.

[6] The addition across the foot of Glos. 165v is the continuation of an entry—a lay holding from Winchcombe Church, Ch. 11—which was squeezed into the space at the end of the chapter.

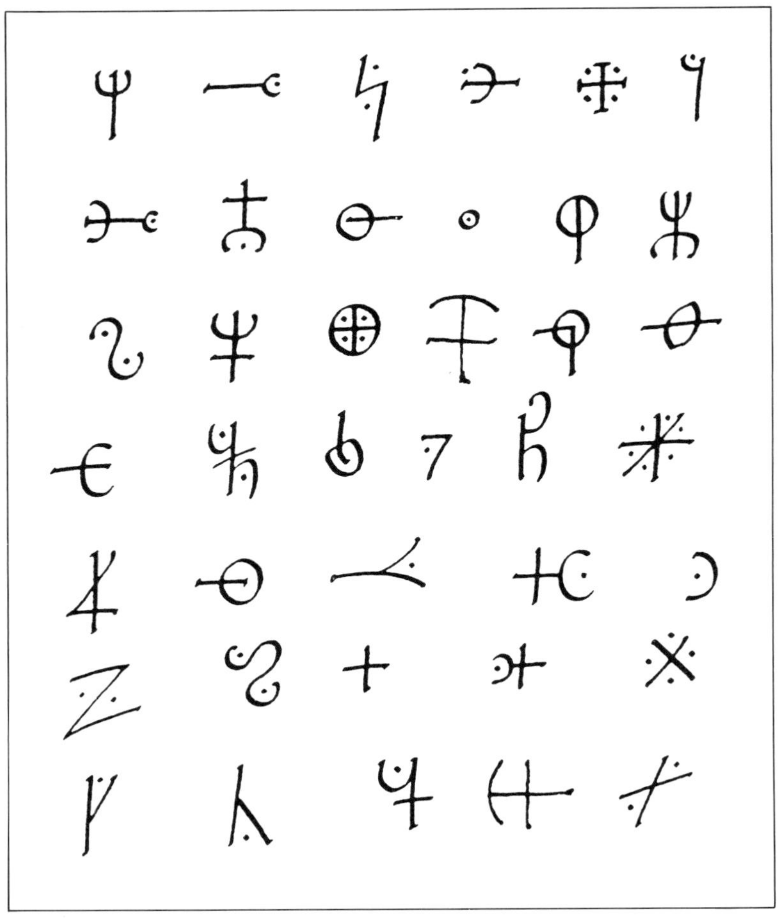

FIG. 6

If such additions were written at some distance from their correct position in the text (for example, at the foot of a column), this was generally—but by no means invariably—indicated by the use of paired transposition signs. There are over 125 sets of these transposition signs in Great Domesday and an example of every type is illustrated in Fig. 6. One such sign was inscribed in the margin beside the information which was out of place, and a generally identical one signalled where it should properly appear (Fig. 7). These signs were sometimes also used where the addition was next to the entry to which it belonged, as well as where entries were simply misplaced and added within the framework of the column or even the county. Occasionally a set of signs was used to correct the order of words within an entry,[7] or to link two entries together as in Wiltshire 68v where it was necessary to show the whereabouts of two hides. Numerous different transposition signs were used, some very elaborate, others simple marks based on the Greek alphabet, particularly the *psi*, and some were rubricated. Every county in Great Domesday, except Hertfordshire, Huntingdonshire, and Staffordshire, has these transposition signs; Lincolnshire has the most with up to twenty-four sets, and the five south-western counties have over thirty sets between them. The scribe seems to have tried deliberately to use different types of signs within each county for clarity: this was particularly necessary where, as in Lincolnshire 357, he needed to draw attention to three separate misplacements on one page. On several occasions the scribe drew a box of ink lines around a marginal addition to show where it belonged, as in Dorset 78 (Fig. 5*d*) and Wiltshire 64v (Fig. 9, Special Study XIV, p. 100 above). In the case of the addition of the slaves in the left margin of

[7] e.g. Oxon. 159, left column.

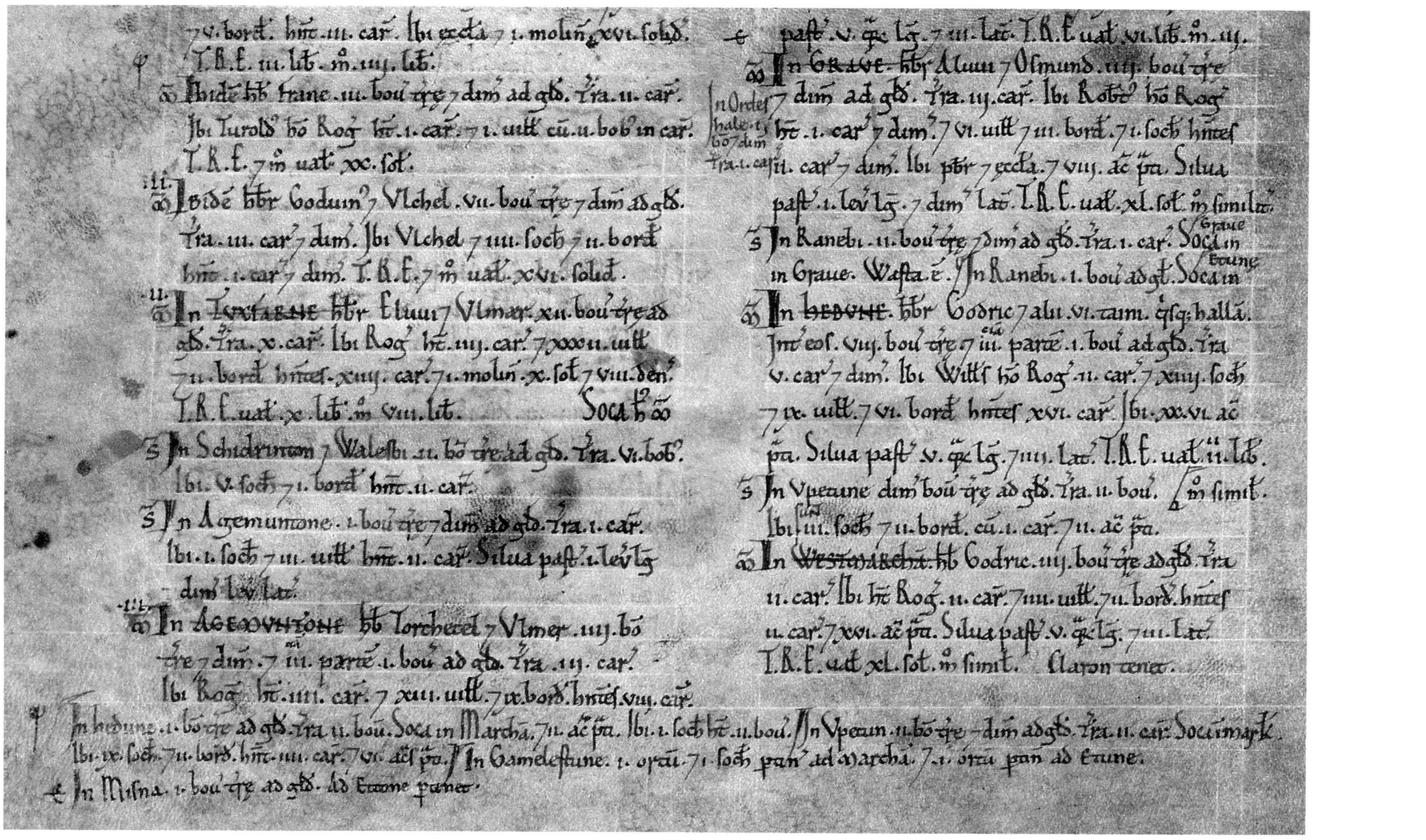

FIG. 7

Additions to Notts. 284v (*slightly reduced*) with two sets of transposition signs. The main scribe had managed to crowd the mention of Ordsall into the centre margin, but he had to write two passages along the bottom of the page and indicate their correct position in each column with transposition signs. The passage he has marked with ⸸ consists of three additions concerning East Markham and Eaton which are divided by the 'gallows' sign (as in Fig. 9 below). The ⸸ above in the left margin indicates where they should properly lie, while the -e beside the lowermost misplaced entry is matched by a similar -e above in the centre margin.

Gloucestershire 166, a double gallows sign (see section 1(*c*) below) was incorporated into the box as well.[1]

Many of these marginal additions were done immediately or very soon after the main text had been written, and probably even before work on the individual county had been completed. In such cases the ink used is identical to that found in the text at that point, and the addition was often rubricated. However, a number are in a different colour or are not rubricated (or both), and so were probably inscribed at a slightly later stage, in several cases by the correcting scribe. This may have been a result of checking the 'original returns'[2] or, in the case of the south-western counties, Exon as suggested above.[3] Some textual additions were no doubt inscribed when information was subsequently brought to light, such as might reveal the existence of a claim or arise as the result of an inquiry.[4]

One type of marginal addition which occurs only in the Devonshire folios is the direct result of a check being made on Exon, and seems to have been written by the correcting scribe. This is the word *par'* (Fig. 18) abbreviating *pariter* 'in parage', 'jointly', and it is written beside many of the entries for manors which exhibit a type of tenure almost invariably involving the land of thegns before 1066.[5] At a time when so many lands had been acquired unlawfully or their tenure contested, it was very important to know the way in which a manor had been held in 1066, although in the case of Devonshire the scribe of Exchequer Domesday did not always think this fact worth including.[6] The information, however, had been given in Exon, so that when the Devonshire folios were checked against it, it was a simple matter to

[1] See also Sussex 16v, where all four corners of the box are formed by partially rubricated gallows signs.

[2] On the subject of the form of the 'original returns', see V. H. Galbraith, *The Making of Domesday Book* (Oxford, 1961), *passim* and esp. ch. xii; P. H. Sawyer, 'The "Original Returns" and Domesday Book', *EHR* 70 (1955).

[3] If other 'circuit volumes' existed these were probably checked too.

[4] In the right margin of Hants 48 is written—in slightly paler ink than that used for the text, but by the main scribe—*Rex W. reddid' eid' ęccl'ę* ('King William gave it back to this church'), the outcome of a claim for alienated church land mentioned in the adjacent entry. There is a marginal *r* (*require* 'look into (this)'; see section 1 (*e*), p. 124 below) written three lines above it in the same colour of ink as the text and, as it does not seem to refer to any omission or problem in the entry, it is likely that it concerned the alienation and that the marginalium below is a direct result of it. See also p. 126, n. 2 below.

[5] It was a form of land tenure whereby a man's estate was not physically divided among his heirs, but enjoyed equally by them, with one heir being responsible to the lord or king for the services due from the land and the other heirs being answerable only to the first. For a discussion of *pariter* and two apparently related terms, see Thorn and Thorn (eds.), *Domesday Book: Devon*, general notes to 1,15.

[6] At least at first: later chapters have more details of the type of previous tenure.

insert the word either in the margin or by interlineation, the latter usually in the form *in parag'*. The ink is paler than that used for the main body of the county and is similar to that found in other additions and corrections to its text.[1]

Another type of marginal addition to the text in Great Domesday is of some of the hundred and wapentake heads, which when properly entered usually occur at the end of the first line of an entry or after the value statement of the preceding one. None of the five south-western counties has them at all[2] and in several other shires they are imperfectly recorded; in Northamptonshire, for instance, about 40 per cent of these heads are missing and in Oxfordshire only a tiny proportion is present. In a number of cases the scribe[3] was able to insert them in the text itself, although sometimes in an entry further on because of lack of space.[4] The fact that they are almost all rubricated suggests that these missing heads were added at only a slightly later date. Some were boxed in by ink lines, as with Winstree Hundred, Herefordshire 186v, illustrated in Fig. 5*e*.

A further marginalium, which seems to have been written by the main scribe of Great Domesday, is the *c* which occurs beside four consecutive entries in Devonshire 101v, and denotes that the revenues of these holdings were reserved for the supply of food and perhaps of clothing to the canons of Exeter. The scribe actually refers to the four entries with the *c*s written beside them as *supra notatae* ('marked above'). It is not clear whether the two *c*s in Yorkshire 329, 379v were intended to convey the same meaning, although it may be significant that part of the land in Nether Poppleton on 329 was given to St Mary's, York.[5]

There are far fewer marginal additions to the text of Little Domesday, perhaps because its scribes did not have to excerpt or condense their material to nearly the same degree as was required of the Exchequer scribe. Moreover, in their case speed of execution may not have been so necessary, so simple errors of omission were not made; and if Little Domesday were a fair copy, then such omissions would have been incorporated. Essex has no such additions of substance; Norfolk has only two[6] and Suffolk only one major insertion in the left margin of 362v, and two lesser ones on 326. However, on a number of occasions in this last county the text extends into the side or bottom margins, often with a line drawn round it.

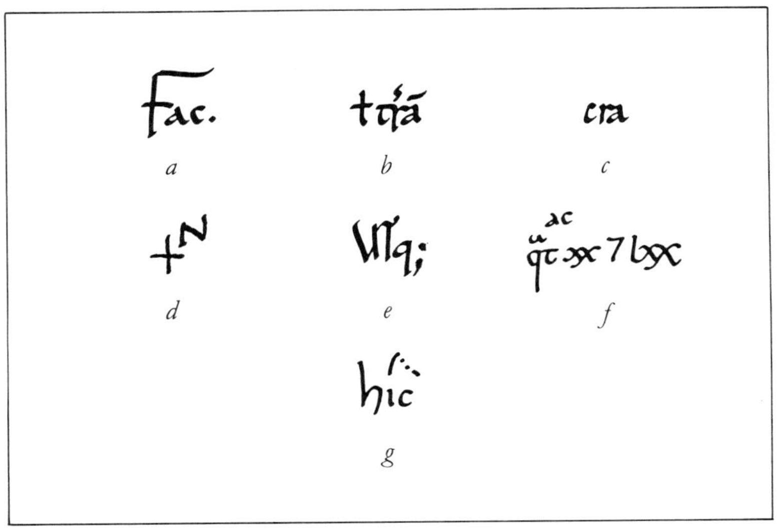

FIG. 8

(*b*) *Miscellaneous Words or Phrases* (Fig. 8)

There are a number of words or phrases which occur only once in the Domesday manuscripts, although the word *Fac* (Fig. 8*a*) occurs on three occasions.[7] According to Welldon Finn, the instance of this word in Wiltshire might be an instruction to a clerk signifying where to start Chapter 2, so that a space should be left at the end of the king's fief for the later inclusion of more of his lands if it became necessary.[8] *Fac* could thus be read as the imperative singular of *facere* 'to do'. This notion seems to fit its occurrence in Berkshire, where it is also written beside Chapter 2 after a space following Chapter 1. The third example, in Hampshire, is also entered beside the first line of the chapter which follows the list of the king's land in the Isle of Wight, although there is no space before it and no sign of the preceding entries having been added. All three *Fac*s certainly appear to have been written by the same person.[9]

In Worcestershire 176 *(ve)l t(er)ra(m)* ('or piece of land') is written in the bottom margin below *i. hid(am)* and indicates an uncertainty (Fig. 8*b*). It is in paler ink and no doubt was inscribed at the same time as the details of woodland in the right margin above. The writer was definitely the main scribe. He also wrote in the margin of Yorkshire 380 the correction *cra* (Fig. 8*c*) to the place-name *Caldeuuelle*: this vill occurs in the form *Cradeuuelle* on 322. Against two of the king's entries in the Summary in Yorkshire 381v is written *+N* (Fig. 8*d*), only the first being actually in the margin. They refer to two holdings that had been relinquished by Nigel Fos-

[1] The check on Exon which produced the added *par'*s (among other corrections) would seem to have been a second check of the Exchequer text, because in the centre margin of Devon. 108v, the first of the two *par'*s added on this folio deliberately avoids an erased memo (see section 1(*f*), p. 126 below): clearly the text opposite was corrected, and the memo erased before the *par'* was written.

[2] This was undoubtedly because they were also missing from Exon and by the time this came to be condensed it was too late to discover in which hundreds all the places lay.

[3] It would seem that these additions in the text were made by the main scribe.

[4] For example, the Wrockwardine Hundred head in the left column of Shrops. 258v.

[5] *Calendar of Charter Rolls*, iii: *1300–1326* (PRO, London, 1908), 113. The *c*s next to two entries in Staffs. 247v have a different meaning; see p. 132, n. 1 below.

[6] Norfolk 158v, 274v.

[7] On Hants 52v, Wilts. 65v, and, with a minuscule *f*, on Berks. 58. It is possible that the *F* on Hants 46v, level with the first line of Ch. 29, is the beginning of *Fac* as it is identical to the *F* of *Fac* on Hants 52v, and the scribe had originally left a small space after the end of the preceding chapter. In the event this proved to be too small for the insertion he had to make, so he was forced to use the central margin. This *F* is quite unlike the two *f*s on Hants 51v (see section 2(*a*), p. 129 below).

[8] R. Welldon Finn, 'The Immediate Sources of the Exchequer Domesday', *Bull. of the John Rylands Lib.* 40 (Manchester, 1957), 68. He believed that more than one scribe wrote Great Domesday, but the 'notes on churches' he mentions (at the end of the king's lands on Wilts. 65v) were definitely done by the main scribe; they are rubricated but were probably added slightly later than the rest of the folio, which suggests a good reason for the space left at the end of Ch. 1.

[9] Of uncertain identity: neither the main nor the correcting scribe uses this form of initial *F*.

sard on 373, and are again probably by the main scribe as he rubricated the text here and the *N* is in red ink. The significance is unknown of two other marginalia in Yorkshire, also probably written by the main scribe: *Vsq(ue)* ('up to [?here]') in the central margin of 300v and in the same colour of ink as the text, which may refer to a check on the column (Fig. 8*e*); and *cht* (or possibly *chr*) on 316, which may be partially erased as it is very faint. Little Domesday also contains two unexplained marginalia of this type (Fig. 8*f*, *g*) which seem to have been written by the same scribe that wrote the nearby text.[1]

A clearer meaning can be attributed to two other marginalia which occur only once each. The word *rex* is written in the same colour ink as the adjacent text in the bottom right corner of Hampshire 51, probably by the main scribe. This insertion may well have been intended to draw attention to the unusual presence of royal land in the middle of this county's folios, as the king's holdings head the account of lands in the New Forest which are here treated in a separate section.[2] Also unique, on the extreme left-hand edge of Gloucestershire 169v the letters *OT* were again probably written by the main scribe as the ink is similar to that of the text. Two of the three holdings in the fief opposite are stated to have been held before 1066 by one Wigot, and it may be that it was this name that was originally inscribed, and that the first three letters were trimmed off during a subsequent rebinding of the manuscript.[3]

(*c*) *The 'Gallows' Sign*

It will be noticed that in most counties in Great Domesday Book (and throughout Little Domesday Book) use is made of the common pennon-shaped sign illustrated in Fig. 9. This 'gallows' sign, as it is usually called, had two functions, for it acts as a *paragraphos* or paragraphing device and also indicates an overrun.

In the first case it was generally placed to the left of the column it served, and in Great Domesday it was almost certainly written by the main scribe. The gallows signs in Little Domesday, as in Exon, were sometimes quite elaborate, and were used to indicate the start of a new entry (Fig. 17, Special Study XIV, p. 110 above), although occasionally one was omitted, as in Little Domesday after a hundred heading.[4] In Great Domesday the use of an enlarged rubricated initial letter generally took the place of the gallows sign as the indication of a new entry. Although in its first function it does

FIG. 9

appear quite frequently in some counties, such as Warwickshire and Berkshire, in the majority it is employed only as a convenient method of subdivision for long entries such as those describing the boroughs.[5] In some counties, for instance Devonshire, the gallows sign was reserved exclusively for its other function, marking where the text overran on to the line below or above, or on to an interlinear line. In these cases the sign was usually upright when the 'overspill' from a line of writing continued on to the line above it, generally as the result of the addition of some detail. When the continuation followed on the line below, the extra phrases were enclosed by two joined triangular pieces (as illustrated) or, occasionally, by the sign upside-down; in this case the continuation would have been written before the next entry was begun. There are several instances in which the scribe failed to use the correct sign. The curious symbol 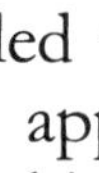 appears very occasionally, as in Sussex 17v and Cheshire 262v. Sometimes in Great Domesday the gallows signs were heightened with a spot of red ink in the triangular part.[6]

(*d*) *Indications of the Administrative Status of a Holding*

Next to the first lines of certain entries is written one of four abbreviations, in the various forms illustrated in Fig. 10. Because they are usually entered within the 'tramlines' formed by the double vertical rulings, it could be argued that they are not marginal at all, but an integral part of the text.[7] In any case they all appear to have been written in by the main scribe at the same time as the entry to which they refer. They consist of *M̄*, *B̄*, *S̄*, or occasionally, in Yorkshire 314–315v, *MN̄R*, *MAN̄R*, *BER'*, *BR̄*; and twice, in Huntingdonshire 206, of *T'*. They are the abbreviations for *manerium* 'manor', *berewica* 'berewick' or 'outlier', *soka* 'soke(land)', and *terra* 'land', and they describe the type of holding in the entry and its relationship with others. The rare *T(erra)* was apparently applied to pieces of land that did

[1] The *q(uat)t(uor) xx ac(rae) 7 lxx* ('fourscore acres and 70') in Suffolk 430 (Fig. 8*f*) does not seem to refer to anything obvious: perhaps the scribe had some measurements, but did not know what was being so described and intended to check up. The *hic* (Fig. 8*g*) is in Essex 70v.

[2] See J. Munby (ed.), *Domesday Book: Hampshire* (Chichester, 1982), note to NF1,1. However, there is no similar word on Hants 52 or 52v which contain the king's lands in the Isle of Wight, also not detailed at the beginning of the county.

[3] What appears to be a tiny E at the foot of Cambs. 191v is the fortuitous result of an ink-blot.

[4] The signs in Little Domesday were done by the scribe of the text at that point and are easily distinguishable from each other; they were designed to catch the eye and are in contrast to the more discreet signs in Great Domesday.

[5] For example, Ches. 262v, Notts. 280, Surrey 143, etc. But not all borough sections had gallows signs: there are none, for example, in Worcs., Devon., Staffs. or Cambs. Holdings such as St Peter of Westminster's 30-hide manor of Longdon (174v) had their paragraphs marked by this sign; and most of the subtenancies of the Bishop of Coutances are thus indicated in Northants 220v–221.

[6] See p. 121, n. 1 above.

[7] Although double vertical rulings are common in manuscripts of this age (*ex inf.* M. Gullick), there seems to be a correspondence between the counties so scored and those containing the *M̄*, *B̄*, *S̄* letters: certainly these letters only occur in those counties ruled with eight verticals. Moreover, every county so ruled has them, except for part of Kent (the second gathering, 8–15, which may have been left over from the first ruling programme, see Gullick, 'Great and Little Domesday Manuscripts', p. 96, Fig. 6, above).

FIG. 10

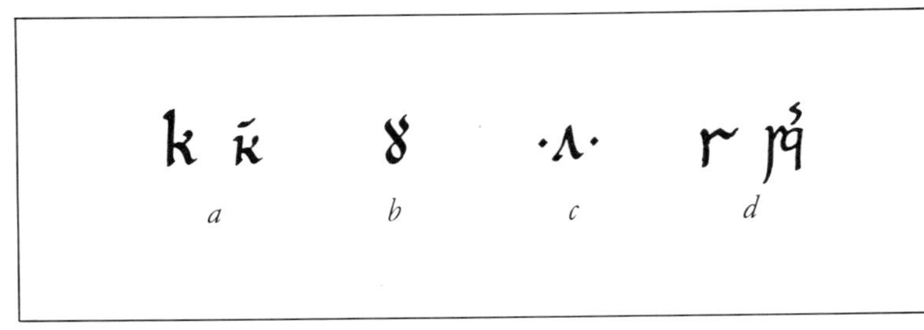

FIG. 11

not fit into the other categories.[1] Sometimes *ii* or *iii* or an even higher number was added above or beside the *M̄* to indicate that a single manor (at 1086) had formerly been two, three, or even more manors before the Conquest (Fig. 12*a*). Often *S̄* and *B̄* were written one above the other and linked by the Tironian *nota* for *et* (*7*), to indicate that a holding was both sokeland and a berewick. Likewise *M̄* linked to *B̄* appears on several occasions. These 'marginalia' occur only in Great Domesday and are limited to certain counties, notably Yorkshire, Lincolnshire, Huntingdonshire, Nottinghamshire, and Derbyshire which probably comprised the northern Circuit VI. They also appear sporadically in those forming the so-called Circuit III: Cambridgeshire, Buckinghamshire, Bedfordshire, Hertfordshire, and Middlesex. The abbreviations seem principally to have been used in the counties that lay in the former Danish areas of the country, to denote a tenurial system with a number of large 'capital' manors on which depended several inferior members of differing status. Even so, in no county are they entered against every holding there,[2] and the reason for this spasmodic insertion is unclear.[3] But the fact that these marginal letters do not appear in the folios for counties in other circuits suggests that in those where they do occur, they had already been entered in the material that preceded the 'circuit volumes' (where and if such existed).[4]

(*e*) *Marginalia Indicating a Matter of Dispute or the Need for Further Information*

Next to a number of entries in Great Domesday is written the letter *k* or *K*, with or without an abbreviation line over it (Fig. 11*a*). This abbreviates the Latin *kalum(p)nia* or *klamor* 'claim' and indicates that a claim was being made about a holding or about some aspect of it. Often, but by no means always,[5] the entry next to which the *k* is written contains details of the claim.[6] The fact that sometimes such details were written in the margin by the main scribe in the same colour of ink as the *k*s,[7] and so apparently at the same time, suggests that all the *k*s were his work. These *k*s occur only in Lincolnshire (seventeen times), Huntingdonshire (fourteen times), Derbyshire (thrice), and Shropshire (once).[8] Of these, both Lincolnshire and Huntingdonshire have appendices listing claims and disputes (called *Clamores* in the former), and the *k*s in the main text sometimes, but not always, refer to entries in these. However, there may be little significance in the correspondence, because, although Yorkshire also has a *Clamores* section, it has no *k*s apart from one ambiguous example. Furthermore, neither Derbyshire nor Shropshire possesses such an appendix. No *k* or similar mark appears in Little Domesday, which has sections called *Invasiones*, 'encroachments', at the end of each of the three counties.[9]

Allied to these *k*s in meaning are two examples of *d* (Fig. 11*b*), which probably abbreviate *disputatio* 'dispute' or *diratiocinandum* 'to be determined, proved, established' and are written against disputed entries in Huntingdonshire 206v and Derbyshire 278.[10] A *k* is also inscribed opposite the Derbyshire example, but since the ink used is not so pale as that of the *d*, they may have been added at different times. Similarly, beside three entries in Hertfordshire 137v and 141 and Staffordshire 249 is written a capital *A* (Fig. 11*c*). These entries contain details of seized or alienated land, so the *A* probably abbreviates a noun or a gerund derived from *arbitrari* 'to decide' or *adjudicare* 'to judge'.[11]

Another marginalium almost certainly contemporary with Domesday Book consists of *r* or *rq*, the latter

[1] *VCH Huntingdonshire*, i (1926), 323.

[2] They are totally absent from several chapters in Yorks., for example.

[3] In later times a particular Domesday vill often appears as the dependency or member of some larger manor and this form of manorial organization may well have existed widely in 1086. But in many counties in Domesday Book no systematic attempt was made either in the text or between the 'tramlines' to record individual holdings as berewicks or sokeland of another manor, although there are occasional references in the text to a 'head' manor (*caput*) or to one holding 'belonging to' or 'being assessed in' another.

[4] It is not clear whether the scribe saw any of this earlier material or only the 'circuit volumes'. On this very complex problem, see Galbraith, *Making of Domesday Book*, ch. xii and esp. 175–6.

[5] See, for example, Lincs. 352, 354, 356, 358.

[6] For example, Hunts. 203v, 204; Derby. 274v, 278.

[7] As Lincs. 340v *Eudo clam(at)* and 348v *Sortebrant calu(m)niat(ur)*.

[8] The letter in the left margin of Yorks. 317v may be a *k* (or perhaps an *b*), if it is not an ink-blot emphasized by letters showing through from the *verso* (the parchment is very thin and transparent here).

[9] Although Exon contains a section entitled *Terrae Occupatae* 'seized lands' for the counties of Devon, Corn., and Som. which corresponds roughly to the *Clamores* of Yorks. and Lincs., there is no sign of a *k* in those counties in Domesday Book; however, this may be because the Exchequer scribe never saw this Exon section.

[10] A *d* with a line through it is also written in the left margin of Yorks. 301v, but it does not seem to have the same meaning.

[11] In the central margin of Derby. 277v the correcting scribe wrote *nescio cuius* ('I do not know whose'), which must refer to the 1086 holder of the manor: it would seem that he had not seen the *Ascuit tenet* ('Hascoit holds (it)') written by the main scribe in a half-line below the entry (before which he had written the first line of the next entry). In other words, the *Ascuit tenet* is original and not an 'answer' to the *nescio cuius*.

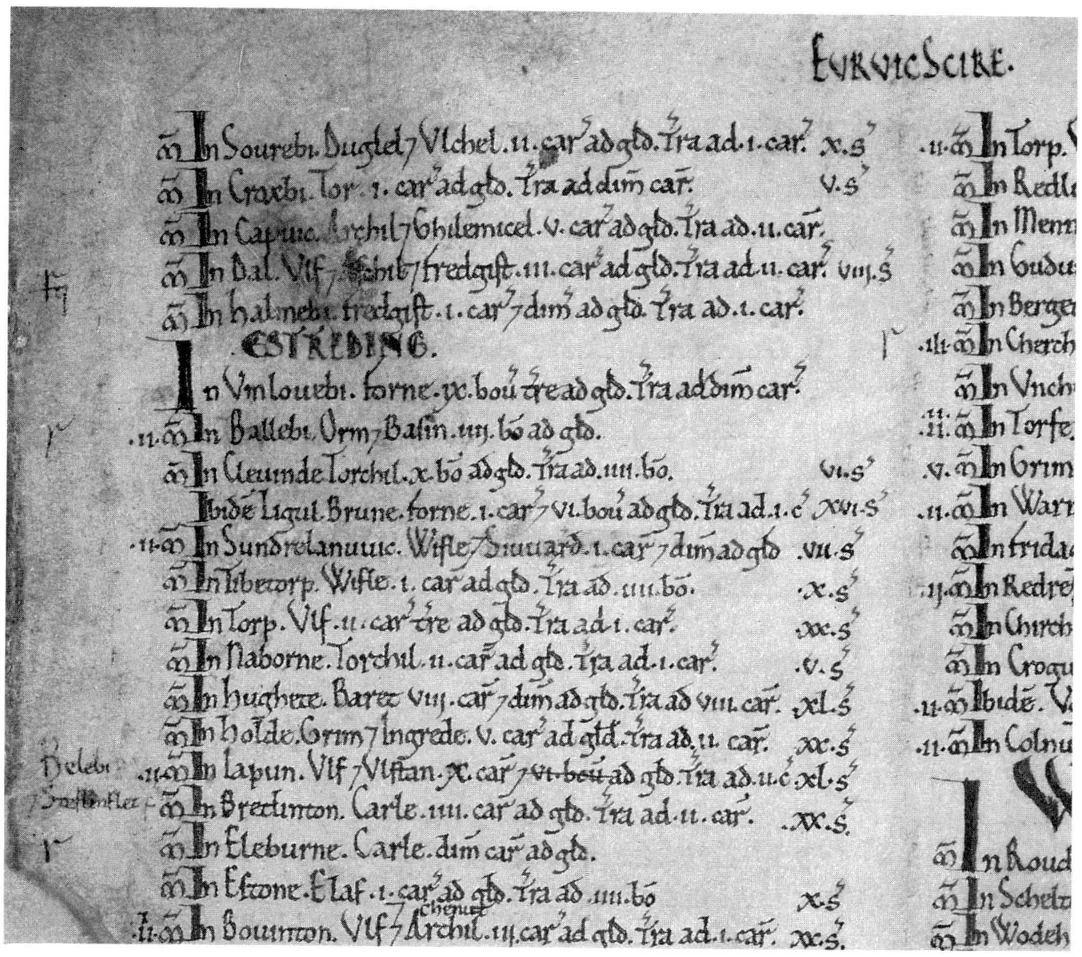

a. The values of manors added to Yorks. 301 after this text had been written, but probably before the county had been completed. Several were not supplied, and ꝛq (once), and r (three times) have been noted in the margin abbreviating *require*, 'inquire'. The marginal addition *Belebi 7 Steflinflet*, (Bielby and Stillingfleet) was written by the main scribe, probably as a reminder to include details of these two places. Evidently none of these requests elicited a reply.

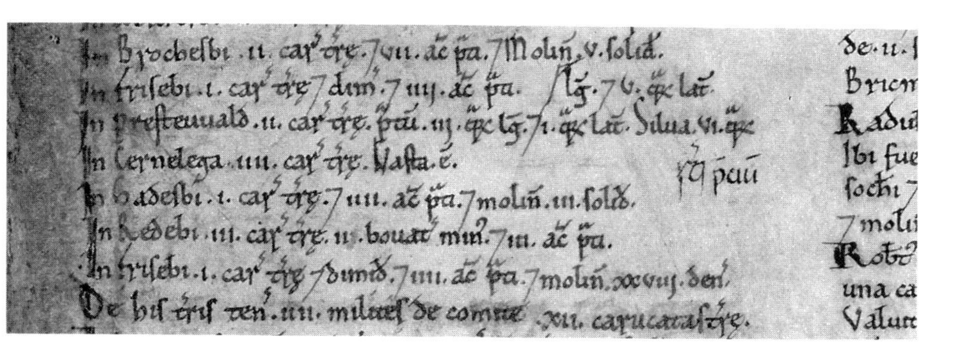

b. Leics. 237. Charley is recorded as 'waste' in this list of the holdings of Earl Hugh. Nevertheless as waste land often had a value, the main scribe has written the abbreviations for *require precium*, 'inquire the value' (in red), to the right of the entry. Once again, this request remained unanswered.

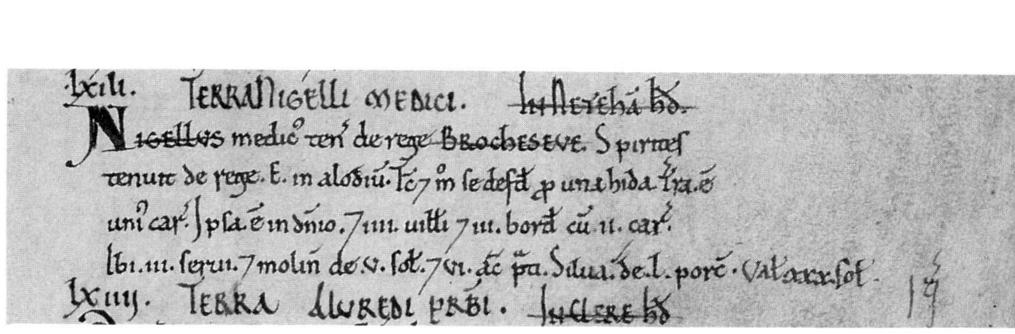

c. During the process of adding the rubrication to Hants 49, the main scribe noticed that the entry for Broxhead lacked a value, so he wrote (in red) ꝛq for *require* next to it. This time the correcting scribe was subsequently able to add the 1086 value of 30*s.* in the margin.

Fig. 12

Requests for information or verification (*slightly reduced*).

often with a 'lightning' type abbreviation sign above it, for *require*, the imperative of *requirere* 'to seek out, to inquire' (Figs. 11*d* and 12). This was sometimes written when an item of information was missing or there was uncertainty about a detail in the entry, and it occurs only in Great Domesday. Often it is clear what was lacking because a space still exists in the text, for example for the missing number of acres of meadow in Leicestershire 230v or for the hidage in Staffordshire 247. The information required was never found or entered in many of these cases, because all work on the production and systematic correction of Domesday Book probably came to an end with King William's death in September 1087. The inscription of such *r*s is haphazard, however, as there are a great many spaces left in entries and no *r* is written beside these. Sometimes, as in the statement of value of Broxhead in Hampshire 49 next to an *rq'* (Fig. 12*c*), there are signs of an insertion in the text; but in several instances the scribe seems to have been questioning the veracity of an item, as with the two separate figures for the carucates in Fridaythorpe in Yorkshire 329v, or with the apparent omission of a hidage in a subholding of Stanstead in Hertfordshire 138v. In about six cases he explains the nature of the query with a fuller phrase, such as *r(e)q(uire) q(uo)t uill(anorum)* ('discover how many villans') in Cambridgeshire 200; *r(e)q(uire) hid(arum) num(erum)* ('find out the number of hides') in Northamptonshire 220; and *r(e)q(uire) de t(er)ra arab(ili) R(ogeri) de Mort(emer) et ep(iscopi)*[1] *baioc(ensis)* ('inquire into the arable land of Roger de Mortimer and of the Bishop of Bayeux') in Lincolnshire 360; see also Fig. 12*b*. Towards the bottom of the left column of Yorkshire 301 an entry which had an *r* written next to it has been erased, presumably because the inquiry revealed that it was incorrect or superfluous.[2]

These *r*s and *rq*s are generally written either in the same colour of ink as the body of the text, suggesting immediate inscription, or in the paler ink of some of the other marginal additions. In a few cases in Great Domesday, however, they are inscribed in the red mercuric sulphide used for the rubrication (Fig. 12*b*).[3] This suggests either that the rubricator checked the text at some stage—although it is not clear whether he was the only person to do so or indeed if he checked the whole manuscript—or that the person checking sometimes mistakenly used the red instead of the black ink.[4] In Oxfordshire 155v, right margin, an *r* in dark brown ink is written opposite an *rq'* in red in the central margin, which points to a separate check by two people: in this case a sentence about five thegns is unfinished.

However, not every *r* abbreviates *require*; for example, the capital R in Cheshire 263, beside the entry concerning a hide of land held by St Chad's Church in King Edward's time, probably stands for *reclamatio* 'claim for restitution'. In this case the R is equivalent to *k*, because the hide in question is later stated to be held in 1086 by Hugh fitzOsbern. Likewise, when an *r* is linked with an *f* it generally seems to have a different meaning, here listed under section 2(*a*) below.

(*f*) *The Scribe's Reminders to Himself*

This particularly interesting group of marginalia occurs only in Great Domesday and is of two main types. First, there are a great many cases, in most counties, where the scribe has erased something in the text by scraping and then, before re-preparation of the surface,[5] he has jotted down in the margin what he wanted to insert there.[6] These notes in turn were generally erased once the final insertion had been made over the erasure, although several are still partially visible in the manuscript. In the right margin of Cornwall 122v the scribe wrote *dim'* and then seems to have erased it when he corrected the tax-assessment in the text to half a ferding. The *petlinge* (Fig. 13*a*) in the right margin of Leicestershire 236 is probably of this type, although it is not actually erased, because the place-name *Petlinge* in the main body of the text is written over an erasure.[7] Secondly, there are several words, often written at the top or bottom of folios, which appear to be the scribe's *aides-mémoire* for something that should be added later. For example, at the top of Lincolnshire 356 he wrote *hvvelle* ('Howell') upside-down (Fig. 13*b*), possibly when (at 355) he was recording details of Gilbert de Ghent's holding there. It may well be relevant that in the top margin of 357 in the next gathering he added details of Kolsveinn's holding in the same place; this addition is certainly later because it is not rubricated. Likewise someone (perhaps this time the correcting scribe) wrote *hennesoure* (Edensor, a place-name) extending into the central margin of Derbyshire

[1] In the manuscript this is *ep̄s*, which abbreviates the nominative *episcopus*, impossible in this phrase.

[2] In two instances at least, the result of an inquiry seems to have been entered by the main scribe: in the case of Hants 48 (see p. 121, n. 4 above) and at the end of a line in the case of *soca* on Lincs. 355v (third line, right-hand column). This suggests strongly that most of, if not all, the *r*s were written at the same time as the main text and probably by the main scribe.

[3] As in Wilts. 65v, Oxon. 154v, 155v, Hants 49, Staffs. 248, and Northants 220, and the *r(e)q(uire) p(re)ciu(m)* ('inquire the value') of Leics. 237 (Fig. 12*b*).

[4] It would seem that in Great Domesday the main scribe did the rubrication (see Gullick, 'Great and Little Domesday Manuscripts', p. 102 above), so it is possible that some at least of the correction by him was done at the time of rubrication.

[5] See Gullick, 'Great and Little Domesday Manuscripts', p. 101 above.

[6] For example, in Shrops. 254v in a holding of Reginald the sheriff at Dawley *Ibi i hida* has been written over an erasure and in the central margin opposite it *[Ibi] i hid'* had been originally jotted down and then partially erased. Also in Shrops. on 255, again in a holding of Reginald, at Eudon, *Silua lx porc'* has been inserted later in slightly paler ink into a space too small for it (the *rc'* of *porc'* had to be interlined) and *silu'*... *porc'* can just be deciphered in the right margin, though erased. In Som. 87 the *lxx* of the present value of the king's manor of Martock is written over an erasure and in the margin next to it (not erased this time) is another *lxx* and the scribe also wrote *septuag'* (*septuaginta*) above it further to emphasize the correction.

[7] This would seem to be the main scribe writing hurriedly and no doubt intending his note to be erased. An erasure in the centre margin of Berks. 58v is also of this type, as are three in the centre margin of Devon. 100v next to entries containing words written over erasures. Because of the number of cases where a partly erased marginal note does correspond to a correction in the text, it may be justifiable to assume that other, total, erasures in the margins beside corrected text are also erased memos. See p. 122, n. 1 above on the sequence of correction at which one, and perhaps all, of these particular alterations to the text took place.

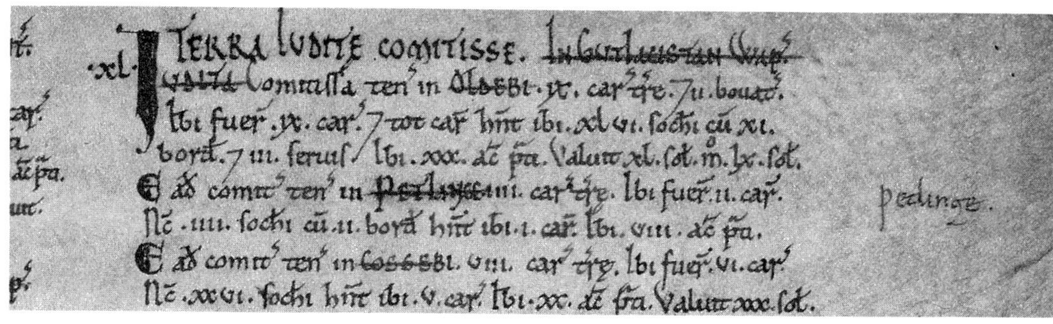

a. The main scribe wrote *petlinge* in the margin of Leics. 236 probably to remind himself to enter this place-name in the text. Later he did so over an erasure, but forgot to erase his reminder. (*slightly reduced*)

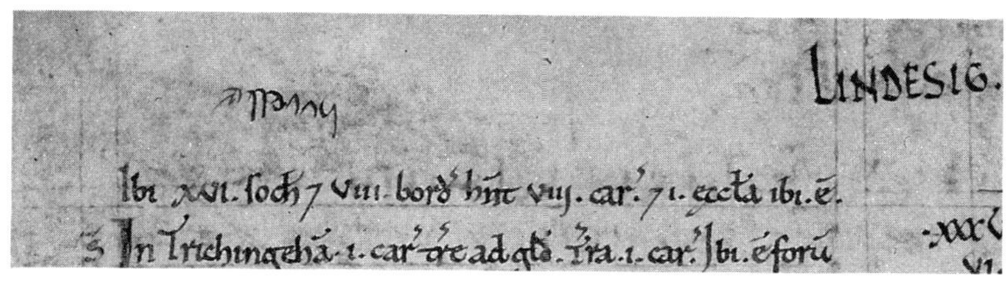

b. On Lincs. 356 the main scribe jotted in *hvvelle* upside-down. Howell is referred to in the text on the previous folio and a holding there was subsequently added at the top of the next, perhaps as a result of this memorandum. (*slightly reduced*)

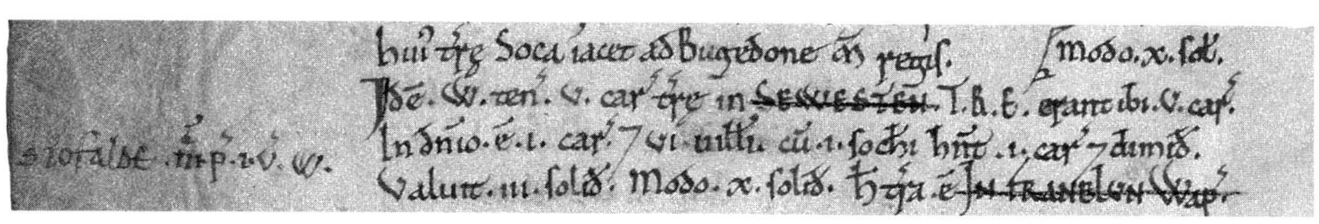

c. Stofalde $\overset{a}{iii}$ *p' i. v'. W*, '[In] "Stofalde" the third part of 1 virgate. Waste [?]', on Leics. 235v. A note, perhaps by the correcting scribe, to add details of this holding when they were available. (*slightly reduced*)

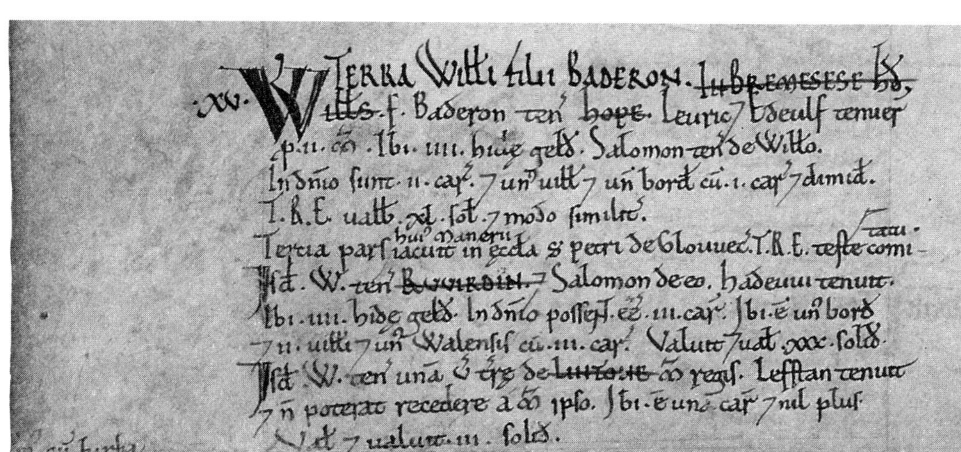

d. The first five letters of *[Wille]lm(us) cu(m) barba*, 'William with a beard', have been trimmed off by a later binder from Herefs. 185v. This may be a reminder by the main scribe to insert details of one of his holdings. (*slightly reduced*)

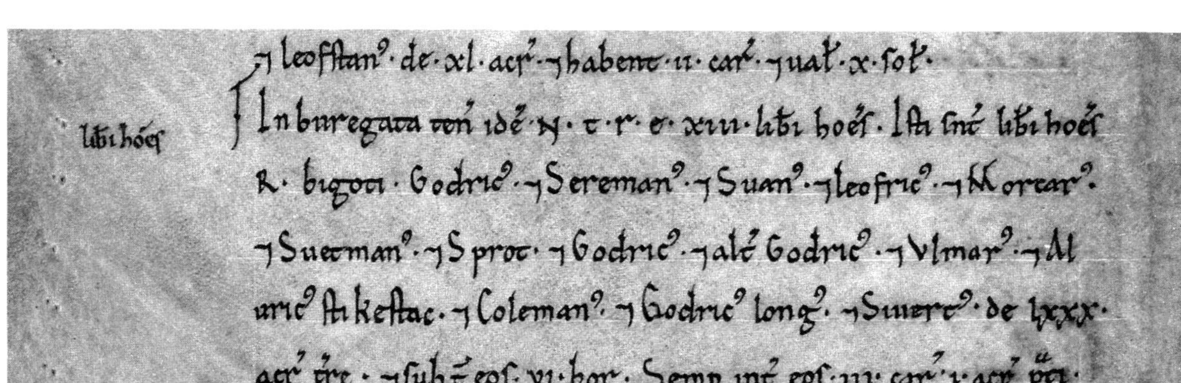

e. A note on Little Domesday Book Suffolk 339v, perhaps added to indicate a subdivision in this chapter: *lib(er)i ho(min)es*, 'free men'. (*slightly reduced*)

FIG. 13

276. The note is in paler ink than the corresponding text; and below it, at the end of Chapter 6, the main scribe added details of Edensor and another manor in the same paler ink. Again, in the left margin of Yorkshire 301 he wrote the place-names *Belebi 7 Steflinflet* (Fig. 12*a*), presumably to remind himself to add them to the king's land when he had ascertained their extent in carucates.[1] Further, at the foot of Herefordshire 183 the scribe wrote *STEPLESHET* (in two lines for some reason, breaking after *STE*). This may have been a note to himself to insert into the space left at the end of the fief any holdings that Nigel the doctor had in the hundred of *Stepleshet* ('Staple').[2] In the left margin of Leicestershire 235v (Fig. 13*c*) is an abbreviated phrase '[In] "Stofalde" the third part of 1 virgate. Waste';[3] this is almost certainly not a proper marginal addition to the text but a reminder, possibly on this occasion by the correcting scribe, to add the details of "Stofalde" when available. There are also marginal references to people, such as [*Wille*]*lm(us) cu(m) barba* (Fig. 13*d*) ('William with a beard', i.e. 'William Beard') in the bottom margin of Herefordshire 185v, although the first letters were lost when the folio was trimmed. *Chetelber* ('Ketilbjorn') is also added at the foot of Lincolnshire 363v. The scribe may have had a note that these two men held land in these counties, but no details.

Possibly of a similar nature are three notes by the scribe who wrote part of the Suffolk entry in Little Domesday. These are the three occurrences of *lib(er)i ho(min)es*, on 333v, 339v (Fig. 13*e*), and 344 and seem to be intended to show the subdivisions of Chapter 7. In the right margin of 336 the scribe writing the text at this point added *de Feudo*, which probably refers to the acquisition by Roger Bigot of Buxhall to 'complete' Baylham.[4]

(*g*) *Marginal Figures*

In several counties, Northamptonshire and Warwickshire in particular, figures are written in the margin

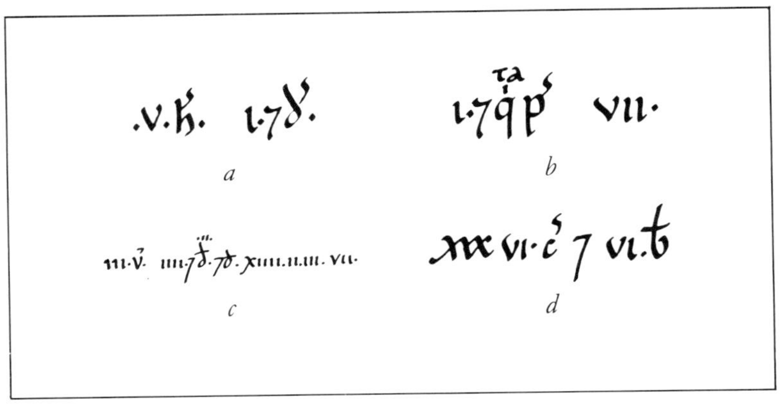

FIG. 14

which seem to refer either to areal or to tax measurements, as a few are followed by a noun-abbreviation, such as *h* for *hida(e)*, or *c* for *carucata(e)*, as in Figs. 14*a*, *d* and 15. The meaning of the figures is far from clear in every case. In Essex there are three sets of figures at the foot of 8 (Fig. 14*c*), 20, and 87, all done by the same scribe. In the first instance these definitely refer to the hidages in the chapter above, and whereas in the second they mostly agree, in the last they have very little correspondence to the hidages in the chapter. Of the two similar sets in Norfolk 261 and 265 which are ostensibly linked with the assessment of the lands of the holders there, only the first one corresponds and then only with the acreages of the free men and sokemen in the subholdings; even so one figure is incorrect.[5] However, in Yorkshire, *xxx vi c' 7 vi b'* is also written at the foot of the left column of 304v (Fig. 14*d*) and it refers to the total carucates and bovates of the main holdings, less the berewicks, of the Bishop of Durham in that column.[6] It was almost certainly written (though rather badly) by the main scribe, though for what purpose is unknown. Against the first two entries for the land of Peterborough Abbey in the right margin of Leicestershire 231 are written *i* and *ii*. The figures in Warwickshire (Fig. 14*b*) seem for the most part to be roughly half the hidages of the manors they appear against and may perhaps refer to the amount of the land that was held in demesne.[7] It is possible also that this is the meaning of the figures in Northamptonshire, all of which are written beside church lands (Fig. 15).[8] The significance of the figures in Oxfordshire, Nottinghamshire, and Suffolk has yet to be grasped, although they seem to be contemporary with Domesday Book because the ink

[1] *Sibiford* is written (again in paler ink than the text) above the heading on Oxon. 160, probably to remind the scribe to include more details of land in Sibford. Land in Sibford (and in Drayton, also in Oxon.) was added in the space left after a chapter in Staffs. 250 (perhaps as late as 1088, although by the main scribe; see Gullick, 'Great and Little Domesday Manuscripts', pp. 106–7 above). They both may have been added in the wrong county by mistake—it is perhaps relevant that they are in the same position, in the penultimate folio of a county, as the *Sibiford* reminder and the repeat of the Drayton entry. Although certain lands do appear elsewhere in Domesday Book in the wrong county, no doubt as a result of confusion at an earlier stage of the Domesday inquiry when the primary division of material was not by county but by fief, this is unlikely to have been the case here. However, there was obviously some confusion in the 'original returns' on the positioning of Sibford because another part, held by Hugh de Grandmesnil, is entered in Northants 224v, although the bulk of the vill must have lain in Oxon. in 1086.

[2] In the left margin of Wilts. 72v the main scribe wrote *laci* (the *l* is faint), probably to remind himself to add the holding of (Roger de) Lacy: it is significant that a joint holding of Roger de Lacy and two others was added later at the foot of the opposite column. See also *Brunetorp* in the bottom margin of Lincs. 341v, *Middeltone antea* in the left margin of Hants 46v, as well as *Stein Ware* in the bottom margin of Herts. 137.

[3] The *W* may not abbreviate *Wasta*, but possibly *Willelmus* 'William (Lovett)', the tenant-in-chief, indicating that the land in "Stofalde" was his.

[4] *Ex inf.* A. R. Rumble.

[5] For a possible reason for these 'lists', see R. Welldon Finn, *Domesday Studies: the Eastern Counties* (London, 1967), 77. He is also unsure whether or not they were written at the same time as Domesday Book.

[6] W. Farrer in *VCH Yorkshire*, ii (1912), 217 n. 8 read *xxxvii c' 7 vi b'*, presumably because he used the faulty Ordnance Survey facsimile, and came to a different conclusion.

[7] This may have been given in the 'circuit volume' containing War. (if such existed), as it was in Exon, or in the 'original returns'; but it was excised in the abbreviation process. It is interesting that most of these figures seem to have been done by the correcting scribe, though those on War. 239v, 244 are in darker ink and may have been inscribed later. But why it should have been thought useful to include those figures for these entries only is a mystery. It is very unlikely, as stated by W. F. Carter in *VCH Warwickshire*, i (1904), 334 n. 8, that the scribe was merely 'trying his pen' here.

[8] Northants 221, 221v, 222, 222v; these were also probably written by the correcting scribe. There is also a *iii* in the right margin of 226 next to the space between Chs. 34 and 35, but it does not seem to be of the same type as the other figures here.

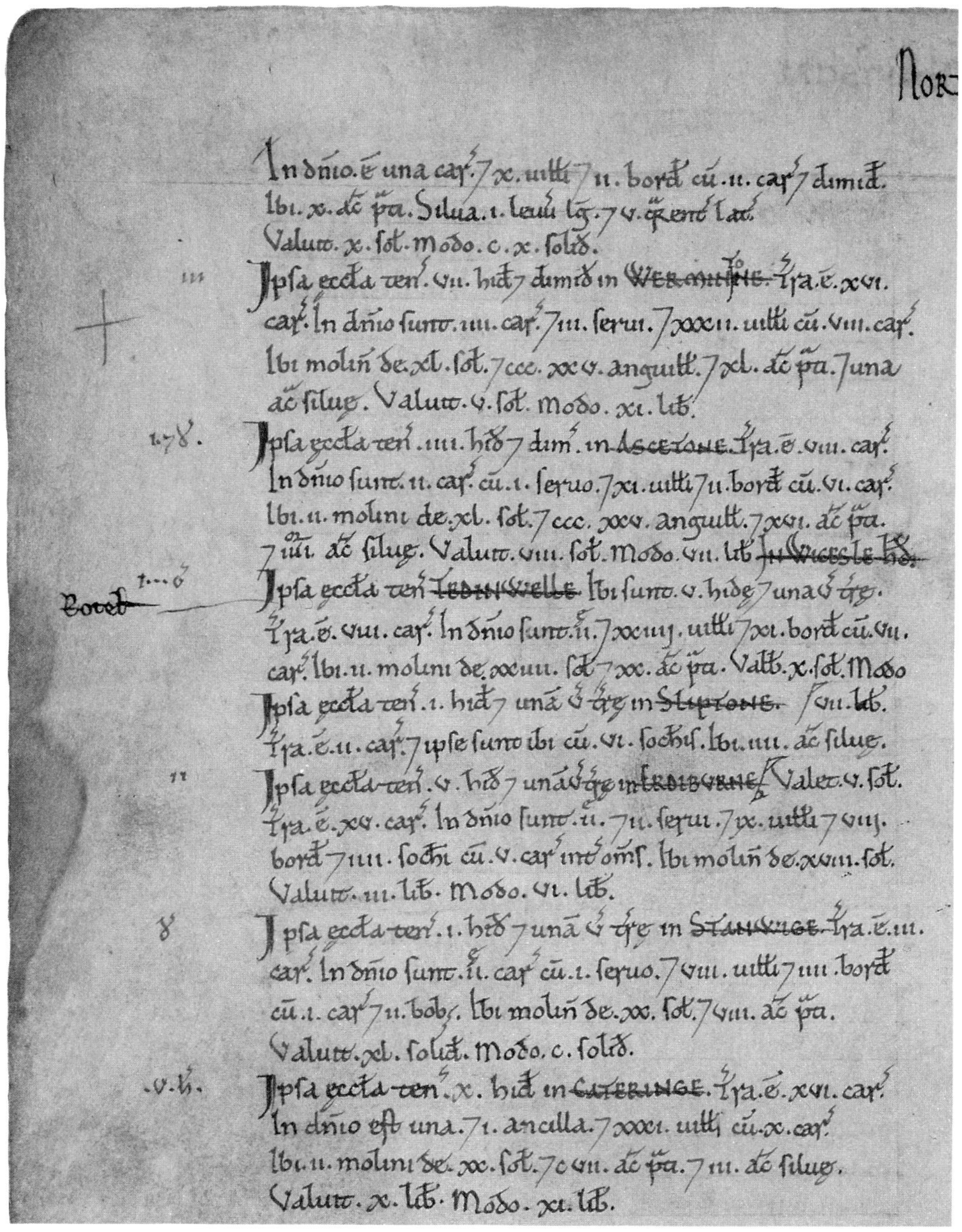

FIG. 15

A miscellany of annotations inscribed against holdings belonging to the Abbey of Peterborough on Northants 221v (*actual size*). The series of neatly-written marginal figures ('3', '$1\frac{1}{2}$', '1 . . .v[irgate]', '2', '$\frac{1}{2}$', and '5 h[ides]'), were perhaps inscribed by the correcting scribe and may indicate the number of hides and virgates held by the Abbey in demesne.

The cross was apparently drawn at the same time as the rubrication as it is in the same red pigment; such crosses were often written next to entries concerned with the Church.

The prominent word *Rotel'*, abbreviating *Roteland*, was added *c.*1300 to show that Tinwell was then in Rutland. This county had increased in extent since 1086.

is the same colour as that of the text in each case. In Bedfordshire the numbers *i* to *vi* single out six consecutive entries on 218v; here the purpose is clear because the text itself states that these six lands were put by Ralph Taillebois in or under the king's administration.

2. ANNOTATIONS INSERTED EITHER IN 1086–1087 OR IN THE MEDIEVAL PERIOD

(*a*) *Letters Concerned with Other Aspects of the Text*

Several views have been put forward concerning the group of letters illustrated in Fig. 16 which must therefore be described in some detail.[1] It is possible that not all of these are to be classed together and that some have different meanings in different counties. The majority occur either beside a chapter heading or beside the first line of a chapter (Fig. 4*a*). But in Yorkshire and Lincolnshire (as also in Exon) *f*s and *fd*s (Fig. 16*a*) appear next to several successive entries within a fief.[2] The

[1] The *f*, the most frequently recurring letter, appears in Yorks., Lincs., Glos., Notts., War., Hants, Derby., Leics., and once in Dorset, as well as throughout Little Domesday. The *n* or *ñ* also occurs in Glos. (Fig. 4*b*) (although the top of the *n* is not always completely joined, so that on occasion it resembles *ii)* as well as in Little Domesday. The *fr* occurs in Derby., Leics., Notts., War. (possibly), Yorks., and in Little Domesday; *fd'* occurs only in Lincs., and *ñf'r* and *rñf* only in Norfolk.

[2] In Yorks. 300, 300v, 301, 301v, 331, 331v whole series of *f*s are written, right down the column, often next to every entry; in several places they seem to have been erased, as if they had served their purpose. In Lincs. 345v, 346 nine *f*s appear beside entries in the fief of Peterborough Abbey, and in the preceding fief (of the Bishop of Lincoln, Lincs. 344, 344v, 345) ten *fd'*s are entered; the ink of the latter is closer in colour to that of the text than the ink used for the *f*s. It is interesting that a series of similar *f*s occurs in Exon next to the first line of almost

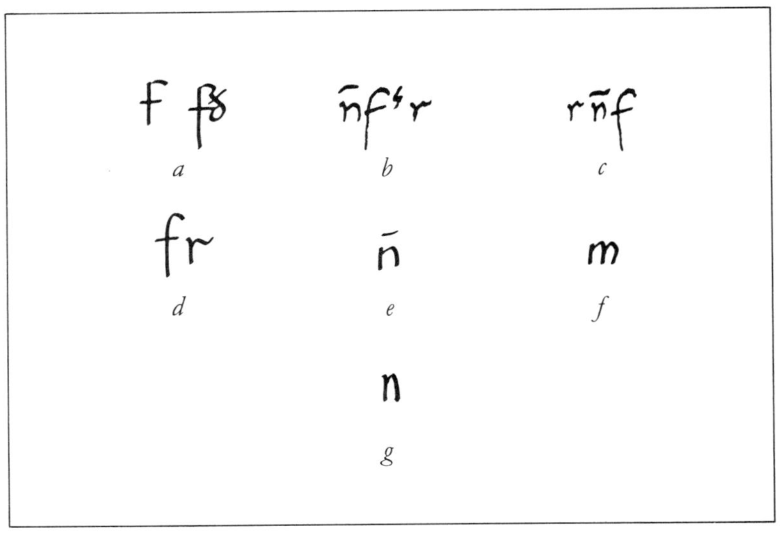

FIG. 16

first interpretation was advanced in 1906 by Charles Johnson[1] and concerned the form in which the information about individual fiefs reached the scribes of both Domesday volumes. He believed that the *n̄f'r* (Fig. 16*b*), which occurs only once (on Norfolk 244v), abbreviated *non fecit retornum* 'has not made a return'; likewise that *rn̄f* (Fig. 16*c*), which also occurs once, on the next folio, was *retornum non fecit*, identical in meaning; that *fr* (Fig. 16*d*) abbreviated *fecit retornum* 'made a return'; that *f* meant *fecit (retornum)*; and that *n̄* (Fig. 16*e*) was short for *non (fecit retornum)*. Such letters, he thought, were intended to show whether a certain tenant-in-chief had, or had not, made a return for his lands to the Domesday commissioners, and these letters were presumably written at the same time as the text. Since the Domesday survey may have relied on two main sources of information, feudal and hundredal, the absence of a return from an individual fief did not mean that it could not be reconstructed from a series of hundred lists as well as from sworn evidence. But the result would have needed checking. Welldon Finn[2] showed that, at least for Norfolk and Suffolk, such letters were not written beside the fiefs of major religious houses, important tenants-in-chief, or those who had been royal officers, reeves, or sheriffs. However, his interpretation is not without difficulties and needs to be more fully worked out. It is possible that the inscription of these letters was haphazard or that if they were in the first draft of Little Domesday some had been left out when the fair copy was made.[3] Certainly it seems odd that one or other of these letters appears beside Chapters 27–42,[4] 44–6, and 48–51 of Norfolk, but not beside Chapters 43 and 47.[5] Finn believed that the *m* or *m̄* (Fig. 16*f*) which occurs in a similar position only in Essex had the same purpose as the *f*s and the other letters, and that it might have stood for 'a return of manors', while *f* represented 'the whole fief'. His first point concerning the *m*s seems likely enough, but if the *f* represents 'the whole fief' this does not explain the strings of *f*s that appear next to successive entries in chapters in Yorkshire (and in Exon also) and, to a lesser extent, in Lincolnshire, when an *m* would be expected.[6]

Galbraith[7] believed in the existence of feudal returns and considered that *n̄f'r* meant *non fecit returnum*, but he also felt that as these letters occur in Great as well as in Little Domesday they should refer to an inquiry made some years after the Domesday inquest and were added 'casually and occasionally'. Certainly the appearance of many of these letters which were written with a thinner pen and in ink of a different colour from that used for the adjacent text suggests later inscription. This may possibly have been as late as 1100 and carried out by a single clerk, as the great majority of the letters in both the Great and Little Domesday volumes are very similarly executed.

On the other hand it is possible that *f* does not abbreviate *fecit* and has nothing to do with making, or not making, returns. It could be short for *feudum* 'fief', 'holding' and be one of the series of later checking marks listed below under section 2(*b*). Perhaps it was inscribed against those holdings which later formed a knight's fee; only detailed study of the later history of these manors, county by county, will prove or disprove this hypothesis.[8] But this view is lent some support by the occurrence in Lincolnshire of *fd'* (*feudum*?) in a similar position to the *f*s in the next chapter of this county.[9] Canon Foster,[10] on the other hand, believed that *f* abbreviated *frithsoca* 'free soke(land)', but his interpretation was apparently based on an *f* in the central margin of 366 referring to an entry in the right column containing the word *frisocam*.[11] In fact, however, the *f* here refers to Chapter 49 in the left column. His view may possibly explain the occurrences of *f*s beside individual entries in Lincolnshire and Yorkshire, but not beside those in Exon, nor those written next to the first entry only in several chapters in a county. Yet there is

every entry in the Count of Mortain's fief in Devon. (210–223) and of most of his Cornish lands (224–265). The appearance of these *f*s in the predecessor of Great Domesday may suggest that they were written at an earlier, rather than a later, date.

[1] C. Johnson, 'Introduction to the Norfolk Domesday', *VCH Norfolk*, ii (1906), 2, and *passim* in the translation footnotes.

[2] Welldon Finn, *Domesday Studies: the Eastern Counties*, 61–3.

[3] It is not certain that Little Domesday *is* a fair copy: it could well be a 'circuit volume' similar to Exon. The greater neatness of the volume may merely be due to a difference in the material from which it was compiled, or to a difference in standards or in the interpretation of their brief by the scribes involved. Moreover, it was probably 'tidied up', and the rubrication was certainly added, when work ceased on Great Domesday without the abbreviation of the three counties contained in Little Domesday having been done. The abbreviation letters could have been in an earlier recension or even in the 'original returns' themselves, and only partially transcribed.

[4] This assumes that the odd letter beside Ch. 32 is an *f* corrected to an *n* as Johnson (*VCH Norfolk*, ii. 176 n. 3) believed, or vice versa.

[5] Similarly in Suffolk, whereas Chs. 40–62, 64–5, 68–70 (and many earlier ones) have either *f* or *fr* or *n* written beside them, no letter appears next to Chs. 63, 66–7.

[6] See p. 129, n. 2 above.

[7] Galbraith, *Making of Domesday Book*, 82.

[8] This interpretation seems to explain better the series of *f*s in Yorks. and Lincs. and in Exon. Almost all the *f*s in Yorks., except for the faintest ones, are indicated in the translation of that county in *VCH Yorkshire*, ii; only once in the footnotes (241 n. 1) does Farrer remark on these marginal letters and there he states that 'This land [of Robert de Tosny] became a part of the fee of Aubigny of Belvoir'.

[9] See p. 129, n. 2 above.

[10] C. W. Foster and T. Longley (eds.), *The Lincolnshire Domesday and the Lindsey Survey*, Lincoln Record Soc. 19 (1924; repr. 1976).

[11] Ibid. 173 n. 3; see also the Index of Subjects under *frigesoca*, p. 312, where reference is made to those entries beside which an *f* is written.

no real reason why the *f* could not have had a different meaning in these two counties. If this interpretation is correct and the *fd'* has a similar meaning to the *f*, the second letter of *fd'* might not be a *d* with an abbreviation line, but an ð (eth).

On two occasions at least, the letters *f* and *r*, although apparently together, were written at different times and may have had different meanings. For example, on 331 of Yorkshire the *r* next to *Chirchebi* in the left column is not very close to the *f* and is in paler ink; as the plough estimate in this entry has been corrected it is possible that the *r* abbreviates *require* and has nothing to do with making a return.[1] Moreover, the *n*s also may have had more than one meaning. There is a view[2] that those marked beside a series of entries dealing with holdings put into the New Forest in Hampshire 51, 51v stand for *nichil* 'nothing' and refer to the lack of value entered for them in 1086 (sc. *nichil valent/reddunt*). Certainly in these particular folios only lands which have no present value have these marginal *n*s. The *nich'* next to the first line of Norfolk Chapter 42, however, cannot have such a meaning, and according to Johnson[3] it meant that no return was made for the land.

(*b*) *Checking Marks* (Fig. 17)

Next to be considered in the second category is a large, amorphous group of marginalia which takes the form of individual letters or signs. They appear to be checking marks made by clerks as they consulted the folios. The ink colour varies, but is often paler than that of the main body of the text at the point where the marks occur. These features make it extremely hard to tell whether the marks were contemporary with Domesday Book or were added between 1086 and the twelfth, or even the fifteenth, century when the manuscripts were still in frequent use.[4] The precise reason for the checking is also unclear in many cases. Although the same sign often occurs against entries of a similar nature in different counties, in others there appears to be no consistency in the use of a certain sign to denote a particular feature which occurs there.

The most common of these signs is the cross (Fig. 17*a*, *b*, *c*) and this seems to have had various functions. On a few occasions it is used as a transposition sign, as described under section 1(*a*) above.[5] Another purpose

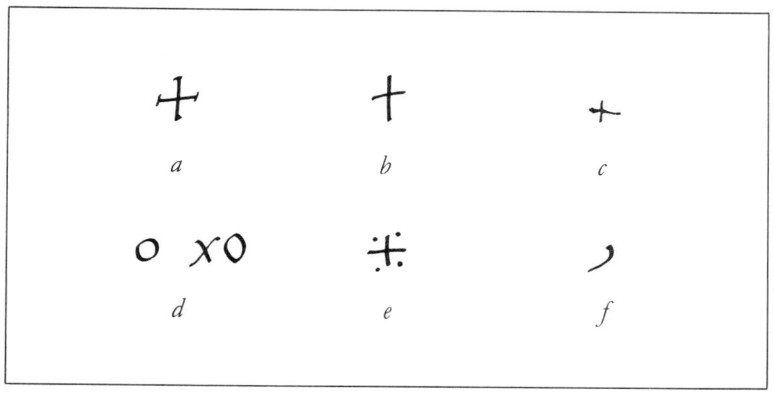

FIG. 17

of a marginal cross was to draw attention to alienated church land. In Somerset there are fourteen of these crosses (Fig. 17*a*), written next to entries concerning land associated with a church in 1066 (most often Glastonbury Abbey), but which by 1086 was held by a lay person.[6] However, by no means all entries recording land taken from a church had crosses marked beside them. In the left margin of Gloucestershire 163v one large cross next to the manor of Stanway is followed by six smaller crosses against six other lands which belonged to Tewkesbury Church, but which appear in the schedule of the king's lands. These Gloucestershire crosses (similar to that in Fig. 17*a*) are executed in red, perhaps suggesting that they were inscribed at the same time as the rest of the rubrication.[7] Sometimes the crosses refer to land held by a church from a lay tenant, such as that next to the left column on Herefordshire 184v, which denotes the manor of Leadon held by St Peter's, Hereford, from Roger de Lacy.[8] Sometimes there is only a tenuous link with the church: the cross next to a holding in Yorkshire 306v (Fig. 17*b*) may refer merely to the fact that the soke belongs to a manor of the Bishop of Durham.[9] Moreover, there are several instances where there is no mention of a church at all in an entry which has a cross beside it.[10] Further study of some of these holdings may reveal that they had belonged at one time to a church, either in Saxon times or after 1086.

The cross also had other meanings. For example, on a few occasions in Hampshire (Fig. 17*c*) a cross is inscribed next to some references to land in the king's forest;[11] see below for another checking mark of this sort. Moreover, on other folios a cross is written next

[1] It is interesting that there is another *r* next to *Cherchebi* on Yorks. 301. Likewise on Yorks. 331v the *r* next to *Chesvic* in the left column is in a darker ink than the *f* preceding it, and again there are signs of a correction in the entry (to the place-name itself), perhaps the result of a *require*. Only on one other occasion in Yorks. is there an *f* and *r* together, on 331v, but here the *r* is the same colour as the *f* and there is no sign of anything erased or added in the entry. However, if the *r* never belongs with the *f* in Yorks., this may support the possibility that the *f*s in Yorks. (and perhaps in Lincs. and Exon too) do not abbreviate *fecit* (*retornum*).

[2] Munby (ed.), *Domesday Book: Hampshire*, note to NF3,5, although more *n*s are visible in the manuscript than he could see on the Ordnance Survey facsimile.

[3] *VCH Norfolk*, ii. 185 n. 3.

[4] See p. 118, n. 7 above.

[5] This may be the purpose of the cross beside the second entry for Pyrton in Ch. 15 of Oxon. 157 because it is in the same colour of ink as the entry (for Ardley) added at the end of the chapter, though there is no corresponding sign beside it.

[6] The Bishop of Coutances, Geoffrey de Mowbray, is counted here as a lay person as his lands form his private fief.

[7] Also the cross in the left margin of Northants 221v and one above the central margin of Oxon. 155v, although these do not refer to church land.

[8] There is also a cross beside the first entry of the land of Barking Church in Surrey 34 and this holding remained with the church until just before the Dissolution: *VCH Surrey*, i (1902), 311 n. 8.

[9] Likewise the one beside the last entry in Hants Ch. 16 (44), land of Wherwell Church, may refer to the exemption from geld of the abbess's house. An entry of a church is also possibly the reason for the cross in Suffolk 305v.

[10] As in Hants 38v (left margin), Derby. 274v, Oxon. 160v, Lincs. 364v, and in Norfolk 131, 147.

[11] In the central margins of Hants 38v, 44v and the right margin of 51 and, perhaps erased, in the central margin of 44 next to the entry for Sway.

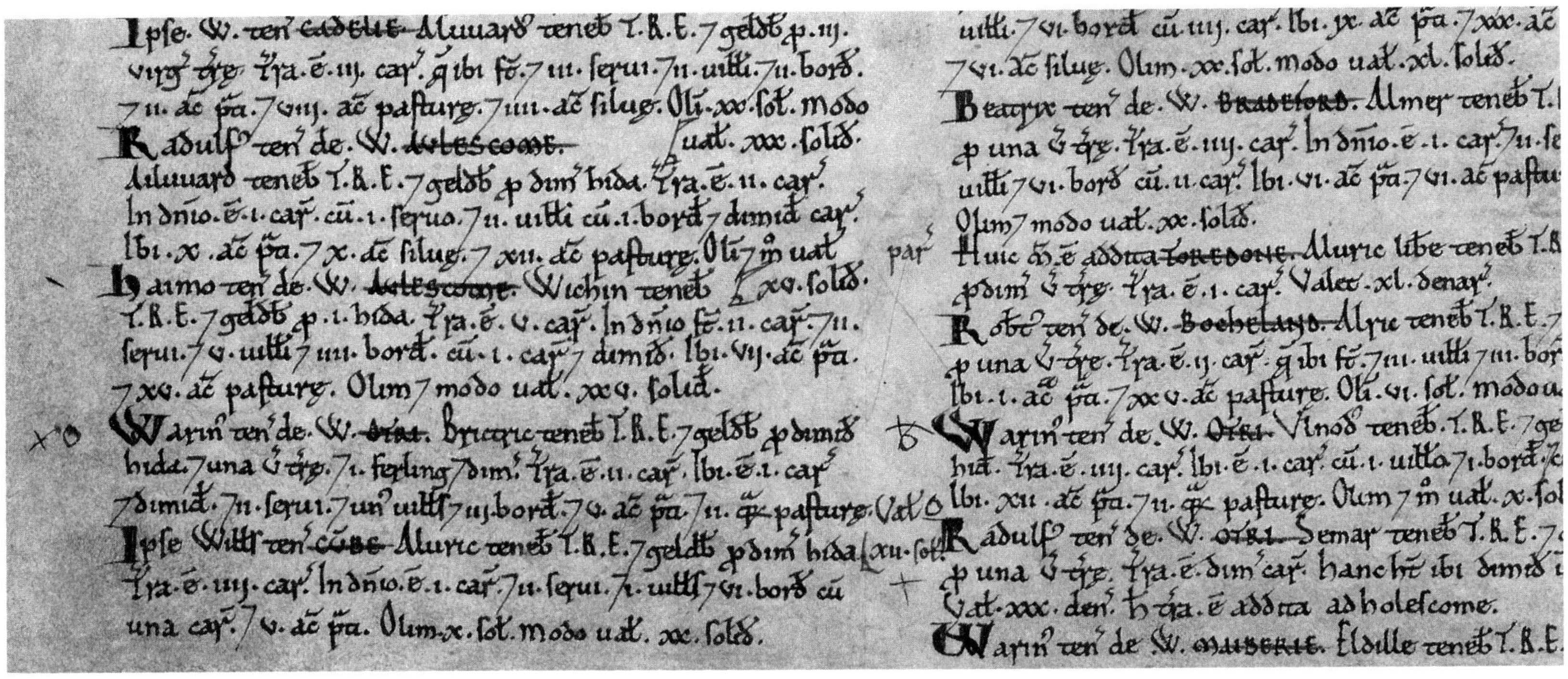

FIG. 18

A group of annotations of various dates on Devon. 110v (*actual size*). *Val' xii sol'*, 'it is worth 12*s*.' was added by the correcting scribe, and with the upside-down 'gallows' sign he has indicated that it should follow *pasturae* at the end of the entry above and to the left. Also written in the centre margin by the correcting scribe, *par(iter)* refers to the entry opposite in the right column, indicating that Ælfric had held the added land in *Toredone* 'in parage' before the Conquest. Probably later on in the Middle Ages the three places here named *OTRI* (Weston and the two holdings in Ivedon) were for some reason singled out by a clerk who inscribed the checking mark ◊ against them. At a slightly later date a further checking mark × was also added beside the same entries: in the centre margin the × next to the first *OTRI* overlaps the ◊.

to holdings in the same vill.[1] The large crosses beside entries in Essex 51v and 63 seem to indicate that these entries are partial duplicates of holdings already entered elsewhere in the county.[2] However, the meaning is not yet clear of a number of crosses, such as the two that appear at the top of some folios[3] or those that are inscribed next to blank lines in the Lincolnshire text.[4]

Finally, there are a great many crosses executed with a stylus without ink, mostly drawn aslant, in the margins of a number of counties, in particular Northamptonshire, Lincolnshire, and Yorkshire.

There are several other marginalia which would appear to be checking marks because they are written beside entries of a similar type. For example, in Devonshire a misshapen *o* occurs beside some, but not all, entries containing the place-names *Otri* and *Aisse* and, once, *Wiche*.[5] This cipher is sometimes coupled with a cross written aslant (Figs. 17*d*, 18), probably done slightly later and with a thinner, scratchier pen.[6] In Yorkshire a cross with dots in the corners (Fig. 17*e*) is written next to several entries containing the heading *Crave* ('Craven')[7] and once on 332, very faintly and possibly erased, next to the chapter heading of Roger de Poitou's lands.[8] A similar sign, but without the dot in the bottom right angle, occurs also in Yorkshire 301v next to a marginal *r*.[9]

A dot appears in the margin beside the first line of entries in several counties and seems to have had various meanings. For instance, in Surrey 32v dots appear next to holdings of which most, if not all, remained in the hands of Chertsey Abbey and might have been marked to signify disputes with tenants.[10]

In Bedfordshire 210, 212, and 216 dots are in-

[1] Small crosses in a paler ink of a blacker colour than that of the text, suggesting later inscription, appear beside two entries on Stafford in Staffs. 248, 248v; two other entries concerning this place have roughly written *c*s beside them (247v).

[2] A. Rumble (ed.), *Domesday Book: Essex* (Chichester, 1983), notes to 25,25 and 30,50. In the right margin of Yorks. 301 there are nine rather faint crosses and on 301v several more, many of them faint and so possibly erased. Some of these Yorks. crosses may refer to the existence of partial or complete duplicate entries elsewhere in the county. See also p. 134, n. 3 below.

[3] On Oxon. 155v and Yorks. 307. The one on Sussex 28v is above a holding given to Battle Abbey; *VCH Sussex*, i (1905), 446 n. 3.

[4] On Lincs. 344, 346; it is possible, though unlikely, that the author of these crosses thought that church land had been omitted here.

[5] *Wiche* represents some six different places in Devon, *Aisse* about seven, and *Otri* and variants no fewer than twelve. Moreover, some *Otri*s had been single manors in 1066 but were divided by 1086; see, for example, Thorn and Thorn (eds.), *Domesday Book: Devon*, general notes to 19,42 and 19,43. These marginal signs may be an attempt to relate and to distinguish them. See Hallam, 'Annotations', p. 138 below, for evidence that some of the *Otri* and *Aisse* entries were used in legal actions in the fourteenth century, although the marks may not have been made then.

[6] An *o* also appears beside *Piteham* in Kent 3v.

[7] On Yorks. 322, 329v, 331v.

[8] Farrer, in *VCH Yorkshire*, ii. 289 n. 35, states that these marks (but only the ones on Yorks. 322, 331v) indicate that the Craven holdings 'had formed part, or subsequently formed part, of the fee' of Roger de Poitou. If this is so, and the identical sign on 329v meant the same, it would seem that the lands in Craven on 329v passed from Osbern d'Arques to Roger after the Domesday survey.

[9] It may indicate that the land is detailed more fully later in the schedule (Yorks. 330), although other land so entered does not have such a sign. The dot in the bottom right square is also missing from the sign on Yorks. 322, but the meaning is different.

[10] Hallam, *Domesday Book through Nine Centuries*, 102–4.

scribed next to four entries concerning the place-name *Tamiseforde*, and in Gloucestershire next to references to Tewkesbury. Meanwhile, in Worcestershire and Herefordshire dots appear next to almost all references to the place-name *Wich(e)*, possibly indicating a check on the salt rights of Droitwich. However, it is not always easy to differentiate between a dot added for a particular purpose and an ink spot, while in Kent it is possible that the dots are in fact merely part of the first letter of the entry. Sometimes two dots appear together next to entries, particularly in Northamptonshire; there the place-name *Langeport* has such pairs of dots on three occasions, but other places have them too.

Meanwhile there are a few comma-type marginal signs which refer to land in the king's forests (Fig. 17*f*). Although those in the central margin of Gloucestershire 166v (Fig. 4*c*) and in the left margin of 167 and 167v exhibit the same dark ink as the text there, these signs may well have been put in the manuscript at the time of one of the royal inquiries into forest rights in the early fourteenth century.[1]

Apart from these, there are several other signs which occur only once or twice and which may or may not belong to this category of checking marks.

(*c*) *Quire Signatures*

A feature of the last ten gatherings of Great Domesday is the group of 'quire signatures'. These are the letters *a* to *k*, running backwards in sequence and written in the same position in the bottom left corner of the verso of the last folio of each of these gatherings (Fig. 19). They were not inscribed by either the main or the correcting scribe, but appear to be in an English hand and contemporary with Domesday Book. They may have been written to indicate the correct order of the exceptional number of gatherings that make up Yorkshire and Lincolnshire, probably as an aid to the binder.[2]

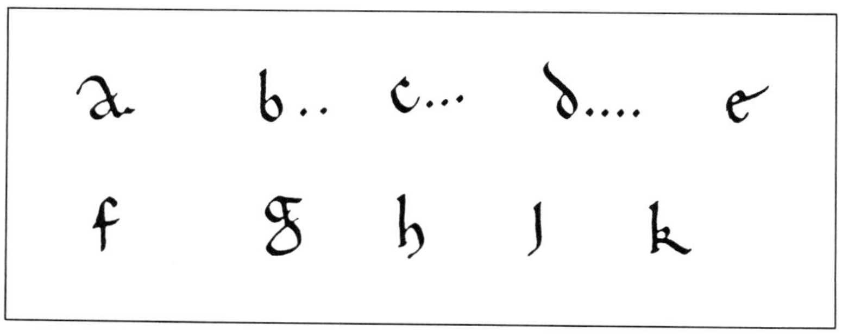

FIG. 19

3. MEDIEVAL ANNOTATIONS DEFINITELY LATER THAN 1086–1087

In this category are several place-names, occurring both in Great and in Little Domesday (and also in Exon). For example, *Gerdelai* is faintly written in the bottom right-hand corner of Northamptonshire 228 and refers to the manor of Yardley Hastings above it. The script suggests a date of insertion from *c*.1300. At about the same time *Todeworthe* (Fig. 20*a*, the final *e* is very faint) was written in the right margin of Wiltshire 69 and refers to the (first) manor of North Tidworth, similarly entered next to it in the text. At the foot of Yorkshire 379, the Summary, is written *Tikhill & Strafford* which also dates from *c*.1300. Tickhill Castle was the administrative centre of the Honour of Tickhill, and the lands listed in the text above were undoubtedly in that Honour in Strafforth Wapentake. The scribe had omitted the Strafforth Wapentake heading and the annotator has supplied it in the bottom margin.[3] In Little Domesday *Tillebyr'* (Fig. 20*b*) was written twice, by two different scribes, in the top margins of Essex 36 and 42 which contain details of Tilbury.[4] It is interesting to observe that the second *Tillebyr* appears to have been written a few decades earlier than the first, towards the end of the thirteenth century as against the first third of the fourteenth. Also at about this time a series of eleven abbreviations for Rutland (*Rotel'*, Fig. 15) was added in the margins of Northamptonshire 219–228v. The county of Rutland was only partly formed at the time of the Domesday survey, a third of its later lands being listed in the Northamptonshire folios as full members of that county.[5] But by the end of the thirteenth century Rutland was regarded as an independent county and it became important for fiscal, judicial, and administrative purposes to indicate which of its lands had been surveyed in Northamptonshire. However, the word *Rotel'* was not added against every Northamptonshire holding which later formed part of Rutland: apart from entries which are no doubt covered by adjacent *Rotel'*s there are two places, Horn and Casterton (220, 229), beside which *Rotel'* probably should have been inscribed.[6] The latest marginal addition, apart from the antiquarian jottings that are discussed in the next section, seems to be *Clarehov* on Yorkshire 380, dating probably from the sixteenth century; the place-name form nearest to this on this folio is *Clareton*, although, unlike the others, it may not refer to a place at all.

4. ANNOTATIONS ADDED BY THE KEEPERS OF DOMESDAY BOOK FROM 1570 ONWARDS

This account of the annotation of the manuscripts is concluded by a brief mention of several extensive mar-

[1] See also Dorset 78v (left margin) and Oxon. 154v (central margin); and see Hallam, *Domesday Book through Nine Centuries*, 66–7 on the forest inquiries.

[2] For a fuller account, see Gullick, 'Great and Little Domesday Manuscripts', pp. 104, 107 above.

[3] *Ex inf.* M. Faull.

[4] Only the first two occurrences of this vill in Essex have such a marginal addition.

[5] Only two of the three wapentakes which were to comprise the county were treated as *Roteland* in 1086 ('Martinsley' and Alstoe), the third, Witchley, being an integral part of Northants. 'Martinsley' and Alstoe were attached to the end of the Notts. survey because their lands were counted as part of the total of two Notts. wapentakes, although with the rubricated heading *Roteland* on 293v. Some of their lands were also surveyed in the circuit that included Lincs. and are duplicated in that county (though with minor differences) where further holdings in Thistleton are recorded which do not appear in the Rutland folios.

[6] It may be relevant that Horn is the only holding of the Bishop of Durham whose fief was added in the space left at the foot of the column and so may have been inadvertently missed by the annotator; and that there is no Witchley Wapentake heading for Casterton, although this royal manor was covered by such a heading on Northants 219v and a *Rotel'* was inserted there.

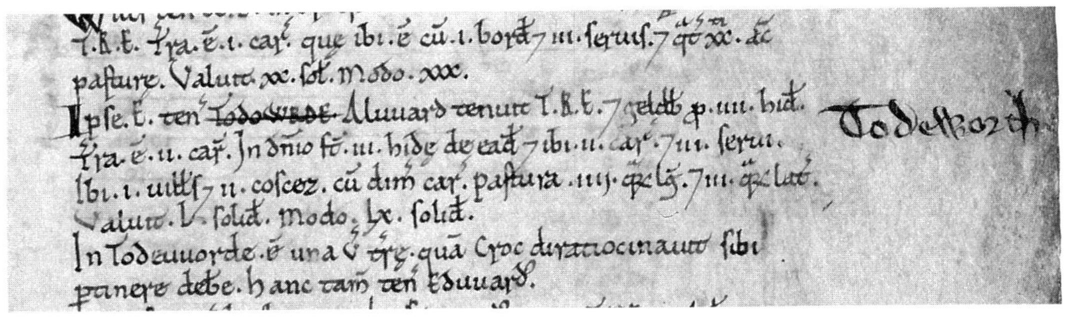

a. Wilts. 69 (*actual size*).

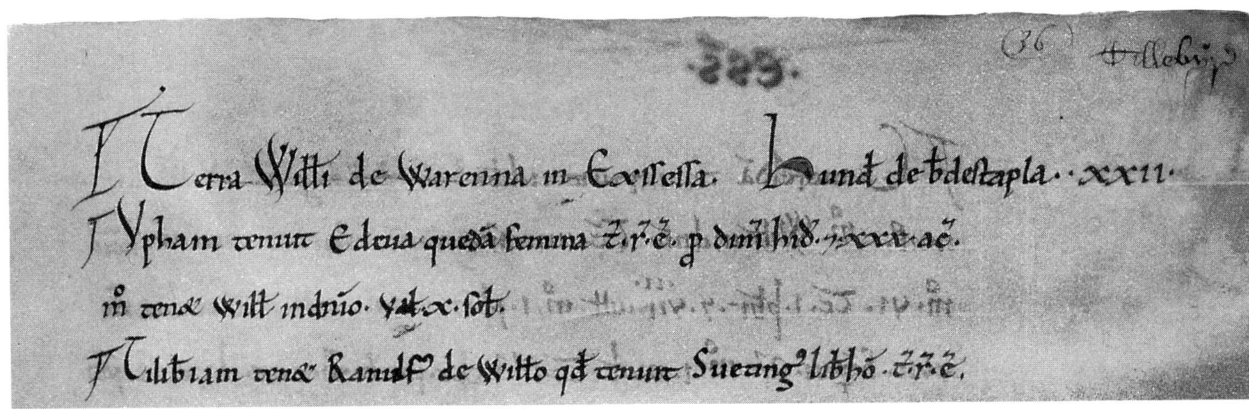

b. Essex 36 (*actual size*).

FIG. 20

ginal notes in Great Domesday, which begins with those done by Arthur Agarde, who, as deputy chamberlain of the Exchequer, was a keeper of Domesday Book from 1570 to 1615.[1] He was a noted scholar and archivist and his interest in Domesday Book and the mensuration it records[2] is shown in his first marginal note, signed and dated 1583, at the bottom of Kent 1 *verso*, which begins 'Look what a sulung is on the following page at this note'. Right on the edge of the folio thus referred to, his drawing of a tiny hand points to the statement that $400\frac{1}{2}$ acres make $2\frac{1}{2}$ sulungs.[3] He also drew a misshapen head, or perhaps a helmet, on Norfolk 128v.[4] The remaining five of his marginal annotations are practical directions. In Herefordshire 179 he instructs the reader that more details (of Archenfield) can be found in the king's land, and on Rutland 293v and 294 he comments on the position of various Rutland lands in other counties.[5]

Perhaps the most important, and certainly the most helpful, annotations done by a keeper were those of Edward Fauconberg who on 3 and 7 January 1659 foliated Great and Little Domesday and noted this fact on a folio at the front of each volume (Figs. 3 and 7, Special Study XVI, pp. 140, 145 below).[6] There are many other antiquarian jottings, both by the keepers and by Abraham Farley, in the preliminary pages of Great Domesday as well as several in the text itself.[7] The last annotation of all is a descriptive heading, written in crayon in the top margin of Cheshire 268v: 'Flintshire & North Wales'. The handwriting is similar to that of Abraham Farley and dates from the mid-eighteenth century.

Although after this the practice of making personal additions to historical documents became unfashionable, a series of oblique pencil marks, some single and others double, appears to have been made in the nineteenth century on the text of Great Domesday, in the *Clamores* sections of Yorkshire and Lincolnshire. These may well be checking marks, but at present their meaning is not clear.[8] Also in hard pencil are six vertical crosses done by one hand in Northamptonshire and Leicestershire; they would appear to be checking marks as they are drawn next to entries containing the place-name *Westone*.[9] Finally, during the 1869 rebinding of the

[1] Hallam, *Domesday Book through Nine Centuries*, 115–17, and 'Annotations', pp. 140–46 below.

[2] This formed part of his lecture to the Society of Antiquaries in 1599 and is preserved in BL MS Cotton Faustina E V, published in T. Gale, *Registrum Honoris de Richmond* (London, 1722), App. II.

[3] It is possible that he indicates other measurements with a hand, but that these have been cut off during the trimming of the leading edge of the manuscript during subsequent rebindings. It may be relevant that a small cross appears next to the entry in Lincs. 336 which concerns the English method of reckoning 120 for 100, which was the subject of the second half of Agarde's annotation on Kent 1 *verso*, referred to above.

[4] There is a third drawing in Domesday Book which probably dates from before Agarde: a much larger hand in the right margin of Cambs. 199 pointing up to where the folio number is now written (although, of course, this would not have been there then). It would seem to indicate an error in the text at this point (a mistaken hundred head); see A. Rumble (ed.), *Domesday Book: Cambridgeshire* (Chichester, 1981), note to 26,51.

[5] On Derby. 272, in English in a mock Domesday script (the rest are in Latin), he gives instructions on where the town of Derby is described; see Hallam, 'Annotations', p. 142, Fig. 4, below. And on Leics. 230v there is the cryptic 'Look in the other book and there you will find a weir' (on Leics. 232v there was a mill—and so perhaps a weir—at Hugh de Grandmesnil's holding at Galby which is below this note).

[6] On folio o in Great Domesday and folio h *verso* in Little Domesday.

[7] See Hallam, 'Annotations', pp. 140–49 below.

[8] For example, there are nine in the left margin and four in the central margin of *Clamores* 373 and nine on 375v; others appear on folios 375, 376, 376v and 377.

[9] Northants 222v, 223, 224, 225v, 227v, and Leics. 235.

manuscripts one of the repairers, J. Kew, wrote his signature on the centre-fold of folios 437/442 in Little Domesday.

Incidental Marks

It only remains to mention briefly a number of pen marks, scribbles, doodles, and ink blots that can be observed throughout both manuscripts, some of them erased or partially erased.[1] There are also smudges of orange paint or ink which mar the folios of several counties. Occasionally it is very hard to tell if a mark is a scribble or a genuine checking mark, such as the marks in the centre margins of Sussex 16v and Hampshire 41v and in the left margin of Bedfordshire 215. It is impossible to tell whether all these were the fault of either the original eleventh-century scribes, or the clerks checking or annotating later: they are in various shades of dark brown and black ink and also in the mercuric sulphide used for the rubrication.

The margins of Great Domesday as well as the text itself are further disfigured by applications, as well as random splashes, of gall. Oak-gall was applied to passages of the text which had been rubbed or were faint and had become hard to read; as it was colourless when first made, splashes sometimes occurred inadvertently and in one or two places it looks as if a large amount of gall was spilt over the page and carelessly wiped away. Unfortunately, over the years this substance has turned a dark brown colour owing to oxidization and what was once legible to the person employing it, is often no longer so.[2] No one is exactly sure when the gall was applied, but the text was evidently more legible to Farley in the 1770s and 1780s than it is today:[3] this may be either because the gall was put on after Farley's day or because it had not oxidized so darkly by that time. A further possibility is that Farley may even have used it himself.

Thus the marginalia of both Great and Little Domesday Book tell us much about the two manuscripts. The numerous additions to the text, small and large, indicate that work on Great Domesday was done in a hurry and before all the information was available. It is also obvious that it was corrected while work on it was still in progress, probably from putative 'circuit volumes' of which Exon at least is an actual specimen, or from the 'original returns' of the several circuits. Both the main scribe and the Norman correcting scribe were responsible for these checks and corrections before William the Conqueror's death in September 1087. Other marginalia show that both manuscripts remained in use as working documents for a long period, and were frequently consulted on questions of original land ownership, taxable values, and manorial appurtenances and rights, for the 'checkers' have left their marks against many entries. Finally, we can appreciate how the keepers of the manuscripts from the sixteenth to the eighteenth centuries regarded Domesday, and enhanced its value to scholars of the time with practical instructions in the margins, and the numbering of the folios themselves.

[1] Some of the doodles are quite elaborate, such as those in the left margin of Wilts. 66v.

[2] For example, gall was applied several times to Lincs. 337, 337v; it is particularly disfiguring on Yorks. 317v, 318. Splashes occur in both these counties too.

[3] In the Ordnance Survey facsimile for Yorks., Farley's text is reproduced for the marginal addition on 317v and also for the last entry on 318, because the gall has almost completely obliterated the original.

[While proofing for the present edition, it was discovered that the lettering obscured by the gall-stains was noticeably clearer in the facsimile than in the manuscript, provided that the extra plate necessary to reproduce their deep yellow-brown colour was left off. Accordingly the publishers decided to favour the legibility of the text at the expense of the true colour of the stains, so that they appear in the facsimile as a dull grey.—Ed.]

AUTHOR'S NOTE

I would like to thank the Hon. Robert Erskine, Dr E. M. Hallam, and my husband, Dr F. R. Thorn, for their many helpful suggestions on the content and layout of this Special Study; also Mr M. Gullick for sharing his views on the scribes of the Domesday manuscripts. I am very grateful to Dr Helen Forde of the Public Record Office for making the manuscripts available to me during their photographing and rebinding, and for the welcome and help given to me by Mr Frank Haynes, Mr Don Gubbins, and Mr John Abbott in the 'cage' at Kew where the manuscripts were being conserved from 1984 to 1986.

C. Thorn

XVI. ANNOTATIONS IN DOMESDAY BOOK SINCE 1100

ELIZABETH M. HALLAM

ONE of the most immediately striking features of the Domesday manuscripts is their excellent state of preservation: they are at first sight, as Sir Francis Palgrave remarked in the 1830s, 'as fresh and perfect as when the scribe put pen to parchment'.[1] But on closer examination, signs of the considerable use made of Domesday throughout its history begin to emerge. The outer corners of the leaves in both volumes are supple and pliable where the oil from human hands has permeated the parchment, particularly on the sheets at the beginning of each county section where the lists of tenants-in-chief are written. Some of the edges of the pages have suffered damage and have needed repair; others appear to have been trimmed. The several rebindings have left their mark in sets of sewing-stations in the centre-folds of the sheets, which have been weakened by the considerable number of perforations.[2] Such signs of wear and tear are a reminder that Domesday Book, although today regarded as a great historical relic and as a museum-piece of international importance, has a long history behind it as a working record.

There are other reminders of the book's uses through the centuries in the many notes and annotations which it contains. Made since 1100, they have for the most part been ignored until now. They fall into two categories: the usually brief marginalia and annotations in the body of the text, and the collection of notes and jottings, some quite substantial, on the pages before and after the main section. The additions to the text were almost all left out in Abraham Farley's magisterial 1783 edition of Domesday Book; and the photozincographic facsimile of 1861–3, although remarkably accomplished for its time, allowed in only a few more. The Victorian makers of the latter blanked out later additions from pages of text, preferring rather to leave spaces or empty pages. Because scholars have worked almost exclusively from these two versions, and very few have been able to consult the original, the purpose and significance of these notes have hitherto been left unexplained.

The end-leaves preceding and following the original text-leaves of Great and Little Domesday, with their annotations, have not always been an integral part of the volumes, but seem to have been included at various rebindings. The folios of Great Domesday now marked i–iv and v–xxii were probably incorporated at the sixteenth-century rebinding, as were many of their equivalents in Little Domesday. In addition, loose leaves and sheets (now mostly leaves) of parchment, bearing notes and annotations by the book's keepers, but also including two thirteenth-century documents, were collected in the front of Great Domesday, and were probably attached to it. These were put into their present order of folios A to H by Robert Rivière, the Victorian binder, in 1869, and were then bound into Great Domesday, probably for the first time.[3] Folio o, however, is an original leaf as it is conjoint with the Kent folio 7. Since one of these pages of memoranda, folio Hv, bears handwriting dating from the 1470s—in a table of contents—the tradition of collecting useful material in the volume dates back at least to this period.

As with the textual annotations, the writings on all the end-leaves were left out of both the 1783 transcription and the 1861–3 facsimile; and they have only ever received brief mention until now.[4] But, like the signs of physical wear to the manuscript, such notes provide a valuable insight into Domesday's changing uses throughout the centuries, and the different ways in which it was regarded by the custodians who wrote them. Those additions and marginalia dating from between 1100 and 1570 are of a practical nature, mainly emphasizing names, facilitating access, and reflecting Domesday's legal uses. From about 1570 and for about two centuries thereafter they become far more copious and detailed, demonstrating the antiquarian interests of the manuscripts' keepers. For the years after the publication of the 1783 edition they are much scarcer as the original Domesday was no longer needed for research and came to be viewed more and more as a venerated and sacrosanct monument of the past.

THE MEDIEVAL ANNOTATIONS

Great Domesday's principal compiler left his work uncompleted, probably on the death of William the Conqueror in September 1087. The draft returns for Essex, Norfolk, and Suffolk had not by then been condensed and were therefore simply appended to the survey, as the volume now called Little Domesday, in what earlier had been intended as their penultimate form. Spaces had been left in Great Domesday for entries for the cities of London and Winchester, but they, like the Eastern

[1] R. H. Inglis Palgrave (ed.), *The Collected Historical Works of Sir Francis Palgrave*, iii (Cambridge, 1921), 321–2.

[2] M. Gullick, 'The Great and Little Domesday Manuscripts', Special Study XIV, pp. 107–9 above; H. Forde, *Domesday Preserved* (HMSO, London, 1986).

[3] The arrangement of all the additional folios to Great Domesday is set out in Appendix III, the Gatherings Chart, pp. 164–5 below.

[4] Public Record Office (abbr. PRO), *Domesday Re-bound* (HMSO, London, 1954), esp. 21, 41; C. Thorn, 'Marginal Notes and Signs in Domesday Book', Special Study XV, pp. 133–5 above.

Circuit returns, were not written into the volume. Some attempt to rectify that omission was later made with the Winchester Domesday, a separate description of tenures in the city made in about 1110 and, like Domesday Book itself, based probably on much earlier lists of holdings. The Winchester Domesday is one of several investigations made in the earlier twelfth century but not connected with the Conqueror's survey. They include lists of holdings in Leicestershire, Lindsey, and Northamptonshire[1] and the summary of the fief of Robert de Bruis which between 1120 and 1129 was added to Great Domesday itself, on blank leaves contained within the Yorkshire section 332v–333 (Fig. 12, Special Study XIV, p. 104 above).[2] The hand is distinctively later than that of the main text; many of the place-names are in a different form from that of 1086–7; and no rubrication has been added.[3] The entry begins: 'This is the fief of Robert de Bruis which was granted after the book of Winchester was written', the 'book of Winchester' being one of the several names given to Domesday in the early twelfth century.[4]

Robert de Bruis, formerly a subtenant of Hugh, Earl of Chester, had served King Henry I well and had been granted the valuable lands enumerated in the Domesday entry during the first decade of the twelfth century, probably shortly after the Battle of Tinchebrai in 1106. Eighty of his manors had come from the king and another thirteen from the fief of William, Count of Mortain, which had been confiscated by the king in 1104.[5] Given the important but not entirely unexceptional nature of the man and his holdings, it might seem unusual that this list should be singled out for copying into Great Domesday's pages, particularly so long after the granting of the lands. But the fact that it was written there demonstrates that the book was in this period both regarded and used as a working document—albeit one of great significance. At the same time, it suggests that the Domesday information about the tenure of individual manors was, like the minutiae about manorial resources and values, gradually going out of date. Yet Domesday was used to settle a number of detailed questions about holdings, rights, and taxable values in Henry I's reign; and, according to King Henry II's treasurer, Richard fitzNigel, it remained in daily use at the Exchequer in the 1170s, as the 'inseparable companion in the Treasury of the royal seal'.[6]

Ways in which it was used in this later period are suggested by another annotation, this time in Little Domesday. Two names, 'Henri De Oilli' and (probably) 'Samson', are carefully written with a stylus on the verso of the last page of text (f. 450v), which contains the colophon on its recto (Fig. 1). The letters are large, and their style and the way in which 'Oilli' is spelt suggest that they date from the middle years of the twelfth century.[7] Henry d'Oilly, lord of the barony of Hook Norton, Oxfordshire, succeeded his father in about September 1142 and died in 1163. As sheriff of Oxfordshire from 1155 to 1160 he had an obvious administrative importance; and the pipe rolls of 1155–63, which contain the royal 'accounts', show that he was excused from paying various debts to the Crown in several counties. A pardon for a geld payment, given by a royal writ, was among these concessions.[8] When such allowances were made to any magnate on his lands, then the sheriff, as the king's principal official in the county, had to be notified, and had also to be informed of the estates involved. Domesday Book, as a list of fiefs and of vills and manors, would have been an invaluable starting-point to the compilers of such instructions.[9] Either as a sheriff, or as someone exempted from making one of these payments, Henry d'Oilly's name was, to a royal administrator, evidently well worth noting in Domesday Book. That it appears in the smaller East Anglian volume, which contains counties outside Henry d'Oilly's range of interest, implies that Great and Little Domesday were being used closely together. The other name, Samson, is more cryptic. There is a possible candidate in the 'Sanson' who appears on the pipe roll of 1158–9, excused by the king's chancellor from paying 40*s*. to the sheriff of Norfolk and Suffolk. In the very same roll, Henry d'Oilly was granted two exemptions; but the identification of this Samson, as the one in Little Domesday, remains tentative.[10]

The twelfth-century annotations in Domesday Book

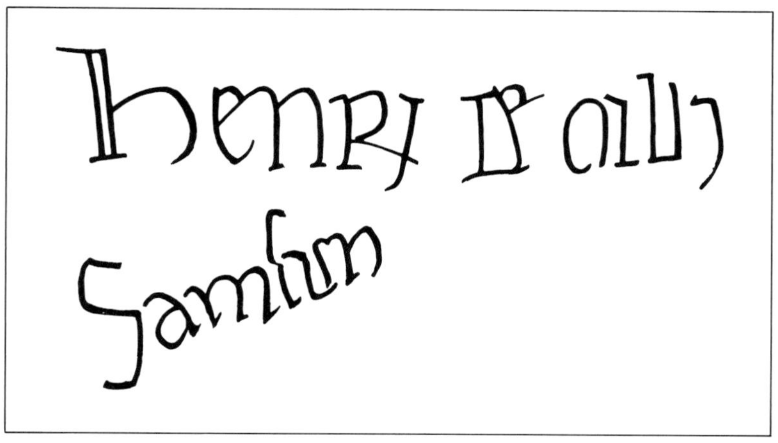

FIG. 1

'Henri De Oilli' and (apparently) 'Samson' written with an uninked stylus re-drawn from LDB 450v.

[1] E. M. Hallam, *Domesday Book through Nine Centuries* (London, 1986), 38.

[2] The dating is through internal evidence. The passage was included by Farley and also appears in the photozincograph.

[3] G. F. Jensen, 'The Domesday Book Account of the Bruce Fief', *EPNS Jnl* 2 (1969–70), 8–17; H. C. Darby and I. S. Maxwell (eds.), *The Domesday Geography of Northern England* (Cambridge, 1962), 457.

[4] Hallam, *Domesday Book through Nine Centuries*, 35.

[5] W. Farrer (ed.), *Early Yorkshire Charters*, ii (Edinburgh, 1915), pp. v–vi, 11.

[6] C. Johnson *et al.* (eds.), *Dialogus de Scaccario* (2nd edn., Oxford, 1983), 63; Hallam, *Domesday Book through Nine Centuries*, 39–42; cf. M. T. Clanchy, *From Memory to Written Record: England 1066–1307* (London, 1979), 18–21.

[7] I am grateful to Mr M. Gullick for discussion of these names. See H. E. Salter (ed.), *The Cartulary of Oseney Abbey*, 3 vols, Oxford Hist. Soc. (1929–31), i. 1, 306; ii. 195; iii. 75.

[8] I. J. Sanders, *English Baronies: A Study of their Origin and Descent, 1086–1327* (Oxford, 1960), 50–4; A. Hughes and J. Jennings (compilers), *List of Sheriffs to 1831*, List and Index Soc. 9 (PRO, 1898), 107; e.g. *Pipe Rolls 2–4 Hen. II*, Pipe Roll Soc. 1 (London, 1884), 23, 27, 35, 36, 81, 140, 149, 150, 185.

[9] Hallam, *Domesday Book through Nine Centuries*, 49; with thanks to Professor W. L. Warren for discussion of this matter.

[10] *Pipe Roll 5 Hen. II*, Pipe Roll Soc. 2 (London, 1885), 12 (Samson), 33, 35 (Henry d'Oilly).

therefore point to its continuing usefulness throughout the first century after it was made, an impression confirmed by the existence of the Herefordshire Domesday. That is an elaborate copy of the Herefordshire folios made in the 1160s, probably for Master Thomas Brown, an important Exchequer official. In it, a copy of the 1086–7 text is annotated in the margins with the geldable values of the manors, and in many cases with updated or replacement place-name forms, which, together with the names of current holders, are all clearly an attempt to bring Domesday's information up to date. But times were changing, and the experiment must have demonstrated that many of Domesday's details were no longer of use, so that the Crown subsequently began to make new surveys of fiefs and of the names of their holders and subtenants instead.[1] As a summary of geldable values, too, Domesday's usefulness was greatly diminished by the late twelfth century. However, as an early and definitive record of manors rightfully belonging to individual holdings, of manorial appurtenances such as churches or mills, of feudal and legal obligations, and of county and of hundred or wapentake boundaries in 1086, Domesday Book remained of value and was extensively cited. Abbreviated versions of its long and complex text, omitting most of the detail, were evidently much in use as finding-aids between the late twelfth and late thirteenth century.[2]

From the 1270s Domesday gained an important new use as the principal proof of ancient demesne tenure. The peasants on any manor listed in the book as the land of William the Conqueror in 1086 or of Edward the Confessor in 1066 could claim valuable legal privileges and light labour-services, in return for which they paid higher taxes to the Crown. Official acceptance of these rights depended very much on whether or not royal interests would be served.[3] Certified copies of complete manorial entries were required in court as proof of such claims, and were widely made for this purpose in the fourteenth and fifteenth centuries. Copies were similarly produced for cases involving ancient rights, tenures, and boundaries, and, although in many such instances Domesday proved irrelevant in practice, legal tradition enshrined it as the essential starting-point. It was also much used in inquiries into royal resources,[4] and all this activity has left its mark in both volumes in the form of marginal annotations and checking marks.

In Little Domesday the most noticeable of the later medieval marginalia are in the Essex section. They are two versions of *Tillebyr'* (Tilbury) apparently written in different hands, the second probably slightly earlier than the first (ff. 36, 42), but both from the reign of Edward I or Edward II (Fig. 20*b*, Special Study XV, p. 134 above). Great Domesday has considerably more of such marginalia, most of which again appear to date from *c.*1300, as with the *Todeworthe* (North Tidworth) on folio 69 (Fig. 20*a*, p. 134 above) and the *Gerdelai* (Yardley Hastings) on folio 228.

At about the same time, the word *Rotel'* (Rutland) was written eleven times in the Northamptonshire folios 219–228v, in order to differentiate those manors which had, since 1086, been moved from Northamptonshire to Rutland (Fig. 15, Special Study XV, p. 129 above). That small and always anomalous county had been represented in Domesday by a description of a mere two wapentakes, appended to the Nottinghamshire folios; later on it had acquired its third wapentake from Northamptonshire. In the late thirteenth and early fourteenth century a number of royal inquiries were made county by county which drew some of their evidence from Domesday Book. Among them were investigations of forest rights (1299–1300 and 1316)—which may have left their traces in the manuscripts in the form of otherwise exceptional checking marks next to forest entries in the Gloucestershire, Dorset, and Oxfordshire folios. There were also surveys of boroughs and manors which were assessed to pay lay subsidies at a higher rate than the counties (1316); and a list was made of royal demesne manors which were liable for tallage (1322).[5] Between 1344 and 1372, moreover, the men of three Rutland vills used Domesday evidence in their struggle to deny their status as ancient demesne tenants and thereby to avoid higher levels of taxation—with ultimate success.[6] The precise occasion when the Rutland manors were marked in the Northamptonshire folios cannot be deduced, but these annotations must have been of considerable value to those making subsequent investigations.

There are yet other annotations in Domesday Book the date, context, and purpose of which are unknown. Among them are a number of circular checking marks which appear in the Devonshire section (Fig. 18, Special Study XV, p. 132 above). One is on folio 101v, next to the entry for the royal manor of Ashreigney (*Aisse*); more are by some of the many *Otri* entries, three of these being on folio 114v and referring to Ivedon and Upottery; and there are others besides. The entries for two of these manors are known to have been used in the later Middle Ages in legal actions turning on Domesday evidence. For example, an extract about one *Otri* was needed in a dispute over labour services in 1377, and the one for Ashreigney in a case involving tolls in 1388.[7] But there is no clear indication that this was the period when the marks were made: another copy of an *Otri* entry was, for example, made as late as 1688.[8]

In assigning the contents list of counties now in the preliminary folios of Great Domesday (f. Hv, Fig. 2) to the later fifteenth century, we are on much firmer ground. Comparison of the handwriting with that of surviving copies from Domesday, datable by their attached writs, shows the list to have been written be-

[1] Hallam, *Domesday Book through Nine Centuries*, 41–2, 48–9.

[2] Ibid. 42–7, 50.

[3] Ibid. 74–113.

[4] Ibid. 64–73.

[5] Ibid. 66–7, 98, 211 (App. III, no. 7); on the checking marks, Thorn, 'Marginal Notes', pp. 131–3 above; also Appendix I, key to marginalia, p. 161 below.

[6] Hallam, *Domesday Book through Nine Centuries*, 99, referring to the vills of Oakham, Langham and Egleston.

[7] Ibid. 99, 102; Thorn, 'Marginal Notes', p. 132 above; C. and F. Thorn (eds.), *Domesday Book: Devon* (Chichester, 1985), general notes to 1,65. 10,1. 16,58. 19,27; 42; 43. 23,18. 34,1.

[8] Hallam, *Domesday Book through Nine Centuries*, 212 (App. IV, no. 17).

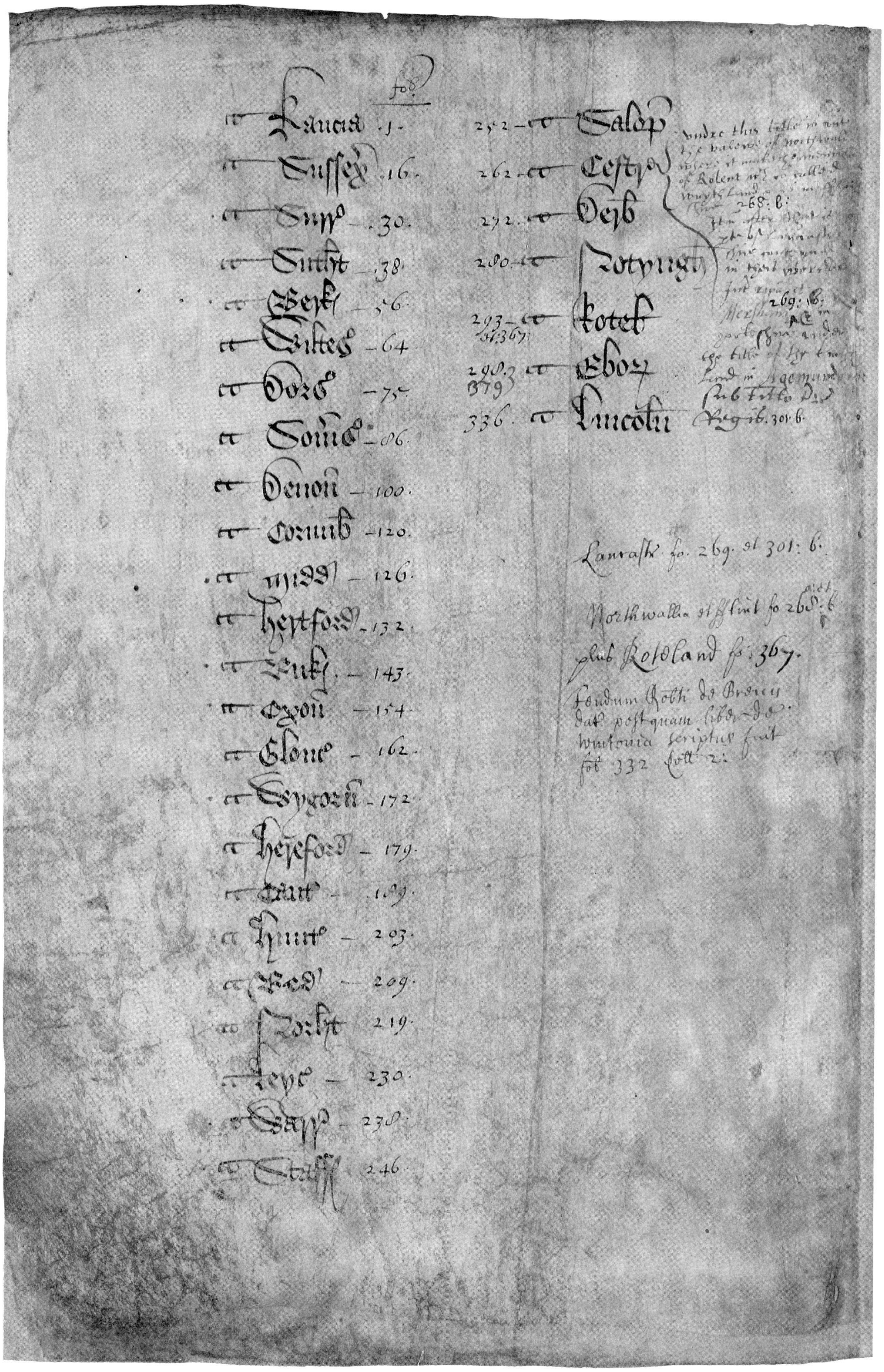

FIG. 2

The list of counties in Great Domesday on folio Hv (*slightly reduced*), written in the late fifteenth century. The foliation numbers were added by Edward Fauconberg on or after 3 January 1659 (Fig. 7). At the top right of the page are a few notes by Arthur Agarde (1570–1615), with another group by Peter le Neve (1684–1712) below.

FIG. 3

The list of the three counties of Little Domesday Book on folio hv (*slightly reduced*) with the foliation numbers added by Edward Fauconberg: his note recording their insertion in this manuscript on 7 January 1659 is to the right. An annotation posssibly by Abraham Farley (1736–91) runs across the centre of the page, and at the bottom a note by Arthur Agarde about the correct nomenclature for an Essex hundred.

tween about 1473 and about 1480.[1] Its author, who regularly made copies from other Treasury of Receipt records besides the book, was probably a clerk working for one of the two deputy chamberlains. Their duties were to care for and to make extracts from the records in their charge and to strike tallies, but it was common practice for such officials to delegate work.[2] The list of the three counties in Little Domesday (f. hv, Fig. 3) looks to be in a slightly later hand, and would appear to conclude the annotations to both manuscripts made by anonymous clerks and scribes during the first five centuries of the book's existence.

[1] PRO C 260/153, no. 21; PRO C 260/154, nos. 7, 17.

[2] For the deputy chamberlains, see J. C. Sainty, *Officers of the Exchequer*, List and Index Soc., special ser., 18 (PRO, 1983), 168, 174.

THE LATER ANNOTATORS

ARTHUR AGARDE

In the reign of Elizabeth I the deputy chamberlains, hitherto visible only as bureaucrats, could for the first time be seen to be working as scholars and archivists. This was greatly due to the abilities and influence of

Arthur Agarde, a lawyer by training, who held one of the two offices between 1570 and 1615. Not only did he continue with his traditional official tasks of caring for and copying the records, but he sorted, indexed, and catalogued them, he explained them to researchers, and he studied them with diligence and interest. Some of his views and theories have been superseded by subsequent record scholars, but it is upon the foundations of his observations that they all have built.[1]

Agarde composed a treatise on records and record-keeping which bring his work at the Treasury of Receipt alive. Written in 1610, its opening pages give an analysis of the many problems of preserving the documents, which are, he says, under constant threat from fire, water, rats, and mice, as well as from their being misplaced or removed. He then describes the records in the four Courts of the Exchequer, among which Domesday has pride of place as 'two of the most ancientest books of record in the realm'. So valuable was this work that it was augmented with further material by Thomas Powell and published in 1631 in his 'Repertory of Records'. The text explains that there are special rules for the care and copying of Domesday Book: no one may place his hands upon the writing, and transcribers must imitate the script of the original.[2] The first precept is probably a very ancient one and is still observed today; the second had been followed by Domesday's custodians since about the 1470s and was to continue into the eighteenth century. Agarde, who had a facility for writing in various styles, developed an elegant minuscule script in which he annotated the manuscript himself and made numerous Domesday copies.[3]

Domesday Book was also singled out from the other records by the security which surrounded it. By the 1620s it was in 'the outer room where the clerks write' at the Tally Court, Westminster,[4] kept in a reinforced iron chest with three locks. The chamberlain and his two deputies held one key each. This safeguard greatly impressed scholars who came to search the record: Sir Henry Spelman, in the first part of his *Archaeologus* (1626), wrote of the three keys and of the substantial fee of 6*s.* 8*d.* which was payable before the book could even be inspected (although he omitted to mention that charges were made for all searches). Extracts, he continued, cost 4*d.* a line; but he praised Agarde for having made him fine copies of Domesday and other records.[5] And although Agarde was bound by the rules to safeguard the book with particular care, equally he was unfailingly willing to explain its contents to visiting researchers and to the antiquarian community at large.

Agarde was an associate of many of the leading scholars of his day, and was one of the early members of the Elizabethan Society of Antiquaries, founded in about 1586. He was a particular friend of the historian and politician Sir Robert Cotton (the creator of the great Cottonian Library), to whom he left many of his manuscripts. Cotton researched in Domesday and other documents with great enthusiasm, and the histories of Huntingdonshire parishes which he wrote into his commonplace book often began with Domesday evidence.[6] Sir George Buck, Master of the Revels, gratefully mentions on the first page of his Domesday collections the help which Agarde had given him in discussing the book's history;[7] and Agarde's name, his imitation eleventh-century script, and his all-pervading influence are in evidence in numerous seventeenth-century compilations of Domesday and other antiquarian materials.[8]

To aid the record-keepers and researchers at the Treasury of Receipt, Agarde wrote two tracts on Domesday. One was a practical guide to the book, containing a long and detailed glossary of obsolete words, alphabetically arranged; lists of castles and of the names of kings, queens, and nobles; and extracts from the *Grand Coustumier de Normandie* and the Inquisitio Eliensis. The manuscript of the latter, Agarde noted, had been lent to him by Cotton on 18 January 1609.[9] It was this work by Agarde which Thomas Powell, the editor of one of Agarde's writings on record-keeping, alluded to as of singular help to searchers in reading and interpreting the book.[10] Agarde's other Domesday treatise, which passed to the Cottonian Library, consists of historical and etymological discussion, and of extracts, bearing on the manuscripts' name and importance, drawn from Richard fitzNigel's *Dialogus de Scaccario*. There is a passage on Danegeld and, again, the extract from the Inquisitio Eliensis.[11] Some of the historical content in this essay proved of lasting value and was much quoted in later works, as was also some of the material contained in a lecture which Agarde delivered to the Society of Antiquaries in 1599. Drawing his evidence from a variety of other records as well as from Domesday, Agarde discussed measurements of land—the hide, the carucate, the bovate, and the Kentish sulung.[12] Although not faultless by modern standards, these writings earned him his rightful place as the founder of modern historical study into Domesday Book.

Agarde's interests and particular preoccupations emerge clearly in his numerous notes and marginalia in the Domesday manuscripts. In both volumes he made an (inaccurate) estimate of the number of pages (Great Domesday, the present f. i *verso*; Little Domesday, f. 451); and he provided helpful hints for later readers,

1 Hallam, *Domesday Book through Nine Centuries*, 114–17.

2 The treatise is PRO IND 17126 (with copies in PRO IND 17128, BL Lansdowne MS 127 and Harley MS 94), printed in part in F. Palgrave (ed.), *Kalendars and Inventories of the Exchequer*, ii (London, 1836), 311–35, and in almost complete form in T. Powell, *The Repertorie of Records* (London, 1631).

3 Hallam, *Domesday Book through Nine Centuries*, 60–1.

4 Society of Antiquaries of London MS 271, ff. 34–5 (I am grateful to Mr I. Gray for this reference); Powell, *Repertorie*, 15, 17.

5 H. Spelman, *Archaeologus in Modum Glosarii*, i (London, 1626), 220.

6 K. Sharpe, *Sir Robert Cotton, 1586–1631: History and Politics in early Modern England* (Oxford, 1979), 17–24; M. McKisack, *Medieval History in the Tudor Age* (Oxford, 1971), 85–94; PRO PROB 11/126, ff. 94v–95v (Agarde's will).

7 BL Lansdowne MS 310, f. 1.

8 BL Stowe MSS 527–31.

9 Bodleian Library, Oxford, MS Gen. Top. C. 22.

10 Powell, *Repertorie*, 133.

11 BL MS Cotton Vitellius C. IX, ff. 229–230v, published in T. Gale, *Registrum Honoris de Richmond* (London, 1722), App. I.

12 Ibid. App. II, from BL MS Cotton Faustina E V.

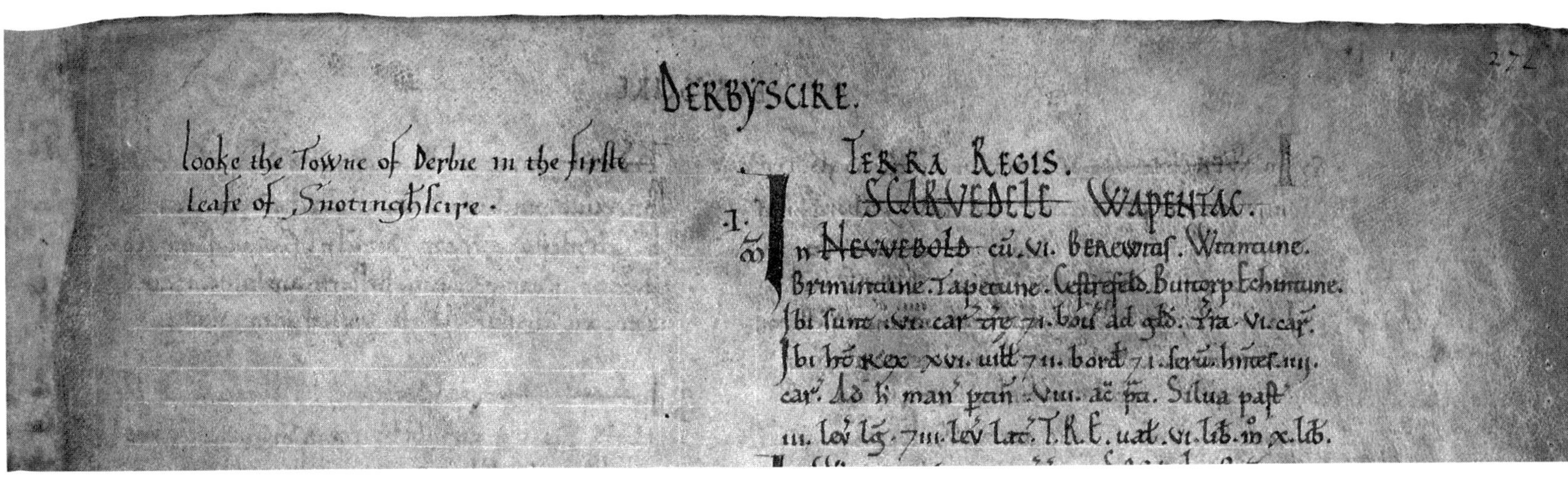

FIG. 4

A helpful note by Arthur Agarde, unusually in English, to resolve a confusion on the opening folio of Derbyshire (272, *slightly reduced*).

as with his directions for finding Dengie Hundred in Little Domesday (f. hv, Fig. 3), for locating the Derby entry at the beginning of the Nottinghamshire quire (Fig. 4) and various Rutland manors in Great Domesday (ff. 272, 293v, 294). A whole page now in the preliminaries of the larger volume (Fig. 5) is covered in notes as to where to find useful information on, for example, the three nights' farm, the names of Anglo-Saxon kings, measurements such as the carucate, and the English method of counting one hundred and twenty for each hundred (a matter also referred to by Agarde on f. 1 *verso*). There are renderings into extended Latin of several words which are heavily abbreviated in the text, and a memorandum, written upside-down and in English, about the loan of the Black Book of the Exchequer to Sir Walter Mildmay on 30 March 1571, and its return on 6 April. Much of the page, which was originally a spare parchment leaf, is written in Agarde's Domesday script. There are yet more of these jottings on folios Dv and Hv, and on folio 462 of Little Domesday, which also has more extensions of abbreviated words.

As well as making these memoranda about his Domesday studies, Agarde used further loose pieces of parchment, some with sewing holes at the head and foot, to inscribe notes about and extracts from other material which bore on the book's history. One text which he quoted was the *Grand Coustumier de Normandie*, a description of the legal customs of the duchy. Its earliest version dated from 1200 to 1220, but it had subsequently been widely augmented and commented upon in its Latin and French versions. On a page which has become folio A, Agarde copied parts of Chapters 28 and 30 in both languages. The texts related to burgage tenure; to alods (lands with no feudal lord) and fiefs; and also to parage, the division of an estate between co-heirs, a form of tenure which is frequently referred to in the Devonshire folios of Domesday.[1]

On what is now folio Ev Agarde expounded and quoted from a number of later records in the Treasury of Receipt. A 'little paper book in the bag of tenures and inquisitions'[2] provided him with material about carucates; the copy of Richard fitzNigel's *Dialogus de Scaccario* in the Black Book of the Exchequer with a note about hides; and a charter of Osbert fitzManners to Anglesey Priory (Cambs.), issued probably in the 1220s or 1230s, with evidence about the selion. He noted that he had put the last document back in its chest in the Treasury,[3] but it cannot now be found. Similarly he stated that he had replaced an extent of the lands of Waleran of Wellesleigh—which he had cited on the hide—in a bag hanging in the Receipt and entitled 'tenures and inquisitions'. However, the original of this extent, dating from 1264, is, together with an inquisition of about the same period, now a part of the Great Domesday preliminaries (f. Fv, Fig. 6). They have been mounted on a single leaf of parchment and incorporated in the volume, probably at the 1869 rebinding, a date consistent with the style of the work. But the extent bears Agarde's handwriting on its dorse (f. F), and he is the most likely original instigator of the somewhat incongruous connection of these documents with Domesday.

Agarde collected references to the book from a variety of other records as well. Still on folio Ev he inscribed an extract from an assize roll of 1277–8, again on the selion, and he noted down the sign which he had written on the document's cover as an identification, a symbol which is still visible today.[4] He quoted a patent roll of 1480–1 on the privileges of ancient demesne tenants;[5] and feet of fines for 1232–3[6] together with a *de banco* (common pleas) roll of 1297–8[7] on the bovate. On the current folio G he gave a copy of *quo warranto* proceedings of 1279–80 in which Domesday was cited, to show that three Somerset manors were not ancient demesne,[8] and on the present folio H, a précis of entries from the hundred rolls of 1275–6 on carucates and the

[1] The manuscript copy to which Agarde referred has not been identified, but for the texts, see *Le Grand Coustumier du Pays et Duché de Normandie* (Rouen, 1539), pp. xlviii, l, lx; W. L. de Gruchy (ed.), *L'Ancienne Coutume de Normandie* (Jersey, 1881), 91, 95–6; see also Thorn, 'Marginal Notes', p. 121, n. 5 above.

[2] Not now identifiable.

[3] Cf. PRO E 40/14480 (confirmation of about the 1240s: see F. Hailstone, *The History of Bottisham and the Priory of Anglesey* (Cambridge, 1873), 202).

[4] PRO JUST 1/1239, m. 9.

[5] PRO C 66/545, m. 23.

[6] PRO CP 25(1)/283/10, no. 104.

[7] PRO CP 40/124, m. 1.

[8] PRO JUST 1/783, m. 48.

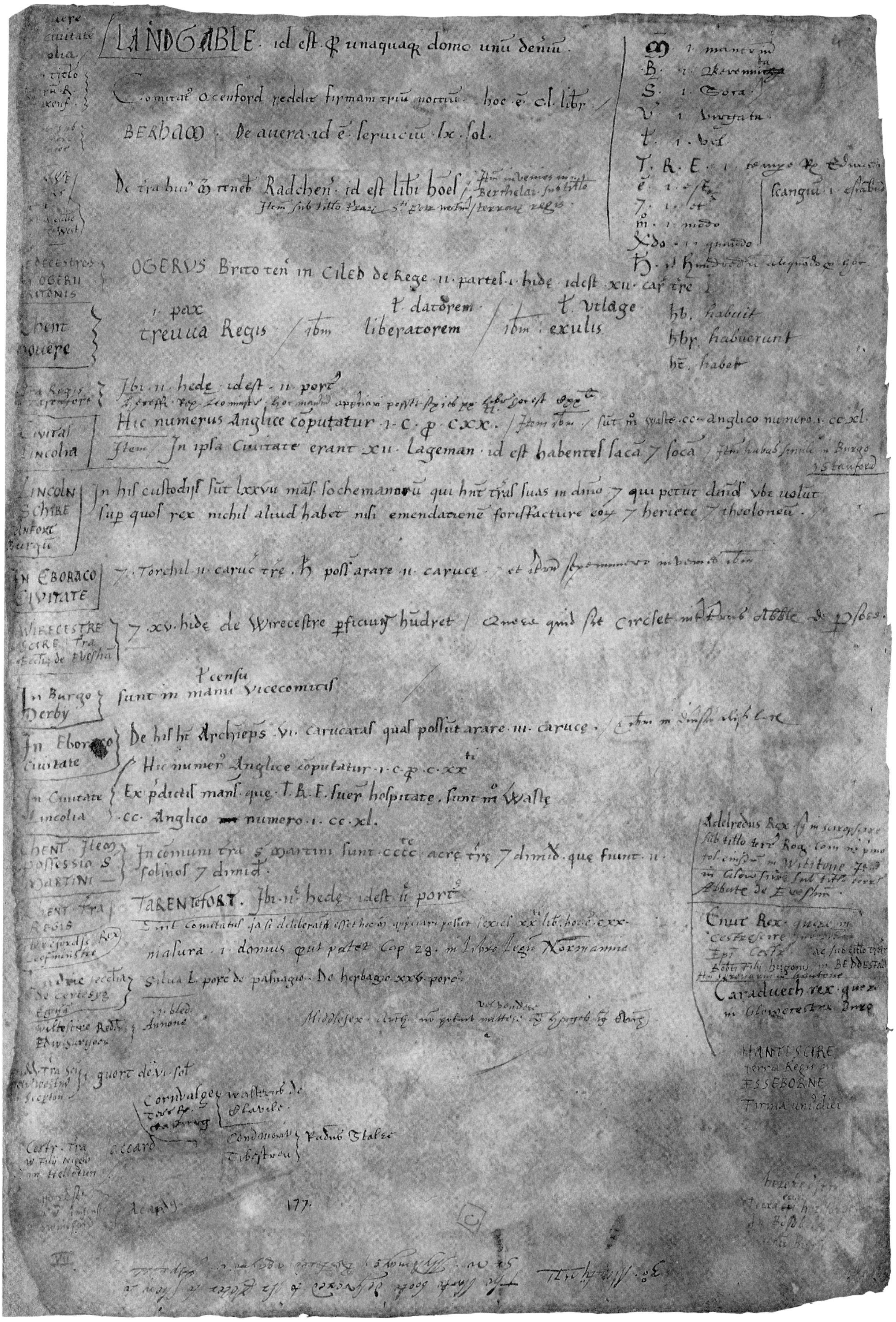

FIG. 5
An extensive collection of jottings on folio C (*slightly reduced*) by Arthur Agarde.

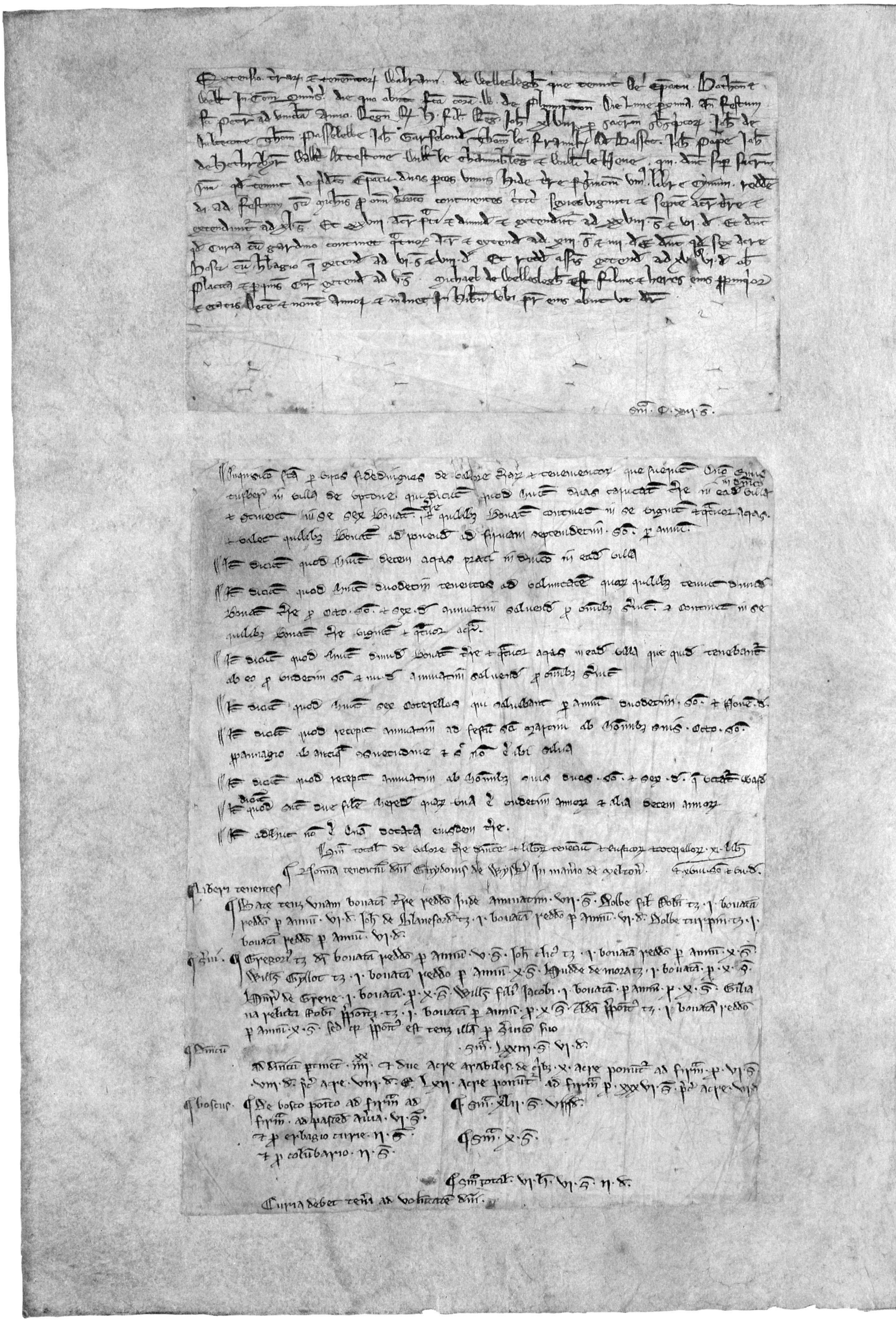

FIG. 6

An extent of 1264, *above*, and an inquisition of similar date, *below*, mounted on to a leaf which is now folio Fv (*slightly reduced*). The dorse of the extent bears Arthur Agarde's handwriting by whom it was presumably brought into association with Great Domesday between 1570 and 1615.

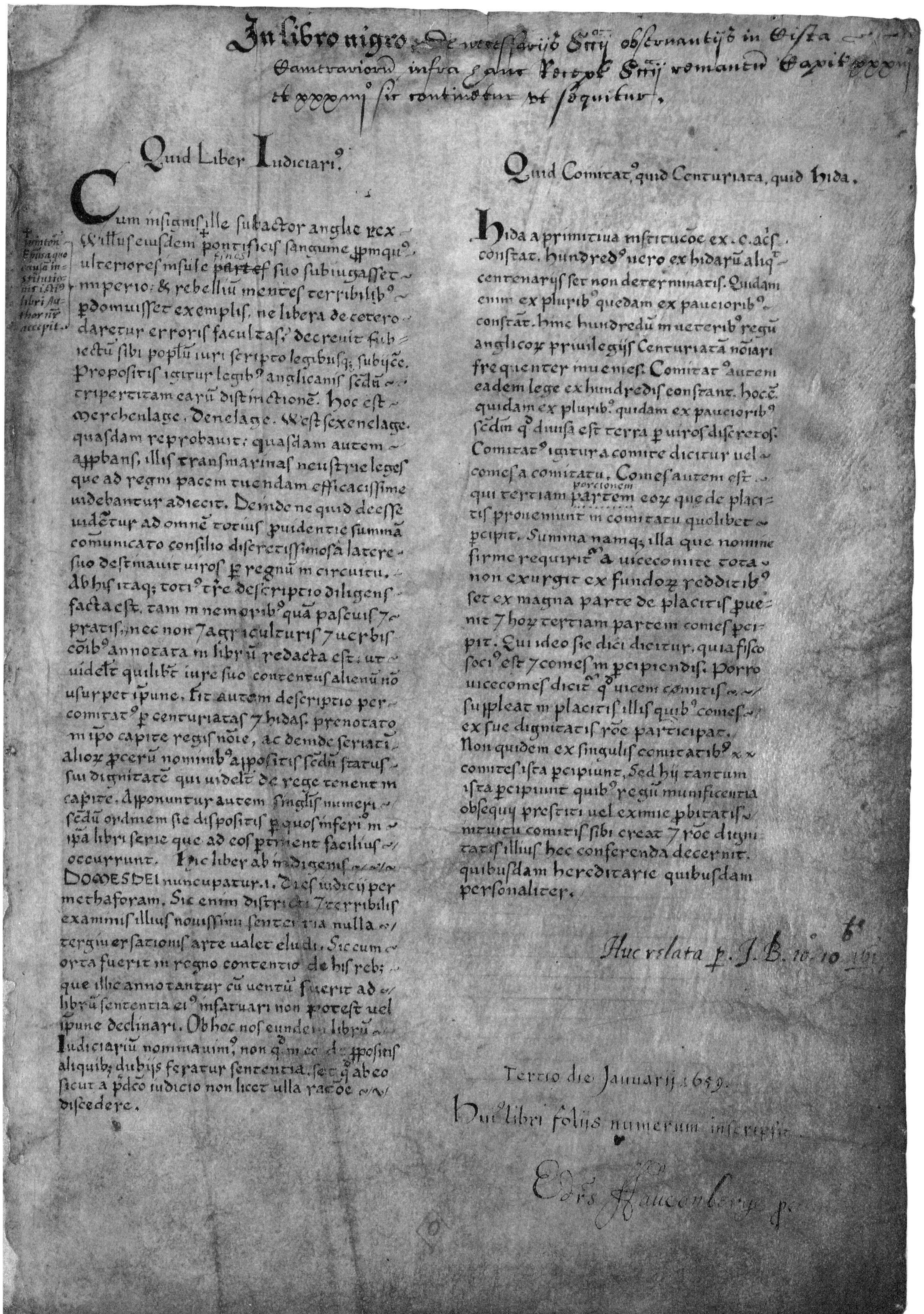

FIG. 7

Folio 0 (*slightly reduced*), which originally was the blank leaf at the beginning of the first gathering of Kent. The two principal columns contain excerpts about Domesday Book from Richard fitzNigel's twelfth-century *Dialogus de Scaccario* written by John Bradshaw on 10 October 1627, with a heading explaining their provenance. This interesting folio also bears the note by Edward Fauconberg stating that he added the foliation numbers to the manuscript on 3 January 1659.

geld.[1] Agarde's commentaries in the preliminary folios and his other jottings in the text of Domesday[2] were to set the pattern for later custodians of the book, several of whom wrote notes of the same kind. But Agarde, in the copiousness of his contributions, left a far greater mark on the Domesday manuscript than any of them, and, indeed, than anyone else since the book had first been made.

John Bradshaw

Arthur Agarde's immediate successor as deputy chamberlain was John Bradshaw, who held the office until his death in 1633,[3] and who, in his work on Domesday, strove to follow in Agarde's footsteps. In 1618 Bradshaw wrote a short tract on Domesday which clearly owed much to Agarde's influence. He began it with the quotation about the book from the *Dialogus de Scaccario* and then explained phrases such as *terra regis*, which he linked with ancient demesne, and TRE: *tempore regis Edwardi*. After discussing other terms such as hide, villein, and bordar, he then noted down from fourteenth- and fifteenth-century plea rolls some references to cases which turned on Domesday evidence. Bradshaw was, however, a modest man who felt himself to be in Agarde's shadow. The import of these later legal records, he remarked diffidently, 'I leave to the judgment of the more learned to be considered of',[4] the 'more learned' being celebrated antiquaries such as Cotton and Spelman, with whom Agarde had mixed on equal terms.

Bradshaw is definitely responsible for one, and probably for a second, annotation in the preliminary pages of Great Domesday, both being excerpts from records. He used the whole of folio o (Fig. 7), at that time still blank, and a part of the original Kent quire, to write out the extracts from the *Dialogus de Scaccario* which Agarde had first noted in his works. These were the passages on the naming of the book and the analysis of the hide,[5] and Bradshaw copied them carefully and accurately, signing his name and the date, 10 October 1627, at the end. But there was also an element of the inappropriate: he inscribed both extracts in quasi-eleventh-century lettering, even though they had been written almost a century after the book. Bradshaw's work is nevertheless well executed and attractive, and proved useful to Domesday's later custodians, many of whom copied it verbatim in their own writings, including Bradshaw's minor textual variations.[6]

The second annotation, this almost certainly by Bradshaw, is on folio ii of Great Domesday, at that time an end-sheet. It gives an extract from a plea roll case of 1253–4, on the subject of the right of presentation to the church of Sandbach, Ches. In the course of these proceedings, an earlier inquisition of 1223–4 was cited, the point at issue being the legal validity of the so-called Domesday roll of Chester. In 1253–4, as thirty years earlier, the justices agreed that the document had perpetual legal validity and could be produced as evidence in court,[7] like Domesday Book itself, after which it was deliberately named. Bradshaw's interest in the Domesday roll clearly stemmed from its title, and he may, indeed, have confused it with the Conqueror's survey. But it had little in common with the book, as it was a roll, begun probably by Ranulf, Earl of Chester (1181–1232), and listing deeds and other useful administrative material of the palatinate of Chester.[8] In Bradshaw's time the original was kept in Chester Castle and was still intact, but later in the seventeenth century its gradual dismemberment began, and today it is represented only by a few fragments. One of these contains charters and deeds relating to the case about the advowson of Sandbach church in 1253–4.[9]

Edward Fauconberg

The next keeper of Domesday Book to make his mark on the manuscripts was Edward Fauconberg, who held the post of deputy chamberlain from 1660 to 1679, having earlier (1655–60) combined it with the higher office of chamberlain.[10] During the Interregnum he introduced a reduction in the fees payable for searches and copies of the records, although their earlier level was resumed after the Restoration.[11] Like Bradshaw, he was a skilled copier of minuscule script, and was respected by scholars and antiquarians for his understanding of Domesday's text. He was also glad to help and advise the less well-informed; and he gave courteous encouragement to Samuel Pepys whom he met in a public house in 1661 and who asked him for information from Domesday 'about the sea, and the dominion thereof' (this is a topic upon which Domesday's information is in fact very circumscribed).[12]

Fauconberg's annotations in Domesday Book were of a highly practical nature: principally, the foliation of both volumes. On folio hv of Little Domesday (Fig. 3) he noted that he had inscribed the numbers in it on 7 January 1659. At that time he signed himself as *camerarius* (chamberlain), but later added the *pro*, presumably after the Restoration when he was demoted to the post of deputy. He had foliated Great Domesday—a few days before his work on the smaller volume—on 3 January 1659, according to his note and signature on folio o (Fig. 7); and he used the information thus gleaned to correct Agarde's estimate (f. i *verso*) of the number of folios in the volume ('*verius* 382 E.F.'). He also inserted

1 PRO SC 5/8/2, mm. 2d, 4d.
2 Thorn, 'Marginal Notes', pp. 133–4 above.
3 Sainty, *Officers*, 176; Hallam, *Domesday Book through Nine Centuries*, 117–18.
4 PRO SP 14/103, nos. 56–7.
5 Johnson *et al.* (eds.), *Dialogus de Scaccario*, 62–4.
6 PRO IND 17176, ff. 91–3.
7 PRO KB 26/152, mm. 10–10d ('rotulus qui vocatur Domisday'); cf. PRO C 66/69, m. 15d ('rotulus qui dicitur Domesday Cestr'').
8 R. Stewart-Brown, 'The Domesday Roll of Chester', *EHR* 37 (1922), 481–500.
9 PRO CHES 38/41/1.
10 Sainty, *Officers*, 19, 176.
11 PRO SP 49/139, f. 12; PRO E 101/337/13; and see PRO C 202/40/2.
12 R. Latham and W. Matthews (eds.), *The Diary of Samuel Pepys, ii: 1661* (London, 1970), 236; Hallam, *Domesday Book through Nine Centuries*, 122.

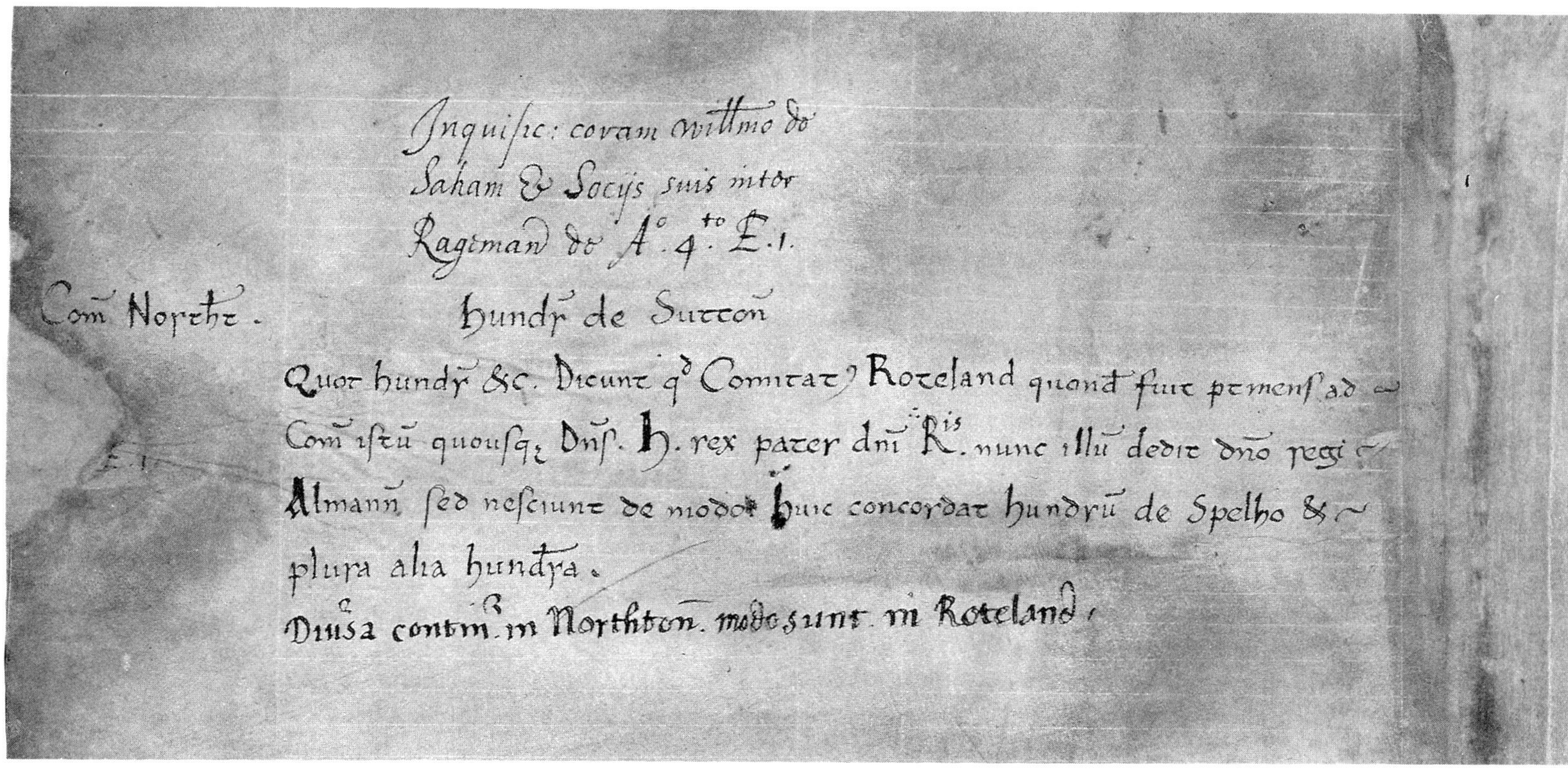

FIG. 8

An inquisition from the hundred rolls of 1275–6 copied on to the blank folio 229v of Northamptonshire (*slightly reduced*) by Peter le Neve.

the new folio numbers into Great Domesday's table of contents (f. Hv, Fig. 2) and into some notes by Arthur Agarde on the same page; and, probably, into Little Domesday's modest list of county names (f. hv, Fig. 3). In addition, he seems to be the author of some fragmentary references, including folio numbers, at the back of Little Domesday (f. 466). This might seem a modest tally in comparison with the long annotations of Agarde, but Fauconberg's contribution was of great value. It immeasurably simplified the work of future deputy chamberlains and scholars, by allowing relatively precise points in the text to be found and identified with dispatch.

A long-serving colleague of Fauconberg was John Lowe, who was a deputy chamberlain from 1666 until 1708. Lowe, a Domesday scholar in the tradition of Agarde, studied the book with great attention, wrote abstracts and indexes of it, and guided the work of many searchers at the Tally Court. Among them was Dr Robert Brady, the leading Tory polemicist during the Exclusion Crisis of the early 1680s, in which the Whigs sought—unsuccessfully—to prevent the future James II from inheriting the Crown on account of his pro-Catholic sympathies. Brady and his Whig opponents waged fierce arguments on the immemoriality or otherwise of the English constitution, focusing particularly on Domesday Book as evidence for and against William I's forcible conquest of England and subsequent enslavement of the Anglo-Saxons. The works of Brady, which cite Domesday as clear evidence for the dispossession of the English by the Conqueror and his men, found little favour after 1688 but are today considered one of the milestones of Domesday scholarship.[1]

[1] PRO IND 17176–7; BL Add. MS 28646; Hallam, *Domesday Book through Nine Centuries*, 123–8.

PETER LE NEVE

Despite Lowe's strong interest in Domesday Book, his hand does not appear anywhere in its pages, unlike that of his fellow deputy chamberlain from 1684 to 1712, Peter le Neve—an eminent and respected antiquary and herald who became Norroy King of Arms in 1704. Little love was lost between the two men: they quarrelled bitterly over what Lowe saw as le Neve's inadequate hours of attendance at the office and over his delegation of tally-striking to a clerk. Lowe also refused to divulge the results of his Domesday inquiries to le Neve,[2] but was clearly unable to prevent him from reading the book, to which his office gave him equal access. Le Neve made numerous searches in it and copies from it, including a transcript of the whole Hertford section for Sir Henry Chauncy's history of that county. Chauncy considered the £15 he paid for it as money very well spent.[3] Le Neve also included Domesday evidence in his treasured antiquarian collections for a history of Norfolk, a work which was eventually written up and published after le Neve's death in 1729 by Francis Blomefield.[4]

Le Neve's hand appears in Great Domesday in four different places. He used a blank page on Northamptonshire 229v (Fig. 8) to inscribe an inquisition from the hundred rolls of 1275–6.[5] The subject was the thorny one of the boundaries of Rutland, and the lettering—inappropriately—imitated that of the book. There are also minor jottings by le Neve in Great Domesday's preliminary folios. On folio iii he noted some appearances in the text of parks for wild beasts and fisheries—with folio numbers; on what is now folio G, the

[2] PRO IND 17175, f. 14; Hallam, *Domesday Book through Nine Centuries*, 128–9.

[3] BL Harley MS 4712, f. 212; Hallam, *Domesday Book through Nine Centuries*, 129. [4] Ibid. 129–30. [5] PRO SC 5/8/3, m. 26.

mention of a weir; and on the present folio Hv (Fig. 2) he made further useful additions to the table of contents, pointing out where material about Lancashire, North Wales and Flintshire, Rutland, and the fief of Robert de Bruis was to be found.

Le Neve also wrote in the Domesday *Abbreviatio*, a magnificent illuminated version of the shortened Domesday text prepared probably in the 1240s for the use of Peter of Savoy, kinsman and adviser of King Henry III.[1] Agarde had made what were, by his standards, discreet annotations in it; le Neve's lettering was far more obtrusive. In the margins of the illustrations of the life and miracles of St Edward the Confessor, he gave descriptions of each scene and references to the appropriate passage in Ailred of Rievaulx's hagiographical biography of the king. He also wrote a less useful memorandum in the front of the volume stating that he, Peter le Neve, one of Queen Anne's deputy chamberlains, believed the book and its illuminations to date from the reign of Henry VII.[2]

In 1712 Peter le Neve was ejected from his office of deputy chamberlain after an unsuccessful machination to gain preferment had rebounded on him. His successors in the next three decades continued to make copies from Domesday—although they abandoned the use of the minuscule script—but showed little inclination for scholarly activity. They had grave problems with the fabric of the Chapter House at Westminster, which became the principal record office for the Treasury of Receipt, and to which Domesday Book was moved in the 1740s. So bad did matters become in the building that in 1751 the main vault collapsed altogether and had to be reconstructed.[3] Committees of the House of Lords set up from 1703 onwards to investigate the state of the nation's archives, and active until 1728, made demands on the State record-keepers for the better sorting, preservation, and listing of their documents. The establishment in 1724 of the new post of keeper of the records at the Chapter House was one result of their inquiries.[4] But meanwhile antiquarians intent on their Domesday studies had to rely heavily on often inaccurate and incomplete copies of the text, and it is no coincidence that the publication of a complete edition of Domesday Book was first widely canvassed at this time.[5]

Abraham Farley

In 1736 Abraham Farley was appointed as one of the deputy chamberlains, a post he was to hold until 1773 when it was combined with the office of joint keeper of the Chapter House records. In or before 1742 he began to work with Domesday Book, and soon came to see himself as a scholar-archivist in the tradition of Agarde and le Neve. Thus he revived le Neve's practice of keeping a register of searches, even using the same volume, and he offered help and advice to antiquarians on Domesday as on the other records in his keeping.[6] He made numerous transcripts from Domesday Book, including one, in 1753, for Philip Carteret Webb, politician, lawyer, and antiquary. It is tempting to see Farley's influence in the important paper which Webb read to the Society of Antiquaries in 1755. In it, Webb gave a sound and balanced account of Domesday Book, made much of the dangers from fire which threatened it, and called for its publication. The Antiquaries endorsed his call with enthusiasm but their funds proved insufficient, and it was not until 1767 that this project was finally to be approved and funded by Parliament. The resulting edition was long in the making, but today, over two centuries after its completion, it still remains the standard version.

The first seven years of its preparation were dogged by inconclusive debate and by several fruitless experiments as how best to reproduce Domesday's text; but in 1774 a method using a specially designed record typeface including Domesday's characteristic elisions was at last approved for the work. In 1770 Farley had been appointed as joint editor with Dr Charles Morton, the under-librarian at the British Museum, and many intense disagreements had arisen between them; in 1774 Farley emerged as the sole editor. It took almost a decade of painstaking effort to bring his *magnum opus* to completion in 1783; and its two volumes, Great Domesday and Little Domesday, were then issued in haste, without even a title-page or table of contents. Despite these omissions, the value of the work was rapidly recognized, and by the time of his death in 1791 Abraham Farley had gained a secure and valued, if not illustrious, reputation.[7]

Farley's transcripts for the parliamentary edition have not survived, but a copy of the Kent folios, which he made for Hasted's history of Kent, is now among the Stowe manuscripts at the British Library, and reveals the meticulousness of his editorial methods.[8] A few minor notes were made in Domesday Book in about the mid-eighteenth century, probably by Farley. The handwriting of these stands out clearly from that of the earlier annotations. Thus the words 'Flintshire & North Wales' are pencilled in on folio 268v, and in Little Domesday there is a memorandum on folio hv (Fig. 3) that Thredling Hundred in Suffolk was represented by the name *Claidone*.

Finally, Farley could be the writer of the words *WERECE'SCIRE* and *WEREC'IRE*, which are inscribed in ink in large, and slightly smudged, red rustic capitals, eleventh-century in style, on folio xxii at the back of Great Domesday (Fig. 9). A further, more tentative,

[1] PRO E 36/284; Hallam, *Domesday Book through Nine Centuries*, 42–4.

[2] PRO E 36/284, ff. 1–2v and facing f. 1.

[3] Hallam, *Domesday Book through Nine Centuries*, 130, 133–4; H. M. Colvin *et al.* (eds.), *A History of the King's Works, v: 1660–1782* (London, 1976), 414–15.

[4] E. M. Hallam, 'Problems with Record-Keeping in Early Eighteenth-Century London', *Jnl of the Soc. of Archivists*, 6 (1979), 219–26.

[5] Hallam, *Domesday Book through Nine Centuries*, 130.

[6] Ibid. 133–4; PRO IND 17175.

[7] Hallam, *Domesday Book through Nine Centuries*, 130–40; M. M. Condon and E. M. Hallam, 'Government Printing of the Public Records in the Eighteenth Century', *Jnl of the Soc. of Archivists*, 7 (1982–5), no. 6 (1984), 348–88, esp. 373–82.

[8] BL Stowe MS 851.

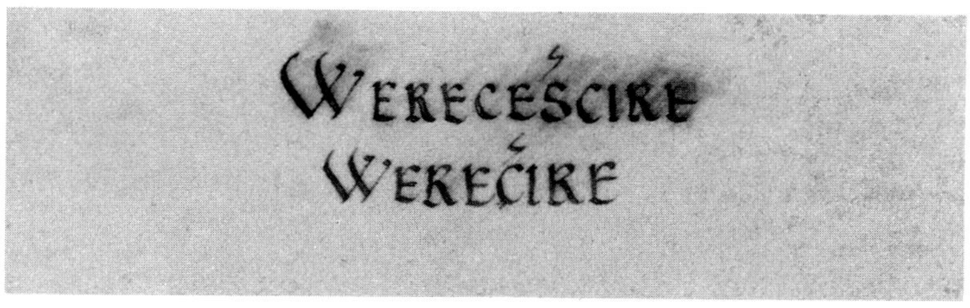

FIG. 9

Two attempts to imitate the rubricated county headings for Worcestershire on f. xxii (*actual size*), the last of the blank leaves added at the end of Great Domesday. Probably made in the 1770s.

WER appears on its *verso*. In 1767–8, when still striving to become the editor of the parliamentary edition, Farley—with Webb's help—had experimented with an engraving of folio 30 (Surrey), a copy of which he had sent to the Lords of the Treasury in support of his application.[1] In the 1770s Owen Manning, to whom Webb gave the plate, had some further engravings made for his history of Surrey; and similarly, Tredway Nash commissioned others for his history of Worcestershire. Farley, with all his experience and interest, was involved with both, but by 1775 he had become so preoccupied with his edition that he had little time or inclination for any rival projects. Manning, infuriated by his delaying tactics, decided to use Farley's colleague, George Rose, to check the proofs instead; Tredway Nash likewise used Rose to verify his Worcestershire engravings, although both Rose and Farley were thanked in his preface.[2] The authorship of the red capitals is therefore uncertain, but they seem very likely to have been connected with the Worcestershire history.

Some marks in Domesday Book are impossible to date: such are the large and disfiguring patches and splashes of gall which were spilt or applied on Great Domesday folios 220, 337, and 337v, among others. The gall when applied was transparent and acted as a clear varnish to improve legibility; now, unfortunately, due to oxidization, these marks have in some cases rendered what is underneath virtually illegible.[3] On folio 187v the writing has become faded, and some of the least legible lines in the right-hand column were carefully retouched in ink, probably at some time in the seventeenth or eighteenth centuries.

THE LAST TWO HUNDRED YEARS

The advent of Abraham Farley's edition of Domesday Book seems considerably to have diminished the concern of the custodians of the original for its safety. By 1807 it had been removed from its chest and was kept in a 'closet' on the Chapter House stairs. When in 1819 the Record Commission, a body set up to supervise and safeguard the public records, reviewed the state of some of the Chapter House documents, it discovered that woodworm had pervaded Domesday's covers and was threatening the parchment itself. Both volumes were rebound, rapidly and lamentably tightly, and during the 1820s were said to have been left 'at large' in the Chapter House.[4] Having escaped the fire at the Houses of Parliament in 1834, by 1846 they had been transferred to a room known as the Library, which was situated above the Chapter House porch. Here they were further endangered by the proximity of the dean and chapter's wash-house and laundry. Eventually, having survived all these hazards unscathed, Domesday Book was in 1859 transferred to the safety and security of the 'treasure-house of the public archives', the new Public Record Office at Chancery Lane.[5]

Within two years, however, Great Domesday was disbound, and first part and then all of it was taken to the Ordnance Survey Department at Southampton. Here, between 1861 and 1863—when it was joined by Little Domesday—a facsimile was made at the behest of Col. Sir Henry James of the Royal Engineers, using a process, at that time at an experimental stage, which he called photozincography. The resulting volumes are attractive and, for their time, remarkably accomplished, but in the retouching process a number of errors were introduced; and many of the marginalia were masked out and all of the preliminary annotations, as already shown, omitted.[6]

Once the facsimile had been made, it was decided that Domesday Book should be rebound in a style 'worthy of the record and of the nation to which it belongs'.[7] Over the next few years a number of designs were suggested, some highly elaborate, such as the scheme which incorporated enamelled bosses depicting William the Conqueror, Queen Victoria, and the penny post. At last, in January 1869, Robert Rivière was commissioned to perform this important task. His covers, considered relatively plain at the time, were of elegantly tooled leather with heavy silver edges. The previous bindings had left much damage at the spine-folds of the sheets, and this was to a degree remedied by Rivière's repairer, J. Kew. Probably the last person to write anything other than folio numbers in Domesday, Kew left his signature in the smaller volume, on the outer spine-fold of folios 437 and 442, where it would be invisible once the volume was bound.[8] Rivière omitted most of the preliminary sheets in Little Domesday, apart from folios h and i; and he similarly removed folios i–iv and v–xxii from Great Domesday, but meanwhile added the previously loose folios A–H.

The photozincographic edition and the 1869 rebinding marked a watershed in the way in which Domesday was regarded by its custodians and by the public at large. Although always the most celebrated of our records and the focus of myths as to its contents, now Domesday as

[1] PRO E 31/6 is his tracing; the engraving was later published with a title-page of 1773 in O. Manning and W. H. Bray, *The History and Antiquities of the County of Surrey*, i (London, 1804), pp. cix, cx.

[2] Condon and Hallam, 'Government Printing of the Public Records', 377, 379; Hallam, *Domesday Book through Nine Centuries*, 135.

[3] Thorn, 'Marginal Notes', p. 135 above.

[4] PRO PRO 36/49, pp. 19–21.

[5] Hallam, *Domesday Book through Nine Centuries*, 150–2.

[6] Ibid. 154–7.

[7] PRO PRO 1/28, 5 March 1864; Hallam, *Domesday Book through Nine Centuries*, 157–60.

[8] Forde, *Domesday Preserved*, 21, 41, with some information provided by the PRO Conservation Department.

an object became a symbol of England's past, a national monument of antiquity. Its octocentenary was triumphantly celebrated in 1886; and during the First and Second World Wars it was given special treatment on its evacuations to Bodmin and to Shepton Mallet prisons.[1] The rebinding of 1953 provided a valuable opportunity for research into the make-up of the volumes. The sheets removed by Rivière were for the most part put back, and the pencilled folio numbers of the preliminary and end pages of both volumes were assigned and written in.[2]

The novocentennial celebrations have brought with them yet further changes to Domesday Book. To make the photographing of the new facsimile possible, in 1984–5 the volumes were again dismantled; and further repairs and research work were carried out. The integrity of the book was left undisturbed, but in 1985 Great Domesday was rebound in two parts and Little Domesday in three. Although this marks a break with a very ancient tradition, it will reduce wear and tear on the manuscripts and has enabled them to be displayed the better. Thus although today it is considered neither necessary nor desirable to annotate manuscripts, their custodians may still, in the work which they carry out upon them, leave an imprint of a quite different kind.[3]

[1] Hallam, *Domesday Book through Nine Centuries*, 161–3, 166–9.

[2] Forde, *Domesday Preserved*, esp. 21, 41–2.

[3] Ibid. 33–47.

AUTHOR'S NOTE

I would particularly like to thank Miss Margaret Condon, Mr Michael Gullick, and Mrs Caroline Thorn for their valuable help and advice on the Domesday manuscripts. I am also indebted to Dr Helen Forde for discussion of the bindings, and to Dr Frank Thorn for his helpful suggestions about the text.

E. M. Hallam

BIBLIOGRAPHY, GLOSSARY AND APPENDICES

BIBLIOGRAPHY

I

EARLY COMPLETE EDITIONS OF DOMESDAY BOOK

Domesday Book, seu Liber Censualis Willelmi Primi Regis Angliae . . ., 2 vols (London, 1783)

This magisterial work, set in specially cast 'record' type, remains the most accurate transcription of both manuscripts. It is usually known as the 'Farley Text', after its author Abraham Farley, Domesday's custodian since 1736 and jointkeeper of the Chapter House records 1773–91. Printed for parliament in 1783, it was reissued in 1817 by the Record Commission with two extra volumes containing certain additional texts associated with Domesday Book as well as indices. Today the 'Farley Text' is more readily available reproduced in the county volumes of the Phillimore edition of Domesday Book (Chichester, 1975–86).

Domesday Book, or the Great Survey of England of William the Conqueror, A.D. 1086, 33 county vols (Ordnance Survey Office 1861–3); 2 complete vols (Ordnance Survey Office, Southampton, 1863)

This was the first complete facsimile reproduction of the folios of both Great and Little Domesday, and was achived by the process of photozincography invented for map making by Sir Henry James, Director of the Ordnance Survey Department 1854–75. For its period this edition was a remarkable achievement and it is only now, 120 years later, that its standards of replication can be surpassed.

II

GENERAL WORKS ON DOMESDAY BOOK

This General Bibliography lists only the principal works concerning Domesday Book and its interpretation. The fullest listing of references is BATES, D., *A Bibliography of Domesday Book* (Woodbridge, 1986)

BALLARD, A., *The Domesday Inquest* (London, 1906; 2nd edn., 1923)

BARING, F. H., *Domesday Tables* (London, 1909)

DARBY, H. C. (ed.), *The Domesday Geography of England*, 6 vols (Cambridge, 1952–75)

DARBY, H. C., *Domesday England* (Cambridge, 1977, 2nd. edn., 1979). The concluding volume of the *Domesday Geography* series

DARBY, H. C., & VERSEY, G. R., *Domesday Gazetteer* (Cambridge, 1975)

ELLIS, H., *A General Introduction to Domesday Book*, 2 vols (London, 1833)

FORDE H., *Domesday Preserved* (HMSO, London, 1986)

GALBRAITH, V. H., *The Making of Domesday Book* (Oxford, 1961)

GALBRAITH, V. H., *Domesday Book: its Place in Administrative History* (Oxford, 1974)

GALBRAITH, V. H., & TAIT, J. (eds.), *Herefordshire Domesday circa 1160–1170*, Pipe Roll Soc., 63, ns 25 (London, 1950)

HALLAM, E. M., *Domesday Book through Nine Centuries* (London, 1986)

HARVEY, S. P. J., 'Domesday Book and Anglo-Norman Governance', *TRHS* 5th ser., 25 (1975), 175–93

HARVEY, S. P. J., 'Recent Domesday studies', *EHR* 45 (1980), 121–33

LENNARD, R. E., *Rural England 1086–1135* (Oxford, 1959)

LOYN, H. R., 'Domesday Book', *Proc. of the Battle Conference 1978*, i (1979), 121–30, 220–2

MAITLAND, F. W., *Domesday Book and Beyond* (Cambridge, 1897), reissued 1960 with Introduction and Bibliographies by E. Miller

PUBLIC RECORD OFFICE, *Domesday Re-bound* (HMSO, London, 1954)

ROUND, J. H., *Feudal England* (London, 1895; 2nd edn., 1964)

SAWYER, P. H. (ed.), *Domesday Book: A Reassessment* (London, 1985)

WELLDON FINN, R., *An Introduction to Domesday Book* (London, 1963)

GLOSSARY

This Glossary contains not only those terms found in Domesday Book but also a number of others commonly used in Medieval Studies, and which may be unfamiliar to the general reader. At the end of certain entries reference is given to the relevant Special Study in this volume where a fuller explanatory treatment is to be found.

ACRE (Lat. *acra*, from *ager*, field). (1) Unlike the modern acre the medieval acre could be used to estimate length as well as area. As a square measure 4 × 40 PERCHES, as a linear measure 66ft. or the length of a cricket pitch. *See* Special Study XI. (2) A unit of assessment to GELD: in some areas 120 geld-acres equalled 1 HIDE.

ALOD, ALLOD (OG. *alod*, latinized). Land held by freehold. *Allodarii* are usually regarded as tenants in freehold. *See* Special Study II.

AMBER (poss. from Lat. *amphora*, a large jar; OG. *einpar*). (1) As a liquid measure, 48 SESTERS. (2) As a dry measure, used for salt: a pennyworth in one entry (GDB 48). *See* Special Study XI.

ANTECESSOR (Lat.). In DB, the preceding landholder, usually the pre-Conquest landholder, from whom the 1086 holder might claim legal title.

ARPENT (Lat. *arepennis*). A term originally meaning 100 square PERCHES imported from France in the eleventh century, and used in GDB particularly for measuring vineyards. *See* Special Study XI.

ASSART, -ING (Lat. *exsartum, -are*). As a noun, a clearing, not yet fully incorporated into the main arable land. As a verb, to make such a clearing.

ASSAY, -ING. The practice of testing the purity of coins, measured by silver content, by melting or 'burning' a sample. *See* FARM (1): BLANCH FARM.

AT FARM. *See* FARM (2).

ÆTHELING (OE.). A term applied to the royal princes of the OE. kingdom, the sons and brothers of the reigning king from whom the next ruler was chosen.

BAILEY (from OFr. *baillier*, to enclose, to control). A defended enclosure. *See* MOTTE.

BEADLE (Lat. *bedellus*; OE. *bydel*). A manorial official, subordinate to the REEVE.

BEREWICK (OE. *berewic*, literally 'barley wick'). An outlying estate, or an estate devoted to some specialized function. *See* Special Study II.

BLANCH, BLANCH FARM. *See* FARM (1).

BLOOM (Lat. *blomae*, *plumbei*). A measure used for iron, probably equivalent to the ingot (Lat. *massa*). *See* Special Study XI.

BODYGUARD. In DB, *heuuard* (OE. *here-weard*, army guard). The duty of providing a bodyguard for a specified period, either for the king or for some other LORD.

BOOKLAND (OE. *bocland*). Land to which the title is a royal charter; the essential factor in bookland tenure is freedom to dispose of the land as the holder wishes. *See* Special Study II.

BOOR (Lat. *burcus*; OE. *gebur*). An inferior peasant: equated in DB with COLIBERT. Archaic in 1086, being replaced by VILLAN.

BORDAR (from OFr. *borde*, a wooden hut). A cottager: a peasant of lower economic status than a VILLAN. Since DB distinguishes bordars from COTTARS and both from COTSETS, there must have been some distinction between them not now readily apparent. All three are also commonly associated with towns. *See* Special Study III.

BOROUGH (OE. *burh*). An urban as opposed to a rural settlement, usually fortified.

BOVATE (from Lat. *bos*, an ox). One-eighth of a CARUCATE; the Anglo-Scand. translation is OXGANG.

BURGESS (from OE. *burh*; OFr. *burgeis*). A townsman usually from the upper stratum of town-dwellers, holding by a special form of tenure characterized by the payment of a money-rent.

BUTSECARL (ON. *batr*, boat + *karl*, man). A seaman; c.f. Anglo-Scand. *batswegen*, which gives Mod. Eng. boatswain, a term of more limited application now than in the eleventh century.

CAPUT (Lat., head). A principal manor. *See* MANOR.

CARTAGE. In DB, *avera* (Lat., property, cattle; OFr. *ovre*, work). The duty of providing carts for the transport of the LORD's goods.

CARUCATE (from Lat. *caruca*, a plough). A ploughland: notionally the area which could be ploughed with an eight-ox team, used in the north and east as a unit of assessment to tax instead of the HIDE.

CASTLE (Lat. *castellum*, *castrum*; OFr. *castel*). The fortified residence of a LORD. *See* Special Study IX.

CEORL (OE.). A peasant or non-noble FREE MAN, with a WERGELD of 200*s*.

CHURCHSCOT. In DB, usually *cirset* (OE. *ciric-sceat*, literally 'church-tax'). An annual render in kind paid to the church; c.f. TITHE. *See* Special Study VIII.

CIRCUIT. The area for which one group of commissioners was responsible, consisting of several shires (usually five). *See* General Introduction, p.3–4.

COLIBERT (Lat. *colibertus*, *quolibertus*, from *libere*, to set free). A FREEDMAN: a former slave, emancipated and (usually) given a small piece of land.

COMMEND, COMMENDATION (from Lat. *commendo*, *-are*, literally 'to put into the hands of'). A form of VASSALAGE.

COMMOTE (OW. *cymwd*). An OW. administrative division, roughly comparable to the English HUNDRED.

CONSTABLE (Lat. *comes stabuli*; OFr. *conestable*, officer of the stable). *See* STALLER.

COTSET (OE. *kotsetla*, a cottage-dweller). A cottager. *See* BORDAR.

COTTAR (from OE. *kot*, a cottage). A cottager. *See* BORDAR.

COUNT (Lat. *comes*, companion). A continental title, denoting a man in authority over a specific area (county) with administrative and judicial powers: used to translate the English EARL.

COURT (Lat. *curia*). Apart from its judicial use, the word also denotes the residence of the LORD (*see also* HALL and MANOR) to which dues were paid.

CROFT (OE., enclosed field). The field or garden belonging to a peasant's house. *See also* TOFT.

CUSTOM, CUSTOMARY DUE (from Lat. *consuetudo*). (1) Fixed RENDERS, financial, administrative or judicial. (2) Deriving from (1), traditional practices, whence the 'customs' of shires and boroughs in DB.

DANEGELD (OE.). Originally the tribute-money paid to the invading Danish armies temp. Æthelræd II. Subsequently used for the HEREGELD.

DEMESNE (Lat. *dominium*; OFr. adj. *demeigne*, owned). Land 'in LORDSHIP' whose produce is devoted to the LORD rather than his tenants: (1) MANORS held in the LORD's personal possession as opposed to those granted to his men; (2) that part of an individual estate exploited directly for the LORD's benefit, as opposed to the part held by the peasants, i.e. the LORD's 'home-farm'. Also expressed as INLAND (OE.), as opposed to WARLAND. *See* Special Studies II and III.

DENARIUS. *See* PENNY.

DICKER (Lat. *decarius*). Literally 'a bundle of ten' used for leather and skins; also gloves, shoes, and in GDB, horseshoes. *See* Special Study XI.

DOMESDAY MONACHORUM. A survey collected within an existing manuscript (now in Canterbury Cathedral library) compiled from DB or from the 'original returns' for the use of the Archbishop and monks of Christ Church, Canterbury.

DRENG (ON. *drengr*, fellow, warrior). In Lancashire and Yorkshire a man personally free, holding land in return for service, including military service.

DUEL (Lat. *duellum*, from *duo*, two). The judicial battle in which accuser and accused fought either in person or through champions, introduced after 1066.

EARL (ON. *jarl*, nobleman, commander). In the OE. period, the chief administrative officers of the king, set over the main divisions of the kingdom (Wessex, Mercia, East Anglia and Northumbria): also the highest rank of the OE. aristocracy after the ÆTHELINGS. It replaces the earlier title *ealdorman* (OE. *ealdor*, lord, + *mann*, man) in the early eleventh century. The title survived the Conquest but the earls of the Norman period had more restricted areas of command (usually a single shire).

ENFEOFFMENT, TO ENFEOFF. *See* FIEF.

ESCHEAT (Lat. *ex* + *cadere*, to fall out; OFr. *cheoir*). To forfeit (land) for some misdemeanour or for lack of heirs.

ESCORT. In DB, *inweard* (OE.). The duty of riding escort to one's LORD, or of providing someone to do so. *See* RADKNIGHT.

EXON DOMESDAY (usually abbr. Exon). The manuscript containing the circuit-return for the five south-western shires, now kept in the Treasury of Exeter Cathedral. *See* General Introduction, p.6.

FARM (Lat. *firma*; OE. *feorm*, tribute). Never an agricultural unit, as in modern usage. (1) A RENDER, originally in kind, but by the eleventh century frequently commuted to money. NIGHT'S FARM: the amount of produce which would support the king and his retinue for one 24-hour period, paid by certain groups of royal estates. BLANCH FARM: (Lat. *blanca*, white) royal dues paid in money ASSAYED for its purity ('white silver', 'white pennies') and usually reckoned as 21 shillings to the pound of silver instead of 20. (2) Land or office held AT FARM: in effect, leased at a specific rent in return for which the tenant, known as the 'farmer', received the profits of the estate or office. *See* Special Study II.

FARTHING. *See* FERDING.

FEALTY (from Lat. *fides*, oath, *fidelitas*, loyalty). (1) The oath sworn by a VASSAL to his LORD in the ceremony of VASSALAGE: usually sworn on holy relics or on the Gospels. (2) The duty owed by a VASSAL to his LORD including tributary service, aid and counsel.

FERDING, FERDINC, FERLING (OE. *feortha*, fourth). (1) A measurement of land, used for fiscal purposes and equalling one-quarter VIRGATE. (2) The subdivision of a SHIRE, usually one of four.

FIEF. In DB, *feudum* (latinized from OG. *fehu*, property). In general a piece of land held in return for military service; in DB, often used as a synonym for HONOUR, which is the collective term for the fiefs of any one individual. From fief comes the verb 'TO ENFEOFF' (to give land in exchange for military service—'IN FEE'); the adjectival 'IN FEE' (land or other property held in exchange for military service—'as a fief'); and the nouns 'feudalism', 'SUBINFEUDATION'. *See* Special Study II.

FOREST (Lat. *foresta*, from *foris*, outside). Land set aside for the king's hunting. Not necessarily wooded.

FRANKPLEDGE (OE. *frith-borh*, peace-pledge). *See* TITHING.

FREEDMAN. *See* COLIBERT.

FREE MAN. In DB, *liber homo* (Lat.). In eastern England a non-noble landholder, usually COMMENDED to a LORD (c.f. SOKEMAN) but sometimes used as an equivalent of THEGN.

FRENCHMAN. In DB, *francus homo*, *francigena* (Lat.). A non-noble immigrant, usually found as a peasant settler of free status: hence *franklin* (Frenchman), a name sometimes given to freeholders in the later Middle Ages.

FURLONG. In DB, *quarentina* (Lat.; OE. *furlang*, from *furh*, furrow, + *lang*, long). The length of a furrow: 40 PERCHES. *See* Special Study X.

FYRD (OE.). The OE. military levy or host.

GELD (OE., money, tax). The English land-tax (DANEGELD, HEREGELD) assessed on the HIDE.

GLEBE (Lat. *gleba*, clod, soil). The land belonging to a village church or priest.

HALL (OE. *heall*, hall). The characteristic feature of a MANOR; the lordly residence to which rents and dues were paid.

HEARTH-TAX. In DB, *fumagium* (Lat., smoke-tax; also *herdigelt*, OE., hearth-tax). A levy on households counted by hearths.

HELVEWECHA (OE. *healf*, half, + *wice*, week). Literally 'half-week', but the meaning of the word (which only occurs in GDB 154v) is obscure.

HEREGELD (OE. *here*, army, + *geld*, tax). An annual tax raised to pay the standing fleet from 1012 to 1051, and reinstituted by William I. *See* GELD.

HERIOT. In DB, *relevium* (Lat., relief; OE. *heregeatu*, literally 'war-gear'). In pre-Conquest England the RENDER in arms and/or money paid at death by a man to his LORD.

HIDE (OE. *hid*, *hida*). The standard unit of assessment to tax, especially GELD. Notionally the amount of land which would support a household: divided into four VIRGATES. *See* Special Studies II and XII.

HOCCUS (derivation uncertain). Possibly a salt-mound, used for drying and purifying salt.

HOMAGE (Lat. *homo*; Fr. *homme*, man). The act of COMMENDATION in which someone became the man or VASSAL of a LORD by placing his clasped hands between those of his LORD and exchanging a kiss. *See* FEALTY.

HONOUR, HONOR (Lat. *honor*, worth). The collection of FIEFS held by a TENANT-IN-CHIEF or a MESNE-TENANT. *See* Special Study II.

HOUSECARL (ON. *huskarl*, a retainer, servant). A Scandinavian term introduced into England in the time of Cnut (1016–35), originally meaning a retainer; but by 1066 it could also be used instead of THEGN when applied to men of Scandinavian descent.

HUNDRED (Lat. *hundredum*; OE. *hund*; OFr. *hundret*, a hundred). An administrative subdivision of the SHIRE with fiscal, judicial and military functions. The men of the hundred are the members of the hundred-court (*see also* WAPENTAKE). The number and size of the hundreds varies greatly from shire to shire, but notionally, and sometimes actually, comprises 100 (or a 'long' hundred of 120) hides.

INCREMENT. In DB, *de cremento* (from Lat. *increscare*, to increase). Increase: usually an additional sum of money added to existing dues.

IN FEE. *See* FIEF.

INLAND. *See* DEMESNE (2).

INQUISITIO COMITATUS CANTABRIGIENSIS (abbr. ICC). An existing document containing a copy of the returns for Cambridgeshire, arranged by HUNDREDS instead of the GDB feudal arrangement and representing a stage in the collection of material for GDB. *See* General Introduction, p.5.

INQUISITIO ELIENSIS (abbr. IE). An existing document (now in Trinity College, Cambridge) containing a copy of the returns for the lands of Ely Abbey extracted from the GDB and LDB material at an early stage. *See* General Introduction, pp.4–5.

KNIGHT. In DB, *miles* (Lat.; OE. *cniht*, a boy or servant). A military retainer. *See also* VASSAL.

LATHE (ON. poet., *lath*, land; OE. *læth*). A sub-division of the SHIRE, exclusive to Kent, similar to the RAPES of Sussex.

LAUND (OFr. *launde*; OCelt. *landa*, a stretch of woodland). A glade or open space among woods.

LEAGUE (Lat. *leuga*). A Gaulish measure of 1½ Roman miles of 1,000 paces. In medieval England one league = 12 FURLONGS, whereas the mile = 8 FURLONGS. *See* Special Study XI.

LIBRUM. In DB, *lib.*, *l.* (Lat., a pound). A money of account amounting to 240 silver pennies which were minted from a pound of silver. *See* Special Study X.

LIVERY (from Lat. *deliberare*, to deliver). The legal process of conveying title to land: the king's *liberator* was the agent who performed this function.

LOANLAND (OE. *lænland*). Land held on a lease, frequently for three lives, i.e. generations. *See* Special Study II.

LORD. In DB, *dominus* (Lat.; OE. *hlaford*, lord; literally 'loaf-giver'). The lord is the holder of the HOMAGE of his VASSALS to whom he gives protection and land in return for support. The lady (OE. *hlafdige*, 'loaf-maker') is the lord's wife.

LORDSHIP. In DB, *dominium* (Lat.). Territory or personnel under the direct authority of a LORD.

LOWY (Lat. *leugata*, square LEAGUE). Probably a square LEAGUE, but also used simply to mean a large property (e.g. the lowy of Tonbridge). *See* Special Study XI.

MANOR (Lat. *manerium*, from *manere*, to dwell; OFr. *manoir*). An estate, varying in size; the estate-centre as opposed to the outlying BEREWICKS. The capital manor (CAPUT) was the administrative centre of the HONOUR where the LORD's chief residence, often his CASTLE, was situated, and where his COURT was held.

MARK (ON. *mǫrk*, mark). (1) A weight defining a unit of account equivalent to two-thirds of a pound (LIBRUM) i.e. in silver 13*s.* 4*d.*; (2) a gold mark which was equivalent to £6. Neither was an actual coin. *See* Special Study X.

MESNE-TENANT (OFr. *mesnie*, retinue). A man holding land of a LORD other than the king.

MESSUAGE (from Lat. *mansio*, dwelling). The unit of a land-tenure within a BOROUGH, comprising a house or houses with appurtenant property. *See* Special Study VI.

MILL (from Lat. *molendinum*). A rotary engine driven by water, in most cases for grinding corn. The windmill does not appear in England for at least a century later than DB. It is possible that mills in the northern regions were 'Norse mills', with the wheel pivoting horizontally, while mills in the south and west were driven by vertically positioned water-wheels. *See* Special Studies I and IV.

MINSTER (Lat. *monasterium*, monastery, church). The mother-church of an area, often in origin a small monastery. The territories assigned to minsters were usually larger than modern parishes. *See* Special Study VIII.

MINT (from Lat. *moneta*). The centres of coin production situated in towns of BOROUGH status. 78 mints are known to exist before 1066, and 64 at the time of the survey. The mint name as well as that of the issuing MONEYER appears on the reverse of every coin. Associated with the mint was the exchange (Lat. *cambium*) where silver bullion and old coin were ASSAYED and bought in for new. *See* Special Study X.

MITTA (OE. *mitte*, measure of capacity). A horse-load, specifically of salt: *See* SUMMA. In the tenth century the salt-tolls of Droitwich were reckoned at 1*d.* on the horse-load and 1*s.* on the cart-load. *See* Special Study XI.

MODIUS (Lat.; OFr. *muid*). (1) A liquid measure used for wine: the Roman *modius* = 8.75 litres, but the DB equivalent is unknown; (2) a dry measure, used (exceptionally) for grain. *See* Special Study XI.

MONEYER (Lat. *monetarius*). An official responsible for the minting of coins, on which his name invariably appeared. Several moneyers operated at important MINTS such as London, Canterbury and Winchester. *See* Special Study X.

MOTTE (OFr., mound, embankment). The mound of earth supporting a timber or stone TOWER. Invariably surrounded by, or attached to, a defended enclosure (BAILEY) to constitute the commonest form of CASTLE in the eleventh century. *See* Special Study IX.

MULTURE (from Lat. *molere*, to grind). A toll paid to the miller for grinding corn.

NIGHT'S FARM. *See* FARM (1).

ORA (ON. *øre*, an ounce). One-eighth of a MARK: a unit of account, usually reckoned as equivalent to 20*d.*, but sometimes as 16*d.* *See* Special Study X.

ORDEAL (OE. *ordal*). The judicial trial, of which several kinds are recorded. The most common are: (1) the ordeal of cold water, in which the suspect was dropped into a specially dug pit filled with holy water; if innocent he sank, if guilty he floated; (2) the ordeal of hot iron, in which the suspect carried a red-hot iron for a specified number of paces. His wounds were bound up for a specific time; if when they were unwrapped they were healed, he was innocent, if they had turned septic, guilty. In both cases, the idea was to appeal to the judgement of God. *See also* DUEL.

OXGANG. *See* BOVATE.

PANNAGE (Lat. *pannagium*). The autumn feed for pigs—acorns and beechnuts. Also, a payment for pasturing pigs: this may be the primary sense of the term in DB.

PARAGE, IN PARAGE (from Lat. *par*, equal). Shared ownership of land by kinsmen: a French usage which is not found in pre-Conquest sources.

PENNY, PENCE. In DB, *d.*, *den.* = *denarius* (Lat.; OE. *pending*, penny). The only actual coin in circulation in the eleventh century. 240 pence were struck from one pound (LIBRUM) of silver. *See* Special Study X.

PERCH (Lat. *pertica*). In the Middle Ages in England, the size of the perch varied from 14 to 18 ft. and could sometimes be 25 to 28 ft. *See* Special Study XI.

PLOUGHLAND (OE. *plog*, plough). The number of ploughlands may: (1) estimate the arable capacity of an estate in terms of the number of eight-ox plough-teams needed to work it; or (2) record an assessment of the dues required from the estate.

PURPRESTURE (Lat. *propestura*; OFr. *pourpresure*). Encroachment, specifically encroachments on land used: (1) in the sense of ASSART; (2) in the sense of illegal encroachment on the land of another.

RADKNIGHT, RADMAN (OE. *radcniht*, riding servant, from OE. *rad*, road). A retainer who performed specific services, including that of riding ESCORT to his LORD. *See* Special Study III.

RAPE (derivation uncertain). One of five (later six) subdivisions of Sussex, each with its LORD and CASTLE. Similar to the Kentish LATHE.

REEVE. In DB, *praepositus* (Lat.; OE. *gerefa*). An administrative officer: used for (1) the king's officials in charge of royal estates; (2) manorial officials of other LORDS in charge of estates; (3) village representatives who oversaw the performance of manorial duties. *See* Special Study III.

RELIEF (Lat. *relevium*; OFr. *relef*). The sum proffered by an heir for succession to his inheritance. In DB sometimes used to translate HERIOT.

RENDER (Lat. *redditum*, from *reddere*, to give). A customary payment usually in kind rather than cash, but sometimes used for manorial values in money.

REVELAND (from OE. *gerefa*, REEVE). Meaning uncertain: perhaps land set aside for the use of a REEVE.

ROUNCEY (Lat. *runcinus*). A cheap riding-horse; at this date probably a harrowing-horse also.

RUSCA (OIr. *rusc*; Gaelic *rusq*, *rusg*). A vessel of straw or bark; thus a measure for butter in Cheshire, size unknown. *See* Special Study XI.

SAKE AND SOKE (OE. *sac* and *soc*). Literally 'cause' and 'suit'; the case heard in a COURT and the duty of attending it. Used to denote the judicial and dominical rights associated with the possession of land, especially BOOKLAND. *See* Special Study II.

SEISIN (OFr.). Lawful possession, usually of land. The phrase 'to be seised of' means 'to possess' or 'to be in possession of'. *See* Special Study II.

SERGEANT, SERGEANTY (from Lat. *serviens*, servant). A tenant who held his land by rendering a specific service, e.g. as a forester or cook; SERGEANTY was the name given to this form of tenure.

SESTER (Lat. *sextarius*). (1) As a liquid measure, used for honey and wine: the size varied but sesters of 24 oz. and 32 oz. are recorded in eleventh-century England. (2) As a dry measure, used for grain: perhaps equivalent to 12 bushels. *See* Special Study XI.

SHERIFF (OE. *scir-gerefa*). The royal officer set over a SHIRE whose duties included judicial and financial functions, as well as the overseeing of royal estates and, in the post-Conquest period, custody of royal CASTLES. The Normans translated the word as *vicecomes* (Lat.), viscount.

SHIRE (OE. *scira*, an area of authority, a county). The main unit of English local administration. The word is used both for the county and for the county- or shire-COURT. The Normans translated the word as *comitatus* (Lat.), county.

SOKE (OE. *soc*). Right of jurisdiction enjoyed by a LORD over specified places and personnel. *See* SAKE AND SOKE.

SOKELAND (OE. *soc*). Used to describe lands appurtenant to a MANOR.

SOKEMAN (OE. *socmann*). A FREE MAN (though often only a peasant) owing service, including suit of COURT, to the LORD of a SOKE (*see* SAKE AND SOKE). *See* Special Study II.

SOLIDUS (Lat.). A money of account amounting to twelve silver PENNIES. The DB abbr. *sol.*, *s.*, stand equally for OE. *scilling*, shilling, which was probably the term in common use.

SORE HAWK (OFr. *sor*, saure). A hawk in its second year which has not moulted and still has red plumage: nowadays a 'red' hawk.

STALLER (ON. *stallari*, a marshal, from *stallr*, a stall or seat). In the OE. period, a high-ranking holder of a recognized office. Sometimes translated in DB as *comes stabuli*, CONSTABLE.

STEERMAN (OE. *stirmann*). In the OE. period, the commander of a ship, especially of the ships provided for the king's service.

STICK (OE. *sticca*, *sticha*, *estika*). A measure for eels: 25 held together by a stick or cord passed through the gills. *See* Special Study XI.

SUBINFEUDATE, SUBINFEUDATION (Lat. *subinfeudatio*, from *feudum*, FIEF). The practice of LORDS in receipt of land from the king entrusting part of it to MESNE-TENANTS. *See* Special Study II.

SULUNG (OE. *sulh*, plough). A Kentish unit of assessment usually regarded as equivalent to two HIDES. *See* Special Study XI.

SUMMA (Gk., latinized *sagma*, saddle). A horse-load, equivalent to MITTA: hence SUMPTER HORSE for pack-horse. No precise equivalent can be given as there was probably local variation. *See* Special Study XI.

SUMPTER HORSE (Gk., latinized *sagma*, saddle). A pack-horse.

TALE, BY TALE. In DB, *ad numerum* (Lat.; OE. *getal*, reckoning, number). Payments made by counting out coins ('telling' them) as opposed to weighing them. *See also* TALLAGE.

TALLAGE (OFr. *tail*). A tax or impost in cash or kind, usually in the sense of a levy by a LORD on unfree peasants.

TENANT-IN-CHIEF (Lat. *tenens-in-capite*, holding in chief). A man who holds his land directly of the king. *See* Special Study II.

THEGN. In DB, *tainus* (OE., latinized, servant, nobleman). A man of noble status as opposed to a peasant (CEORL), having a WERGELD of 1,200*s*. A king's thegn was COMMENDED to the king; a median thegn to some other LORD. The nobility of pre-Conquest England was ranked according to the HERIOT they paid in the following descending order: EARL, king's thegn, median thegn.

THEGNLAND (OE.). Land belonging to a THEGN; sometimes apparently used as the equivalent of LOANLAND.

THIRD PENNY. The portion of the dues (particularly the judicial renders including penalties) from the SHIRE and HUNDRED apportioned to the EARL. The other two PENNIES went to the king.

THRAVE (of Scand. origin, e.g. Dan. *trave*). Two shocks of twelve sheaves each of reaped corn. *See* Special Study XI.

TIMBER (OFr. *timbre*). A bundle of 40 pelts. *See* Special Study XI.

TITHE. In DB, *decima* (Lat.; OE. *teotha*, a tenth). A render to the church amounting to one-tenth of the annual produce. In the eleventh century one-third of the tithe was paid to the church of the MANOR and two-thirds to the mother-church (MINSTER) on which the manorial church was dependent.

TITHING (OE. *teotha*, a tenth). The subdivision of a HUNDRED, notionally ten men, the main function of which was to organize sureties so as to ensure that its members appeared in court when summoned: later the system was known as FRANKPLEDGE.

TOFT (OE.; ON. *topt*, homestead). A peasant's house or cottage, to which belonged his garden or field. *See* CROFT.

TOLL AND TEAM (OE. *toll*, tax + *team*, cattle). The right to receive tolls on merchandise and probably to hold a market.

TOWER (Lat. *turris*). The tower of a CASTLE, especially the upstanding donjon (Lat. *dominium*), or keep. The tower, or the MOTTE in a motte and bailey, is used symbolically for the whole building since it represents the LORD's authority (also Lat. *dominium*). *See* Special Study IX.

TRE (abbr. for Lat. *Tempore Regis Edwardi*). The formula commonly used in DB to indicate the position 'in the time of King Edward', i.e. before the Conquest in 1066. In EXON a more exact phrase is sometimes used: 'the day when King Edward was alive and dead', i.e. 5 January 1066.

TRW (abbr. for Lat. *Tempore Regis Willelmi*). The formula used today (by analogy with TRE) to indicate the position after the Conquest, 'in the time of King William', more especially in 1086 when the survey was being compiled.

TURBARY (OE. *torvelande*). A place from which turves were taken; the right to cut turves of peat.

VASSAL, VASSALAGE (Lat. *vassus*; OCelt. *gwas*, a boy or servant). A man, usually of noble rank, who subordinates himself to a LORD.

Vassalage is the status of a vassal, which was entered by COMMENDATION in the ceremony of HOMAGE, sealed by the oath of FEALTY. The relationship might be personal or, if the vassal received a FIEF, tenurial.

VAVASOUR (OFr.). In eleventh-century Normandy, a retainer of lower status than a VASSAL.

VILL (Lat. *villa*, village; OE. *tun*, township). (1) The unit of local administration at its lowest level: GELD for instance was levied on the SHIRE, HUNDRED and vill, in that descending order. Not necessarily a village in the modern sense: a vill represents an area of land rather than the site of a specific settlement, and may contain more than one settlement. (2) In DB occasionally used of urban sites which were not fully fledged BOROUGHS *See* Special Study V.

VILLAN (Lat. *villanus*, a villager, which translates OE. *tunsman*). A peasant of higher economic status than a BORDAR and living in a village. Notionally unfree because subject to the manorial COURT. *See* Special Study III.

VIRGATE (Lat. *virgata*, from *virga*, a rod). One-quarter of a HIDE: the equivalent of the English YARDLAND.

WAPENTAKE (ON. *vapnan tak*, 'the taking up of weapons' laid aside during peaceful assemblies after agreement). In northern and eastern England, a division of the SHIRE with the same functions exercised by the HUNDRED in the south and west.

WARA (OE.). The obligations (especially for the payment of GELD) owed by an estate to the royal service; literally 'defence', hence the common formula in DB, *x se defendit pro y hidae* to indicate liability to GELD.

WARLAND (*see* WARA). Land which owes service (as opposed to the exempt DEMESNE or INLAND): thus land held by peasants and tenants as opposed to their LORD.

WARNODE (ODan. *værned*, assurance, pledge). The service (specifically GELD) owed by WARLAND; the land which owes this service.

WASTE. In DB, *wasta* (Lat.; poss. OE. *wæste*, uninhabited, desolate; OFr. *wast*). Land which does not RENDER dues either because it has been physically devastated, or because the dues have been attached to some other MANOR, or because they have been withheld. Some manors described as 'waste' are nevertheless credited with values and with population or other appurtenances in DB. Land on which GELD was not paid is also sometimes described as 'waste'.

WEIGHED AND BURNT. Coin which has been ASSAYED. *See* FARM (1): BLANCH FARM, also Special Study X.

WERGELD (OE. *wer*, man + *geld*, money). Originally the recompense paid to the kin of a slain man by the kin of the slayer to avert the blood-feud: the amount varied according to the rank of the slain man, 1,200*s*. for a THEGN, 200*s*. for a CEORL. By the tenth century the wergeld was used to assess the amount of judicial fines.

WEY (OE. *wæge*). A measure for cheese (40*d*. worth in GDB 58v): later weys varied between 175 and 196 pounds.

YARDLAND. *See* VIRGATE.

YOKE. In DB, *iugum* (Lat.; OE. *ioclet*). One-quarter of a SULUNG in Kent. Oxen were yoked in pairs and a full plough-team would have consisted of four pairs of oxen.

APPENDIX I

THE MARGINALIA OF GREAT DOMESDAY BOOK

A KEY TO THE SYSTEM OF REFERENCE USED IN THE TRANSLATIONS

All marginalia are printed in the margins of the translation-pages as close as possible to the positions they occupy in the MS. Passages of text, phrases or single words are translated in full. Those insertions that were certainly inscribed at the time of writing and checking the MS in 1086–7 are printed in the same roman type as the main text and are left undated. Marginal text of demonstrably later insertion is printed in *italic*, and author and date, where these are known, are included within square brackets.

The following table sets out the system of symbols employed for the various categories of marginalia found in Great Domesday Book.

A marginal sign not indicated in the translation-pages is the very common 'gallows' sign which is employed as a paragraphing device in the left-hand margin of the column. It can also appear towards the ends of lines, usually within the column, when it marks the point where overrunning text is carried over onto the line above or below (see right). Likewise the many crosses and obliques made with an uninked stylus are also omitted; such marks are seldom visible in the facsimile and their purpose is in any case unknown.

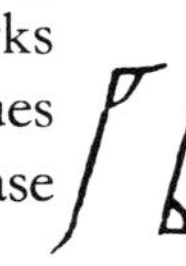

For a full account of all these marginalia, see C. Thorn, 'Marginal Notes and Signs in Domesday Book', Special Study XV. For an account of the writing of GDB, see M. Gullick 'The Great and Little Domesday Manuscripts', Special Study XIV; and for the later additions, see E. M. Hallam, 'Annotations in Domesday Book since 1100', Special Study XVI.

TRANSPOSITION SIGNS

Main Scribe of Domesday Book

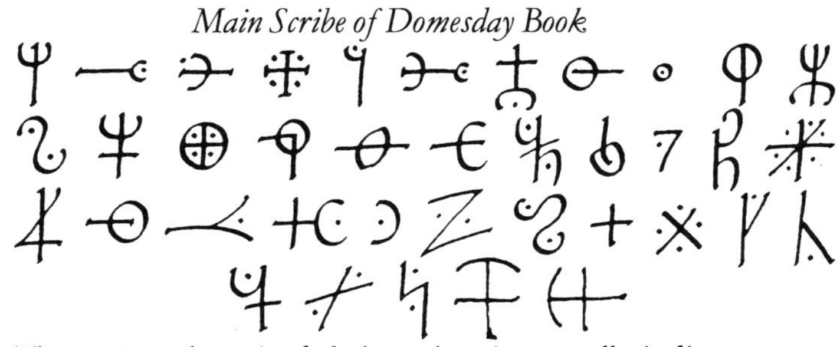

§ These 38 cyphers (and their variants) generally indicate matter that had been inserted out of order in the MS. They usually occur in pairs, one sign being drawn beside the misplaced passage, and the corresponding one indicating where it should properly lie. Both are indicated by §. Occasionally such signs were used to link entries referring to the same vill or manor, or to correct the order within an entry.

On folios where more than one pair of transposition signs occurs, they are distinguished by a suprascript number, e.g. §[1] relates to the other §[1] on the same page, §[2] to §[2], and so on.

In the cases where corresponding signs are inscribed on adjacent folios, the folio number is indicated suprascript, e.g. §[f.357]

(Frequent)

INDICATIONS OF ADMINISTRATIVE STATUS

Main Scribe of Domesday Book

In a number of counties the following abbreviations (and their variants) occur immediately next to the first line of certain entries. They all appear to have been written at the same time as the text to which they refer.

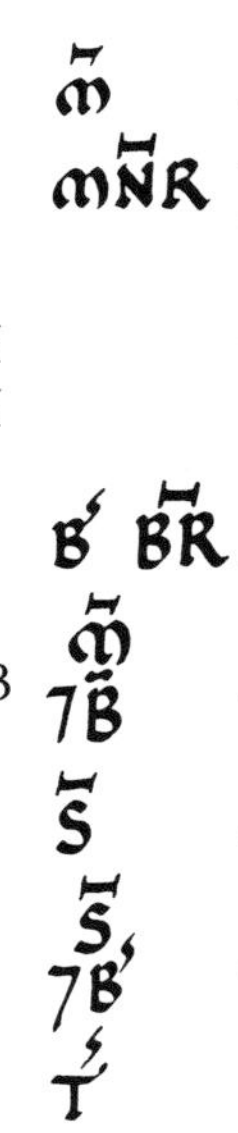

M	*Manerium*, 'manor'. Sometimes a numeral is added above, or beside, indicating that a single holding had been two or more separate manors before 1066. The latter is transcribed in the translation-pages as 2M, 3M, etc.	(Beds., Bucks., Cambs., Derby., Herts., Hunts., Lincs., Middx., Notts., Yorks.)
2M		
3M		
B	*Berewica*, 'berewick'.	
MB	*Manerium et Berewica, Berewicae.*	
S	*Soca*, 'sokeland'.	
SB	*Soca et Berewica.*	
T	*Terra*, 'land'	(Hunts. only)

OTHER SIGNS AND ABBREVIATIONS

Various Periods

Various marginal additions were inscribed in the MS at the time of writing and checking and also during the medieval period by clerks consulting its folios.

[1], [2], [3], etc., marginalia which are attributable to some identifiable purpose and/or period as listed below. Typical examples are given in each section.

☐ a marginalium which cannot at present be so attributed.

⬚ a marginalium so faint in the MS (largely due to erasure or to wear) that it is not apparent in the facsimile.

☒ unintentional marks, such as slips of the pen, doodles, blots or accidental offsets from the opposite page, inserted only where such a mark could be mistaken for a deliberate marginal sign.

[1] REQUESTS FOR INFORMATION OR VERIFICATION

Period of Domesday Book

Certain details of some entries were not available as the main scribe wrote the text and he therefore left spaces for their inclusion later on. The returns for other entries also contained apparently incorrect information. Occasionally he inscribed the marginal notes *rq'*, *r* against such entries (sometimes in red) to show that further enquiry was needed.

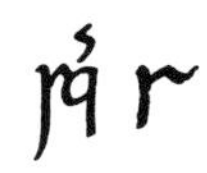

abbreviations for *require*, 'enquire'. When the missing detail was asked for specifically, e.g. *r qt' t'ra*, 'enquire how much land' (Staffs. 247), the phrase is translated as '[1] how much land'. (Frequent)

2 REMINDERS FOR CORRECTIONS AND ADDITIONS TO BE ENTERED IN THE TEXT

Period of Domesday Book

These are words, phrases or names (or their abbreviations) which were noted by both the main and the correcting scribe in the margin during the course of their work as *aides-mémoire*. There are two types:

(i) A note of the correction to be inserted over an existing erasure once the parchment had been re-prepared for it. These notes were usually erased after the correction had been inserted, although some are still partially visible.

(ii) A note of some matter to be added later. Many of these were never written into the text. Where possible these words or phrases are translated and the abbreviations of names extended, when tentatively with [?].

(Frequent)

3 EXPLANATORY ADDITIONS OUTSIDE THE TEXT

Period of Domesday Book

During the process of checking the MS details were sometimes added, such as certain hidages or carucages or the way in which a manor had been held TRE. These were written in the margins, mostly by the correcting scribe, but no attempt was made to incorporate them into the text. Examples are:

 '5 hides'

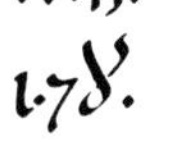 '1½'  '½'  '7'
(usually hides, virgates; or carucates, bovates)

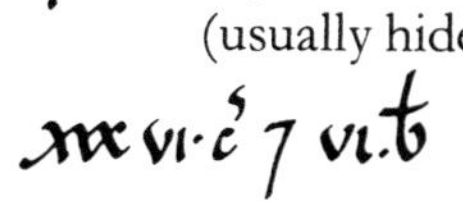 '36 carucates and 6 bovates'

(Leics., Northants, Notts., Oxon., War., Yorks.)

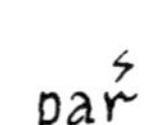 *pariter*, 'in parage' (Devon.)

 *TRE*, 'in the time of King Edward' (Hants 44)

All are translated *in situ*.

4 INDICATIONS OF DISPUTED LAND

Period of Domesday Book

Sometimes properties were the subject of a dispute over ownership, and this was usually noted either within an entry when it was written, or soon afterwards in the margin. However, some claims may have been missed or may have arisen subsequently, and attention was drawn to them, as well as to some of those already documented in the text, by one of the following marginal abbreviations:

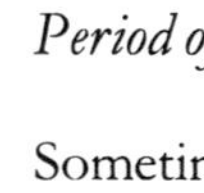 either *kalum(p)nia* or *klamor*, 'claim'. (Derby., Hunts., Lincs., Shrops.)

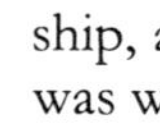 capital A, probably some part of *arbitrari*, 'to decide' or *adjudicare*, 'to judge'. (Herts., Staffs.)

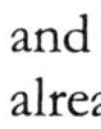 probably *disputatio*, 'dispute', or some part of *diratiocinari*, 'to determine', 'to prove'. (Derby., Hunts.)

 probably *reclamatio*, 'claim for restitution'. (Ches.)

5 QUIRE SIGNATURES

Period of Domesday Book

A series of consecutive letters *a–k*, indicating to the binder the correct order of quires (gatherings) in Yorks. and Lincs. only.

5 COMMENTS ON MATTER IN THE TEXT

Period of Domesday Book or later

Marginalia of this type date either from 1086 to 1087 or from later during the medieval period.

 Written by the main scribe apparently against holdings relinquished by Nigel Fossard. (Yorks.)

 Indicating alienated church land or land held by a church from a lay tenant. Sometimes in red and therefore by the main scribe. (Glos., Herefs., Som.)

 Inscribed mostly against chapter headings or the first lines of chapters, and sometimes against groups of successive entries. *f, fd'* = possibly *feudum*, 'fief', 'holding', indicating a knight's fee in later times. For other interpretations, e.g. *f, fr* = *fecit returnum*, 'has made a return', or the negative *n* = *non fecit returnum*, or *f* = *frithsoca*, 'free sokeland', see discussion in Thorn, 'Marginal Notes', p.129–31 above. Period unknown. (Frequent)

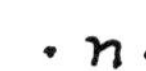

 A different *n*, probably = *nichil*, '[it renders] nothing', indicating holdings put into the New Forest with no recorded value at 1086. Period unknown. (Hants.)

7 THE CHECKING MARKS OF CLERKS CONSULTING THE MANUSCRIPT

Various periods

Domesday Book continued to be used as a working document throughout the medieval period. The following are some of the many marks and signs employed by persons consulting the MS.

 Drawn beside entries which mention a church, or are concerned in some way with ecclesiastical matters. Some are probably erased. (Frequent)

 Unobtrusive dots (one or two) relating certain entries to others. (Frequent)

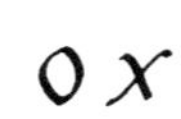 Similar to the preceding, but limited to Devon.

 Next to entries which contain references to land in the king's forest. Probably late, even 14th century. (Dorset, Glos., Oxon.)

 Similar to the preceding, but limited to Hants.

 Drawn next to certain entries in Craven Wapentake in Yorks., and also beside the heading of Roger de Poitou's land, probably to show that these lands formed part of Roger's fee in 1086 or later. (Yorks.)

 Possibly indicates that land so marked was detailed more fully later in the county folios. (Yorks.)

 Drawn next to certain entries in Yorks., and possibly indicating land given to a church. (Yorks.)

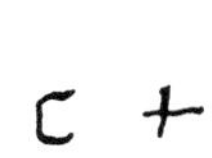 Drawn next to entries concerning the city of Stafford or containing references to it. (Staffs.)

 Drawn in hard pencil next to entries containing the place-name *Westone*. (Leics., Northants)

 Single or double oblique lines drawn in pencil next to certain entries in the *Clamores*. (Lincs., Yorks.)

8 RARE MARGINALIA NOT COVERED BY THE ABOVE CATEGORIES

All periods

In a MS with as complex a history as GDB there are inevitably a number of 'special cases' among the annotations made in its margins. The following are rare or even unique examples which nevertheless can be attributed to some definite purpose or period.

 *canonicis*, 'for the canons', written by the main scribe against four manors reserved for the support of the canons of Exeter, as noted in the text immediately beneath. (Devon. 101v)

 Perhaps abbreviating some part of *facere*, 'to do', and indicating where the next section of text should be started after a space had been left at the end of the previous section. (Berks. 58, Hants 52v, Wilts. 65v)

 *Usque*, 'up to [here?]', possibly indicating the position reached during a check on the column. (Yorks. 300v)

nescio cuius 'I do not know whose', written by the correcting scribe against an entry in which he had mistakenly thought that the holder's name was missing. (Derby. 277v)

rex Perhaps written by the main scribe to draw attention to the presence of royal land in an unusual position in the county. (Hants 51)

 A marginal note by the main scribe to correct the name-form *Caldeuuelle* in the adjacent text to *Cradeuuelle*. (Yorks. 380)

 Drawings, probably added in the sixteenth or seventeenth centuries. (Cambs. 199, Kent 2)

Caroline Thorn

APPENDIX II

METHODS OF TEXTUAL ABBREVIATION IN GREAT DOMESDAY BOOK

As was the normal practice in most Latin manuscripts and documents produced in western Europe during the medieval period, the text of Great Domesday Book was written in an abbreviated form, economical of both time and parchment. The basic symbols and methods of abbreviation employed in the manuscript are the conventional ones of the period, but some shortened forms are peculiar to the technical terms used in the Domesday records.

The precise shape normally given to a few of the conventional abbreviation-symbols by the main scribe who wrote nearly the whole of Great Domesday Book may be taken as characteristic features of his writing therein. These idiosyncratic shapes are as follows: the second form of the overline (see 1, below); both the symbols for *et* (see 2); and the first form of the abbreviation for *-bus* (see 4). For the benefit of readers of the present facsimile edition, a representative selection of the main types of abbreviation found in Great Domesday Book is listed below with, in the case of complete words but not of syllables, an extension in Latin and a translation in English.

1. CONTRACTION AND SUSPENSION

The most common method of shortening words was to contract and/or suspend their length by the omission of letters. Such shortening was indicated by the use of the 'overline', a horizontal line above or attached to the letter after which other letters had been omitted. Two different forms of the overline were used in Great Domesday Book. The first is a short horizontal line curving upwards at its right-hand end; when placed above a vowel this most usually signifies the omission of the letter *m*; it was also often attached to the ascenders of the letters *b*, *d*, *h*, and *l*.

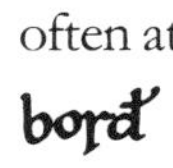	*bordarius*	bordar
	comes	count, earl
	*cum*	with
	*se defendit*	it is assessed
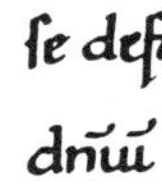	*dominium*	demesne
	*episcopus*	bishop
	*hida*	hide
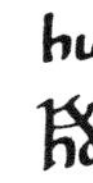	*hundredum, hundret*	hundred
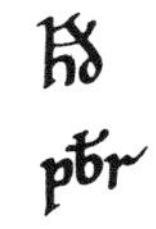	*presbiter*	priest
	*villanus*	villan

The second form of the overline is a short horizontal line having an oblique hairline attached to each end, one rising, the other descending; this form was more often used above a consonant. When written at speed it can develop into a narrow s-shape.

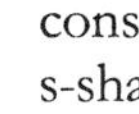	*caruca*	plough
	*denarius*	penny
	*tenet*	he, she, it holds
	*terra*	land

2. THE ABBREVIATIONS FOR *ET*

The word which occurs most frequently in Great Domesday Book is Latin *et*, 'and'. In the vast majority of instances this was represented by the Tironian *nota*, the symbol ⁊ which originated in the Roman system of shorthand writing developed by Cicero's secretary Tiro. Often, as a consequence of the speed at which it was written, this was given a very long descender in Great Domesday Book and there is an overlap with the letters on the following line. In the most formal parts of the text at the beginning of a county, and in some rubrics, the alternative medieval abbreviation for *et*, the ampersand, sometimes occurs, but this is very rare in comparison to the *nota*.

⁊	*et* (usual)	and
& &	*et* (rare)	

3. SIGLA

Complete words were sometimes represented only by their initial letter, written in capital form. In some chapters, a tenant-in-chief's forename was abbreviated in this way when it was mentioned several times in successive entries.

B̃	*Berewica*	berewick
m̃	*Manerium*	manor
s̃ s̃	*Sanctus*	Saint
s̃	*Soca*	soke
T.R.E.	*Tempore Regis Edwardi*	TRE, 'in the time of King Edward'
v̄	*virgata*	virgate

4. RECURRENT FINAL SYLLABLES

Certain final syllables which occurred very frequently as Latin inflexions were symbolized in a conventional manner.

bꝫ b'	*-bus*	
oꝝ oꝝ	*-orum*	
᷑	(supracript) *-ur*	
ꝰ	(supracript) *-us*	

Some space was also saved by the use of ligatures of final *-ns* and *-nt* (ns nt), and of both initial and medial *TR* (TR).

5. SUPRASCRIPT LETTERS

The abbreviation-sign sometimes took the form of one letter written above another. In most cases the supraspcript letter is the final one of the word or syllable which has been shortened. The form of suprascript *a* is usually open-topped.

mᵒ	*modo*	now
pᵃtũ	*pratum*	meadow
uᵒ	*vero*	truly
qᵃ qᵉ qⁱ qᵒ	*qua, que, qui, quo*	
qᵃꝝ	*quarentena*	furlong

This method of abbreviation was also used with numerals, sometimes involving two suprascript letters.

iiᵒ iiᵉ iiᵒˢ	*duo, due, duos*	two
iiiiᵒʳ	*quattuor*	four
viiiᵗᵒ	*octo*	eight
xxᵗⁱ	*viginti*	twenty
xxxᵗᵃ	*triginta*	thirty
qᵗ xxᵗⁱ	*quater viginti*	eighty

6. OTHER COMMON ABBREVIATIONS

a. Words or syllables associated with the letter *p*.

ꝑ	*per*	through; also as the syllable *per-*
p̄	*pre-*	the syllable *pre-*
ꝓ	*pro*	for; also as the syllable *pro-*

b. Words or syllables associated with the letter *q* (*see also* 5, above).

ꝗ	*quam*	than, which
q̄do q̄do	*quando*	when
nunꝗ	*nunquam*	never
postꝗ	*postquam*	after
qͥa	*quia*	because
qꝫ	*-que*	and
qđ	*quod*	which
q̄m	*quoniam*	since

c. Miscellaneous Common Words and Names.

.ē.	*est*	he, she, it is
.ēē.	*esse*	to be
fuer̄	*fuerunt*	they were
hƀt	*habet*	he, she, it has
hoēs	*homines*	men
hō	*homo*	man
Iohs̄	*Johannes*	John
n̄	*non*	not
sꝫ	*sed*	but
t̄c	*tunc*	then
ꝉ	*vel*	or
Witts	*Willelmus*	William

Alexander R. Rumble

APPENDIX III

THE ARRANGEMENT OF FOLIOS BY GATHERINGS IN GREAT DOMESDAY BOOK

The manuscript is made up from forty-seven gatherings of parchment (sometimes called quires) consisting of irregular numbers of sheets and half-sheets as set out in the diagram below. Certain additional sheets were bound into the beginning and end of the volume in later times and are here indicated by broken lines. The *recto* of a folio is signified by the folio number only, and the *verso* by the number followed by v.

† indicates that one side of the folio is blank, ‡ that it is blank on both sides.

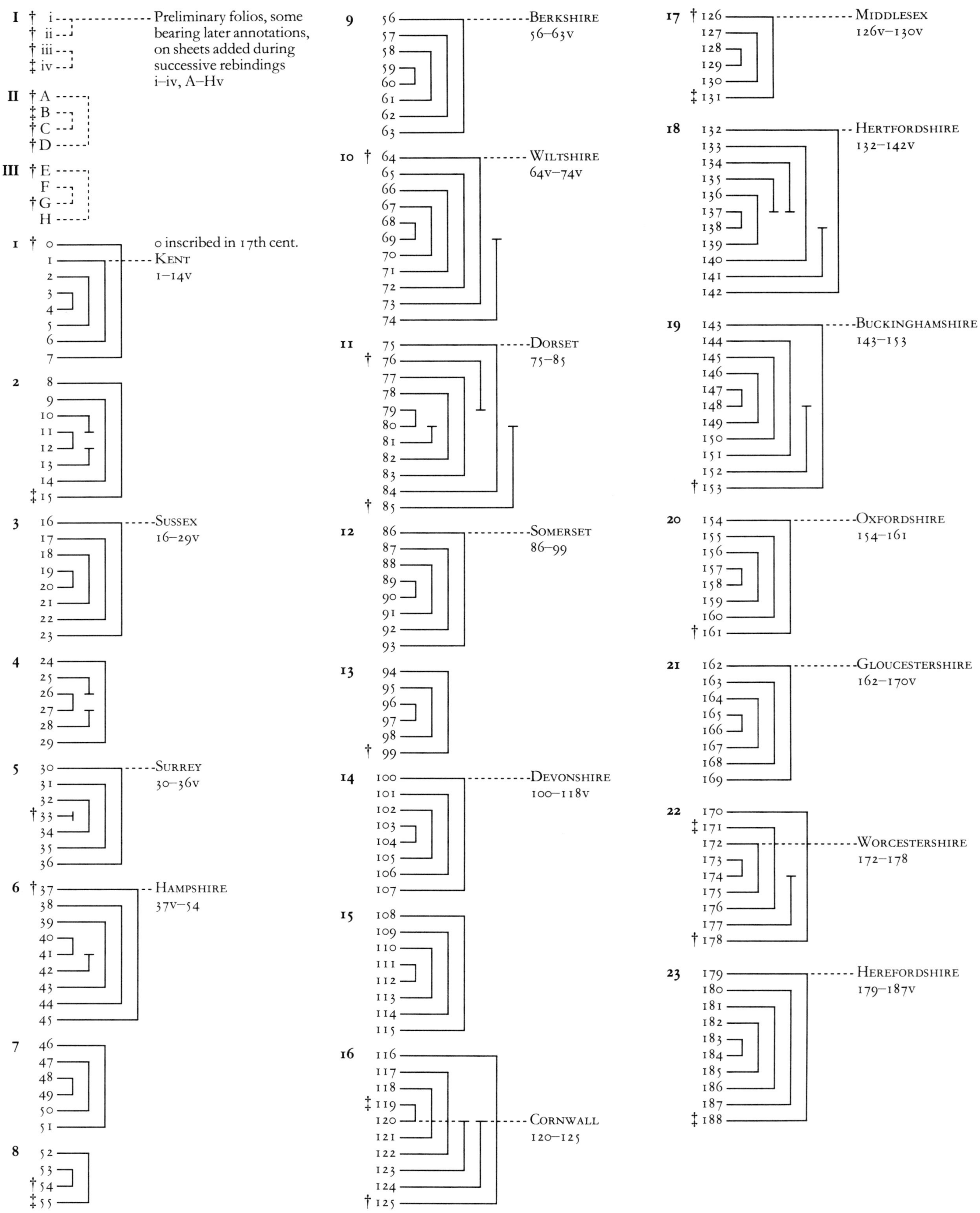

24 189, 190, 191, 192, 193, 194, 195, 196 — CAMBRIDGESHIRE 189–202v

25 197, 198, 199, 200, 201, 202

Volume 2 of the 1986 rebinding of the MS begins here

26 203, 204, 205, 206, 207, 208 — HUNTINGDONSHIRE 203–208v

27 209, 210, 211, 212, 213, 214, 215, 216, 217, 218 — BEDFORDSHIRE 209–218v

28 219, 220, 221, 222, 223, 224, 225, 226, 227, 228, 229 — NORTHAMPTONSHIRE 219–229

229v inscribed in 18th cent.

29 230, 231, 232, 233, 234, 235, 236, †237 — LEICESTERSHIRE 230–237

30 238, 239, 240, 241, 242, 243, 244, ‡245 — WARWICKSHIRE 238–244v

31 246, 247, 248, 249, 250, ‡251 — STAFFORDSHIRE 246–250v

32 252, 253, 254, 255, 256, 257, 258, 259 — SHROPSHIRE 252–260v

33 260, ‡261, †262, 263, 264, 265 — SHROPSHIRE (cont.); CHESHIRE 262v–269

34 266, 267, 268, 269, †270, ‡271 — 'BETWEEN THE RIBBLE AND THE MERSEY' 269v–270

35 272, 273, 274, 275, 276, 277, 278, ‡279 — DERBYSHIRE 272–278v

36 280, 281, †282, 283, 284, 285, 286, 287, 288 — NOTTINGHAMSHIRE 280–293

37 289, 290, 291, 292, 293, †294, ‡295, ‡296 — RUTLAND 293v–294

38 ‡297, 298, 299, 300, 301, 302, 303, 304, 305, 306 — YORKSHIRE 298–333

39 307, 308, 309, 310, 311, 312, †313, 314

40 315, 316, 317, †318, 319, 320, 321, 322

41 323, 324, 325, 326, 327, 328, 329, 330

42 331, 332, †333, ‡334, ‡335, 336, 337, 338, 339, 340 — YORKSHIRE (cont.); 332v, 333 inscribed in 12th cent.; LINCOLNSHIRE 336–371v

43 341, 342, 343, 344, 345, 346, 347, 348

44 349, 350, 351, 352, 353, 354, 355, 356

45 357, 358, 359, 360, 361, 362, 363, 364

46 365, 366, 367, 368, 369, 370, 371, ‡372

47 373, †374, 375, 376, 377, ‡378, 379, 380, 381, †382 — 'CLAMORES' for YORKS. and LINCS. 373–382

IV ‡v, ‡vi, ‡vii, ‡viii, ‡ix, ‡x — Sheets added during successive rebindings v–xxii

V ‡xi, ‡xii, ‡xiii, ‡xiv, ‡xv, ‡xvi

VI ‡xvii, ‡xviii, ‡xix, ‡xx, ‡xxi, xxii

xxii inscribed in 18th cent.

DOMESDAY BOOK STUDIES

INDEX

In common with all parts of the present edition of Domesday Book, the English counties and their abbreviations given in this index are those that existed prior to the restructuring of the counties in 1974.

C

D

E

F

M

Q

R

S

T

U

V

W

Y

GLOUCESTERSHIRE

THE

GLOUCESTERSHIRE DOMESDAY

ALECTO HISTORICAL EDITIONS
LONDON
1989

ISBN for Gloucestershire volumes: 0 948459 29 8
ISBN for this volume: 0 948459 93 x

Printed in England

ALECTO HISTORICAL EDITIONS
46 Kelso Place, London W8 5QG, England

CONTENTS

PREFACE

THIS is the ninth volume of the Alecto County Edition of Domesday Book to be published. In the manuscript, the section for Gloucestershire occupies nine folios, of which eight constitute one complete gathering and the ninth is the first folio of the gathering which follows containing Worcestershire. Gloucestershire comes fifteenth in the order of counties, and the spacing and style of the main scribe's writing suggest that its folios were written about two-thirds of the way through the programme in which the thirty counties were inscribed.

Gloucestershire has a special relationship with the Domesday survey, since it was at the Christmas court in Gloucester itself, in 1085, that the whole procedure was set in motion. The king's court had been accustomed to meet here since the early tenth century, when Æthelræd and Æthelflæd, the ealdorman and his wife, made the city their capital for the administration of Mercia. The king's hall and chamber are mentioned specifically in the very first entry on the opening folio 162 of the Gloucestershire section, where it is stated that it was here, before the Conquest, that the city had rendererd its annual dues which included '12 sesters of honey according to the measure of the same borough, and 36 dickers of iron, and 100 rods of iron, drawn out for nails for the king's ships'. To add to this heterogeneous collection 'certain other small customary dues' were also gathered together here on the same occasion. The building was perhaps at 'Kingsholm', which was the site of a manor-house that survived until the sixteenth century. It is likely that it was in this place that the court met in 1085, though it is also possible that the new castle, built since 1066, was used for the purpose instead.

Throughout this edition the names and extent of the counties are those which obtained prior to the restructuring of the counties in 1974. Since their traditional boundaries had remained virtually unchanged since the time of the Domesday survey, there seemed little purpose in following recent, arbitrary innovations which have neither historical justification nor useful function in this context. In this volume and on the associated county map we therefore ignore the loss of the considerable territory that now forms half of the invented county of Avon, and return it to its rightful position as the south-western corner of Gloucestershire as it had been for a thousand years or more.

The three volumes that constitute each part of the County Edition are designed to be mutually supportive and are separated in this way for the reader's convenience. For instance, it is desirable for the facsimile folios to be present in one book and the parallel translations in another so that both can be consulted side by side. For the same reason the key to the symbols employed in the translations for Great Domesday's marginal notes and signs (Appendix I), and the list of abbreviations found in the manuscript (Appendix II) are best incorporated in the third volume, *Domesday Book Studies*, so that they, too, can be used in conjunction with the folios of translations and facsimile to which they refer. A fourth separate element is the large-scale county map which is provided as a loose-leaf folded sheet in order to be spread out near at hand if required.

Besides the book containing the facsimile folios and the maps, the division of text into two further self-contained volumes reflects the character and scope of their contents. *Domesday Book Studies* (which is common to the entire County Edition) is a book of essays on topics concerning Domesday Book in general, while this volume contains all matter specific to the locality in question. The translations are put at the end, unusually after the indices, where they are easiest to find and where their pages can be matched with the facsimile of the manuscript by the same folio numbers without disrupting the pagination of the rest of this book.

In a project so closely bound up with local history, place-name identification will constitute a salient feature affecting all its aspects, especially in the translations, indices and maps where their occurrences must always be consistent. By chance, the present publication was first set in motion towards the end of a period when the place-names recorded in Domesday Book had come under particular scrutiny, but not always with unanimously accepted results. The only recourse was to log every mention of a name on to a card index and enter into it all dissident opinion. This organized body of raw material was then submitted to F. R. Thorn, appointed for his special knowledge of the Domesday hundreds and place-names, and who has also established their position on the map. Dr Thorn in turn wishes to acknowledge the generous assistance with the Gloucestershire place-names afforded him by J. S. Moore and to his wife Caroline for help at every stage of writing, mapping and indexing.

Those responsible for the making of the facsimile and for the production of the edition are noticed in the acknowledgements printed in the accompanying *Domesday Book Studies,* other than W. S. Cowell Ltd of Ipswich who have typeset this particular volume. Special mention should also be made of Westerham Press for the complex task of setting the translations to match the Latin text of the manuscript with such success. The database for the manipulation of the place- and personal names for the Indices has been developed by James Brennan. The design and typography for this, as for the rest of the work, is by Ian Mortimer, I. M. Imprimit, London.

Our thanks are due especially to Elaine Shaughnessy who has controlled the editing of this volume overall, to Basil Harley for guiding the diverse elements through the press, to Brian Martin for overseeing production at Westerham Press, and also to the following for their diligence in the accomplishment of its various parts:

Bibliography: Dr David Bates, for rearranging his *Domesday Bibliography* already published; editing, Patricia Gibson.

Indices: Jenny Page for keying-in the material for the database from which both Indices are derived; Douglas Matthews for the compilation of the Index of Persons; Cyril Simsa and Jenny Page for editing.

Translation: initial standardization, Eric Hemming, Paul Francis and Stephen Wilson; copy-preparation at Oxford University Press, George Tulloch; editing, David Walker, Christine Shaw, Caroline Thorn; typesetting at Westerham Press, Clive Logsdon.

Map: assistance with the design, Tom Phillips; compilation and editing, Frank Thorn, Des Seal, Cyril Simsa; drafting, Marcus Dadds; overseeing production at Cook Hammond and Kell Ltd, Jackie Hoy.

Finally, at Alecto, for the myriad incidental activities that such a project requires, we must thank Sarah Burton, Caroline Juler, Henrietta Pearson and Emma Wells-Cole.

Ann Williams, *Editor-in-Chief*

R. W. H. Erskine, *General Editor*

The following is a list of abbreviations which are used throughout this edition. References to publications are given in their abbreviated form if they occur in the county bibliography.

AntJ	*Antiquaries Journal*
ArchJ	*Archaeological Journal*
ASE	*Anglo-Saxon England*
BAR	British Archaeological Reports
BL	British Library
CA	*Current Archaeology*
DB	Domesday Book
EconHR	*Economic History Review*
EETS	Early English Text Society
EHR	*English Historical Review*
EPNS	English Place-Name Society
Exon	Exeter Domesday Book
GDB	Great Domesday Book
HMSO	Her Majesty's Stationery Office
JBAA	*Journal of the British Archaeological Association*
JMH	*Journal of Medieval History*
LDB	Little Domesday Book
MA	*Medieval Archaeology*
MS, MSS	Manuscript(s)
MS	*Mediaeval Studies*
NGR	National Grid Reference
N & Q	*Notes and Queries*
PBA	*Proceedings of the British Academy*
PRO	Public Record Office
TRHS	*Transactions of the Royal Historical Society*
VCH	*The Victoria Histories of the Counties of England*

INTRODUCTION

AN INTRODUCTION TO THE GLOUCESTERSHIRE DOMESDAY

ANN WILLIAMS

GLOUCESTERSHIRE has an intimate association with the Domesday survey, which was set in motion by the 'deep speech' of the Christmas court which met at Gloucester in 1085. If the county has not received the same attention as its neighbour, Worcestershire, this is perhaps due to the fact that only now is the *Victoria County History* producing its volume on the Gloucestershire Domesday. A translation of the Gloucestershire folios appeared in 1812, and the text was published by Rudder in 1799 as well as in the Ordnance Survey photozincograph.[1] The gap left by the absence heretofore of a *VCH* volume has been in part filled by A. S. Ellis on the Domesday landholders, by C. S. Taylor's analysis of the Domesday text, and latterly by David Walker's study of the town and shire at the time of Domesday.[2] The Domesday text for Gloucestershire, in the printed version devised by Abraham Farley, has been available, with a rather free translation, in the volume for Gloucestershire in the Phillimore edition, by J. S. Moore.[3] The notes to this volume have been of immense value in the preparation of the present study and translation.

A debt must also be acknowledged to the work on pre-Conquest Gloucestershire of C. S. Taylor, H. P. R. Finberg and Della Hooke, evidence of which will be found throughout this essay. Taylor's studies on the religious houses of the shire have been of particular help.[4] Finberg's contributions to the early history of the shire, both in his *Gloucestershire Studies* and in the volume on the West Midlands which he produced for the University of Leicester's hand-list of Anglo-Saxon charters, are invaluable.[5] Last but not least, many of the opinions expressed herein on the early history and administration of the shire originate in the studies of Della Hooke on the West Midland landscape.[6]

The boundaries of the territory called Gloucestershire in the eleventh century differ considerably from those of the modern county as it existed before the boundary changes of 1974 which regrettably changed the face of England. In the eleventh century, Gloucestershire's western edge was encroaching upon its neighbour, Herefordshire, a process to be observed in Domesday itself.[7] Moreover, the penetration of Wales by English and Normans in the eleventh century had resulted in the annexation to Gloucestershire of the territory which later formed the county of Monmouth.[8] The southern boundary with Somerset has proved more stable, though the growth of Bristol drew the former Somerset districts of Bedminster and Knowle into Gloucestershire. To the north and east, where the shire abuts on Worcestershire, Warwickshire, Oxfordshire and Wiltshire, the boundaries were drawn to respect the possessions of religious houses, in particular the privileged territory of the bishopric of Worcester.[9] This had the result of producing 'islands' of land physically within one shire but administratively within another. These anomalies were smoothed out over succeeding centuries and a summary of the changes,

[1] Bawdwen, *Dom. Boc. A Translation of the Record called Domesday*; Rudder, *New History of Gloucestershire*; James (director), *Domesday Book: or the Great Survey of England*.

[2] Ellis, 'On the Landholders of Gloucestershire'; Taylor, *Analysis of the Domesday Survey of Gloucestershire*; Walker, 'Gloucester and Gloucestershire'.

[3] Moore (ed.), *Domesday Book: Gloucestershire*.

[4] C. S. Taylor, 'Berkeley Minster', *Trans. of the Bristol and Gloucestershire Archaeol. Soc.* (abbr. *TBGAS*) 19 (1894–5), 70–84; *idem*, 'Deerhurst, Pershore and Westminster'.

[5] Finberg (ed.), *Gloucestershire Studies*; H. P. R. Finberg, *The Early Charters of the West Midlands* (Leicester, 1961).

[6] D. Hooke, *Anglo-Saxon Landscapes of the West Midlands: The Charter Evidence*, BAR Brit. ser. 95 (1981); D. Hooke, *The Anglo-Saxon Landscape: the Kingdom of the Hwicce* (Manchester, 1985).

[7] Finberg, 'Bishop Athelstan's Boundary', *Early Charters*, 225–7.

[8] F. Thorn, 'The County Boundary', *Domesday Book: Gloucestershire*, ed. Moore.

[9] See A. Williams, 'An Introduction to the Worcestershire Domesday', *The Worcestershire Domesday*, eds. A. Williams and R. W. H. Erskine (London, 1988), 2, 15–17.

prepared by Frank Thorn, will be found in the Phillimore edition, and it is upon his revised version of this that the map and indices associated with the present volume are based.[1]

GLOUCESTERSHIRE IN THE DOMESDAY SURVEY

MANORIAL RESOURCES AND DUES

Gloucestershire belonged to the West Midlands circuit (Circuit V) which also included Worcestershire, Herefordshire, Shropshire, Cheshire and possibly Staffordshire, and the language and formulae used therefore show some of the idiosyncracies also found in the Domesday accounts of these shires.[2]

Throughout Domesday Book a prominent place in each manorial entry is given to its assessment to geld, expressed in terms of the number of hides at which it was assessed. In Gloucestershire the hides are often said to be geldable (*geldantes*), since there are frequent references to exemptions, details of which are sometimes given. At Mitcheldean, King Edward had remitted geld on the whole manor, assessed at two hides and two and a half virgates, since the pre-Conquest tenants, Godric, Alric and Earnwig, had been wardens of the forest. The same king had remitted the geld on two hides of the ten-hide manor of Hampnett for Archbishop Ealdræd of York, the pre-Conquest tenant. Other exemptions to religious houses or ecclesiastical persons are mentioned, but it was not only the church which enjoyed such privileges; Edward had also remitted geld on six hides of the fifteen-hide manor of Lechlade to the layman Siward Barn. It is clear in fact that demesne was often (perhaps always) exempt; this is specifically stated in the accounts of Preston (near Cirencester), Cow Honeybourne, Temple Guiting (f.167v), Stratton, Siddington and Sherborne. Defaults are also recorded, as at Daglingworth (f.166v), where Ralph, the 1086 tenant, had kept back the geld on three hides of the five and a half hides in the estate, and at Deerhurst (f.165), where Gerard the chamberlain had withheld geld and service on eight hides at Kemerton and three hides at Boddington.

The rate at which the geld was levied is never recorded in Domesday, presumably because it could be varied from time to time as the king willed. Only in exceptional cases are actual payments recorded, as at Upper Slaughter, a three-hide estate of which one hide paid annually 10*s*. geld for the king's use (*ad opus regis*); a rate of 3*s*. 4*d*. (a quarter of a mark) per hide per year. The hidage is by the eleventh century an estimate of fiscal liability rather than acreage, but the two are obviously related; hence the curious entry for the unnamed manor held by Gosmer of the Bishop of Coutances, assessed at one hide in which there are only sixty-four acres 'when it was ploughed'. A variation in the hidation formula occurs at Chedworth and Churcham, where the hides are said to be 'in woodland and open land' (*inter silvam et planum*). The Latin is a direct translation of the Old English formula *on wudu and on felda* found in pre-Conquest charters. In this phrase the original meaning of *feld* ('open country') has been modified to mean 'land cleared from the woodland' or 'open land beside woodland'.[3]

The number of ploughs in demesne and those held by the men of the manor are regularly recorded. In some shires, but not those of Circuit V, the total for ploughlands is also given. However it is sometimes stated that more ploughs 'could be there'. Some discussion has taken place in recent years over the significance of the plough and ploughland figures, and it has been debated whether, as was once thought, they relate to the agricultural capacity of the manor, or are yet another fiscal calculation of some kind. To this question the Gloucestershire folios contribute no obvious insights, though no statistical calculations, which might throw light on the matter, have been made, due to the innumeracy of the present author.

The most common non-arable appurtenances are meadow and woodland. Meadow is

[1] See p.1, n.8 above.

[2] For the circuits, see H. R. Loyn, 'A General Introduction to Domesday Book', *Domesday Book Studies*, eds. A. Williams and R. W. H. Erskine (London, 1987), 3–4.

[3] Hooke, *Anglo-Saxon Landscapes*, 175.

normally measured in acres, though occasionally cash-renders are substituted, as at Sezincote, where, in 1086, the only revenue from the manor was 12*d.* from its meadow. The meadow at Lechlade paid £7. 7*s.* as well as hay for the oxen, and that at Kempsford paid £9 and pasturage for the oxen. The connection of meadow with winter-fodder for the plough-oxen is mentioned again at Haresfield where there was 'meadow sufficient for the ploughs'. Woodland was measured in leagues and furlongs, both length and breadth being commonly given. Like meadow, its cash render was sometimes substituted, as at Newent and Bisley. At Highnam there was woodland 'enough for the manor', and at Little Sodbury 'a small amount'. At Temple Guiting, a most unusual entry, there was woodland and pasture rendering forty hens. Brushwood (*broca*) is recorded at Deerhurst. Pasture is commonly recorded in many shires alongside meadow and woodland, but it rarely occurs in the shires of Circuit V. At Temple Guiting the pasture is mentioned in the same breath as woodland and, in this case, pasturage of pigs on the acorns and beech-mast is probably intended. An unspecified amount of pasture rendering 2*s.* is recorded at Shipton Moyne. A vineyard is recorded at Stonehouse, measured, as is customary in Domesday, by the French arpent (*arpenz*).

Farm-animals are rarely mentioned in Domesday Book. Though livestock statistics were collected, they were omitted from the final recension and occur only in unusual contexts. Draught-animals are mentioned twice in the entry for Bishop's Cleeve. Sheep were kept at Kempsford, for a sheepfold rendering 120 weys of cheese is recorded, and also at Cirencester, where the queen had received the sheep's wool. Cows, pigs and hens are recorded among the renders of some manors.

The salt industry of Droitwich in Worcestershire is well-attested in the Gloucestershire folios, since many of the manors in the shire had interests there. The most common industrial appurtenances, however, here as elsewhere, were water-mills. Their renders are usually expressed in cash (*£. s. d.*) but the mill at Rudford rendered only corn, 'as much as could be sold'. Mills had a useful sideline in fishing, and renders of eels are common. Fisheries are also plentiful in Gloucestershire, as one would expect from a shire with a large frontage on the Severn, and fisheries there and on the Wye are recorded. St Peter's, Gloucester had sixteen salmon annually from its burgesses in the city. Some renders in cash and kind are recorded from individual tenants and groups of tenants. Six men at Pucklechurch paid 100 *massae* of iron and a man at Batsford paid six ploughshares. Ploughshares were also rendered by a burgess at Gloucester attached to the manor of Quenington, and a smith, attached to Quenington but apparently also in Gloucester, paid 2*s.* Another Gloucester burgess, attached to Woodchester (f. 170v), rendered twenty horseshoes (or perhaps twenty pairs of horseshoes). These references, coupled with the thirty-six dickers of iron and 100 drawn rods rendered by the city of Gloucester to the king, indicate a well-established iron industry in the shire, probably based, as later, on the Forest of Dean. The well-wooded areas of the shire produced other items; honey renders are recorded at Bisley and at Deerhurst.

Of particular interest are the food-rents due from some of the royal manors. Cheltenham before the Conquest paid £9. 5*s.* and 3,000 loaves for dogs (presumably hunting-dogs); in 1086 it paid £20, twenty cows, as many pigs and 16*s.* for bread. Identical renders were owed from the king's holding at 'Barton' (in Gloucester). Cirencester before the Conquest owed three and a half *modii* of wheat, three *modii* of malt, six and a half sesters of honey, £9. 5*s.* and 3,000 loaves for dogs; in 1086 it rendered the same as Cheltenham and 'Barton'. Such renders are very ancient and represent the 'farm' (*feorm*) or food-rent due to the king. Food-rents of this type are mentioned in the laws of Ine (688–726), where the *feorm* of a ten-hide estate is reckoned as ten vats of honey, 300 loaves, twelve ambers of Welsh ale, thirty of clear ale, two full-grown cows or ten wethers, ten geese, twenty hens, ten cheeses, an amber full of butter, five salmon, twenty pounds of fodder and 100 eels.[1] The original *raison d'être* was to supply the needs of the royal household for

[1] F. L. Attenborough, *The Laws of the Earliest English Kings* (Cambridge, 1922; reiss. 1963), 59 (Ine 70. i).

one twenty-four-hour period. The night's farm rendered from Westbury-on-Severn before 1066 and for four years afterwards was an old food-rent; Bitton continued to pay its night's farm in 1086.

Renders of this kind were paid by groups of estates, or by multiple estates of which Westbury-on-Severn is typical: manors consisting of a central vill, where the lord's hall was situated, with a group of dependent vills or berewicks whose dues were rendered at and to the central hall. The same system is found in Wales and is exemplified in the Gloucestershire folios by the entries for the holdings of Waswic the reeve, Elmui, Bleio and Iudichael (f.162). Each held a group of villages, and they rendered jointly forty-seven sesters of honey, forty pigs, forty-one cows and 28*s.* for hawks. These villages were part of the great estate or castlery of Chepstow ('Strigoil'), based on the castle of 'Strigoil' built by Earl William fitzOsbern. The four groups of villages held by Waswic, Elmui, Bleio and Iudichael, all of whom, as their names show, were Welsh, have been identified as the commotes of Brynbuga (Usk), Edeligion, Caldicot and Llebenydd.[1] Chepstow, or 'Strigoil', to which these commotes were appurtenant, is entered among the royal boroughs and is described as a 'town' (*villa*). The revenues were divided between the king (£12) and William de Eu (£9), as the successor of Ralph de Limesy, who received it from Earl William. The lands belonging to Chepstow are assessed, not in hides, as in the rest of Gloucestershire, but in carucates; their renders are partly in cash, but partly also in the dues characteristic of food-rents: pigs, honey, loaves and ale.

It is clear that such dues were by the mid eleventh century being commuted into money-rents. The practice of assigning food-rents and other dues to an individual in return for an annual fixed cash-rent was known as 'farming' the estate. The distinction between farming in this sense and direct exploitation is nicely pointed by the entry for Tockington: 'this manor paid no farm TRE but he to whom it belonged lived off it' (f.164). Ælfsige of Faringdon and Godwine of Stanton held the two royal manors at Great Barrington of the king at farm. It is likely that the value of the manor, given at the end of each entry, is in fact the sum for which it could be farmed, rather than the total of the actual renders from it. This interpretation would explain entries such as that for Tetbury and Tetbury Upton: 'these two manors TRE were worth £33; now they are at farm for £50'.

Dues of whatever kind, and services such as ploughing, harrowing, scything and reaping (mentioned in the entry for Deerhurst) were due to the hall, the central point of the manor. Possession of a hall, indeed, seems to be one of the distinguishing characteristics of a manor. Halls are not often mentioned in Domesday, but the hall (*aula*) at Tewkesbury is recorded, with the sixteen bordars who lived around it, and Chedworth's hall received salt-tolls. The court (*curia*) at Tewkesbury is probably identical with its hall; 'court' could be applied both to the building and to the lord's court which met there. The eight burgesses at Gloucester who belonged to Tewkesbury served its court.

Population

The usual categories of rural population, villans, bordars and slaves, appear in Gloucestershire but, as in the rest of the West Midlands circuit, a remarkable variety of other peasants are recorded. The most exceptional entry is perhaps that for Hidcote Bartrim, where 'the wives of 4 villans lately dead have one plough'. Half-villans are recorded in several places; these are men holding half the normal villan-tenement of a virgate (yardland). Female slaves are recorded as well as male; they were perhaps mostly dairymaids, as the male slaves were mostly ploughmen. The *coliberti* who are mentioned on ten Gloucestershire manors are usually regarded as freed slaves, endowed with small amounts of land. Some simply appear with a share in the common

[1] Moore (ed.), *Domesday Book: Gloucestershire*, notes to W2.

ploughs of the vill, but the eighteen coliberts who lived at Barton (in Bristol) TRE held fourteen ploughs between them, and the twenty coliberts at Westbury on Trym had ten ploughs. The two coliberts at Pucklechurch must have had some resources in order to pay a rent of 34*d*. Most of the Gloucestershire coliberts are associated with royal or ecclesiastical estates, but the freeing of slaves was a pious act, carried out by laymen as well as ecclesiastics; at Hailes, William Leofric had freed twelve slaves. Like cottars and cotsets, who appear in other shires, another category called coliberts may have provided specialist craftsmen as well as labourers, though no examples from Gloucestershire can be cited. References to specialists are infrequent, though there was a smith at Pinbury, and five potters paying 44*d*. at Haresfield Court.

The upper ranks of the peasantry are represented by the radknights, *francigene*, free men and *homines*, all of whom belong to a stratum of non-noble free men, equivalent to the later franklins or yeomen. The radknights or radmen as a group appear only in the West Midlands circuit, though this seems to be a function of the way in which information was compiled rather than their actual distribution in eleventh-century England.[1] Their name means 'riding-men' and their primary duty was probably to act as escort to their lords. They can be equated with the men described in pre-Conquest sources as *geneatas*, whose obligations included fighting in the lord's warband and agricultural services.[2] About 1050, a survey of the manor of Tidenham was compiled which describes the services due from the *geneatas* on this multiple estate:[3] 'the *geneat* must labour either on the estate or off the estate, whichever he is bidden, and ride and furnish carrying-service and supply transport and drive herds and do many other things.'

Oddly enough in view of the existence of this survey, so close in date to Domesday itself, no radknights are recorded at Tidenham in Domesday Book, either before or after the Conquest. The duties of the radknights who are recorded, however, resemble those of the Tidenham *geneatas*. The radknights of Tewkesbury ploughed and harrowed for their lord's hall, and those at Deerhurst ploughed, harrowed, scythed and reaped 'for the use of the lord' (*ad opus domini*). They were not, however, entirely dependent upon their lords, but had land, ploughs, and dependents of their own. At Berkeley, for instance, ten radknights held seven hides and seven ploughs, and nineteen radknights held forty-eight ploughs 'with their own men'. At Berkeley and Deerhurst, they are specifically equated with free men. Free men and radknights are not, however, identical, since free men are recorded by that name at Cirencester, Sevenhampton, Deerhurst and Edgeworth; like the radknights of Berkeley, the free men of Sevenhampton had 'men' of their own. *Homines* ('men') are also mentioned, but it is not always clear what the word means. The 'men' at Brawn and Upton St Leonards, both berewicks of 'Barton' (in Gloucester), were probably villans. Brawn, with three men, was assessed at three virgates, and Upton, assessed at one hide, had four men; one virgate was the usual tenement for a villan. On the other hand, the 'men' of Meysey Hampton and Bisley are specifically distinguished from other categories of population, including, in the case of Bisley, radknights. The Bisley men, twenty-three of them, paid 44*s*. and two sesters of honey, and the five men at Doynton paid 5*s*. The men of Pucklechurch, who paid 100 *massae* of iron and the man at Batsford who paid six ploughshares have already been mentioned; they were perhaps specialized craftsmen.

The *francigene* (literally 'French-born') are distinguished from the other free men by their foreign origin, but their status seems analogous. Round considered them sergeants, holding land in return for some specific service. Some of the Gloucestershire Frenchmen were quite comfortably off; one at Ullington (now in Worcestershire) held one and a half hides of land, and another at Daglingworth held with his men half a hide and a plough.

Knights (*milites*) are a distinct category on two grounds; their service is military service and they are assumed to be noble. There has been considerable discussion over the status and

[1] *VCH Dorset*, iii (1968), 15.

[2] F. M. Stenton, *Anglo-Saxon England* (3rd edn., Oxford, 1971), 473. The 'old geneat' Byrhtwold was among the warriors killed at the Battle of Maldon in Essex in 991 (E. V. Gordon (ed.), *The Battle of Maldon* (London, 1937), 61).

[3] A. J. Robertson (ed.), *Anglo-Saxon Charters* (2nd edn., Cambridge, 1956), no. 109.

position of the knights in Domesday Book who are unnamed, and who have been entered along with manorial populations.[1] The word 'knight' is of English origin, from *cniht*, meaning 'retainer'. It was used to translate the Latin *miles*, which in the eleventh century meant a trained warrior who fought on horseback, but also increasingly a man of noble rank. When used with a Christian name, *miles*, like OE *beorn* and *cild*, both of which could mean 'warrior', implied status. It is not quite clear that this was the primary meaning of *miles* when used by itself. It is true that the unnamed *miles* who held *Aldritone* (Frampton) of Winchcombe Abbey is in the position of any other mesne-tenant, and that his name may have been omitted by accident, but the *milites* of Adlestrop are enumerated with the other inhabitants of the manor, most of whom were certainly of peasant status and some at least unfree. Like the other free tenants, however, knights could have land, ploughs and men of their own. At North Cerney, belonging to Gilbert fitzTurold, four of Gilbert's knights, with their men, held seven ploughs and a mill rendering 8*s*., while at Ampney Crucis a knight held the land of four villans.

It remains true, however, that even if it be shown that some knights were poorly endowed with land, their status need not be affected by this. It is not certain that they had no other resources than those recorded in Domesday Book. A lord might retain his men in his own household, or provide some of them with estates on which they could support themselves; or he could combine the two expedients, providing both a stipend and the rent from small parcels of land. The apparently 'poor' knights of Domesday may be household retainers enriched in this way.

The officials known as reeves are frequently mentioned in the Gloucestershire folios. The word, from OE *gerefa*, was applied to men of widely differing status and function. Sæwine, the pre-Conquest reeve of Bristol, who held the manor of Clifton, represents the upper stratum. He was presumably the port-reeve of Bristol with responsibility for collecting the king's dues and overseeing mercantile transactions within the town. The duties of the port-reeve are recorded in the laws of Æthelræd II and Edmund: to collect toll, to ensure the purity of the coinage and prevent counterfeiting, and to act as witness to sales.[2] They also had judicial responsibilities. In the 990s, the reeves of Buckingham and Oxford were accused of malpractice in allowing Christian burial to thieves, although the king upheld them.[3]

Similar responsibilities were laid upon the reeves of royal estates, especially those which, like Cheltenham, were heads of hundreds. The reeves of hundredal manors would have collected the geld from the hundreds concerned, and probably presided over the hundred courts. They also managed the estates and ensured the payment of their dues. The reeves of these manors, and those of the other royal estates at Alveston, Thornbury, Avening, Old Sodbury, Naas and Tockington had improved their charges with additional ploughs, mills, slaves and villagers between the Conquest and 1086. The office of reeve was both onerous and lucrative and it is likely that the men who held the office were king's thegns of some wealth. The entries for Chedworth and Arlington, both royal manors in 1086, are followed by a note saying that before 1066 the reeves paid 'what they wished', but that now they paid £40 in blanched pennies. Both manors were tenanted in 1066, Arlington by Cynewig Chelle, who was certainly a king's thegn, and Chedworth by Wulfweard, who may have been, if he is to be identified with Wulfweard White. It is probable that Cynewig and Wulfweard held these manors as royal reeves.[4]

Other lords than the king employed men to manage their estates. The reeve who held the lands of one and a half villans and five bordars at Newent, belonging to the Abbey of Sainte-Marie of Cormeilles, was probably the church's steward. Where reeves are listed among the other inhabitants of the vill, as at Quenington and Brockworth, they are probably the village

[1] S. P. J. Harvey, 'The Knight and the Knight's Fee', *Past and Present*, 49 (1970), 3–43.

[2] A. J. Robertson (ed.), *The Laws of the Kings of England from Edmund to Henry I* (Cambridge, 1925; reiss. New York, 1974), 15, 73, 77 (III Edmund 5, IV Æthelred 3, 7).

[3] P. H. Sawyer (ed.), *Anglo-Saxon Charters: An Annotated List and Bibliography*, R. Hist. Soc. Guides and Handbooks, 8 (London, 1968) (henceforward cited by number preceded by S.), S.883, dated 995.

[4] Arlington was a royal estate in 1008 (Sawyer (ed.), S.920; see P. H. Sawyer (ed.), *Charters of Burton Abbey* (Oxford, 1979), no. 31).

headmen, who organized the performance of labour-services and the payment of dues owed by the peasants.

Priests and Churches

Domesday is not a sure guide to the number of churches in existence in 1086. It appears to record them only sporadically and perhaps only when they made some particular contribution to manorial revenues. The two churches at Deerhurst, St Mary's and Holy Trinity, both of which are undoubtedly pre-Conquest in origin and standing to this day, are not mentioned.

Deerhurst was in origin a minster, as were the churches at Berkeley and Tewkesbury; the minster at Tewkesbury still existed in 1086.[1] In the account in Domesday Book of the manor of Tewkesbury, the land of the church is entered separately. It was a substantial endowment, consisting of twenty-four and a half hides of land in five estates. Each entry has a red cross placed against it in the margin; the cross for Stanway, the first estate to be entered, is larger than the rest, and a minster (*monasterium*) is recorded; perhaps this was the minster church of Tewkesbury itself, abandoned when the Benedictine abbey was established in 1102. A second church is recorded at Clifford Chambers (now in Warwickshire), one of the berewicks of the manor of Tewkesbury. This is presumably an estate church, built by the holder of Tewkesbury in King Edward's time, Beorhtric son of Ælfgar, or, since Clifford Chambers had been held by Beorhtric's family for three generations, one of his ancestors. Edgar (959–75) permitted thegns holding bookland who had a church to which a graveyard was attached to pay one-third of their demesne-tithes to that church, the remainder going to the local minster, and this legislation was repeated in the code of Cnut (1016–35).[2] St Mary's, Deerhurst, was likewise the minster church, while Holy Trinity, built in 1055 by Oda of Deerhurst, served the secular estate.[3]

Deerhurst, Berkeley and Tewkesbury were not the only minsters in Gloucestershire in the pre-Conquest period. Twyning was the site of a minster in the eighth century, though no sign of a church is apparent from the account of the manor. The minster at Beckford (now in Worcestershire) also had disappeared long before the survey, though a church still existed, whose tithes were given by Earl William fitzOsbern to the Abbey of Cormeilles.[4] Churches are recorded at Tidenham, Ashton under Hill, Littleton-on-Severn, Ampney Crucis and Frampton Cotterell, the last being built after 1066. This list cannot be exhaustive. Mention of a priest implies a church, and therefore some forty-two more churches can be added to this meagre total, including that at Bishop's Cleeve, where a minster dedicated to St Michael is mentioned as early as Offa's reign.[5]

The church at Stow-on-the-Wold, attached to Maugersbury is of particular interest, since its dedication, to St Edward, is actually recorded in Domesday.[6] A hide of land attached to the church was freed of geld by Æthelræd II (978–1016). The charter of Æthelræd conveying this land to Evesham Abbey still exists, though its authenticity has been doubted.[7] The dedication, however, is undoubtedly to Æthelræd's brother and predecessor, Edward the Martyr, murdered at Corfe Castle (Dorset) in 978.

Towns and Boroughs

The description of the city of Gloucester opens the shire account. It is not, unfortunately, a very exhaustive survey. There is no estimate of the total number of burgesses or tenements; the only messuages recorded are those which were once tributary to the royal farm, but have since been

[1] For Deerhurst and Berkeley, see pp.27–9, 32–3 below.
[2] Robertson (ed.), *Laws of the Kings of England*, 21, 165 (II Edgar 2, I Cnut 11).
[3] See pp.28–9 below.
[4] Sawyer (ed.), S.172, S.1431.
[5] Ibid. S.141.
[6] Moore (ed.), *Domesday Book: Gloucestershire*, note to 12,1.
[7] Sawyer (ed.), S.935, dated 1016.

alienated. The building of the castle had resulted in the destruction of sixteen houses, and fourteen more are described as 'waste', that is, they paid no dues. Seventy-one burgesses are recorded among the appurtenances of various manors within the shire. This rather unsatisfactory description can be supplemented by the account of Gloucester in the satellite text known as Evesham K, preserved in the archive of Evesham Abbey.[1] It was compiled about 1100 and is clearly based on Domesday material which has been updated. According to this account, there were, before 1066, 300 burgesses in the king's demesne, paying a total rent of £8. 10*s*. a year. 'Now' (in *c*.1100) ninety-seven burgesses live in their own inherited property (i.e. they are presumably the descendants of the pre-Conquest tenants) and ninety-seven, both French and English, in tenements which they have bought. A further twenty-four burgesses had dwelt 'within the castle' (presumably in the houses destroyed when it was built) and eighty-two messuages are 'waste'.

No total is given for the number of burgesses in 1100, but the number assigned to individual lords amounts to 312, of which 194 were in the king's demesne, sixty in that of the Archbishop of York, six belonged to the Bishop of Worcester, and fifty-two to St Peter's, Gloucester. Added to these must be the inhabitants of the houses attached to particular manors, 194 in all. Ten churches are recorded. Clearly Gloucester was a substantial town in the late eleventh century. The Domesday account, brief though it is, gives some impression of its activities. There was a mint, from which the king had £20, and the renders of the borough, in iron and iron rods,[2] indicate some form of metal-working industry. The fact that the iron rods were to provide nails for the king's ships may imply that shipbuilding was also being carried on in the city. Fishing was clearly important: Roger of Berkeley held a fishery which had once been in the royal demesne, and St Peter's, Gloucester not only had four mills and a fishery, but also received sixteen salmon annually from its burgesses, as well as a rent in cash. The city had its own weights and measures; the honey which it rendered to the king TRE was reckoned by the borough's measure, as opposed to the honey rendered by the manor of Deerhurst, which was reckoned by the king's measure.[3] The king's *minister*, Robert, mentioned in the account of Gloucester, was probably the port-reeve; he may be identical with Robert Despenser, whose brother, Urse d'Abetot, was Sheriff of Worcester.[4] Both the castle and the king's hall, with its chamber, are mentioned; the hall appears again in the Worcestershire folios, which record that half a hide at Droitwich was attached to the hall of Gloucester. This royal hall was probably on the site of the later manor-house of 'Kingsholm', which survived to the sixteenth century, though latterly in a ruinous state. Its name is preserved in that of Kingsholm Square in Gloucester.[5] The mention of the chamber is interesting and may be connected with the city's duty to supply clothing as well as lodging, since the English glossed the word 'chamberlain' (*camerarius*) not only as *burthegn*, from OE *bur*, 'bower' or 'private room', but also as *hrægIthegn*, from *hrægl*, 'clothing, raiment'.[6] Chamberlains were, however, responsible for cash as well as for clothing and other personal possessions of the king.

Winchcombe receives even more summary treatment than Gloucester. It is called a borough, but how long it had been so is a matter of conjecture. No details are given, but twenty-one burgesses are recorded among the appurtenances of various manors. Its hundred, with which it rendered £20 after the Conquest, may be 'Greston' in which the town lay, or the reference may be to the *ferding* of Winchcombe wherein Evesham Abbey held fifty-six hides.[7] The three neighbouring hundreds added (apparently) after 1066 are those of 'Witley', Kiftsgate and "Celfledetorn". Roger d'Ivry, who had added 60*s*. to the borough's renders, may have been its port-reeve.

[1] Translated and discussed in Moore (ed.), *Domesday Book: Gloucestershire*, Appendix.

[2] See p.3 above.

[3] GDB 166.

[4] For whom, see Williams, 'Introduction to the Worcestershire Domesday', 29–30.

[5] H. Hurst, 'Excavations at Gloucester, Third Interim Report: Kingsholm', *AntJ* 55 (1975), 286.

[6] S. Keynes, *The Diplomas of Æthelred II 'the Unready' 978–1016* (Cambridge, 1980), 159.

[7] Moore (ed.), *Domesday Book: Gloucestershire*, note to B1, and see pp.13–14 below.

Like Gloucester, Winchcombe is more fully surveyed in Evesham K. Sixty burgesses are recorded there in 1066, fifty-two of whom continued to live in their hereditary property, while eight more were immigrants. The Abbot of Winchcombe had forty burgesses and forty-one more belonged to other lords. Several mills are recorded.

Gloucester and Winchcombe are at least described in the Domesday account of the shire, if only inadequately. Bristol is not surveyed at all, though it is called a borough in the Exon Domesday.[1] Various details can be gleaned from incidental references. The pre-Conquest port-reeve, Sæwine, has already been mentioned. Two houses in Bristol were attached to the royal manor of Westbury on Trym and ten houses to Bishopsworth (Som.), which belonged to the Bishop of Coutances (sometimes, as here, called St-Lo), Geoffrey de Mowbray.[2] His interest in the borough was considerable, for he received thirty-three marks of silver and one mark of gold from it, acccording to the testimony of the burgesses, recorded in the account of the manor of Barton (in Bristol). This manor (which represents the king's interest) paid, with the borough, 110 marks of silver to the king. It seems therefore that Bishop Geoffrey of Coutances held the third penny (usually the earl's share) of the borough of Bristol. The 'Church of Bristol' held three hides of land in Mangotsfield, a berewick of Barton. This was presumably St Peter's, the oldest church in Bristol.

Cirencester was the head of its hundred and before 1066 paid a render in kind characteristic of a royal farm. It is described as a *villa regia* in 999, and may have been the centre of an old administrative unit such as that based on Winchcombe.[3] A new market had been established by 1086, but there are no other indications of burghal status, though burgesses were established there by 1133.[4] Cirencester in 1086 was in the same stage of development as Tewkesbury, which had thirteen burgesses and a market established by Queen Matilda, and Berkeley, which possessed a market in which dwelt seventeen men (*homines*). All three developed into boroughs, but in 1086 the process was only beginning.

The Machinery of the Survey

The actual making of the Domesday survey is still reflected in the Gloucestershire folios. In the account of Woodchester, held illegally by Edward of Salisbury, it is stated that 'no one has rendered account of this manor to the king's commissioners, nor did any of them (presumably the manorial jury) come to his *descriptio*'. Here the two main processes, a written account submitted to the circuit commissioners, subsequently checked against the witness of the men of the vill, are clear. As a result of this dereliction, Woodchester could not be surveyed; only the shire's testimony that Edward held it illegally and that Earl Godwine had bought it from Azur for his wife Gytha are recorded. This last information presumably came from the shire also, since the sale would have been conducted in its witness. Similarly, there was no one to render account of two manors in Longtree Hundred held by Earl Hugh of Chester. As a result, only the hidage, the pre-Conquest tenants, and the two (unnamed) men who held of Earl Hugh in 1086 are recorded; and the land was valued by the shire court at £8. All this information, except the value, which is said to be only an estimate, could have been derived from geld records. Lastly there was no one to answer for a hide of land in 'Swineshead' Hundred held by Roger fitzRalph; here the only details recorded are two slaves, and the value was assessed at 10*s*.

The shire court's testimony is mentioned in other contexts. It affirmed for instance that two and a half virgates held by William fitzBaderon belonged to the royal demesne of Westbury-on-Severn, and supported the claim of Roger de Lacy to half a hide at Edgeworth against Earl Hugh. It also declared that King Edward had leased Guiting Power to Alwine the sheriff and not given it outright 'as a gift'. In these instances we see the collective memory of the shire at work.

[1] Exon 141v. [2] GDB 88. [3] See pp. 13–14 below. [4] Finberg (ed.), *Gloucestershire Studies*, 65.

The testimony of the hundred court is appealed to in the case of Windrush, held by Ælfsige of Farringdon in 1086; it had been wrongfully placed in Salmonsbury Hundred, but the men of Barrington Hundred successfully maintained that it should lie there.[1]

Individual testimony was also taken. Roger of Berkeley stated that Earl William had assigned the tenants of Cromhall and their service to the reeve of Berkeley (i.e. to himself). Roger de Lacy and the Abbot of Malmesbury claimed the king's gift as their title to two fisheries at Madgetts. A man of Sigar de Chocques claimed that three of the five hides at Yanworth were quit of geld. Other evidence of title adduced includes livery of seisin, as at Dyrham, where Durand the sheriff had given seisin of three hides to the Church of St Mary, Pershore. Henry de Ferrers produced not only the testimony of the shire but the king's sealed writ as proof of the exemption from geld of six hides at Lechlade. Evesham Abbey claimed the authority of Æthelræd II for the exemption of one of the nine hides at Maugersbury from geld, and may even have produced the charter concerned.[2]

THE HISTORY OF THE SHIRE

The Kingdom of the Hwicce

The area now called Gloucestershire lies in the south-western corner of the old kingdom of Mercia, which stretched, at its greatest extent, from the Thames to the Humber, and from the Fens to the borders of Wales. It was, however, not the Mercians but the West Saxons who first brought this area under English control. In 577, the West Saxon kings Cuthwine and Ceawlin 'fought against the Britons and killed three kings, Coinmail, Condidan and Farinmail, at the place which is called Dyrham, and they captured three of their cities, Gloucester, Cirencester and Bath'.[3]

West Saxon control was not maintained beyond 628 when the kings Cynegils and Cwichhelm lost the Battle of Cirencester to the Mercian Penda.[4] It was probably Penda who incorporated the area of Gloucestershire, with what was later Worcestershire and the western third of Warwickshire, into the kingdom of the Hwicce, with its own royal line, within the Mercian hegemony (see map opposite).[5] The centre of the Hwiccian kingdom was Worcester where a bishopric was established in 679 or 680. At about the same time, Osric, king of the Hwicce, founded a monastery at St Peter's, Gloucester.

The Hwiccian kings may have been related to the Bernician rulers of Northumbria, though it has been suggested that they formed a junior line of the Mercian royal house.[6] The family survived until the end of the eighth century, but is then heard of no more, unless Coenwulf, king of the Mercians (796–821), was indeed of Hwiccian descent.[7] The territory continued to be known as the province of the Hwicce until the tenth century, perhaps because it was more or less co-extensive with the episcopal see of Worcester. In the eighth century, the rulers of Mercia began to take an interest in the Hwiccian area. It was Offa who, by tradition, founded Winchcombe Abbey, and his successor Coenwulf transformed it into a double-house (for both monks and nuns) of which his daughter Cwoenthryth was abbess. From this time onwards, Winchcombe became the *eigenkirche* or proprietary church of the Mercian royal house.[8] Since such churches are the key to much of our understanding of Dark Age history, a word of explanation is in order. The founder of a religious community was not acting purely out of piety, though pious motives must not be belittled. He (or she) retained control over the foundation,

[1] GDB 165v.
[2] See p.7 above.
[3] D. Whitelock *et al.* (eds.), *The Anglo-Saxon Chronicle: A Revised Translation*, (London, 1965), *s.a.* 577.
[4] Ibid. *s.a.* 628.
[5] Stenton, *Anglo-Saxon England*, 43.
[6] Finberg, 'The Princes of the Hwicce', *Early Charters*, 167–80.
[7] S. R. Bassett, 'A Probable Mercian Royal Mausoleum at Winchcombe, Gloucestershire', *AntJ* 65 (1985), 84. See p.13, n.6 below.
[8] For Winchcombe, see the previous note, and also W. Levinson, *England and the Continent in the Eighth Century* (Oxford, 1949), 249–58.

and not merely in the capacity of advocate (lay representative). The appointment of the community's head was, if not in the gift of, at least heavily influenced by the wishes of the founder and his heirs, and the house's resources were to some extent still at his disposal. Such resources were considerable. In the first place the spiritual benefits must not be under-rated. Not only were prayers offered for the benefit of the founder and his kin, but he and they were usually buried in the church, as Coenwulf was at Winchcombe. Their names were recorded in the

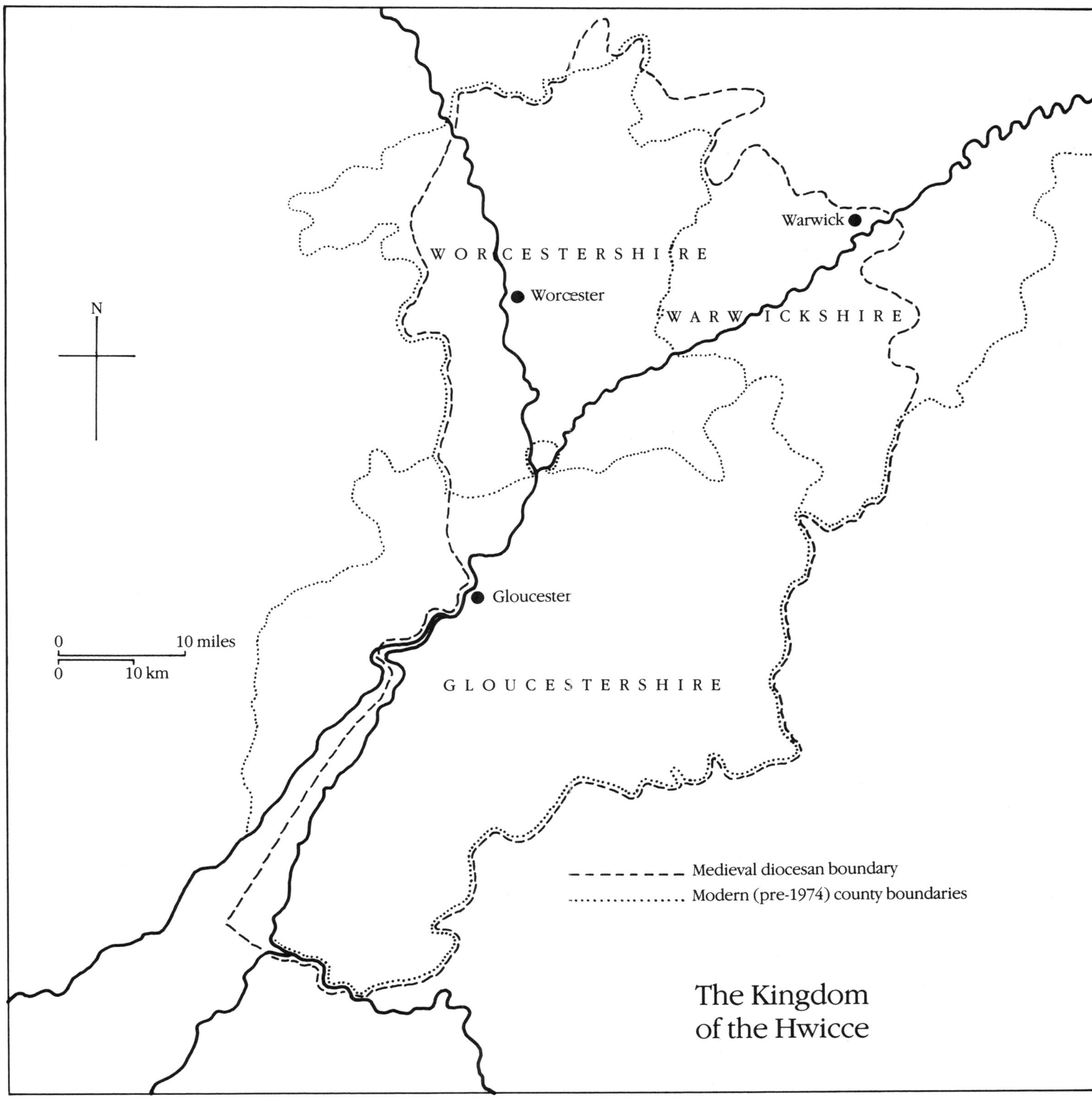

obituary-list and cycle of remembrance; no small advantage for an aristocracy as zealous for fame as that of pre-Conquest England. Even sainthood itself was not an impossible ambition: such a cult grew up in the tenth century around the Mercian prince Cynehelm, canonized as St Kenelm. These cults of royal princes fostered feelings of local self-identity even after the loss of political independence.[1]

In a more practical vein, the proprietary church provided employment and, if need be, refuge for the founder's kin. The educated priests and monks of the community could be used as a kind of secretariat; specifically, they preserved the family's records and title-deeds. It was at

[1] D. Rollason, 'The Cults of Murdered Royal Saints in Anglo-Saxon England', *ASE* 11 (1983), 1–22.

Winchcombe that the archives of Coenwulf's descendants were kept until the end of the ninth century. The Church of Winchcombe, therefore, was not only a religious centre, but a focus of Mercian political control in the south-west of their kingdom.

The West Saxon Supremacy

The power of the Mercian kings was on the wane in the ninth century. In 825 they lost the overlordship of the southern English to Wessex after the Battle of *Ellendun* (near Wroughton in Wiltshire). Succession disputes between rival branches of the royal kin weakened the kingdom, and to these problems were added, from the 830s, the Viking incursions. In 874 King Burgred fled to Rome, where he died, and his successor, Ceolwulf II, was forced to acquiesce in the Danish settlement of the East Midlands. Ceolwulf was the last independent ruler of Mercia. The date of his death is unknown, but in 886 'all the English people that were not under subjection to the Danes' submitted to Alfred, King of Wessex (871–99). The rule of English Mercia was entrusted to a Mercian ealdorman, Æthelræd, who married Æthelflæd, Alfred's daughter. Husband and wife exercised joint authority, and when Æthelræd died in 911, Æthelflæd continued to rule until 918 as Lady of the Mercians.

West Saxon sources call Æthelræd an ealdorman, but in Mercia he (and later his widow) exercised the functions of a king.[1] The Lords of Mercia made their capital, not at Tamworth in Staffordshire, the old centre of Mercian royalty, but at Gloucester. Possibly Tamworth was too close to the Danish frontier, which followed the line of Watling Street. It is from their time that Gloucester began to regain the prominence it had enjoyed in the Roman period. Their residence was probably in the Anglo-Saxon palace at 'Kingsholm', and it may have been here that the Mercian *witan* met in 896.[2] At Gloucester also was founded the 'new minster' of St Oswald's, to which in 909 Æthelflæd translated the relics of this Northumbrian royal saint.[3] Both she and her husband were buried at Gloucester, perhaps in the recently excavated crypt at the eastern end of the tenth-century church of St Oswald.[4] The town was probably fortified at this time, as part of the programme for defence against the Danes begun by Alfred and continued by his successors.

The Origins of the Shire

After the death of Æthelflæd in 918, Mercia was absorbed into the kingdom of the West Saxons. Edward the Elder (899–924), Alfred's son and successor, seems to have intended that his eldest (but possibly illegitimate) son Athelstan should become king of the Mercians, while Ælfweard, his second son, became king of the West Saxons. Ælfweard, however, died soon after his father and Athelstan became king of both peoples. One of the consequences of this union was the extension to the Midlands of the West Saxon unit of administration, the shire. The Midland shires (with the exception of the anomalous Rutland) take their names from the chief town of their region, and for good reason. One of the major assets of the West Saxons in their struggle with the Danes was the series of fortified strongholds, called *burhs*, begun by Alfred and continued by Edward and Æthelflæd. These *burhs* not only provided refuge for the local population and garrison, but also bases from which to launch attacks into Danish-held territory. The shires of the West Midlands probably originate in the areas assigned for the support and manning of such *burhs*.

[1] For instance, he and his widow issued charters in their own names, see Sawyer (ed.), S.217–225.

[2] Ibid. S.1441.

[3] Oswald was a member of the royal family of Bernicia (northern Northumbria) who ruled from 635 to 641; he may therefore have been related to the Hwiccian kings.

[4] C. Heighway and R. Bryant, 'A Reconstruction of the Tenth-Century Church of St Oswald, Gloucester', *The Anglo-Saxon Church: Papers . . . in Honour of Dr H. M. Taylor*, eds. L. A. S. Butler and R. K. Morris, Council for British Archaeology Research Report, 60 (London, 1986), 193.

The principles on which this support was assessed are set out in the Burghal Hidage,[1] a document dating from the reign of Edward the Elder. Each pole of wall (five and a half yards) required four men to defend it. The relationship was expressed in hides, reckoning one man to one hide, and thus the Burghal Hidage, which records the hidages assigned to each *burh*, allows the length of its walls to be calculated. In those cases where the actual walls are still standing, these calculations are remarkably accurate. Thus Wareham in Dorset was assessed at 1,600 hides, implying walls 2,200 yards long and in fact the defences here measure 2,180 yards.

Gloucester does not figure in the Burghal Hidage, though both Worcester and Warwick appear in one of the two versions in which it has been preserved. It has been argued elsewhere that the shire of Worcester was created early in the tenth century, either by Æthelflæd or by Edward the Elder.[2] Since Worcestershire forms the central portion of the province of the Hwicce, some reorganization of the remainder of its territory must have been carried out at this time. The shire of Gloucester, however, is said to have been created a century later, by Eadric 'Streona', ealdorman of Mercia (1007–17), by the amalgamation of 'Gloucestershire' and 'Winchcombeshire'.[3] Even then, the area west of the Severn and the Leadon belonged to Herefordshire until 1021.[4]

Winchcombe and its 'shire' have been extensively studied. It seems to have been a compact block of territory in the north-east of the modern county, including the hundreds of 'Greston', 'Witley', Kiftsgate, "Celfledetorn", 'Holford', Cheltenham, Tibblestone, Salmonsbury and Barrington. This is presumably the area described as the *ferding* of Winchcombe (f.166), in which Evesham Abbey had fifty-six hides. Using the Domesday hidage and also the reconstructions of the Gloucestershire hundreds prepared by J. S. Moore,[5] the hidage of 'Winchcombeshire' can be calculated as 667½. Its origins are difficult to ascertain. Though it is mentioned only around the year 1000, it may be much older. It could be the territory assigned, in the eighth century or earlier, to the royal church of Winchcombe; it could even be the patrimony of the Hwiccian kings of the seventh century.[6] On the other hand it may be of tenth-century date, perhaps associated with the fortification of Winchcombe as a *burh*. We do not, however, know when this took place, for the first reference to Winchcombe as a borough is in Domesday Book itself. In 918 a Viking host raiding in the Severn estuary was put to flight by 'the men of Hereford and of Gloucester and from the nearest *burhs*'. The *burhs* are not named, but it is possible that Winchcombe was one of them.[7]

Another possible scenario for the creation of 'Winchcombeshire' is the establishment of a reformed Benedictine monastery there, in the reign of Edgar (959–75). Winchcombe was probably re-founded *c*.970; its first abbot was Germanus, formerly a monk of Fleury-sur-Loire. He and his monks were expelled in the reaction which followed Edgar's death in 975, but the community had been re-established by the 980s.[8] It is possibly at this time that the cult of St Kenelm became established. In the hagiographical tradition Kenelm was said to have been a son of Coenwulf of Mercia, murdered by his jealous sister Cwoenthryth. The Mercian prince Cynehelm does indeed attest charters of Coenwulf in the period between 803 and 811, but the details given in the hagiographical tradition (which seems to date from the mid eleventh century) are not consistent with what is known from ninth-century sources.[9] However the unreliability of the eleventh-century *passio* of St Kenelm does not mean that no such person ever existed, nor that some local cult had not grown up around him. Cults of murdered royal saints

1 Translated and edited in S. Keynes and M. Lapidge, *Alfred the Great* (Harmondsworth, 1983), 193–4, 339–41.

2 See Williams, 'Introduction to the Worcestershire Domesday', 10–11.

3 T. Hearne (ed.), *Hemingi Chartularium Ecclesiae Wigorniensis* (henceforward *Hemming's Cartulary*), i (London, Oxford, 1723), 280–1. Hemming, a monk of Worcester, compiled his work in the 1090s.

4 See p.1, n.7 above.

5 Moore (ed.), *Domesday Book: Gloucestershire*, 'Gloucestershire Hundreds and Welsh Commotes'.

6 Bassett, 'Mercian Royal Mausoleum', 84. I am grateful to Dr Bassett for discussing this topic with me, and for giving me a copy of his paper. His forthcoming study of Winchcombe and its land will throw much-needed light on the matter and is eagerly awaited.

7 Whitelock *et al.* (eds.), *Anglo-Saxon Chronicle*, *s.a.* 918.

8 D. Knowles *et al.* (eds.), *The Heads of Religious Houses in England and Wales, 940–1216* (Cambridge, 1972), 78.

9 Rollason, 'Murdered Royal Saints', 9–10; A. Thacker, 'Kings, Saints and Monasteries in Pre-Viking Mercia', *Midland Hist.* 10 (1985), 9–12.

were not uncommon and some had clear political functions, serving as foci for local feeling. The veneration of Kenelm, at a house particularly associated with this family, may have served to keep alive the memory of Mercian independence under West Saxon rule.

Whatever its origins, the fact that Domesday describes the territory of Winchcombe as a *ferding* ('quarter') implies that there were three other such divisions within Gloucestershire.[1] One was probably the territory known in the later Middle Ages as the 'Seven Hundreds' of Cirencester.[2] There were in fact nine hundreds at the time of Domesday, totalling 659¼ hides and comprising 'Bradley', "Wacrescumbe", 'Brightwells Barrow', Bibury, Rapsgate, Bisley, Longtree, "Gersdones" and Cirencester itself. Cirencester was the site of a church, dedicated to St Mary, and paid, as we have seen, an ancient food-rent. It was clearly a place of some standing. Another late territory is the 'Seven Hundreds' of 'Grumbalds Ash', the Domesday constituents of which are the hundreds of "Letberge", Brentry, "Grimboldestou", Bagstone, "Edredestane", 'Langley', 'Swineshead' and Pucklechurch; a total of 314½ hides.[3] The focus of this group in the later Middle Ages seems to have been Bristol, but an earlier centre may have been Bath, which lay within Mercia until the late ninth century.[4] However, Pucklechurch was a royal estate; Edmund (939–46) was stabbed there in a brawl in 946.[5]

The last *ferding* was centred on Gloucester itself. It may originate in the 300 hides which Osric, king of the Hwicce, gave to his new foundation of St Peter's, Gloucester, in *c*.679;[6] an area probably corresponding to the later hundreds of 'Whitstone', Berkeley and the 'Kings Barton' portion of 'Dudstone'. The hundred of "Blachelaue", between those of Berkeley and 'Dudstone', may belong here also. The Domesday hidage of these hundreds adds up to 292¼ hides, but Berkeley (which is not named as a hundred until the twelfth century) was made up of the lands which had once belonged to the minster church; their core consisted of a block of territory assessed at ninety-six and a half hides. If only this part of Berkeley is included, the *ferding* of Gloucester would contain 257 hides.

It is difficult to say how old such units really are. It is tempting to connect the *ferdings* of Gloucester, Cirencester and "Grimboldestou" (?Bath) with the cities belonging to Coinmail, Condidan and Farinmail captured in 577, but there is no real evidence for this assumption. It is equally possible that they were created in the tenth century as a response to the needs of protecting the area against Danish attack. It has also been suggested that they might have provided 'a means of financing the provision of ships', an intriguing idea which deserves more detailed study than can be attempted here.[7]

It is obvious that some individual hundreds are based on older territorial divisions. Cheltenham Hundred, for instance, was made up in 1086 of four vills: Cheltenham itself, a royal estate of ten hides; Prestbury, also assessed at ten hides and held by the Bishop of Hereford; Leckhampton, where there were two manors, totalling seven hides; and Swindon, assessed at three hides; thirty in all. There was a minster at Cheltenham in the ninth century, held by the Bishop of Hereford of the Bishop of Worcester; its site may have been at Prestbury (whose name means 'the priests' *burh*').[8] The coincidence of an old minster and a royal vill suggests an old unit of administration. A similar picture presents itself in "Wacrescumbe" Hundred. There were seventy-two hides here in 1086, thirty of which lay in the manor of Withington and its outliers, held by the Bishop of Worcester. In 774, an earlier bishop of this see granted to Abbess Æthelburh a life lease on twenty-one hides belonging to the minster of Withington.[9] Æthelburh was a member of the Hwiccian royal house, and the minster had been founded by Oshere, king of the Hwicce and Æthelræd, king of the Mercians in the period 674–704. Withington itself

[1] GDB 166 (the Abbey of Evesham held fifty-six hides in the *ferding* of Winchcombe).

[2] H. M. Cam, 'Early Groups of Hundreds', *Liberties and Communities in Medieval England: Collected Studies in Local Administration and Topography* (Cambridge, 1944; repr. London, 1963), 95–6; the 'Seven Hundreds' are first recorded in 1189.

[3] Ibid. 96–7.

[4] Bath was the site of a Mercian *witan* in the time of Burgræd, in 864, but is included among the West Saxon *burhs* in the time of Edward the Elder (899–924); B. Cunliffe, 'Saxon Bath', *Anglo-Saxon Towns in Southern England*, ed. J. Haslam (Chichester, 1984), 349.

[5] Whitelock *et al.* (eds.), *Anglo-Saxon Chronicle*, *s.a.* 946.

[6] See p.29 below.

[7] Hooke, *Kingdom of the Hwicce*, 77.

[8] Sawyer (ed.), S.1431.

[9] Ibid. S.1255.

was an ancient entity which may go back to a Romano-British estate.[1] Its pre-Conquest bounds include three hides at Whittington, which still lay in the hundred in the eleventh century, though it no longer belonged to the Church of Worcester. It seems that the core of "Wacrescumbe" Hundred was an old royal and minster site, which was just possibly a survival from the Romano-British past.

In the County Hidage, sometimes dated to the early eleventh century, the assessments of several shires, including Gloucestershire, are recorded. Neither the precise date, nor the purpose of the list are known. It survives in four versions, here called A, B, C and D.[2] The best text, A, assigns 3,400 hides to Gloucestershire, but B gives only 2,000 hides and both C and D give 2,400 hides. The discrepancies are hard to reconcile. At the time of Domesday, Gloucestershire contained thirty-nine hundreds, but several were very small, and some fragmentation had perhaps taken place in the course of the century. Tidenham and Wyvern were perhaps originally one unit, and the same may be true of Kiftsgate, 'Witley' and "Celfledetorn"; "Letberge" and Brentry; and "Langebrige" and Botloe. The total hidage of Gloucestershire in Domesday is in the region of 2,391 hides (Maitland made it 2,400), which is close to the figure in the C and D versions of the County Hidage. Moreover, if the four *ferdings* which have been discussed are reckoned as three units of 700 hides and one of 300 (Gloucester), the same assessment of 2,400 hides is reached. The Gloucestershire hundreds vary greatly in hidage, and none even approximate to the ideal 100 hides; hence the difference in assessments.

Gloucestershire in the Eleventh Century

At whatever date it was formed, Gloucestershire was part of the ealdordom of Mercia. In the 990s, this ealdordom lapsed, though Leofwine was appointed to the ealdordom of the Hwiccian shires.[3] In 1007 the whole of Mercia was reunited in the hands of Eadric 'Streona' ('the grasping') (1007–17). He acquired a bad reputation as a turncoat and traitor, based largely upon his activities during the Danish invasion and conquest which brought Cnut to the throne of England. In 1017 Cnut had him murdered and gave his office to Leofwine of the Hwicce.

In Leofwine's former territory, Cnut created two earldoms, one in Worcestershire for his nephew Hakon, and one in Gloucestershire for his brother-in-law, Elaf, whose sister, Gytha, married Godwine, Earl of Wessex.[4] Elaf was thus uncle to two future kings, Swein Estrithson of Denmark and Harold Godwineson of England. Though these earldoms lapsed with the death or departure of their earls, they had a permanent effect on the political geography of the area, for Gloucestershire did not revert to the earldom of Mercia, held by the descendants of Leofwine. In 1044, it formed, with Herefordshire, Somerset, Oxfordshire and Berkshire, the earldom of Elaf's nephew, Swein Godwineson (1044–50). On Swein's disgrace, Herefordshire, probably with Gloucestershire and Oxfordshire, became the earldom of Ralph 'the Timid', Edward the Confessor's nephew, who was succeeded on his death in 1057 by Harold Godwineson, now also Earl of Wessex after the death of Godwine in 1053. This association of Gloucestershire with the Earls of Wessex rather than the Mercian family was important for the history of the shire in the Norman period.[5]

The removal of Gloucestershire and Herefordshire from the earldom of Mercia was not the only effect of the Danish wars of Æthelræd II's reign. It is easy to underestimate the effects of the Danish conquest of Cnut. Five major battles were fought in 1016, culminating in the Danish victory at Ashingdon in Essex. The death-rate among the English aristocracy must have been

[1] H. P. R. Finberg, 'Roman and Saxon Withington', *Lucerna* (London, 1964), 21–65.

[2] Discussed in C. P. Lewis, 'English and Norman Government and Lordship in the Welsh Borders, 1039–1087' (unpubl. D.Phil. thesis, Oxford Univ., 1985), 41–7. A: Morris, *Old English Miscellany*, 145; B: BL Cotton Vespasian A xviii, f.112v; C: BL Cotton Claudius B vii, f.204v; D: T. Gale (ed.), *Scriptores XV*, 748.

[3] For Leofwine, see A. Williams, '"Cockles amongst the Wheat": Danes and English in the Western Midlands in the First Half of the Eleventh Century', *Midland Hist.* 11 (1986), 7–8.

[4] For Elaf's career, see Williams, '"Cockles amongst the Wheat"', 9.

[5] See p.33 below.

crippling, and more were murdered by Cnut in 1017, or banished, or fled abroad to escape such fates. There was sustained fighting in the western shires in the years 1015–16 and it was at Olney (Bucks.), near Winchcombe, that Cnut and Edmund Ironside met after Ashingdon to partition the kingdom. The heavy taxation raised by successive kings to finance these wars took its toll and even the Bishop of Worcester was reduced to selling church plate to meet his church's obligations. Lesser houses also felt the pinch; in 1022 Eadric, Abbot of St Peter's, Gloucester, leased two of the church's manors in return for £15 in gold, with which he could redeem the rest of his house's land from 'the great heregeld levied throughout England'.[1]

The succession of Cnut and the appointment of Danish earls, not only in East Anglia and Northumbria, but also in the south-western shires of Mercia, brought an influx of Danes to replace the slaughtered and exiled English nobles. Of the Danish names recorded in Gloucestershire on the eve of the Norman Conquest, some are common: Asgot, Bondi, Eskil, Grim, Healfdane, Harold, Ketil, Saxi, Swein, Thorbiorn, Thorkil, Thorsten, Tovi, Ulf and Ulfkil. Others are rare: Aswith, Auti, Balki, Ebbi, Elaf, Forne, Hemming, Huscarl and Vigot. The name Thorbert is of particular interest as an Anglo-Scandinavian hybrid, made up of ON *Thor-* and OE *-beorht*. Of course not all the men who bore these names in 1066 were Danes, and not all of those who were came from Denmark; they could just as well have been Anglo-Danes from the eastern and northern shires. Some may have been Englishmen with fashionable Danish names. But some men of undoubted Danish descent did hold land in Gloucestershire: Earnsige son of 'Ocea' had a Danish father and an English mother, and Strang, who held one of the three estates at Shipton Moyne, is actually called a Dane in Domesday.[2] The existence of men like Earnsige and Strang, whose background can be amplified beyond the bare facts given by Domesday, should raise questions about other thegns with Danish or Anglo-Scandinavian names about whom we are less well-informed.

THE HOLDERS OF LAND

The Pre-Conquest Lay Tenants

Identification of the men named in Domesday as holders of land in King Edward's day is difficult. Making allowances for joint tenancies, and for some tentative identifications (most of which cannot, for reasons of space, be detailed here) some 173 named individuals held land in Gloucestershire on the eve of the Norman Conquest. In Table 1 below this information is summarized, with the position in 1086 included for comparison. At first sight, the table below seems to confirm the often-repeated view that the Norman Conquest saw the replacement of a large number of modestly endowed thegns by a small, rich and close-knit baronage. On closer examination, however, some reasons for scepticism may be put forward.

Table 1: Size of holdings in Gloucestershire before and after the Conquest

	1066	*1086*
Less than 5 hides	101	22
Between 5 and 9 hides	33	8
Between 10 and 19 hides	27	16
Between 20 and 39 hides	8	14
40 hides and over	4	7
Total of holders	173	67

In the first place, contemporary sources indicate that England on the eve of the Conquest was possessed of an aristocracy not only rich, but also highly stratified. Nobles are defined in the law codes as men with a 1,200*s*. wergeld, as opposed to the peasants, whose wergeld was 200*s*.

[1] Sawyer (ed.), S.1424.

[2] See pp.24, 26 below.

Within this upper class of thegns, however, finer distinctions existed. The laws of Cnut reveal a threefold classification in the shires of western and southern England, into earls, king's thegns, and median thegns.[1] At the apex of this society were the comital families, some of whom were connected by blood or marriage to the ruling house.[2] Few Norman barons could match the wealth of Harold Godwineson or Leofric of Mercia. Next came the king's thegns, on whom to a large extent the exercise of royal authority rested. Lastly came the median thegns, men commended to a lord other than the king. Status did not depend solely upon birth. This was a service aristocracy; the OE word *thegn* itself had the meaning 'servant', like the Latin *minister* which was used as its equivalent.[3] Service enabled a man to improve his status: a *ceorl* could acquire a thegn's rank by an earl's gift.[4] Service to the king conveyed a higher honour than service to a lesser lord, hence the use of titles indicating function, like *staller*, a Danish office implying a connection with the royal court, and borne by men of considerable wealth and influence.[5] Wealth itself was also important in determining rank. The Ely records mention in passing that possession of forty hides of land conferred upon the holder the rank of a *procer*, one of the 'better men' of the shire; a distinction which has social implications, for the Abbot of Ely endowed his brother Guthmund with land to this amount so that he could marry the lady of his choice.[6]

Birth, office, wealth, all conferred rank. This is the society which we should expect to find mirrored in Domesday Book. To a certain extent, this expectation is fulfilled. The earls are clearly visible, and a fair estimate of their vast wealth can be made. King's thegns and thegns commended to other lords are also in evidence. There are, however, difficulties. Surnames, in the sense of heritable names used to distinguish members of a family, were only just in the process of formation in 1066, a process which was further advanced in Normandy than in England.[7] It is thus not easy to identify the English tenants, especially if they bear very common Christian names, and to be certain that all their land has been traced. This leads to an underestimation of the wealth of men with common names. To take an example from Gloucestershire, Godric, who held a small estate of only one and a quarter hides at Windrush, is described as King Edward's thegn. It is highly unlikely that this is all the land he possessed, but the rest of his holding cannot be identified because his name is so ordinary. It appears on a dozen occasions within the Gloucestershire folios; the land concerned amounts to thirty-five and a half hides. The possibility that only one Godric held all of it cannot be ruled out, neither can it be assumed without further evidence.[8] Nor do we know if this Godric of Windrush held land outside Gloucestershire.

The last point is an important one, for it is clear that some of the men who held only small amounts of land within Gloucestershire were rich and powerful thegns holding estates spanning several counties. Such were Vigot of Wallingford who held one and three-quarter hides of land in Gloucestershire, Bondi the staller (three hides), Thorkil White (five hides), Wulfweard White (seven hides), and Siward Barn (seventeen hides). These men can be recognized by their distinctive bynames or by the fact that their estates are known to have come into the hands of particular Norman successors.[9] The presence of these men warns against the assumption that all the anonymous Ælfrics, Eadrics and Leofwines held nothing but their Gloucestershire lands.

[1] N. P. Brooks, 'Arms, Status and Warfare in Late-Saxon England', *Ethelred the Unready: Papers from the Millenary Conference*, ed. D. Hill, BAR Brit. ser. 59 (1978), 81–104.

[2] For a study of one of the most powerful, see A. Williams, 'Land and Power in the Eleventh Century: The Estates of Harold Godwineson', *Proc. of the Battle Conference 1980*, iii (1981), 171–87.

[3] H. R. Loyn, 'Gesiths and Thegns in England from the Seventh to the Tenth Century', *EHR* 70 (1955), 529–49, discusses the significance of the use of the word *thegn* for noblemen from the time of Alfred onwards.

[4] So Archbishop Wulfstan claimed in one of his homilies; quoted in F. M. Stenton, 'The Thriving of the Anglo-Saxon Ceorl', *Preparatory to Anglo-Saxon England*, ed. D. M. Stenton (Oxford, 1970), 388–9.

[5] K. Mack, 'The Staller', *JMH* 12 (1986), 13–35.

[6] E. O. Blake (ed.), *Liber Eliensis*, Camden Soc. 3rd ser., 92, R. Hist. Soc. (London, 1962), 167, 424–5.

[7] J. C. Holt, *What's in a Name? Family Nomenclature and the Norman Conquest*, The Stenton Lecture, 1981 (Reading, 1982).

[8] The Godric who held Windrush is probably identical with the Godric who held Siddington, which he shared with Leofwine, for another manor at Windrush was also held by Leofwine. Moreover, both Windrush and Siddington passed to Roger de Lacy.

[9] Thus Vigot's land passed to Miles Crispin, Bondi's to Henry de Ferrers, Thorkil's to Hugh l'Asne (see further p.36 below). Wulfweard and Siward are identified by their bynames.

A complication of a different kind is illustrated by Domesday's treatment of the manor of Windrush, held by Ælfsige of Faringdon. It appears twice, once under the name of Ælfsige, and once under that of the Church of Winchcombe. The entry in Ælfsige's name says that the three and a half hides at Windrush were held TRE by Wulfric, Tovi and Leofwine as three manors, and they could go where they would (f.170v). The entry for the Church of Winchcombe, however, says that the estate had been given to the abbey by Bolli, who could go with the land where he would; Wulfric, Tovi and Leofwine are represented merely as tenants with two hides, five virgates and one virgate respectively (f.165v). Wulfric's portion of the manor appears yet a third time, under the fief of Roger de Lacy (f.167v). The three apparently independent thegns of the first entry turn out to be no such thing; they are actually subtenants, holding of someone else. It is not absolutely clear that it is Bolli they hold of, but it is likely. This assumption can to a certain extent be supported by the entries concerning Baunton. There were two manors in this vill; one (three and three-quarter hides) was held in 1066 by Ketil and in 1086 by his son Eadric, the other (two and a quarter hides) was held in 1066 by Bolli and in 1086 by Geoffrey Orlateile. This is the only other reference to Bolli in the Gloucestershire folios; the name is not common and the same man is probably involved. When we then discover that Ketil held land in Windrush (five virgates), it becomes likely that Bolli was the lord both of Windrush and Baunton, and that Ketil, as well as Wulfric, Leofwine and Tovi, was his tenant.

TABLE 2: Pre-Conquest tenants holding ten hides or more

	Hides	Virgates		Hides	Virgates
Beorhtric son of Ælfgar	160		Ketil	14	
Alwine the sheriff	50		Thorsten	14	
Countess Gode	47		Almær	13	
Earnsige son of 'Ocea'	42		Beorhtric	11	2
Siward	38	2½	Dunning	11	
Asgot	35	1½	Rotlesc	11	
Earl Harold	35		Alric	10	1
Wulfweard	34	2	Earl Tosti	10	
Ulf	33		Beorhtmær (1)	10	
Baldwin son of Herluin	26		Beorhtmær (2)	10	
Ælfstan of Boscombe	24	2	Cola	10	
Earl Ralph	20		Dene	10	
Dunna	19		Huscarl	10	
Tovi	17		John the Dane	10	
Siward Barn	15		Leofwine	10	
Cynewig Chelle	15		Saxi	10	
Eadnoth	15		Strang the Dane	10	
Elaf	15		Wulfweard	10	
Eadric	14	2	Baldwin	10	
Queen Edith	14				
			Total: 39 tenants hold 875 hides, 1 virgate		

Now these indications emerge only because there was in 1086 a dispute over the tenure of Windrush between Winchcombe and Ælfsige; Ælfsige claimed to hold it of the king, whereas Winchcombe maintained that he held of the church. It is a reminder that the men named as the pre-Conquest holders of land are not necessarily holding independently; they may be tenants of a lord who is not, for one reason or another, named by Domesday Book.[1] They may in fact be the equivalents, not of the Norman tenants-in-chief, with whom they are frequently compared, but of the Norman mesne-tenants, who are much more numerous. The contrast between the tenurial patterns of 1066 and those of 1086 may therefore be less than at first appears. This assertion is borne out to an extent by comparing Table 2 above and Table 4 on p.37: in 1066, thirty-nine men

[1] See further on this topic, P. H. Sawyer, '1066–1086: A Tenurial Revolution?', *Domesday Book: A Reassessment*, ed. P. H. Sawyer (London, 1985), 76–7; D. R. Roffe, 'An Introduction to the Nottinghamshire Domesday', *The Nottinghamshire Domesday*, eds. A. Williams and R. W. H. Erskine (forthcoming); D. R. Roffe, 'An Introduction to the Derbyshire Domesday', *The Derbyshire Domesday*, eds. A. Williams and R. W. H. Erskine (forthcoming).

held estates of ten hides or over, amounting to $875\frac{1}{4}$ hides (one third of the total hidage); in 1086, thirty-seven men held estates of ten hides or over, amounting to $931\frac{1}{2}$ hides (just over one third of the total hidage).

Bearing these caveats in mind, let us examine what the Gloucestershire folios have to tell about the landholders of 1066. Pride of place must go to the comital families, beginning with the earl in whose *scir* ('sphere of influence') the county lay: Harold Godwineson, in his capacity as Earl of Hereford. He held the third penny of the revenues of Winchcombe, a perquisite due to his office, but his lands in the shire were not large; thirty-five hides at Alveston, Naas, Chipping Campden and Bromsberrow. His mother Gytha held the unhidated (because unsurveyed) manor of Woodchester, bought for her by her husband, Earl Godwine, 'so that she could live off it while she stayed at Berkeley. She was unwilling to use up anything from that manor because of the destruction of the abbey'. This passage has been taken to imply that Earl Godwine was responsible for the church's demise, but other interpretations are possible.[1] Tosti, Harold's brother and Earl of Northumbria, held an estate of ten hides at Southrop.

To these lands must be added those held by the men commended to the two earls. Eight of Harold's thegns appear by name, and an unnamed thegn held five hides at Weston-sub-Edge. A few can be identified elsewhere. Asgot, who held twenty-one hides at Kempsford is probably identical with Asgot, Earl Harold's man, who held eight and a quarter hides at Taplow (Bucks.).[2] He may also be identical with the Asgot who was William Leofric's predecessor in Gloucestershire, Berkshire and Essex.[3] Alwig, who held two hides at Oldland as Harold's man, is presumably the same Alwig who held five hides at Tytherington, since both manors passed to Osbern, Bishop of Exeter. The Ealdræd who held two hides at Harry Stoke of Harold is presumably the Ealdræd who held Wapley (no hidage recorded), for both manors passed to Geoffrey, Bishop of Coutances; he was still holding Wapley in 1086 as Geoffrey's tenant. Tovi *Widenesci*,[4] described as Earl Harold's housecarl, held four hides at Great Barrington. By 1086 it had passed to Ælfsige of Faringdon, who had also succeeded a Tovi at Windrush. This Tovi was associated with Wulfric and Leofwine, and they were probably holding of Bolli;[5] a Leofwine was also holding three hides of Earl Harold at Didmarton. It will be remembered that another manor at Windrush was held by Godric, King Edward's thegn.[6]

Earl Tosti's man, Elaf, held seven hides in Driffield. His name is very unusual and he can probably be identified with the tenant of eight hides in Preston (near Cirencester), especially since both manors passed to Regenbald of Cirencester. Regenbald held two other manors, at Ampney St Mary and Norcote, held by Godric TRE. This Godric may be the brother of Elaf; Elaf and his brother held seven hides in North Cerney, though this estate passed to Gilbert fitzTurold.

The prominence of the West Saxon earls is striking in view of the almost total absence of the Mercian family. An unnamed thegn who held five hides at Weston-sub-Edge is described as the man of Leofric, presumably the earl, who died in 1057. Leofric's son and successor, Ælfgar, is said to have put the manor of Ullington in Pebworth (both now in Worcestershire).[7] Pebworth was a divided vill; six and a quarter hides had been held by Wulfgeat and Wulfweard, who are probably the two unnamed thegns who held the other manor there, assessed at two and a quarter hides.[8] They may have been Earl Ælfgar's men. Coventry Abbey, founded by Earl Leofric and Lady Godgifu, held the ten-hide manor of Long Marston (now in Warwickshire).

Traces of Earl Harold's immediate predecessor in the earldom of Hereford, Ralph 'the Timid', are still visible in Domesday. His mother Gode, Edward the Confessor's sister, held forty-seven hides of land in the shire, presumably in the king's hand in 1086, since she herself died in 1049. Ralph begins to sign the charters of his royal uncle in 1050, and his rise must be

[1] See pp.32–3 below.
[2] GDB 144.
[3] See p.25 below.
[4] His byname may mean 'the Wend'; the Wends were Slavonic people, neighbours of the Danes, living on the south shores of the Baltic Sea. See G. Tengvik, *Old English Bynames* (Uppsala, 1938), 136.
[5] See p.18 above.
[6] See p.17 above.
[7] GDB 167.
[8] GDB 169.

associated with the disgrace of Swein Godwineson in 1049. His later nickname 'the Timid' stems from his disastrous defeat at the hands of Gruffydd ap Llewelyn in 1055, when, according to the Chronicle, 'the English fled because they were on horseback'. Ralph, trained in continental styles of warfare, had apparently made a premature attempt to introduce cavalry into England. His wife bore the Danish name Gytha, and probably came from the English Danelaw. She held no land in Gloucestershire, but a very considerable estate in the East Midlands. Their son received the Danish name Harold. Most of Ralph's recorded land also lay in the eastern shires, but in Gloucestershire he held Sudeley and Toddington (twenty hides), both of which passed by 1086 to his son Harold.

The second rank of the English aristocracy, the king's thegns, is well represented in the Gloucestershire folios: Alweard who held five hides in Doynton, Cynewig Chelle who held five hides in Arlington, Wulfgar who held eight hides in Tockington, Dene who held ten hides in Coberley and Godric who held one and a quarter hides in Windrush are all described as King Edward's thegns, while Rotlesc who held eleven hides in Beckford (now in Worcestershire) is called the king's housecarl. Eight other men are said to hold of King Edward, including Thorkil White. Cynewig's name is very rare, occurring only four times in Domesday; twice in Gloucestershire, where he held Saintbury (ten hides) as well as Arlington; once in Oxfordshire, where he held two hides at "Asce", and once in Wiltshire, where he held six hides at Ashton Gifford.[1] He was probably holding Arlington as the king's reeve. Dene's name is also unusual, occurring twelve times in Domesday, of which all but two are in Lincolnshire and Nottinghamshire. It is therefore likely that the two southern references, in Gloucestershire and Wiltshire, are to the same man, who held six hides in Corton (Wilts.), as well as his ten hides in Gloucestershire. Rotlesc's name is unique in Domesday, and von Feilitzen suggested that it is a corruption of Hrosskell, found in Nottinghamshire and Yorkshire.[2]

It is unclear why some men are singled out as king's thegns, while others, whose wealth suggests that they were the king's men, are not. The richest thegn in Gloucestershire is not so distinguished. Beorhtric son of Ælfgar possessed 313 hides of land in the south-western shires, half of which (160 hides) lay in Gloucestershire. The centre of his wealth was the great hundredal manor of Tewkesbury,[3] assessed in Domesday at ninety-five hides, though the assessment of its constituent elements amounts to 106 hides. Of this, forty-five hides (forty-six and a half in fact) were in demesne, twenty hides (twenty-four and a half) belonged to the church, and thirty hides were tenanted, though unfortunately the tenants are not named. The whole manor was 'exempt and free from all geld and royal service' except the personal service of its lord. Attached to this manor were six estates, amounting to thirty-four and a quarter hides, held by thegns who had 'put themselves and their lands in Beorhtric's power'. Four are named, Liut of Kemerton (now in Worcestershire), Dunning of Alderton with Dixton, and Hermar and Alwine of Stoke Orchard.

In the manor of Tewkesbury we see a great multiple estate, its constituent elements united not by geography but by ties of lordship. The dependent estates, or berewicks, are attached to the central manor, where the lord's hall and court lie. The hall is mentioned in the Domesday account; sixteen bordars lived 'around' it and were presumably manorial servants. Nine radknights in the berewicks owed agricultural services to the lord's court, and eight burgesses in Gloucester owed service there. The lands of the thegns who had commended themselves to Beorhtric would, in the eastern shires, have been described as sokeland of Tewkesbury and the services of the commended thegns probably included the duty of attending the lord's court. Since the whole manor (apart from the lands of the commended thegns) was 'quit and free of all geld and royal service', the duties of Tewkesbury's tenants were discharged, not to the king's

[1] GDB 70v.

[2] O. von Feilitzen, *The Pre-Conquest Personal Names of Domesday Book* (Uppsala, 1937), 294, 350.

[3] Apart from Tewkesbury (106 hides) Beorhtric held five manors in Glos., totalling 54 hides; his men held another 6½ hides. In Dorset he held just under 66½ hides, in Devon., just under 57 hides. He had lesser amounts in Cornwall (17¾ hides), Wilts. (10 hides) and Worcs. (2 hides).

officers, but to their lord, Beorhtric son of Ælfgar. Such arrangements are not unknown, but in all other recorded instances are made for the benefit of ecclesiastical houses, the most famous being the triple-hundred of 'Oswaldslow', belonging to the Bishop of Worcester.[1] It would be hard to find another pre-Conquest layman in such a position, but it is difficult to be sure how singular Beorhtric was in this respect. His honour is preserved for us because it passed almost intact into the hands of Queen Matilda. Had the integrity of other English lay estates been similarly preserved, other nobles of Beorhtric's power might have been found. Indeed, within the shire of Gloucester itself, there are indications of a very similar estate to that of Tewkesbury, also in lay hands.[2] Tewkesbury then appears unique, but its singularity may lie simply in the nature of the evidence.

Tewkesbury's importance lies partly in the fact that it is in origin the endowment of a minster church which has at some point been secularized. The Church of Tewkesbury in Domesday holds twenty hides (actually twenty-four and a half) of land; the site of the minster was at Stanway, where Domesday records a *monasterium*, a word which can mean both monastery and minster. Little is known of this church.[3] The medieval Abbey dates from 1102, when the Norman Abbot of Cranborne in Dorset transferred his community to Tewkesbury, of which Cranborne became a cell. Virtually all that we know of the pre-Benedictine church there comes from the unreliable *Chronica* of Tewkesbury Abbey, compiled much later,[4] which says much of the monks' beliefs about their community's origins, but with little regard to historical accuracy. However, even garbled traditions may contain a grain of truth and it is worth investigating this tradition, with a view to discovering what, if anything, it contains of value.

The *Chronica* ascribes the foundation of Tewkesbury to the eponymous hermit 'Theokus' ('Tewk'), on the site of whose retreat two ealdormen (*duces*), Oddo and Doddo, founded a monastery at a date which appears to be 715. This is not a very promising tale, but it illustrates the kind of material used by the compiler of the *Chronica* and his highly imaginative presentation thereof. He goes on to tell us that though Oddo and Doddo were the founders of Tewkesbury, they were buried at Pershore in Worcestershire, because Doddo had entered the monastic life there. Their brother Almaric, however, was buried at Deerhurst, in a little chapel built against the door of the priory there, and his tomb is 'still' shown, bearing an inscription, which is quoted thus: 'Doddo *dux* had this royal hall (*regiam aulam*) consecrated in the church in honour of St Mary the Virgin for love of his brother Almaric'. This inscription is clearly based upon the genuine inscription on the foundation-stone of the chapel of Holy Trinity, Deerhurst, built by Oda, who really was an earl, for the soul of his brother Ælfric, not in the early eighth century, but in 1056.[5] The Tewkesbury writer has simply appropriated Oda (the second founder of Pershore) and his brother Ælfric, added a third brother, Doddo, shifted the whole story back three and a half centuries, and added the mythical 'Tewk', thus producing a monastic foundation for his house in the days of Bede.

Given this evidence of the chronicler's inventiveness, it seems unlikely that his account of Beorhtric and his family would be of any value. Since, however, it is our only source for Beorhtric's antecedents, it is worth examining. The story of the chronicler runs as follows: in the reign of Athelstan (924–39) lived a nobleman called *Haylwardus* (Æthelweard), 'sprung from the illustrious stock of King Edward the Elder', who on account of his fair colouring was called *Snew* (snow). In the time of Æthelræd (II) and St Dunstan (i.e. between 978 and 988), he and his wife *Alfgiva* (Ælfgifu) founded a monastery at Cranborne, of which Tewkesbury was made a cell. *Haylwardus* was killed at the Battle of Ashingdon in Essex (1016—a merciful release given his implied age) leaving a son *Algar* (Ælfgar), the father of Beorhtric.

When dealing with material like this the question to ask is not so much 'is it true?' as 'what

[1] See Williams, 'Introduction to the Worcestershire Domesday', 15–18.

[2] See the discussion of the church and manor of Deerhurst, pp.27–9 below.

[3] See *VCH Gloucestershire*, viii (1968), 154.

[4] BL Cotton Cleopatra C iii, f.220; printed in J. Caley and H. Ellis (eds.), *Dugdale's Monasticon Anglicanum*, ii (London, 1830), 59.

[5] See p.28 below.

does it mean?' There was indeed a tenth-century nobleman called Æthelweard who might accurately be described as 'sprung from the illustrious stock of King Edward': Æthelweard the Chronicler, ealdorman of the Western Shires, who died in about 998, was a descendant of King Æthelræd I, brother of Alfred.[1] According to William of Malmesbury, he refounded the Abbey of Pershore.[2] But Æthelweard was a very common name. In 988, Oswald, Archbishop of York and Bishop of Worcester, granted three hides at Clifford Chambers (now in Warwickshire) for three lives to a thegn called Æthelweard.[3] Now Clifford Chambers, assessed at seven hides, was one of the estates attached to Tewkesbury in 1066, and had been held at that date by Beorhtric son of Ælfgar. It seems the Tewkesbury chronicler may have been right to give Beorhtric a grandfather called Æthelweard, even if he got the wrong one.

We may go a little further. In the eighteenth century, transcripts were made of two eleventh-century charters, now lost. The first is a confirmation of Æthelræd II of grants made to Cranborne Abbey by Ælfgifu, widow of Ailward (Æthelweard) 'Meaw', the founder, with the consent of her son, Ælfgar; the second is a gift of this Ælfgar to the same house.[4] The lands recorded in these charters lay at Cranborne and Dewlish (both in Dorset), held in 1066 by Beorhtric son of Ælfgar; Wimborne St Giles (Dorset) and Loosebeare (Devon.), held by Cranborne Abbey in 1066; Medland (Devon.), held in 1066 by a thegn called Ælfstan; and Ashton (Dorset), which does not appear in Domesday.

Ælfgar son of 'Meaw' is said by the twelfth-century chronicler Florence of Worcester to have been one of the Englishmen who fought on the Danish side at the Battle of Sherston in Wiltshire in 1086; the others were Eadric 'Streona' and Ælfmær 'Darling', whose presence (but not that of Ælfgar) is confirmed by the account of the battle in the Anglo-Saxon Chronicle.[5] Ælfgar 'Meaw' or *Mæw* ('seagull') attests charters of Æthelræd II between 999 and 1009, being associated in the witness-lists with one Æthelmær and his father Æthelwold; such associations sometimes indicate kinship.[6] This Æthelmær is probably Æthelmær the Stout, whose son Æthelweard was one of the English nobles murdered at Cnut's orders in 1017;[7] his father would then be Æthelwold the Stout, who was one of the witnesses to a lawsuit held in London in 989–90, attesting immediately before Ælfgar, described as 'the Honiton man'.[8] One might suspect that this Ælfgar is Ælfgar 'Meaw'; especially since Honiton (in South Molton, Devon.), was held in 1086 by Odo fitzGamelin, whose manor of Great Torrington in the same shire had belonged to Beorhtric son of Ælfgar.[9] If Ælfgar of Honiton was indeed Beorhtric's father, then the royal connections alleged by the Tewkesbury chronicler may have some foundation, for the Anglo-Saxon Chronicle records the death, in 962, of another Ælfgar, described as 'the king's kinsman in Devon'. Though the details of the chronicler's story may be incorrect, its general tenor seems to reflect reality.

A man of Beorhtric's standing might be expected to attract the allegiance of lesser thegns, and some of his men appear in the pages of Domesday. To those already mentioned may be added Ebbi, who held two and a half hides at Iron Acton. Like Liut of Kemerton, Ebbi's name does not appear elsewhere in Domesday Book; but Dunning, who held Alderton with Dixton (eleven hides) can be traced elsewhere. His name is uncommon, and he is probably the Dunning who in Worcestershire held three and three-quarter hides at Eckington and two and a quarter hides at

[1] See A. Campbell (ed.), *The Chronicle of Æthelweard* (London, 1962), pp.xii–xvi, 1–2.

[2] N. E. S. A. Hamilton (ed.), *Willelmi Malmesbiriensis Monachi De Gestis Pontificum Anglorum*, Rolls Ser. 52 (London, 1870), 298.

[3] Sawyer (ed.), S.1356; Finberg, *Early Charters*, 236; preserved in the early eleventh-century portion of Hemming's Cartulary, which is probably to be dated before 1013.

[4] Calendared in C. R. Hart, *The Early Charters of Eastern England* (Leicester, 1966), 253–4; see also Keynes, *Diplomas of Æthelred II*, 227 n.265.

[5] B. Thorpe (ed.), *Florentii Wigorniensis Chronicon ex Chronicis*, i (London, 1868), 177.

[6] Keynes, *Diplomas of Æthelred II*, 209–10.

[7] Whitelock *et al.* (eds.), *Anglo-Saxon Chronicle*, *s.a.* 1017.

[8] Sawyer (ed.), S.877.

[9] GDB 116v. Beorhtric also preceded Odo at Little Weare (a berewick of Great Torrington), Delley, Broadhembury, Shapcombe, Plymtree and 'Dart'. Three Frenchmen who held 3 virgates at Great Torrington are also identified by Exon Domesday (f.376) as Walter de Claville, Goscelm and Ansgar de Montacute, three brothers who had Beorhtric son of Ælfgar as their *antecessor* (GDB 112v/Exon 397). In Ansgar's fief, the pre-Conquest tenant is named, not as Beorhtric, but as Alric, and it seems likely that Alric was in fact Beorhtric's tenant. If this is so then it is possible that the Alweald who held Honiton (in South Molton) TRE also held of Beorhtric son of Ælfgar.

Birlingham of the Abbey of Westminster, both of which passed to Urse d'Abetot.[1] He is possibly also the Dunning who held Donningstone (Devon.), which preserves his name; he continued to hold this manor in 1086.[2] The Annals of Winchcombe record that Dunning gave to that church the church-scot of two virgates at Alderton and two virgates at Dixton, in 1059.[3] It so happens that in 1066, Winchcombe Abbey held land in part of Alderton (later called Frampton) and three hides at Twyning, another part of which (later called The Mythe) belonged to Beorhtric's manor of Tewkesbury. Perhaps Winchcombe's lands in both these vills were benefactions made by Dunning's lord.

Beorhtric son of Ælfgar was the richest thegn in Gloucestershire in King Edward's day, and no other pre-Conquest landowner at that date can be shown to possess comparable wealth. Two men held more than forty hides of land, Alwine the sheriff and Earnsige son of 'Ocea'.[4] Alwine's name is very common and it is not even certain if the Domesday form represents OE Ælfwine or Æthelwine. Moreover it is evident that the Domesday scribes had difficulty distinguishing the elements *-wine* and *-wig* in personal names, so that in the manuscript *Aluui* may represent Alwine as well as Alwig.[5] It seems that this has happened in Gloucestershire, for in the account of the royal manor of Awre, the sheriff's name is given as Alwig. Bearing these problems in mind, the holdings of Alwine the sheriff can be reconstructed. Guiting Power was leased by King Edward to Alwine for his lifetime and, after his death, King William gave his widow and his land to Richard *iuvenis*, whose successor, William Goizenboded, held it in 1086. William also held half a hide at Westbury-on-Severn which Alwine had given to his wife, and it is therefore probable that the Alwine who held six other manors which had passed into William's possession is Alwine the sheriff. This amounts in all to twenty-seven and a half hides of land. One of the manors was at Aylworth, a vill divided in 1086 between William Goizenboded and Gilbert fitzTurold; Gilbert's predecessor is also called Alwine and held four hides there. In addition to this, Alwine (*Aluui*) the sheriff held leasehold tenements at 'Morwent' (in Hartpury) (three virgates) and Upton St Leonards (one hide), both members of the royal manor of 'Barton' (in Gloucester). The tenement at Upton was held in 1086 by Humphrey of Maidenhill and appears again under his name.[6] Humphrey's only other manor, a hide at Sezincote, had been held by Alwine (*Aluui*) TRE, and another manor at Sezincote, also held by Alwine, passed to Urse d'Abetot. Alwine (*Aluui*) had also been reeve of the royal manor of Awre, and had abstracted from it its berewicks of Purton, Etloe and Bledisloe (seven hides in all). Purton had passed to Earl William fitzOsbern, who added it to the royal manor of Naas. Etloe was held in 1086 by Roger of Berkeley, who had also succeeded Alwine at Dodington (three hides and 'two parts of half a hide'). Roger was holding the remaining portion of Dodington (one and a half hides and 'the third part of half a hide') of the Bishop of Coutances, but the pre-Conquest tenant here is named as Wulfnoth. Bledisloe was held by William fitzBaderon in 1086. This William also succeeded Alwine at Cirencester (two hides). Cirencester of course was a royal manor, and William fitzBaderon's holding appears in the account of Cirencester as two hides held TRE by a free man who 'paid 20*s.* farm and served the sheriff (presumably Alwine) throughout England'. William fitzBaderon's manor of Huntley had also been held by Alwine, as tenant of the Bishop of Worcester, and he had succeeded Alwine at Evington (five virgates), a berewick of the manor of Deerhurst belonging to the Abbey of Westminster.

William fitzBaderon also held two and a half virgates which the shire court maintained ought to belong to the king's manor of Westbury-on-Severn. No pre-Conquest tenant is named in the entry, but as we have seen, Alwine the sheriff had given land here to his wife. Alwine therefore held a total of just over fifty hides in Gloucestershire. His name is too common to identify his holdings in other shires.

[1] GDB 174v.

[2] GDB 105.

[3] R. R. Darlington, 'Winchcombe Annals 1048–1181', *A Miscellany for Doris Mary Stenton*, eds. P. M. Burnes and C. F. Slade, Pipe Roll Soc. 76 (1962), 116.

[4] See Table 2, p.18 above.

[5] von Feilitzen, *Pre-Conquest Personal Names*, 415.

[6] GDB 170, but here the name of the previous tenant is Pain (*Pagen*), a Norman name very unusual before the Conquest. He may have been Alwine's tenant.

Earnsige on the other hand has a name so rare as to occur only twelve times in Domesday Book. Moreover these occurrences are confined to the neighbouring shires of Gloucester, Hereford and Worcester, which suggests that only one man is involved. Among the Gloucestershire estates held by Earnsige were two manors in Lower Swell, one held in 1086 by Drogo fitzPons of Ralph de Tosny and one held by William de Eu. According to the Evesham Chronicle, land at Swell had been bequeathed to the abbey by a rich English woman, Ealdgyth, as partial recompense for her theft of a tooth and armbone from the relics of St Ecgwine, the founder. The bequest was disputed by her son Earnsige, and only when he had expended his resources in riotous living was he forced to mortgage part of the estate to Abbot Æthelwig.[1] A charter of King Edward, granting to Evesham three hides at Swell, forfeited by Earnsige son of 'Oce', is still extant;[2] this estate at Upper Swell is found in the abbey's possession in Domesday. The mention of Earnsige's father 'Oce' enables us to identify him further with the Earnsige who held Astley (Worcs.), assessed at six hides, and held in 1086 by Ralph de Tosny, for this estate had formerly been in the possession of 'Ocea' the Dane.[3]

Earnsige held another manor in Gloucestershire as the predecessor of Drogo fitzPons: the ten-hide manor of Frampton on Severn, one hide of which, at Painswick, was held by Roger de Lacy. He also preceded Drogo at Hamnish in Herefordshire (one hide), and Roger de Lacy at Tedstone Wafre (one hide) in the same county. He is probably the holder of the Herefordshire manor of Brimfield (three virgates), held in 1086 by Roger de Mortimer. In Gloucestershire, Earnsige's manors at Upper Siddington, Aston Somerville (now in Worcestershire), Eyford and Miserden (twenty-two hides in all) passed to Hacoit Musard. He thus held in all fifty and three-quarter hides, the bulk of which lay in Gloucestershire. As to his antecedents, it is clear that he was of mixed English and Danish descent; his father, known only by his nickname 'Ocea' (from OE *yce*, 'toad'), was a Danish settler from the time of the Scandinavian kings.[4]

Earnsige's lands were divided in 1086 between several Norman successors, each of whom had other English predecessors apart from him. All the lands of William Leofric, not only in Gloucestershire, but in Berkshire and Essex also, had belonged to one Englishman, Asgot.[5] Asgot's case is of interest since it is possible to reconstruct his family's holdings. Two of William Leofric's Berkshire manors lay in Childrey and Coleshill. At Childrey there were two other manors, one (ten hides) held by Turstin fitzRolf and one (thirteen hides) by Roger de Lacy. Coleshill likewise contained three manors (all of eight hides), held by William, Turstin and the Abbey of Nunnaminster, Winchester, which had received its share from Roger de Lacy's father, Walter.[6] Turstin's predecessor in both cases was Beorhtric, who also held both Turstin's other manors in the shire, at Upton (ten hides) and Sparsholt (two and three-quarter hides); he is probably the Beorhtric who held another manor in Sparsholt (two hides) which passed to Hascoit Musard.[7] The Lacys' predecessor at both Childrey and Coleshill was Edmund, who also held Roger's manor of Enborne (three and a quarter hides). Asgot, Beorhtric and Edmund are presumably the three thegns who held the hide of Coleshill which lay in Wiltshire and which was held in 1086 by William Leofric, Turstin fitzRolf and Roger de Lacy.[8] They are probably also the three free men who held the manor of Sparsholt (sixteen hides) which was in the king's hands in 1086.[9]

The tenure of Asgot, Beorhtric and Edmund at Childrey and Coleshill suggests that they are kinsmen, probably brothers, who have shared out a common inheritance. Asgot appears in conjunction with Beorhtric in Gloucestershire also, for both held estates at Leckhampton.

[1] W. D. Macray (ed.), *Chronicon Abbatiae de Evesham* (abbr. *Chron. Evesham*), Rolls Ser. 29 (London, 1863), 94.

[2] Sawyer (ed.), S.1026.

[3] GDB 176v; Hearne (ed.), *Hemming's Cartulary*, i. 255-6. See Williams, '"Cockles amongst the Wheat"', 14.

[4] Tengvik, *Old English Bynames*, 339, connects *Ucc(e)a*, *Oce(a)* with OE 'toad, frog', and suggests that 'the nickname is likely to denote a big, coarse person'.

[5] William Leofric also held one estate in Oxfordshire, an unnamed manor of 3 hides $1\frac{2}{3}$ virgates (f.160) for which no pre-Conquest tenant is given. His land in Berkshire is entered in the name of William fitzRichard, but the account of the hide at Coleshill which lay in Wiltshire (f.72v) shows that this is an error for William Leofric.

[6] GDB 59v, 62v, 63.

[7] GDB 61v.

[8] GDB 72v.

[9] GDB 57.

Beorhtric also appears as the predecessor of Turstin fitzRolf at Coates (one hide) and Hasfield (one and a half hides); these manors were held of Westminster Abbey. Edmund also appears in Gloucestershire as the predecessor of Roger de Lacy at Stratton (five hides). Beorhtric preceded Turstin fitzRolf at Alvington and Little Marcle (nine hides) in Herefordshire, the former now in Gloucestershire; at Newton Valence (ten hides) in Hampshire, and at Little Kimble (ten hides) in Buckinghamshire. Edmund also held land in Buckinghamshire at Wraysbury (twenty hides) which had passed to Robert Gernon in 1086.[1] Asgot is probably the man of Earl Harold who held eight and a quarter hides at Taplow (Bucks.), and twenty-one hides at Kempsford (Glos.). There are two reasons for this identification. Firstly, Beorhtric is described as Earl Harold's man in the Herefordshire entries already referred to (though in Bucks. and Hants he appears as King Edward's thegn). Secondly the identification of Earl Harold's thegn Asgot with the predecessor of William Leofric would explain the latter's tenure of the unidentified manor of "Schilcheham" in Essex, far from his other estates, for Harold had been Earl of East Anglia from 1046 to 1053, and had retained land and men there even after relinquishing the earldom.[2]

Asgot then held a total of ninety-four and a half hides in four shires, Beorhtric sixty-eight hides in five shires, and Edmund forty-nine hides in three shires; in addition to which the three held jointly another seventeen hides, a grand total of 228½ hides.[3] One of Asgot's manors was at Hailes, and he can thus be identified as Asgot (Osgod) of Hailes who at some time in the 1050s witnessed a grant of Bishop Ealdræd to St Mary's, Worcester in company with the 'leading men' of the shire.[4] It is of interest that William Leofric freed twelve slaves at Hailes. Old English wills frequently specify slaves who are to be manumitted and it is possible that William, who is probably Asgot's son, was fulfilling one of his father's bequests.

Baldwin son of Herluin is also known from sources other than Domesday. He is identified by his patronymic only in the entry for Coln Rogers,[5] but he can be identified as the predecessor of Hugh de Grandmesnil at Lower Quinton and Weston-on-Avon (both now in Warwickshire), for much of Hugh's land in other shires had come from Baldwin.[6] He held at least twenty-six hides of land in Gloucestershire. Baldwin's name is not English and suggests, as does that of his father, a North French or Flemish origin. According to Hemming, the Worcester monk who wrote in the 1090s, Herluin had been in the service of Beorhtheah Bishop of Worcester (1033–8), whom he accompanied when the bishop conducted Gunnhild, daughter of Cnut and Emma, to her marriage with Henry, son of the Emperor Conrad II.[7] Beorhtheah gave Herluin a manor at Leopard in Worcestershire, which Baldwin still held in 1086 as the tenant of Hugh de Grandmesnil. Baldwin followed his father in service to the Bishops of Worcester, for he was steward to Ealdræd, from whom he received the manor at Weston-on-Avon.[8] The family may have come from Flanders in the time of Cnut, and may have been connected with Queen Emma, who spent the time of her exile there in the reign of Harold I (1035–40).

Baldwin held thirty-two and a half hides in Warwickshire and thirty-one and three-quarter hides in Northamptonshire as well as his Gloucestershire lands. In Buckinghamshire, Thorgisl, who held five hides at Stowe, is described as the man of Baldwin son of Herluin, and the Alwine who was co-tenant of Baldwin at Thurlaston in Leicestershire (six carucates) was probably his man also: co-tenancies in Domesday sometimes disguise dependent tenures, and Alwine also held Thrupp Grounds (Northants) of Baldwin. At the least Baldwin held eighty-six and a quarter hides of land and may have held more.

1 GDB 105v, 47v, 151, 145v.

2 LDB 93, 103. For Harold's interests in East Anglia, see Williams, 'Land and Power', 173–4.

3 Asgot held 62 hides as William Leofric's predecessor (25 in Glos., 30 in Berks., and 7 in Essex), plus (probably) the land (3 hides 1⅔ virgates) in Oxon.; plus Taplow (Bucks.) and Kempsford in Glos. (29¼ hides); Beorhtric held 4½ hides of land in Glos. (possibly more if he is the pre-Conquest tenant of Wheatenhurst and Woodchester), 33 hides in Berks., 9 hides in Herefs., 10 hides in Hants and 10 hides in Bucks.; and Edmund held 5 hides in Glos., 21 hides in Wilts. and 20 hides in Bucks.

4 Sawyer (ed.), S.1408. *Osgod* is the English spelling of the Scandinavian name *Asgot*.

5 Coln Rogers is not named as such in DB, but can be identified from later sources as the unnamed holding of 10 hides in 'Bradley' Hundred on f.163.

6 See *VCH Warwickshire*, i (1904), 275. The lands lay in Bucks., Northants, and Leics. as well as War.

7 Hearne (ed.), *Hemming's Cartulary*, 267.

8 Sawyer (ed.), S.1407.

Ælfstan of Boscombe, who held twenty-four and a half hides in Gloucestershire, was even richer, with at least 241 hides of land in eight shires.[1] Most of his land passed to William de Eu. He is called a king's thegn in Bedfordshire and Hertfordshire, and the charter by which the king granted him Sevington (Wilts.) is preserved in the Abingdon Cartulary.[2] He may be identical with the Alstan who was Sheriff of Bedfordshire, and who witnessed a St Albans deed between 1053 and 1066.[3] Of the remaining thegns, John the Dane is worth consideration. He was the predecessor of Matthew de Mortagne at Shipton Moyne, Gloucestershire (ten hides), and he also appears as Matthew's predecessor in Dorset (holding fourteen and three-quarter hides) and Somerset (five and a half hides). It is in the Somerset folios that he is called 'the Dane', holding Yatton (twenty hides) as well as the land which passed to Matthew.[4] Since Matthew de Mortagne also held the manor at Shipton Moyne which had belonged to Strang the Dane (mentioned nowhere else in Domesday), it seems likely that John and Strang were kinsmen. They may indeed be the same man; 'John' is perhaps the 'Christian' name of Strang. John held just over fifty hides of land in three shires.

Of the king's thegns we have been considering, some can be shown to have men commended to them, and it may be presumed that not all of these have been indicated in Domesday. The recording of pre-Conquest subtenants is sporadic in Domesday and it was not always considered relevant to include them. It seems likely that many of the men who held only small amounts of land in Gloucestershire and elsewhere were in fact tenants of other lords. Only detailed examination of the estates of Englishmen over several shires will reveal the patterns of pre-Conquest commendation and land tenure, a task which at the present time of writing has scarcely begun.

TABLE 3: Ecclesiastical tenants in 1086

	Hides	Virgates		Hides	Virgates
Church of Worcester	145		Bath Abbey	10	
Archbishop Thomas of York	112*		Coventry Abbey	10	
St Peter's, Gloucester	97*		Abbey of Saint-Evroul	10	
Winchcombe Abbey	78		Troarn Abbey	10	
Saint-Denis, Paris	60†		Abingdon Abbey	7	2
Westminster Abbey	59†		Osbern Bishop of Exeter	7	
Evesham Abbey	55		Abbey of Sainte-Marie, Cormeilles	6	
Church of Hereford	30		Malmesbury Abbey	5	
Pershore Abbey	22		Church of Lambeth	4	
Glastonbury Abbey	20		Church of Cirencester	2‡	
Eynsham Abbey	14		Abbey of Sainte-Marie, Lyre	1	1
La Trinite, Caen	11				
			Total: 23 tenants hold 775 hides, 3 virgates		

* The archbishop's total includes 49 hides formerly belonging to St Peter's, Gloucester.
† The lands of Saint-Denis and Westminster had been the endowment of the Church of Deerhurst.
‡ Regenbald, who may have been Dean of Cirencester, held $20\frac{1}{4}$ hides.

The Ecclesiastical Tenants

About a third of the total hidage of Gloucestershire, 796 hides out of 2,396, was in the hands of the Church in 1086 (see Table 3 above). This proportion is common to most of the shires of southern and western England. The richest ecclesiastical landholder was, as one might expect, the episcopal Church of Worcester, in whose diocese the shire lay. Archbishop Thomas of York, whose see had been associated with that of Worcester before the Conquest, followed; half his honour had belonged to the Gloucester Churches of St Peter and St Oswald, and had been retained by Thomas's predecessor, Ealdræd, who had rebuilt the Church of St Peter. St Peter's

[1] In Beds., Herts., Wilts., Som., Berks., Dorset, and Hants. Von Feilitzen, *Pre-Conquest Personal Names*, 180 n.2, relates virtually all the DB references to *Alstan* to Ælfstan of Boscombe.
[2] Sawyer (ed.), S.999, dated 1043.
[3] Ibid. S.1235.
[4] GDB 82v, 89v, 98; Exon 450.

was, despite this, the third richest church in the shire, followed by the Abbey of Winchcombe, Saint-Denis of Paris, Westminster Abbey and Evesham Abbey; the remaining ecclesiastics held more modest estates.

Of the religious houses situated outside the shire, little need be said of the English churches, which will be discussed within the context of their own shires. The continental houses with land in Gloucestershire include La Trinite, Caen, founded by Duchess (later Queen) Matilda, which received its possessions here by a royal grant in 1082.[1] Saint-Evroul, founded by Hugh de Grandmesnil in 1050, likewise received its manor at Roel from King William in 1081.[2] The Abbey of Troarn was also founded in 1050, by Roger de Montgomery, and probably received its Gloucestershire lands from Roger after his appointment as Earl of Shrewsbury in 1071. The Abbeys of Lyre and Cormeilles were founded by William fitzOsbern, Lyre in 1046 and Cormeilles about 1060. Both received considerable gifts in lands, churches and tithes from William and his son and successor as Earl of Hereford, Roger de Breteuil. Any gifts from William must pre-date his death in February 1071, and those of Roger his rebellion and forfeiture in 1075. William was buried at Cormeilles, which received from Roger the manor of Newent for the repose of his father's soul. Duntisbourne Leer was given to the Abbey of Lyre by Roger de Lacy, and the gift must have been relatively recent, for Roger's father Walter died only in 1085.

All these benefactions, which involve quite small amounts of land, represent the distribution by the victors of the spoils of war. The Abbey of Saint-Denis, however, though confirmed in its lands by King William in 1069, had acquired its estates before the Conquest.[3] This ancient house had been the special favourite of succeeding dynasties of Frankish kings since the sixth century and tradition alleged that English kings, from Offa onwards, had endowed it also.[4] These early grants are of dubious authenticity, but the abbey had certainly received Taynton (Oxon.) from King Edward; both the king's writ notifying the shire court of the grant and the charter which he commanded to be written have survived. The king's interest in Saint-Denis may have been stimulated by the fact that his physician Baldwin (later Abbot of Bury St Edmunds) was a monk of that house.[5]

Saint-Denis received from Edward half the hundred of Deerhurst, the other half going to the king's own foundation of Westminster. Deerhurst was a hundredal manor, originally assessed at 119 hides, of which Westminster received fifty-nine hides and Saint-Denis sixty hides. The structure of the manor, like that of Tewkesbury which it closely resembles, is still visible in Domesday Book. Westminster was holding the capital manor, Deerhurst itself, with four berewicks, Hardwicke (whose name means 'dairy-farm'), Bourton-on-the-Hill, Todenham and Sutton-under-Brailes (now in Warwickshire). Attached to this core were the lands of tenants, whose names are recorded for 1066 and 1086; the pre-Conquest tenants are described as radknights, glossed as 'free men', who owed agricultural services *ad opus domini*. At least one of these men can be identified as a king's thegn: Alwine (Alwig), predecessor of William fitzBaderon at Evington.[6] The holding of Saint-Denis consisted of a number of vills in Deerhurst Hundred, plus some smaller pieces of land; no tenants, pre- or post-Conquest, are named.

No churches are mentioned in the manor, either in the Westminster entry, or in that for Saint-Denis. Yet St Mary's, Deerhurst, which still stands, is substantially a pre-Conquest building, the earliest elements of which may date to the beginning of the ninth century.[7]

[1] H. W. C. Davis *et al.* (eds.), *Regesta Regum Anglo-Normannorum 1066-1154*, i (London, 1913), no. 149.

[2] Ibid. no. 140.

[3] Sawyer (ed.), S.133; see M. Gelling, *The Early Charters of the Thames Valley* (Leicester, 1979), 101; Sawyer (ed.), S.318, S.686, S.1186.

[4] Sawyer (ed.), S.1028, S.1105.

[5] The charter is discussed in Gelling, *Early Charters of the Thames Valley*, 142–4, which prints and translates the note appended to it in the name of Baldwin, monk of Saint-Denis, who 'received' the charter and the gift of Taynton (Oxon.) for the abbey's benefit: he is the Abbot Baldwin (of Bury St Edmunds) holding land at Deerhurst in 1086.

[6] See p.23 above.

[7] H. M. and J. Taylor, *Anglo-Saxon Architecture*, i (Cambridge, 1965), 193–209; an even earlier date for the fabric of St Mary's is claimed by E. Gilbert, 'The First Stone Church at Deerhurst', *TBGAS* 87 (1968), 71–95, who believes that it may date back as far as the fifth century.

Moreover, there is a second church, dedicated to Holy Trinity, which is known to have been founded in 1056, and which is also of pre-Conquest fabric. The history of the community at Deerhurst goes back to 804, when Æthelric son of Æthelmund left four estates to the minster of Deerhurst as his burial fee; one was Todenham, still part of the manor in 1086.[1] It was clearly a minster, and there is no reference to any reform in the tenth century, though Archbishop Ælfheah (St Alphege) is said to have begun his ecclesiastical career as a monk at Deerhurst.[2] There need not, however, have been a monastic community there at the time.

The next reference to Deerhurst is the building of Holy Trinity in 1056. The foundation-stone of this little church records that 'Earl Oda had this royal hall built and dedicated in honour of the Holy Trinity for the soul of his brother Ælfric which left the body in this place. Bishop Ealdræd dedicated it the second of the Ides of April in the fourteenth year of the reign of Edward king of the English', that is, 12 April 1056.[3] The death of Ælfric is recorded in 1053, and that of Oda, which also happened at Deerhurst, in 1056. Both brothers were buried in the Church of Pershore in Worcestershire.[4]

Oda, whom William of Malmesbury describes as a kinsman of King Edward, was briefly Earl of western Wessex during the exile of Godwine in 1051–2.[5] When Godwine was reinstated, Oda seems to have been compensated with an earldom in Worcestershire. Traces of his tenure in that shire are recorded in Domesday Book, which reveals that he had held Longdon (Worcs.), a thirty-hide manor which belonged in 1066 to Westminster Abbey, and that part of Mathon (now in Herefordshire) had belonged to two of Oda's thegns, Ælfweard and Merewine.[6] Since Westminster's land in Worcestershire had once belonged to the Abbey of Pershore, Longdon must have been given to that house by Oda.

Pershore was an ancient foundation, dating back perhaps to the seventh century.[7] It was one of the houses reformed in the tenth century by St Oswald. William of Malmesbury claims that it was the ealdorman Æthelweard the Chronicler, whose sphere of authority was western Wessex, who re-founded the abbey; William calls Æthelweard 'Earl of Dorset'.[8] The church burnt down in 1002 and all its records were lost. Its surviving cartulary contains only one early charter, a grant of Æthelræd II giving land at Mathon to Leofwine, ealdorman of the Hwicce, in 1014.[9] Land at Mathon, which belonged to Pershore in 1086, had been held by two of Earl Oda's thegns.[10]

The post-Conquest 'Annals of Pershore' are now lost, and only a few fragments are preserved in the writings of the antiquary, John Leland.[11] They name Oda as the restorer of the abbey's fortunes after its spoliation, attributed to Ælfhere, ealdorman of Mercia (956–83), said to be the father of Oda. The abbey was certainly functioning in the 1020s, for Beorhtheah, who succeeded to the bishopric of Worcester in 1033, had previously been Abbot of Pershore. Oda, however, was not the son of Ælfhere of Mercia. If William of Malmesbury is correct in calling him a kinsman of King Edward, it is possible that he was descended from Æthelweard of the western shires, who was descended from King Æthelræd I. Æthelweard died *c.*998, and his son Æthelmær succeeded him as ealdorman of the western shires. Æthelmær founded the Abbey of Eynsham in Oxfordshire, endowing the house with, *inter alia*, fourteen hides at Mickleton (Glos.), still held by the church in 1086.[12] The ealdorman Æthelweard outlawed by Cnut in 1020 was probably Æthelmær's son-in-law and successor. Oda and his brother Ælfric may have been

[1] Sawyer (ed.), S.1187.

[2] He was the Bishop of Winchester (984–1006) before his translation to Canterbury, and was martyred by the Danes who captured that city in 1012.

[3] Taylor and Taylor, *Anglo-Saxon Architecture*, 209–11.

[4] Whitelock *et al.* (eds.), *Anglo-Saxon Chronicle*, *s.aa.* 1053, 1056.

[5] W. Stubbs (ed.), *Willelmi Malmesbiriensis Monachi De Gestis Regum Anglorum*, Rolls Ser. 90, i (London, 1887), 243.

[6] GDB 174v (Longdon, Worcs., held by Westminster Abbey in 1086); the tenure of Oda is mentioned in passing in the account of Bushley (Worcs.), in the Herefordshire folios (f.180v). For Mathon (5 hides), see GDB 175v, 184v, 186v. Merewine and Ælfweard each held half a hide.

[7] Its founder is usually assumed to be Oswald, brother of Osric, king of the Hwicce, who founded St Peter's, Gloucester (Sawyer (ed.), S.70).

[8] Stubbs (ed.), *Willelmi Malmesbiriensis*, i. 243.

[9] Sawyer (ed.), S.932.

[10] See n.6 above.

[11] See Robertson (ed.), *Anglo-Saxon Charters*, 456–8.

[12] Sawyer (ed.), S.911, and see p.22, n.1 above. For Ælfhere's dealings with Pershore, see A. Williams, '"Princeps Merciorum Gentis": the Family, Career and Connections of Ælfhere, Ealdorman of Mercia, 956–83', *ASE* 10 (1982), 168–9.

Æthelmær's sons or grandsons. If Oda's forebears had been ealdormen of the west, Edward's promotion of him to this office in 1051 would represent an attempt to revive an older comital family to replace the dangerous kin of Godwine; especially as Godwine's rise to power as earl of the whole of Wessex coincided with the disgrace of the younger Æthelweard in 1020.[1]

Oda's grants to Pershore and his burial at that house represent the continuing interest in the abbey of the founder's kin. But what of Deerhurst? Since Oda died there, it was presumably his place of residence, and the building of Holy Trinity looks like the construction of an estate church to serve a secular holding, while the minster continued to control another part of the manor. At Tewkesbury also there were two churches; the ancient minster at Stanway, to which the twenty hides of the church belonged, and the estate church at Clifford Chambers (now in Warwickshire).[2] C. S. Taylor suggested that the division of the hundred of Deerhurst between Westminster and Saint-Denis is a reflection of the former division between the secular holding of Oda and the land of the old minster. The Westminster share was the capital manor, which Holy Trinity was built to serve, and the Saint-Denis portion the minster's endowment.[3] This is perhaps why no tenants are recorded on the Saint-Denis estate. It appears that Oda died without heirs and that his land passed to his kinsman, the king, who used it to endow his own foundation at Westminster, which by 1066 held two-thirds of the lands of Pershore, as well as half the manor of Deerhurst. The Church of Deerhurst, however, was given to Saint-Denis, with its land.

The relationship between Deerhurst and Pershore is analogous to that between Tewkesbury and Cranborne, discussed above.[4] In each case an old minster and its associated multiple estate is in the hands of a king's thegn, whose family are also the founders and sponsors of a reformed Benedictine abbey. Deerhurst was probably the centre of the lands of Oda as Tewkesbury was for those of Beorhtric son of Ælfgar; a manor of 119 hides is no mean endowment. Since Oda died in 1056, his former estate cannot be reconstructed from Domesday, but he held at least 154 hides (119 at Deerhurst, thirty at Longdon, Worcs., and five at Mathon, Herefs.). It is likely that the men who held lands attached to Deerhurst and Longdon were Oda's men; this is certainly the case with Ælfweard of Longdon, who held land at Mathon as Earl Oda's thegn.[5] Oda and Beorhtric stand out as the dominating figures in the region.[6]

The religious houses of Gloucestershire itself are not well provided with pre-Conquest records. Like Pershore, both St Peter's, Gloucester, and Winchcombe Abbey experienced disastrous fires which destroyed their archives. St Peter's burnt down in 1122 with the loss of 'all the treasures that were there except a few books and three mass vestments'.[7] Its history therefore rests upon a late compilation made in the time of Abbot Frocester (1382–1412), the basic authenticity of which has been defended by Finberg.[8] The abbey is said to have been founded by Osric, king of the Hwicce, in 679, and endowed with 300 hides of land, perhaps identical with the later *ferding* of Gloucester.[9] It was originally a double monastery, whose abbesses were members of the Hwiccian royal kin, but by the ninth century was probably staffed by secular priests. The post-Conquest 'History' claims that it was re-established as a Benedictine monastery by Archbishop Wulfstan in 1022.[10] The first abbot, Eadric, is castigated for dissipating the abbey's wealth, in particular for selling off the manors of Down Hatherley and Badgeworth 'in perpetual inheritance'. In fact, the charter quoted shows that the estates were leased for life only, but as all too often happened, they were subsequently lost to the church; in 1066

[1] Williams, '"Cockles amongst the Wheat"', 2 and n.14.

[2] See pp.21-2 above.

[3] Taylor, 'Deerhurst, Pershore and Westminster', 244.

[4] See pp.20–2 above.

[5] For Ælfweard of Longdon, see Williams, 'Introduction to the Worcestershire Domesday', 7.

[6] Beorhtric son of Ælfgar seems to have had some interest in the estate of Longdon (Worcs.), for after 1066 Earl William attached three virgates at Pull (Worcs.), a member of Longdon, to Beorhtric's manor of Bushley (Worcs.) (f.180v) and he is probably therefore the Beorhtric who held Longdon TRE (f.174v). Moreover Kemerton and Boddington, which were members of Tewkesbury, are said to have paid geld and done service in Deerhurst Hundred (ff.163v, 166). There may therefore have been some connection between Oda and Beorhtric, but of what nature one cannot tell.

[7] Finberg, *Early Charters*, 11.

[8] Finberg, 'The Early History of Gloucester Abbey', *Early Charters*, 153–66.

[9] Sawyer (ed.), S.70.

[10] W. H. Hart (ed.), *Historia et Cartularium Monasterii Sancti Petri Gloucestriae*, Rolls Ser. 33, i (London, 1863), 8; see also D. Whitelock, *Sermo Lupi ad Anglos* (3rd edn., Exeter, 1963), 12 and note, who dates the refoundation to the time of Cnut, before the death of Archbishop Wulfstan in 1023.

Down Hatherley was attached to the royal manor of 'Barton' (in Gloucester) and Badgeworth passed to Ælfstan of Boscombe and thence to William de Eu. The abbey did acquire the manors of Churcham and Highnam, but in a manner rather unfortunate; they were given by *Wlfinus le Rue* (?Wulfwine the Red) in reparation for having slain six priests between Churcham and Gloucester.

Eadric died in 1058, and was succeeded by Wilstan, a monk of Worcester. In the same year the church was rebuilt and re-dedicated by Ealdræd, Bishop of Worcester, but there was a price on this action, for Ealdræd retained three of the manors of St Peter's as recompense: Oddington, Northleach and Standish, a total of forty-nine hides. Ealdræd became Archbishop of York in 1060, and as a result, these manors passed in 1069 to his Norman successor in the archiepiscopal see, Thomas of Bayeux, who held them at the time of Domesday. King William had ordered their return in 1070, but they were not restored until 1095.[1]

Abbot Wilstan died on a pilgrimage to Rome in 1072, and was succeeded by the Norman Serlo, formerly a monk of Mont-Saint-Michel, who died in 1104. He was a close friend of the Englishman Æthelwig, Abbot of Evesham.[2] It was in his time that the church received a small bequest of land at Duntisbourne Abbots from the widow of Walter de Lacy (died 1085).

As well as the three manors of St Peter's, Archbishop Thomas held all the lands of St Oswald's, Gloucester, consisting of three manors at Swindon (three hides), Widford (two hides) and North Cerney (four hides), the second of which is now in Oxfordshire. St Oswald's seems to have been acquired along with the lands of Archbishop Stigand of Canterbury; four other manors belonging to Stigand were held by Thomas. Stigand, a notorious pluralist, had retained the bishopric of Winchester after his elevation to the see of Canterbury, and the lands may have been connected with Winchester, for Walkelin, nephew of the Norman bishop, held one of these estates of Archbishop Thomas.

St Oswald's, though poorly endowed by the time of Domesday, had an illustrious history. It was founded, as we have seen, by the Lords of Mercia, Æthelræd and Æthelflæd, and the finds from the recent excavations suggest a fine and richly furnished building.[3] In 909 the relics of the Northumbrian royal saint, Oswald, were translated from Bardney in Lincolnshire, and the church dedicated in his honour. Æthelræd and Æthelflæd were both buried at Gloucester, and it has been suggested that their tombs were not in St Peter's, but in St Oswald's, possibly in the building tentatively identified as a crypt at the eastern end of the earliest building there.[4] St Oswald's was and remained a community of secular clerks. The ecclesiastical disfavour shown to this kind of foundation in the monastic reform of the tenth century may have contributed to its later obscurity, though colleges of secular canons regained some popularity in the eleventh century.

The history of the Church of Cirencester is even more obscure. The community, of secular canons, existed in the time of Edward the Confessor, holding only two hides of land, at the royal manor of Cirencester. It was dedicated to St Mary. King William made a small grant of a villan and part of the woodland at Painswick (f.167v) and this seems to have been its total endowment in 1086. In Domesday, however, the holding of the church is followed by that of Regenbald the priest, called Regenbald of Cirencester in the Berkshire folios.[5] Twelfth-century sources call him Dean of Cirencester but this may be a consequence of Henry I's grant of all Regenbald's land to his newly established priory of Augustinian canons at Cirencester, established in 1133.[6] Regenbald was very rich; in the reign of King William he held some ninety hides of land in Berkshire, Herefordshire, Dorset, Somerset, Wiltshire and Buckinghamshire as well as Gloucestershire. Some of this must have been acquired after 1066, but much of it came from King Edward whose chaplain he had been. A writ of Edward, addressed to 'my bishops and my

[1] Davis *et al.* (eds.), *Regesta*, i, no. 36.

[2] Macray (ed.), *Chron. Evesham*, 90.

[3] For some idea of the decoration, see J. K. West, 'A Carved Slab Fragment for St Oswald's Priory, Gloucester', *Studies in Medieval Sculpture*, ed. F. H. Thompson, Soc. of Antiquaries Occasional Papers, ns 4 (1983).

[4] See p.12, n.4 above.

[5] GDB 63.

[6] C. D. Ross (ed.), *The Cartulary of Cirencester Abbey* (London, 1964), ii. 497. Henry I's charter is no. 28 (i. 21–4).

earls . . . in all the shires in which Regenbald my priest has lands and men' grants him various judicial and financial rights and proclaims that 'the fine payable to him be equivalent to that of a diocesan bishop in all things'.[1] Regenbald is described as 'chancellor' in Domesday, and may have exercised this function even before the Conquest. In Gloucestershire Regenbald held twenty and a quarter hides of land. Two of his manors (Ampney St Mary and Norcote) had belonged to Godric, and two (Driffield, and Preston near Cirencester) to Elaf, Earl Tosti's thegn and possibly Godric's brother. Regenbald also held the Church of Cheltenham, with one and a half hides of land, and one hide at Elmstone Hardwicke, belonging to Deerhurst.[2] His brother held two hides at Ampney St Peter of St Peter of Gloucester, and his son Alweald held two hides at Aldsworth. The pre-Conquest tenant of Aldsworth was called Balki, a very rare name found only here and in Suffolk; he may have been connected with Harold Godwineson, Earl of East Anglia from 1046–53, since other lands of Harold and his family are found in Regenbald's possession.[3]

Though the Abbey of Bath lay in Somerset, not Gloucestershire, its land in this shire is of sufficient interest to warrant mention. In 1086, Bath possessed only two manors in the shire, Olveston and Cold Ashton (ten hides in all), but it had formerly held the hundredal manor of Tidenham, assessed at thirty hides, which was in the king's hand in 1086, having been held by Archbishop Stigand. The lease granting Stigand the estate for life is extant; in return Stigand paid ten marks of gold and £20 of silver, and an annual rent of a mark of gold, six porpoises and 30,000 herrings.[4] These are presumably the 'monks' supplies' mentioned in the Domesday account of the manor. The huge render of herrings is obviously related to the fisheries recorded in Domesday: eleven in demesne and forty-two belonging to the villans on the Severn; and on the Wye, one in demesne and two and a half belonging to the villans, to which Earl Roger had added two more. Roger's father, Earl William, had given two fisheries on the Severn and half a fishery on the Wye to Walter de Lacy and two fisheries on the Wye to Ralph de Limesey.[5]

The Domesday account of Tidenham can be compared with a pre-Conquest survey of the manor, compiled about 1050.[6] Like Domesday, this gives the hidage of the manor as thirty hides, but whereas Domesday assigns ten hides to the demesne, the Tidenham survey gives only nine, with twenty-one hides occupied by tenants. Unlike Domesday, the survey names the vills dependent upon the central manor, and gives for each the number of peasant holdings (yardlands) and fisheries; the vills concerned are Stroat, a lost 'Middeltun' near Beachley, Sedbury (*Kingestune*), Bishton and Lancaut. Each yardland paid 12*d.* rent and 4*d.* in alms; and from each weir, every other fish belonged to the lord of the manor, as well as 'every rare fish which is of any value', defined as sturgeon, porpoise, herring or sea-fish. No one could sell fish without informing the lord, if he was at the estate. Part of the land 'above the dyke' (Offa's Dyke) was let to Welsh 'sailors' who were presumably also fishermen.

The Tidenham survey also describes the services due from the peasants upon the estate. It does not give population statistics, but fifty-four yardlands, or peasant holdings, are recorded, which should be compared with the Domesday figures of forty-eight peasants (thirty-eight villans and ten bordars).[7] The survey divides the peasant population into *geneatas* and *geburas*. As we have seen, the *geneatas* are the equivalent of radknights, though none are recorded in the Domesday account of Tidenham.[8] Domesday elsewhere equates *geburas* with the semi-free *coliberti*, but the Old English *gebur* seems to have suffered a downgrading in the twenty years that elapsed between the Conquest and the production of Domesday Book; the services due from the Tidenham *geburas* are those associated with villans. They were quite heavy; each *gebur* had to

[1] Sawyer (ed.), S.1097.

[2] Regenbald had amassed quite a collection of churches, at Wellington, Milborne Port and Frome (Som.), Avebury and Pewsey (Wilts.), Shrivenham, Cookham and Bray (Berks.), and Passenham (Northants), as well as Cheltenham (and presumably Cirencester); see F. Barlow, *The English Church, 1000–1066* (London, 1963), 134–5.

[3] See p.33 below.

[4] Sawyer (ed.), S.1426.

[5] Walter de Lacy's fisheries are presumably among the four and a half held by his son Roger (f.167v) while those of Ralph de Limesy had passed to William de Eu (f.166v).

[6] Sawyer (ed.), S.1555.

[7] Twelve bordars had been added to the manor by Roger de Breteuil and three villans had been given away by Earl William, illustrating the kind of changes which could take place in a comparatively short time.

[8] See p.5 above.

plough half an acre a week and another acre as church-scot; in the latter case he had to supply seed to sow it also, but in the former he merely had to fetch the seed from the lord's barn. He had to supply materials for building weirs and for fencing, fence one pole of the hedge belonging to the manor house (*burh*), reap one and a half acres, mow half an acre and do 'other work' as required. He had moreover to pay 6*d.* and half a sester of honey every Easter, at Lammas six sesters of malt, and at Martinmas a ball of good net yarn which was presumably connected with the obligations to do with the fishing rights. For every seven pigs owned by each *gebur*, three were owed to the abbey and nevertheless payment was still required for feeding the animals on the mast from the woodland.

The last community to be discussed is that of Berkeley. The abbey there may have been defunct in 1066, and the great multiple estate which had been its endowment was in the king's hands. It consisted of a capital manor, Berkeley itself, assessed at five hides and having the lands of seven radknights, assessed at seven hides, attached to it; twenty-two berewicks, with a total assessment of 124 hides; and five other manors, amounting to sixteen hides of land; a grand total of 152 hides. No church is mentioned in the Domesday account of the manor, but Bernard the priest had held five hides, which, as J. S. Moore has shown, lay at Hinton and 'Hinworthy' in the nearby parish of Slimbridge, both of which contain the element *hiwan*, 'a religious community'. The nunnery probably lay at Oldminster in Hinton, and Bernard was its last chaplain.[1]

Though Berkeley is not called a hundred in Domesday, the twelfth-century hundred of Berkeley (i.e. the jurisdictional area then known as Berkeley Hernesse) consisted of the lands attached to the manor in 1086, and C. S. Taylor maintained that 'there can be no reasonable doubt that Berkeley Hundred does represent the possessions of the ancient minster'.[2] There was a community there in the early ninth century, probably a double monastery, if Florence of Worcester is correct in describing Ceolburh as its abbess in 807.[3] Ceolburh's son Æthelric son of Æthelmund bequeathed to her the manor of Stoke (later Stoke Bishop) and the minster of Westbury on Trym, with reversion to the Church of Worcester, provided that the bishop thereof protected her against any claims from 'the Berkeley people'.[4] There was indeed a dispute, for in 824 Bishop Heahberht was involved in a lawsuit about it with the *familia* of Berkeley.[5] Stoke Bishop was also the subject of a later disagreement, and in 883 Ealdorman Æthelræd made a grant of privileges to the community at Berkeley, now under the authority of an abbot, in return for twelve hides at Stoke Bishop, which were leased to Cynewulf son of Ceoluht, with reversion to Worcester (which held the estate in 1066).[6] It is possible that Cynewulf son of Ceoluht was a kinsman of Ceolburh, and that the dispute concerned the narrow line between the personal possessions of the founding family and the lands which they assigned to the support of their church. Æthelræd's charter is witnessed *inter alia* by Æthelhun, Abbot of Berkeley, who, according to Florence of Worcester, succeeded to the bishopric of Worcester in 915 and died in 922.

Nothing more is heard of the community of Berkeley until the record of its demise in Domesday Book, recorded in the account of the manor at Woodchester, which Earl Godwine bought from Azur for his wife Gytha 'so that she could live off it while she stayed at Berkeley' for she did not wish to consume anything from that manor 'because of the destruction of the abbey'. The passage has been taken to imply that Godwine was responsible for the end of the community and Walter Map, the twelfth-century historian and gossip, has a splendid tale of Godwine setting one of his handsome nephews to seduce the nuns, so that the king dissolved the nunnery because of their misconduct and gave its lands to Godwine.[7] As Freeman pointed out this is a variation on the story of Swein Godwineson's abduction of the Abbess of Leominster,

[1] Moore (ed.), *Domesday Book: Gloucestershire*, note to 1,18.
[2] Taylor, 'Berkeley Minster', 79.
[3] Thorpe (ed.), *Florentii Wigorniensis*, *s.a.* 807. Her death is recorded in the *Anglo-Saxon Chronicle* for this year; it calls her an abbess, but it is Florence who adds 'of Berkeley'.
[4] Sawyer (ed.), S.1187.
[5] Ibid. S.1433.
[6] Ibid. S.218.
[7] W. Map, *De Nugis Curialium*, ed. M. R. James, *Anecdota Oxoniensia*, 14 (1914), 201.

though there is a connection between Godwine and some of the Berkeley land.[1] It is not even certain whether all religious life had in fact ceased. In 1130, Roger of Berkeley (a descendant of the Domesday tenant) accounted for the clothing of three nuns, and when the Church of Berkeley and its possessions were given to Reading Abbey by Queen Adeliza in 1147–50, the prebends of two nuns were included.[2] A nun called Cwenhild, possibly a member of the community, was holding nine hides at Naunton (near Bourton-on-the-Water) in 1086. Whether the nunnery had been completely destroyed and, if so, whether Earl Godwine should be held responsible are matters which remain uncertain.

The Norman Conquest

As we have seen, Gloucestershire was part of the earldom of Hereford, held in 1066 by Harold Godwineson. Like all the possessions of Harold and his kin, the earldom was forfeit to the new king, William the Conqueror, as were all the lands, personal and comital, of Harold. The early stages of Norman rule in Gloucestershire are illuminated by a writ of the Conqueror, in English, issued before his departure to Normandy in February 1067.[3] It announces the king's gift of lands at Latton and Eysey, formerly the possession of King Harold (the royal title is actually used), to Regenbald, William's priest. Though both manors are in Wiltshire, part of Latton lay in Gloucestershire, and the writ is therefore addressed to the leading men of both shires: the Bishops Herman of Sherborne and Wulfstan of Worcester, 'Earl' Eustace (the Count of Boulogne), Eadric, Beorhtric and all the king's thegns of Wiltshire and Gloucestershire.

Of this document, Round wrote: 'we see here then, I think, the Conqueror, in his first days as an English king, addressing his subjects, in a part of the realm not yet under Norman sway, and doing so in their own tongue, and in the form to which they were accustomed'.[4] The writ shows, firstly, the early distribution of at least some of Harold's estates, but the recipient is equally important, for he is our old friend Regenbald of Cirencester, entering the employ of the new king; one of the Englishmen who not only survived the Conquest but profited from it.

The appearance of Eustace of Boulogne in the address is of particular interest. Apart from this writ, nothing is known of Eustace's movements between his appearance at Duke William's side in the Battle of Hastings, bearing the papal banner, and his abortive attack on Dover in the late summer of 1067.[5] Since this raid was launched from Boulogne, it might be assumed that Eustace was one of the Frenchmen to whom the Conqueror distributed largesse when they returned home after his coronation. William of Poitiers, however, reports that after the Dover raid Eustace forfeited the fiefs he had received from William, which were presumably in England.[6] The writ we have been examining suggests that Eustace received not only land but office in the west; in fact, that he was the first 'Norman' Earl of Hereford. Round explains William's choice of Eustace 'as being, from his previous connexion with England, less obnoxious than a Norman was likely to prove', for Eustace was Edward the Confessor's brother-in-law.[7] Since it was Eustace's running battle with the men of Dover which provoked the rebellion of Earl Godwine in 1051, this may seem a little disingenuous, but it was certainly the English thegns of the south-east who invited him to lead their rebellion in the summer of 1067.

If Eustace was indeed appointed to Harold's earldom in Hereford, it would be entirely

[1] It was at Beverston, one of the members of Berkeley, that Godwine made his rendezvous with his sons Swein and Harold when they rebelled against King Edward in 1051 (Whitelock *et al.* (eds.), *Anglo-Saxon Chronicle*, *s.a.* 1051).

[2] *Pipe Roll 31 Henry I*, Pipe Roll Soc. 31 (London, 1929), 133; see Kemp, 'Churches of Berkeley Hernesse', 101–2; B. R. Kemp, *Reading Abbey Cartularies*, Camden Soc. 4th ser., 31, R. Hist. Soc. (London, 1986), 225f.

[3] Davis *et al.* (eds.), *Regesta* i, no. 9; for the date, see Darlington, 'Æthelwig, Abbot of Evesham', 17 n.6. It survives only as a copy in the Cirencester Cartulary (Ross (ed.), *Cartulary of Cirencester Abbey*, i. 20–1, no. 26) but there seems no reason to doubt its authenticity.

[4] J. H. Round, 'Regenbald, Priest and Chancellor', *Feudal England* (London, 1895), 423.

[5] For Eustace's part in the Battle of Hastings, see D. M. Wilson (ed.), *The Bayeux Tapestry* (London, 1985), plate 68 and pp.194–5; for the Dover incident, see R. Foreville (ed.), *Guillaume de Poitiers, Histoire de Guillaume le Conquérant* (Paris, 1952), Chs. 47–8.

[6] See J. Le Patourel, *The Norman Empire* (Oxford, 1976), 29, 40 n.3.

[7] Round, 'Regenbald', 424.

consistent with King William's other early arrangements in the area. He restored to Alvred of Marlborough the lands of his uncle Osbern Pentecost, which had been seized by Earl Harold in 1051 and made gifts to those Normans who had settled in the west in the time of Edward the Confessor.[1] Eustace could be regarded as having some prior interest in the earldom of Hereford. He had married as his first wife, Gode, sister of Edward the Confessor. She was then the widow of Drogo, Count of the Vexin, by whom she had two sons, Walter, who received the family's continental possessions, and Ralph, who we have seen was Earl of Hereford from 1050 to 1057.[2] Though his earldom passed to Harold Godwineson, Ralph left a son, another Harold, apparently still a minor in 1066.[3] It may be that Eustace, as one of the few remaining kinsmen of this young man, was the obvious choice to receive his stepson's earldom.

Eustace seems, however, to have abandoned his charge, possibly after the rebellion of Eadric the Wild, in which a large part of Herefordshire was devastated.[4] A parallel suggests itself with Gherbod the Fleming, who was given the earldom of Chester in 1070 but could not hold it, and returned to Flanders; or with Aubrey de Couci, who abandoned his earldom of Northumbria in 1080 and lost his English lands as a result. Eustace subsequently made his peace with William and received a large estate in England, which formed the basis of the honour of Boulogne; both he and his second wife, Ida of Lorraine, appear as tenants in 1086. Eustace does not seem to have held any of the land of his first wife, Gode, except Lambeth (Surrey), part of which he gave to St Andrew's, Rochester.[5] Harold himself was holding several of his father's manors in 1086, including Sudeley and Toddington, in Gloucestershire. He held in all forty-four hides of land in Gloucestershire, Worcestershire (f.177) and Warwickshire (f.244).

The Anglo-Saxon Chronicle implies that no wholesale redistribution of land took place before the king's return from Normandy at the end of 1067, when he 'gave away every man's land'. In the earlier months of that year, those English who had submitted to the new king were allowed to buy back their estates. A reference in Gloucestershire may be related to this process. In 1086, Beorhtric was holding two estates at Leckhampton, one of which had belonged to him in King Edward's day, while the other had been held by Ordric; both had been conceded to Beorhtric by King William 'when he went into Normandy'. No date is given, but this could be the king's first, triumphal return in 1067, in which case Beorhtric was one of those who salvaged at least part of their fortune by speedy submission to the new king. This Beorhtric is in fact the kinsman of Asgot and Edmund, whose pre-Conquest holdings have already been discussed.[6] He was probably not the only member of his family to survive. As we have seen, a large part of Asgot's land went to William Leofric, who has no other predecessor. Since he has an English byname, William was presumably at least half English, and it is likely that he is Asgot's son, perhaps by a Norman woman.

It is tempting to identify this Beorhtric with the Beorhtric named in the Latton and Eysey writ, rather than Beorhtric son of Ælfgar, as suggested by Round.[7] The lands of Beorhtric son of Ælfgar all passed into Norman hands, though we do not know how early; the process must have begun at least before 1071, since some manors are found in the possession of Earl William fitzOsbern.[8] The Eadric named in the writ is certainly the pre-Conquest Sheriff of Wiltshire, who appears in Domesday as the holder of a hide of land belonging to the royal manor of Chippenham (Wilts.), most of which passed to Roger of Berkeley by 1086.[9] How long Eadric continued in office is not known, but by 1081 he had been replaced by Edward of Salisbury.

It might be assumed that the pre-Conquest Sheriff of Gloucestershire also survived and

[1] GDB 186 (Burghill and Brinsop).

[2] See pp.19–20 above.

[3] The manor of Ebury (Middx.) belonged to Harold son of Ralph TRE, but both it and he were in the wardship of Queen Matilda in 1066 (f.129v).

[4] Whitelock *et al.* (eds.), *Anglo-Saxon Chronicle*, *s.a.* 1067.

[5] *VCH Surrey* i (1902), 312 n.2; GDB 34. Gode herself was dead by 1049, see D. Bates, 'Lord Sudeley's Ancestors: the Family of the Counts of Amiens, Valois and the Vexin in France and England during the Eleventh Century', *The Sudeleys: Lords of Torrington*, The Manorial Soc. of Great Britain (1987), 38. I am grateful to Dr Bates for allowing me to read this paper in advance of publication.

[6] See pp.24–5 above.

[7] Round, 'Regenbald', 425.

[8] See, for example, GDB 180v (Bushley).

[9] GDB 64v, 72v. Eadric's name is very common and he cannot be further identified but must have held other land, for that in Wiltshire was held of him by a tenant *Celein* (possibly OE *Ceolsige*).

continued in office after the Conquest, since Domesday tells us that it was King William who on the death of Alwine gave his land and widow to Richard *iuvenis*.[1] If Alwine did continue as sheriff, however, it is odd that he was not included in the address of the Latton and Eysey writ. Richard *iuvenis*, his successor in the land, held a manor in Worcestershire before the Conquest, and must have been one of Edward the Confessor's Normans. His Worcestershire estate, like his Gloucestershire lands, passed to William Goizenboded, who held no other land. It can probably be assumed that William was Richard's son. It has been doubted whether his mother was Alwine's widow, since if she were, he would have been a minor in 1086;[2] but this objection seems to rest on von Feilitzen's identification of Alwine the Sheriff of Gloucestershire with Æthelwine, Sheriff of Warwickshire, who was alive at least as late as 1072.[3] This identification has been challenged, and if the Gloucestershire Alwine is a different individual, his death may have taken place much earlier, perhaps even before the Conquest. The marriage of his widow with a Norman settler of the Confessor's reign would accord well with the early policy of William I, which was to adapt as far as was feasible to pre-existing arrangements. William Goizenboded's byname ('cursed, or foretold, by a witch') is English, and points to an English parent.

Beorhtric, William Leofric and William Goizenboded may thus all be Englishmen or Anglo-Normans who survived the Conquest in possession of their or their families' lands, or at least some part of them. To this group may be added Ketil and his son Eadric, Dunna and Ælfsige of Faringdon. In 1086, Ketil and Eadric held some ten and a half hides of land in Gloucestershire, all of which had belonged to Ketil in King Edward's time. This represents the whole of Ketil's lands in the shire except for three and a half hides which went to William fitzBaderon.[4] Dunna was less fortunate; of the nineteen hides which he possessed he retained only two, the remainder going to Osbern Giffard, who also held Dunna's lands in Berkshire, Somerset and Wiltshire.[5] Dunna had held his manor at Brimpsfield of Earl Harold, and perhaps his connection with the dead king led to his dispossession. Not all of Harold's men, however, were so unfortunate. Ælfsige of Faringdon had held two hides at Littleworth (Berks.) of Harold in 1066, which seems to be his whole estate before the Conquest apart from five hides at Longney (Glos.), but since his name is very common, it is impossible to be certain of this.[6] By 1086, Ælfsige had acquired control, either as a king's thegn or at farm, of thirty-four hides of land in Gloucestershire, Berkshire, and Oxfordshire, nearly all of which had belonged to Harold TRE.[7] His son, Ælfwig, had a house in Wallingford (Berks.), and a hide of land at Milton-under-Wychwood (Oxon.), of the fee of Earl William, which must have been acquired before the earl's death in February 1071. This estate was still held by Ælfwig's grandson, Robert of Astrop, in the late twelfth century; he gave it to the monks of Bruern.[8] Ælfsige, like Regenbald, prospered through service to the new king, by 'acting as one of those King's reeves who were found useful by William as agents among his new subjects'.[9]

These survivors represent an early stage in William I's treatment of his new kingdom. It seems that his original intention was to maintain an amalgam of Norman incomers and native English magnates. This policy was overturned by the series of English rebellions between 1067 and 1071. Though frequently dismissed as the draggled tail-end of the Norman Conquest, these rebellions were both dangerous in themselves and far-reaching in their effects; for it was their aftermath which saw the wholesale dispossession of English lords and the redistribution of their estates. The process began at the end of 1067, a year which saw rebellion in the south-east, the West Country and the Marches of Wales.

1 GDB 167 (Guiting Power).

2 Moore (ed.), *Domesday Book: Gloucestershire*, note to 34,8.

3 He witnessed a charter of Robert of Stafford in that year: R. W. Eyton, 'The Staffordshire Chartulary', *Collections for a History of Staffordshire*, 2 (1881), 178.

4 Ketil's lands in 1086 lay in Windrush, Daglingworth, Baunton and Alkerton; the 3½ hides held by William fitzBaderon lay at Daglingworth and were held TRE by Ketil and Alric. Ketil's name does not occur elsewhere in the Gloucestershire folios.

5 GDB 62, 98, 72v. Dunna held one manor in Somerset in 1086, Buckland Dinham (12 hides).

6 GDB 57v. He is described as King Edward's thegn in the *Vita Wulfstani* which recounts the consecration by Bishop Wulfstan of Worcester of the church which Ælfsige had built at Longney: R. R. Darlington (ed.), *The Vita Wulfstani of William of Malmesbury*, Camden Soc. 3rd ser., 40, R. Hist. Soc. (London, 1928), 40.

7 In Oxon. he held the royal manors of Langford and Shipton-under-Wychwood at farm (f.154v).

8 *VCH Oxfordshire*, i (1939), 388.

9 *VCH Berkshire*, i (1906), 293.

It was largely the Mercian thegns of the north and west, who had not taken part in the Hastings campaign, who participated in the English risings which provoked the savage 'harrying of the north' in the winter of 1070–1. Some Gloucestershire landholders were involved. Mærle-Sveinn, who held Tarlton, was one of the earliest rebels, fleeing to Scotland with Edgar Ætheling in the summer of 1067.[1] His Gloucestershire manor passed, like his great possessions in the north, to Ralph Paynel. Another northern magnate with land in Gloucestershire was Siward Barn, lord of Lechlade. He was one of those who held out to the end, in the marshes of Ely.[2] When this last stand failed, Siward left England, and, it is said, was one of those who took service in the Varangian Guard of the Emperor at Constantinople.[3] Mærle-Sveinn and Siward were great magnates, who made an impact upon the historical sources of the time, but many lesser thegns must have been ruined in the English revolts, of whose fate nothing can be ascertained. The Gloucestershire folios record the outlawry of one Wulfweard, whose little estate at Gloucester was given by Earl William to his cook (f.162v), presumably because, like many Englishmen of the time, he had 'gone to York', but we know no more about him.

The defeat of the rebels and the redistribution of their lands was presided over in the southern shires of Mercia by Earl William fitzOsbern, appointed to the earldom of Hereford in 1067. He was killed at the Battle of Cassel, in Flanders, in February 1071, and his lands and office passed to his son, Roger de Breteuil. Roger, however, rebelled in 1075, and lost both earldom and lands, after which the earldom lapsed. The first Norman settlers in the west were probably fitzOsbern's men, some of whom still held in 1086, like Ansfrid de Cormeilles, Durand of Gloucester, Hugh l'Asne, Gilbert fitzTurold and William fitzNorman. Others were involved in the rebellion of Earl Roger, and forfeited their lands; or had died, like Roger de Pitres, and been succeeded by their heirs.

The means whereby the massive transference of land from English to Norman hands was accomplished is still obscure. It seems that one expedient was to grant to each Norman the lands of a named English predecessor or several named predecessors, who are called *antecessores*; it is from these *antecessores* that title was derived.[4] Thus, in Gloucestershire, Henry de Ferrers (unsuccessfully) claimed 'Alverston' because it had belonged to one of his usual *antecessores*, Bondi the staller; whereas Osbern Giffard held 'Oldbury' even though it had not belonged to his *antecessor* Dunna. This practice accounts for the single manors and small estates in Gloucestershire in the hands of men whose main holdings lay elsewhere. Siward Barn, who held Henry de Ferrers' only manor in Gloucestershire, also preceded him in Derbyshire and elsewhere; Eadric, who had held four of the seven manors belonging to Ernulf de Hesdin, is found as Ernulf's predecessor in Wiltshire, Hampshire, Somerset and Dorset; Thorkil, who held the Gloucestershire manor of Hugh l'Asne at Brockworth, is Thorkil White, his predecessor in Herefordshire; Miles Crispin holds the Gloucestershire lands of his usual predecessor, Vigot of Wallingford; William de Eu those of Ælfstan of Boscombe; Sigar de Chocques, the lands of Countess Gode; and Matthew de Mortagne those of John the Dane. This principle must have made the task of redistribution easier, but the instances where the lands of one Englishman were divided amongst several Normans, like those of Earnsige son of 'Ocea', show that other factors were involved.

It is not always possible to determine even approximately when a 1086 landholder received his honour, but since Humphrey the chamberlain was associated with Queen Matilda, his lands were probably acquired before her death in 1083. It is unlikely that Roger de Montgomery received any of his lands in the west before his appointment as Earl of Shrewsbury in 1071[5], and

[1] Whitelock *et al.* (eds.), *Anglo-Saxon Chronicle*, *s.a.* 1067.

[2] Ibid. *s.a.* 1071.

[3] For Siward at Constantinople, see J. Godfrey, 'The Defeated Anglo-Saxons take Service with the Byzantine Emperor', *Proc. of the Battle Conference 1978*, i (1979), 69 and the references there cited.

[4] Not all the *antecessores* of the 1086 tenants were English, nor all pre-Conquest tenants, since much redistribution had taken place by 1086; thus William fitzBaderon's *antecessor* was his uncle Wihanoc and one of William de Eu's *antecessores* was Ralph de Limesy.

[5] See J. F. A. Mason, 'Roger de Montgomery and his Sons, 1067–1102', *TRHS* 5th ser., 13 (1963), 9.

the same is probably true of Hugh d'Avranches, nicknamed Hugh 'the fat', who received the earldom of Chester in the same year. Hugh de Grandmesnil probably also arrived in the 1070s, rather than the 1060s.

TABLE 4: 1086 tenants holding ten hides or more

	Hides	Virgates		Hides	Virgates
Roger de Lacy	70	2	Harold son of Earl Ralph	20	
William Goizenboded	59	3	Drogo fitzPons	20	
Ansfrid de Cormeilles	48	1½	Turstin fitzRolf	19	
Ernulf de Hesdin	46	2½	Roger of Berkeley	18	
Ralph de Tosny	41		Osbern Giffard	18	
William de Eu	40	2½	Geoffrey, Bishop of Coutances	17	
Roger d'Ivry	40	2	Humphrey the chamberlain	15	3
William fitzBaderon	38	½	Robert d'Oilly	15	
Durand of Gloucester	35	3	Henry de Ferrers	15	
Robert de Tosny	33		Ælfsige of Faringdon	12	2
Earl Hugh	31	2	Gilbert, Bishop of Lisieux	12	
Hascoit Musard	30		Ketil and Eadric	10	2
William Leofric	25	½	William fitzGuy	10	
Sigar de Chocques	25		Roger de Beaumont	10	
Matthew de Mortagne	24		Robert Despenser	10	
Hugh l'Asne	23		Walter fitzPons	10	
Hugh de Grandmesmil	22	3	Walter the crossbowman	10	
Walter fitzRoger	22	1	Beorhtric	10	
Gilbert fitzTurold	21				

Total: 37 tenants hold 931 hides, 2½ virgates

One early honour was that of Walter de Lacy, once believed to have been a follower of William fitzOsbern.[1] Since many of his English predecessors were Harold Godwineson's men, however, his fief is likely to have been created quite early, out of the possessions of the dead king. Walter's lands in Herefordshire, Gloucestershire, Shropshire, Oxfordshire, Berkshire, Wiltshire, and Worcestershire comprised the later honour of Weobley in Herefordshire; his brother Ilbert de Lacy held an honour of comparable size, based on Pontefract (Yorks.).[2] Walter died in 1085, and his lands were held in 1086 by his son Roger, whose lands in Gloucestershire made him the richest man in the shire (see Table 4 above). Several of his English predecessors appear in other shires also: Eadwig, who had held Wormington, is probably the Herefordshire thegn Eadwig Cild, seventeen of whose manors in that shire passed to the Lacys, including Weobley which became the *caput* of their honour; Earnsige son of 'Ocea' held both Painswick (Glos.) and Tedstone Wafre (Herefs.); and the manor of Oxenhall (Glos.) was held of Earl Harold by Thorkil, presumably the same Thorkil six of whose Herefordshire manors went to the Lacys, since four of them were held by Thorkil of Earl Harold. As we have seen, Edmund of Stratton was one of Roger de Lacy's predecessors in Berkshire.[3]

Ansfrid of Cormeilles, who held the third largest lay fee in Gloucestershire after Roger de Lacy and William Goizenboded, was one of Earl William's men. Like most of William's vassals, he held land in Herefordshire also, and in fact Tarrington in that shire became the *caput* of his honour, though the bulk of his land lay in Gloucestershire. He married a niece of Walter de Lacy, from whom he received Winstone and Duntisbourne Abbots. Durand of Gloucester, the Domesday sheriff, was also connected with Earl William. His brother, Roger de Pitres, had been sheriff under the earl but was dead before the time of Domesday. Roger's son, Walter, was also holding land in Gloucestershire and elsewhere, and was eventually Durand's heir. Their lands, in Herefordshire, Gloucestershire, Wiltshire and Hampshire, passed to Walter's son Roger, father of Miles of Gloucester, Earl of Hereford.[4] Three more of Earl William's men held land in

[1] For the Lacys, see Wightman, *Lacy Family*; cf. C. P. Lewis, 'The Norman Settlement of Herefordshire under William I', *Proc. of the Battle Conference 1984*, vii (1985), 203–5.

[2] The lands of Ilbert lay in Yorks., Lincs., Notts., Bucks., Oxon., Berks. and Surrey.

[3] See p.25 above.

[4] Walker, '"Honours" of the Earls of Hereford'.

Gloucestershire in 1086, Hugh l'Asne, Gilbert fitzTurold and William fitzNorman, but their main holdings were in Herefordshire.

Other Herefordshire barons were William fitzBaderon and Drogo fitzPons. William was custodian of the royal castle at Monmouth, as successor to his paternal uncle, Wihanoc. The family was Breton, from Epiniac and La Boussac, near Dol, and William was therefore a particularly appropriate choice to guard the Welsh March.[1] Other Bretons in the shire include Joscelin, who held the little manor of Charfield; and Hascoit Musard, whose Gloucestershire lands were insignificant in comparison to his estates elsewhere, in Buckinghamshire, Berkshire, Oxfordshire, Warwickshire, and Derbyshire. Drogo fitzPons seems to be associated with Ralph de Tosny of whom he held lands in Herefordshire as well as Gloucestershire; he also appears as a tenant-in-chief in both those shires, and in Worcestershire also. Both Ralph de Tosny and his brother Robert held land in Gloucestershire, but their main interests were elsewhere.

Ernulf de Hesdin and William de Eu, both of whom held over forty hides of land in Gloucestershire, were Wiltshire magnates. William de Eu, as the Gloucestershire and Dorset folios make clear, had some connection with Ralph de Limesey, but whether of kinship or marriage is not known.[2] It was in succession to Ralph that William de Eu had £9 from the customary dues of Chepstow (now in Monmouthshire), which Ralph had received from Earl William. The other major landowner in Gloucestershire was Roger d'Ivry, whose main holdings lay in Oxfordshire. He was closely connected with Robert d'Oilly, whose lands came mostly through his marriage to an Englishwoman, the daughter of Vigot of Wallingford; they are said to have been oath-brothers.[3] Both Robert and his son-in-law, Miles Crispin, held land in Gloucestershire, though their estates were comparatively small.

Of the men whose main wealth was in Gloucestershire, William Goizenboded, Ansfrid of Cormeilles, Durand of Gloucester, William Leofric and Harold son of Earl Ralph, three were of English descent. William the chamberlain, who held land in Buckinghamshire and Bedfordshire as well as Gloucestershire, may have had some connection with Harold son of Earl Ralph, since Queen Edith had given him Harold's Middlesex manor of Ebury (now in south-west London), at farm for £3 a year. He held it of the king after her death in 1075, but lost it in 1082 to Geoffrey de Mandeville, the Domesday tenant.[4]

Of the Gloucestershire landholders perhaps the most interesting is Roger de Berkeley. Though as a tenant-in-chief he is fairly small beer, with only twenty-five hides of land, three of which lay in Wiltshire, he was also holding at farm the great manor of Berkeley, assessed at 152 hides, for which he was paying no less than £170 in assayed silver annually. He claimed the 'little castle' built by Earl William at Sharpness, presumably the origin of the present Berkeley Castle.[5] He also held Etloe, part of the royal manor of Awre (no hidage recorded). Roger's position clearly grew out of his status as a royal official; he was the reeve of the royal estate of Barton (in Bristol). His brother Ralph was holding a small estate (six hides) in Gloucestershire and Somerset.[6]

Roger's grandson, Roger III, lost Berkeley itself, but retained one of its members, Dursley, which became the *caput* of his honour.[7] Berkeley was given by Henry II to Robert fitzHarding of Bristol for services rendered to the Angevin cause in the civil wars of Stephen's reign.[8] This

[1] William fitzBaderon was holding 2½ virgates which the shire court said should belong to the royal manor of Westbury-on-Severn (f.167). He also held, by force, 1 virgate at Newent of the Abbey of Cormeilles (f.166). In the account of the royal manor of Westbury, it is stated that lands in Newent and other places had been taken away from the manor, and were held by the Abbot of Cormeilles, Osbern and William, son(s) of Richard. The portions of the manor in the possession of Cormeilles and Osbern fitzRichard present no problems and are easily traceable, but 'William fitzRichard' has proved a stumbling-block. In view of William fitzBaderon's connection with at least 3½ virgates of Westbury's land, it is obvious that 'scribal error' is involved; what the scribe intended to write was 'Osbern fitzRichard and William fitzBaderon'.

[2] R. W. Eyton, *A Key to Domesday: An Analysis and Digest of the Dorset Survey* (London, 1878), 76; R. W. Eyton, *Domesday Studies: An Analysis and Digest of the Somerset Survey*, i (London, 1880), 64.

[3] R. Lennard, *Rural England 1086–1135* (Oxford, 1966), 65.

[4] GDB 129v.

[5] GDB 64v, 72v. Roger also held 2 carucates of land belonging to Chepstow, and 1½ hides and the 'third part of ½ hide' at Dodington from the Bishop of Coutances.

[6] GDB 99/Exon 464v.

[7] I. J. Sanders, *English Baronies* (Oxford, 1960), 114.

[8] Finberg, 'Three Studies in Family History', *Gloucestershire Studies*, 146.

Robert fitzHarding was the grandson of Eadnoth the staller, who served three kings, Edward, Harold and William and was killed in 1068, defending the West Country against the invasion of the sons of Harold Godwineson from Ireland.[1] Since it has been doubted whether this descent is really true, it is worth setting out some of the evidence. In the twelfth century, Robert gave to the Church of St Augustine's, Bristol the manor of Fifehead Magdalen (Dorset), with the consent of Earl Ranulph of Chester.[2] In 1086 this estate had been held by Ranulph's predecessor, Earl Hugh of Chester, in succession to his usual *antecessor*, Eadnoth the staller. Not only does this show that Robert was a descendant of Eadnoth, it indicates that Hearding, though not actually mentioned in Domesday, was probably still holding Fifehead as the earl's tenant in 1086.[3]

The family of Hearding son of Eadnoth thus survived the lean years, when the lands of once-wealthy thegns passed to foreigners, and, in the words of Henry of Huntingdon, 'it was a disgrace to be called an Englishman'.[4] Though his father's lands were used to endow the Earl of Chester, Hearding kept some estates in Gloucestershire; he was holding Wheatenhurst (five hides) in pledge from Beorhtric in 1086. William of Malmesbury describes him as a litigious man, and one can imagine why. His son, Robert, however, made his fortune as reeve of Bristol and a prosperous merchant, which enabled him to finance Henry II's bid for the English throne, and won him the manor of Berkeley Castle.

One more Englishman who held land in Gloucestershire must be mentioned. Thorvald (*Turold*), who held five hides at Meysey Hampton of Earl Roger de Montgomery, is described as the nephew of Vigot, presumably (since the name is rare) Vigot of Wallingford. Vigot's lands passed mostly to Robert d'Oilly, his son-in-law, and Miles Crispin, but his Middlesex manors went to Earl Roger, which may account for his nephew's appearance as the earl's tenant.[5] Thorvald also held of Earl Roger at 'Eaton Mewsey' (now Castle Eaton, Wilts.), Penton Mewsey and Houghton (both Hants), and Loseley (Surrey); all these manors and Meysey Hampton are tenurially associated in the later Middle Ages.[6] He also held, in all likelihood, Burpham and Worplesdon (both Surrey), and Milston (Wilts.), of the earl.[7] All of these manors, except Meysey Hampton, were held TRE by Osmund, who may be Thorvald's father. Thorvald's lands held of the earl amount to thirty-five hides. His cousin Ealdgyth was married to Robert d'Oilly and her daughter was the wife of Miles Crispin.[8] Another cousin, Alfred, also described as Vigot's nephew, held Littlestoke and Checkendon (both Oxon.), eight hides in all, as a tenant-in-chief in 1086; both belonged TRE to Wulfræd, perhaps his father.[9] Though Vigot's son, Toki of Wallingford, had been killed at the Battle of Gerberoy in 1079, the family remained well established, though at a lower level of society than had been their fortune in the reign of King Edward.[10]

Though the Norman Conquest was a disastrous experience for the English aristocracy, in which many of them lost their lands if not their lives, its effects should not be overestimated. The English who survived were poorer both in terms of their own pre-Conquest wealth, and that of the Normans who supplanted them. They suffered a depression in status, few of them holding as tenants-in-chief of the king. They became mesne-tenants of Norman lords or of ecclesiastical houses, who had once been king's thegns. They and their children had to adapt to a new social order. But they did not vanish. At the level of the shire, indeed, they may still have been a significant force, given that the great magnates, after the Conquest as before, must often have had business elsewhere. Last but not least, it should be remembered that we do, after all, speak not French, but English.

[1] Whitelock *et al.* (eds.), *Anglo-Saxon Chronicle*, *s.a.* 1068.

[2] Caley and Ellis (eds.), *Dugdale's Monasticon*, vi (1) (1830), 366; W. Farrer, *Honors and Knights' Fees*, ii (London, 1924), 286–7.

[3] GDB 80; *VCH Dorset*, iii. 57.

[4] Henry of Huntingdon, *Historia Anglorum*, ed. T. Arnold, Rolls Ser. 74 (London, 1879), 209.

[5] GDB 129.

[6] Lewis, 'English and Norman Government', 216–17.

[7] GDB 34v, 68v; Mason, 'Roger de Montgomery', 9.

[8] E. A. Freeman, *A History of the Norman Conquest, its Causes and its Results*, iv (2nd edn., Oxford, 1871), 734.

[9] GDB 160.

[10] Whitelock *et al.* (eds.), *Anglo-Saxon Chronicle*, *s.a.* 1079. He was apparently the king's squire, for he was killed while bringing the king a fresh horse. See M. Chibnall, *Anglo-Norman England 1066–1166* (Oxford, 1986), 35.

HUNDREDS AND WAPENTAKES

F. R. THORN

UNDER William I, as under the English kings, vills were grouped together for taxation, judicial and other obligations into 'hundreds' or, in former Danish areas, into 'wapentakes'. These administrative units, intermediate in size between the vill and the shire, and laid down before civil parishes came into existence, usually consisted of a single unified tract of territory (in 1086 varying widely between twenty and 300 hides in extent) which could belong to a variety of tenants-in-chief. Often a lord (particularly the king or a church) was paramount in a hundred; or the lordship of the hundred was attached to a particular manor by a system that was developed in the later medieval period. Some hundreds contained a single large manor only, and these and others had but a single tenant-in-chief. A few had isolated detachments and fewer still were ecclesiastical hundreds geographically scattered but owing suit to their church, however remote, and not to some local meeting-place. Vills were sometimes divided by hundred boundaries and the members of large manors were often in several different hundreds. Many of the hundred-names, if not replaced in 1086 by those of manors, refer to the meeting-places, 'moots', which were often at road-junctions, river-crossings, beside barrows or mounds, on hilltops or near isolated trees in a prominent position.

Hundreds cannot be described or mapped on the basis of Domesday Book alone, for the boundaries of estates and hundreds are never indicated, nor can every estate be allocated with certainty to a particular hundred, especially when it is mentioned in passing or is the dependency of some composite manor. The composition of hundreds can be partly restored from internal evidence by noting those places that fall directly beneath a hundred heading in the text and by identifying hundredal groupings which in many counties are inscribed in a standard sequence. However, the later history of the manor and of the hundred as well as geographical probability must also be employed and the hundredal rubrication itself examined, for it can be shown to be sometimes incorrect or deficient. The scribe's not infrequent errors are of only a few types and easily allowed for, and some restoration of missing headings can be made from the evidence of the text; but a decision sometimes has to be made to restore a hundred heading above a place from later evidence alone.

If these restorations are not made, Domesday will seem to allocate such a place to a different hundred, of which it will appear, owing to its geographical position, to be an improbable detachment. Allowance must be made for the fact that places lying close to the boundary of a hundred in 1086 may well be found in an adjacent hundred in the thirteenth-century surveys which are the first to show the composition of hundreds in detail.

Strictly speaking, it is impossible to map eleventh-century hundred boundaries. The hundred is the sum of exploited land and woodland, while 'waste', 'forest', moor and bog are either to be regarded as being outside the hundred, or the hundred boundary through them is ill-defined. Expansion of arable land, assarting, and drainage have all tended to change boundaries considerably. Compared with the number of vills surveyed in Domesday Book, charters with boundary clauses are few, their interpretation difficult and their relation to Domesday estates often indirect. Few estate maps survive from the Middle Ages and the first accurate hundred maps, dating from the early nineteenth century, are at the end of a process of change which may have left the 1086 pattern scarcely recognizable. But by using the evidence, whether certain, probable or supplemented, for the composition of the eleventh-century hundreds, lines can be drawn between manors—which may well contain more than one place and extend over more than one modern parish—according to the hundred in which they probably lay in 1086. In this way it is possible to recover something that approximates to the eleventh-century topography and administrative divisions.[1]

THE HUNDREDS OF GLOUCESTERSHIRE

THE Gloucestershire that is described in Domesday Book had been created out of the former kingdom of Mercia in the early eleventh century by the amalgamation of two 'counties', one based on Gloucester and the other on Winchcombe. This combination was soon after amplified by the transfer from Herefordshire of some land that lay between the river Wye

[1] Apart from works cited in individual articles in the series, documents and discussions concerning the hundredal system will be found in O. S. Anderson, *The English Hundred-Names* (Lund, 1934); *Inquisitions and Assessments Relating to Feudal Aids with other Analogous Documents, Preserved in the Public Records Office A.D. 1284–1431* (abbr. *Feudal Aids*), 6 vols. (HMSO, London, 1899–1920); F. Liebermann, *Die Gesetze der Angelsachsen*, 3 vols. (Halle, 1903–16); H. R. Loyn, *The Governance of Anglo-Saxon England, 500–1087* (London, 1984); A. J. Robertson (ed.), *The Laws of the Kings of England from Edmund to Henry I* (Cambridge, 1925); F. M. Stenton, *Anglo-Saxon England* (3rd edn., Oxford, 1971).

and the rivers Severn and Leadon. The fusion of Gloucestershire and 'Winchcombeshire' is attributed to Eadric 'Streona' who was Ealdorman of Mercia from 1007 to 1017.[1]

The County Hidage, dating from early in the eleventh century, seems to assign 2,400 hides to this enlarged Gloucestershire;[2] the county was thus, like almost all the other 'Mercian' shires, a multiple of 1,200 hides based on a 'county town'. However, the areas that were, or were to become, Gloucestershire and 'Winchcombeshire' may have been laid down in the tenth century. Although neither appears in the appendix to the Burghal Hidage, which perhaps dates from 915, 1,200 hides dependent on the *burh* of Worcester and 2,400 hides on that of Warwick are found there.[3] Since Gloucester and Winchcombe were involved with these adjacent areas, they must have been apportioned their hides at the same time.

The analogy with Worcestershire (1,200 hides divided into twelve hundreds) might suggest that Gloucestershire had once contained twenty-four hundreds; but there seem to have been about forty in 1086, ranging in size from "Letberge" (six hides) to Salmonsbury (178 hides). About fifteen hundreds contained less than fifty hides[4] and if any original neat pattern of twenty-four hundreds existed, it seems that a complex process of fission and amalgamation had taken place by 1086. Exactly how many hundreds there were in 1086 is uncertain. Both Berkeley and Tewkesbury manors were the centres of great multiple estates whose members, united by tenure and not by geography, were later considered to form hundreds named from their head manors, although the names of their hundreds were omitted by the scribe of Great Domesday. This may have been deliberate, for in the early part of Chapter 1[5] he incorporates the hundred-name (where it is not the same as the manor-name) in the first sentence of the entry: e.g. 'In Bledisloe Hundred King Edward held Awre'. But in three clear instances in this chapter—Cheltenham, Westbury-on-Severn, Lydney—where the hundred was named from the royal manor, he seems intentionally to have omitted the hundred-name. This caused him some confusion: having begun 'In 'Langley' Earl Harold held . . .', he realized that 'Langley' was a hundred-name and so had to interline *Hund'*.[6] Earlier he had written 'In Cirencester Hundred King Edward had five hides of land' and in so doing omitted the name of the holding: it was actually the important royal manor of Cirencester.[7] If there is indeed a pattern to this omission of hundred-names in the *Terra Regis* section, it may be that both 'Barton' (in Gloucester), tentatively assigned here to 'Dudstone' Hundred, and Barton (in Bristol), assumed to lie in 'Swineshead' Hundred, were, in 1086, the *capita* of small royal hundreds, as they were in later times.[8]

There may also have been a separate hundred of Winchcombe in 1086. Domesday Book says that Winchcombe 'rendered £6 as farm TRE . . . Afterwards, it rendered £20 with the whole hundred of the same vill'.[9] Sometimes towns were treated as hundreds, as for example Cambridge in 1066, Gloucester in 1316[10] and Winchcombe itself from time to time; but the increase in value from £6 to £20 suggests that a separate hundred had been added to the borough revenue: this is likely to have been 'Greston' in which Winchcombe was situated. Unfortunately the moot of 'Greston' has not been located; if it had lain in Winchcombe, it would be easy to explain the fact that the hundred was alternatively named from the borough, for some of the later references to the hundred of Winchcombe are clearly to 'Greston'.[11] The same entry also states that 'Durand the sheriff added 100*s*. and Roger d'Ivry 60*s*. Now with the three hundreds associated with it, it renders £28 at 20(*d*.) to the ora'. The fact that three sums of money are involved (£20 plus 100*s*. plus 60*s*.) suggests that the revenue from two hundreds had been added to the existing sum of £20. This £20 itself appears, as we have seen, to be composed of £6 (which was the value of the borough TRE and may have increased later) plus the value of the 'whole hundred of the same vill'. The three hundreds may well have been 'Greston', 'Holford', later amalgamated with it, and Tibblestone.

This dependency of more than one hundred on a single vill is found in other counties, most notably Oxfordshire, and may be the remnant of a much older structure.[12] However, both in this case and in the other Gloucestershire instance—the two hundreds dependent on the royal manor of "Langeberge"—the phrasing suggests that the arrangement is quite recent. "Langeberge", with its member *Mene*, appears to be the solitary constituent of Kiftsgate Hundred. *Mene* can be identified as Meon (represented today by Meon Hill, Meon Hall and Lower Meon, now War.) and "Langeberge" itself was probably close by unless the hun-

[1] T. Hearne (ed.), *Hemingi Chartularium Ecclesiae Wigorniensis* (henceforward *Hemming's Cartulary*), i (London, Oxford, 1723), 280; Finberg (ed.), *Gloucestershire Studies*, 25; H. P. R. Finberg, *The Early Charters of the West Midlands* (2nd edn., Leicester, 1972), 228–35; A. Williams, 'An Introduction to the Gloucestershire Domesday', p.13 above.

[2] F. W. Maitland, *Domesday Book and Beyond* (Cambridge, 1897), 456. The DB total also seems to be roughly 2,400 hides.

[3] D. Hill, 'The Burghal Hidage: the Establishment of a Text', *MA* 13 (1969), 84–92; S. Keynes and M. Lapidge (eds. and trans.), *Alfred the Great* (Harmondsworth, 1983), 193–4, 339–41.

[4] These figures are taken from Taylor, *Analysis of the Domesday Survey of Gloucestershire*.

[5] The first normal hundred head (at the end of a line) occurs above Thornbury on f.163v.

[6] GDB 163.

[7] GDB 162v.

[8] For example, the hundred of *Bertona Regis iuxta Gloucestriam* is mentioned in 1316 (*Feudal Aids*, ii (1900), 274) and the *Libertas Berton' Regis iuxta Bristoll'* in 1334 (R. E. Glasscock (ed.), *The Lay Subsidy of 1334*, Brit. Acad. Records of Social and Economic Hist. ns 2 (London, 1975), 91).

[9] GDB 162v.

[10] *Feudal Aids* (1900), ii. 264: 'In the hundred of Gloucester is the borough of Gloucester and there is no other vill in the hundred'. In Shropshire DB a hundred dependent on Shrewsbury is called both Shrewsbury Hundred and the City Hundred (*hundredum civitatis*).

[11] O. S. Anderson, *The English Hundred-Names: The South-Western Counties* (abbr. *EHNSW*) (Lund, Leipzig, 1939), 16–18.

[12] H. M. Cam, *Liberties and Communities in Medieval England: Collected Studies in Local Administration and Topography* (Cambridge, 1944; repr. London, 1963), 64–90.

dred was divided.[1] Meon Hill itself stretches south towards Chipping Campden and there are farms on it called Longlands and Long Hill in Mickleton parish.[2] Because the name Kiftsgate occurs twice (once in Mickleton and once on the boundary of Weston Subedge and Chipping Campden parishes),[3] the site of the moot is uncertain, but the size of the 'hundred' (a mere eight hides) is worthy of notice.[4] Since Kiftsgate is later the name of a hundred that amalgamated "Celfledetorn", Kiftsgate and 'Witley', it is possible that Kiftsgate had in 1086 just been established as the new centre of a hundredal grouping based on a royal manor. Kiftsgate may thus be the intended designation of the combined hundred, and the two hundreds placed in "Langeberge" by the sheriff may be "Celfledetorn" and 'Witley'. It would be even more explicable if the sheriff were reuniting hundreds that were formerly a unit.

Apart from naming them, Domesday says little else about the hundreds other than to record that Sevenhampton, though attached to Prestbury, lay outside the hundred of Cheltenham;[5] that by the judgement of the men of the hundred Winchcombe Abbey's manor of Windrush lay in Barrington Hundred not in Salmonsbury;[6] and that eight hides in Kemerton (now Worcs.) and three hides in Boddington had always rendered geld and done other services in Deerhurst Hundred.[7] The rest of Windrush seems also to have been in Barrington Hundred in 1086,[8] but the dispute may have been no more than academic since Salmonsbury Hundred (178 hides) and Barrington Hundred (twenty-three hides) could once have been a single 200-hide unit.

Reconstruction of the 1086 hundreds depends primarily on the evidence of Domesday, but for Gloucestershire the Domesday information can be cross-checked against a genuine 'satellite text', Evesham K,[9] and also against an abundance of thirteenth- and fourteenth-century material.[10] In many counties of Domesday Book the names of the hundreds are entered in the same order in most fiefs or in every fief.[11] This fact is invaluable in identifying mistaken or missing heads, but it does not apply to Gloucestershire. Such an order would anyway be difficult to perceive in a county that consists of so many small fiefs: thirty-four chapters contain but a single hundred heading, a further fourteen contain only two, and the largest chapter, apart from the *Terra Regis*, is Chapter 78 comprising only fifteen hundred-names.[12]

TABLE 1: The Hundreds of Gloucestershire

Modern Name	Form(s) found in Domesday Book	Number on map
Bagstone	*Bachestanes*	XXXIII
Barrington	*Bernินton-e, Berniton-e*	XIX
*Berkeley		XXVII
Bibury	*Becheberie, Begeberie, Begebriges*	XXIII
Bisley	*Biselege, Biseleie*	XXII
"Blachelaue"	*Blacelew, Blachelaue, Blachelawes,*[1] *Blacheleu, Blachelew*	XXI
Bledisloe	*Blideslau, Blideslawe, Bliteslau*	XX
Botloe	*Botelau, Botelewes, Boteslau*	VI
'Bradley'	*Bradeleg-e, Bradelei*	XIV
Brentry	*Bernintreu*	XXXV
'Brightwells Barrow'	*Bricstuoldes, Brictuoldesberg, Brictwoldesberg, Bristoldesberg*	XXXI
"Celfledetorn"	*Celflede, Celfledetorn-e, Celfleode, Ceolflede*	I
Cheltenham	*Cilteham, Ciltenham, Cliteham*	XII
Cirencester	*Cirecestre*[2]	XXIX
Deerhurst	*Derhest-e*	VII
'Dudstone'	*Dodestan, Dudestan-es, Dunestan-e*	XI
"Edredestane"	*Ederestan, Edredestan-e, Hedredestan*	XXXIX
"Gersdones"	*Gersdon-es, Gersdunes*	XXX
'Greston'	*Gretestan-e, Gretestanes*	V
"Grimboldestou"	*Grimboldestou, Grimboldestowes*	XXXIV
'Holford'	*Holeford-es, Holiforde*	IX
Kiftsgate	*Cheftesihat*	II
"Langebrige"	*Langebrige, Tolangebriges*	X
'Langley'	*Langelei, Langenei*	XXXII
"Letberge"	*Letberg-e*	XXXVI
Longtree	*Langetreu, Langetrew-es*	XXVIII
Lydney	*Ledenei*	XXIV
Pucklechurch	*Pulcecerge, Pulcrecerce*	XXXVIII
Rapsgate	*Respiet, Respiget-e*	XVIII
Salmonsbury	*Salemanesberie, Salmanesberie, Salemones, Salemonesberie, Salesmanesberie*	XV
'Swineshead'	*Sineshouedes, Suinheue*	XXXVII
*Tewkesbury		IV
Tibblestone	*Tedboldestan, Tetboldestane-s*	VIII
Tidenham	*Tedeneham*	XXVI
"Wacrescumbe"	*Wacrescumbe*	XIII
Westbury	*Westberie-s*	XVI
'Whitstone'	*Witestan*	XVII
'Witley'	*Widelei, Wideles, Witelai*	III
Wyvern	*Tuiferde, Twiferde*	XXV

* Does not occur as a hundred-name in the text, but assumed to have been a manorial hundred in 1086.

[1] In the facsimile the suprascript *H* above the *c* of *BLACELAWES* is not completely clear.

[2] It is not certain how the abbreviated form *Cirecestr'* should be expanded.

[1] GDB 163. "Langeberge" itself can scarcely be Longborough, despite the arguments of Warmington, 'Domesday Manor of Langeberge cum Mene'; see Moore (ed.), *Domesday Book: Gloucestershire*, note to 1,12.

[2] NGR SP 1641 and SP 1542 respectively.

[3] Respectively Kiftsgate Court (NGR SP 1743) and the Kiftsgate Stone (NGR SP 1339). The former is normally regarded as an antiquarian revival (Smith, *Place-Names of Gloucestershire* (abbr. *PNGlos.*), i (1964), 230), yet it makes better topographical sense and there is a Spelsbury Barn (OE *spell*, 'speech' and *beorg*, 'hill'), perhaps the moot site, close by at NGR SP 173433.

[4] The DB phrasing is ambiguous, but Evesham K (see n.9 below) makes it clear that the eight hides are shared between "Langeberge" and Meon.

[5] GDB 165. The point would not normally need making, since in most counties berewicks (except for some lands of some churches) are members of the hundreds in which they are geographically situated. In Gloucestershire, however, most are in the hundred of the head manor; see pp.44–5 below. Thus on f.164v the additional information about Aycote – 'it belongs to Bibury' – is equivalent to a hundred head: it belonged to Bibury manor and so was in Bibury Hundred.

[6] GDB 165v.

[7] GDB 166. Joined to the manor of Tewkesbury by Gerard the chamberlain and never returned to Deerhurst; see p.47 below.

[8] The "Gersdones" hundred heading above the second entry for Windrush in Ch. 78 (f.170v) is probably an error; see p.43 below.

[9] Transcribed and edited in H. B. Clarke, 'The Early Surveys of Evesham Abbey: An Investigation into the Problem of Continuity in Anglo-Norman England' (unpubl. Ph.D. thesis, Birmingham Univ., 1977). Discussed and partly calendared in Moore (ed.), *Domesday Book: Gloucestershire*, Appendix.

[10] In addition to *Feudal Aids* and the *Lay Subsidy Rolls*, one can consult with profit the *Rotuli Hundredorum*, 2 vols. (Record Commission, London, 1812–18), and *The Book of Fees*, 2 vols. and Index (HMSO, London, 1920–31).

[11] This is discussed in P. H. Sawyer, 'The "Original Returns" and Domesday Book', *EHR* 70 (1955), 177–97; see esp. p.181.

[12] These figures include a few restored hundred heads.

Thus no chapter contains any figure that approaches all forty hundreds; nor could this be so, since some hundreds are tied to particular holders, especially churches. On the other hand, some patterns do emerge: several hundreds end one chapter and begin another as if the compiler looked for an estate of the next fief-holder in the hundred check-list on which he had just been working;[1] sometimes hundreds are in inverse order in adjacent chapters.[2]

Both internal and later evidence suggest that the rubrication itself is nearly complete. There are about 250 hundred heads and apart from seven that are absent from the land of the king (five of them identical with the name of the relevant manor), a mere five more seem to be missing from the other seventy-seven chapters.[3] A single hundred head normally governs a block of manors, but on two occasions Domesday Book eliminates all doubt about the hundred in which an unnamed place lay by inserting *in eodem hundredo* ('in the same hundred') or *in ipso hundredo* ('in this hundred').[4] In three cases error may be suspected. There seems to be no good tenurial reason and no later evidence for placing part of Sezincote (Ch. 53) in "Celfledetorn" Hundred rather than with the rest of the vill in 'Witley'. A portion of Latton (now all in Wilts.), if correctly identified, probably lay in "Gersdones" Hundred not in Salmonsbury; while a "Gersdones" hundred head seems to have been placed in error above the second entry for Windrush in Chapter 78: it probably lay in Barrington, like the rest of the vill.[5]

Thus the Gloucestershire folios provide good evidence on which to base a map: most vills can be allocated to hundreds with certainty, and lines can be drawn between them which normally follow parish boundaries where it can be assumed that the vill and the later parish were co-extensive. On the other hand, a number of estates and some entire later parishes, not named in Domesday Book, but implicitly included in the entry for some other manor, can only be placed in their probable 1086 hundred on the basis of later evidence: for example, Cranham[6] in Rapsgate Hundred, Stroud[7] in Bisley Hundred, as well as Prescott[8] in Tewkesbury Hundred. A few problems of detail remain, especially in the Bristol area.[9]

The pattern that emerges is complex, both in terms of the boundary of the county and the limits of individual hundreds. While in the centre and the south-east of the shire there is a characteristic patchwork of large, geographically unified hundreds with a variety of tenancies—lay, ecclesiastical and royal—the arrangement on the northern boundary, in the area around Bristol and west of the river Severn, is quite different. The complicated interweaving of hundreds in these parts does not seem to have had a single cause, nor to have arisen at any one time: rather, 1086 seems to catch a moment in the kaleidoscopic changes produced by the conflicting tendencies of old units to fragment and new ones to accrete.

In the north of the county much of the disruption of other hundreds is caused by the intrusion of scattered parts of the great multiple estates of Deerhurst and Tewkesbury. Both vills were royal *tunas* with minster churches and one or both may have been ancient centres of administration of large tracts of Mercian territory. By 1086 they had parted company in terms of tenure: Tewkesbury, perhaps at one time the 100-hide endowment of a minster church, had returned to royal hands, while Deerhurst, like Pershore (Worcs.), had been divided between two churches, in this case St Peter of Westminster and Saint-Denis of Paris.[10] The original Tewkesbury Hundred, while still having some detached portions, may have been more compact: Domesday seems to imply that to the basic 100 hides[11] had been added others acquired, perhaps by commendation, by its TRE holder, Beorhtric. These additional thirty-five and a quarter hides lay in Ashton under Hill (now Worcs.), Kemerton (now Worcs.), Boddington, Wincot (now War.), Alderton, Dixton, 'Hentage' (in Alderton), Twyning and Stoke Orchard, and these vills are in most cases both marginal to, or separated from, the main body of the hundred and divided or disputed with other hundreds (listed below in Table 2).[12] Even

[1] See Chs. 5–6; 23–4; 42–3; 54–5; 59–60. This does not mean that the order of hundreds dictated the order of these chapters: for example, Ch. 6 had to be the land of the Bishop of Coutances, as the land of the last bishop before the lands of the churches were detailed. It merely means that the scribe began the second of each of these chapters with land in the same hundred as had finished the preceding chapter.

[2] In Chs. 6–9 Pucklechurch and 'Langley' Hundreds alternate in the order Ch. 6: Pucklechurch . . . 'Langley'; Ch. 7: 'Langley', Pucklechurch; Ch. 8: Pucklechurch; Ch. 9: 'Langley'.

[3] Ignoring the seven missing in Ch. 1, hundred heads may need to be supplied as follows: 'Dudstone' above 'Barton' (in Gloucester) (f.162v); 'Swineshead' above Barton (in Bristol) (f.163); for both see p.41 above. More certainly, 'Dudstone' should be added above Churchdown (f.164v); Wyvern above Madgetts (f.167v); Cirencester above Baunton (f.168v); 'Greston' above Sudeley (f.169); and Botloe above Pauntley etc. (f.170). This list agrees with Moore (ed.), *Domesday Book: Gloucestershire*, except that he uses Twyford as his chosen form for Wyvern Hundred, and restores a Barrington hundred head above Windrush (f.165v), when the information is in fact included in the latter part of the entry.

[4] GDB 162v, 166v.

[5] A minor scribal slip is the omission of *Hund'* after *In Grimboldestou* on f.166.

[6] NGR SO 8912.

[7] NGR SO 8505.

[8] NGR SO 9829.

[9] The exact boundary of "Letberge" Hundred (which probably included Cattybrook, Easter Compton and Over, NGR ST 5883, 5782, 5882) is hard to determine because of the tenurial complexity of Almondsbury parish; see J. S. Moore, 'The Gloucestershire Section of Domesday Book: Geographical Problems of the Text, Part 1', *Trans. of the Bristol and Gloucestershire Archaeol. Soc.* (abbr. *TBGAS*), 105 (1987), 114–16. Likewise the 1086 bounds of Kingsweston (in Bristol) are uncertain: the adjacent Shirehampton and Lawrence Weston, unnamed in DB, have been assumed to lie in Brentry Hundred where they certainly did later (Glasscock (ed.), *Lay Subsidy of 1334*, 102); see E. S. Lindley, 'The Anglo-Saxon Charters of Stoke Bishop', *TBGAS* 78 (1959), 97, 102. The boundaries of all the hundreds have been checked against those given on the maps of C. and J. Greenwood, *A Map of the County of Gloucestershire from an Actual Survey made in the year 1823* (London, 1824), and of Isaac Taylor, *Map of the County of Gloucester* (Ross, 1777), the latter reproduced in *A Gloucestershire and Bristol Atlas*, ed. W. L. King (London, 1961).

[10] See Williams, 'Introduction', p.27 above.

[11] These 100 hides probably consisted of the 95 summarized on f.163 plus 5 hides at Oxenton (f.163v).

[12] See also *VCH Gloucestershire*, vi (1965), 186.

those members of the core of ninety-five hides that lay in other counties—Hanley Castle (Worcs.) and Shenington (Oxon.)—may have been quite recent accretions: the four hides of Hanley Castle seem to be needed to make up the 1,200 hides of Worcestershire in 1086. Deerhurst's scattered pattern is expected, being that of a major ecclesiastical hundred,[1] but it is even better understood if it had once formed a 200-hide unit with Tibblestone Hundred or a 300-hide unit with both Tibblestone and Tewkesbury Hundreds.[2] In the south of the county, the multiple royal estate of Berkeley, also based on a minster church, and assessed at nearly 150 hides in Domesday Book, may also have progressively drawn members out of their geographical hundreds, especially in the area around Bristol.

Any simple, original pattern of hundreds is also distorted by the existence in 1086 of other scattered one-owner hundreds, usually attached to a church. In the south, Brentry Hundred held by the Bishop of Worcester had probably been combined from the members of existing territorial hundreds, while Bibury, also in large part held by the Bishop of Worcester, and "Langebrige", held mainly by Gloucester Church, may once have been entirely ecclesiastical hundreds—though, if that were so, parts had been alienated by 1086. Bibury Hundred, despite being of mixed tenure in Domesday Book, was a liberty of the Bishop of Worcester[3] and had probably been severed from some larger unit. "Langebrige" had perhaps been cut off from Botloe or from Westbury Hundred: its outlier at Preston (in Dymock) was no doubt in the hundred as a result of its association with Highnam. "Wacrescumbe" Hundred may also have been a hundred of the Bishop of Worcester,[4] and Cheltenham a breakaway unit of thirty hides based on a small minster church. This process continued after 1086, when the Bishop of Worcester made his portion of Tibblestone Hundred, centred on Bishop's Cleeve, into a separate hundred.

Unusual in other counties, but quite common in Gloucestershire, was the tendency for the solitary manor of a tenant-in-chief, usually a church, which lay in one hundred to become attached to a hundred in which the tenant had more or larger manors. Similarly, the members of a manor may have been counted with their *caput* in its hundred, rather than in the hundred where they actually lay—this being a parallel, though on a smaller scale, to the arrangement of Deerhurst, Tewkesbury and Berkeley Hundreds. Thus Lark Stoke and Lower Lark Stoke (both now War.), Hidcote Bartrim and part of Weston-on-Avon (now War.), though lying geographically in "Celfledetorn"

[1] Compare the Domesday hundreds of 'Oswaldslow' (Worcs.), Leominster (Herefs.) and 'Bishop Giso's Hundred' (Som.). Sutton-under-Brailes (now War.) and Little Compton (now War.) are detached parts of Deerhurst Hundred surrounded by other counties.

[2] See *VCH Gloucestershire*, vi. 238; viii (1968), 243. In *Feudal Aids*, ii. 252, 289, Deerhurst and Tibblestone Hundreds are treated as one.

[3] See *VCH Gloucestershire*, vii (1981), 1.

[4] See Williams, 'Introduction', pp. 14–15 above.

TABLE 2: Places in Gloucestershire divided between hundreds in 1086

Vill or land-unit	Hundreds between which divided, including number on map
*Alderton	Tewkesbury and 'Greston' Hundreds, IV and V (Alderton and Frampton)
Ashton under Hill (now Worcs.)	Tewkesbury and Tibblestone Hundreds, IV and VIII
*Coberley	'Bradley' and Rapsgate Hundreds, XIV and XVIII (Upper Coberley and Coberley)
*Colesbourne	"Wacrescumbe" and Rapsgate Hundreds, XIII and XVIII (Little Colesbourne and Colesbourne)
Condicote	'Witley' and Salmonsbury Hundreds, III and XV
Duntisbourne Abbots	Rapsgate and Cirencester Hundreds, XVIII and XXIX
*Haresfield	'Dudstone' and 'Whitstone' Hundreds, XI and XVII (Haresfield and Haresfield Court)
*Hidcote	"Celfledetorn" and 'Witley' Hundreds, I and III (Hidcote Boyce and Hidcote Bartrim)
Kemerton (now Worcs.)	Tewkesbury and Deerhurst Hundreds, IV and VII
*Lemington	Tewkesbury and Deerhurst Hundreds, IV and VII (Lower Lemington and Lemington)
Sezincote	"Celfledetorn" and 'Witley' Hundreds, I and III
*Stoke	"Letberge" Hundred, XXXVI (Stoke Gifford)[1], and 'Swineshead' Hundred, XXXVII (Harry Stoke)
Stoke Orchard	Tewkesbury and Tibblestone Hundreds, IV and VIII
*Swell	'Witley' and Salmonsbury Hundreds, III and XV (Upper Swell and Lower Swell)
Tidenham	Tidenham and Wyvern Hundreds, XXVI and XXV
*Twyning	Tewkesbury and 'Greston' Hundreds, IV and V (The Mythe and Twyning)
*Walton	Tewkesbury and Deerhurst Hundreds, IV and VII (Walton Cardiff and Deerhurst Walton)
Wapley	'Swineshead' and Pucklechurch Hundreds, XXXVII and XXXVIII
Weston-on-Avon (now War.)	"Celfledetorn" and 'Witley' Hundreds, I and III
Wincot (now War.)	'Witley' and Tewkesbury Hundreds, III and IV
Woodchester	"Blachelaue" and Longtree Hundreds, XXI and XXVIII
Places probably divided in 1086, but one part is not named in Domesday Book	
*Coln	Deerhurst Hundred, VII (Coln St Dennis), and 'Bradley' Hundred, XIV (†Coln Rogers)[2]
Ruddle	Westbury Hundred, XVI (Ruddle), and Bledisloe Hundred, XX[3]
In the following places the same piece of land is disputed between adjacent hundreds	
Boddington	three hides disputed between Tewkesbury and Deerhurst Hundreds, IV and VII, on ff. 163v, 166
Kemerton (now Worcs.)	eight hides disputed between Tewkesbury and Deerhurst Hundreds, IV and VII, on ff. 163v, 166
Stoke Orchard	three hides less one virgate disputed between Tewkesbury and Tibblestone Hundreds, IV and VIII, on ff. 163v, 165
Windrush	three and a half hides disputed between Salmonsbury and Barrington Hundreds, XV and XIX, on f. 165v.[4]

* Domesday vill now represented by two or more modern settlements, lying in adjacent hundreds. In the cases of Alderton and Twyning, one of the settlements (Frampton and The Mythe respectively) acquired a more specific name after 1086. It is not certain how many of the places listed above were already represented by separate settlements in the late eleventh century.

† Implied but not named in Domesday Book.

[1] The five hides of Stoke Gifford are recorded twice in D B, once as an unnamed member of the large manor of Westbury on Trym (in Bristol) (f. 164v), which lay in Brentry Hundred, XXXV, and once as a separate named holding in "Letberge" Hundred, XXXVI (f. 168v). Thus the Stoke Gifford portion of this divided vill was further disputed between two hundreds.

[2] Corresponds to the unnamed royal manor of ten hides on f. 163.

[3] The unnamed half-hide held by Walter the crossbowman, entered immediately below the named entry for Ruddle on f. 169.

[4] Windrush is additionally said to be divided between Barrington and "Gersdones" Hundreds, XIX and XXX, but this is probably an error in rubrication.

Hundred, seem to have become attached to 'Witley' Hundred where Evesham Abbey had its major holding of Willersey.[1] Both Twyning and Snowshill (held by the Church of Winchcombe) were isolated geographically from their hundreds ('Greston' and 'Holford') and probably only connected to them by tenure. Notgrove and Cold Aston were attached to "Wacrescumbe", though geographically separate from it, since they were members of Withington held by Worcester Church. Upper Coberley, as a portion of Northleach held by the Archbishop of York, was a remote part of 'Bradley' Hundred, while Wapley, as a member of Bitton manor, though detached from 'Swineshead' Hundred, depended on it.[2] Aycote, as a manor of the Bishop of Worcester, though surrounded by Rapsgate Hundred, belonged to Bibury. Widford (Oxon.) seems to have become attached to Barrington Hundred by the desire of the Archbishop of York to keep his one Oxfordshire estate with his Gloucestershire holdings or because his subtenant, St Oswald of Gloucester, wished its land to remain in the county.

The result is that several hundreds, which may well once have been continuous, were left truncated or broken up: "Celfledetorn", 'Witley' and Tibblestone by the intrusion of Worcestershire and parts of Deerhurst and Tewkesbury Hundreds. Coln Rogers, the unnamed ten hides held by the king in 'Bradley' Hundred,[3] may once have been connected to the rest of Salmonsbury Hundred, but in 1086 was severed by Coln St Dennis, a member of Deerhurst Hundred. "Letberge" Hundred lying to the north of Bristol may have been the remaining splinter of an original hundred, dismembered when parts of Berkeley Hundred were drawn from it and Brentry Hundred was created. The interlacing of Rapsgate and Cirencester Hundreds in the lands of the modern parish of Duntisbourne Abbots was particularly complicated. In 1086, as a result of this continuous process of change, large numbers of vills were divided by or disputed between hundreds (listed above in Table 2). In most cases this was because a portion of the vill was or had become part of a single-owner hundred: most notably of the hundreds of Deerhurst and Tewkesbury. Some vills however, for example Woodchester, were divided only because they lay close to the boundaries of 'normal' hundreds.[4]

Not only were internal boundaries complicated, but the boundary between Gloucestershire and the counties of Worcestershire, Warwickshire and Oxfordshire was equally complex—with many projections, detachments and interpenetration—and for many similar reasons. The sequence of events is difficult to determine and to date, but the border was not simply drawn, as has often been said, so as to include in Worcestershire lands of the Churches of Worcester, Evesham, Pershore and Westminster. All these churches also held land in Gloucestershire in 1086, much of it in the north of the county. Rather, the county boundary was drawn so as to allocate 1,200 hides to Worcestershire and 2,400 hides jointly to Gloucestershire and 'Winchcombeshire', and in so doing followed the boundaries of existing administrative units (the hundreds) some of which were already discrete. In the case of the lands of Worcester Church it is possible to date a partial redrawing of their hundreds, which must also have affected the lands of Evesham, Pershore and Westminster Churches, interspersed with them. There exists a charter—the Altitonantis, dating from 964[5]—which created for Worcester Church a 300-hide ship-soke: the hundred of 'Oswaldslow'. This was done by adding to the monks' fifty hides of Cropthorne (Worcs.), which formed the hundred of "Cuthburgelawe", other lands which had previously been subject to 'royal exactions',[6] and most of which might have been expected geographically to form a part of 'Winchcombeshire'. This new unit was added to "Wlfereslawe", an already scattered episcopal hundred in the heart of Worcestershire, and to a third hundred, "Winburgetrowe", created from Bredon (Worcs.), Blockley (then Worcs., but now in Glos.)[7] and Tredington (now War.), also episcopal lands, which would appear to have lain in the ambit of 'Winchcombeshire' and Warwickshire. Perhaps it is significant that there is no mention of counties in the charter, but whether the reorganization preceded or followed the laying down of the county boundary (in the latter case radically altering it), the assessment of each county seems to have remained the same.[8]

Incidental details complicate even this picture: Icomb, lying well within Gloucestershire, was divided

[1] See p.42, n.5 above. Upper Swell, also held by Evesham Church, was detached from 'Witley', but by the intrusion of a part of Condicote. This latter was itself a berewick of Oddington (f.164v) and so in Salmonsbury Hundred. Part of Wincot (War.) (f.167) lay in 'Witley' Hundred for no apparent reason, unless it too had been church land.

[2] Lasborough, though continuous with Longtree Hundred, projects from it in a way that suggests it had been drawn into the hundred, probably since it had the same holder as Rodmarton (f.166v).

[3] GDB 163.

[4] The division of Woodchester between "Blachelaue" and Longtree Hundreds is not recorded after Domesday (*VCH Gloucestershire*, xi (1976), 152). The exact division is unclear, but the brook that joins the river Frome outside Stroud would be a natural demarcation. One part was not hidated, but the relative values suggest a nearly equal split.

[5] P. H. Sawyer (ed.), *Anglo-Saxon Charters: An Annotated List and Bibliography*, R. Hist. Soc. Guides and Handbooks, 8 (London, 1968), no. 731.

[6] This probably means that they lay in 'normal' hundreds, but ecclesiastical hundreds that were not liberties were also subject to normal taxation, dues and services. The added lands included Overbury (Worcs.), Pendock (Worcs.), Teddington (now Glos.), Mitton (now Glos.), Sedgeberrow (Worcs.), Evenlode (now Glos.), Daylesford (now Glos.), part of Icomb (now Glos.), together with Northwick (in Blockley, now Glos.) and Dorn (now Glos.), not named in DB, all of which were close to the 1086 county boundary of Gloucestershire, or formed projections into it or islands within it.

[7] This occupied the same 'island' of land with Dorn and Northwick, but they were in different constituents of 'Oswaldslow' since they were held separately by the bishop and the monks.

[8] See A. Williams, 'An Introduction to the Worcestershire Domesday', *The Worcestershire Domesday*, eds. A. Williams and R. W. H. Erskine (London, 1988), 10–11, 15–16, and F. R. Thorn, 'Hundreds and Wapentakes', ibid. 35.

with Worcestershire,[1] Bickmarsh (now Worcs.) with Warwickshire, Wickhamford (Worcs.) with Worcestershire (although the one hide may not have been detached from Gloucestershire), and Latton (Wilts.), if correctly identified, with Wiltshire.[2] Fixed though the county boundary in 1086 may appear, it too was evolving: the royal portion of Woodchester was effectively in Wiltshire (although it did not stay there), because its farm had been placed there by Edward.[3] Likewise Kingswood, as an unnamed member of the Wiltshire manor of Chippenham, had at some point been withdrawn from the county and placed in Wiltshire, where it remained until 1844. The four hides of Great Barrington held by Ælfsige of Faringdon had probably, like lands in Oxfordshire, been added to his manor of Faringdon (Berks.) and were soon, if not already, counted as a part of Berkshire, where they remained until the nineteenth century.[4] In 1190 part of Minety (Wilts.) was purchased with Cirencester from Richard I by the Abbot and convent of Cirencester and from that time at least lay in Gloucestershire; it is not certain if it was an outlying part of Cirencester Hundred—and therefore in Gloucestershire—in 1086.[5]

In the Forest of Dean area Domesday Book catches hundred and county boundaries in flux.[6] The Gloucestershire 'hundreds' that lay west of the Severn and Leadon—Botloe, "Langebrige", Westbury, Bledisloe, Lydney, Wyvern, Tidenham—had, it seems, been considered part of Herefordshire until 1020 and remained a part of Hereford diocese until 1541.[7] Soon after 1086, a group of manors deemed to lie in Bromsash Hundred, Herefordshire, were drawn into Gloucestershire: they were 'Newarne' (in East Dean), Redbrook, Ruardean, Staunton, 'Whippington' (in Staunton), and Alvington which had been a detachment of that hundred. 'Newarne', though listed in the Herefordshire folios, had already in effect been transferred to Gloucestershire by Roger de Pitres,[8] and Kingstone (in Weston under Penyard, Herefs.) was in an equivocal position, rendering geld and doing service in Gloucestershire, but also attending pleas in Herefordshire.[9]

Pinched between the Forest and the Severn, this area was and remains marginal land. Wyegate and Hewelsfield had been taken into the Forest; Mitcheldean and English Bicknor at either end of the Forest were free of geld for guarding it.[10] Like the arrangements on the Somerset edge of Exmoor, administration was based on a series of smallish manors, mostly royal, which had not yet combined or developed into hundreds.[11] Tidenham and Wyvern had perhaps once been a single unit before Tidenham was acquired by the Church of Bath; they later recombined and, following the transfer of the Herefordshire land to Gloucestershire, a new hundred of St Briavels was created to the north of them. Westbury-on-Severn appears to have originated as a multiple estate and had had a number of dependencies—Kyre (Worcs.), Clifton upon Teme (Worcs.), Newent (Glos.), Kingstone (in Weston under Penyard, Herefs.), Edvin Loach (now Herefs.)—some of them a considerable distance away where the northern boundaries of Herefordshire and Worcestershire met, although these may not have been original members of the estate.[12]

Royal manors were important in the Gloucestershire land between the Severn and the Wye; they also named a

[1] The Worcestershire portion was 'Church Icomb', usually called just Icomb on modern maps (NGR SP 2122), while the Gloucestershire portion was Icomb Place and Icomb Proper (NGR SP 2122, SP 2022 respectively). The distinction has ceased to have much value now that both parts are in the same county.

[2] Moore (ed.), *Domesday Book: Gloucestershire*, note to 71,1. Latton may have been included in Glos. in error by a misdivision of inquest material at an earlier stage, since Humphrey the cook does not appear as a separate landholder in Wilts. (although he is joint holder of Widhill (Wilts.) with Theobald). But the shape of the county boundary suggests that a part of Latton may once have lain in Glos., though in "Gersdones" Hundred rather than in Salmonsbury.

[3] GDB 164. Probably Edward of Salisbury, Sheriff of Wiltshire.

[4] See F. R. Thorn, 'Hundreds and Wapentakes', *The Berkshire Domesday*, eds. A. Williams and R. W. H. Erskine (London, 1988), 31.

[5] *VCH Gloucestershire*, ii (1907), 80, n.12. Five hides at Minety had been granted in the mid ninth century to Malmesbury Abbey by Æthelwulf, King of the West Saxons (Sawyer (ed.), *Anglo-Saxon Charters*, nos. 320, 322). This suggests that the land lay in Wessex, not Mercia, at that stage, but it is uncertain whether the five hides then included the portion that later lay in Gloucestershire. The outline of Minety is indicated on the Wiltshire map in the present series.

[6] The exact line of the boundary between Gloucestershire and Herefordshire in 1086 in the area of the Forest of Dean is at present unclear, because the changes that produced the modern boundaries were made soon after 1086. A fuller study of tenures is needed to refine it. However, the fact that Wyegate, St Briavels and Allaston were in Gloucestershire in 1086 helps to define the southern boundary of Herefordshire. On the less certain eastern edge of the Forest, for the purpose of this study, it has been assumed that the later parishes of Abinghall, Flaxley and Littledean (not separately mentioned in DB) lay in Gloucestershire in 1086: see *VCH Gloucestershire*, x (1972), 1.

[7] Finberg, *Early Charters*, 225–7. Lea, mentioned in the Herefordshire folios (f.182v), was later partly in Gloucestershire (a detached part of that county took in most of the centre of the village). This was so from at least 1334 (Glasscock (ed.), *Lay Subsidy of 1334*, 104, 122) until the nineteenth century, but it is not clear if the village was so divided in 1086.

[8] GDB 181.

[9] GDB 182v. It had been a member of Westbury-on-Severn (f.163).

[10] The bulk of the Forest of Dean no doubt lay in Herefordshire, for it intruded on a number of Herefordshire manors and is probably represented by the £15 which William fitzNorman pays 'for the forests which he holds' (f.181). If *Sapina*, mentioned in the Gloucestershire entry for the manor of Westbury-on-Severn (f.163), means 'fir-wood', then it might be that the Forest had been an appurtenance of Westbury-on-Severn before 1066. Against this it can be urged that *sap(p)inus*, 'fir', 'spruce', perhaps 'conifer', is a masculine noun elsewhere in Latin, that *sapina* is not otherwise found in DB and is surprisingly specific where *foresta* might have been expected. Moreover, the word has a capital *S* and is rubricated as if it were a place-name. It could be a metathesis of *Sapian* which is a possible early form of (Lower) Sapey (Worcs.), one of the unnamed constituents of the ten hides of Clifton upon Teme mentioned earlier in this same Westbury-on-Severn entry; see n.12 below. The form *Sapian* is found in a charter (Sawyer (ed.), *Anglo-Saxon Charters*, no.121) and in Hearne (ed.), *Hemming's Cartulary*, i. 251. In this edition it has been treated as a place-name of uncertain identification, "Sapina".

[11] Lydney (f.164) was only recently a royal manor. Bledisloe lay in the royal manor of Awre.

[12] The ten hides of Clifton upon Teme included parts at Little Stanford, Shelsley Walsh, Hamcastle, Lower Sapey and Tenbury Wells. Kyre and Clifton upon Teme had been possessions of Worcester Church. See Hearne (ed.), *Hemming's Cartulary*, i. 251, 255, and Moore, 'Gloucestershire Section of Domesday Book', 118–21.

number of hundreds in the core of the county.[1] Even when this was not so, the hundred moot was sometimes within the bounds of a royal manor. This was certainly the case with 'Langley' which had its moot in Alveston, Longtree which had its moot in Avening, and Botloe which had its moot in Newent. The pattern may have applied more generally: the moot of 'Dudstone' was probably in 'Barton' (in Gloucester), and that of 'Swineshead' in Bitton. The hundred of Salmonsbury appears to have been attached to the royal manor of Lower Slaughter, since manor and hundred made a single joint payment. The hundred of Bledisloe probably depended on Awre, while royal manors such as "Langeberge" and Winchcombe probably each served as the *caput* of a hundred even though they did not name it. Furthermore, each dominated a group of hundreds, some of whose members would otherwise have lacked a royal presence.[2] This lends support to the notion that many hundreds were at some time appurtenances of manors, frequently royal ones, even though it is unclear whether the arrangement was original or subsequent to the creation of the hundred.[3]

In this and in other ways fragmentary hints in Domesday Book allow a fascinating glimpse of earlier administrative arrangements. Winchcombe, which had been a county, is once called a *ferding* (a 'quarter') and it is stated that all fifty-six hides of Evesham Church lay there, in the hundreds of Salmonsbury and 'Witley'.[4] Other evidence, especially from charters, suggests that 'Winchcombeshire' had contained the Domesday hundreds of 'Greston', 'Witley', Kiftsgate, "Celfledetorn", 'Holford', Cheltenham, Tibblestone, Salmonsbury, "Wacrescumbe" and Barrington, and that Mitton and Daylesford (parts of 'Oswaldslow' Hundred, Worcs., in 1086) and no doubt other lands, had once been included.[5] One *ferding* implies three others and it may be that the seven hundreds of Cirencester and the seven hundreds of 'Grumbalds Ash', centred perhaps on Bitton or Bristol (though only evidenced after Domesday), were in reality older units. A final *ferding*, smaller than the rest, depended perhaps on Gloucester.[6] But these *ferdings* cannot pre-date the laying down of the shire and before them the administrative structure may have consisted of large areas of land dependent on royal *tunas*, having minster churches. These tracts of land may later have been hidated and divided into hundreds, some of which were soon severed entirely from their *capita*, while others—separated partly on geographical lines, partly by tenure and so to some extent interwoven—remained grouped in twos or threes.[7] Deerhurst, Tewkesbury and Tibblestone may once have been 300 hides dependent on Tewkesbury; Berkeley, "Blachelaue" and 'Whitstone' perhaps three hundreds associated with Berkeley.[8] However, although tenure seems important in defining the shape of hundreds, so is geography: the rivers, both major and minor, the western escarpment of the Cotswolds and the Fosse Way all play their parts.

The relationship of the 1086 hundreds to those of the later Middle Ages is detailed below in Table 3. Nearly all the changes are of name or due to amalgamation or division: only in the Forest of Dean area was there a larger reorganization.[9] Some individual transfers took place; most were of minor importance,[10] but some represent the resolution of disputes mentioned or implied in Domesday Book. Thus the three hides at Boddington and eight hides of Kemerton (now Worcs.) which Gerard had joined to Tewkesbury Hundred but which, it was stated, had always rendered geld and services in Deerhurst,[11] none the less remained in Tewkesbury Hundred. Gerard's holding at Bourton-on-the-Hill,[12] though not said to be a source of dispute in 1086, was also put into Tewkesbury Hundred.[13] In 1086 Bernard and Reginald held seven hides of Bishop's Cleeve at Stoke Orchard in Tibblestone Hundred and were refusing to do service to St Mary's of Worcester. Bernard's three hides had already in effect been transferred to Tewkesbury Hundred, and remained there.[14]

SOUTH WALES

By 1086 the Normans had penetrated the Welsh border at every point and were holding portions of Wales. The area that Gloucestershire Domesday Book calls 'Wales' was only briefly surveyed, though more

[1] Useful information is contained in Anderson, *EHNSW*, 1–34; in Smith, *PNGlos.*, and in the *VCH Gloucestershire* topographical volumes.

[2] See p.41 above. Neither 'Witley' nor "Celfledetorn" Hundreds, which were probably attached to the royal manor of "Langeberge", themselves contained any holdings of the king.

[3] See Cam, *Liberties and Communities*, 64–90. The most ancient and important royal manors were probably those such as Cheltenham, 'Barton' (in Gloucester), Cirencester, Bitton, Westbury-on-Severn and Awre, which were characterized by food renders or payments of a part or the whole of a night's farm.

[4] GDB 166.

[5] Finberg, *Early Charters*, 228–35.

[6] See Cam, *Liberties and Communities*, 91–106, and Williams, 'Introduction', p.14 above. The transfer of part of Herefordshire after 1020 will have added about 200 hides.

[7] On this aspect of hundredal history, see P. H. Hase, 'The Development of the Parish in Hampshire, particularly in the Eleventh and Twelfth Centuries' (unpubl. Ph.D. dissertation, Cambridge Univ., 1975).

[8] It has already been suggested that Salmonsbury and Barrington were a 200-hide unit; and that Tidenham/Wyvern, "Langebrige"/ Botloe (or Westbury) and "Celfledetorn"/'Witley' may once have been single units.

[9] See Hart, 'Hundred of St Briavels'; *idem*, 'Metes and Bounds of the Forest of Dean'.

[10] Prestbury was transferred from Cheltenham Hundred to Deerhurst Hundred, Doynton to 'Langley and Swineshead' Hundred from Pucklechurch. Didcot (unnamed but in Tibblestone Hundred in 1086, Moore (ed.), *Domesday Book: Gloucestershire*, note to 1,59) was absorbed by Tewkesbury Hundred. Stanley Pontlarge, apparently in Tewkesbury Hundred in 1086, was subsequently in 'Holford and Greston', *VCH Gloucestershire*, vi. 186.

[11] GDB 166.

[12] GDB 163v.

[13] *VCH Gloucestershire*, vi. 185–6, 203–4. All three are here mapped in Deerhurst Hundred. The portion of Boddington that was transferred to Tewkesbury Hundred lay at Barrow (NGR SO 8824); the portion remaining in Deerhurst Hundred was at Hayden and Withy Bridge (NGR SO 9023, 9024); *VCH Gloucestershire*, viii. 170.

[14] GDB 163v, 165; *VCH Gloucestershire*, vi. 186. The holding has here been mapped in Tibblestone Hundred.

TABLE 3: The Domesday Hundreds of Gloucestershire, showing the places from which they were named, and their approximate relationship to the hundreds of the fourteenth century

Modern Name and number on map	Place from which named, with NGR if known and if not indexed below	Approximate relationship to the hundreds of the fourteenth century[1]
Bagstone, XXXIII	Bagstone in Wickwar parish (ST 6887)	Part amalgamated with "Grimboldestou", XXXIV, and "Edredestane", XXXIX, to form 'Grumbalds Ash';[2] remainder to Thornbury[3]
Barrington, XIX	Domesday manor of Great Barrington (royal)	Absorbed by Salmonsbury, XV
*Berkeley, XXVII	Domesday manor (royal)	Continued as Berkeley
Bibury, XXIII	Domesday manor (Abbey of Worcester)	Absorbed by 'Brightwells Barrow', XXXI
Bisley, XXII	Domesday manor (Earl Hugh). The moot was probably at the Wittantree (SO 902074)	Continued as Bisley
"Blachelaue", XXI	Name lost, site unknown	Absorbed by 'Whitstone', XVII
Bledisloe, XX	Domesday manor (royal)	Enlarged by the addition of Lydney, XXIV
Botloe, VI	Botloe's Green in Newent parish (ST 7228)	Continued as Botloe
'Bradley', XIV	Name lost. The moot was perhaps at Stowell Cross (SP 0913)	Enlarged by the addition of "Wacrescumbe", XIII
Brentry, XXXV	Brentry in Henbury parish (ST 5779)	Renamed Henbury
'Brightwells Barrow', XXXI	Probably named from the barrow which also named Barrow Elm Farm (SP 1604) in Hatherop parish, where the moot later was	Enlarged by the addition of Bibury, XXIII
"Celfledetorn", I	Name lost, site unknown	Absorbed by Kiftsgate, II
Cheltenham, XII	Domesday manor (royal)	Continued as Cheltenham
Cirencester, XXIX	Domesday manor (royal)	Renamed 'Crowthorne',[4] and enlarged by the addition of "Gersdones", XXX
Deerhurst, VII	Domesday manor (Abbey of St Peter of Westminster/ Abbey of Saint-Denis of Paris)	Divided into Westminster and Deerhurst Hundreds respectively according to tenure
'Dudstone', XI	Site uncertain, but probably near Kingsholm on the northern edge of Gloucester (SO c.834190)[5]	Enlarged by the addition of "Langebrige", X, but split into 'Dudstone' and 'Kings Barton' Hundreds[6]
"Edredestane", XXXIX	Name lost, site unknown. The moot was possibly at Dodington Ash (ST 7578) adjacent to Old Hundred (ST 765786) in Tormarton parish	Mostly amalgamated with Bagstone, XXXIII, and "Grimboldestou", XXXIV, to form 'Grumbalds Ash'[2]
"Gersdones", XXX	Name lost; site uncertain, but possibly near Down Ampney (SU 0996)	Amalgamated with most of Cirencester, XXIX, to form 'Crowthorne'[4]
'Greston', V	Name lost, site unknown	Amalgamated with 'Holford', IX, to form 'Holford and Greston' Hundred
"Grimboldestou", XXXIV	Site lost, but connected with the later name of the hundred, 'Grumbalds Ash'[2]	Amalgamated with part of Bagstone, XXXIII, and part of "Edredestane", XXXIX, to form 'Grumbalds Ash'[2]
'Holford', IX	Named from a ford in a deep hollow, probably near Ford (SP 0829) in Temple Guiting parish	Amalgamated with 'Greston', V, to form 'Holford and Greston' Hundred
Kiftsgate, II	Possibly represented by Kiftsgate Stone (SP 135390) on the boundary of Weston Subedge and Chipping Campden parishes; more probably by Kiftsgate Court in Mickleton parish (SP 1743)[7]	Enlarged by the addition of "Celfledetorn", I, and 'Witley', III
"Langebrige", X	Name lost, site unknown. Possibly an early name for Over Causeway, the long causeway which carries the A40 trunk road from Highnam to Gloucester (SO 8118)	Absorbed by 'Dudstone', XI
'Langley', XXXII	Name lost, but the site was in Alveston, near Wolfridge and Greenhill (ST 6387)	Amalgamated with 'Swineshead', XXXVII, to form 'Langley and Swineshead' Hundred. Part lost to Thornbury[3]
"Letberge", XXXVI	Name lost, site unknown. From Middle English *lete* (a 'court' or 'leet') and *beorg* ('hill')	Partly absorbed by Thornbury[3]
Longtree, XXVIII	Longtree Barn in Avening parish (ST 8796)	Continued as Longtree
Lydney, XXIV	Domesday manor (royal)	Mostly absorbed by Bledisloe, XX; part went to St Briavels Hundred[8]
Pucklechurch, XXXVIII	Domesday manor (Abbey of Gloucester)	Continued as Pucklechurch
Rapsgate, XVIII	Rapsgate in Colesbourne parish (SO 994110)	Continued as Rapsgate
Salmonsbury, XV	Salmonsbury Camp in Bourton on the Water parish (SP 1720)	Enlarged by the addition of Barrington, XIX
'Swineshead', XXXVII	Name lost; site uncertain, but perhaps in or near Bitton (ST 6869). Swineford (ST 6968) nearby in Somerset may be a related name	Amalgamated with 'Langley', XXXII, to form 'Langley and Swineshead' Hundred. Part lost to 'Barton Regis' Hundred[9]
*Tewkesbury, IV	Domesday manor and borough (royal)	Continued as Tewkesbury
Tibblestone, VIII	The Tibble Stone stood at the crossroads of the Stow-Tewkesbury and Cheltenham-Evesham roads (SO 963338)[10]	Northern part continued as Tibblestone; southern part became the hundred of Bishop's Cleeve[11]
Tidenham, XXVI	Domesday manor (royal in 1086, but formerly held by the Abbey of Bath)	Absorbed by Wyvern, XXV, and taken into the lordship of 'Strigoil' (Chepstow)[12]
"Wacrescumbe", XIII	Name lost, but the site lay in the bounds of Withington, probably at SP c.037170[13]	Absorbed by 'Bradley', XIV
Westbury, XVI	Domesday manor of Westbury-on-Severn (royal)	Continued as Westbury, but reduced by losses to St Briavels Hundred[8]
'Whitstone', XVII	A field name in Hardwicke parish (ST c.800118)	Enlarged by the addition of "Blachelaue", XXI
'Witley', III	Name lost, site uncertain, but survived as a hundred-name into the next century[14]	Absorbed by Kiftsgate, II
Wyvern, XXV	Wyvern Pond and Wyvern Farm in Woolaston parish[15]	Enlarged by the addition of Tidenham, XXVI, and taken into the lordship of 'Strigoil' (Chepstow)[12]

* Does not occur as a hundred-name in Domesday Book, but assumed to have enjoyed hundredal status in 1086.

NOTES TO TABLE 3

[1] Information, which occasionally conflicts, is derived from *Feudal Aids*, ii, and Glasscock (ed.), *Lay Subsidy of 1334*.
[2] The site of 'Grumbalds Ash' might be the same as "Grimboldestou", with substitution of OE *aesc* ('ash-tree') for *stou* ('place, meeting-place'); see Anderson, *EHNSW*, 29; Smith, *PNGlos.*, iii (1964), 22.
[3] Thornbury Hundred was formed from the manors of Thornbury and Gaunt's Earthcott from 'Langley' Hundred, XXXII, Iron Acton and Tytherington from Bagstone, XXXIII, Marshfield from "Edredestane", XXXIX, and 'Lee' (in Almondsbury) from "Letberge", XXXVI.
[4] 'Crowthorne' is a lost name, but may have been near 'Court Hall' in Daglingworth or Stratton parishes near Cirencester (Anderson, *EHNSW*, 26; Smith, *PNGlos.*, i. 66). The hundred is called Cirencester in 1316 (*Feudal Aids*, ii. 270).
[5] Dudstone in Hempstead parish (SU 817167 on the six-inch OS sheet 33NW of 1903 and 1921) is probably an antiquarian revival: Smith, *PNGlos.*, ii (1964), 135; see Anderson, *EHNSW*, 13.
[6] 'Kings Barton' Hundred contained the Domesday manors of 'Barton' (in Gloucester), Harescombe, Sandhurst, Upton St Leonards and (?)Wotton (in Gloucester), all with the exception of the last held by the king in 1086.
[7] See p.42, n.3 above.
[8] St Briavels Hundred was formed from parts of the hundreds of Westbury and Lydney, XVI and XXIV, and from the manors of Ruardean and Staunton which lay in Herefordshire in 1086.
[9] 'Barton Regis' Hundred near Bristol (not to be confused with the 'Kings Barton' Hundred near Gloucester discussed above, n.6) included Barton (in Bristol), Clifton (in Bristol) and Mangotsfield.
[10] The stone now stands outside the Teddington Hands garage (also SO 963338).
[11] It was 'Tibblestone with the Liberty of Cleeve' in 1316 (*Feudal Aids*, ii. 274), 'Cleeve Hundred' in 1334 (Glasscock (ed.), *Lay Subsidy of 1334*, 93).
[12] *VCH Gloucestershire*, x. i; *Calendar of the Patent Rolls 1364–7*, 275. Wyvern Hundred, incorporating Tidenham, was withdrawn from the county during the reign of Henry III (1216–72), becoming part of the Marcher lordship of 'Strigoil' (Chepstow). It was returned to the county by the Act of Union 1536 and put in Westbury Hundred.
[13] Sawyer (ed.), *Anglo-Saxon Charters*, no. 1556. The only known later form is *Wacrescymbe* from Hemming (early twelfth century); see Smith, *PNGlos.*, i. 163; Anderson, *EHNSW*, 5.
[14] *Wichtele* Hundred in the Pipe Roll for 1169; see Anderson, *EHNSW*, 17.
[15] OE *twi* and *fyrde* ('double ford') referring to a double stream crossing made by the Roman road, now the A48, south-west of Woolaston. The name was 'Twyford' in the Middle Ages. The modern name, assimilated to the name of the river Wye, was represented by Wyvern Pond (now filled in) at ST 584989 in the north-east quadrant of the road junction, and by Wyvern Farm (ST 585988); see Smith, *PNGlos.*, iii. 263; Anderson, *EHNSW*, 5.

---

extensively than land similarly dependent on Shropshire and Cheshire. Particular lands are specified as lying 'between the Wye and the Usk', or 'beyond the Usk', but only a few names are given—Chepstow, Caerleon, Portskewett, Dinham, Llanvair Discoed, Caerwent, Caldicot, and Rogerstone—though a few others can be easily deduced from the evidence of Domesday Book.[1] Further information about land in the jurisdiction of Caerleon Castle and dependent on Monmouth Castle is found in the Herefordshire folios.[2] The number of unnamed villages mentioned,[3] their size in ploughlands and their value, suggest that 'Wales' was an extensive area. The successive phases of conquest, their dating and their extent, however, are not yet well understood.[4] It is probable that Earl William fitzOsbern, who governed Gloucestershire and Herefordshire as a palatine earldom until his death in 1071 and who is named in Domesday Book as a builder of castles and a grantor of lands, partly consolidated the gains of Earl Harold and of Edward the Confessor, inheriting both land and client kingdoms, and partly extended them. The geographical spread of those Domesday vills that can be identified from their later manorial history, together with the foundation of monasteries and grants to churches, especially to his preferred foundations of Cormeilles and Lyre, all suggest that Earl William controlled from Gloucestershire and from Herefordshire an area that corresponded to much of the later county of Monmouthshire. This involved the domination of the whole of the cantref of Gwent Is Coed and of the eastern part of Gwent Uwch Coed. It is probable that he established the 'Strigoil' lordship (held in 1086 by William de Eu) based on Chepstow Castle, and that the four groups of Welsh villages under Welsh reeves were the commotes of Brynbuga (Usk), Edeligion, Caldicot and Llebenydd. The commote of Teirtref, certainly under Norman control by 1074, may well be represented by the men who had been transferred to the customary dues of King Gruffydd. Thurstan's six carucates beyond the Usk, together with his lands in the castlery of Caerleon, probably accounted for a further part of the commote of Edeligion. If Teirtref was dependent on Gloucestershire it was surrounded on three sides by Welsh land colonized from Herefordshire: in the north by the commote of Ewias, held in 1086 by Roger de Lacy, in the east by Archenfield, which had been taken over during the reign of Edward the Confessor, and in the south by Monmouth Commote, much of which would have been in the lordship of Monmouth Castle in 1086. The major Norman thrust into south and west Wales took place in the reign of William Rufus and the exact extent of Norman domination in 1086 is unclear and disputed.[5] The associated map has been drafted to show its maximum likely extent.[6]

[1] The one carucate held by St Michael was at Llanfihangel Rogiet (NGR ST 4587); that belonging to St Dewy was at Dewstow (NGR ST 4688).

[2] Caerleon's castlery is probably included in error in Herefordshire, by misdivision of inquest material: William d'Ecouis is not entered as a landholder in Gloucestershire. Monmouth itself had probably been established in the Welsh commote of Ergyng (Archenfield), though its castlery extended into Gwent; see Moore (ed.), *Domesday Book: Gloucestershire*, notes to S2 and E35–6.

[3] Many of these unnamed places are tentatively identified in Moore (ed.), *Domesday Book: Gloucestershire*, notes to W2–7, 9–19.

[4] See J. E. Lloyd, 'Wales and the Coming of the Normans', *Trans. of the Honourable Soc. of Cymmrodorion* (1899–1900), 122–79; J. E. Lloyd, *A History of Wales from the Earliest Times to the Edwardian Conquest*, 2 vols. (London, 1911); F. and C. Thorn (eds.), *Domesday Book: Herefordshire* (Chichester, 1983), Introductory Notes 1–2.

[5] See P. Courtney, 'The Norman Invasion of Gwent: A Reassessment', *JMH* 12 (1986), 297–313.

[6] The construction of the boundaries of the eleventh-century Welsh commotes and cantrefs, mainly on the basis of later evidence, is taken from M. Richards, *Welsh Administration and Territorial Units, Medieval and Modern* (Cardiff, 1969), and from Moore (ed.), *Domesday Book: Gloucestershire*.

BIBLIOGRAPHY

INDICES

TO THE DOMESDAY FOLIOS

BIBLIOGRAPHY

The following bibliography, arranged in date order, is derived by kind permission from D. Bates, *A Bibliography of Domesday Book*, published by Boydell and Brewer Ltd for the Royal Historical Society, 1986. Dr Bates has added certain entries to this county list in order to update it, and to include appropriate references which are cited in the 'General Studies' section of his original work.

GLOUCESTERSHIRE

1. M. Hale, *The Primitive Organisation of Mankind, Considered and Examined According to the Light of Nature* (London, 1677). Made use of DB statistics from Glos. to demonstrate an increase in population in later times at pp.236–7.

2. S. Rudder, *A New History of Gloucestershire* (Cirencester, 1779). Contains a text of the DB folios for the county.

3. W. Bawdwen, *Dom. Boc. A Translation of the Record called Domesday, so far as Relates to the Counties of Middlesex, Hertford, Buckingham, Oxford and Gloucester* (Doncaster, 1812). Bawdwen produced a rather unsatisfactory translation of the whole of DB (British Library, Add. MS 27769), of which only sections were published.

4. H. James (director), *Domesday Book: or the Great Survey of England of William the Conqueror, A.D. MLXXXVI. Facsimile of the Part Relating to Gloucestershire*. Photozincographed by Her Majesty's Command at the Ordnance Survey Office, Southampton (Southampton, 1862).

5. E. A. Fuller, 'Tenures of Land, by the Customary Tenants in Cirencester', *Trans. of the Bristol and Gloucestershire Archaeol. Soc.* 2 (1877–8), 285–319. Some discussion of DB for Cirencester and its relationship to the record of customs and services in the Cirencester cartulary of *c.*1155.

6. A. S. Ellis, 'On the Manorial History of Clifton', *Trans. of the Bristol and Gloucestershire Archaeol. Soc.* 3 (1878–9), 211–31. See 19.

7. A. S. Ellis, 'On the Landholders of Gloucestershire Named in Domesday Book', *Trans. of the Bristol and Gloucestershire Archaeol. Soc.* 4 (1879–80), 86–198. Also printed as *Some Account of the Landholders of Gloucestershire Named in Domesday Book, A.D. 1086* (privately printed, 1880). Of variable quality. A collection of material about the DB tenants.

8. H. Barkly, 'On an Alleged Instance of the Fallibility of Domesday in Regard to "Ancient Demesne"', *Domesday Studies: being the Papers read at the Meetings of the Domesday Commemoration 1886*, ed. P. E. Dove, 2 vols. (London, 1888–91), ii. 471–83. Deals with Nympsfield and a supposed contradiction between charter evidence and DB.

9. C. S. Taylor, *An Analysis of the Domesday Survey of Gloucestershire* (Bristol, 1889). A large-scale analysis of the contents of Glos. DB in the manner of Eyton's work on Dorset and Somerset. The treatment of statistics is not always reliable.

10. C. S. Taylor, 'The Pre-Domesday Hide of Gloucestershire', *Trans. of the Bristol and Gloucestershire Archaeol. Soc.* 18 (1893–4), 288–319.

11. J. J. Mercier, 'A History of Kemerton', *Trans. of the Bristol and Gloucestershire Archaeol. Soc.* 19 (1894–5), 24–40. Kemerton is in Glos. DB, but the place was transferred to Worcs. in 1931.

12. F. H. Baring, 'The Hidation of Some Southern Counties', *EHR* 14 (1899), 290–9.

13. A. Hall, 'Bibury', *N & Q* 9th ser., 5 (1900), 384. Suggests identification of *Alvredintune* with Ablington in Bibury. But see 50.

14. C. S. Taylor, 'Deerhurst, Pershore, and Westminster', *Trans. of the Bristol and Gloucestershire Archaeol. Soc.* 25 (1902), 230–50. Deals mainly with Deerhurst Hundred.

15. A. Harvey, *Bristol: A Historical and Topographical Account of the City* (London, 1906). A brief discussion of the DB entry.

16. C. S. Taylor, 'The Northern Boundary of Gloucestershire', *Trans. of the Bristol and Gloucestershire Archaeol. Soc.* 32 (1909), 109–39. Reprinted in shortened form in *Gloucestershire Studies*, ed. H. P. R. Finberg (Leicester, 1957), 17–51.

17. M. L. Bazeley, 'The Forest of Dean and its Relations with the Crown during the Twelfth and Thirteenth Centuries', *Trans. of the Bristol and Gloucestershire Archaeol. Soc.* 33 (1910), 153–286. Discusses DB evidence. See 28, 30.

18. W. St C. Baddeley, *Place-Names of Gloucestershire: A Handbook* (Gloucester, 1913). Superseded by 39.

19. C. S. Taylor, 'Note on the Entry in Domesday Book Relating to Westbury-on-Severn', *Trans. of the Bristol and Gloucestershire Archaeol. Soc.* 36 (1913), 182–90. See 6.

20. C. S. Taylor, 'The Norman Settlement of Gloucestershire', *Trans. of the Bristol and Gloucestershire Archaeol. Soc.* 40 (1917), 57–88.

21. F. T. S. Houghton, 'The Family of Muchgros', *Trans. of the Birmingham Archaeol. Soc.* 47 (1921), 8–34. For the DB holdings of the Mussegros family in Glos. and other counties.

22. A. H. Thompson, 'The Jurisdiction of the Archbishops of York in Gloucestershire', *Trans. of the Bristol and Gloucestershire Archaeol. Soc.* 43 (1921), 85–180. For DB and the lands of the former monastery of St Oswald's, Gloucester.

23. C. Oman, 'Concerning Some Gloucestershire Boundaries', *Essays in History Presented to Reginald Lane Poole*, ed. H. W. C. Davis (Oxford, 1927), 86–97.

24. L. Landon, 'The Barony of Little Easton and the Family of Hastings', *Trans. of the Essex Archaeol. Soc.* ns 19 (1930), 174–9. On the DB estates of Walter the deacon.

25. E. A. Fuller, 'Medieval Cirencester', *Trans. of the Bristol and Gloucestershire Archaeol. Soc.* 54 (1932), 107–15.

26. R. R. Darlington, 'Æthelwig, Abbot of Evesham', *EHR* 48 (1933), 1–22, 177–98. For the estates of Evesham Abbey and DB-related material in the Evesham cartularies. See further 50, 52.

27. L. E. W. O. Fullbrook-Legatt, 'Saxon Gloucestershire', *Trans. of the Bristol and Gloucestershire Archaeol. Soc.* 57 (1935), 110–35. Contains material on DB place-names and hundreds.

28. G. B. Grundy, 'The Ancient Woodland of Gloucestershire', *Trans. of the Bristol and Gloucestershire Archaeol. Soc.* 58 (1936), 65–155; 59 (1937), 205–9. For maps and discussion of DB woodland. See 30.

29. C. E. Hart, 'The Origin and the Geographical Extent of the Hundred of St Briavels in Gloucestershire', *Trans. of the Bristol and Gloucestershire Archaeol. Soc.* 66 (1945), 138–65. Reprinted in C. E. Hart, *The Extent and Boundaries of the Forest of Dean and Hundred of St Briavels* (Woodgate near Coleford, 1947), 1–28.

30. C. E. HART, 'The Metes and Bounds of the Forest of Dean', *Trans. of the Bristol and Gloucestershire Archaeol. Soc.* 66. 166–207. Reprinted in Hart, *Extent and Boundaries*, 29–70. Uses DB evidence to discuss and map the Forest of Dean, which is not mentioned in DB. See also 28.

31. R. H. HILTON, 'Winchcombe Abbey and the Manor of Sherborne', *Univ. of Birmingham Hist. Jnl* 2 (1949–50), 31–52.

32. H. C. DARBY and I. B. TERRETT (eds.), *The Domesday Geography of Midland England* (Cambridge, 1954; 2nd edn., 1971; repr. 1978). Changes in the second edition are small but significant.

33. H. P. R. FINBERG, *Roman and Saxon Withington: A Study in Continuity*, Dept. of Eng. Local Hist. Occasional Papers, 8 (Leicester, 1955; repr. 1959).

34. H. P. R. FINBERG, *Gloucestershire: An Illustrated Essay on the History of the Landscape* (London, 1955). Revised as *The Gloucestershire Landscape* (London, 1975).

35. H. P. R. FINBERG, 'The Genesis of the Gloucestershire Towns', *Gloucestershire Studies*, ed. Finberg, 52–88.

36. D. WALKER, 'Miles of Gloucester, Earl of Hereford', *Trans. of the Bristol and Gloucestershire Archaeol. Soc.* 77 (1958), 66–84. See pp.81–2 for *Alwintune* in Herefs. DB as Alvington (Glos.).

37. D. WALKER, 'The "Honours" of the Earls of Hereford in the Twelfth Century', *Trans. of the Bristol and Gloucestershire Archaeol. Soc.* 79 (1960), 174–211. For the DB holdings of Durand, Sheriff of Gloucester, and his nephew Walter fitzRoger in Glos. and other counties.

38. W. E. WIGHTMAN, 'The Palatine Earldom of William fitz-Osbern in Gloucestershire and Worcestershire (1066–1071)', *EHR* 77 (1962), 6–17.

39. A. H. SMITH, *The Place-Names of Gloucestershire*, 4 vols., EPNS 38–41 (Cambridge, 1964–5).

40. D. C. DOUGLAS, 'The Domesday Tenant of Hawling', *Trans. of the Bristol and Gloucestershire Archaeol. Soc.* 84 (1965), 28–30. Brief discussion of the DB holdings of the Chocques ('de Cioches') family.

41. W. E. WIGHTMAN, *The Lacy Family in England and Normandy, 1066–1194* (Oxford, 1966).

42. H. B. CLARKE, 'The Norman Conquest of the West Midlands', *Vale of Evesham Hist. Soc. Research Papers*, 1 (1967), 17–26.

43. B. R. KEMP, 'The Churches of Berkeley Hernesse', *Trans. of the Bristol and Gloucestershire Archaeol. Soc.* 87 (1968), 96–110. Several points about DB Berkeley.

44. C. J. BOND, 'The Estates of Evesham Abbey: A Preliminary Survey of their Medieval Topography', *Vale of Evesham Hist. Soc. Research Papers*, 4 (1973), 1–62.

45. D. C. COX, 'The Vale Estates of the Church of Evesham, *c.*700–1086', *Vale of Evesham Hist. Soc. Research Papers*, 5 (1975), 25–50.

46. C. J. BOND, 'The Medieval Topography of the Evesham Abbey Estates: A Supplement', ibid. 51–60.

47. D. WALKER, 'Gloucester and Gloucestershire in Domesday Book', *Trans. of the Bristol and Gloucestershire Archaeol. Soc.* 94 (1976), 107–16.

48. B. HARVEY, *Westminster Abbey and its Estates in the Middle Ages* (Oxford, 1977).

49. C. C. DYER, *Lords and Peasants in a Changing Society: The Estates of the Bishopric of Worcester, 680–1540* (Cambridge, 1980). For landholdings in Glos., War., and Worcs.

50. J. S. MOORE (ed.), *Domesday Book: Gloucestershire* (Chichester, 1982). Text, translation and valuable notes. An appendix describes the sections of the Evesham and Worcester satellites and surveys which are relevant to Glos. DB. See also 26, 52.

51. A. WARMINGTON, 'The Domesday Manor of Langeberge cum Mene', *EPNS Jnl* 16 (1983–4), 38–49. Identifies as Longborough. Cf. 39, 50.

52. H. B. CLARKE, 'The Domesday Satellites', *Domesday Book: A Reassessment*, ed. P. H. Sawyer (London, 1985), 50–70. For DB-related material in the Evesham cartularies. See also 26, 50.

INDEX OF PLACES

NOTES

In this edition, the place-names found in the translation, on the county map, and in the following Index of Places are all interrelated and have been established according to strict editorial policy. The central source for each of these three elements has been a specially compiled card-index containing a card for every mention of a place-name in Domesday Book: this index itself has been adjusted as research progressed. Thus the separate disciplines of identification, map-making, indexing, and rendering the Latin into readable English have all contributed to this compendium of Domesday place-names and to the manner of the presentation of each category. However, a word of caution is appropriate here, because the reader should be aware that the simple exchange of a Domesday name for even the most obvious modern equivalent does not necessarily mean that the original settlement lay precisely at that location, nor that it had a similar territorial form.

It is important to realize that the place-names of Domesday Book do not represent modern religious, social, administrative or agricultural units such as parishes, townships, villages, hamlets or farms, except by coincidence. They stand for estates or taxable units that may not in reality have been either independent or self-supporting. No bounds are given and these estates, depending on their size, may well have extended over more than one modern parish, be interlaced with other holdings, or possess a number of widely scattered members. Most Domesday estates will have contained several settlements, all of which had names in 1086, but which the survey leaves unnamed and whose statistics it engrosses with others. Frustratingly, Domesday says nothing that allows us to determine the centre, the extent, or the form of the estate.

Many Domesday estate-names will doubtless have been those actually current in the locality concerned; but others are 'booknames'—administrators' designations and often very general in scope—such as the name of a valley, hill, river or tract of land. These were probably known by more specific names on the ground, but Domesday Book does not record them. Especially where a vill is shown to have been in divided ownership in 1086, or where the Domesday unit is the fragment of some great multiple estate of pre-Conquest times, Domesday may well retain the 'charter' or 'book' name of its more extensive predecessor even though other evidence may indicate that a more precise appellation was almost certainly in use at the time.

The Domesday name may now be represented by a parish name, or by that of a township, hamlet or isolated farm. It may no longer survive as a settlement-name at all, but only as that of a river, wood, hill, road or bridge. The name may even have become lost before it appeared on any map; and finally it may have escaped identification altogether, either because the place designated scarcely survived the eleventh century or because the form in which Domesday transmits the place-name is corrupt and so far unintelligible.

A Domesday place can only be considered to be satisfactorily identified when the proposed name has passed a number of tests. Is the evolution of the 1086 name-form to the suggested modern equivalent philologically acceptable? Does it lie in the hundred indicated or implied by the text, or reconstructed from it? Do the details of land, equipment, resources and industry given by the entry in Domesday Book accord with what could have been practicable within the proposed area? Can the estate be identified among the possessions of the 1086 holder's heir or successors in later centuries? In practice, by no means all published identifications satisfy these requirements and the accuracy and reliability of identifications varies considerably from county to county. Much depends on the quality of the work of the eighteenth and nineteenth century 'antiquarian' pioneers and of the sections on Domesday in the relevant volume of the *Victoria County Histories*. The standard of more recent work, the existence of a county volume among the publications of the English Place-Name Society, or of 'topographical' volumes from the *Victoria County History* make the identifications of some counties more secure than those of others. The evidence so gathered will have been reviewed for H.C. Darby's monumental series on Domesday Geography (1952–77) and for the Phillimore edition of Domesday Book (1975–86), but with varying thoroughness. For the present publication, it has been impractical to re-examine every item of this complex and widely scattered evidence afresh, but in cases where modern published identifications conflict or where there are other obvious reasons for doubt, the evidence has been rescrutinized.

In the following Index of Places, a system of square-bracketed editorial additions and of single or double inverted commas imply varying degrees of certainty in identification, and are set out in the key below. A further key precedes the translation in this volume and contains the related conventions employed there. Among the symbols on the county map, of which this index is also the gazetteer, will be found a system of circles, complete, broken or interlinked, which serves the same function, besides a full treatment of the county- and hundred-boundaries in 1086.

By far the greater part of the evidence for the identification of place-names is derived from Great Domesday Book itself. However, occasionally a holding was entered without its eleventh-century name, or the name given has been replaced by a later one, and where possible these have been supplied from the testimony of certain other documents that are directly related to the making of Domesday Book or to its use. Such documents deemed admissable as evidence in this context are, for example, the Exon Book for the south-western counties, Evesham A for Worcestershire, and the Herefordshire Domesday. However, there is no source other than the Domesday folios accepted for identifications in this volume.

F.R.Thorn

GENERAL

1. Scope of Index

The Index refers to all place-names found in the text written at the time of the compilation of Great Domesday Book, 1086–7, including all contemporary corrections, notes and additions in the margins. Insertions added to the MS in medieval and later times are not indexed, but identifications are incorporated which have been assisted by the evidence of any secondary documents that might exist as indicated in the introduction to these notes above.

Only references to the folios and translation supplied with this volume are indexed. A section listing any named holdings in this county which are recorded in the folios of other shires will be found on the associated county map.

2. Use of suprascript numbers

Where a place-name occurs more than once on a folio, its incidence is indicated by a suprascript number.

Note that occasionally a named entry can be followed immediately by further reference(s) to the same vill, usually designated by terms such as *ibi*, 'there'; *ibidem*, 'in the same place'; *in eadem villa*, 'in the same vill'. Such entries are not indexed as the place-name itself is absent.

3. Use of "...."

Double inverted commas indicate a name found only in Domesday Book and for which there is no known later equivalent, or of which the form may be corrupt. The name so enclosed is printed in Roman type.

4. Use of '....'

Single inverted commas indicate the latest or most typical known form of a name which remained in use beyond the eleventh century, but which either has not survived into modern times at all, or which only appears on twentieth-century maps as the name of a feature such as a river, hill, wood etc., rather than a place of habitation. This also applies to names without a continuous history and which have only recently been revived for antiquarian reasons.

MODERN PLACE-NAMES (ROMAN TYPE)

5. Authority

The modern place-names are consistent with those marked on the particular 1:100,000 Ordnance Survey grey base-map employed as the background for each associated county map. Note that place-names can vary from edition to edition of OS maps and their absence from this particular map does not mean they are necessarily lost.

6. Modern counties

Throughout this edition the county-boundaries are regarded as those that existed prior to the reconstructing of the counties in 1974.

7. National Grid Reference

Four-figure National Grid References are given for modern place-names which represent settlements recorded in Domesday Book. Note that these NGRs do not necessarily pin-point the precise location of such settlements in 1086 for the reasons set out in the introduction to these notes above.

8. Common prefixes and suffixes: Great, Little, etc.

Modern places which are distinguished by common prefixes such as Old, Great and Little, Upper, Middle and Lower, Nether and Over, East and West, North and South have their main entry indexed under the relevant place-names in the same way as those with distinguished suffixes such as All Saints, St Andrews and Abbots.

9. Use of 'or', 'and'

Where a place is designated by two or more prefixes or suffixes and linked by 'or', e.g. Great or Little, All Saints or St Andrew, it is uncertain which of these two modern places represents the holding in question or whether both did so. Where prefixes are linked by 'and', e.g. East and West, St Peter and St Martin, the inference is that both modern places lie within the territory of a single estate of 1086.

10. Use of 'in', 'near'

In the event of two or more places in one county having the same name, they are distinguished by the addition of the parish-names in square brackets, e.g. [in Compton]. The only exception is when the parish- and place-name are the same, or where the place-name forms part of the parish-name. In these cases one will be followed by the parish-name, [in Compton], while the other will be related to a prominent nearby town or feature, [near Wallingford].

11. Choice of representative names distinguished by affixes

In a given locality a single place-name in Domesday Book may now be represented by a number of variant names distinguished by different prefixes or suffixes. Where a major derivative name signifying a village or hamlet still exists, such as Great, Little, Higher, Lower, St Mary, St Peter, this is preferred to minor or dependent variant names, such as Park, Moor, Gate, Green, Manor. Similarly minor settlement-names, where only they survive, are preferred to non-settlement names such as those of fields, hills, woods, streams, marshes.

Where the name in Domesday Book is represented on modern maps only by the name of a minor feature, the principal element alone is used in the index and in the translation, so that Weston Farm, Lodge, Hall, Bridge, Wood etc., appear only as Weston.

12. Places now 'lost'

A number of places named in Domesday Book either no longer exist as distinct settlements or have disappeared altogether due to urban development, inundation by reservoirs, coastal erosion, rural depopulation, and other causes. These 'lost' places are treated variously, both in the translation and in this index, according to the circumstances that have caused them to disappear.

a. Places which have been absorbed into an area of urban development, but have given their name to a distinct suburb or district. These are designated as 'in' the relevant town or city which is enclosed in square brackets, e.g. Knowle [in Bristol].

b. Places absorbed into urban development, as above, but of which the name has not survived as that of a distinct suburb or district. These are designated as 'in' the relevant town or city in square brackets, also as above, but the place-name is enclosed within single inverted commas, e.g. 'Tessall' [in Birmingham].

c. Places now lost underwater have their names enclosed in single inverted commas and are followed by an indication of their former whereabouts in square brackets if known, e.g. 'Syndercombe' [in Clatworthy Reservoir].

d. Names of places lost in rural areas are enclosed in single or double inverted commas as set out in 3 and 4 above. However, they may also be designated as being 'in' the parish to which they belonged when this is known. e.g. "Sortelai" [in Quainton], 'Ashden' [in Compton].

e. Those lost places which can be reliably located have been plotted on the accompanying county map. Those which can only be approximately located are included in the Index and the translation but are not mapped.

13. Use of names other than Domesday derivatives

All modern names used in this edition are derived from those of 1086 with only the following exceptions:

a. Where the name of the Domesday Book estate has been entirely superseded by a more recent name that covers the same extent, e.g. Reigate (Surrey) for 'Churchfield'; Padstow (Corn.) for *Lanwenehoc*.

b. Where the later name of the Domesday Book estate is derived from the TRE or TRW holder or his title, e.g. Dodington (Som.) for 'Stowey'; Bishopstone (Herefs.) for 'Mansell'.

c. Where the name is that of a river covering a multitude of settlements that lay on its banks, e.g. Ottery (Devon.); Winterbourne, Cerne or Piddle (Dorset).

d. Where the holding is unnamed in Domesday Book, but its name can be reliably established from any other contemporary documents, such as those mentioned in the introduction to these notes above.

PLACE-NAMES IN DOMESDAY BOOK *(ITALIC TYPE)*

14. Variant forms

All variant forms found in these county folios of Domesday Book are indexed.

15. Abbreviation

Place-names that are specifically shortened in the MS with abbreviation-marks are given in their extended form.

OTHER

16. Use of *u*, *v*, *w*

Since *u* and *v* are used indiscriminately in this MS, as in others of the period, they are here transposed to be closest to the modern spelling of the place-names. Double-*u* (*uu*) is always transposed as *w*, except in names enclosed in double inverted commas (see 3 above) where the scribe's original orthography is maintained.

17. Use of hyphenated endings

Where the spelling of a name varies only by the addition of a final letter or letters, the shorter version is given followed by the variant ending after a hyphen. Thus *Evelai*, *Evelaia* appears as *Evelai-a*; *Heiford*, *Heiforde* as *Heiford-e*; *Winewic*, *Winewiche* as *Winewic-he*.

18. Page and folio references

References to the pages of editorial matter in this volume are printed in **bold**, and are followed by the references to the folio numbers of the facsimile and the translation, which are identical for both.

19. Recto and Verso

Folio numbers without suffix indicate the *recto* of the folio, while suffix 'v' indicates the *verso*.

20. Use of ‡

A double-dagger ‡ before a main entry refers to the errata section printed at the end of these indices.

GLOUCESTERSHIRE

A

Æ

B

EDITOR'S NOTE

The region now called Monmouthshire remained a disputed territory between England and Wales for many centuries, and is therefore distinguished from Wales in this index.

INDEX OF PERSONS AND ECCLESIASTICAL BODIES

NOTES

1. TRE, TRW

Most of the entries in Domesday Book record two distinct categories of landholder: those English or Anglo-Scandinavian owners who held land before the Conquest (TRE, *tempore regis Edwardi*, 'in the time of King Edward'), and those who dispossessed them after 1066 (TRW, *tempore regis Willelmi,* 'in the time of King William')—or more particularly twenty years later at the time of the Conqueror's survey. It is usual for the Church to maintain continuity of ownership throughout both periods, but it is rare for an individual to do so. Since Domesday Book is a description of the situation at the time of its compilation in 1086–7, the circumstances obtaining TRE are invariably entered in the past tense, TRW in the present.

2. Use of * †

Prefixed asterisks * indicate references to the names of English or Anglo-Scandinavian landholders or churches mentioned only in a TRE context. Daggers † signify those which are stated to have continued their tenancy from the TRE to the TRW period. Names found only TRW have no prefixed symbol.

3. The Kings

The references to King Edward and to King William are divided for convenience into categories which encompass various aspects of kingship. The references to King Edward implied by the abbreviation TRE are not indexed. Where the text shows that someone in the TRE period *tenuit de rege Edwardo*, 'held of King Edward', the references are indexed under the category of King Edward 'as lord'.

References to the equivalent TRW phrase *tenet de rege*, 'holds of the king', are not indexed as it was not used systematically and was anyway superfluous because in feudal theory current after the Conquest all land was technically held of the king.

4. Abbeys and Churches

The terms *Abbatia,* 'Abbey', and *Æcclesia,* 'Church' are sometimes used interchangeably in Domesday Book for large monastic institutions. In this index, 'Abbey' is always used for the Benedictine houses, both in England and on the continent, while 'Church' is reserved for secular houses, i.e. colleges of priests, non-monastic bishoprics, minsters, etc. Only churches recorded as owning land are indexed here.

5. Personal Names TRE

All TRE names are standardized in accordance with O. von Feilitzen, *The Pre-Conquest Personal Names of Domesday Book* (Uppsala, 1937) with the following exceptions: Alfred, Edgar, Edith, Edmund, Edward, Edwin, Harold, Morcar, Siward, Stigand, Swein and Waltheof.

Old English forms are used in preference to Scandinavian variants. When no Old English form is attested, names are standardized first to their Anglo-Scandinavian, then to their Old Danish, Old Swedish, and finally Old Norse forms.

6. Personal Names TRW

There is no authority equivalent to von Feilitzen for TRW names, and their transposition into modern forms by individual historians has seldom been consistent. For this edition the editors have retained what they perceive to have become the 'accepted' forms of certain names despite inconsistencies. Thus, for example, *Albertus Lotharingensis* becomes Albert of Lorraine, not the Lotharingian, whilst *Walterius Flandrensis* remains Walter the Fleming, not of Flanders, in the style used for most non-Norman continentals. However, a policy of standardization has been established for the aspects of nomenclature which follow.

Modern anglicized forms of Christian names are preferred, e.g. Gilbert for *Giselbertus*, Geoffrey for *Goisfridus,* Hugh for *Hugo*, Ralph for *Radulfus.*

Continental and English toponymics appear in the modern form of the place-name e.g. Robert d'Oilly not *Robert de Oilgi*, Roger of Westerham not *Roger de Oisteram.* As in these examples, 'de' is used for continental places of origin, 'of' for English names.

Continental patronymics are expressed with the prefix 'fitz', e.g. Hugh fitzBaldric. The equivalent English or Anglo-Scandinavian names are expressed as 'son of', e.g. Swein son of Azur. This rule is also applied to patronymics in TRE names.

Ambiguous TRW personal names which are attested in both Anglo-Scandinavian and Continental sources are given their Continental forms unless the manuscript specifically identifies any person so named as English.

TRW names with obscure Latin forms or with no modern equivalent appear in the Index as they do in the manuscript, but without the *-us* ending, e.g. Otbert for *Otbertus*, Winemar for *Winemarus.*

7. Titles

Main entries are indexed under the toponymic, and the personal name(s), where known, are supplied in square brackets, e.g. Mortain, [Robert], Count of; Coutances, [Geoffrey de Mowbray], Bishop of. If these name(s) occur explicitly in the folios of this country, the square brackets are left off.

8. Occupational Names

Examples: Alwine the huntsman, Gilbert the cook, Regenbald the priest. Although Domesday Book describes many of these persons with other descriptive suffixes—for instance Regenbald occurs variously in different counties as 'the priest', 'the chaplain', 'the king's chaplain', and 'of Cirencester'—only that or those which occur in the folios of this particular county are listed here.

9. Cross-indexing

All patronymics, non-titular toponymics, rank-names, bynames and occupational names are cross-indexed with the main entry under the Christian name. Examples:

Main Entry	Cross-reference
Eudo fitzHubert	Hubert, *see* Eudo fitzHubert
Alvred of Lincoln	Lincoln, *see* Alvred of Lincoln
Leofwine Cild	Cild, *see* Leofwine Cild
Alwine Cobbold	Cobbold, *see* Alwine Cobbold
Gilbert the cook	cook, *see* Gilbert the cook

In the case of Abbeys, main entries will be found under the place-name with the dedication cross-indexed: Ramsey, Abbey of St Benedict (main entry); St Benedict, Ramsey, Abbey of.

Secular churches are indexed under Church with a cross-reference to the dedication, and also to the place-name: Church of Saint-Remy of Rheims (main entry); Saint-Remy of Rheims, Church of; Rheims, Church of Saint-Remy of.

10. Folio References

Only one reference to a name is indexed per folio. The frequent use of *idem*, 'the same man', is not indexed as the name itself is not present. References are linked by a hyphen when the consecutive entries for a holder's fief cover more than one folio.

Folio numbers without suffix indicate the recto of the folio, while suffix 'v' indicates the verso.

GLOUCESTERSHIRE

A

Æ

B

C

D

TRANSLATION

TRANSLATION

NOTES TO THE TRANSLATION

SOURCE AND STANDARDIZATION

The translations in the County Edition of Domesday Book are based in the main upon those that appear in the *Victoria Histories of the Counties of England*, of which publication commenced in 1900 and is still in progress. The translator of the relevant county folios of Domesday Book in volume one of *VCH Gloucestershire* (forthcoming) is G. Walker. Alecto Historical Editions are grateful to the publishers of *VCH* for permission to make use of this translation.

In order that the translations contained in each of the county volumes can be served by a common system of indices, the text of all sources has been standardized so that place- and personal names as well as technical terms and certain common phrases are consistent throughout. The opportunity has also been taken to correct such errors as may have become apparent as a result of subsequent research.

For a detailed statement of the policies governing the treatment of names, see the notes which precede the 'Index of Places' and the 'Index of Persons and Ecclesiastical Bodies' above.

METHODS OF RELATING THE TRANSLATION TO THE FACSIMILE

Throughout the folios of Great Domesday Book there is considerable variation in the number of lines written per page, in the depth and width of the columns, and in the spaces that separate the numbered chapters. In order to assist the use of the facsimile and this translation together, the type-size and the lay-out of the pages of the translation have been designed to match the configuration of the MS text as closely as possible.

The MS was foliated in the seventeenth century on only the *recto* side of each page. In the translation the *verso* is also foliated with the number followed by v.

● to the left, within the column, signifies the presence of one of the larger rubricated initial letters that commonly begin each entry. This device is provided to enable the reader more easily to relate passages in the translation to those in the facsimile by counting the spots on the former against the more prominent initials in the latter.

Typography

Roman type is reserved for the original text of Great Domesday, including all corrections and marginal additions made to the MS at the time of its compilation in the late eleventh century.

Italic type is used for all matter added subsequently during the Middle Ages and up to recent times.

The use of upper and lower case is the same as in the MS:

FULL CAPITALS represent the large rustic capitals used for county- and chapter-headings, which are all written in red.

Large and Small Capitals represent matter written in black rustic capitals within the text and usually through-lined in red. Those not written in capitals, whether intentionally or in error, are here transposed in lower case.

MARGINALIA

The translations of those passages entirely written in the margin are printed as close as is possible to the position they occupy in the MS, in smaller type where necessary. A complete key to the system of symbols employed here for the marginal notes and signs found in the MS, such as § for the transposition signs, M, B, S, etc. preceding ● in certain counties, and [1], [2], [3], [ ], [⋮], [☒], etc., is given in Appendix I, 'The Marginalia of Great Domesday Book', in the associated *Domesday Book Studies* volume, pp. 160–2.

EDITORIAL CONVENTIONS

Square brackets are reserved for editorial insertions.

[*sic*] — indicates a scribal error in the MS, here reproduced in the translation. The only exception is incorrect chapter numbering.

[. . .] — signifies a gap in the MS text, either left blank by the scribe for an insertion to be added later, or as a result of erasure. Three full points within the brackets are the standard length in the translations regardless of the actual extent of the gap in the MS.

† 7 hides † — Daggers enclose the tentative translation of a passage, phrase or numeral which is obscure in the MS, owing either to slips of the pen, to unclear alteration by the scribe, or to the worn condition of the parchment.

<u>7 hides</u> — Underlining indicated words or passages marked for deletion in the MS: the same convention is followed in the translation where no correction has been added suprascript. In the latter case, only the corrected text is given.

|it is worth 12*s*.| — Bars within the text enclose the full extent of a passage of which part is written in the margin, where a note will be found to that effect in square brackets.

[?]Weston — The modern equivalent given for a Domesday place-name which is probable, but not certain.

[?Weston] — A place left unnamed in Domesday Book, but which can be tentatively identified from internal evidence or from the evidence of other related documents.

Weston [in Parishbrook] — Where a county contains two or more modern places with the same name, they are differentiated by indicating the parish 'in' which each of them lies.

Weston [near Oldborough] — In the above instance, when one of the place-names is the same or partially the same as the name of the parish in which it lies, giving the awkward Weston [in Weston], its situation is instead indicated as being 'near' a prominent town or feature.

[Great or Little] Weston — The use of 'or' indicates that it is uncertain which of two or more modern places now represent the Domesday place-name, or whether all did so.

[Great and Little] Weston — The use of 'and' indicates that two or more modern places lie within the territory of the same Domesday estate.

Weston [Oxon.] — County abbreviations indicate that a locality recorded in the folios of this county lies within the boundaries of another in modern times. Throughout this edition the modern county boundaries are taken to be those that obtained prior to the restructuring of the counties in 1974.

NOTES TO THE TRANSLATION

Use of Inverted Commas

"Celverdescote" Double inverted commas indicate a place-name found only in Domesday Book and for which there is no known later equivalent, or of which the form may be corrupt.

Hundred- and wapentake-names are similarly treated, but a typical form is used if there are variants.

'Sculthorp' Single inverted commas indicate the latest or most typical known form of a name which remained in use beyond the eleventh century, but which either has not survived into modern times at all, or which only appears on twentieth-century maps as the name of a feature such as a river, hill, wood, etc., rather than as a place of habitation. This also applies to names without a continuous history and which have only recently been revived for antiquarian reasons.

Hundred- and wapentake-names which are antiquarian revivals are similarly treated. Single inverted commas also indicate such names derived from places which had disappeared before the compilation of the first OS one-inch maps in the early nineteenth century, either because they never were the names of inhabited communities, or because they had fallen into disuse by that time. In such cases the name-form adopted is the latest, most or a regularized form.

EDITOR'S NOTES

Anomalous Tenses

In the section which constitutes 'The Land of the King' on ff. 162v–164 the tenses of the verbs in certain passages are confused in the original. This anomaly arose because the king's holdings were described with the pre-Conquest tenant at the beginning of each entry, and it is not always clear whether the details that follow relate to the TRE or to the TRW period. Wherever there is doubt the verbs are omitted in this translation.

Wrong Chapter-Headings

In the Gloucestershire folios the numbering or the order of the introductory list of landholders on f. 162v sometimes differs from the rubricated chapter-headings in the text.

On f. 166v, left column, three chapters are out of numerical order because the scribe mistakenly entered the fiefs of Earl Roger, Earl Hugh and the Count of Mortain before he had completed the ecclesiastical section. For a detailed account of the stages of writing this much-adjusted passage, see Caroline Thorn, 'Marginal Notes and Signs in Domesday Book', pp. 114–17, figs. 1–4, in the associated *Domesday Book Studies* volume.

Further on, in the heading of Hugh l'Asne's fief at the end of f. 169 the LX of the correct number LXIII is separated from the III by the decorative ascender of the initial H of his name. On looking back, it seems that the scribe saw only the LX when he came to inscribe the next chapter-heading over the page (that of Miles Crispin which should be LXIIII), and therefore wrongly numbered it LXI. This error caused the sequence of numbers in the text to be three digits behind those in the list until he rectified his mistake on the last folio, 170.

For the sake of simplicity these scribal errors are noticed here only and are not signalled by [*sic*] in this translation.

• IN THE TIME of King EDWARD the city of Gloucester rendered £36 by tale, and 12 sesters of honey according to the measure of the same borough, and 36 dickers of iron, and 100 rods of iron, drawn out, for nails for the king's ships, and certain other small customary dues in the hall and in the king's chamber.

This city now renders the king £60 at 20[*d.*] to the ora, and the king has £20 from the mint.

• In the king's demesne land Roger of Berkeley holds 1 house and 1 fishery in this vill, and it is out of the king's hand. Baldwin held this TRE.

Bishop Osbern holds the land and messuages which Eadmær held; he pays 10*s.* with other customary dues.

Geoffrey de Mandeville holds 6 messuages. TRE these rendered 6*s.* 8*d.* with other customary dues.

William [fitz]Baderon [holds] 2 messuages rendering 30*d.*

William the scribe, 1 message rendering 51*d.*

Roger de Lacy, 1 message rendering 26*d.*

Bishop Osbern, 1 message rendering 41*d.*

Berner, 1 message rendering 14*d.*

William the Bald, 1 message rendering 12*d.*

Durand the sheriff, 2 messages rendering 14*d.*

The same Durand holds 1 message rendering 26*d.*, and in addition 1 message which renders no customary dues.

Hadewin holds 1 message which pays rent but withholds other customary dues.

Gosbert [holds] 1 message, Dunning 1 message, Widard 1 message. Arnulf the priest [holds] 1 message which pays rent and withholds other customary dues.

• All these messuages rendered the royal customary dues TRE. Now King William has nothing from these, nor does Robert, his minister.

These messuages were in King Edward's farm on the day on which he was alive and dead. Now they have been removed from the king's farm and customary dues. TRE the whole of the king's demesne in the city was for lodging or clothing. When Earl William received it at farm, it was for clothing in the same way.

Where the castle stands were 16 houses which are not there now, and in the fortified area of the city 14 houses have been destroyed.

• Earl William built the CASTLE of CHEPSTOW [Mon.], and in his time it rendered only 40*s.* from ships going into the woodland. In the time of his son, Earl Roger, however, the vill itself rendered £16, and Ralph de Limesy had half. Now the king has £12 from it.

• All together from the renders of Caerleon [Mon.] and 1 plough [*sic*] which is there, and from 7 fisheries in the Wye and the Usk, come £7. 10*s.*

• In WALES are 3 hardwicks, Llanvair Discoed [Mon.], and Portskewett [Mon.] and Dinham [Mon.]. In these are 8 ploughs, and 11 half-villans and 15 bordars with 6 ploughs. For these 3 hardwicks Roger d'Ivry wished to have 100*s.*

• Under Waswic the reeve are 13 vills; under Elmui 14 vills; under Bleio are 13 vills; under Iudichael are 14 vills.

§ These render 47 sesters of honey and 40 pigs and 41 cows and 28*s.* for hawks. The whole of this is worth £9. 10*s.* 4*d.*

For a piece of waste land Walter the crossbowman renders 1 sester of honey and 1 pig.

Berdic the king's jester has 3 vills, and there are 5 ploughs. He pays nothing.

Morin [has] 1 vill; Cynesige 1; the son of Waswic 1; Sessisbert 1; Abraham the priest 2 vills: these men have 6 ploughs, and they pay nothing. Earl William placed these within the customary dues of King Gruffydd, with the leave of King William.

§ Under the same reeves are 4 vills made waste by King Caradoc.

• In the king's alms is 1 vill which renders to the church for his soul on the feast of St Martin 2 pigs and 100 loaves with beer.

1 carucate of land belongs to St Michael, and 1 carucate to St David. These render no service except to the saints.

One Beluard of Caerwent has half a carucate of land and pays nothing.

From the pannage come 66 pigs, and they are valued at 44*s.* All these render £40. 12*s.* 8*d.* Durand the sheriff gave these same things to William de EU for £55 at farm.

• Walter the crossbowman holds 2 carucates of land of the king, and has there 3 ploughs, and 3 slaves and 3 female slaves. This is worth 20*s.*

Gerard has 2 carucates of land, and there are 2 ploughs. It is worth 20*s.*

Ows the king's reeve [has] 2 carucates of land, and there are 4 ploughs. It is worth 20*s.* There is in the king's demesne 1 carucate of land which Dagobert held.

Joscelin the Breton holds 5 carucates of land in Caerwent [Mon.], and there are 2 ploughs, with 2 Welshmen. It is worth 20*s.*

The Bishop of Coutances holds 5 carucates of land of the king, and one of his men [holds] of him. There are 2 ploughs in demesne; and 3 [ploughs] of the villans. It is worth 40*s.*

Roger of Berkeley holds 2 carucates of land at Rogerstone [Mon.], and has there 6 bordars with 1 plough. It is worth 20*s.*

Durand the sheriff holds of the king in Caerwent [Mon.] 1 estate called Caldicot [Mon.]. There he has in demesne 3 ploughs; and 15 half-villans and 4 slaves and 1 knight. All these have 12 ploughs. There is a mill rendering 10*s.* The whole of this is worth £6.

William de EU has, as he says, £9 as customary dues from Chepstow [Mon.]. But Gerard and other men say that he has no more by right from the £10 of customary dues of Chepstow, even if it should be valued at £100.

• In Wales the same William has in fief 3 fisheries in the Wye [which] render 70*s.*, and in the same fief Earl William gave Ralph de Limesy 50 carucates of land as it is done in Normandy. Hugh and other livery-officers attest that he granted it to Ralph thus. Now William de EU says that he has only 32 carucates of this land. There are in demesne 8 ploughs; and the men have 16 ploughs. There are 2 mills rendering 10*s.* The whole is worth £12. 10*s.*

Roger de Lacy holds in the fief of Chepstow [Mon.] as much inhabited land with 1 mill as is worth 36*s.*

Turstin fitzRolf has 17 ploughs [*sic*] between the Usk and the Wye. 4½ of these are in demesne; the others are the men's. There are 11 bordars, and a mill rendering 7*s.* The whole is worth £9. The king's reeves claim 5½ carucates of this land, saying that Turstin took them without any grant.

The same Turstin has 6 carucates of land beyond the Usk, and there his men have 4 ploughs, and a mill rendering 15*s.*, and [there is] half a fishery rendering 10*s.* The whole is worth 54*s.* 6*d.*

Alvred d'Epaignes has in fief 2 carucates of land, and there are 2 ploughs in demesne. The same Alvred has in Wales 7 vills which belonged to Earl William, and to Roger, his son, in demesne. These render 6 sesters of honey and 6 pigs and 10*s.*

• The BOROUGH of WINCHCOMBE rendered £6 as farm TRE. Earl Harold had the third penny of this [£6], that is, 40*s*. Afterwards, it rendered £20 with the whole hundred of the same vill. Durand the sheriff added 100*s*., and Roger d'Ivry 60*s*. Now with the 3 hundreds associated with it, it renders £28 at 20[*d*.] to the ora.

HERE ARE NOTED THE LANDHOLDERS OF GLOUCESTERSHIRE

• I KING WILLIAM
II The Archbishop of York
III The Bishop of Worcester
IIII The Bishop of Hereford
V The Bishop of Exeter
VI The Bishop of Saint-Lo
VII The Church of Bath
VIII The Abbey of Glastonbury
IX The Abbey of Malmesbury
X The Abbey of Gloucester
XI The Abbey of Winchcombe
XII The Abbey of Evesham
XIII The Abbey of Abingdon
XIIII The Abbey of Pershore
XV The Abbey of Coventry
XVI The Abbey of Cormeilles
XVII The Abbey of Lyre
XVIII The Abbey of Eynsham
XIX The Abbey of Westminster
XX The Church of Saint-Denis of Paris
XXI The Church of Lambeth
XXII The Church of Saint-Evroul
XXIII The Church of LA TRINITE, Caen
XXIIII The Church of Troarn
XXV The Church of Cirencester
XXVI Regenbald the priest
XXVII Earl Roger
XXVIII Earl Hugh
XXIX The Count of Mortain
XXX Gilbert Maminot, Bishop of Lisieux
XXXI William de Eu
XXXII William fitzBaderon
XXXIII William the chamberlain
XXXIIII William Goizenboded
XXXV William fitzGuy
XXXVI William Froisseloup
XXXVII William fitzNorman
XXXVIII William Leofric
XXXIX Roger de Lacy
XL Roger de Beaumont
XLI Roger d'Ivry
XLII Roger of Berkeley
XLIII Ralph, his brother
XLIIII Ralph Paynel
XLV Ralph de Tosny
XLVI Robert de Tosny
XLVII Robert Despenser
XLVIII Robert d'Oilly
XLIX Richard the legate
L Osbern Giffard
LI Geoffrey Orlateile
LII Gilbert fitzTurold
LIII Durand the sheriff
LIIII Drogo fitzPons
LV Walter fitzPons
LVI Walter fitzRoger
LVII Walter the deacon
LVIII Walter the crossbowman
LIX Henry de Ferrers
LX Ernulf de Hesdin
LXI Harold son of Ralph
LXII Hugh de Grandmesnil
LXIII Hugh l'Asne
LXIIII Miles Crispin
LXV Urse d'Abetot
LXVI Hascoit Musard
LXVII Turstin fitzRolf
LXVIII Ansfrid de Cormeilles
LXIX Humphrey the chamberlain
LXX Humphrey of Maidenhill
LXXI Humphrey the cook
LXXII Sigar de Chocques
LXXIII Matthew de Mortagne
LXXIIII Joscelin the Breton
LXXV Roger fitzRalph
LXXVI The wife of Gerwy
LXXVII Baldwin
LXXVIII Ælfsige and other thegns of the king

THE LAND OF THE KING

• King EDWARD held CHELTENHAM. There were 8½ hides. 1½ hides belong to the church. Regenbald holds them. In demesne were 3 ploughs; and 20 villans and 10 bordars and 7 slaves with 18 ploughs. The priests, 2 ploughs. There, 2 mills rendering 11*s*. 8*d*. To this manor King William's reeve added 2 bordars and 4 villans, and 3 mills – 2 of these are the king's, the third the reeve's – and there is 1 plough more. TRE it rendered £9. 5*s*. and 3,000 loaves for the hounds. Now it renders £20 and 20 cows and 20 pigs and 16*s*. for loaves.

• In 'BARTON' [in Gloucester] King Edward had 9 hides. 7 of these were in demesne, and there are 3 ploughs; and 14 villans and 10 bordars with 9 ploughs. There are 7 slaves. Of this manor 2 free men hold 2 hides, and they have there 9 ploughs. These men cannot separate themselves nor the land from the manor. There is a mill rendering 4*s*. King William's reeve added 8 bordars and 2 mills and 1 plough. TRE it rendered £9. 5*s*. and 3,000 loaves for the hounds. Now it renders £20, 20 cows, 20 pigs and 16*s*. for loaves.

Archbishop Ealdræd leased 1 member of this manor, BRAWN. There are 3 virgates of land and 3 men. Miles Crispin holds it.

Alwig the sheriff leased another member, called UPTON ST LEONARDS. There is 1 hide of land, and there are 4 men. Humphrey holds it.

The same Alwig leased a third member, called 'MORWENT' [in Hartpury]. There are 3 virgates of land. Nigel the physician holds it.

• IN 'DUDSTONE' HUNDRED a certain thegn, Eadmær, had 3 manors, Haresfield and Down Hatherley and Sandhurst. This man could give and sell his land to whom he wished. This land was assessed at 2 hides. In demesne were 8 ploughs; and 4 villans and 4 bordars and 30 slaves with 5 ploughs. There is sufficient meadow for the ploughs.

• In HARESCOMBE Wigflæd held 3 free virgates of land, like Eadmær. She had 2 ploughs there, and 2 bordars and 5 slaves, and meadows for the ploughs.

• In BROOKTHORPE Ælfric held 3 virgates of land. [. . .] He had 2 ploughs, and 1 villan, 3 bordars [and] 4 slaves. Earl Harold took these 5 lands after the death of King Edward. Roger d'Ivry put these same [lands] to farm for £46. 13*s*. 4*d*.

• In the same HUNDRED, adjoining the city, Wulfweard had half a hide of King Edward quit, and there are 2 ploughs, and 4 slaves. Earl William gave this to one of his cooks, for Wulfweard was outlawed.

• IN CIRENCESTER HUNDRED King Edward had 5 hides of land. There are in demesne 5 ploughs; and [he has] 31 villans with 10 ploughs. There are 13 slaves and 10 bordars, and 3 mills rendering 30*s*., meadows, and 2 woods rendering 50*s*., and there are 2 free men having 2 ploughs. The queen had the wool from the sheep. TRE this manor rendered 3½ modii of wheat and 3 modii of malt, and 6½ sesters of honey, and £9. 5*s*., and 3,000 loaves for the hounds. Now it renders £20. 5*s*., 20 cows, 20 pigs, and 16*s*. for loaves, and from the new market 20*s*., of which ST MARY'S has the third penny.

In Cirencester 1 free man held 2 hides of land and paid 20*s*. in farm, and did service for the sheriff throughout the whole of England. Earl William put this land outside the farm and gave it to one of his men.

• IN 'SWINESHEAD' HUNDRED there were TRE 36 hides at farm in BITTON, with 2 members, Wapley and Winterbourne. In demesne were 5 ploughs; and 41 villans and 29 bordars with 45 ploughs. There are 18 slaves, with 1 mill. TRE this manor rendered the farm of 1 night, and now it does the same.

• IN SALMONSBURY HUNDRED King Edward held LOWER SLAUGHTER. There were 7 hides, and in demesne 3 ploughs; and 9 villans and 11 bordars with 8 ploughs. 7 slaves there, and 2 mills rendering 1 mark of silver, meadows rendering 10*s*., and from 1 of these hides 10*s*., and 5*s*. for the hounds.

From this manor the sheriff paid what he wished TRE. Therefore they do not know [how] to value it. Now the sheriff has added there 1 plough, and 5 bordars with 1 plough. Now he pays from this manor and from the hundred £27 by tale.

● In WESTBURY-ON-SEVERN [were] 30 hides. There King Edward had 5 ploughs in demesne; and 32 villans and 15 bordars with 28 ploughs. There is 1 slave.

This manor rendered the farm of 1 night TRE; the same for 4 years TRW. Afterwards 6 hides were taken away from this manor in Kyre ['Little Kyre' and Kyre Magna, Worcs.], and 10 hides in Clifton upon Teme [Worcs.], 8 hides in Newent and Kingstone [in Weston under Penyard, Herefs.], [and] 1 hide in Edvin Loach [Herefs.].

Now the Abbot of Cormeilles and Osbern and William fitzRichard hold these lands, and yet from what remains the sheriff finds the whole farm. The men of the shire, however, say that "Sapina" lay in Westbury-on-Severn in the farm of King Edward.

● In KIFTSGATE Hundred King Edward held "LANGEBERGE" [?War.], with 1 member called MEON [Meon and Lower Meon, War.]. In each were 8 hides. In demesne, 3 ploughs; and 10 villans and 4 bordars with 6 ploughs, and a mill rendering 5*s*., and 6 slaves. Meadow rendering 10*s*. TRE the sheriff paid from this manor whatever it produced at farm. Now it renders £15 with the 2 hundreds which the sheriff placed there.

● In BLEDISLOE Hundred King Edward held AWRE. There are 5 hides, and in demesne 1 plough; and 12 villans and 8 bordars with 14 ploughs. There is 1 slave, and a mill rendering 30*d*., and a salt-pan rendering 30 summae of salt, and a church with 1 virgate of land.

This manor rendered half of the farm of a night TRE, and now it does the same. In the same manor there lies waste half a hide and accordingly it only renders £12. Yet the sheriff pays the whole farm.

☒ Outside the manor are 3 members which were always within it, and ought to be, as the men of the shire bear witness, that is, Purton, Etloe [and] Bledisloe. In these are 7 hides, and in demesne 1 plough; and 20 villans and 3 bordars with 13 ploughs, and 2 slaves, and a fishery.

Purton is in the fief of Earl William. Roger of Berkeley holds Etloe. William fitzBaderon holds Bledisloe. Alwig the sheriff put these outside the farm.

● In 'LANGLEY' HUNDRED Earl Harold held ALVESTON. There were 10 hides. In demesne [is] 1 plough; and 23 villans and 5 bordars with 22 ploughs, and 2 slaves. The reeve has added there 2 ploughs, and 5 slaves. It renders £12 by weight.

● IN BERKELEY King Edward had 5 hides, and in demesne [are] 5 ploughs; and 20 villans and 5 bordars with 11 ploughs, and 9 slaves, and 2 mills rendering 12*s*. There are 10 radknights having 7 hides and 7 ploughs. There is 1 market in which 17 men dwell, and they pay rent in the farm.

These BEREWICKS pertain to BERKELEY:

● In Hill 4 hides; in [?]Alkington 4 hides; in Hinton 4 hides; in Cam 6 hides, and another 11 hides; in Gossington 4 hides; in Dursley 3 hides; in Coaley 4 hides; in Uley 2 hides; in Nympsfield 3 hides; in Wotton-under-Edge 15 hides and half a virgate; in Symonds' Hall half a hide; in Kingscote 4½ hides; in Beverston 10 hides; in Ozleworth half a hide; in Almondsbury 2 hides; in Horfield [in Bristol] 8 hides; in Kingsweston [in Bristol] 7 hides and 1 virgate; in Elberton 5 hides; in Cromhall 2 hides; in Arlingham 9 hides; in Ashleworth 3 hides.

All these members, written above, pertain to Berkeley. All together [. . .].

In these [lands] TRE [were] in demesne 49½ ploughs; and 242 villans and 142 bordars with 126 ploughs. There are 127 slaves. There are 19 free men, radknights, having 48 ploughs with their men. There are 22 coliberts and 15 female slaves. There are 8 mills rendering 57*s*. 6*d*.

● In this manor TRE 2 brothers held 5 hides in CROMHALL, having in demesne 2 ploughs; and 6 villans and 5 bordars having 6 ploughs. These 2 brothers could turn where they would with their land. Then it was worth £4; now £3. These men Earl William commended to the reeve of Berkeley so that he might have their service; so says Roger. From this manor with all its appurtenances Roger pays at farm £170 assayed and weighed. ☒

● Roger himself has of the land of this manor 2 hides in Slimbridge, 1 hide in Clingre, 1 hide in Hurst [Hurst and Old Hurst], [and] 7 hides in Newington Bagpath. There are in demesne 10 ploughs; and 13 villans and 21 bordars with 22 ploughs. There are 16 slaves, and a mill rendering 5*s*. The whole was worth £9 TRE; now £11. 10*s*.

The same Roger holds 5 hides, the land of Bernard the priest. There he has 3 ploughs, and 2 villans and 6 bordars with 5 ploughs. It is and was worth 60*s*.

● In SHARPNESS are 5 hides pertaining to Berkeley which Earl William put outside [the farm] to build a little castle. Roger claims these.

● In "EDREDESTANE" Hundred Queen Edith held MARSHFIELD. There are 14 hides. In demesne [are] 5 ploughs; and 36 villans and 13 bordars with 30 ploughs. There are 18 slaves. A priest has 1 of these hides. TRE it rendered £35; now £47.

● In BARTON in BRISTOL were 6 hides. In demesne [are] 3 ploughs; and 22 villans and 25 bordars with 25 ploughs. There are 9 slaves and 18 coliberts having 14 ploughs. There are 2 mills rendering †27*s*.† When Roger received this manor from the king he found there 2 hides, and 2 ploughs in demesne; and 17 villans and 24 bordars with 21 ploughs. 4 slaves and 13 coliberts with 3 ploughs. In 1 member of the same manor, Mangotsfield, 6 oxen in demesne. Of the same land, the Church of Bristol holds 3 hides, and 1 plough is reckoned there. 1 radknight holds 1 hide, and has 1 plough, and 4 bordars with 1 plough. This manor and BRISTOL render to the king 110 marks of silver. The burgesses say that, besides the king's farm, Bishop Geoffrey has 33 marks of silver and 1 mark of gold.

● In 'BRADLEY' HUNDRED Baldwin son of Herluin had 1 manor in which were 10 hides. The Bishop of Bayeux held this manor. Now it is in the king's hand and pays geld. In demesne are 2 ploughs; and 7 villans and 5 bordars with 6 ploughs. There are 5 slaves, and 2 mills rendering 20*s*. There is a priest. TRE it was worth £12; now £6.

● In CIRENCESTER HUNDRED Almær had HULLASEY, in which were 3½ hides. The Bishop of Bayeux held it. Now it is in the king's hand. In demesne is 1 plough; and 4 villans and 4 bordars with 3 ploughs. It was worth £4; now 50*s*. ☒

7 ● In TEWKESBURY were 95 hides TRE. Of these, 45 are in demesne, and were quit of all royal service and geld except the service of the lord himself whose manor it was. In the capital manor were in demesne 12 ploughs, and all together 50 slaves and female slaves, and 16 bordars lived around the hall, and [there were] 2 mills rendering 20*s*., and 1 fishery, and 1 salt-pan at Droitwich [Worcs.] pertaining to the manor.

At Southwick 3 hides; in Tredington 6 hides; in Fiddington 6 hides; in Pamington 8 hides; in Natton |3½ hides;| in Walton Cardiff 3 hides; [. . .] in Aston on Carrant 6 hides. |[partly in margin]|

There were 21 villans and 9 radknights having 26 ploughs, and 5 coliberts and 1 bordar with 5 ploughs. These radknights ploughed and harrowed at the lord's court.

In Gloucester were 8 burgesses paying 5*s*. 4*d*. and serving at court.

7 In the whole of Tewkesbury are 120 acres of meadow, and woodland 1½ leagues long and as much broad.

[7] At Tewkesbury are now 13 burgesses paying 20*s.* a year. The market which the queen established there renders 11*s.* 8*d.* There is 1 plough more, and 22 slaves and female slaves all together. [There is] 1 fishery, and 1 salt-pan at Droitwich [Worcs.].

● Three radknights belonged there TRE. One of them held 6 hides in Aston on Carrant. Now Gerard holds them. Another held 3 hides in Walton Cardiff. Now Ralph holds them. The third held 2 hides in Fiddington. Now Bernard holds them.

In these 11 hides are 10 ploughs in demesne; and 4 villans and 1 bordar and 9 slaves with 1 plough. There are 18 acres of meadow. The whole was worth £10 TRE; now as much.

● At OXENTON TRE was a hall and 5 hides pertaining to Tewkesbury. There are 5 ploughs in demesne; and 5 villans and 2 radknights having 7 ploughs, and 12 slaves and female slaves all together. There are 24 acres of meadow. At Winchcombe 3 burgesses pay 40*d.* All this is and was worth £8.

This land listed below belongs to the Church of Tewkesbury.

[6] ● IN STANWAY [Stanway and Wood Stanway] are 7 hides belonging to the church. There are 2 ploughs in demesne; and 8 villans and 2 bordars with 8 ploughs. There is a minster, and 5 slaves and female slaves all together, and a salt-pan at Droitwich [Worcs.], and 8 acres of meadow, [and] woodland 3 furlongs long and 1 broad. TRE it was worth £8; now £7.

[6] ● In TADDINGTON, 4 hides. There are 2 ploughs, and 11 villans and 1 radknight with 2 ploughs, and 3 bordars and 9 slaves. It was worth £6; now 100*s.*

[6] ● In LOWER LEMINGTON, 3 hides. There are 2 ploughs, and 8 villans with 4 ploughs, and 6 slaves and 1 bordar. It was worth 60*s.*; now 40*s.*

[6] ● In GREAT WASHBOURNE, 3 hides. There are 2 ploughs, and 6 villans with 3 ploughs, and 1 bordar and 9 slaves with a female slave. It was and is worth 60*s.*

[6] ● In FIDDINGTON, 2 hides. There is 1 villan and 2 coliberts with 2 ploughs. It is and was worth 10*s.* 1 of these hides was quit land.

[6] ● In NATTON, 1 hide of quit land, and there is 1 plough. It is worth 10*s.*

[6] ● In STANLEY PONTLARGE, 4½ hides. There is 1 plough, and 4 villans with 2 ploughs, and 3 bordars and 5 slaves. This land was quit. It was worth £4; now 40*s.*

All the land belonging to the church paid geld for 20 hides TRE.

[7] ● To the same manor of Tewkesbury belonged, besides the demesne, 4 hides which are in Hanley Castle [Worcs.]. TRE there were in demesne 2 ploughs, and 40 villans and bordars all together, and 8 slaves and female slaves all together, and a mill rendering 16*d.* Woodland in which there was an enclosure. This land belonged to Earl William. Now it is in the king's farm in Hereford. TRE it was worth £15; now £10.

● In Forthampton 9 hides belonged to this manor. There are 2 ploughs in demesne, and 20 villans and bordars all together, and 6 slaves and female slaves all together. There is woodland. It was worth £10 TRE; now £8. Earl William held these 2 estates, and they paid geld with Tewkesbury.

● In Shenington [Oxon.] 10 hides belonged to the same manor. There are 4 ploughs, and 8 villans and 4 bordars and 5 radknights with 8 ploughs. There are 12 slaves, and a mill rendering 3*s.* This land paid geld for 7 hides. TRE it was worth £20; now £8. It is in the king's hand. Robert d'Oilly holds it at farm.

● In CLIFFORD CHAMBERS [War.], 7 hides belonging to the same manor. 3 ploughs in demesne there; and 14 villans with 5 ploughs, and a mill rendering 12*s.*, and 2 acres of meadow. All together there were 13 slaves and female slaves, and a church and a priest with 1 plough. It was worth £8; now £6. The queen gave this land to Roger de Bully, and it paid geld for 4 hides in Tewkesbury.

The 50 hides described above have made quit and freed from all geld and royal service the 95 hides which belonged to Tewkesbury.

[7] This manor of Tewkesbury, when it was complete TRE, was worth £100; when Ralph received it, £12, since it had been dismembered and broken up; now it is valued at £40, but Ralph pays £50.

[7] Beorhtric son of Ælfgar held this manor TRE and at that time he had these lands of other thegns, listed below, in his power.

● In ASHTON UNDER HILL [Worcs.] 1 thegn held 4 hides, and it was a manor. Now Gerard holds it and has 1 plough there, and 2 villans with 1 plough. It is and was worth 40*s.*

● In KEMERTON [Worcs.] Liut held 8 hides, and it was a manor. Now Gerard holds it and has 3 ploughs there, and 14 villans with 6 ploughs. There are 8 slaves, and 3 mills rendering 15*s.* It was worth £8; now £6. 3 hides in Boddington belong to this manor. The same Gerard holds them, and has there 2 ploughs, and 4 villans with 3 ploughs, and there are 3 slaves, and a mill rendering 8*s.*, and 8 acres of meadow. It is and was worth 40*s.*

● In WINCOT [War.] 1 thegn held 3 hides. The queen gave this land to Regenbald the chaplain. There are 3 villans with half a plough. It was worth 40*s.*

● In ALDERTON Dunning held 6½ hides, and in Dixton 4½ hides, and in [?]'Hentage' [in Alderton] 1 thegn held 1 hide. Humphrey holds these lands of the king, and has 4 ploughs in demesne there; and [there are] 5 villans and 8 bordars with 3 ploughs, and 1 radknight with 1 plough, and in Winchcombe 1 burgess; and 12 acres of meadow are reckoned there. TRE the whole was worth £11; now £6.

● In THE MYTHE 4 villans held 2 hides, and 1 thegn half a hide. There are 4 ploughs, and 3 acres of meadow. The queen gave this land to John the chamberlain. It is and was worth 35*s.*

● In STOKE ORCHARD Hermar and Alwine held 3 hides, less 1 virgate. Now Bernard holds them of the king, and has 1 plough in demesne there, and 4 acres of meadow. It was worth 60*s.*; now 40*s.*

● Those who held these lands TRE submitted themselves and their lands under the power of Beorhtric.

IN 'LANGLEY' HUNDRED

● BEORHTRIC son of Ælfgar held Thornbury. TRE there were 11 hides, and 4 ploughs in demesne; and 42 villans and 18 radknights with 21 ploughs, and 24 bordars and 15 slaves and 4 coliberts. 2 mills rendering 6*s.* 4*d.* there, [and] woodland 1 league long and 1 broad. A market rendering 20*s.* there. Now the reeve has added a mill there rendering 8*d.* This manor belonged to Queen Matilda. Humphrey pays from it £50 by tale. In this manor is 1 meadow rendering 40*s.*, and at Droitwich [Worcs.] 40 sesters of salt or 20*d.*, and a fishery at Gloucester rendering 58*d.*

IN "EDREDESTANE" HUNDRED

● The same Beorhtric held OLD SODBURY. TRE there were 10 hides, and 4 ploughs in demesne; and 12 villans with 5 ploughs, and 4 bordars and 18 slaves, and a park, and a mill rendering 5*s.* Now the reeve has added 1 mill rendering 40*d.* There is woodland 1 league long and 1 broad.

From this manor Humphrey pays £16. 10*s.* To this manor belongs 1 virgate in Droitwich [Worcs.] which rendered 25 sesters of salt. Urse the sheriff oppressed the men to such an extent that now they cannot render the salt.

IN LONGTREE HUNDRED

● The same Beorhtric held AVENING. TRE there were 10 hides, and 8 ploughs in demesne; and 24 villans and 5 bordars and 30 slaves with 16 ploughs. There were 4 mills rendering 19*s.* 2*d.* Now the reeve has added 1 mill rendering 40*d.* There is woodland 2 leagues long and half a league broad. There is a hawk's eyrie. It is worth £27.

IN 'BRIGHTWELLS BARROW' HUNDRED

● The same Beorhtric held FAIRFORD. TRE there were 21 hides, and [he had] 56 villans and 9 bordars with 30 ploughs. There was a priest, who held 1 virgate of the demesne, and 3 mills rendering 32*s.* 6*d.* In demesne are only 13 hides and 1 virgate. Queen Matilda held this manor. Humphrey pays £38. 10*s.* by tale. From the land of this manor the queen gave 4 hides to John the chamberlain. There are 2 ploughs, and 9 villans and 4 bordars with 4 ploughs. There are 14 slaves. It renders £9 at farm.

● The queen herself gave Baldwin 3 hides and 3 virgates of the same land, and he has 2 ploughs there, and 5 slaves, and 1 free man having 1 plough, and 2 bordars. It is worth £4.

Those who held these 2 estates TRE were not able to withdraw from the capital manor.

In Botloe Hundred

● King Edward held Dymock. There were 20 hides, and 2 ploughs in demesne; and 42 villans and 10 bordars and 11 coliberts having 41 ploughs. A priest there holding 12 acres, and 4 radknights with 4 ploughs. Woodland there 3 leagues long and 1 broad. From this manor the sheriff paid what he wished TRE. King William held it in his demesne for 4 years. Afterwards Earl William had it and [then] Roger, his son. The men of the shire do not know by what means. Now it renders £21.

In Bledisloe Hundred

● Earl Harold held Naas. There were 5 hides, and in demesne 1 plough; and 10 villans and 2 bordars with 9 ploughs. TRE it was not at farm. Earl William joined it to 2 other manors, namely Poulton [in Awre] and Purton. In these there were 9 hides, and 2 ploughs in demesne; and 15 villans and 2 bordars and 2 slaves with 9 ploughs. 1 fishery there. Now the reeve has added in Poulton [in Awre] 1 plough. Purton is claimed for the king's farm. All together they render £11.

● In Lydney Earl William made 1 manor out of 4 estates which he received from their lords. From the demesne of the Bishop of Hereford, 3 hides. From the demesne for the sustenance of the monks of Pershore, 6 hides where there were 6 villans with 4 ploughs. From 2 thegns he received 3½ hides. There are in demesne 3 ploughs, and 8 bordars, and a mill rendering 40*d*. [There is] woodland 1 league long and a half broad. All together it renders £7.

● In Tidenham Hundred the Abbot of Bath had 1 manor called Tidenham. 30 hides were reckoned there. 10 of these were in demesne. There were 38 villans having 38 ploughs, and 10 bordars. In the Severn, 11 fisheries in demesne, and 42 fisheries of the villans. In the Wye, 1 fishery, and 2½ fisheries of the villans. Earl Roger added 2 fisheries in the Wye. There is woodland 2 leagues long and half a league broad, and there are 12 bordars more.

● From this land Earl William gave 1 virgate of land to his brother, Bishop Osbern, with 1 villan, and to Walter de Lacy he gave 2 fisheries in the Severn and half [a fishery] in the Wye with 1 villan. To Ralph de Limesy he gave 2 fisheries in the Wye with 1 villan. To the Abbey of Lyre he gave half a hide of land and the church of the manor, with tithe.

This manor did not pay rent TRE, except for the sustenance of the monks. Archbishop Stigand was holding it when Earl William received it. Now it renders £25 at 20[*d*.] to the ora, and in blanch money. There is now a mill rendering 40*d*.

In Rapsgate Hundred

● Wulfweard held Chedworth. There were 15 hides in woodland and field and meadow, and 7 ploughs in demesne TRE; and 16 villans and 3 bordars with 6 ploughs, and 3 mills rendering 14*s*. 2*d*., and a toll of salt which came to the hall. There the sheriff has added 8 villans and 3 bordars having 4 ploughs.

In Bibury Hundred

● Cynewig Chelle, a thegn of King Edward, held Arlington. ☒ There were 5 hides, and 4 ploughs in demesne; and 12 villans and 1 bordar with 6 ploughs; and 16 slaves and female slaves all together, and 2 mills rendering 20*s*. Woodland 1 league long and a half broad. The reeves of these 2 manors paid what they wished TRE. Now they pay £40 of blanch money at 20[*d*.] to the ora. Earl Roger held them.

In Tibblestone Hundred

● Rotlesc, a housecarl of King Edward, held Beckford [Worcs.]. There were 11 hides, and 3 ploughs in demesne; and 34 villans and 17 bordars having 30 ploughs. There are 12 slaves and 4 female slaves. From this manor Earl William gave 3 hides to Ansfrid de Cormeilles in which there were 12 villans with 5 ploughs.

● Thorbert, a thegn of Earl Harold, held Ashton under Hill [Worcs.]. There are 8 hides, and 4 ploughs in demesne; and 10 villans and 4 bordars with 6 ploughs. There are 8 slaves and 3 female slaves. Earl William made 1 manor of these 2 vills and they were not [held] at farm until Roger d'Ivry put them at farm for £30. The earl himself gave to the Abbey of Cormeilles the tithes and the churches with 2 villans and 3 virgates of land.

The men of the shire, when questioned, said that they had never seen the king's writ which said this land had been given to Earl William.

In 'Langley' Hundred

● Wulfgar, a thegn of King Edward, held Tockington. There were 8 hides, and 5 ploughs in demesne; and 20 villans and 12 bordars and 10 slaves with 20 ploughs. This manor did not ☒ render farm TRE but the person who owned it lived off it. Earl William held it in demesne and there the reeve added 1 plough, and a mill rendering 8*d*. Now it renders £24 of blanch money at 20[*d*.] to the ora.

In 'Dudstone' Hundred

● Eadric Lang, a thegn of Earl Harold, held Hempsted [in Gloucester]. ☒ There were 5 hides, and in demesne 3 ploughs; and 6 villans and 8 bordars with 6 ploughs. 6 slaves there, and half a fishery. Earl William took this manor in demesne and it was not at farm. But now the sheriff has put it [at farm] for 60*s*. by tale.

In Longtree Hundred

● Gytha, the mother of Earl Harold, held Woodchester. Earl Godwine bought it from Azur and gave it to his wife so that she could live off it while she stayed at Berkeley. She was unwilling to use up anything from that manor because of the destruction of the abbey. Edward holds this land in the farm of Wiltshire, unjustly as the shire says, since it does not pertain to any farm. No one gave any account of this manor to the king's commissioners, nor did any of them come to this registration. This land renders £7.

In Wyvern Hundred

● Beorhtric held 3 hides in Madgetts, and they paid geld. In demesne there the king has 2 fisheries. Roger de Lacy has 1 fishery with half a hide. The Abbot of Malmesbury has 1 fishery with half a hide and this by the king's gift, as they say. William de Eu has 2 hides, and he claims these 4 fisheries. These fisheries are in the Wye, and they rendered £4.

In "Gersdones" Hundred

● Eadnoth held Down Ampney TRE. There are 15 hides paying geld. Of these King Edward pardoned Eadnoth 5 hides, as the shire says, and afterwards this manor paid for 10 hides. In demesne [are] 4 ploughs; and a priest and 19 villans and 3 bordars with 10 ploughs. There are 12 slaves. This manor belonged to the Bishop of Bayeux and was worth £20. Now it renders £26 to the king's farm.

In Barrington Hundred

● Tovi the Wend, a housecarl of Earl Harold, held Great Barrington. There are 4 hides. In demesne are 2 ploughs; and 10 villans and 5 bordars with 5 ploughs. There are 4 slaves, and a mill rendering 5*s*. It is and was worth £7. Ælfsige of Faringdon holds it in the king's farm.

● Æthelmær held 4 hides in Great Barrington as a manor TRE. In demesne is 1 plough; and 7 villans and 3 bordars with 4 ploughs. There are 6 slaves, and a mill rendering 5*s*. It was worth 100*s*.; now 60*s*. Godwine of Stanton holds it in the king's farm.

II. THE LAND OF ARCHBISHOP THOMAS

● Archbishop Stigand held Churchdown. There were 15½ hides, and 2 ploughs in demesne; and 18 villans and 5 bordars and 7 radknights with 30 ploughs. There is woodland half a league long and 3 furlongs broad. Then it was worth £13; now £12.

● The same Stigand held Hucclecote [in Gloucester]. There were 4 hides, and in demesne 2 ploughs; and 11 villans and 5 bordars with 11 ploughs. There is a mill rendering 32*d*., and woodland 1 league long and a half broad. Then, as now, worth £4.

● The same Stigand held Bishop's Norton. There were 5½ hides, and in demesne 2 ploughs; and 15 villans with 15 ploughs, and 4 slaves, and a mill rendering 32*d*. Then, as now, worth £4.

Archbishop Thomas now holds these 3 manors. Walkelin, a nephew of the Bishop of Winchester, holds Bishop's Norton of him.

In Salmonsbury Hundred

● Archbishop Ealdræd held [Lower and Upper] Oddington, with the Berewick of Condicote. There were 10 hides, and 2 ploughs in demesne; and 16 villans and 2 radknights and 4 bordars with 14 ploughs. This land never paid geld TRE. It was worth £6; now £10. Archbishop Thomas holds it. St Peter of Gloucester had it in demesne until King William came to England.

In Cheltenham Hundred

● Archbishop Stigand held Swindon. There were 3 hides, and 2 ploughs in demesne; and 7 villans and 2 bordars and they have 7 ploughs. There are 4 slaves. Then it was worth £3; now £4. 10*s*. Archbishop Thomas holds this manor from the land of St Oswald and it pays geld.

In "Wacrescumbe" Hundred

● Gundulf held and holds in Shipton Solers 1 manor of 1 hide, and it pays geld, and there is 1 plough in demesne, and it is worth 8*s*. He holds it of Archbishop Thomas.

● Pinn held 1 manor of 1 hide in Hampen, and it paid geld. Ansgar holds it of Archbishop Thomas, and he has 1 plough in demesne. It was worth 20*s*.; now 10*s*.

[2] In 'Bradley' Hundred

● St Peter of Gloucester held Northleach, and Archbishop Ealdræd held it with the abbey. There were 24 hides. In demesne are 4 ploughs; and 33 villans and 16 bordars with 30 ploughs. There are 4 slaves, and 2 mills rendering 7*s*. 4*d*.

Stowell belongs to this manor. There are 2 ploughs in demesne; and 5 villans with 5 ploughs, and a mill rendering 40*d*., and 4 slaves and 2 female slaves; and in Upper Coberley is 1 hide belonging to this manor.

Of this land of this manor Walter fitzPons holds 1 manor of 12 hides which belonged to the same manor TRE. There are 2 ploughs in demesne at Farmington; and 25 villans with 12 ploughs, and 4 slaves.

The whole manor was worth £18 TRE. Archbishop Thomas put it at farm for £27. The hide of Upper Coberley is valued at 20*s*.; what Walter holds is worth £14. Archbishop Thomas claims it.

● Archbishop Stigand held Compton Abdale. There were 9 hides. There are 2 ploughs, and 5 acres of meadow, and 22 villans and 5 bordars with 11 ploughs. There are 5 slaves, and a mill rendering 5*s*. TRE it was worth £9; now £7. Archbishop Thomas holds it. A man of Roger d'Ivry holds 1 manor of 3 hides belonging to this manor. The archbishop himself claims this.

In 'Whitstone' Hundred

● Archbishop Ealdræd held Standish. It belonged to the demesne of St Peter of Gloucester. There were 15 hides TRE. In demesne are 3 ploughs; and 9 villans and 14 bordars with 16 ploughs, and 7 radknights having 17 ploughs. There are 8 slaves, and half a fishery, [and] woodland half a league long and 1 furlong broad. TRE the whole manor was worth £16; now £12. Archbishop Thomas holds it and it pays geld in the same way.

Of this land of this manor the Abbot of Gloucester holds 1 hide and ought by right to hold it. Earl Hugh holds 1 hide unjustly. Durand the sheriff holds 3 hides which Earl William gave to his brother Roger. Archbishop Thomas claims these.

In Barrington Hundred

● St Oswald of Gloucester held Widford [Oxon.]. There were 2 hides TRE, and 2 ploughs in demesne; and 4 villans and †3† bordars with 2 ploughs. There are 4 slaves, and 8 acres of meadow, and a mill rendering 10*s*. TRE it was worth 40*s*.; now 60*s*. Ranulph holds it of the same saint. As it was then, so it is now.

In Rapsgate Hundred

● St Oswald held North Cerney, a manor of 4 hides, TRE. The same saint still holds it and has 2 ploughs in demesne; and 6 villans and 2 bordars with 5 ploughs. There is 1 slave, and a mill rendering 7*s*., and 2 acres of meadow. Then it was worth 100*s*.; now £4.

In "Langebrige" Hundred

● Ulfkil held Lassington, a manor of 2 hides. Now Roger holds it of Archbishop Thomas. This land pays geld. In demesne is 1 plough; and 5 villans and 2 bordars with 3 ploughs. There are 3 slaves, and 20 acres of meadow. It was worth 40*s*.; now |30*s*.| |[in margin]|

III. THE LAND OF THE CHURCH OF WORCESTER

In Brentry Hundred

● St Mary of Worcester held and holds Westbury on Trym [in Bristol]. There were and are 50 hides. In demesne are 2 ploughs; and 8 villans and 6 bordars with 8 ploughs. There are 4 slaves and 1 female slave.

These members belong to this manor: Henbury [in Bristol], Redwick, Stoke Bishop [in Bristol], Yate. In these are 9 ploughs in demesne; and 27 villans and 22 bordars with 26 ploughs. There are 20 slaves and 2 female slaves and 20 coliberts with 10 ploughs, and a mill rendering 20*d*.

To this manor belong 6 radknights having 8 hides and 8 ploughs. They could not be separated from the manor. And in Bristol 2 houses rendered 16*d*.

● Of this land of this manor Turstin fitzRolf holds 5 hides in Aust, and Gilbert fitzTurold 3½ hides in Compton Greenfield, and Constantine 5 hides in Itchington. In these lands are 5 ploughs in demesne; and 16 villans and 12 bordars with 12 ploughs. There are 11 slaves. Of the same land of this manor Osbern Giffard holds 5 hides and he does no service. The whole manor with its members was worth £24 TRE.

Now the demesne of St Mary is worth £29. 14*s*. 6*d*.; what the men hold, £9.

In Rapsgate Hundred

● The church itself held Colesbourne, and Swein [held] of it. He could not withdraw. There are 8 hides paying geld. Walter fitzRoger holds it of the church. In demesne is 1 plough; and 18 villans and 2 bordars with 5 ploughs. There are 2 slaves, and 3 acres of meadow, and 2 mills rendering 7*s*. 6*d*. Then it was worth £8; now £4.

● The church itself held Aycote, and Æthelric [held] of it. It belongs to Bibury. There is 1 hide. In demesne are 2 ploughs; and 2 villans and 4 bordars with 2 ploughs. There are 2 slaves, and 8 acres of meadow, and a mill rendering 64*d*. It was worth 20*s*.; now 30*s*. Ordric holds it of the bishop.

In Bibury Hundred

● The church itself held Bibury. There are 21 hides. In demesne
[2] are 4 ploughs; and 19 villans and 2 bordars with 11 ploughs. There are 3 radknights having 4 hides and 4 ploughs, and a priest having 3 hides and, with his men, 4 ploughs. There are all together 11 slaves and female slaves, and 2 mills rendering 17*s*., and 10 acres of meadow.

● Of the same land of this manor Durand holds of the bishop 1 manor of 3 hides and 1 virgate in Barnsley, and Eudo [holds] 7 virgates as a manor in the same place. In these are 5 ploughs in demesne; and 12 villans with 6 ploughs. There are 12 slaves. The whole manor was worth £18 TRE; and now the same. Bishop Wulfstan holds it, and it pays geld.

In "Wacrescumbe" Hundred

● The church itself holds Withington. There are 30 hides. 3 of these have never paid geld. In demesne are 2 ploughs; and 16 villans and 8 borders with 7 ploughs. There are 6 slaves, and 10 acres of meadow, [and] woodland 1 league long and a half broad, and in Cassey Compton is 1 plough, and 2 villans and 2 borders with 1 plough, and 2 slaves, and a mill rendering 5*s*.

In the same manor are 4 radknights having 2 hides and 3 virgates, and they have 2 ploughs, and [there is] a priest having half a hide and 1 plough. In Gloucester 4 burgesses pay 7½*d*.

● Of this land of this manor Morin holds of the bishop 3 hides in Foxcote, Ansketil [holds] 2 hides in Little Colesbourne and Hilcot, Robert 4½ hides in Dowdeswell and Pegglesworth, Schelin 5 hides in Notgrove, [and] Drogo 10 hides in Cold Aston.

In these lands are 16 ploughs in demesne; and 51 villans and 7 borders with 28 ploughs. There are 41 slaves, and 3 mills rendering 13*s*. 4*d*. In Winchcombe 1 burgess pays 3*s*. In certain places [are] meadow and woodland but not much.

The whole manor was worth £38 TRE; now £33 among them all. Bishop Wulfstan holds this manor.

IN TIBBLESTONE HUNDRED

● The church itself held BISHOP'S CLEEVE. There are 30 hides. In demesne are 3 ploughs; and 16 villans and 19 borders with 16 ploughs. There are 8 slaves, and 1 pack-horse. There a priest has 1 hide and 2 ploughs, and [there is] 1 radknight having 1 hide and 2 ploughs. There is a very little wood.

● Of this land of the same manor Durand the sheriff holds of the church 6 hides in Southam, Ralph [holds] 4 hides in 'Sapperton' [in Bishops Cleeve], [and] Turstin fitzRolf 6 hides in Gotherington. In these lands are 8 ploughs in demesne; and 22 villans and 7 borders with 13 ploughs. There are 20 slaves, and 3 pack-horses, and a mill rendering 12*d*., and a certain amount of meadow. Of the same land Bernard and Reginald hold 7 hides in Stoke Orchard, and they are not willing to do service to ST MARY. The whole of this manor was worth †£36† TRE; now £26 among them all. Bishop Wulfstan holds this manor.

IIII. THE LAND OF THE CHURCH OF HEREFORD

IN CHELTENHAM HUNDRED

● THE BISHOP OF HEREFORD held PRESTBURY. There are 30 hides. In demesne are 3 ploughs; and 18 villans and 5 borders with 9 ploughs. There is a priest and 1 radknight with 2 ploughs, and in Winchcombe 1 burgess paying 18*d*., and 11 slaves and female slaves all together. There are 20 acres of meadow, and woodland 1 league long and a half broad.

To this manor belongs 1 vill outside this HUNDRED, SEVENHAMPTON. There are 20 hides of the above-mentioned 30 hides; [. . .] and there are 2 ploughs, and 21 villans with 11 ploughs. There are 3 free men having 7 ploughs with their men.

Of these 20 hides Durand holds 3 hides of the bishop. The whole manor was worth £12 TRE; now £16. Robert, the bishop of the same city, holds this manor.

V. THE LAND OF BISHOP OSBERN

IN 'SWINESHEAD' HUNDRED

● The BISHOP of EXETER holds OLDLAND. Alwig, a man of Earl Harold, held it and he could go where he would. There are 2 hides; one pays geld, the other does not. In demesne are 2 ploughs; and 1 villan and 6 bordars with 1 plough. There are 2 slaves, and 10 acres of meadow. Then it was worth £4; now 20*s*.

IN BAGSTONE HUNDRED

● The same bishop holds TYTHERINGTON. Alwig held it TRE. There are 5 hides, and 2 ploughs are in demesne, and 1 villan and 5 bordars and 2 slaves, and 20 acres of meadow. [There is] woodland half a league in length and breadth. It was worth 100*s*.; now 40*s*.

VI. THE LAND OF THE BISHOP OF COUTANCES

IN BAGSTONE HUNDRED ☒

● The BISHOP of SAINT-LO holds IRON ACTON, and Ilger [holds] of him. There are 2½ hides. In demesne is 1 plough; and 4 villans and 5 bordars and 1 slave and 2 female slaves with 1½ ploughs. There is half a mill rendering 16*d*., and 10 acres of meadow and 1 furlong of woodland. It is and was worth 40*s*. Ebbi, a man of Beorhtric son of Ælfgar, held this manor.

IN 'SWINESHEAD' HUNDRED

● The same bishop holds HAMBROOK, and Oswulf [holds] of him. Algar held it of King Edward, |[in margin]| and he could go where he would. There are 2 hides. |There is land for 5 ploughs.| In demesne are 2 ploughs; and 2 villans with 2 ploughs, and 2 slaves, and 6 acres of meadow. It was worth 100*s*.; now 60*s*.

● The same bishop holds 1 manor of 1 hide, and Goismer [holds] of him. In this hide when it is ploughed there are only 64 acres of land. There is 1 plough in demesne. It was worth 20*s*.; now 16*s*.

● The same bishop holds HARRY STOKE, and Theobald [holds] of him. Ealdræd held it of Earl Harold, and could go where he would. There are 2 hides; one pays geld, the other does not. In demesne is 1 plough; and 2 villans and 1 bordar with 1 plough. There are 6 slaves, and 5 acres of meadow. It was worth 40*s*.; now 20*s*.

IN PUCKLECHURCH HUNDRED

● The same bishop holds DOYNTON, and Robert [holds] of him. Alweard, a thegn of King Edward, held it. There are 5 hides paying geld. In demesne are 3 ploughs; and 14 villans and 8 bordars with 8 ploughs. There are 10 slaves, and 2 mills rendering 10*s*. 10*d*., and 2 men paying 5*s*., and 12 acres of meadow, [and] woodland half a league long and a half broad. It is and was worth £8.

● The same bishop holds WAPLEY, and Ealdræd [holds] of him. The same man held it TRE. There is 1 hide, and in demesne 1 plough, and 2 slaves. It is and was worth 20*s*.

IN "LETBERGE" HUNDRED

● The same bishop holds 'LEE' [in Almondsbury], and Robert [holds] of him. Algar held it TRE. There is 1 hide paying geld, and 2 ploughs in demesne; and 3 bordars and 2 slaves with 1 plough. It is and was worth 20*s*. [2]

IN 'LANGLEY' HUNDRED

● The same bishop holds GAUNT'S EARTHCOTT, and Robert [holds] of him. Cuthwulf held it TRE. There are 2 hides paying geld, and 2 ploughs are in demesne, and 2 bordars and 4 slaves and |4 villans|, and 10 acres of meadow, and woodland [. . .]. It is and was |[in margin]| worth 40*s*.

IN "EDREDESTANE" HUNDRED

● The bishop himself holds DODINGTON, and Roger [holds] of him. Wulfnoth held it TRE. There are 1½ hides and the third part of half a hide. In demesne is 1 plough; and 4 villans and 1 bordar with 1 plough. There are 3 slaves. It is and was worth 30*s*. [2]

VII. THE LAND OF THE CHURCH OF BATH

IN 'LANGLEY' HUNDRED

● ST PETER of BATH held OLVESTON. There are 5 hides. Of these, 3 pay geld and 2 [hides] do not pay geld by gift of King Edward and King William. In demesne are 2 ploughs; and 9 villans and 6 bordars and a priest and 1 radknight with 10 ploughs. There are 7 slaves, and meadows and woodland to maintain the manor. It was worth 100*s*.; now £4. The church itself still holds it.

IN PUCKLECHURCH HUNDRED

● The church itself holds COLD ASHTON. There are 5 hides. Of these, 2 are quit of geld by gift of King Edward and King William. But 3 pay geld. In demesne is 1 plough; and 3 villans and 3 bordars and 1 radknight. Among them all [they have] 3 ploughs. There is 1 colibert, and a mill rendering 50*d*., and 6 acres of meadow. It is and was worth £4.

VIII. THE LAND OF THE CHURCH OF GLASTONBURY

IN PUCKLECHURCH HUNDRED

● ST MARY of GLASTONBURY holds PUCKLECHURCH. There are 20 hides. In demesne are 6 ploughs; and 23 villans and 8 bordars with 18 ploughs. There are 10 slaves, and 6 men render 100 ingots of iron, less 10, and in Gloucester 1 burgess pays 5*d*., and 2 coliberts pay 34*d*., and there are 3 Frenchmen, and 2 mills rendering 100*d*. There are 60 acres of meadow, and woodland half a league long and a half broad. It was worth £20; now £30.

IX. THE LAND OF THE CHURCH OF MALMESBURY

IN 'LANGLEY' HUNDRED

● ST MARY of MALMESBURY holds LITTLETON-ON-SEVERN. There are 5 hides. Of these, 2½ pay geld, the others are quit. In demesne are 2 ploughs; and 13 villans and 2 bordars with 8 ploughs. There is a church and a priest, and 20 acres of meadow. It was worth 60*s*.; now 100*s*.

X. THE LAND OF ST PETER OF GLOUCESTER

In 'Dudstone' Hundred

● St Peter of Gloucester held TRE the manor of 'Barton' [in Gloucester] with the members belonging to it: Barnwood [in Gloucester], Tuffley [Tuffley and Lower Tuffley, in Gloucester], 'Morwent' [in Hartpury]. There are 22 hides, less 1 virgate. There are 9 ploughs in demesne; and 42 villans and 21 bordars with 45 ploughs.
[2] There are 12 slaves, and a mill rendering 5s., and 120 acres of meadow, and woodland 5 furlongs long and 3 broad. It was worth £8; now £24.

This manor was always quit of geld and from all royal service.

In "Blachelaue" Hundred

● The same church itself held Frocester. There are 5 hides. In demesne are 4 ploughs; and 8 villans and 7 bordars with 7 ploughs. There are 3 slaves, and 10 acres of meadow, and woodland 3 furlongs long and 2 furlongs broad. It was worth £3; now £8.

In "Grimboldestou" Hundred

● The church itself holds Boxwell. There are 5 hides. In demesne are 2 ploughs; and 12 villans and 1 radknight having 12 ploughs. There are 8 slaves, and a mill rendering 5s. It was worth 70s.; now 100s.

In 'Brightwells Barrow' Hundred

● The church itself holds Coln St Aldwyns. There are 4 hides. In demesne are 3 ploughs; and 11 villans and 7 bordars with 12 ploughs. There are 4 slaves. It was worth £6; now £8. 2 mills rendered 25s.

In Bibury Hundred

● The church itself holds Aldsworth. There are 11 hides. In demesne are 3 ploughs; and 21 villans and 5 bordars and 2 Frenchmen with 15 ploughs. There are 6 slaves. It was worth 100s.; now £8.

In 'Witley' Hundred

● The church itself holds Buckland. There are 10 hides. In demesne are 3 ploughs; and 22 villans and 6 bordars with 12 ploughs.
☒ There are 8 slaves, and 10 acres of meadow. It was worth £3; now £9.

In Tibblestone Hundred

● The church itself holds Hinton on the Green [Worcs.]. There are 15 hides. In demesne are 2 ploughs; and 30 villans and 7 bordars with 16 ploughs. There are 11 slaves and 1 Frenchman.

It was worth £3; now £10. This manor is quit of geld and of all public service except to the church.

In "Langebrige" Hundred

● The church itself holds Highnam. There are 7 hides. In demesne
[1] are 3 ploughs; and 22 villans and 4 bordars with 7 ploughs. There are 8 slaves, and 30 acres of meadow, [and] sufficient woodland for the manor. It was worth 40s.; now £4.

● The church itself holds Preston [in Dymock]. There are 2 hides. In demesne are 2 ploughs; and 8 villans and 4 bordars with 8 ploughs. There are 4 slaves. It was worth 30s.; now £4.

In Botloe Hundred

● The church itself holds Upleadon. There are 4 hides. In demesne are 2 ploughs; and 8 villans and 1 bordar with 8 ploughs. There are 4 slaves, and a mill rendering 4s., and 10 acres of meadow, [and] woodland 2 leagues long and 2 furlongs broad. It is worth scarcely 30s.

☒ In Westbury Hundred

● The church itself holds Churcham and 'Morton' [in Churcham]. In both woodland and field [are] 5 hides. In demesne are 2 ploughs; and 7 villans and 2 bordars with 6 ploughs. [There is] woodland 1 league long and 1 broad. There the church had its hunting in 3 enclosures TRE and in the time of [King] William. It was worth 20s.; now 40s.

In "Gersdones" Hundred

● In Ampney St Peter the brother of Regenbald holds 2 hides. There are 2 ploughs, and 5 villans with 3 ploughs, and 4 slaves, and 24 acres of meadow, and a mill rendering 5s. It was worth 40s.; now scarcely 20s.

In Cirencester Hundred

● With King William's consent the wife of Walter de Lacy gave to St Peter for the soul of her husband Duntisbourne Abbots, a manor of 5 hides. In demesne [are] 3 ploughs; and 8 villans with 5 ploughs. There are 16 slaves, and a mill rendering 2s. It is worth £4.

TRE St Peter of Gloucester had from its burgesses 19s. 5d. and 16 salmon. Now it has as many salmon and 50s. There is a mill rendering 12s., and 4 fisheries for the sustenance of the monks.

XI. THE LAND OF THE CHURCH OF WINCHCOMBE

In Salmonsbury Hundred

● The Church of St Mary of Winchcombe holds Sherborne. There are 30 hides. 10 of these are free [and] pertain to the court. There are 5 ploughs in demesne; and 40 villans and 7 bordars with 22 ploughs. There are 12 slaves, and 4 mills rendering 40s., and 30 acres of meadow. TRE it was worth £20; now £14.

● The church itself holds Bledington. There are 7 hides. In demesne are 2 ploughs; and 8 villans and 4 bordars with 5 ploughs, and 8 slaves and 2 female slaves. There is a mill rendering 5s., and 30 acres of meadow. It was worth £4; now £3.

In 'Greston' Hundred

● The church itself holds Twyning. There are 3 hides paying geld. In demesne are 2 ploughs; and 24 villans and 8 bordars with 27 ploughs. There are 8 slaves and 2 female slaves, and 40 acres of meadow, [and] woodland 2 furlongs long and 1 broad. It was worth £8; now £7.

● The church itself holds Frampton Court. There is 1 hide, and in demesne 4 ploughs, and 6 slaves and 2 female slaves. This land was free and quit of all geld and royal service. It was worth 40s.; now 50s.

☒ ● The church itself holds Frampton, and a certain knight [holds] of the abbot. There are 2½ hides. In demesne are 2 ploughs; and 1 villan with 1 plough, and there can be 3 [ploughs] more. There are 4 slaves. It is and was worth 30s.

● The church itself holds Naunton [in Toddington], and 2 knights [hold] of the abbot. There are 3½ hides. In demesne are 3 ploughs and 3 slaves; and 2 villans with 1 plough, and 6 more
☒ [ploughs] could be there. It is and was worth 40s.

● The church itself holds Stanton. There are 3 hides. In demesne are 2 ploughs; and 14 villans with 7 ploughs. There are 3 bordars and 6 slaves, and 6 acres of meadow, [and] woodland 1 league long and a half broad. It is and was worth £3.

● The church itself holds Charlton Abbots. There are 2 hides free and quit. In demesne is 1 plough; and 4 villans and 2 bordars with 4 ploughs. There are 6 slaves, and a mill rendering 20d., and 2 acres of meadow. It is and was worth 20s.

In 'Holford' Hundred

● The church itself holds Snowshill. There are 7 hides paying geld. In demesne are 3 ploughs; and 12 villans and 2 bordars with 6 ploughs. There are 6 slaves. It is and was worth 100s.

In "Celfledetorn" Hundred

● The church itself holds Cow Honeybourne [Worcs.]. There are 10 hides. Of these, 2 [are] in demesne, and 8 [liable] for service. In demesne are 5 ploughs; and 15 villans with 5 ploughs. There are 9 slaves and 3 female slaves. It was worth £6; now £8.

● The church itself holds Admington [War.]. There are 3½ hides. In demesne are 2 ploughs; and 13 villans with 6 ploughs. There are 4 slaves and 2 female slaves. It was worth £4; now £3.

● The church itself holds Hidcote Boyce. There are 2 free hides. In demesne is 1 plough, with 1 slave. It is and was worth 40s.

TRE this church was assessed in Gloucestershire at 60 hides.

● Ælfsige of Faringdon holds of the abbey itself 3½ hides in Windrush. Bolla held it and gave it to the abbey. He could go with this land where he would. In demesne are 5 ploughs; and 1 villan and 7 bordars with 1 plough, and 10 slaves, and 1½ mills §

XII. THE LAND OF ST MARY OF EVESHAM

In Salmonsbury Hundred

● The Church of St Mary of Evesham holds Maugersbury near Stow-on-the-Wold. There were 8 hides TRE, and a ninth hide belongs to the Church of St Edward. King Æthelræd gave it there quit. In demesne are 3 ploughs; and 12 villans and 1 free man and a priest having among them 7 ploughs. There are 6 slaves, and a mill rendering 8s., [and] a certain amount of meadow. TRE it was worth 100s.; now £7.

● The church itself holds Adlestrop. There are 7 hides. In demesne are 2 ploughs; and 10 villans and 2 bordars with 3 ploughs. There are 4 slaves, and 1 knight with 2 ploughs. There is little meadow. It was worth £4; now 100s.

● The church itself holds Bourton-on-the-Water. There are 10 hides. In demesne are 6 ploughs; and 16 villans and 8 bordars and 2 free men with 7 ploughs.

§ rendering 12s. 6d. All together it is worth £8. Wulfric held 2 hides of this land as a manor, and Tovi 5 virgates as a manor, and Leofwine 1 virgate as a manor. This manor which Ælfsige holds of the abbot unjustly lay in Salmonsbury Hundred after Bolla died. Now it lies in Barrington Hundred by the judgement of the men of the same hundred.

There is a priest with half a plough. It was worth £8; now £12.

● The church itself holds BROADWELL. There are 10 hides. There are 6 ploughs in demesne; and 25 villans and 8 bordars and 1 free man and a priest. Among them all they have 12 ploughs. In Gloucester 4 burgesses, and in Winchcombe 1 [burgess], pay 27*d.* The whole was worth £8; now £12.

There are 13 slaves

IN 'WITLEY' HUNDRED

● The church itself holds UPPER SWELL. There are 3 hides, and 9 villans and 2 bordars and a priest. Among them all [they have] 4 ploughs. There are 6 slaves. It was worth £4; now £5. In demesne are 3 ploughs. There are 3 mills [rendering] 20*s.*

● The church itself holds WILLERSEY. There are 8 hides, 1 at Wickhamford [Worcs.]. There are 3 ploughs in demesne; and 16 villans and 4 bordars and a priest with 6 ploughs. There are 2 slaves, and little meadow. It was worth £4; now 100*s.*

● The church itself holds WESTON-ON-AVON [War.]. There are 3 hides and 1 free [hide]. In demesne are 2 ploughs; and 5 villans and a priest with 2 ploughs. It was worth 20*s.*; now 40*s.*

● The church itself holds STOKE [Lark Stoke and Lower Lark Stoke, War.]. There are 2 hides. In demesne is 1 plough; and 7 villans and 2 bordars with 2 ploughs. There is 1 slave. It is and was worth 40*s.*

● The church itself holds HIDCOTE BARTRIM. There are 3 hides. In demesne is 1 plough and 2 slaves; and the wives of 4 villans who have recently died have 1 plough. It is and was worth 20*s.*

The abbot has these 2 vills commended to 2 of his knights.

● In the ferding of WINCHCOMBE, ST MARY of EVESHAM had 56 hides TRE.

XIII. THE LAND OF ST MARY OF ABINGDON

IN 'GRESTON' HUNDRED

● THE CHURCH OF ST MARY of ABINGDON holds DUMBLETON. There are 7½ hides. In demesne are 4 ploughs; and 13 villans and 8 bordars with 8 ploughs. There are 6 slaves, and a mill rendering 6*s.* TRE it was worth £12; now £9. This manor paid geld TRE.

XIIII. THE LAND OF ST MARY OF PERSHORE

IN RAPSGATE HUNDRED

● THE CHURCH OF ST MARY of PERSHORE holds COWLEY. There are 5 hides paying geld. In demesne are 2 ploughs; and 14 villans and 1 bordar with 7 ploughs. There are 5 slaves, and a mill rendering 50*d.*, and 6 acres of meadow, and woodland 3 furlongs long and 1 broad. It is worth 100*s.*

IN "GRIMBOLDESTOU" [HUNDRED]

● The church itself holds HAWKESBURY. There are 17 hides. In demesne [are] 5 ploughs; and 18 villans and 25 bordars with 15 ploughs. There are 2 slaves and 7 coliberts. There are 3 mills rendering 19*s.* 2*d.*, and 10 acres of meadow, [and] woodland 2 leagues long and 1 broad. It was worth £16; now £10.

XV. THE LAND OF ST MARY OF COVENTRY

IN "CELFLEDETORN" HUNDRED

● THE CHURCH OF ST MARY of COVENTRY holds LONG MARSTON [War.]. There are 10 hides. In demesne are 3 ploughs; and 15 villans and 3 bordars with 12 ploughs. There are 6 slaves, and meadow rendering 10*s.* It was worth £8; now 100*s.*

XVI. THE LAND OF SAINTE-MARIE OF CORMEILLES

IN BOTLOE HUNDRED

● THE CHURCH OF SAINTE-MARIE of CORMEILLES holds NEWENT. King Edward held it. 6 hides there did not pay geld. Earl Roger gave it to this church for the soul of his father with the consent of King William. In demesne are 3 ploughs; and 9 villans and 9 bordars with 12 ploughs. There is a reeve having 1½ villans and 5 bordars. Among them all they have 5 ploughs, and a mill rendering 20*d.* There are 2 slaves, and 2 mills rendering 6*s.* 8*d.* From the woodland, 30*d.*

Of this land Durand holds 1 hide of the abbot, and has there 1 plough, and 5 bordars and 2 slaves with 2 ploughs. There are 2 enclosures of which the king has seisin. The whole manor was worth £4 TRE; now 100*s.* Durand's hide [is worth] 12*s.* Of the land of this manor William fitzBaderon holds 1 virgate by force.

XVII. THE LAND OF SAINTE-MARIE OF LYRE

IN RAPSGATE HUNDRED

● THE CHURCH OF SAINTE-MARIE of LYRE holds DUNTISBOURNE LEER. There is 1 hide and 1 virgate. In demesne is 1 plough, and 2 bordars. It is and was worth 20*s.* Roger de Lacy gave this land to the church itself. Eadmær held it TRE.

XVIII. THE LAND OF THE CHURCH OF EYNSHAM

IN "CELFLEDETORN" HUNDRED

● The CHURCH of EYNSHAM holds MICKLETON. There are 14 hides. In demesne are 5 ploughs; and 20 villans and 7 bordars with 10 ploughs. There are 8 slaves and 2 female slaves, and 24 measures of salt from Droitwich [Worcs.]. It is and was worth £10. The same church held it TRE. [7]

XIX. THE LAND OF ST PETER OF WESTMINSTER

IN DEERHURST HUNDRED

● THE CHURCH OF ST PETER OF WESTMINSTER holds DEERHURST. There are 59 hides.

In the capital manor were 5 hides TRE. There are 3 ploughs, and 20 villans and 8 bordars with 10 ploughs. There are 6 slaves, and 60 acres of meadow, [and] woodland 2 leagues long and half a league broad. It is and was worth £10. To this manor belong these BEREWICKS: Hardwicke 5 hides; Bourton-on-the-Hill 8 hides; Todenham 7 hides; Sutton-under-Brailes [War.] 5 hides; all together 25 hides. There are 13 ploughs in demesne; and 45 villans and 27 bordars with 21 ploughs. There are 37 slaves, and 4 mills rendering 20*s.*, and 20 acres of meadow, woodland 1 league long and a half broad, and water-meadow 3 furlongs long and 1 broad.

Of the land of this manor, radknights, that is free men, held TRE, who, however, all ploughed and harrowed, mowed |and reaped| for the lord's work. |[partly in margin]|

At Elmstone Hardwicke Beorhtric [. . .] 1 hide. Reinbald holds it.

At 'Ellings' [in Tirley] Godric [held] 2 hides. At Wightfield Eadwig [held] 1 hide. At Todenham Eadwig [held] 1 hide. Walter Ponther holds these.

At Boddington 2 hides. At Bourton-on-the-Hill 2 hides. Wulfwig held these. At Kemerton [Worcs.] half a hide. Leofwine held it. Gerard holds these lands. Abbot Baldwin holds half a hide in the same place.

At Evington Alwig [held] 1 hide and 1 virgate. At Oridge Street Leofwine [held] half a hide. At Tirley Eadric [held] 2½ virgates. William fitzBaderon holds these.

At Tirley Eadric [held] 2½ virgates. At Kemerton [Worcs.] Alwine [held] half a hide. Abbot Baldwin holds these.

At Hasfield Beorhtric [held] 1½ hides. Turstin fitzRolf holds them.

At Lemington Auti [held] 3 hides. Gilbert fitzTurold holds them.

At Moreton-in-Marsh Alfrith [held] half a hide. The same man holds it himself.

● In these lands 11½ ploughs are in demesne; and 14 villans and 27 bordars with 7 ploughs. There are 14 slaves, and 20 acres of meadow. [2]

Besides these, Gerard the chamberlain holds 8 hides in Kemerton [Worcs.] and 3 hides in Boddington, which always paid geld and did other services in Deerhurst Hundred. But after Gerard had them he neither rendered geld nor service.

TRE the whole manor gave as farm £41, and 8 sesters of honey according to the king's measure; now it is worth £40. Of these, £26 belong to the demesne manor and £14 to the men.

⊠

XX. THE LAND OF SAINT-DENIS OF PARIS

IN DEERHURST HUNDRED

● THE CHURCH OF SAINT-DENIS holds these vills in DEERHURST HUNDRED: Uckington 5 hides; Staverton 3 hides; Coln St Dennis and Calcot 5 hides; Little Compton [War.] 12 hides; Preston on Stour [War.] 10 hides; Welford-on-Avon [War.] 15 hides. In these lands 15 ploughs are in demesne; and 75 villans and 12 bordars with 39 ploughs. There are 38 slaves, and 4 mills rendering 40*s.*, and 36 acres of meadow, [and] woodland 2½ leagues long and 1 league and 2 furlongs broad. [2]

Of this above-mentioned land, 5 free men hold 4½ hides. To the same manor belong 2½ hides beyond the Severn. In Woolstone 5 hides; in The Leigh 1 hide; in Deerhurst Walton 1 hide; in Kemerton [Worcs.] half a hide. In these lands are 5 ploughs in demesne; and 5 villans and 18 bordars with 9 ploughs. 1 free man lives there. There are 38 acres of meadow, [and] woodland half a league long and 2 furlongs broad. To this manor belong 30 burgesses in Gloucester paying 15*s.* 8*d.*, and 2 burgesses in Winchcombe paying 10*d.* TRE the whole manor was worth £26. 10*s.*; now £30.

XXI. THE LAND OF THE CHURCH OF LAMBETH

In "Celfledetorn" Hundred

[2] ● The Church of St Mary of Lambeth holds Aston Subedge. Countess Gode held it TRE. There are 4 hides. In demesne are 3 ploughs; and 6 villans and 1 knight with $3\frac{1}{2}$ ploughs. There are 6 slaves and 3 female slaves. It was worth 100*s.*; now £4.

XXII. THE LAND OF SAINT-EVROUL

In 'Holford' Hundred

● The Church of Saint-Evroul holds Roel of the king. Wulfweard held it TRE. There are 10 hides. In demesne are 4 ploughs; and 16 villans and 2 bordars with 6 ploughs. There are 3 slaves. It is and was worth £10. This manor has never paid geld.

XXIII. THE LAND OF THE CHURCH OF THE NUNS OF CAEN

In Cirencester Hundred

● The Church of the nuns of La Trinite of Caen holds Pinbury of the king. There are 3 hides. In demesne are 3 ploughs; and 8 villans and a smith with 3 ploughs. There are 9 slaves, and a mill rendering 40*d.* It is and was worth £4.

In Longtree Hundred

● The church itself holds Minchinhampton. Countess Gode held it TRE. There are 8 hides. In demesne are 5 ploughs; and 32 villans and 10 bordars with 24 ploughs. There is a priest and 10 slaves, and 8 mills rendering 45*s.*, and 20 acres of meadow, [and] woodland 2 leagues long and half a league broad. It is worth £28.

XXIIII. THE LAND OF THE CHURCH OF TROARN

In Longtree Hundred

● The Church of Saint-Martin of Troarn holds Horsley by gift of King William. Gode, the sister of King Edward, held it. There

[2] are 10 hides. In demesne are 4 ploughs; and 6 villans and 5 bordars with 6 ploughs, and 1 radknight, and in Gloucester 1 house rendering 6*d.*

§1 There is a mill rendering 50*d.* It was worth £12; now £14.

XXVII. THE LAND OF EARL ROGER

In "Gersdones" Hundred

[2] ● Earl Roger holds Meysey Hampton, and Thorvald, the nephew of Vigot, [holds] of him. §2

XXVIII. THE LAND OF EARL HUGH

In Bisley Hundred

● Earl Hugh holds Bisley, and Robert [holds] of him. There are 8 hides. In demesne are 4 ploughs; and 20 villans and 28 bordars with 20 ploughs. There are 6 slaves and 4 female slaves. There are 2 priests and 8 radknights having 10 ploughs, and 23 other men paying 44*s.* and 2 sesters of honey. There are 5 mills rendering 16*s.*, and woodland rendering 20*s.*, and in Gloucester 11 burgesses paying 66*d.* It was worth £24; now £20.

§3 In Longtree Hundred the same earl holds Westonbirt. Alnoth held it TRE. There are 3 hides paying geld. In this hundred Leofwine held 1 hide.

● In the same place the earl himself holds 1 hide at Througham. Leofnoth held it of King Edward and could go where he would. This land pays geld. There are 4 bordars with 1 plough, and 4 acres of meadow. It is worth 20*s.*

● In the same place the earl himself holds half a hide which Roger de Lacy claims in Edgeworth by witness of the shire. It is worth 10*s.*, and it pays geld.

In 'Witley' Hundred

● The earl himself holds Chipping Campden. Earl Harold held it. There are 15 hides paying geld. In demesne [are] 6 ploughs; and 50 villans and 8 bordars with 21 ploughs. There are 12 slaves, and 2 mills rendering 6*s.* 2*d.* There are 3 female slaves. It was worth £30; now £20.

In Longtree Hundred

§3 ● The earl himself holds 2 manors of 4 hides paying geld, and 2 of his men [hold] of him. Alnoth and Leofwine held them TRE. There has been no one to answer for these lands, but they are valued by the men of the shire at £8.

XXIX. THE LAND OF THE COUNT OF MORTAIN

In 'Witley' Hundred

[6] ● The Count of Mortain holds Longborough. Tovi held it TRE. There are 2 hides. In demesne are 2 ploughs; and 3 villans and 1 bordar with 1 plough, and 4 slaves. It was worth £4; now 40*s.*, and it pays geld.

§1 XXV. THE LAND OF THE CHURCH OF CIRENCESTER

In Cirencester Hundred

● The Church of Cirencester holds of the king 2 hides in alms, and held them of King Edward quit of all customary dues. There are 6 acres of meadow. This is and was worth 40*s.*

XXVI. THE LAND OF REGENBALD THE PRIEST

In "Gersdones" Hundred

§1 XXVI

● Regenbald holds Ampney St Mary of the king. Godric held it TRE. There are 4 hides and 1 virgate. In demesne [are] 2 ploughs; and 8 villans and 1 bordar with 6 ploughs, and a priest. There are 8 slaves, and 2 mills rendering 10*s.*, and 20 acres of meadow. It is and was worth 100*s.*

● The same Regenbald holds Driffield. Elaf held it of Earl Tosti. There are 7 hides. In demesne [are] 4 ploughs; and 8 villans and 2 bordars and a priest with 5 ploughs. There are 15 slaves, and a mill rendering 5*s.*, and 20 acres of meadow. It is and was worth £8.

In Cirencester Hundred

● The same Regenbald holds 1 hide in Norcote. Godric held it TRE. In demesne is 1 plough; and 2 villans and 2 bordars with 2 ploughs. There are 6 slaves. It is worth 40*s.* This thegn could go where he would.

● The same Regenbald holds Preston [near Cirencester]. Elaf held it TRE. There are 8 hides paying geld besides the demesne. In demesne are 4 ploughs; and 7 villans and 6 bordars with 6 ploughs. There are 9 slaves, and 12 acres of meadow. It is and was worth £8. Elaf himself could go where he would.

XXX. THE LAND OF GILBERT, BISHOP OF LISIEUX

In Longtree Hundred

● Hugh Maminot holds Rodmarton of Gilbert, Bishop of Lisieux, and he himself [holds] of the king. There are 2 hides. In demesne are 2 ploughs; and 1 villan and 2 bordars and a priest with 1 plough. There are 2 slaves. It was worth £4; now £3. Leofwine held it of King Edward.

● The same Hugh holds Lasborough of the bishop himself. Leofwine held it. There are 5 hides. In demesne is 1 plough; and 5 villans and a priest with 2 ploughs. There are 7 slaves. It was worth £10; now 50*s.*

In "Grimboldestou" Hundred

● The same Hugh holds Little Sodbury of the same bishop. Alweard held it TRE. There are 5 hides paying geld. In demesne are 2 ploughs; and 4 villans and 2 bordars with 2 ploughs. There are 4 slaves, and 20 acres of meadow, [and] a small amount of woodland. It was worth £8; now £4.

XXXI. THE LAND OF WILLIAM DE EU

In "Blachelaue" Hundred

[6] ● William de Eu holds Stonehouse. Tovi held it TRE. There were 7 hides. There are 2 ploughs in demesne; and 21 villans and 9 bordars with 20 ploughs. There are 4 slaves, and 2 mills rendering 17*s.* 6*d.* There are 2 arpents of vineyard. It is and was worth £8. This manor pays geld.

In Lydney Hundred

● The same William holds 'Alverston' [in Woolaston]. Bondi held it TRE. There are 3 hides paying geld. There is nothing in demesne; but 5 villans and 3 bordars have 3 ploughs. There is a fishery rendering 12*d.*, and 10 acres of meadow, [and] woodland half a league long and a half broad. It was worth 20*s.*; now 30*s.* Henry de Ferrers claims it because Bondi held it. Ralph de Limesy, the predecessor of William, held it.

● The same William holds 2 hides in the same place paying geld, and there are 2 villans with 2 ploughs. Wulfnoth held it. It is and was worth 10*s.*

● The same William held Wyegate, and Ralph de Limesy [held it] before him. Ælfstan held it TRE. Now, by the king's order, it is in his

[7] forest. There were 6 hides, and they paid geld and were worth 60*s.* Now there is only a fishery rendering 10*s.*

In Wyvern Hundred

[2] ● The same William holds Woolaston. Beorhtric son of Ælfgar held it. There are 2 hides. There is nothing in demesne, except 5 villans with 5 ploughs. There is 1 fishery in the Severn rendering 5*s.*, and a mill rendering 40*d.* It is and was worth 20*s.* This land pays geld.

[2] ● The same William holds in Tidenham $1\frac{1}{2}$ virgates paying geld. Archbishop Stigand held them. There is 1 villan with 1 plough, and 2 fisheries. It is and was worth 10*s.*

In Cirencester Hundred

● The same William holds Daglingworth. Ælfstan held it TRE. There are $5\frac{1}{2}$ hides paying geld. In demesne are 2 ploughs; and 6 villans and 4 bordars with $5\frac{1}{2}$ ploughs. There are 7 slaves, and a mill rendering 8*s.* Ralph holds this manor of William and it pays geld, but he himself retains the geld on 3 hides. 1 Frenchman holds half a hide of this land and has 1 plough there with his men. The whole was worth £10 TRE; now £8.

● The same William holds 1 hide in Tarlton, and Herbert [holds] of him. Leofric held it TRE and could go where he would. In demesne is 1 plough and 4 slaves. It was worth 40*s.*; now 20*s.*

In Longtree Hundred

§2 Leofnoth held it. There are 5 hides. In demesne is 1 plough, and 4 villans and 2 bordars and a priest and 2 other men. Among them all they have $2\frac{1}{2}$ ploughs. There are 6 slaves. It was worth £8; now £3.

There is a priest with half a plough. It was worth £8; now £12.

● The church itself holds BROADWELL. There are 10 hides. There are 6 ploughs in demesne; and 25 villans and 8 bordars and 1 free man and a priest. Among them all they have 12 ploughs. In Gloucester 4 burgesses, and in Winchcombe 1 [burgess], pay 27*d*. The whole was worth £8; now £12. There are 13 slaves

IN 'WITLEY' HUNDRED

● The church itself holds UPPER SWELL. There are 3 hides, and 9 villans and 2 bordars and a priest. Among them all [they have] 4 ploughs. There are 6 slaves. It was worth £4; now £5. In demesne are 3 ploughs. There are 3 mills [rendering] 20*s*.

● The church itself holds WILLERSEY. There are 8 hides, 1 at Wickhamford [Worcs.]. There are 3 ploughs in demesne; and 16 villans and 4 bordars and a priest with 6 ploughs. There are 2 slaves, and little meadow. It was worth £4; now 100*s*.

● The church itself holds WESTON-ON-AVON [War.]. There are 3 hides and 1 free [hide]. In demesne are 2 ploughs; and 5 villans and a priest with 2 ploughs. It was worth 20*s*.; now 40*s*.

● The church itself holds STOKE [Lark Stoke and Lower Lark Stoke, War.]. There are 2 hides. In demesne is 1 plough; and 7 villans and 2 bordars with 2 ploughs. There is 1 slave. It is and was worth 40*s*.

● The church itself holds HIDCOTE BARTRIM. There are 3 hides. In demesne is 1 plough and 2 slaves; and the wives of 4 villans who have recently died have 1 plough. It is and was worth 20*s*.

The abbot has these 2 vills commended to 2 of his knights.

● In the ferding of WINCHCOMBE, ST MARY of EVESHAM had 56 hides TRE.

XIII. THE LAND OF ST MARY OF ABINGDON

IN 'GRESTON' HUNDRED

● THE CHURCH OF ST MARY of ABINGDON holds DUMBLETON. There are $7\frac{1}{2}$ hides. In demesne are 4 ploughs; and 13 villans and 8 bordars with 8 ploughs. There are 6 slaves, and a mill rendering 6*s*. TRE it was worth £12; now £9. This manor paid geld TRE.

XIIII. THE LAND OF ST MARY OF PERSHORE

IN RAPSGATE HUNDRED

● THE CHURCH OF ST MARY of PERSHORE holds COWLEY. There are 5 hides paying geld. In demesne are 2 ploughs; and 14 villans and 1 bordar with 7 ploughs. There are 5 slaves, and a mill rendering 50*d*., and 6 acres of meadow, and woodland 3 furlongs long and 1 broad. It is worth 100*s*.

IN "GRIMBOLDESTOU" [HUNDRED]

● The church itself holds HAWKESBURY. There are 17 hides. In demesne [are] 5 ploughs; and 18 villans and 25 bordars with 15 ploughs. There are 2 slaves and 7 coliberts. There are 3 mills rendering 19*s*. 2*d*., and 10 acres of meadow, [and] woodland 2 leagues long and 1 broad. It was worth £16; now £10.

XV. THE LAND OF ST MARY OF COVENTRY

IN "CELFLEDETORN" HUNDRED

● THE CHURCH OF ST MARY of COVENTRY holds LONG MARSTON [War.]. There are 10 hides. In demesne are 3 ploughs; and 15 villans and 3 bordars with 12 ploughs. There are 6 slaves, and meadow rendering 10*s*. It was worth £8; now 100*s*.

XVI. THE LAND OF SAINTE-MARIE OF CORMEILLES

IN BOTLOE HUNDRED

● THE CHURCH OF SAINTE-MARIE of CORMEILLES holds NEWENT. King Edward held it. 6 hides there did not pay geld. Earl Roger gave it to this church for the soul of his father with the consent of King William. In demesne are 3 ploughs; and 9 villans and 9 bordars with 12 ploughs. There is a reeve having $1\frac{1}{2}$ villans and 5 bordars. Among them all they have 5 ploughs, and a mill rendering 20*d*. There are 2 slaves, and 2 mills rendering 6*s*. 8*d*. From the woodland, 30*d*.

Of this land Durand holds 1 hide of the abbot, and has there 1 plough, and 5 bordars and 2 slaves with 2 ploughs. There are 2 enclosures of which the king has seisin. The whole manor was worth £4 TRE; now 100*s*. Durand's hide [is worth] 12*s*. Of the land of this manor William fitzBaderon holds 1 virgate by force.

XVII. THE LAND OF SAINTE-MARIE OF LYRE

IN RAPSGATE HUNDRED

● THE CHURCH OF SAINTE-MARIE of LYRE holds DUNTISBOURNE LEER. There is 1 hide and 1 virgate. In demesne is 1 plough, and 2 bordars. It is and was worth 20*s*. Roger de Lacy gave this land to the church itself. Eadmær held it TRE.

XVIII. THE LAND OF THE CHURCH OF EYNSHAM

IN "CELFLEDETORN" HUNDRED

● The CHURCH of EYNSHAM holds MICKLETON. There are 14 hides. In demesne are 5 ploughs; and 20 villans and 7 bordars with 10 ploughs. There are 8 slaves and 2 female slaves, and 24 measures of salt from Droitwich [Worcs.]. It is and was worth £10. The same church held it TRE. [7]

XIX. THE LAND OF ST PETER OF WESTMINSTER

IN DEERHURST HUNDRED

● THE CHURCH OF ST PETER OF WESTMINSTER holds DEERHURST. There are 59 hides.

In the capital manor were 5 hides TRE. There are 3 ploughs, and 20 villans and 8 bordars with 10 ploughs. There are 6 slaves, and 60 acres of meadow, [and] woodland 2 leagues long and half a league broad. It is and was worth £10. To this manor belong these BEREWICKS: Hardwicke 5 hides; Bourton-on-the-Hill 8 hides; Todenham 7 hides; Sutton-under-Brailes [War.] 5 hides; all together 25 hides. There are 13 ploughs in demesne; and 45 villans and 27 bordars with 21 ploughs. There are 37 slaves, and 4 mills rendering 20*s*., and 20 acres of meadow, woodland 1 league long and a half broad, and water-meadow 3 furlongs long and 1 broad.

Of the land of this manor, radknights, that is free men, held TRE, who, however, all ploughed and harrowed, mowed |and reaped| for the lord's work. |[partly in margin]|

At Elmstone Hardwicke Beorhtric [. . .] 1 hide. Reinbald holds it.

At 'Ellings' [in Tirley] Godric [held] 2 hides. At Wightfield Eadwig [held] 1 hide. At Todenham Eadwig [held] 1 hide. Walter Ponther holds these.

At Boddington 2 hides. At Bourton-on-the-Hill 2 hides. Wulfwig held these. At Kemerton [Worcs.] half a hide. Leofwine held it. Gerard holds these lands. Abbot Baldwin holds half a hide in the same place.

At Evington Alwig [held] 1 hide and 1 virgate. At Oridge Street Leofwine [held] half a hide. At Tirley Eadric [held] $2\frac{1}{2}$ virgates. William fitzBaderon holds these.

At Tirley Eadric [held] $2\frac{1}{2}$ virgates. At Kemerton [Worcs.] Alwine [held] half a hide. Abbot Baldwin holds these.

At Hasfield Beorhtric [held] $1\frac{1}{2}$ hides. Turstin fitzRolf holds them.

At Lemington Auti [held] 3 hides. Gilbert fitzTurold holds them.

At Moreton-in-Marsh Alfrith [held] half a hide. The same man holds it himself.

● In these lands $11\frac{1}{2}$ ploughs are in demesne; and 14 villans and 27 bordars with 7 ploughs. There are 14 slaves, and 20 acres of meadow. [2]

Besides these, Gerard the chamberlain holds 8 hides in Kemerton [Worcs.] and 3 hides in Boddington, which always paid geld and did other services in Deerhurst Hundred. But after Gerard had them he neither rendered geld nor service.

TRE the whole manor gave as farm £41, and 8 sesters of honey according to the king's measure; now it is worth £40. Of these, £26 belong to the demesne manor and £14 to the men.

[X]

XX. THE LAND OF SAINT-DENIS OF PARIS

IN DEERHURST HUNDRED

● THE CHURCH OF SAINT-DENIS holds these vills in DEERHURST HUNDRED: Uckington 5 hides; Staverton 3 hides; Coln St Dennis and Calcot 5 hides; Little Compton [War.] 12 hides; Preston on Stour [War.] 10 hides; Welford-on-Avon [War.] 15 hides. In these lands 15 ploughs are in demesne; and 75 villans and 12 bordars with 39 ploughs. There are 38 slaves, and 4 mills rendering 40*s*., and 36 acres of meadow, [and] woodland $2\frac{1}{2}$ leagues long and 1 league and 2 furlongs broad. [2]

Of this above-mentioned land, 5 free men hold $4\frac{1}{2}$ hides. To the same manor belong $2\frac{1}{2}$ hides beyond the Severn. In Woolstone 5 hides; in The Leigh 1 hide; in Deerhurst Walton 1 hide; in Kemerton [Worcs.] half a hide. In these lands are 5 ploughs in demesne; and 5 villans and 18 bordars with 9 ploughs. 1 free man lives there. There are 38 acres of meadow, [and] woodland half a league long and 2 furlongs broad. To this manor belong 30 burgesses in Gloucester paying 15*s*. 8*d*., and 2 burgesses in Winchcombe paying 10*d*. TRE the whole manor was worth £26. 10*s*.; now £30.

XXI. THE LAND OF THE CHURCH OF LAMBETH

[2] In "Celfledetorn" Hundred

● The Church of St Mary of Lambeth holds Aston Subedge. Countess Gode held it TRE. There are 4 hides. In demesne are 3 ploughs; and 6 villans and 1 knight with $3\frac{1}{2}$ ploughs. There are 6 slaves and 3 female slaves. It was worth 100*s*.; now £4.

XXII. THE LAND OF SAINT-EVROUL

In 'Holford' Hundred

● The Church of Saint-Evroul holds Roel of the king. Wulfweard held it TRE. There are 10 hides. In demesne are 4 ploughs; and 16 villans and 2 bordars with 6 ploughs. There are 3 slaves. It is and was worth £10. This manor has never paid geld.

XXIII. THE LAND OF THE CHURCH OF THE NUNS OF CAEN

In Cirencester Hundred

● The Church of the nuns of La Trinite of Caen holds Pinbury of the king. There are 3 hides. In demesne are 3 ploughs; and 8 villans and a smith with 3 ploughs. There are 9 slaves, and a mill rendering 40*d*. It is and was worth £4.

In Longtree Hundred

● The church itself holds Minchinhampton. Countess Gode held it TRE. There are 8 hides. In demesne are 5 ploughs; and 32 villans and 10 bordars with 24 ploughs. There is a priest and 10 slaves, and 8 mills rendering 45*s*., and 20 acres of meadow, [and] woodland 2 leagues long and half a league broad. It is worth £28.

XXIIII. THE LAND OF THE CHURCH OF TROARN

In Longtree Hundred

● The Church of Saint-Martin of Troarn holds Horsley by gift of King William. Gode, the sister of King Edward, held it. There
[2] are 10 hides. In demesne are 4 ploughs; and 6 villans and 5 bordars with 6 ploughs, and 1 radknight, and in Gloucester 1 house rendering 6*d*.
§1 There is a mill rendering 50*d*. It was worth £12; now £14.

XXVII. THE LAND OF EARL ROGER

In "Gersdones" Hundred

[2] ● Earl Roger holds Meysey Hampton, and Thorvald, the nephew of Vigot, [holds] of him. §2

XXVIII. THE LAND OF EARL HUGH

In Bisley Hundred

● Earl Hugh holds Bisley, and Robert [holds] of him. There are 8 hides. In demesne are 4 ploughs; and 20 villans and 28 bordars with 20 ploughs. There are 6 slaves and 4 female slaves. There are 2 priests and 8 radknights having 10 ploughs, and 23 other men paying 44*s*. and 2 sesters of honey. There are 5 mills rendering 16*s*., and woodland rendering 20*s*., and in Gloucester 11 burgesses paying 66*d*. It was worth £24; now £20.

● In the same place the earl himself holds 1 hide at Througham. Leofnoth held it of King Edward and could go where he would. This land pays geld. There are 4 bordars with 1 plough, and 4 acres of meadow. It is worth 20*s*.

● In the same place the earl himself holds half a hide which Roger de Lacy claims in Edgeworth by witness of the shire. It is worth 10*s*., and it pays geld.

§3 In Longtree Hundred the same earl holds Westonbirt. Alnoth held it TRE. There are 3 hides paying geld. In this hundred Leofwine held 1 hide.

In 'Witley' Hundred

● The earl himself holds Chipping Campden. Earl Harold held it. There are 15 hides paying geld. In demesne [are] 6 ploughs; and 50 villans and 8 bordars with 21 ploughs. There are 12 slaves, and 2 mills rendering 6*s*. 2*d*. There are 3 female slaves. It was worth £30; now £20.

In Longtree Hundred

§3 ● The earl himself holds 2 manors of 4 hides paying geld, and 2 of his men [hold] of him. Alnoth and Leofwine held them TRE. There has been no one to answer for these lands, but they are valued by the men of the shire at £8.

XXIX. THE LAND OF THE COUNT OF MORTAIN

In 'Witley' Hundred

[6] ● The Count of Mortain holds Longborough. Tovi held it TRE. There are 2 hides. In demesne are 2 ploughs; and 3 villans and 1 bordar with 1 plough, and 4 slaves. It was worth £4; now 40*s*., and it pays geld.

§1 XXV. THE LAND OF THE CHURCH OF CIRENCESTER

In Cirencester Hundred

● The Church of Cirencester holds of the king 2 hides in alms, and held them of King Edward quit of all customary dues. There are 6 acres of meadow. This is and was worth 40*s*.

XXVI. THE LAND OF REGENBALD THE PRIEST

In "Gersdones" Hundred

§1 XXVI

● Regenbald holds Ampney St Mary of the king. Godric held it TRE. There are 4 hides and 1 virgate. In demesne [are] 2 ploughs; and 8 villans and 1 bordar with 6 ploughs, and a priest. There are 8 slaves, and 2 mills rendering 10*s*., and 20 acres of meadow. It is and was worth 100*s*.

● The same Regenbald holds Driffield. Elaf held it of Earl Tosti. There are 7 hides. In demesne [are] 4 ploughs; and 8 villans and 2 bordars and a priest with 5 ploughs. There are 15 slaves, and a mill rendering 5*s*., and 20 acres of meadow. It is and was worth £8.

In Cirencester Hundred

● The same Regenbald holds 1 hide in Norcote. Godric held it TRE. In demesne is 1 plough; and 2 villans and 2 bordars with 2 ploughs. There are 6 slaves. It is worth 40*s*. This thegn could go where he would.

● The same Regenbald holds Preston [near Cirencester]. Elaf held it TRE. There are 8 hides paying geld besides the demesne. In demesne are 4 ploughs; and 7 villans and 6 bordars with 6 ploughs. There are 9 slaves, and 12 acres of meadow. It is and was worth £8. Elaf himself could go where he would.

XXX. THE LAND OF GILBERT, BISHOP OF LISIEUX

In Longtree Hundred

● Hugh Maminot holds Rodmarton of Gilbert, Bishop of Lisieux, and he himself [holds] of the king. There are 2 hides. In demesne are 2 ploughs; and 1 villan and 2 bordars and a priest with 1 plough. There are 2 slaves. It was worth £4; now £3. Leofwine held it of King Edward.

● The same Hugh holds Lasborough of the bishop himself. Leofwine held it. There are 5 hides. In demesne is 1 plough; and 5 villans and a priest with 2 ploughs. There are 7 slaves. It was worth £10; now 50*s*.

In "Grimboldestou" Hundred

● The same Hugh holds Little Sodbury of the same bishop. Alweard held it TRE. There are 5 hides paying geld. In demesne are 2 ploughs; and 4 villans and 2 bordars with 2 ploughs. There are 4 slaves, and 20 acres of meadow, [and] a small amount of woodland. It was worth £8; now £4.

XXXI. THE LAND OF WILLIAM DE EU

In "Blachelaue" Hundred

[6] ● William de Eu holds Stonehouse. Tovi held it TRE. There were 7 hides. There are 2 ploughs in demesne; and 21 villans and 9 bordars with 20 ploughs. There are 4 slaves, and 2 mills rendering 17*s*. 6*d*. There are 2 arpents of vineyard. It is and was worth £8. This manor pays geld.

In Lydney Hundred

● The same William holds 'Alverston' [in Woolaston]. Bondi held it TRE. There are 3 hides paying geld. There is nothing in demesne; but 5 villans and 3 bordars have 3 ploughs. There is a fishery rendering 12*d*., and 10 acres of meadow, [and] woodland half a league long and a half broad. It was worth 20*s*.; now 30*s*. Henry de Ferrers claims it because Bondi held it. Ralph de Limesy, the predecessor of William, held it.

● The same William holds 2 hides in the same place paying geld, and there are 2 villans with 2 ploughs. Wulfnoth held it. It is and was worth 10*s*.

● The same William held Wyegate, and Ralph de Limesy [held it] before him. Ælfstan held it TRE. Now, by the king's order, it is in his
[7] forest. There were 6 hides, and they paid geld and were worth 60*s*. Now there is only a fishery rendering 10*s*.

In Wyvern Hundred

[2] ● The same William holds Woolaston. Beorhtric son of Ælfgar held it. There are 2 hides. There is nothing in demesne, except 5 villans with 5 ploughs. There is 1 fishery in the Severn rendering 5*s*., and a mill rendering 40*d*. It is and was worth 20*s*. This land pays geld.

[2] ● The same William holds in Tidenham $1\frac{1}{2}$ virgates paying geld. Archbishop Stigand held them. There is 1 villan with 1 plough, and 2 fisheries. It is and was worth 10*s*.

In Cirencester Hundred

● The same William holds Daglingworth. Ælfstan held it TRE. There are $5\frac{1}{2}$ hides paying geld. In demesne are 2 ploughs; and 6 villans and 4 bordars with $5\frac{1}{2}$ ploughs. There are 7 slaves, and a mill rendering 8*s*. Ralph holds this manor of William and it pays geld, but he himself retains the geld on 3 hides. 1 Frenchman holds half a hide of this land and has 1 plough there with his men. The whole was worth £10 TRE; now £8.

● The same William holds 1 hide in Tarlton, and Herbert [holds] of him. Leofric held it TRE and could go where he would. In demesne is 1 plough and 4 slaves. It was worth 40*s*.; now 20*s*.

In Longtree Hundred

§2 Leofnoth held it. There are 5 hides. In demesne is 1 plough, and 4 villans and 2 bordars and a priest and 2 other men. Among them all they have $2\frac{1}{2}$ ploughs. There are 6 slaves. It was worth £8; now £3.

● The same William holds Shipton Moyne as Ralph de Limesy held it. Wulfwig held it TRE. There are 2 hides. In demesne are 2 ploughs, and 2 bordars and 8 slaves. It is and was worth 40*s*. Wulfwig himself could go where he would. Hugh holds it of William.

● The same William holds Culkerton, and Herbert [holds] of him. Scirweald held it TRE. There are 3 virgates and 5 acres. In demesne is 1 plough, and 3 slaves. It is and was worth 35*s*. Ralph de Limesy held this land but it did not belong to Ælfstan.

In 'Dudstone' Hundred

● The same William holds Badgeworth. Ælfstan held it. There are 8 hides. In demesne are 6 ploughs; and 20 villans and 14 bordars with 24 ploughs. There are 17 slaves, and a mill rendering 12*d*., [and] woodland 2 leagues long and 1 broad. It was worth £15; now £13.

In Salmonsbury Hundred

● The same William holds Lower Swell. Earnsige held it TRE. There are 3 hides paying geld. It was worth 40*s*.; now 10*s*.

☒ XXXII. THE LAND OF WILLIAM FITZBADERON [6]

In Cirencester Hundred

● William fitzBaderon holds 2 hides in Cirencester, and Hugh holds of him. In demesne is 1 plough; and 1½ villans and 4 bordars with 1 plough. There are 2 slaves. It was worth 100*s*.; now 70*s*. Alwig held ☒ this land.

● The same William holds Daglingworth. Ketil and Ælfric held it and could go where they would. There are 3½ hides. In demesne are 1½ ploughs; and 1 villan and 2 bordars with 1 plough. There is 1 slave. It was worth £10; now 70*s*.

● The same William holds 1 hide in Siddington. Aswith held it TRE and could go where he would. In demesne is 1 plough, and 4 slaves. It is and was worth 24*s*.

In Longtree Hundred

● The same William holds Westonbirt. Beorhtsige held it TRE. There are 3 hides. In demesne are 2 ploughs; and 2 villans and 3 bordars with 2 ploughs. There are 4 slaves, and 6 acres of meadow. It was worth £6; now £3.

In Botloe Hundred

● The same William holds Tibberton. There are 5 hides. Wulfhelm held it of King Edward and he could go where he would. In demesne are 3 ploughs; and 10 villans and 8 bordars with 8 ploughs. There are 4 slaves, and woodland 3 leagues long and 1 broad. It was worth £6. 10*s*.; now 100*s*.

● The same William holds Huntley. Alwine held it of Archbishop Ealdræd and could go where he would. There are 2 hides. In demesne is 1 plough; and 4 villans and 6 bordars with 3 ploughs. There is 1 slave, [and] woodland 2 leagues long and 1 broad. It was worth 40*s*.; now 30*s*.

In Westbury Hundred

☒ ● The same William holds Longhope. Forne and Wulfheah held it of King Edward, and these thegns could go where they would. There are 5 hides paying geld. In demesne are 2 ploughs; and 12 villans and 1 bordar with 12 ploughs. There are 3 slaves, and a mill rendering 17*d*. It was worth £8; now 100*s*.

● The same William holds Stears. Wulfheah held it TRE. It was worth 10*s*.; now 5*s*. There is 1 hide and it does not pay geld.

● The same William holds 2½ virgates, and he has there 1 villan and 1 bordar. His predecessor Wihanoc held them, but the shire affirms that this land belonged to the king's demesne farm in Westbury-on-Severn. It is worth 3*s*.

● The same William holds Newnham. There is 1 hide, and 3 villans and 3 bordars paying 20*s*. This land does not pay geld. There is woodland 2 furlongs long and 1 broad.

In Lydney Hundred

● The same William holds St Briavels. Ælfhere held it TRE. There are 6 hides paying geld. In demesne are 2 ploughs; and 3 villans and 5 bordars with 2 ploughs. There are 3 slaves, and a mill rendering 5*s*., and 20 acres of meadow, and half a fishery in the Wye, [and] woodland 1 league long and a half broad. It was worth £4; now 40*s*.

[7] ● The same William held Hewelsfield. Wulfheah held it TRE. There
§ are 3 hides. By the king's order this land is in the forest. It was worth 30*s*.

XXXIII. THE LAND OF WILLIAM THE CHAMBERLAIN [6]

In 'Witley' Hundred

● William the Chamberlain holds Wincot [War.]. Wynric held it TRE. There are 3 hides. In demesne are 3 ploughs; and 2 villans and 2 bordars with 1 plough. There are 4 slaves. It is and was worth £4. This manor pays geld.

In "Wacrescumbe" Hundred

§ ● The same William [fitzBaderon] holds Hampen, and Geoffrey [holds] of him. Eadwig held it. There are 5 hides. In demesne are 2 ploughs; and 6 villans with 3 ploughs. There are 4 slaves. This land pays geld. It was worth 100*s*.; now 60*s*.

XXXIIII. THE LAND OF WILLIAM GOIZENBODED

In "Celfledetorn" Hundred

● William Goizenboded holds Pebworth [Worcs.] of the king. Wulfgeat and Wulfweard held it TRE as 2 manors. There are 6 hides and 1 virgate. In demesne is 1 plough, and 1 bordar and 1 slave. It was worth £7; now £4. 10*s*.

● The same William holds Ullington [Worcs.]. A thegn held it TRE. There are 5 hides. In demesne are 2 ploughs; and 2 villans and a Frenchman holding 1½ hides with 1 plough. Earl Ælfgar placed this manor in Pebworth [Worcs.]. It was worth 100*s*.; now 40*s*.

● The same William holds Lower Clopton [War.]. Huscarl held it TRE. There are 10 hides. In demesne [are] 3 ploughs; and 12 villans and 4 bordars and 1 radknight with 9 ploughs. In Winchcombe [is] 1 burgess. It was worth £8; now 100*s*.

In 'Witley' Hundred

● The same William holds Ebrington. Beorhtmær held it. There are 10 hides. In demesne [are] 4 ploughs; and 18 villans and 4 bordars with 14 ploughs. There are 8 slaves and 3 female slaves, and 2 mills rendering 15*s*. It was worth £12; now £7.

In Salmonsbury Hundred

● The same William holds 'Caldicott' [in Hawling], and Ranulph [holds] of him. Alwine held it TRE. There are 3 hides paying geld. In demesne [are] 3 ploughs, and 8 slaves and female slaves all together. It was worth 60*s*.; now 40*s*.

● The same William holds Aylworth. Alwine held it TRE. There is 1 hide paying geld. In demesne [is] 1 plough, and 2 slaves. It was worth 6*s*.; now 3*s*.

In 'Holford' Hundred

● The same William holds Farmcote. Alwine held it. There are 3 hides paying geld. In demesne [are] 2 ploughs; and 4 villans with [2] 4 ploughs, and 13 slaves and female slaves all together. Geoffrey holds it of William. It was worth £10; now £3.

● The same William holds Guiting Power. King Edward held it and he leased it to Alwine his sheriff, so that he should have it for his lifetime. But it was not a gift, as the shire bears witness. On the death of Alwine, King William gave his wife and land to a certain young man, Richard. Now William, the successor of Richard, holds this land thus. There are 10 hides. Of these, 9 pay geld. In demesne are 4 ploughs; and 4 villans and 3 Frenchmen and 2 radknights and a priest with 2 bordars. Among them all they have 5 ploughs. All together [there are] 11 slaves and female slaves, and 2 mills rendering 14*s*. There 5 salt-pans render 20 summæ of salt. In [2] Winchcombe 2 burgesses pay 11*s*. 4*d*. It was worth £16; now £6.

● The same William holds Castlett. Alwine held it. There are ☒ 2 hides paying geld. In demesne [are] 2 ploughs, and 4 slaves, and a mill rendering 5*s*. It was worth 40*s*.; now 10*s*.

In Botloe Hundred

● The same William holds Taynton. Alwine held it. There are 6 hides. In demesne is 1 plough; and 9 villans and 7 bordars with 9 ploughs. It was worth £6; now £3.

In Barrington Hundred

● The same William holds 2 hides in Little Barrington, and Ralph [holds] of him. Alwine held them TRE. In demesne is 1 plough, and 1 slave, and a mill rendering 40*d*., and 6 acres of meadow. It is and was worth 40*s*.

In Westbury Hundred

● The same William holds half a hide of land and half a fishery. Alwine the sheriff held it and gave it to his wife. These were, however, [part] of the king's farm in Westbury-on-Severn.

In 'Greston' Hundred

● The same William holds 1 hide in Dumbleton. Sæwine held it TRE and could go where he would. It was worth 20*s*.; now 12*s*.

XXXV. THE LAND OF WILLIAM FITZGUY [6]

In "Grimboldestou" Hundred

● William fitzGuy holds Dyrham of the king. Ælfric held it TRE. There are 7 hides paying geld. In demesne is 1 plough; and 13 villans and 13 bordars with 2 ploughs. There are all together 8 slaves and female slaves, and 3 mills rendering 15*s*., and 6 acres of meadow. It was worth £12; now £8.

● The same William held 3 hides of this manor of which Durand the sheriff had given seisin to St Mary of Pershore, by order of the king; these Earl William had given to Turstin fitzRolf with this manor.

[6] ## XXXVI. THE LAND OF WILLIAM FROISSELOUP

In 'Dudstone' Hundred

● William Froisseloup holds [?]Wotton [in Gloucester] of the king. Godric held it. There are 2 hides. In demesne are 2 ploughs, and 4 bordars and 4 slaves. It was worth 30*s*.; now 60*s*.

In 'Witley' Hundred ● The same William holds in Condicote half a hide paying geld. There was 1 plough, and 4 slaves. It was worth 20*s*.; now 3*s*. Beorhtric held it TRE.

In 'Greston' Hundred

● The same William holds 1 hide in 'Littleton' [in Dumbleton]. Godric held it. In demesne are 2 ploughs, and 2 bordars and 3 slaves, and a mill rendering 4*s*. It was worth 40*s*.; now 30*s*., and it pays geld.

[6] ## XXXVII. THE LAND OF WILLIAM FITZNORMAN

In "Langebrige" Hundred

● William fitzNorman holds Moorcroft [Moorcroft and Upper Moorcroft]. Wulfheah held it TRE. There is 1 hide. In demesne is 1 plough, with 2 bordars. It was worth 8*s*.; now 10*s*. This land does not pay geld.

In Westbury Hundred

● The same William holds English Bicknor. Morganau held it TRE. There is half a hide. In demesne is half a plough, with 6 bordars. It was worth 5*s*.; now 10*s*.

● The same William holds in Mitcheldean 2 hides and 2½ virgates of land. 3 thegns, Godric, Alric and Earnwig, held these TRE. In demesne are 3 ploughs. There are 38 bordars having 7½ ploughs, and 3 of them pay 8*s*. It was worth 33*s*.; now 44*s*. King Edward granted these lands quit of geld in return for guarding the forest.

In Botloe Hundred

● The same William holds Taynton. Wulfgar held it of King Edward. This land is free. [. . .] There are 6 bordars with 1 plough. It is and was worth 20*s*.

[7] 1 virgate of land in the same place belongs to the forest and renders 12*d*.

In Bledisloe Hundred

● The same William holds 1 hide and half a virgate of land. Siward and Wynstan held them. In demesne are 2 ploughs; and 17 bordars with 5 ploughs. It was worth 15*s*.; now 30*s*.

XXXVIII. THE LAND OF WILLIAM LEOFRIC

In Cheltenham Hundred

[6] ● William Leofric holds Leckhampton of the king. Asgot held it TRE. There are 3 hides paying geld. In demesne are 2 ploughs; and 2 villans and 8 bordars with 1 plough. There are 4 slaves, [and] woodland 1 furlong long and 1 broad. It is and was worth 40*s*.

In 'Greston' Hundred

● The same William holds Hailes. Asgot held it TRE. There are 11 hides. In demesne are 3 ploughs; and 9 villans and 11 bordars with 8 ploughs. There were 12 slaves whom William made free. There is a mill rendering 10*s*., [and] woodland 1 league long and a half broad. It was worth £12; now £8. This manor pays geld.

In "Wacrescumbe" Hundred

● The same William holds Whittington. Asgot held it. There are 3 hides and they pay geld. In demesne are 2 ploughs; and 6 villans and 1 radknight and 4 bordars with 4 ploughs. There is a mill rendering 10*s*., [and] woodland 1 league long and a half broad. It was worth 100*s*.; now 60*s*.

● The same William holds in Shipton Oliffe 3 hides less 1 virgate, and they pay geld. Geoffrey holds them of him. Asgot held them. In demesne are 2 ploughs; and a priest and 1 villan and 4 slaves without a plough. It was worth 40*s*.; now 20*s*.

In 'Bradley' Hundred

● The same William holds Turkdean, and Geoffrey [holds] of him. Asgot held it. There are 5 hides and 1½ virgates. [There is] nothing in demesne. There are 2 villans and 3 bordars with 1 plough. This land pays geld. It was worth £4; now 10*s*.

XXXIX. THE LAND OF ROGER DE LACY

In Botloe Hundred

[6] ● Roger de Lacy holds Kempley [Kempley and Kempley Green] of the king. Eadric and Leofric held it TRE as 2 manors and they could go where they would. There are 3 hides. In demesne are 3 ploughs; and 10 villans and 7 bordars with 12 ploughs. There are 7 slaves. It was worth £4; now 100*s*.

● The same Roger holds Oxenhall. Thorkil held it of Earl Harold and he could go where he would. There are 3 hides. In demesne are 2 ploughs; and 5 villans and 3 bordars with 5 ploughs. There are 2 slaves, and in Gloucester 3 burgesses paying 15*d*. It is and was worth 40*s*.

● The same Roger holds Carswalls, and Odo [holds] of him. [2] Wulfhelm held it TRE and he could go where he would. There is 1 hide and 1 virgate. In demesne is 1 plough; and 3 villans and 1 bordar with 3 ploughs. It is and was worth 20*s*.

In Salmonsbury Hundred

● The same Roger holds Icomb Place, and Ralph [holds] of him. Healfdene held it. There are 2 hides. In demesne are 2 ploughs; and 2 villans and 2 bordars with 1 plough. There are 4 slaves and 3 female slaves. It is and was worth 40*s*. This land pays geld.

● The same Roger holds Wyck Rissington, and Hugh [holds] of him. There are 8 hides paying geld. Alweard and Eskil and Alweard and Wulfwig held them as 4 manors. In demesne are 7 ploughs; and 4 villans with 2 ploughs. There are 12 slaves and 2 female slaves. There is a mill rendering 10s. It is and was worth £7 and £10 [*sic*].

In 'Holford' Hundred

● The same Roger holds Temple Guiting. There are 10 hides paying geld besides the demesne which does not pay geld. Beorhtric, a thegn of King Edward, held it. In demesne are 5 ploughs; and 25 villans and a priest and 7 radknights with 18 ploughs. There are 18 slaves and female slaves all together, and 3 mills rendering 24*s*., and a salt-pan [2] rendering 20*s*. and 12 summae of salt; and in Winchcombe 3 burgesses paying 32*d*., and in Gloucester 2 burgesses paying 10*d*. From the woodland and pasture, 40 hens. It is and was worth £10.

In Rapsgate Hundred

● The same Roger holds Duntisbourne Abbots, and Gilbert [holds] of him. Cyneweard, a thegn of King Edward, held it and he could go where he would. There are 2 hides. In demesne is 1 plough; and 2 villans and 2 bordars with 1½ ploughs. There are 2 slaves. It is and was worth 40*s*.

In Bisley Hundred

● The same Roger holds Painswick. There is 1 hide paying geld. Earnsige held it. In demesne is 1 plough; and 35 villans and 16 bordars and a priest and 3 radknights. Among them all they have 52 ploughs. There are 11 slaves, and 4 mills rendering 24*s*., [and] woodland 5 leagues long and 2 broad. It was worth £20; now £24. The thegn himself could go where he would. In this land St Mary of Cirencester holds 1 villan and part of the woodland. King William granted it this. It is worth 10*s*.

● The same Roger holds Edgeworth. There are 1½ hides paying geld. Alwine held them. In demesne are 4 ploughs; and 4 villans and 3 bordars with 2 ploughs. There are 2 free men with 2 ploughs. There are 15 slaves, and a mill rendering 30*d*., and 2 acres of meadow, [and] woodland 1 league long and a half broad. It is and was worth £6.

● The same Roger holds half a hide with 1 fishery in the Wye, and there is 1 villan with 1 plough. This land is called Madgetts. It is and was worth 20*s*. Beorhtric held it.

● The same Roger holds half a hide in Tidenham. Archbishop Stigand held it. There is 1 villan with 1 plough, and 4½ fisheries. It is and was worth 20*s*.

In 'Brightwells Barrow' Hundred

● The same Roger holds Quenington. There are 8 hides. 3 free men, Dodda, and another Dodda, and Alweald, held them as 3 manors and they could go where they would, and they paid geld. In demesne are 3 ploughs; and 20 villans and 7 bordars and a priest and a reeve. Among them all they have 12 ploughs, and [there are] 2 radknights with 1 plough. There are 12 slaves, and 2 mills rendering 20*s*., and 10 acres of meadow. In Gloucester 1 burgess renders 4 iron tips for ploughshares, and 1 smith pays 2*s*. It was worth £8; now £10.

● The same Roger holds Eastleach Turville, and William [holds] of him. There are 5 hides. Ealdwine held it TRE. In demesne are 2 ploughs; and 12 villans and 1 bordar with 5 ploughs. There are 5 slaves, and 8 acres of meadow. It is and was worth £6.

● The same Roger holds Williamstrip, and William [holds] of him. There are 2 hides. Dunning held it TRE. In demesne are 2 ploughs; and 3 villans and 3 bordars with 1 plough. There are 6 slaves. It is and was worth 100*s*.

In Barrington Hundred

● The same Roger holds Windrush, and Ralph [holds] of him. There are 2 hides. Wulfric held it TRE. In demesne is 1 plough; and 3 villans and 2 bordars with 1 plough. There are 5 slaves, and a mill rendering 5*s*., and 10 acres of meadow. It was worth 100*s*.; now £4.

[X]

● In the same place the same Roger holds 1 hide and 1 virgate, and Hugh [holds] of him. Godric, a thegn of King Edward, held them. In demesne is 1 plough, and 2 bordars and 1 slave, and a mill rendering 3*s*., and 8 acres of meadow. It is and was worth 24*s*.

IN CIRENCESTER HUNDRED

● The same Roger holds STRATTON. There are 5 hides paying geld besides the demesne. Edmund held it TRE. In demesne are 3 ploughs; and 16 villans and 7 bordars with a priest having 9 ploughs. There are 5 slaves, and 2 mills rendering 20*s*. It was worth £8; now £6.

● The same Roger holds SIDDINGTON, and his mother holds it as her dower-land. There are 6 hides. Godric and Leofwine held it as 2 manors. In demesne are 3 ploughs; and 9 villans and 6 bordars and a priest with 7 ploughs. There are 2 slaves, and a mill rendering 10*s*. It was worth £8; now £9.

● The same Roger holds COATES. There are 1½ hides. Leofwine held it. Now Gerard holds it of Roger. In demesne are 2 ploughs; and 2 villans with a priest having 2½ ploughs. There are 9 slaves. It was worth £4; now £3.

IN SALMONSBURY HUNDRED

● The same Roger and his mother hold UPPER SLAUGHTER. There are 3 hides. Offa and Leofwine held it as 2 manors and could go where they would. In demesne are 4 ploughs, and 4 bordars and 8 slaves, and a mill rendering 12*s*. It is and was worth £6. Of these 3 hides, 1 hide paid geld each year at 10*s*. for the king's use.

IN 'GRESTON' HUNDRED

● The same Roger holds WORMINGTON; Walter fitzErcold [holds] of him. There are 5 hides paying geld. Eadwig held it. In demesne are 2 ploughs; and 6 villans with 2 ploughs. There are 2 slaves, and a mill rendering 8*s*., and 10 acres of meadow. It was worth 100*s*.; now £4.

XL. THE LAND OF ROGER DE BEAUMONT [6]

IN "CELFLEDETORN" HUNDRED

● ROGER de Beaumont holds DORSINGTON [War.], and Robert [holds] of him. There are 10 hides. Saxi held it. In demesne [are] 3 ploughs; and 8 villans with 5 ploughs, and 6 slaves. It was worth £8; now 100*s*.

XLI. THE LAND OF ROGER D'IVRY [6]

IN 'BRADLEY' HUNDRED

● ROGER d'IVRY holds HAMPNETT. There are 10 hides. Archbishop Ealdræd held it. Out of these 10, King Edward gave him 2 hides quit [of geld], as they say. In demesne are 3 ploughs; and 10 villans with a priest and 1 bordar with 5 ploughs. There are 11 slaves, and in Winchcombe 10 burgesses pay 65*d*. It was worth £8; now £6.

IN LONGTREE HUNDRED

● The same Roger holds TETBURY. There are 23 hides paying geld. Siward held it TRE. In demesne are 8 ploughs; and 32 villans and 2 bordars and 2 radknights with a priest having among them all 14 ploughs. There are 19 slaves, and a mill rendering 15*d*., and pasture rendering 10*s*., and 10 acres of meadow.

● The same Roger holds TETBURY UPTON. There are 2 hides and 1 virgate paying geld. Ælfric held it of King Edward. In demesne are 2 ploughs; and 5 villans and 3 bordars with 3 ploughs. There are 8 slaves.

These 2 manors were worth £33 TRE; now they are at farm for £50.

● The same Roger holds CULKERTON, and Ansketil [holds] of him. Ælfric held it. There are 1½ hides. In demesne [are] 2 ploughs, and 4 slaves. It was worth 20*s*.; now 30*s*.

● The same Roger holds HAZELTON [in Rodmarton]. There are 3 hides and 3 virgates paying geld. Alnoth held it TRE. In demesne are 4 ploughs; and 7 half-villans and 1 bordar with 3 ploughs, and 17 slaves, and half a mill rendering 30*d*., and 15 acres of meadow. A certain man, Roger, held this manor of the Bishop of Bayeux for £16. Afterwards the bishop gave it to the same Roger with the farm.

XLII. THE LAND OF ROGER OF BERKELEY

IN RAPSGATE HUNDRED [6]

[X] ● ROGER of Berkeley holds COBERLEY. There are 10 hides. Dene, a thegn of King Edward, held it. In demesne are 2 ploughs; and 19 villans and 4 bordars with 5 ploughs. There are 4 slaves, and 5 acres of meadow, [and] woodland 3 furlongs long and 2 broad. It was worth £7; now £8.

IN "EDREDESTANE" HUNDRED

● The same Roger holds DODINGTON. There are 3 hides and 2 parts of half a hide. Alwine held it TRE. In demesne is 1 plough; and 7 villans and 4 bordars with 4 ploughs. There are 4 slaves, and 10 acres of meadow. It is and was worth £3.

IN PUCKLECHURCH HUNDRED

● The same Roger holds SISTON. Anna held it. There are 5 hides paying geld. In demesne are 2 ploughs; and 8 villans and 10 bordars with 4 ploughs. There are 4 slaves, and 8 acres of meadow. It is and was worth 100*s*.

XLIII. THE LAND OF RALPH OF BERKELEY [6]

IN PUCKLECHURCH HUNDRED

● RALPH, the brother of this Roger, holds WAPLEY of the king. There is 1 hide. Godric held it. In demesne is 1 plough, and 4 slaves. It is and was worth 20*s*.

IN "BLACHELAUE" HUNDRED

● The same Ralph holds LEONARD STANLEY. There are 4½ hides. Godric and Wihtnoth held it as 2 manors. In demesne are 2 ploughs; and 6 villans and 14 bordars with 12 ploughs. There are 5 slaves, and 10 acres of meadow. It was and is worth 100*s*.

XLIIII. THE LAND OF RALPH PAYNEL [6]

IN CIRENCESTER HUNDRED

● RALPH Paynel holds TARLTON, and Ralph [holds] of him. There are 4½ hides paying geld. Mærle-Sveinn held it. In demesne are 3 ploughs; and 10 villans and 1 bordar with 3 ploughs. There are 10 slaves. It was worth £10; now 100*s*.

IN LONGTREE HUNDRED

Roger d'Ivry held 1½ virgates of land of Ralph Paynel which they have both relinquished.

XLV. THE LAND OF RALPH DE TOSNY

IN 'WITLEY' HUNDRED

● RALPH de Tosny holds CHARINGWORTH, and Roger [holds] of him. There are 10 hides. Beorhtmær held it. In demesne [are] 3 ploughs; and 13 villans and 1 radknight with 6 ploughs, and 9 slaves and female slaves all together. It was worth £8; now £6.

IN SALMONSBURY HUNDRED

● The same Ralph holds ICOMB [Place or Proper], and Roger [holds] of him. There are 10 hides paying geld. In demesne [are] 3 ploughs; and 12 villans and 2 bordars with 7 ploughs. There are 8 slaves. It is and was worth £6.

IN BOTLOE HUNDRED

● The same Ralph holds BROMSBERROW. There are 5 hides. Earl Harold held it. In demesne is 1 plough; and 11 villans and 8 bordars with 14 ploughs. There is 1 slave, [and] woodland 2 leagues long and 1 broad. It was worth £8; now 100*s*.

IN "GERSDONES" HUNDRED

● The same Ralph holds HARNHILL, and Roger [holds] of him. There [2] are 5 hides. Alric and Alwine and Wulfric held them as 3 manors.

● The same Ralph holds 'AMPNEY' [in Driffield] and CERNEY WICK, and Roger [holds] of him. There are 4 hides. 4 thegns held them as 4 manors and could go where they would. In demesne [are] 10 ploughs, and 1 villan and 1 bordar. There are 21 slaves, and a mill rendering 5*s*., and 30 acres of meadow. It was worth £10; now £6.

IN SALMONSBURY HUNDRED

● The same Ralph holds LOWER SWELL, and Drogo [holds] of him. Earnsige held it. There are 7 hides paying geld. In demesne are 4 ploughs; and 10 villans with 6 ploughs, and a mill rendering 7*s*. 6*d*. It was worth £8; now £7.

XLVI. THE LAND OF ROBERT DE TOSNY [6]

IN SALMONSBURY HUNDRED

● ROBERT de Tosny holds GREAT RISSINGTON. Ulf held it. There are [X] 13 hides paying geld. In demesne are 3 ploughs; and 23 villans and 6 bordars with 10 ploughs. There are 8 slaves and female slaves all together, and a mill rendering 10*s*., and 1 burgess in Gloucester paying 3*d*. It was worth £12; now £10.

IN "GRIMBOLDESTOU" HUNDRED

● The same Robert holds HORTON. There are 10 hides paying geld. Ulf held it. In demesne are 3 ploughs; and 11 villans and 8 bordars with 8 ploughs. There are 7 slaves, and a mill rendering 6*s*., and 20 acres of meadow, [and] woodland 2 leagues long and 1 broad. It was worth £12; now £7.

IN BISLEY HUNDRED

● The same Robert holds SAPPERTON [near Cirencester] and FRAMPTON MANSELL. In the one [are] 5 hides, and in the other 5 hides. Ulf held them. In demesne are 7 ploughs; and 17 villans and 9 bordars with 10 ploughs. There are 13 slaves, and 2 mills rendering 6*s*., [and] woodland half a league long and 2 furlongs broad. These 2 manors together were worth £14 TRE; now £16.

XLVII. THE LAND OF ROBERT DESPENSER [6]

IN 'GRESTON' HUNDRED

● ROBERT Despenser holds CHILDSWICKHAM [Worcs.]. There are 10 hides paying geld. Baldwin held it. In demesne are 3 ploughs; and 32 villans and 10 bordars with 12 ploughs. There is 1 slave, and 2 mills rendering 10*s*., and 10 acres of meadow. In Winchcombe [is] 1 burgess paying 16*d*. It was worth £12; now £16.

6 ## XLVIII. THE LAND OF ROBERT D'OILLY

IN SALMONSBURY HUNDRED

● ROBERT d'Oilly holds LITTLE RISSINGTON. There are 10 hides paying geld. Siward held it. In demesne [are] 4 ploughs; and 12 villans and 2 bordars with 5 ploughs. There are 8 slaves, and 2 mills rendering 20*s*. It was worth £10; now £8.

IN 'BRADLEY' HUNDRED

● The same Robert holds TURKDEAN. There are 5 hides and 2½ virgates paying geld. Siward held it. In demesne are 4 ploughs; and 12 villans with 6 ploughs. All togther there are 8 slaves and female slaves. It was worth £6; now 100*s*.

IN SALMONSBURY HUNDRED

2 ● Roger d'Oilly holds NAUNTON [near Bourton-on-the-Water] of Osbern fitzRichard. There are 5 hides paying geld. Thorsten held it. In demesne [are] 2 ploughs; and 8 villans with 4½ ploughs. It is worth £3.

XLIX. THE LAND OF RICHARD THE LEGATE

IN "EDREDESTANE" HUNDRED

6 ● RICHARD the legate holds TORMARTON of the king. There are 8 hides. [. . .] Alric held it of King Edward. In demesne are 6 ploughs; and 20 villans and 4 bordars and a priest and 1 radknight. Among them all they have 12 ploughs. There are 12 slaves. It was worth £12; now £15.

L. THE LAND OF OSBERN GIFFARD

IN 'LANGLEY' HUNDRED

6 2 ● OSBERN Giffard holds ROCKHAMPTON of the king. There are 3 hides paying geld. Dunna held it TRE. In demesne are 2 ploughs; and 6 villans and 7 bordars with 3 ploughs. There are 5 slaves, and 20 acres of meadow, and a salt-pan at Droitwich [Worcs.] rendering 4 summae of salt, [and] woodland 1 league long and a half broad. It is worth £6

IN "LETBERGE" HUNDRED

● The same Osbern holds STOKE GIFFORD. There are 5 hides paying geld. Dunna held it. In demesne are 4 ploughs; and 8 villans and 3 bordars and a priest with 8 ploughs. There are 4 slaves. It was worth £6; now £8.

IN RAPSGATE HUNDRED

● The same Osbern holds BRIMPSFIELD. There are 9 hides paying geld. Duns held it of Earl Harold. In demesne are 3 ploughs; and 16 villans and 6 bordars and a priest with 12 ploughs. There are 8 slaves and 4 female slaves, and 2 mills rendering 64*d*. In Gloucester [are] 5 burgesses paying 2*s*. It is and was worth £12.

● The same Osbern holds 'OLDBURY' [in Elkstone], but it did not
2 pertain to the land of the man Duns which Osbern holds, as the shire says. [. . .] Æthelric held it and could go where he would. There is 1 hide and 1 plough. It is and was worth 10*s*.

LI. THE LAND OF GEOFFREY ORLATEILE

6 ● GEOFFREY Orlateile holds of the king in BAUNTON 2 hides and 1 virgate paying geld. Bolli held them. There is nothing in demesne. There are 2 villans and 8 bordars with 3 ploughs. It is and was worth 40*s*. There are 8 acres of meadow.

LII. THE LAND OF GILBERT FITZTUROLD

IN CIRENCESTER HUNDRED

6 ● GILBERT fitzTurold holds 1 hide of the king in COATES, and Oswulf [holds] of him. Cyneweard held it TRE. In demesne are 2 ploughs, and 3 bordars and 6 slaves. It was worth 40*s*.; now 30*s*.

● The same Gilbert holds half a hide in TREWSBURY, and Osweard [holds] of him. Alweard held it. In demesne is 1 plough. It was worth 10*s*.; now 15*s*.

IN RAPSGATE HUNDRED

● The same Gilbert holds NORTH CERNEY. There are 7 hides. 2 thegns, Elaf and his brother, held it as 2 manors and could go where they would. In demesne are 4 ploughs; and 7 villans and 6 bordars with 5 ploughs. There are 6 slaves, and a mill rendering 8*s*., and 6 acres of meadow, [and] woodland 2 furlongs long and 1 broad. There 4 knights of Gilbert with their men have 7 ploughs, and a mill rendering 8*s*. The whole was worth £14 TRE; now £12.

● The same Gilbert holds RENDCOMB. There are 5 hides paying geld. Ælfric held it. In demesne is 1 plough; and 3 villans and 7 bordars with 3 ploughs. There are 7 slaves, and 1 Frenchman holds the land of 2 villans, and [there is] a mill rendering 8*s*., and 4 acres of meadow. It was worth £7; now 100*s*.

X ● The same Gilbert holds RENDCOMB, and Walter [holds] of him. There are 3 hides paying geld. In demesne are 2 ploughs; and 4 villans and 3 bordars with 2 ploughs. There are 6 slaves, and a mill rendering 5*s*., and 3 acres of meadow. It is and was worth £6.

In Salmonsbury Hundred ● The same Gilbert holds AYLWORTH, and Walter [holds] of him. Alwine held it. There are 4 hides paying geld. In demesne [are] 2 ploughs; and 3 villans with 2 ploughs, and 6 slaves and female slaves all together. It is and was worth 40*s*.

● The same Gilbert holds [Lower and Upper] HARFORD. Ælfhere held it. There is 1 hide paying geld. In demesne [are] 2 ploughs; and 4 villans and 1 bordar with 2 ploughs, and 2 slaves, and a mill rendering 5*s*. It is and was worth 40*s*.

LIII. THE LAND OF DURAND OF GLOUCESTER

IN WESTBURY HUNDRED

6 ● DURAND the sheriff holds 1 manor of 3 hides. Alweald held it, and it paid geld. In demesne is 1 plough; and 4 villans and 3 bordars with 4 ploughs. There are 2 slaves. It was worth 60*s*.; now 40*s*.

IN "GERSDONES" HUNDRED

● The same Durand holds 1 hide in ASHBROOK, and a certain knight of his [holds] of him. In demesne [is] 1 plough, and 1 bordar and 1 slave. It is and was worth 10*s*.

IN CIRENCESTER HUNDRED

● The same Durand holds 2 hides in DUNTISBOURNE ROUSE, and Ralph [holds] it of him. Wulfweard held it of King Edward as a manor. In demesne are 2 ploughs; and 3 villans and 1 bordar with 1 plough. There are 4 slaves, and 2 acres of meadow. It is and was worth 40*s*.

IN LONGTREE HUNDRED

● The same Durand holds CULKERTON, and Roger d'Ivry [holds] of him. There are 2 hides and 2½ virgates. Grim held it. In demesne are 2 ploughs; and 6 villans with 3 ploughs. It is and was worth £4.

IN "GRIMBOLDESTOU" HUNDRED

● The same Durand holds DIDMARTON, and Ansketil [holds] of him. There are 3 hides paying geld. Leofwine held it of Earl Harold. In demesne are 3 ploughs; and 8 bordars with 1 plough, and 4 slaves, and 6 acres of meadow. It was worth 30*s*.; now 40*s*.

IN 'DUDSTONE' HUNDRED

2 ● The same Durand holds WHADDON. There are 5 hides. 5 brothers held them as 5 manors, and they could go where they would and were equals. In demesne are 5 ploughs; and 1 villan and 7 bordars with 5 ploughs. TRE it was worth £8; now 100*s*.

IN "CELFLEDETORN" HUNDRED

● The same Durand holds SEZINCOTE, and Walter [holds] of him. There are 2½ hides. Leofwine and Leofwig held it as 2 manors. In demesne are 2 ploughs, and 4 bordars. It was worth 40*s*.; now 60*s*.

IN SALMONSBURY HUNDRED

● The same Durand holds ICOMB PROPER, and Walter [holds] of him. There are 2 hides paying geld. Thorsten held it. In demesne [are] 2 ploughs; and 2 villans and 2 bordars with 1 plough, and 6 slaves and female slaves all together. It was worth 30*s*.; now 40*s*.

IN "WACRESCUMBE" HUNDRED

● The same Durand holds SHIPTON SOLERS, and Ralph [holds] of him. Eadwig held it. There are 3½ hides paying geld. In demesne are 2 ploughs; and 3 villans with 2 ploughs, and 4 slaves, and 10 acres of meadow. It was worth £4; now 40*s*.

IN 'WHITSTONE' HUNDRED

● The same Durand holds in HARESFIELD COURT 7 hides paying geld. 2 brothers, Godric and Eadric, held them as 2 manors and could go where they would. In demesne are 3 ploughs; and 9 villans and 11 bordars with 9 ploughs. There are 4 slaves, and 5 potters pay 44*d*. [There is] woodland half a league long and 3 furlongs broad. It is and was worth £6.

● The same Durand holds MORETON VALENCE. There are 3 hides paying geld. Auti held it. In demesne is 1 plough; and 4 villans and 6 bordars with 3½ ploughs. There are 4 slaves, and 20 acres of meadow. It was worth £4; now 40*s*.

IN 'GRESTON' HUNDRED

● The same Durand holds 'LITTLETON' [in Dumbleton], and Ralph [holds] of him. There is half a hide paying geld. Leofnoth held it as 1 manor. There is 1 plough. It is and was worth 10*s*.

IN 'WITLEY' HUNDRED

● In CONDICOTE Osbern holds of Durand 1½ hides. It is and was worth 20*s*.

LIIII. THE LAND OF DROGO FITZPONS

IN "BLACHELAUE" HUNDRED

6 ● DROGO fitzPons holds FRAMPTON ON SEVERN of the king. There are 10 hides paying geld. Earnsige held it. In demesne are 3 ploughs; and 10 villans and 8 bordars with 6 ploughs. There are 9 slaves, and a mill rendering 10*s*., and 10 acres of meadow, [and] woodland 1 league long and 3 furlongs broad. In Gloucester, 1 burgess paying 6*d*. It is and was worth 100*s*. Of this manor Roger de Lacy holds 1 hide unjustly.

IN 'BRIGHTWELLS BARROW' HUNDRED

● The same Drogo holds EASTLEACH MARTIN. There are 10 hides paying geld. Cola held it. In demesne are 4 ploughs; and 15 villans and 4 bordars with 9 ploughs. There are 9 slaves, and a mill rendering 10*s*., and 10 acres of meadow. It was worth £8; now £10.

LV. THE LAND OF WALTER FITZPONS

IN 'BRIGHTWELLS BARROW' HUNDRED

6 ● WALTER fitzPons holds SOUTHROP of the king. There are 10 hides paying geld. Earl Tosti held it. In demesne are 4 ploughs; and 16 villans and 6 bordars and a priest with 8 ploughs. There are 12 slaves, and a mill rendering 10*s*., and 20 acres of meadow. It was worth £12; now £15.

[6]
LVI. THE LAND OF WALTER FITZROGER

In Barrington Hundred

● Walter fitzRoger holds Great Barrington of the king. There are 8 hides. [. . .] Thorsten and Eadwig held it as 2 manors. In demesne are 4 ploughs; and 14 villans and a priest and 2 bordars with 9 ploughs. There are 14 slaves, and a mill rendering 10*s*., and 20 acres of meadow. It is and was worth £8.

In "Gersdones" Hundred

● The same Walter holds South Cerney. There are 14 hides and 1 virgate. Archbishop Stigand held it. In demesne are 2 ploughs; and 25 villans and a priest and 9 bordars with 10 ploughs. There are 4 slaves, and 100 acres of meadow, and there were 3 mills rendering 30*s*. It was worth £16; now £12.

This manor is claimed for the Church of St Mary of Abingdon, but the whole shire bore witness that Archbishop Stigand had held it for 10 years while King Edward was alive. Earl William gave this manor to Roger the sheriff, the father of Walter.

LVII. THE LAND OF WALTER THE DEACON

In 'Witley' Hundred

[6] ● Walter the deacon holds Sezincote of the king. There are 4½ hides. Godwine held it and could go where he would. In demesne [are] 2 ploughs; and 8 villans with 6 ploughs, and 10 slaves. It is and was worth £3.

LVIII. THE LAND OF WALTER THE CROSSBOWMAN

In Westbury Hundred

● Walter the crossbowman holds Bulley of the king. There are 4 hides paying geld. Tovi held it of King Edward. In demesne are 2 ploughs; and 4 villans and 6 bordars with 4 ploughs. There are 4 slaves, and 10 acres of meadow. In Gloucester 1 burgess pays 18*d*. It was worth 60*s*.; now 40*s*.

● The same Walter holds Ruddle. There is 1 hide paying geld. Tovi held it. In demesne is 1 plough; and 2 villans and 4 bordars with 2 ploughs. It was worth 40*s*.; now 10*s*.

In Bledisloe Hundred

● The same Walter holds half a hide which does not pay geld. Palli held it. There is a mill. It is worth 19*s*.

In 'Langley' Hundred

● The same Walter holds Frampton Cotterell. There are 5 hides paying geld. Ælfstan of Boscombe held it. In demesne is 1 plough; and 10 villans and 11 bordars with 5 ploughs. There are 5 slaves, and 2 mills rendering 5*s*. And there is a church which was not [there before]. It was worth £8; now £3.

LIX. THE LAND OF HENRY DE FERRERS

In 'Brightwells Barrow' Hundred

[6] ● Henry de Ferrers holds Lechlade. Siward Barn held it. There were 15 hides TRE paying geld. But the king himself granted 6 hides quit of geld. The whole shire bears witness to this, and the man himself who bore the king's seal. In demesne are 4 ploughs; and 29 villans and 10 bordars and 1 Frenchman holding the land of 1 villan. Among them all they have 16 ploughs. There are 13 slaves, and 3 mills rendering 30*s*., and a fishery rendering 200 eels, less 25. From the meadows, £7. 7*s*., besides the hay for the oxen. In Winchcombe 2 burgesses pay 16*d*., and 1 in Gloucester pays nothing. The whole manor was worth £20 TRE; and now the same.

LX. THE LAND OF ERNULF DE HESDIN

In 'Brightwells Barrow' Hundred

[6] ● Ernulf de Hesdin holds Kempsford. There are 21 hides paying geld. Asgot held it of Earl Harold. In demesne are 6 ploughs; and 38 villans and 9 bordars and 1 radknight with 18 ploughs. There are 14 slaves, and 4 mills rendering 40*s*. and 40*d*., and from the meadows £9 besides pasture for the oxen, and from the sheep-fold 120 weys of cheese. In Gloucester 7 burgesses pay 2*s*. The whole was worth £30 TRE; now £66. 6*s*. 8*d*.

● The same Ernulf holds Hatherop. There are 7 hides. Wulfweard White held it. In demesne are 6 ploughs; and 23 villans with 10 ploughs. There are 12 slaves, and a mill rendering 15*s*. It was worth £8; now £12.

In "Gersdones" Hundred

● The same Ernulf holds in 'Ampney St Nicholas' 4 hides and 2½ virgates. Alric and Godric held them as 2 manors. [. . .] In demesne are 3 ploughs; and 7 villans and 2 bordars with 2 ploughs. There are 4 slaves. The whole was and is worth £6.

In "Grimboldestou" Hundred

● The same Ernulf holds Oldbury on the Hill. There are 5 hides paying geld. Eadric held it. In demesne are 3 ploughs; and 4 villans with 4 ploughs, and there are 9 slaves, and 1 Frenchman [2]
having 1 plough. There are 6 acres of meadow. It is and was worth £10.

● The same Ernulf holds Badminton. There are 4 hides paying geld. Eadric held it. In demesne are 2 ploughs; and 6 villans and 8 bordars with a priest have 13 ploughs. There are 9 slaves, and 8 acres of meadow. It is and was worth £10. [X]

● The same Ernulf holds Acton Turville. There are 5 hides paying geld. Eadric held it. In demesne are 3 ploughs; and 4 villans and 3 bordars with 4 ploughs. There are 15 acres of meadow. It is and was worth 100*s*.

In 'Swineshead' Hundred

● The same Ernulf holds Hanham, and Humbald [holds] of him. Eadric held it. There is half a hide [. . .]. In demesne are 2 ploughs, with 8 bordars and 4 slaves. It is and was worth 40*s*.

LXI. THE LAND OF HAROLD SON OF EARL RALPH

● Harold son of Earl Ralph holds Sudeley of the king. Ralph [6]
his father held it. There are 10 hides paying geld. In demesne are 4 ploughs; and 18 villans and 8 bordars with 13 ploughs. There are 14 slaves and female slaves all together, and 6 mills rendering 52*s*., [2]
[and] woodland 3 leagues long and 2 broad.

● The same Harold holds Toddington. His father held it. There are 10 hides paying geld. In demesne are 3 ploughs; and 17 villans and 7 bordars and 2 free men have among them all 8 ploughs. There are 10 slaves and female slaves all together, and 2 mills rendering 20*s*. From 1 salt-pan, 50 mittae of salt. These 2 manors are and were worth £40.

LXII. THE LAND OF HUGH DE GRANDMESNIL [6]

In "Celfledetorn" Hundred

● Hugh de Grandmesnil holds Pebworth [Worcs.]. There are 2 hides and 1 virgate. 2 thegns held it as 2 manors. There are 3 ploughs, and 1 villan and 1 bordar and 7 slaves.

● The same Hugh holds Broad Marston [Worcs.]. There are 2 hides [. . .].

● The same Hugh holds Upper Quinton [War.]. There are 2 hides. 1 thegn held it. In demesne [are] 2 ploughs; and 5 villans and 1 bordar with 3 ploughs. There are 4 slaves and 1 female slave. They were worth £7; now £4.

● The same Hugh holds Lower Quinton [War.], and Roger [holds] of him. There are 12 hides. Baldwin held it TRE. In demesne [are] 3 ploughs; and 17 villans and 2 bordars with 9 ploughs. There are 6 slaves. It was worth £7; now £6.

● The same Hugh holds Weston-on-Avon [War.], and Roger [holds] of him. There are 4 hides. Baldwin held it. In demesne [are] 2 ploughs; and 6 villans with 3 ploughs. There are 4 slaves and 5 female slaves, and a mill rendering 10*s*. It was worth £7; now £6.

● The same Hugh holds Willicote [Willicote and Little Willicote, War.], and his clerk [holds] of him. There are 2½ hides. In demesne [are] 2 ploughs; and 2 villans and 1 bordar with 1 plough. There are 4 slaves and 1 female slave. It was worth 40*s*.; now 30[*s*.]. Leofric held it.

LXIII. THE LAND OF HUGH L'ASNE [6]

In 'Dudstone' Hundred

● Hugh l'Asne holds of the king Brockworth. There are 5 hides. Thorkil held it of King Edward. In demesne are 2 ploughs; and 8 villans and 6 bordars and a priest and 2 free men and a reeve. Among them all they have 15 ploughs. There are 4 slaves, and a mill rendering 2*s*., [and] woodland 1 league long and a half broad. It was worth £6; now 100*s*.

● The same Hugh holds Shipton Solers. There are 5 hides paying geld. Wulfweard held it. In demesne are 2 ploughs; and 4 villans and 1 bordar with 2 ploughs. There are 5 slaves, and a mill rendering 10*s*. It was worth £4; now £3. In "Wacrescumbe" Hundred

In 'Bradley' Hundred

● The same Hugh holds Salperton. There are 10 hides paying geld. Wulfweard held it. In demesne are 3 ploughs; and 10 villans and a priest with 7 ploughs, and 11 slaves and female slaves all together, and 5 acres of meadow. It was worth £9; now £7.

|In Cirencester Hundred| |[partly in margin]|

● The same Hugh holds Bagendon, and Gilbert [holds] of him. There are 3 hides paying geld. Wulfweard held it. In demesne are 3 ploughs; and 5 villans with 3 ploughs, and 6 slaves, and a mill rendering 10*s*., and 8 acres of meadow. It is and was worth £4.

6 LXI. THE LAND OF MILES CRISPIN

In 'Dudstone' Hundred

● Miles Crispin holds in Brawn 3 virgates of land. Vigot held them. [. . .] In demesne [is] 1 plough; and 7 bordars with 2 ploughs, and half a fishery. It was worth 40s.; now 30s.

In Longtree Hundred

● The same Miles holds Cherington, and Geoffrey [holds] of him. Hemming held it of King Edward. There are 2 hides paying geld. In demesne are 3 ploughs; and 3 villans and 8 bordars with 3½ ploughs. There are 12 slaves, and a mill rendering 30d., and 4 acres of meadow. It is and was worth £4. or 2

In "Grimboldestou" Hundred

● The same Miles holds Alderley. Vigot held it. There is 1 hide. In demesne are 2 ploughs; and 7 villans and 5 bordars with 7 ploughs. There are 4 slaves, and a mill rendering 10s., and 12 acres of meadow. It is and was worth 100s.

6 LXII. THE LAND OF URSE D'ABETOT

In 'Witley' Hundred

● Urse of Worcester holds in Sezincote 1 hide. Alwine held it as a manor, and it paid geld. In demesne [is] 1 plough, and 4 slaves. It was worth 40s.; now 10s.

LXIII. THE LAND OF HASCOIT MUSARD

In 'Witley' Hundred

6 ● Hascoit Musard holds of the king Saintbury. Cynewig Chelle held it. There are 10 hides. In demesne [are] 3 ploughs; and 18 villans and 3 bordars with 9 ploughs, and 10 slaves and female slaves all together, and a mill rendering 6d. It was worth £12; now £10.

● The same Hascoit holds 1 hide in Sezincote, and it pays geld. Wulfwine held it as a manor. There is 1 plough, and 1 bordar. It is and was worth 10s.

In Salmonsbury Hundred

● The same Hascoit holds Eyford. There are 5 hides paying geld. Earnsige held it. In demesne are 2 ploughs; and 12 villans and 1 bordar with 5 ploughs. All together there are 8 slaves and female slaves. It is worth £4.

In 'Greston' Hundred

● The same Hascoit holds Aston Somerville [Worcs.]. There are 6 hides paying geld. Earnsige held it. In demesne are 3 ploughs; and 12 villans with 4 ploughs, and 9 slaves and female slaves all together. There is a mill rendering 8s., and 20 acres of meadow. It is and was worth £6.

In Cirencester Hundred

● The same Hascoit holds Upper Siddington. There are 10 hides paying geld, besides the demesne. Earnsige held it. In demesne are 3 ploughs; and 8 villans and 10 bordars with a priest having 5½ ploughs. There are 7 slaves, and 20 acres of meadow. It was worth £10; now £8.

In Bisley Hundred

● The same Hascoit holds Miserden. There is 1 hide paying geld. Earnsige held it. In demesne are 3 ploughs; and 8 villans and 5 bordars and a priest and 1 radknight. Among them all they have 9 ploughs. There are 10 slaves, and 8 acres of meadow, [and] woodland 1 league long and a half broad. It was worth 100s.; now £7.

LXIIII. THE LAND OF TURSTIN FITZROLF

In "Gersdones" Hundred

6 ● Turstin fitzRolf holds of the king Ampney Crucis. There are 7 hides. Tovi held it of King Edward. In demesne are 3 ploughs; and 8 villans and a priest with 8 ploughs. There are 8 slaves. Of this land Tovi holds the land of 2 villans, and a certain knight the land of 4 villans. Half a hide and 4 acres of meadow belong to the church. It was worth £8; now £6.

● In the same place Turstin himself holds 1 hide. Wulfwig held it as a manor and could go where he would. In demesne [are] 2 ploughs, with 1 bordar. It was worth 40s.

In Cirencester Hundred

● The same Turstin holds in Coates 1 hide. Beorhtric held it as a manor of King Edward. In demesne is 1 plough; and 3 villans with 3 ploughs. There are 6 slaves, and 4 acres of meadow. It is and was worth 50s. Gerwy holds it of Turstin.

In "Grimboldestou" Hundred

● The same Turstin holds Hillesley, and Bernard [holds] of him. There is 1 hide. Ælfric held it. In demesne are 2 ploughs; and 5 half-villans and 7 bordars with 2 ploughs. There are 8 slaves, and 3 mills rendering 18s., and 8 acres of meadow. It was worth 40s.; now 60s.

In Bagstone Hundred

● The same Turstin holds Tortworth. There is 1 hide. Alweald held it. In demesne are 2 ploughs; and 6 villans and 7 bordars with 7 ploughs. There are 6 slaves, and 3 mills rendering 15s., and 10 acres of meadow. Woodland 1 league long and a half broad renders 5s. It was worth £7; now 100s.

In "Blachelaue" Hundred

● The same Turstin holds King's Stanley. There are 5 hides. Tovi held it of King Edward. In demesne are 2 ploughs; and 8 villans and 6 bordars with 10 ploughs. There are 4 slaves, and 2 mills rendering 35s., and 10 acres of meadow, [and] woodland 1 league long and a half broad. It is and was worth 100s. Tovi holds 2 hides of this land in alms of King William. ☒

● The same Turstin holds Fretherne. Auti held it. There are 3 hides paying geld. In demesne is 1 plough; and 3 villans and 3 bordars with 2 ploughs, and 1 slave. It was worth 60s.; now 30s.

6 LXV. THE LAND OF ANSFRID DE CORMEILLES

In Bisley Hundred

§ ● Ansfrid de Cormeilles holds Winstone. There are 5 hides. Wulfweard held it. In demesne are 3 ploughs; and 10 villans and 4 bordars and 1 Frenchman with 8 ploughs. There are 8 slaves, and a mill rendering 20d. It is and was worth £7. ☒

In "Celfledetorn" Hundred

● The same Ansfrid holds Weston-sub-Edge. 2 thegns held it, one the man of Earl Harold, the other of Leofric. There are 10 hides [held] as 2 manors, and [the men] could go where they would. In demesne [are] 4 ploughs; and 18 villans and 1 bordar with 9 ploughs, and 12 slaves. They were worth 100s.; now £7.

● The same Ansfrid holds 5 hides in Burnt Norton. 2 thegns held them as 2 manors and they could go where they would. In demesne [are] 4 ploughs; and 9 villans and 2 bordars with 4 ploughs, and 10 slaves. They were worth £4; now £6.

In 'Witley' Hundred

● The same Ansfrid holds Batsford. Beorhtmær held it. There are 3 hides. In demesne [are] 3 ploughs; and 10 villans with 6 ploughs, and 16 slaves, and 1 man rendering 6 ploughshares. It was worth £8; now £6.

In 'Greston' Hundred

● The same Ansfrid holds Postlip. Godric held it. There are 3 hides paying geld. In demesne are 2 ploughs; and 3 villans and 5 bordars with 2 ploughs. There are 11 slaves, and 2 mills rendering 15s., [and] woodland 1 league long and 1 broad. It was worth 100s.; now £4.

In "Wacrescumbe" Hundred

● The same Ansfrid holds in Shipton Solers 3 virgates of land. Bil held it as a manor, and it paid geld. In demesne is 1 plough. It is and was worth 10s. This Bil could go where he would. ☒

In 'Bradley' Hundred

2 ● The same Ansfrid holds Winson. Eadric and Leofric and Alric held it as 3 manors and could go where they would. There are 5 hides paying geld. In demesne are 4 ploughs; and 9 villans and 4 bordars with 5 ploughs. There are 10 slaves and female slaves all together, and a mill rendering 7s. 6d., and 15 acres of meadow. It was worth £8; now £7.

In Cirencester Hundred

§ ● The same Ansfrid holds 1 hide in Duntisbourne Abbots. Almær held it as a manor and could go where he would. In demesne is 1 plough, and 1 villan and 2 bordars and 5 female slaves. It was worth 40s.; now 20s.

In Rapsgate Hundred

2 ● The same Ansfrid holds Elkstone. 2 Leofwines held it as 2 manors. There are 4½ hides, and in Colesbourne 1½ hides. Alwine held them as a manor, and these 3 thegns could go where they would. [. . .] In demesne are 2 ploughs; and 5 villans and 2 bordars with 3½ ploughs. There are 4 slaves, and 10 acres of meadow, [and] woodland half a league long and 2 furlongs broad.

1 knight holds half of this manor of Ansfrid, and has 2 ploughs there, and 5 villans and 2 bordars with 3 ploughs.

And another knight holds Colesbourne of him, and has half a plough there, and [there are] 2 villans and 2 bordars with 1 plough, and a mill rendering 50d. This was worth £8; now £7. 10s.

● The same Ansfrid holds Syde, and Turstin [holds] of him. Leofwine held it of King Edward. There are 3 hides paying geld. In demesne are 2 ploughs; and 1 villan with a priest and 3 bordars with 1 plough, and 6 slaves, and 4 acres of meadow. It was worth £4; now 40s.

● The same Ansfrid holds 2½ virgates in Duntisbourne Abbots, and Bernard [holds] of him. Almær held them as a manor and could go where he would. There is 1 bordar. It is and was worth 4s.

● The same Ansfrid holds PAUNTLEY, $1\frac{1}{2}$ hides, and KILCOT, 1 hide, and KETFORD, 1 hide, and HAYES, 1 hide. All together [there are] $4\frac{1}{2}$ hides. Wulfhelm and Alweard and Wicga held them as 4 manors. $1\frac{1}{2}$ hides [are] free from geld. [. . .] In demesne are 2 ploughs; and 7 villans and 3 bordars with 7 ploughs. There are 2 slaves, and a mill rendering 7*s.* 6*d.* It was worth £3. 10*s.*; now £4. Those who held these lands could go where they would.

These lands, and WINSTONE and DUNTISBOURNE ABBOTS, entered above, Ansfrid had of Walter de Lacy when he married his niece. But the other lands he holds of the king.

LXIX. THE LAND OF HUMPHREY THE CHAMBERLAIN

IN 'WITLEY' HUNDRED

● HUMPHREY the chamberlain holds of the king LONGBOROUGH. There are 4 hides paying geld. Alstan and Blæcmann and Eadric and Alric held it as 4 manors and could go there they would. In demesne were 4 ploughs; and 3 villans and 5 bordars with 3 ploughs. There are 9 slaves. It was worth £16; now 100*s.*

IN "GERSDONES" HUNDRED

● The same Humphrey holds in AMPNEY CRUCIS 1 hide. Alwig held it of King Edward as a manor. In demesne [are] 2 ploughs, and 4 slaves and 1 bordar, and a mill rendering 5*s.* It is and was worth 25*s.*

IN CIRENCESTER HUNDRED

● The same Humphrey holds 1 hide in PRESTON [near Cirencester]. Alwine held it as a manor. In demesne is 1 plough and 2 slaves; and 3 bordars with 1 plough. It is and was worth 30*s.* The man who held it could go where he would.

● The same Humphrey holds 1 hide in NORCOTE. Alweard held it as a manor. In demesne are 2 ploughs; and 2 bordars with half a plough. It is and was worth 40*s.* William holds these 2 estates of Humphrey. Those who held them could go where they would.

● The same Humphrey holds 2 hides in SIDDINGTON, and Ansketil [holds] of him. Alweard held them as a manor. In demesne is 1 plough; and 2 bordars with half a plough, and a mill rendering 5*s.* It is and was worth 40*s.* The man who held them could go where he would.

IN BAGSTONE HUNDRED

● The same Humphrey holds IRON ACTON. Harold held it, the man of Alwig Hiles, who could go where he would. There are $2\frac{1}{2}$ hides. In demesne is 1 plough; and 3 villans and 3 bordars with half a plough. There are 2 slaves, and $1\frac{1}{2}$ mills rendering 64*d.*, and 5 acres of meadow. It is and was worth 40*s.*

● The same Humphrey holds WICKWAR. There are 4 hides. 3 men
as 3 manors of Beorhtric son of Ælfgar held it TRE and could go where they would. In demesne were 3 ploughs; and 9 villans and 14 bordars with 9 ploughs. There are 5 slaves, and 20 acres of meadow and 6 furlongs of woodland. It was and is worth £12.

The queen gave Humphrey these 2 vills, Iron Acton and Wickwar.

IN "GERSDONES" HUNDRED

● The same Humphrey holds 1 virgate of land in ASHBROOK, and William [holds] of him. Alwine held it as a manor. There is 1 villan. It is and was worth 2*s.*

LXX. THE LAND OF HUMPHREY OF MAIDENHILL

IN 'DUDSTONE' HUNDRED

● HUMPHREY of Maidenhill holds UPTON ST LEONARDS. Paganus held it. There is 1 hide. In demesne [is] 1 plough and 3 slaves; and 4 bordars with 2 ploughs. It was worth 30*s.*; now 20*s.*

IN 'WITLEY' HUNDRED

● The same Humphrey holds 1 hide in SEZINCOTE. Alwig held it as a manor, and it paid geld. In demesne were 2 ploughs and 6 slaves, and 1 bordar, and it was worth 50*s.*; now only 12*d.* because of the meadows.

LXXI. [THE LAND] OF HUMPHREY THE COOK

IN SALMONSBURY HUNDRED

● HUMPHREY the cook holds in LATTON [Wilts.] 1 hide, and has 1 plough there, with 4 bordars, and it is worth 15*s.*, and it pays geld. Osbern of Cherbourg held it. Ordric held it as a manor TRE.

LXXII. THE LAND OF SIGAR DE CHOCQUES

IN 'HOLFORD' HUNDRED

● SIGAR de Chocques holds of the king HAWLING. Countess Gode held it. There are 10 hides paying geld. In demesne are 3 ploughs, and 20 villans and 5 bordars with 9 bordars [*sic*]. There are 6 slaves and 3 female slaves. There is woodland. It was worth £7; now £8.

IN 'BRADLEY' HUNDRED

● The same Sigar holds HAZLETON [near Andoversford]. Gode held it. There are 10 hides. King William granted 3 of these hides quit of geld, as the shire attests. In demesne are 3 ploughs; and 14 villans and a priest with 10 ploughs. There are 6 slaves. It was worth £8; now £7.

● The same Sigar holds YANWORTH. Gode held it. There are 5 hides. 3 of these are quit of geld by [grant of] King William, as Sigar's man says. In demesne are 3 ploughs; and 14 villans and 2 bordars with 7 ploughs. There are 7 slaves, and a mill rendering 40*d.*, [and] woodland 3 furlongs long and 2 broad. It was worth £7; now £6.

LXXIII. THE LAND OF MATTHEW DE MORTAGNE

IN LONGTREE HUNDRED

● MATTHEW de Mortagne holds of the king SHIPTON MOYNE. Strang the Dane held it. There are 10 hides paying geld. In demesne are 2 ploughs; and 4 villans and 2 bordars with 4 ploughs. There are 4 slaves, and a mill rendering 10*s.* From the pasture, 2*s.* It was worth £15; now £8.

● The same Matthew holds SHIPTON MOYNE, and Rumbald [holds] of him. There are 10 hides paying geld. John held it TRE. In demesne are 3 ploughs; and 4 villans and 8 bordars with 4 ploughs. There are 4 slaves, and a mill rendering 12*s.* From the pasture, 2*s.* It was worth £15; now £8.

● The same Matthew holds 1 hide there, and Rumbald [holds] of him. Alwine held it and could go where he would, and afterwards Reinbert the Fleming had it. In demesne is 1 plough; and 1 villan and 1 bordar with half a plough. It was worth 20*s.*; now 14*s.*

LXIIII. THE LAND OF JOSCELIN THE BRETON

IN BAGSTONE HUNDRED

● JOSCELIN the Breton holds of the king CHARFIELD. Ælfhild held it of King Edward. There are 3 hides. In demesne are 2 ploughs; and 4 villans and 7 bordars with 4 ploughs. There are 4 slaves, and a mill rendering 10*s.*, and 8 acres of meadow, [and] woodland half a league long and wide. It was worth £4; now 40*s.*

LXXV. THE LAND OF ROGER FITZRALPH

IN 'SWINESHEAD' HUNDRED

● ROGER fitzRalph holds 1 manor, called CLIFTON [in Bristol], which Sæwine, reeve of Bristol, held of King Edward, and he could go where he would with this land, nor did he give any farm for it. There are 3 hides. In demesne are 3 ploughs; and 6 villans and 6 bordars with 2 ploughs. There are 3 slaves, and 8 acres of meadow. It was worth 100*s.*; now 60*s.*

IN 'SWINESHEAD' HUNDRED

● Roger has 1 manor of 1 hide of land and he has 2 slaves there. This is valued at 10*s.* There has been no one to answer for this land.

● Walter has 1 manor of 1 virgate of land. It was worth 20*d.*; now 2*s.*

LXXVI. THE LAND OF THE WIFE OF GERWY

IN 'HOLFORD' HUNDRED

● THE WIFE OF GERWY de Loges holds of the king 4 hides in TEMPLE GUITING. 3 thegns, Wulffrith, Tovi and Thorbiorn, held it as 3 manors, and it paid geld. In demesne is 1 plough; and 1 villan with half a plough. It was worth 40*s.*; now 20*s.*

LXXVII.

IN "GERSDONES" HUNDRED

● BALDWIN holds of the king 3 virgates of land in AMPNEY CRUCIS. Alwine held them TRE. There is 1 plough, with 2 bordars. It is and was worth 10*s.*

LXVIII. THE LANDS OF THE KING'S THEGNS

IN BARRINGTON HUNDRED

● ÆLFSIGE of Faringdon holds of the king 3½ hides in WINDRUSH. Wulfric and Tovi and Leofwine held them as 3 manors and could go where they would. In demesne are 5 ploughs; and 1 villan and 7 bordars with 1 plough. There are 10 slaves, and 1½ mills rendering 12*s*. 6*d*. It was worth £3; now £8.

IN "GERSDONES" HUNDRED

● KETIL holds of the king 1 hide and 1 virgate in WINDRUSH. He himself held them TRE. There is 1 plough, and 4 slaves. It is and was worth 20*s*.

IN RAPSGATE HUNDRED

● The same Ketil holds 3½ virgates in DUNTISBOURNE ABBOTS. He himself held them TRE. There is 1 plough, and 2 bordars and 2 slaves. It was worth 10*s*.; now 15[*s*.].

IN LONGTREE HUNDRED

2 ● OSWEARD holds of the king RODMARTON. There are 3 virgates paying geld. He himself held it TRE. There is 1 plough. It was worth 20*s*.; now 10*s*.

IN CIRENCESTER HUNDRED

● EADRIC son of Ketil holds BAUNTON of the king. His father held it TRE. There are 3 hides and 3 virgates paying geld. In demesne are 2 ploughs; and 3 villans with 1 plough, and 4 slaves, and 15 acres of meadow. It is and was worth 60*s*.

IN 'DUDSTONE' HUNDRED

● EDWARD holds of the king half a hide as a manor, and has there in demesne 1 plough; and 6 bordars with 2 ploughs. It is worth 30*s*.

IN "CELFLEDETORN" HUNDRED

● EDITH holds of the king BICKMARSH [Worcs.]. She herself held it TRE. There is 1 hide, and in demesne 2 ploughs, and 1 villan and 1 bordar and 4 slaves. It is and was worth 20*s*.

IN SALMONSBURY HUNDRED

● CWENHILD the nun holds of the king 9 hides in NAUNTON [near Bourton-on-the-Water]. Of these, 4 hides paid geld. Æthelmær held them as a manor. In demesne are 4 ploughs; and 7 villans with 5 ploughs, and now 1 plough is reckoned [there], and [there is] a mill rendering 5*s*., and 13 slaves and female slaves all together. It was worth £8; now £5.

IN CHELTENHAM HUNDRED

● BEORHTRIC holds of the king 4 hides in LECKHAMPTON, and it pays geld. He himself [held] 2 hides TRE and Ordric held the other 2. King William, when he was setting out for Normandy, gave them both to the same Beorhtric. In demesne he has 1 plough; and 9 bordars with 3 ploughs, and 2 slaves and 1 female slave. [There is] woodland 2 furlongs long and 2 broad. It is worth 30*s*.

IN 'HOLFORD' HUNDRED

● ALWEALD holds of the king PINNOCK. He himself held it TRE. There are 4 hides. One of these did not pay geld. In demesne are 4 ploughs; and 11 villans and 5 bordars with 4 ploughs. There are 8 slaves, and a mill rendering 30*d*. In Winchcombe 1 burgess pays 8*d*. [There is] woodland half a league long and 1 furlong broad. It is and was worth £4.

IN BIBURY HUNDRED

● ALWEARD son of Regenbald holds ALDSWORTH. Balki held it. There are 2 hides paying geld. In demesne is 1 plough; and 4 villans and 2 bordars with 2 ploughs, and 1 slave. It was worth 40*s*.; now 30*s*.

IN 'WHITSTONE' HUNDRED

● ÆLFSIGE holds of the king LONGNEY. There are 5 hides paying geld. He himself held it TRE. In demesne are 2 ploughs; and 6 villans and 12 bordars with 9 ploughs. There are 4 slaves, and 10 acres of meadow and a fishery. It was worth 100*s*.; now 60*s*.

IN 'SWINESHEAD' HUNDRED

● DUNS holds of the king BITTON. He himself held it TRE. There are 2 hides. One of these paid geld, the other belonged to the church. In demesne are 2 ploughs; and 5 villans and 2 bordars with 5 ploughs. There are 4 slaves, and 10 acres of meadow. It was worth £6; now £3.

IN "BLACHELAUE" HUNDRED

● BEORHTRIC holds of the king WOODCHESTER. He himself held it TRE. There is 1 hide paying geld. There are 16 villans and 12 bordars with 16 ploughs. [There is] nothing in demesne. In Gloucester 1 burgess renders 20 [pieces of] iron. There is a mill rendering 10*s*. It is and was worth 100*s*.

● HEARDING holds in pledge from Beorhtric WHEATENHURST. Beorhtric himself held it TRE. There are 5 hides paying geld. In demesne is 1 plough; and a priest and 2 villans and 6 bordars with 5 ploughs. There are 3 slaves, and a mill rendering 10*s*., and 10 acres of meadow. It was worth 100*s*.; now 30*s*.

● EADRIC son of Ketil holds ALKERTON. His father held it TRE. There are 4½ hides paying geld. In demesne is 1 plough; and 6 villans and 4 bordars with 8 ploughs. There are 3 slaves, and a mill rendering 10*s*., and 10 acres of meadow. [There is] woodland 1 league long and a half broad. It is and was worth £3.

IN BOTLOE HUNDRED

● MATOC holds of the king RUDFORD. He himself held it TRE. There are 2 hides. [. . .] In demesne [are] 2 ploughs; and 3 villans and 4 bordars with 3 ploughs, and a mill rendering as much grain as it is possible to make a profit from. It is and was worth 40*s*.

GLOUCESTERSHIRE

THE

GLOUCESTERSHIRE DOMESDAY

FOLIOS AND MAPS

Gloucestershire: Folios 162–170

ALECTO HISTORICAL EDITIONS
LONDON
1988

ISBN for Gloucestershire volumes: 0 948459 29 8
ISBN for this volume: 0 948459 63 8

Printed in England

ALECTO HISTORICAL EDITIONS
46 Kelso Place, London W8 5QG, England

This volume of the
County Edition
of
Great Domesday Book
is limited to
one thousand copies

This is set number
444

DEDICATED

BY GRACIOUS PERMISSION

TO

HER MAJESTY

THE QUEEN

PREFACE

The Facsimile Folios

The original manuscript of Great Domesday Book was made up of 47 separate gatherings, or quires. Each gathering consisted of a number of parchment sheets folded one inside the other and sewn into a booklet, the folios having previously been written so that they read consecutively in the manner of a modern newspaper. Sometimes an extra half-sheet was attached by a guard stitched inside the gathering or folded outside round the spine. The present facsimile replicates the arrangement of the folios of this county exactly, and their position in the manuscript is shown diagrammatically in Appendix III at the end of the *Domesday Book Studies* volume.

An exceptional quantity of notes and signs were added in the margins of Great Domesday Book, both at the time of its compilation and also subsequently when the manuscript was in use as a working document. The high quality of this facsimile has made it possible for the vast majority of these marginalia to be reproduced for the first time. Their date and purport are signalled in the margins of the translation by a system of symbols of which the key is to be found in *Domesday Book Studies* as Appendix I.

The Latin text is heavily abbreviated, especially since the repetitive contents of Great Domesday Book were expressed by standard formulae. A guide to the system of abbreviation employed in this particular manuscript is given in Appendix II.

The translations will be found at the end of the accompanying county volume. Each page has been laid out to match the arrangement of its corresponding folio and bears the same folio number. This correlation provides a convenient method of reference between the facsimile and its translation and also enables the Indices to serve both.

The Maps

Two maps are supplied with this volume; a general map of Domesday England and a large-scale county map. The former is a distribution map of all the settlements mentioned in Domesday Book overlaid by the outlines of the counties and the locations of the boroughs, bishops' sees, and land-owning monasteries throughout the kingdom at that time.

The county map marks a considerable advance on previous attempts to plot the topographical information contained in Domesday Book, because its unprecedented scale enables both ancient and modern features to be related. For the method of determining the boundaries of the hundreds or wapentakes, see the article devoted to the subject in the volume containing the Introductions and Translation, and for a statement of the policy governing the identification of place-names see the Notes to the Index of Places in the same book. Throughout this edition the configurations of the counties are those that existed prior to their restructuring in 1974, since before that date there has been relatively little change to their number or extent since the time of Domesday Book.

R. W. H. Erskine, *General Editor*

Gloucestershire: Folios 162–170

Tempore Regis Edwardi reddebat ciuitas de Glowecestre. xxxvi. lib numeratas. 7 xii. sextaria mellis ad mensurā eiusdē burgi. 7 xxxvi. dicras ferri. 7 c. uirgas ferreas ductiles ad clauos nauiū regis. 7 quasdā alias minutas consuetudines in aula 7 in camera regis.

Modo reddit ipsa ciuitas regi. lx. lib. de xx. in ora.

7 De moneta hē rex. xx. lib.

In dnica terra regis ten Rogeri de berchelai unā domū 7 unā piscariā in ipsa uilla. 7 est extra manū regis. Hanc Balduin tenuit. T.R.E.

Osbn eps ten terrā 7 mansiones quas Edmarus tenuit reddt. x. solid cū alia consuetudine.

Gausfrid de Manneuile ten. vi. mansion. hę T.R.E. reddeb vi. solid 7 viii. denar cū alia csuetud.

Witts baderon. ii. mansion. de. xx. denar.

Witts scriba. i. mansion ten de. li. denar.

Rogeri de laci. i. mansion de. xxvi. denar.

Osbn eps. i. mansion de. xli. denar.

Berner. i. mansion de. xiiii. denar.

Witts caluus. i. mansion de. xii. denar.

Durand uicecom. ii. mansion de. xiiii. den.

Ist durand ten. i. mansion de. xxvi. den.

7 adhuc unā mansion que nulla csuetud redd.

Hadeuuin ten. i. mans. que dat gablū. sed aliā csuetud retinet.

Hosbt. i. mansionē. Dunning. i. mans. Widard. i. mans.

Arnulf pbr. i. mans. que redd gablū. 7 aliā csuet retin.

Omīs istę mansiones reddeb regalē csuetud. T.R.E.

Modo rex W. nichil inde hē. nec Rotbt minister ei.

Istę mansion fuer in firma regis. E. die qua fuit uiuus 7 mortuus. Modo ū sunt ablatę de firma 7 csuetud regis.

T.R.E. erat dnīu regis in ciuitate totū hospitatū t uestitū.

Qdo comes W. ad firmā recep. simit uestitū fuit.

Sedecī dom erant ubi sedet castellū. que modo desunt.

7 in Burgo ciuitatis sunt Wastatę. xiiii. domus.

Castellū de Estrighoiel fecit Witts comes. 7 eius tēpore reddeb. xl. sot tantū de nauib in siluā euntib. Tēpore ū Rogerii comit filii ei. reddēd ipsa uilla. xvi. lib. 7 medietatē habeb Rad de limesi. Modo hē rex inde. xii. lib.

Int reddītione de carleion. 7 i. carucā que ibi ē 7 vii. piscarias in Waie 7 huscha. exeunt. vii. lib 7 x. solid.

In Wales sunt. iii. harduices. Lamecare 7 Poteschiuuet 7 Dinan. In his sunt. viii. car. 7 xi. uitti dimidii. 7 xv. bord cū vi. car. Ex his. iii. harduicis uoleb habere. c. solid Rog de Jurei.

Sub Wasuuic ppositō sunt. xiii. uillę. Sub Elmui. xiiii. uillę. Sub Bleio sunt. xiii. uillę. Sub Idhel sunt. xiiii. uillę. Hi reddunt. xl vii. sextaria mellis. 7 xl. porc. 7 xli. uaccas. 7 xxviii. solid p accipitrib. Tot hoc uat. xv. lib 7 x. sot 7 iiii. den.

De una Wasta tra. redd Walt balistari. i. sext mett 7 i. porc.

Berdic ioculator regis hē. iii. uillas. 7 ibi. v. car. nil redd.

Morin. i. uilla. Chenefis. i. filii Wasuuic. i. Sessisbert. i. Ibrahā pbr. ii. uillas. hi hnt. vi. car. 7 nichil reddunt. hos misit. W. comes ad csuetud Grifin regis. licentia regis. W.

7 Sub eisd ppositis sunt. iiii. uillę Wastatę p rege Caraduech.

In elemosina regis ē una uilla. que p anima ei redd ecclę ad festū S marini. ii. porc 7 c. panes cū ceruisa.

Ad scm Michaelē. ē. i. carucata træ. 7 ad scm Deuuin una carucata. hę non reddt seruitiū nisi scis.

Wi Beluard de Caruen hē dimid car træ. 7 nichil redd.

Sexaginta 7 vi. porci exeunt de pasnag. 7 appciant xl. iiii. sot. Ħ omīa redd. xl. lib 7 xii. sot 7 viii. den.

Durand uicecom ded hęc ead Witto de ... p. lv. lib ad firmā.

Walteri balistari ten de rege. ii. carucat træ. 7 ibi hē iii. car. 7 iii. seruos 7 iii. ancillas. Vat ħ. xx. sot.

Girard hē. ii. caruc træ. 7 ibi. ii. car. Vat. xx. sot.

Ouus ppositus regis. ii. caruc træ. 7 ibi. iiii. car. Vat. xx. sot.

Ibi. ē in dnio regis. i. caruc træ quā tenuit Dagobt.

Gozelin brito ten. v. caruc træ in caruen. 7 ibi sunt. ii. car cū. ii. Walensib. Vat. xx. sot.

Eps Cstantiensis ten de rege. v. caruc træ. 7 de eo un hōo. Ibi sunt. ii. car in dnio. 7 iii. uillanos. Vat. xl. sot.

Roger de Berchelai ten. ii. car træ ad Strigoielg 7 ibi hē vi. bord cū. i. car. Vat xx. sot.

Durand uicec ten de rege In caruen. i. trā Caldecote nom. Ibi hē in dnio. iii. car. 7 xv. dimid uittos. 7 iiii. seruos. 7 un militē. hi omīs hnt. xii. car. Ibi molin de. x. solid. hoc totū uat. vi. lib.

Witts de ow. hē de Strigoielg. xv. lib p csuetud ut dicit. Sed Girard 7 alii hoēs dicū nil plus habe illū iuste de. x. lib. De csuetud Strigoielg. eā si appcaret.

In Wales. hē isd W. in feudo. iii. piscarias c. lib. in Waie. reddt. lxx. solid. 7 in eod feudo ded Witts com Rad de limesi. L. carucatas træ sic fit in Normannia. hoc testant hugo 7 alii libatores qđ tra Rad ccessit. Modo dic W. de ow. n se habe de hac tra nisi. xxii. car. Ibi sunt in dnio. viii. car. 7 hoēs hnt. xvi. car. Ibi. ii. molini de. x. sot. Tot uat. xii. lib 7 x. sot.

Rog de laci ten in feudo de Strigoielg tant træ hospitatę cū uno molino. qđ uat. xxxvi. solid.

Turstin fili Rolf hē int huschā 7 Waiā. xvii. carucas. De his sunt in dnio. iiii. 7 dimid. alię sunt hōum. Ibi. xi. bord sunt. 7 molin de vii. solid. Vat. xv. lib tot. De hac tra. v. caruc 7 dimid. calumniant ppositi regis. dicentes qđ eas Turst sine dono suscep.

Ist Turstin hē vi. caruc træ ult huschā. 7 ibi hoēs hnt. iiii. car. 7 molin redd. xv. sot. 7 dimid piscaria de. x. sot. Tot uat. liiii. sot 7 vi. den.

Alured hispan hē in feudo. ii. carucat træ. 7 ibi. ii. car in dnio. Isd. A. hē In Wales vii. uillas. que fuer Witti comitis 7 Rog filii ei in dnio. hę reddt vi. mett sextaria. 7 vi. porc. 7 x. solid.

GLOWECSCIRE.

BURGUS de WINCELCUMBE reddeb T.R.E. vi. lib
de firma. De his habeb heraldus com iii. den' id est xl. sol.
Postea redd. xx. lib cu toto hund eid uillæ. Durand
uicecom apposuit. c. sol. 7 Roger de Iurei. lx. sold.
Modo adiunctis iii. hund. redd. xxviii. lib de xx. in Ora.

Hic Annotant Terrã Tenentes In Glowecscire.

TERRA REGIS.

REX EDWARDUS tenuit CHINTENEHAM. Ibi erant viii. hide 7 dim.
Ad eccla ptin. i. hid 7 dim. Reinbald ten eam.
In dnio. erant. iii. car. 7 xx. uitti 7 x. bord 7 vii. serui. cu. xviii.
car. Pbri. ii. car. Ibi. ii. molini de. xi. sol 7 viii. denar.
Huic m accreuit ppositus regis W. duos bord 7 iiii. uittos
7 iii. molinos. hoz. ii. sunt regis. tciu ppositi. 7 i. car plus. e ibi.
T.R.E. reddeb. ix. lib 7 v. sol. 7 ter mille panes canib.
Modo redd. xx. lib. 7 xx. uaccas. 7 xx. porc. 7 xvi. sol p panib.

In BERTUNE habuit rex. E. noue hid. De his erant vii. in dnio.
7 ibi. iii. car. 7 xiiii. uitti 7 x. bord cu. ix. car. Ibi. vii. serui.
De hoc m ten. ii. libi hoes. ii. hid. 7 hnt ibi. ix. car. Ipsi se
n possunt seu tra separare a manerio. Ibi molin de. iiii. sold.
Ppositus W. regis accreuit viii. bord 7 ii. molinos. 7 i. caruca.
T.R.E. reddeb. ix. lib. 7 v. sold. 7 ter mille panes canib.
Modo redd. xx. lib. xx. uaccas. xx. porc. 7 p panib. xvi. sol.
De hoc m prestitit Aldred archieps. i. mebru BREWERE.
Ibi sunt. iii. uirg tre. 7 iii. hoes. Milo crispin tenet.
Alter mebru noe OPTUNE prestitit Aluui uicecom. Ibi
una hida tre. 7 ibi sunt. iiii. hoes. Hunfrid ten.
Terciu mebru noe MERWEN prestitit isd Aluui. Ibi sunt
iii. uirg tre. Nigell medicus tenet.
IN DUDESTAN HUND habuit qda tain Edmær. iii. maner.
Hersefel. 7 Athelai. 7 Sanher. Iste ho poterat dare 7 uende tra
sua cui uoluisset. p. ii. hid se defdb h tra. In dnio erant
viii. car. 7 iiii. uitti 7 iiii. bord. 7 xxx. serui. cu. v. car.
Ibi pti sufficiens carucis.
In HERSECOME teneb Wiflet. iii. uirg tre. libas sic 7 Edmer.
Ibi habeb. ii. car. 7 ii. bord. 7 v. seruos. 7 prata carrucis.
In BROSTORP tenuit Aluric. iii. uirg tre.
Hic habeb ii. car. 7 un uittm. iii. bord. iiii. seruos.
Has. v. tras abstulit Heraldus com post morte regis. E.
Has easd Rog de Iurei posuit ad firma p. xlvi. lib. 7 xiii. sol. 7 iiii. den.
In eod HUND iuxta ciuitate habuit Uluuard dimid hida.
de rege. E. quieta. 7 ibi. ii. car 7 iiii. serui.
Hanc dedit W. com cuida coquo suo. Uluuard eni utlag fact. e.
In CIRECESTRE HD habuit rex. E. v. hid tre.
Ibi in dnio. v. car. 7 xxxi. uittm cu. x. car. Ibi. xiii. serui.
7 x. bord 7 iii. molini de. xxx. sold. Prata. 7 ii. siluas de. l. sol.
7 ibi. ii. libi hoes. ii. car hntes. Lana ouiu regina habeb.
T.R.E. reddeb hoc m. iii. modios frumti 7 dimid. 7 brasii. iii. mod.
7 mell. vi. sextar 7 dimid. 7 ix. lib. 7 v. sol. 7 ter mille pan canib.
Modo redd. xx. lib. 7 v. sol. xx. uaccas. xx. porc. 7 p pan. xvi. sol.
7 De nouo foro. xx. sol. quoz ht S MARIA tciu den.
In Cirecestre un lib ho teneb. ii. hid tre. 7 reddeb. xx. sol in
firma. 7 p tota anglia uicecomita seruitiu faciebat.
Witts com hanc tra misit extra firma. 7 cuida suo hoi dedit ea.
In SUINHEVE HD. erant T.R.E. ad firma. xxvi. hide in
BETUNE. cu. ii. mebris Wapelei 7 Wintreborne.
In dnio erant. v. car. 7 xli. uitts. 7 xx ix. bord. cu. xl v. car.
Ibi. xviii. serui. cu. i. molino.
Hoc m T.R.E. reddeb firma uni noctis. 7 m similit facit.
In SALEMANESBERIE HD tenuit. E. rex SCLOSTRE.
Ibi erant. vii. hide. 7 In dnio. iii. car. 7 ix. uitti 7 xi. bord
cu. viii. car. Ibi. vii. serui. 7 ii. molini de una marka argti.
Prata de. x. sol. 7 de una ex his hid. x. sold. 7 canib. v. solid.

De hoc m̃ reddeb qđ uoleb uicecom T.R.E. Id ne sciũt appciari.
Modo uicecom accreũ ibi .i. car. 7 v. borđ cũ .i. car.
Reddit nc de m̃ ipso 7 de hund. xx vii. lib. ad numerũ.

In WESBERIE .xxx. hidę. Ibi habeb. E. rex .v. car
in dnio. 7 xxx ii. uittos 7 xv. borđ cũ xx viii. car.
Ibi .i. seruus.
Hoc m̃ reddeb una nocte de firma T.R.E. Similit T.R.W.
p .iiii. annos. Postea ablatę sunt de isto m̃ vi. hidę
In chire. 7 in Cliftone .x. hidę. In Noent 7 Chingestune.
viii. hid. In Ladeuent .i. hid.
Has tras ten m abb de Cormelies. 7 Osbn. 7 Witts .f. Ricardi.
7 tam de remanentia inuen uicecom totã firmam.
Dnt duo hões de comitatu qđ Sapina iacuit in Wes
berie ad firmã regis. E.

In CHETESILAT hđ tenuit. E. rex LINGEBERGE.
cũ uno mẽbro noe MENE. In utroq; erant .viii. hidę.
In dnio .iii. car. 7 x. uitti 7 iii. borđ cũ .vi. car. 7 molin
de .v. sol. 7 vi. serui. Prat de .x. sol.
T.R.E. reddeb uicecom de hoc m̃ qđ exibat ad firmã.
Modo reddt .xv. lib. cũ .ii. hund quos ibi uicec apposuit.

In BLITESLAU hđ tenuit. E. rex AURE. Ibi .v. hidę.
7 In dnio .i. car. 7 xii. uitti 7 viii. borđ cũ .xiiii. car. Ibi
un seruus. 7 molin de .xxx. denar. 7 salina de .xxx. sũmis
salis. 7 Eccta cũ .i. uirg træ.
Hoc m̃ reddeb dimid firmã noctis T.R.E. 7 m similit facit.
De eod m̃ iacet Wastata dimid hida. 7 đđ n reddt nisi
.xii. lib. Vicecom tam reddt totã firmã.
Extra m̃ sunt .iii. mẽbra que sep in eo fuer. 7 esse debent
ut testant hões de comitatu. Id est Pertone. Etlau. Bliteslau.
In his sunt .vii. hidę. 7 in dnio .i. car. 7 xx. uitti 7 iii. borđ
cũ .xiii. car. 7 ii. serui 7 piscaria.
Pertone .ẽ. in feudo Witti comitis. Etelau ten Rog de berchelai.
Bliteslau ten Witts filii baderon. Aluui uicecom misit h ex firm.

In LANGELEI hund tenuit heraldus com ALWESTAN. Ibi erant .x. hidę.
In dnio .i. car. 7 xxiii. uitti 7 v. borđ cũ .xx ii. car. 7 ii. serui.
Ibi pposit accreuit .ii. car. 7 v. seruos. Reddt .xii. lib ad pensũ.

In BERCHELAI habuit. E. rex .v. hid. 7 in dnio .v. car.
7 xx. uitti 7 v. borđ cũ .xi. car. 7 ix. serui. 7 ii. molini
de .xii. solid. Ibi .x. radchenistres. hntes .vii. hid. 7 vii. car.
Ibi un forũ in quo manent .xvii. hões. 7 reddt censũ in firma.
Hę BEREWICHE ptin ad BERCHELAI.
In Hilla .iiii. hidę. In Almintune .iiii. hidę. In Hinetune
.iiii. hidę. In Camma .vi. hidę. 7 alię .xi. hidę. In Gosintune
.iiii. hidę. In Dersilege .iii. hidę. In Couelege .iiii. hidę.
In Euuelege .ii. hidę. In Nimdesfelle .iii. hidę. In Vutune
.xv. hidę 7 dimid .v. In Simondeshale dimid hida.
In Chingescote .iiii. hidę 7 dimid. In Beurestane .x. hidę.
In Osleuuorde dimid hida. In Almodesberie .ii. hidę.
In Horefelle .viii. hidę. In Westone .vii. hidę 7 una .v.
In Eldbertone .v. hidę. In Cromale .ii. hidę. In Erlingehã
.ix. hidę. In Esceleuuorde .iii. hidę.
Hec supdicta mẽbra oma ptinent ad Berchelai.
Int totu
In his. T.R.E. in dnio .xl ix. car. 7 dimid. 7 cc. xl. ii. uitti.
7 c xl. ii. borđ cũ .c. xx vi. car. Ibi .c. xx. vii. serui.
Ibi .xix. libi hões radchenist. hntes .xl viii. car. cũ suis hõib.
Ibi .xxii. colibti. 7 xv. ancillę.
Ibi .viii. molini de .L. vii. sol 7 vi. denar.

In isto m̃ tenuer .ii. frs T.R.E. in CROMHAL .v. hidas.
hntes in dnio .ii. car. 7 vi. uitti. 7 v. borđ hntes .vi. car.
Hi .ii. frs cũ tra sua se poterant uertere quo uolebant.
Tc ualeb .iiii. lib. m .iii. lib. Hos W. com comdauit
pposito de berchelai. ut eor habeet seruitiũ. sic dic Rogg.
De hoc m̃ cũ omib, ad eũ ptinentib, reddt Rogeri
ad firmã .c lxx. lib. arsas 7 pensatas.

Ipse Rogeri ht de tra hui m̃ in hellinbruge .ii. hid.
Ad Claenhangare .i. hid. Ad hirslege .i. hid. Ad Neueton
.vii. hid. Ibi sunt in dnio .x. car. 7 xiii. uitti 7 xxi. borđ.
cũ .xx ii. car. Ibi .xvi. serui. 7 Molin de .v. solid.
Tot T.R.E. ualeb .ix. lib. Modo .xi. lib 7 x. solid.
Isd Rogeri ten trã Bernardi pbri .v. hid. Ibi ht .iii. car.
7 ii. uittos. 7 vi. borđ. cũ .v. car. Val 7 ualuit .lx. sol.

In HESSE sunt .v. hidę ptinent ad Berchelai. qs
W. com misit ext ad faciendũ un castellulũ. h Roger calumniat.

In TEDEDESTANE hđ tenuit Eddid regina
MERESFELDE. Ibi .xiiii. hidę. In dnio .v. car. 7 xxx vi.
uitti 7 xiii. borđ cũ .xxx. car. Ibi .xviii. serui.
Pbr ht una ex his hid.
T.R.E. reddeb .xxx v. lib. modo .xl vii. lib.

In BERTUNE apud BRISTOU erant .vi. hid. In dnio
.iii. car. 7 xxii. uitti 7 xx v. borđ cũ .xx v. car. Ibi .x.
serui. 7 xviii. colibti. hntes .xiiii. car. Ibi .ii. molini
de .xx. solid. Qdo Roger recep hoc m̃ de rege. inuen
ibi .ii. hid 7 ii. car. in dnio. 7 xvii. uitti 7 xxiiii. borđ
cũ .xxi. car. Ibi .iij. seruos. 7 xiii. colibtos cũ .iii. car.
In uno mẽbro ejd m̃ manegodesfelle .vi. boues in dnio.
De ead tra ten eccta de Bristou .iii. hid. 7 i. car habet ibi.
Vn Radchenist ten .i. hid. 7 ht .i. car. 7 iiii. borđ cũ .i. car.
Hoc m̃ 7 BRISTOU reddt regi .c 7 x. mark argenti.
Burgenses dnt qđ eps .G. ht .xxx iii. mark argenti
7 unã mark auri. pter firmã regis.

In BRADELEI hđ habuit Balduin .f. Herlouini m̃
un in quo erant .x. hidę. Hoc m̃ tenuit eps baiocsis.
m est in manu regis 7 geldat. Ibi sunt in dnio .ii. car.
7 vii. uitti 7 v. borđ cũ .vi. car. Ibi .v. serui. 7 ii. molini
de .xx. solid. Ibi pbr. T.R.E. ualeb .xii. lib. Modo .ix. lib.

In CIRECESTRE hđ habuit Elmar HUNLAFESED.
in quo erant .iii. hidę 7 dim. Eps baiocsis tenuit. m est
in manu regis. In dnio .ẽ. i. car. 7 iiii. uitti 7 iii. borđ
cũ .iii. car. Valuit .iii. lib. m .L. sol.

In TEODECHESBERIE fuer T.R.E. quat xx. 7 xv. hidę.
Ex his sunt in dnio .xl v. 7 erant quietę ab omi ser
uitio regali 7 geldo. pter seruitiũ ipsius dni cui erant.
In capite m̃ erant in dnio .xii. car. 7 L. int seruos
7 ancillas. 7 xvi. borđ circa aulã manebant. 7 ii. mo
lini de .xx. solid. 7 una piscaria. 7 una salina ap Wichã
ptin ad m̃.
Ap Sudwichã .iii. hid. In Trotintune .vi. hidę. In Fiten
tone .vi. hidę. In pamintonie .viii. hidę. In Natone .iii. hidę 7 dim.
In Waltone .iii. hidę. In Estone .vi. hidę.
Ibi erant uitti .xxi. 7 ix. Radchenist. hntes .xx vi. car.
7 v. colibti 7 un borđ cũ .v. car. Hi Radchenist
arabant 7 herciabant ad curiã dni.
In Glouuecestre erant .viii. burgses. reddtes .v. solid
.iiii. den. 7 seruientes ad curiã.
In tota Teodechesberie sunt .c xx. ac pti. 7 silua una
leuga 7 dimid long. 7 tantd lat.

· Ap Teodekesberie sunt m̃. xiii. burgses reddẽtes. xx. sol
p ann̄. Mercatũ qđ regina cõstituit ibi. reddit. xi. solid
7 viii. denar. Ibi. ẽ una car plus. 7 xcii. int̃ seruos
7 ancillas. Vna piscaria 7 una salina ap Wichã.
Ibi. iii. Radchenist̃. T.R.E. p̃tineb. Vn eoꝝ tenebat
In Estone. vi. hid. Modo ten Girard. Alt̃ tenebat
In Waltone. iii. hid. Modo ten Radulf. Terci teneb
In Treintone. ii. hid. Modo ten Bernard.
In his. xi. hid sunt. x. car in dn̄io. 7 iiii. uitti 7 i. bord
7 ix. serui. cũ una car. Ibi. xviii. ac p̃ti.
Tot T.R.E. ualb. x. lib. Modo tantd.
Ap ~~Oxendone~~. T.R.E. erat aula. 7 v. hide p̃tinẽs
ad Teodekesbie. Ibi sunt. v. car in dn̄io. 7 v. uitti
7 ii. radchenist̃ hñtes vii. car. 7 int̃ seruos 7 ancitt.
xii. Ibi xx iiii. ac p̃ti. Ap ~~Wicecobe~~. iii. burgses
redd. xl. den. Tot hoc uat 7 ualuit. viii. lib.
~~Hec Subscripta t̃ra p̃tin eccle de Teodekesberie.~~
+ In ~~Stanwege~~. sunt. vii. hide. p̃tin eccle.
Ibi. ii. car in dn̄io. 7 viii. uitti 7 ii. bord cũ. viii.
car. Ibi monaster. 7 int̃ seruos 7 ancillas. v. 7 ap Wichã
una salina. 7 viii. ac p̃ti. Silua. iii. q̃x lg. 7 una lat.
T.R.E. ualb. viii. lib. Modo. vii. lib.
+ In ~~Tatintone~~. iiii. hide. Ibi sunt. ii. car. 7 xi. uitti
7 un Radchen cũ. ii. car. 7 iii. bord. 7 ix. serui.
Valeb. vi. lib. modo. c. sol.
+ In ~~Limentone~~. iii. hide. Ibi sunt. ii. car. 7 viii. uitti
cũ. iiii. car. 7 vi. serui. 7 un bord.
Valuit. lx. sol. modo. xl. solid.
+ In ~~Wassborne~~. iii. hide. Ibi sunt. ii. car. 7 vi. uitti
cũ. iii. car. 7 i. bord. 7 ix. serui cũ ancitt.
Valuit 7 uat. lx. solid.
+ In ~~Fifhide~~. ij. hidæ. Ibi un uitts 7 ii. coliba cũ. ii.
car. Vat 7 ualuit. x. sol. Vna ex his hid q̃eta t̃ra fuit.
+ In ~~Aitone~~. i. hida. q̃eta t̃re. 7 ibi. i. car. Vat. x. sol.
+ In ~~Stanlege~~. iii. hide 7 dimid. Ibi. ẽ. i. car. 7 iiii.
uitti cũ. ii. car. 7 iii. bord 7 v. serui. H t̃ra q̃eta fuit.
Valuit. iiii. lib. modo. xl. solid.
Tota t̃ra p̃tin eccle geldab p. xx. hid. T.R.E.
In eod m̃ de ~~Teodekesberie~~ p̃tineb. iiii. hide sine
dn̄io quæ sunt in Hanlege. Ibi T.R.E. erant in dn̄io
ii. car. 7 int̃ uittos 7 bord. xl. 7 int̃ seruos 7 ancillas
viii. 7 molin de xvi. den. Silua in qua. ẽ haia.
H t̃ra fuit W. comitis. m̃. ẽ ad firma regis in hereford.
T.R.E. ualuit. xv. lib. modo. x. lib.
In Fortemetone. ix. hide. p̃tineb huic m̃. Ibi. ii. car.
in dn̄io. 7 xx. int̃ uittos 7 bord. 7 vi. int̃ seruos 7 ancitt.
Ibi silua. Valuit. x. lib. T.R.E. m̃. viii. lib.
Has. ii. t̃ras tenuit W. com. 7 geldb ꝓpt Tedekesbie.
In ~~Senendone~~. x. hide p̃tin eid m̃. Ibi sunt. iiii.
car. 7 viii. uitti 7 iiii. bord. 7 v. radchenist̃ cũ. viii. car.
Ibi. xii. serui. 7 molin de. iii. sol. H t̃ra geld p. vii. hid.
T.R.E. ualb. xx. lib. modo. viii. lib. In manu regis. ẽ.
Robt de olgi ten ad firmã.
In ~~Clifort~~. vii. hide p̃tin eid m̃. Ibi. iii. car in dn̄io.
7 xiiii. uitti cũ. v. car. 7 molin de. xii. sol. 7 ii. ac p̃ti.
Ibi erant int̃ seruos 7 ancitt. xiii. 7 eccta 7 p̃br cũ. i. car.
Valb. viii. lib. Modo. vi. lib. Hanc t̃rã dedit regina
Rogerio de busli. 7 geldb p. iiii. hid in ~~Tedechesberie~~.
Quat xx. 7 xv. hidas quæ p̃tin ad Tedechesberie. q̃nq
q̃inta hide sup memoratæ faciebant q̃etas 7 libas ab omi
geldo 7 regali seruitio.

Maneriũ istud Tedekesberie cũ erat tot simul T.R.E. ualb. c. lib.
Xdo Radulf recep. xii. lib. q̃a destruct 7 cõfusũ erat. Modo
appciat. xl. lib. Tam Radulf reddit. l. lib.
Hoc m̃ tenuit Brictric fili Algar. T.R.E. 7 has subscriptas
t̃ras alioꝝ teinoꝝ ipso t̃pr in sua potestate habuit.
In ~~Essetone~~ tenuit un tein. iiii. hid. 7 m̃ erat.
Modo ten Girard. 7 ibi ht. i. car. 7 ii. uittos cũ. i. car.
Vat 7 ualuit. xl. solid.
In ~~Chenemertone~~ tenuit. ~~Lec~~. viii. hid. 7 m̃ erat. Modo
ten Girard. 7 ibi ht. iii. car. 7 xiiii. uitt cũ. vii. car. Ibi. viii.
serui. 7 iii. molini de. xv. solid. Valuit. viii. lib. modo. vi. lib.
Ad hoc m̃ adiacent. iii. hide in Boxwelle. Isd Girard ten.
7 ibi ht. ii. car. 7 iiii. uitt cũ. iii. car. 7 ibi. iii. serui. 7 molin
de. viii. solid. 7 viii. ac p̃ti. Vat 7 ualuit. xl. sol.
In ~~Wenecote~~ tenuit un tein. iii. hid. Regina dedit hanc
t̃rã Rainaldo capellano. Ibi sunt. iii. uitti. cũ dimid car.
Valuit. xl. solid.
In ~~Alrestone~~ tenuit Duning. vi. hid 7 dimid. 7 In Bricle
done. iiii. hid 7 dim. 7 In Hundeuuic. i. hid tenuit. i. tein.
Has ten t̃ras Hunfrid de rege. 7 ibi ht. iiii. car in dn̄io.
7 v. uitti 7 viii. bord cũ. iii. car. 7 un Radchenist cũ. i. car.
7 In Wicecobe un burgsis. 7 ibi hnt. xii. ac p̃ti.
Tot T.R.E. ualb. xi. lib. Modo. vi. lib.
In ~~Tuninge~~ teneb. iiii uitti. ii. hid. 7 un tein dimid hid.
Ibi sunt. iiii. car. 7 iii. ac p̃ti. Regina dedit hanc t̃rã Johi camer.
Vat 7 ualuit. xxx v. solid.
In ~~Stoches~~ tenuer Hermer 7 Aluuin. iii. hid. una v min.
Modo ten Bernard de rege. 7 ht ibi. i. car in dn̄io. 7 iiii. acs
p̃ti. Valuit. lx. solid. modo. xl. solid.
Qui T.R.E. has t̃ras tenebant. 7 se 7 t̃ras suas sub Brictrici
potestate summiser. ~~In Langelei Hd.~~
~~Brictric~~ fili Algar tenuit ~~Turneberie~~. Ibi T.R.E. erant
xi. hide. 7 iii. car in dn̄io. 7 xl ii. uitti. 7 xviii. radchenistre
cũ. xxi. car. 7 xx iiii. bord. 7 xv. serui. 7 iiii. coliba. Ibi. ii. mo
lini de. vi. solid 7 iiii. den. Silua de. i. lev lg. 7 una lat.
Ibi forũ de. xx. solid. Modo accreuit p̃posit molin ibi de. viii. den.
Hoc m̃ fuit reginæ Mathildis. Hunfrid reddit de eo. l. lib ad numer.
In hoc m̃ est un p̃tũ de. xl. solid. 7 ad Wiche. xl. sext salis.
uel. xx. den. 7 piscaria de Glouuecestre de. l. 7 viii. denar.
Isd Brictric tenuit ~~Sopeberie~~. ~~In Edredestan Hund.~~
Ibi T.R.E. erant. x. hide. 7 iiii. car in dn̄io. 7 xii. uitti cũ. v.
car. 7 iiii. bord 7 xviii. serui. 7 un parcus. 7 molin de. v. sol.
Modo creuit p̃posit. i. molin de. xl. denar. Ibi silua
de una leuua lg. 7 una lat.
Hunfrid reddit de hoc m̃. xvi. lib 7 x. solid.
Ad hoc m̃ p̃tin una v in Wiche quæ reddeb. xx v. sext
salis. Vrsus uicecom ita uastauit hoes. qđ m̃ redde n possunt sal.
Isd Brictric tenuit ~~Avenninge~~. Ibi ~~In Langetreu Hd.~~
T.R.E. erant. x. hide. 7 in dn̄io. viii. car. 7 xxiiii. uitti 7 v.
bord 7 xxx. serui. cũ. xvi. car. Ibi. iiii. molini de. xix. sol
7 ii. den. Modo creuit p̃posit un molin de. xl. denar. Ibi
silua. ii. leuuis lg. 7 dimid leuua lat. Ibi. ẽ aira accipitris. Vat. xx. vii. lib.
Isd Brictric tenuit ~~Hersefelde~~. ~~In Bristoldesberg Hd.~~
Ibi T.R.E. erant. xxi. hida. 7 l vi. uittos 7 ix. bord cũ. xxx. car.
Ibi p̃br qui teneb unã v t̃re de dn̄io. 7 iii. molini de. xxii.
solid. 7 vi. den. In dn̄io non sunt nisi. xiii. hide 7 una v.
Hoc m̃ tenuit Mathildis regina. Hunfrid reddit. xxx viii. lib.
7 x. sol ad numerũ. De t̃ra hui m̃ dedit regina. iiii. hid
Johi camerario. Ibi sunt. ii. car. 7 ix. uitti 7 iiii. bord cũ. iii. car.
Ibi. xiiii. serui. Reddit. ix. lib de firma.

Ipsa regina dedit Balduino .iii. hid 7 iii. virg de eade tra.
7 ibi ht .ii. car. 7 v. seruos. 7 un liberu hoem hntem .i. car.
7 ii. bord. Val. iiii. lib.
Qui has .ii. tras tenuer T.R.E. n poterant recede a capite m.

In Botelau hd.

Rex. E. tenuit Dimoch. Ibi erant .xx. hide 7 ii. car
in dnio. 7 xl. ii. uitti. 7 x. bord. 7 xi. colibti hntes .xl. i.
car. Ibi pbr tenens .xii. acras. 7 iiii. Radchenistre
cu .iiii. car. Ibi silua .iii. leuu lg. 7 una lat.
De hoc m reddeb uicecom qd uoleb T.R.E.
Rex. W. tenuit in dnio suo .iiii. annis. Postea habuit
eu com. W. 7 Rogeri fili ei. hoes de comitatu nesciunt
quomodo. Modo redd .xxi. lib. In Bliteslau hd.

Heraldus com tenuit Nest. Ibi erant .v. hide. 7 in dnio .i. car.
7 x. uitti 7 ii. bord cu .ix. car. T.R.E. non fuit ad firma.
Comes u W. adiunx illu .ii. aliis m. scilicet Pontune
7 Pertune. In his erant .x. hide 7 ii. car in dnio. 7 xv.
uitti 7 ii. bord. 7 ii. serui. cu .ix. car. Ibi .i. piscaria.
Modo creuit ppost in Pontune .i. car. Pertune e in
calumnia ad firma regis. Int tot redd .xi. lib.

In Lindenee fecit com W. un m de .iiii. tris quas
ab aliis dnis accepit. De dnio epi de hereford .iii. hid.
De dnico uictu monachoru de Pisore .vi. hid. ubi erant
vi. uitti cu .iiii. car. De duob teinis accep .iii. hid 7 dim.
Ibi sunt in dnio .iii. car. 7 viii. bord. 7 molin de .xl. den.
Silua .i. leuua lg. 7 dimid lat. Int tot redd .vii. lib.

In Tedeneha hund habuit abb de Bade un man
rioe Tedeneha. Ibi habebant .xxx. hide. haru .x. erant
in dnio. Ibi erant .xxviii. uitti hntes .xxviii. car. 7 x. bord.
In Sauerna .xi. piscariae in dnio. 7 xl ii. piscariae uillanoru.
In Waia .i. piscaria. 7 uillanoru .ii. piscariae 7 dimidia.
Rogeri comes creuit in Waia .ii. piscarias. Ibi e silua
.ii. leuu lg. 7 dimid leuua lat. 7 xii. bord plus sunt.
W. com dedit de hac tra fri suo. O. epo una v tre cu .i.
uitto. 7 Walterio de Laci dedit .ii. piscar in Sauerna.
7 dimid in Waia. cu uno uitto. Rad de Limesi dedit
ii. piscar in Waia cu uno uitto. Abbatiae de Lira
dedit dimid hid tre 7 ecclam m cu decima.
Hoc m n reddeb censu T.R.E. nisi uictu monachis.
Stigand archieps teneb illu. qdo com W. accep eu.
Modo redd .xxv. lib. de .xx. in ora. 7 albas.
Ibi e m molin de .xl. denarus. In Respiet hund.

Wiuuard tenuit Cedorde. Ibi .xv. hide int siluam 7 pla
num 7 pratu. 7 vii. car in dnio T.R.E. 7 xvi. uitti 7 iii. bord
cu .vi. car. 7 iii. molini de .xiii. solid 7 ii. denar. 7 de melle
neu sat qd ueniet ad aula. Ibi creuit uicecom .viii.
uittos. 7 iii. bord hntes .iiii. car. In Begeberie hd.

Chenuichelle ten regis. E. tenuit Alvredintune.
Ibi erant .v. hid p. 7 iiii. car in dnio. 7 xii. uitti
7 un bord cu .vi. car. 7 xvi. int seruos 7 ancillas.
7 ii. molini de .xx. solid. Silua .i. leuua lg. 7 dim lat.
Horu .ii. maneriou ppositi qd uoleb reddeb T.R.E.
Modo redd .xl. lib albor numor de .xx. in ora.
Rog com tenuit. In Tetboldestane hd.

Rofles huscarle. R.E. tenuit Beceford. Ibi erant
xi. hide. 7 iii. car in dnio. 7 xxxiiii. uitti 7 xvii. bord
hntes .xxx. car. Ibi .xii. serui. 7 iiii. ancille.
De hoc m dedit W. com .iii. hid Ansfrido de Cormelus.
in quib erant .xii. uitti cu .v. car.

Turbertus ten heraldi com tenuit Estone. Ibi sunt
viii. hide 7 iii. car in dnio. 7 x. uitti 7 iiii. bord
cu .vi. car. Ibi .viii. serui. 7 iii. ancille.
De his .ii. uitlis fec com W. un m. 7 n erat ad firma
donec Rog de Iurei misit ad .xxx. lib firme.
Decima u 7 ecclas cu .ii. uittis 7 iii. virg tre. dedit
ipse com abbatiae de Cormelus.
Hoes de comitatu in qsta dixer se nunq uidisse
breue regis qui hanc tra dixeret data e. comiti W.

Wlgar ten regis. E. tenuit In Langenei hd.
Tochintune. Ibi fuer .viii. hide. 7 v. car in dnio.
7 xx. uitti 7 xii. bord 7 x. serui. cu .xx. car.
Hoc m n redd firma T.R.E. sed inde uiueb cui erat.
Com W. tenuit in dnio. 7 ibi creuit ppositus .i. car.
7 molin de .viii. denar.
Modo redd .xxiii. lib. candidoru numoru de .xx. in ora.

Edric lang ten heraldi com tenuit In Dodestan hd.
Hechanestede. Ibi erant .v. hide 7 in dnio .iii. car.
7 vi. uitti 7 viii. bord cu .vi. car. Ibi .vi. serui.
7 dimid piscaria. Hoc m cep W. com in dnio. 7 non
fuit ad firma. Sed m uicecom posuit eu ad .lx. sol. nuo.

Gueda mat heraldi com tenuit Udecestre. In Langetreu hd.
Goduin emit ab Azor 7 ded sue uxori. ut inde uiueret donec
ad Berchelai maneret. Noleb eni de ipso m aliqd comedere.
p destructione abbatiae. Hanc tra ten Eduuard in firma
de Wiltescire. iniuste ut dicit comitat. qa non ptin ad aliq
firma. De quo m nemo legatus regis reddid ratione. nec
aliqs eoru uenit ad hanc descriptione. H tra redd .vii. lib.

Brictric tenuit .iii. hid in Modiete. In Tuiferde hd.
7 geldab. In dnio ht rex ibi .ii. piscarias. Roger de Laci
ht una piscar cu dimid hida. Abb de Malmesberia ht
una piscar cu dimid hida. 7 hoc dono regis sic dicunt.
Willi de Ow ht .ii. hid. 7 ipsas .iiii. piscarias calumniat.
He piscariae sunt in Waia. 7 reddeb .iiii. lib. In Bersdon hd.

Ednod tenuit Omenel T.R.E. Ibi .xv. hide geld.
De his pdonauit rex. E. Ednodo .v. hid. ut dicit scira.
7 postea reddeb de .x. hid. hoc m. In dnio .iii. car.
7 pbr 7 xix. uitti 7 iii. bord cu .x. car. Ibi .xii. serui.
hoc m fuit epi baiocsis. 7 ualb .xx. lib. Modo redd
xxvi. lib in firma regis. In Bebuitone hd.

Tovi Widenesci huscarle heraldi com tenuit Bebuitone.
Ibi .iiii. hide. In dnio sun .ii. car. 7 x. uitti 7 v. bord cu .v.
car. Ibi .iiii. serui. 7 molin de .v. solid.
Val 7 ualuit .vii. lib. Elsi de Ferendone ten in firma regis.

Elaves tenuit in Bebuitone .iii. hid p m. T.R.E.
In dnio e .i. car. 7 vii. uitti 7 iii. bord cu .iii. car.
Ibi .vi. serui. 7 molin de .v. sol. Valuit .c. solid. m .lx. solid.
Goduin de Stantone ten in firma regis.

II. TERRA THOME ARCHIEPI.

Stigand archieps tenuit Circesdvne. Ibi erant xv. hidę 7 dimid. 7 ii. car in dnio. 7 xviii. uilli 7 ix. bord 7 vii. radchenist. cu xxx. car. Ibi silua dimid leuua lg. 7 iii. qz lat. T.R.E. ualb. xiii. lib. Modo. xii. lib.

Ipse Stig tenuit Hochilicote. Ibi erant. iiii. hidę. 7 in dnio. ii. car. 7 xi. uilli 7 v. bord cu. xi. car. Ibi. e molin de. xxxii. den. 7 silua. i. leuua lg. 7 dim lat. Te 7 m uat. iiii. lib.

Ipse Stig tenuit Nortune. Ibi erant. v. hidę 7 dim. 7 in dnio. ii. car. 7 xv. uilli cu. xv. car. 7 iiii. serui. 7 molin de. xxxii. den. Te 7 m uat. iiii. lib.

Hos. iii. man ten m Thomas archieps.

Nortune ten Walchelin de eo. nepos epi de Wintoni.

Eldred archieps ten Otintune. In Salmanesberie hd.
7 sub Berew Condicote. Ibi erant. x. hidę. 7 ii. car in dnio. 7 xvi. uilli 7 ii. radchenist. 7 iiii. bord cu. xiiii. car. H tra nunq geldau. T.R.E. Valb. vi. lib. m. x. lib. Thomas archieps ten. Scs petrus de Glouuecestre habuit in dnio. donec .W. in anglia uenit. In Celfledetorn hd.

Stigand archieps tenuit Svindone. Ibi erant iii. hidę. 7 ii. car in dnio. 7 vii. uilli 7 ii. bord. 7 hnt vii. car. Ibi sunt. iii. serui. Te ualb. iii. lib. m. iii. lib 7 x. solid. Hoc m ten Thomas arch. de tra S Osuualdi. 7 geldat. In Wacrescube hd.

Gundulf tenuit 7 ten in Schipetune. un m de una hida. 7 geld. 7 ibi. i. car in dnio. 7 ual. viii. solid. De Thoma arch ten.

Pin tenuit. i. m de. i. hida in Bagepine. 7 geld. Ansger ten de Thoma arch. 7 ht. i. car in dnio. Valuit. xx. sol. Modo. x. solid. In Bradelege hd.

Scs petrus de Glouuec tenuit Lecce. 7 Eldred archieps tenuit cu abbatia. Ibi erant. xxiiii. hidę. In dnio sunt iiii. car. 7 xxxiii. uilli 7 xvi. bord cu. xxx. car. Ibi sun iiii. serui. 7 ii. molini de. vii. solid 7 iiii. den.
Ad hoc m adiacet Scanuuelle. Ibi sunt. ii. car in dnio. 7 v. uilli cu. v. car. 7 molin de. xl. den. 7 iiii. serui. 7 ii. ancillę. 7 in Culberlege. e una hida pan huic m.
De hac tra hui m ten Walt fili ponti un m de. xii. hid. q iacuit in eod m T.R.E. Ibi sunt. ii. car in dnio ap Tormentone. 7 xxv. uilli cu. xii. car. 7 iiii. serui.
Tot m T.R.E. ualb. xviii. lib. Thomas arch misit ad firma p xxvii. lib. hida de Culberlege. pcat. xx. solid.
Qd Walt ten. uat. xiii. lib. Thomas arch caluniat.

Stigand archieps tenuit Cvntvne. Ibi erant. ix. hidę. Ibi sunt. ii. car 7 v. ac pti. 7 xxii. uilli 7 v. bord cu. xi. car. Ibi. v. serui. 7 molin de. v. solid.
T.R.E. ualb. ix. lib. modo. vii. lib. Thomas arch tenet.
Vn ho Rog de Laci ten un m de. iii. hid pan huic m. hoc ipse arch caluniat. In Wirestan hd.

Eldred archieps tenuit Standis. De dnio S petri de Glouuecestre fuit. Ibi erant. xv. hidę. T.R.E. In dnio sunt. iii. car. 7 ix. uilli 7 xiiii. bord cu. xvi. car. 7 vii. radchenist. hntes. xvii. car. Ibi. viii. serui. 7 dim piscaria. Silua dim leuua lg. 7 una q lat.
Tot m T.R.E. ualb. xvi. lib. modo. xii. lib. Thomas arch ten. 7 similit geldat.
De hac tra hui m ten abb de Glouuec. i. hid. 7 iure debt tene.

Hugo com ten una hid in ipsa. Durand uicecom ten. iii. hid. qs .W. com ded fri ei Rogerio. Has caluniat arch Thomas.

Scs Osuuald de Glouuec tenuit Widiforde. In Bernitone hd.
Ibi T.R.E. erant. ii. hidę. 7 ii. car in dnio. 7 iiii. uilli 7 iii. bord cu. ii. car. Ibi. iiii. serui. 7 viii. ac pti. 7 molin de. x. solid. T.R.E. ualb. xl. sol. m. lx. sol. Rannulf ten de eod Sco. Q ualis tc fuit. talis. e modo. In Respigete hd.

Scs Osuuald tenuit in Cerneī. un m de. iii. hid. T.R.E. Ipse Scs ten adhuc. 7 ht. ii. car in dnio. 7 vi. uilli 7 ii. bord cu v. car. Ibi. i. seru. 7 molin de. vii. sol. 7 ii. ac pti. Te ualuit. c. sol. Modo. iiii. lib. In Langebrige hd.

Vlchetel tenuit Lessedvne. m de. ii. hid. Modo ten Rog de Thoma arch. H tra geld. In dnio. e una car. 7 v. uilli 7 ii. bord cu. iii. car. Ibi. iii. serui. 7 xx. ac pti. Valuit. xl. sol. m. xx. sol.

III. TERRA ECCLE DE WIRECESTRE. In Bernintreu hd.

Sca Maria de Wirecestre tenuit 7 ten Bvregberie. Ibi fuer 7 sunt. l. hidę. In dnio sunt. ii. car. 7 viii. uilli 7 vi. bord cu. viii. car. Ibi. iiii. serui 7 una ancilla.
Ad hoc m ptin h mebra. Henberie. Redeuuiche. Stoche. Giete. In his sunt. ix. car in dnio. 7 xxvii. uilli 7 xxii. bord. cu. xxvi. car. Ibi. xx. serui 7 ii. ancillę. 7 xx. coliba cu. x. car. 7 molin de. xx. den.
Ad m ptin. vi. radchenist hntes. viii. hid. 7 viii. car. n poterant a m separari. 7 In Bristou. ii. dom reddeb. xvi. den.
De hac tra hui m ten Turstin fili Rolf. v. hid In Austreclive. 7 Gislebt fili Turold. iii. hid 7 dimid In Contone. 7 Constantin. v. hid In Icetune. In his trib sunt. v. car in dnio. 7 xvi. uilli 7 xii. bord cu. xii. car. Ibi. xi. serui.
De ead tra hui m ten Osbn gifard. v. hid. 7 nullu seruitiu facit.
Tot m cu mebris suis. T.R.E. ualb. xxiiii. lib.
Modo dniu S Mariae uat. xxx. lib. 7 xiii. sol. 7 vi. den.
Qd hoes ten. ix. lib. In Respigete hd.

Ipsa eccla tenuit Colesborne. 7 Suein de ea. n poterat recedere. Ibi. viii. hidę geld. Walteri. f. Rog ten de eccla. In dnio. e una car. 7 xviii. uilli 7 ii. bord cu. v. car. Ibi. ii. serui. 7 iii. ac pti. 7 ii. molini de vii. solid. 7 vi. denar. Te ualuit. viii. lib. Modo. iiii. lib.

Ipsa eccla ten Alcote. 7 Alric de ea. In Begeberie iacet. Ibi una hida. In dnio sunt. ii. car. 7 ii. uilli 7 iiii. bord cu ii. car. Ibi. ii. serui. 7 viii. ac pti. 7 molin de. lxiiii. den. Valuit. xx. sol. modo. xxx. solid. Ordric ten de epo.

Ipsa eccla tenuit Bechesberie. In Bechesberie hvnd.
Ibi. xxi. hida. In dnio sunt. iiii. car. 7 xix. uilli 7 ii. bord cu. xi. car. Ibi. iii. radchenist hntes. iiii. hid 7 iiii. car. 7 pbr hns. iii. hid. 7 cu suis. iii. car. Ibi. xi. int seruos 7 ancillas. 7 ii. molini de. xvii. solid. 7 x. ac pti.
De ead tra hui m ten Durand de epo un m de. iii. hid 7 una v in Berneslei. 7 Eudo. vii. uirgat ibid p m.
In his sunt. v. car in dnio. 7 xii. uilli cu. vi. car. Ibi. xii. serui. Tot m T.R.E. ualuit. xviii. lib. 7 m similit.
Vlstan eps ten. 7 geldat. In Wacrescube hd.

Ipsa eccla ten Widindvne. Ibi. xxx. hidę. Tpe ex his nunq geldauer. In dnio sunt. ii. car. 7 xvi. uilli 7 viii.

Isd. W. ten SCIPTONE. sic Rad de limesi teneb. Wlui tenuit T.R.E.
Ibi. ii. hide. In dnio sunt. ii. car. 7 ii. bord 7 viii. serui. Val 7 ualuit
xl. sol. Ipse Wluui poterat ire quo uellet. Hugo ten de Witto.
Isd. W. ten CULCORTORNE 7 Herbt de eo. Sciruold tenuit
T.R.E. Ibi. iii. uirg 7 v. acre. In dnio. e una car. 7 iii. serui.
Val 7 ualuit. xxxv. sol. Hanc tra tenuit Rad de limesi. sed n fuit Alestani.
Isd. W. ten BEIEWRDE. Alestan tenuit. In DUDESTANES hd.
Ibi. viii. hide. In dnio sunt. vi. car. 7 xx. uitti 7 xiiii. bord
cu. xxiiii. car. Ibi. xvii. serui. 7 molin de xii. denar. Silua. ii. leuu
lg 7 una lat. Valuit. xv. lib. Modo: xiii. lib. In SALEMANES
Isd. W. ten SUELLE. Ernesi tenuit T.R.E. BERIE hd.
Ibi. iii. hide geld. Valuit. xl. sol. modo. x. sol.

.XXXII. TERRA WILLI FILII BADERON. In CIRECESTRE hd.

Wills filius BADERON ten. ii. hid in CIRECESTRE. 7 Hugo ten
de eo. In dnio. e una car. 7 un uitts 7 dimid. 7 iiii. bord cu. i. car.
Ibi. ii. serui. Valuit. c. solid. modo. lxx. solid. Aluui tenuit hanc tra.
Isd Witts ten DUNTESBORNE. Chetel 7 Aluric tenuer. 7 poteran
ire quo uoleban. Ibi. iii. hide 7 dimid. In dnio. i. car 7 dimid est.
7 un uitts 7 ii. bord cu. i. car. Ibi. i. seru. Valuit. x. lib. m. lxx. sol.
Isd. W. ten in SUDTONE. i. hid. Osuuid tenuit. T.R.E. 7 potuit
ire quo uoluit. In dnio. e. i. car. 7 iiii. serui. Val 7 ualuit xxiiii. sol.
Isd. W. ten WESTONE. Bricsi tenuit T.R.E. In LANGETREU hd.
Ibi. iii. hide. In dnio sunt. ii. car. 7 ii. uitti 7 iii. bord cu. ii. car.
Ibi. iiii. serui. 7 vi. ac pti. Valuit. vi. lib. modo. iii. lib.
Isd. W. ten TEBRISTON. Ibi. v. hide. Vlfelm tenuit de rege. E. In BOTELAU
7 poterat ire quo uellet. In dnio sunt. iii. car. 7 x. uitti hund
7 viii. bord cu. viii. car. Ibi. iiii. serui. 7 Silua. iii. leuu lg.
7 una lat. Valuit. vi. lib. 7 x. sol. Modo: c. solid.
Isd. W. ten HUNTELEI. Aluuin tenuit de Aldred archiepo.
7 poterat ire quo uoleb. Ibi. ii. hide. In dnio. e una car. 7 iiii.
uitti 7 vi. bord cu. iii. car. Ibi. i. seru. Silua. ii. leuu lg. 7 i. lat.
Valuit. xl. solid. Modo: xxx. solid. In WESTBERIE hund.
Isd. W. ten HOPE. Forne 7 Vlfeg ... tenuer de rege. E. 7
Ibi. v. hide geld. 7 poteran ipsi teini ire quo uoleb. In dnio sun
.ii. car. 7 xii. uitti 7 un bord cu. xii. car. Ibi. iii. serui. 7 molin
de. xviii. denar. Valuit. viii. lib. modo. c. sol. sol.
Isd. W. ten STAURE. Vlfeg tenuit T.R.E. Valuit. x. sol. m. v.
Ibi. e una hida 7 n geldat.
Isd. W. ten. ii. uirg 7 dimid. 7 ibi ht. i. uittm 7 i. bord. Ante
cessor ei Wihanoc tenuit. sed comitat affirmat hanc tra
ee. de dnica firma regis in Westberie. Val. iii. sol.
Isd. W. ten NEVNEHAM. Ibi. i. hida 7 iii. uitti 7 iii. bord.
redditeS. xx. sol. H tra n geldat. Silua ibi. ii. qrc lg. 7 una lat.
Isd. W. ten LEDENEI. Alfer tenuit In LEDENEI hund.
T.R.E. Ibi. vi. hide geld. In dnio sunt. ii. car. 7 iii. uitti 7 v.
bord cu. ii. car. Ibi. iii. serui. 7 molin de v. sol. 7 xx. ac pti
7 in Waie dimid piscar. Silua. i. leuu lg. 7 dimid lat.
Valuit. iiii. lib. Modo: xl. solid.
Isd. W. tenuit HIWOLDESTONE. Vlfeg tenuit T.R.E.
Ibi. iii. hide. H tra iussu regis. e in foresta. Valb xxx. sol.

.XXXIII. TERRA WILLELMI CAMERARII. In WITELAI hd.

Wills camerari ten WENECOTE. Wenric tenuit. T.R.E.
Ibi. iii. hide. In dnio sunt. iii. car. 7 ii. uitti 7 ii. bord cu. i. car.
Ibi. iiii. serui. Val 7 ualuit. iiii. lib. Hoc m geldat.
Isd. W. ten HASEDENE. 7 Goisfrid de eo. Eduui In WACRESCUBE hd.
tenuit. Ibi. v. hide. In dnio sunt. ii. car. 7 vi. uitti cu. iii. car. Ibi
iiii. serui. H tra geldat. Valuit. c. sol. modo: lx. sol.

.XXXIIII. TERRA WILLI GOIZENBODED. In CEOLFLEDE hd.

Wills Goizinboded. ten PEBEWORDE de rege.
Vluiet 7 Vluuard tenuer T.R.E. p. ii. m.
Ibi. vi. hide 7 una v. In dnio. e una car. 7 i. bord
7 un seruus. Valuit. vii. lib. m. iiii. lib.
Isd. Witts ten WENITONE. Vn tain 7 x. sol.
tenuit T.R.E. Ibi. v. hide. In dnio sunt. ii. car. 7 ii.
uitti 7 un francig ten. i. hid 7 dimid. cu. i. car.
Hoc m misit Algar com in pebeuuorde. Valuit. c. sol.
Isd. W. ten CLOPTUNE. Huscarle tenuit m. xl. sol.
T.R.E. Ibi. x. hide. In dnio. iii. car. 7 xii. uitti 7 iiii.
bord 7 un Radchenist cu. ix. car. In Wicelcobe
Valuit. viii. lib. Modo: c. solid. un burgsis.
Isd. Witts ten BRISTENTUNE. In WITELAI hd.
Brismar tenuit. Ibi. x. hide. In dnio. iiii. car.
7 xviii. uitti 7 iiii. bord cu. xiiii. car. Ibi. viii. serui
7 iii. ancille. 7 ii. molini de. xv. solid. hund.
Valuit. xii. lib. modo. vii. lib. In SALESMANESBERIE
Isd. W. ten CALLICOTE. 7 Rannulf de eo. Aluuin
tenuit. T.R.E. Ibi. iii. hide geld. In dnio. iii. car.
7 viii. int seruos 7 ancillas. Valuit. lx. sol. m. xl. sol.
Isd. W. ten ALEWRDE. Aluuin tenuit. T.R.E. Ibi
una hida geld. In dnio. i. car. 7 ii. serui. Valuit. vi. sol.
Isd. W. ten TERNECOTE. In HOLEFORD hd. m. iii. sol.
Aluuin tenuit. Ibi. iii. hide geld. In dnio. ii. car.
7 iiii. uitti cu. iiii. car. 7 xiii. int seruos 7 ancillas.
Goisfrid ten de Witto. Valuit. x. lib. m. iii. lib.
Isd. W. ten GETINGE. Rex. E. tenuit. 7 accomo
dauit eu Aluuino uicecomiti suo ut in uita sua haberet.
non tam dono dedit ut comitat testat. Mortuo u
Aluuino: rex W. dedit Ricardo cuida iuueni uxore
ei 7 tra. Nc Witts successor Ricardi ita ten hanc tra.
Ibi. x. hide. haru. ix. geldant. In dnio sunt. iiii.
car. 7 iiii. uitti 7 iii. francig. 7 ii. Radchenist. 7 pbr
cu. ii. bord. int oms hnt. v. car. Int seruos 7 an
cillas. xi. 7 ii. molini de. xiiii. solid. Ibi. v. sa
line reddit. xx. sumas salis. In Wicelcobe. ii. bur
genses reddit. xi. sol 7 iiii. denar.
Valuit. xvi. lib. Modo: vi. lib.
Isd. W. ten CATESLAI. Aluuin tenuit. Ibi. ii. hide
geld. In dnio. ii. car. 7 iiii. serui. 7 molin de. v. solid.
Valuit. xl. solid. modo. x. solid. In BOTELAU hd.
Isd. W. ten TETINTON. Aluuin tenuit. Ibi. vi. hide.
In dnio. e una car. 7 x. uitti 7 vii. bord cu. ix. car.
Valuit. vi. lib. modo. iii. lib. In BERNINTONE hd.
Isd. W. ten. ii. hid in BERNINTONE 7 Radulf de eo.
Aluuin tenuit T.R.E. In dnio. e. i. car. 7 un seruus.
7 molin de. xl. den. 7 vi. ac pti. Val 7 ualuit. xl. sol.
Isd. W. ten dimid hid tre. 7 dimid piscaria In WESTBERIE hd.
Aluuin uicecom tenuit. 7 uxori sue dedit. H tam
fuer de firma regis in Westberie. In BRETESLAU hd.
Isd. W. ten in DUNBENTUNE. i. hid. Sauuin tenuit. T.R.E.
7 potuit ire quo uoluit. Valuit. xx. solid. modo: xii. solid.

.XXXV. TERRA WILLI FILII WIDON. In BRICTWOLDESTOU hd.

Wills fili Widonis ten de rege DIRHAM. Aluric
tenuit. T.R.E. Ibi. vii. hide geld. In dnio. e una car. 7 xiii.
uitti 7 xiii. bord cu. ii. car. Ibi. viii. int seruos 7 ancillas.
7 iii. molini de. xv. solid. 7 vi. ac pti. Valuit. xii. lib.
Modo. viii. lib.
Isd Witts tenuit. iii. hid huic m. quib durand uicecom saisierat
S. MARIA de persore iussu regis. quas W. com dederat
Turstino filio Rolf cu hoc m.

·XXXVI. TERRA WILLI FROISSELEW. IN DUDESTAN HD.

WILLS froisseleuu. ten de rege VLETONE. Godric tenuit. Ibi .ii. hide. In dnio sunt .ii. car. 7 iiii. bord 7 iiii. serui. Valuit .xxx. sol. m .lx. sol.

In Witelei HD. Isd .W. ten In CONNICOTE dim hid. geld. Ibi erat .i. car 7 iiii. serui. Valuit .xx. sol. modo .iii. solid. Brictric tenuit .T.R.E. IN GRETESTAN HD.

Isd .W. ten in LITENTUNE .i. hida. Godric tenuit. In dnio sunt .ii. car. 7 ii. bord. 7 iii. serui. 7 molin de .iiii. solid. Valuit .xl. sol. Modo .xxx. sol. 7 geld.

·XXXVII. TERRA WILLI FILII NORMAN. IN LANGEBRIGE HD.

WILLS filius Norman ten MORCOTE. Vlfegh tenuit .T.R.E. Ibi .i. hida. In dnio .e. una car. cu .ii. bord. Valuit .viii. sol. modo .x. sol. H tra geld.

Isd Wills ten BICANOFRE. Morganau tenuit .T.R.E. IN WESTBERIE HD. Ibi dimid hida. In dnio .e. dim car. cu .vi. bord. Valuit .v. sol. modo .x. sol.

Isd .W. ten in DENE .ii. hid. 7 .ii. virg tre 7 dimid. Has tenuer .iii. teini. Godric Elric 7 Ernui .T.R.E. In dnio sunt .iii. car. Ibi .xxxviii. bord hntes .vii. car 7 dimid. 7 tres ex eis reddt .viii. solid. Valuit .xxxiii. sol. modo .xliiii. solid.

Has tras cessit rex .E. qetas a geldo. p foresta custod.

Isd .W. ten TATINTON. Vlgar tenuit de rege .E. IN BORTELAU HD. H tra liba est. Ibi sunt .vi. bord. cu .i. car. Val 7 ualuit .xx. solid.

Ibid una v tre iacet ad forestā. 7 redd .xii. den.

Isd .W. ten .i. hid 7 dimid v tre. IN BLIDESLAWE HD. Siuuard 7 Winstan tenuer. In dnio sunt .ii. car. 7 xvii. bord cu .v. car. Valuit .xv. sol. m .xxx. sol.

·XXXVIII. TERRA WILLI LEURIC. IN CILTEHĀ HD.

WILLS Leuric ten de rege LECHANTONE. Osgot tenuit .T.R.E. Ibi .iii. hide geld. In dnio sunt .ii. car. 7 ii. uitti 7 viii. bord cu .i. car. Ibi .iiii. serui. Silua una qx lg. 7 una lat. Val 7 ualuit .xl. sol.

Isd .W. ten HELLE. Osgot tenuit .T.R.E. IN GRETESTAN HD. Ibi .xi. hide. In dnio sunt .iii. car. 7 x. uitti 7 xi. bord cu .viii. car. Ibi erant .xii. serui. quos Wills liberos fecit. Ibi molin de .x. solid. Silua una leuua lg. 7 dimid lat. Valuit .xii. lib. m .viii. lib. hoc m geldat. IN WACRESCUBE HD.

Isd .W. ten WITETUNE. Osgot tenuit. Ibi .iii. hide 7 geld. In dnio sunt .ii. car. 7 vi. uitti 7 un Radchen 7 iiii. bord cu .iiii. car. Ibi molin de .x. sol. Silua una leuua lg. 7 dimid lat. Valuit .c. sol. m .lx. sol.

Isd .W. ten in SCIPETUNE .iii. hid. una v min. 7 geld. Goisfrid ten de eo. Osgot tenuit. In dnio sunt .ii. car. 7 pbr 7 i. uitts. 7 iiii. serui. sine car. Valuit .xl. sol. Modo .xx. sol. IN BRADELEG HD.

Isd .W. ten TURGHEDENE. 7 Goisfrid de eo. Osgot tenuit. Ibi .v. hide 7 una v 7 dimid. In dnio nichil. Ibi sunt .ii. uitti 7 iii. bord cu .i. car. H tra geld. Valuit .iiii. lib. modo .x. sol.

·XXXIX. TERRA ROGERII DE LACI. IN BORTELAU HUND.

ROGERIUS de Laci ten de rege CHEUENEHELEI. Edric 7 Leuric tenuer .T.R.E. p .ii. m. 7 poterant ire quo uolebant. Ibi .iii. hide. In dnio sunt .iii. car. 7 x. uitti 7 vii. bord cu .xii. car. Ibi .vii. serui. Valuit .iiii. lib. modo .c. sol.

Isd Rog ten HORSENEHAL. Turchil tenuit de Heraldo com. 7 poterat ire quo uoleb. Ibi .iii. hide. In dnio sunt .ii. car. 7 v. uitti 7 iii. bord cu .v. car. Ibi .ii. serui. 7 In Glouuecestre .iii. burgses. de .xv. den. Val 7 ualuit .xl. solid.

Isd Rog ten CRASOWEL. 7 Odo de eo. Vlfel tenuit .T.R.E. 7 poterat ire quo uellet. Ibi .i. hida 7 una v. In dnio .e. una car. 7 iii. uitti 7 un bord cu .iii. car. Val 7 ualuit .xx. solid.

Isd Rog ten LECUBE. 7 Radulf de eo. Haldene tenuit. IN SALEMANESBERIE HD. Ibi .ii. hide. In dnio sunt .ii. car. 7 ii. uitti 7 ii. bord cu .i. car. Ibi .iiii. serui 7 iii. ancille. Val 7 ualuit .xl. sol. H tra geld.

Isd Rog ten RISEDUNE. 7 Hugo de eo. Ibi .viii. hide geldantes. Aluuard 7 Aschil 7 Aluuard 7 Vluui tenuer p .iiii. m. In dnio sunt .vii. car. 7 iiii. uitti cu .ii. car. Ibi .xii. serui 7 ii. ancille. Ibi molin de .x. solid. Val 7 ualuit .vii. lib 7 x. lib. IN HOLEFORD HD.

Isd Rog ten GETINGE. Ibi .x. hide geld pter dniu qd n geld. Brictric tenuit tein regis .E. In dnio sunt .v. car. 7 xxv. uitti 7 pbr 7 vii. radchen cu .xviii. car. Ibi .xviii. int seruos 7 ancillas. 7 iii. molini de .xxiiii. solid. 7 salina de .xx. sol. 7 xii. sumas salis. 7 in Wincelcube .iii. burgses de .xxxii. den. 7 In Glouuec .ii. burgses de .x. den. De silua 7 pastura .xl. gallinas. Val 7 ualuit .x. lib. IN RESPIGETE HD.

Isd Rog ten LANESBORNE. 7 Gislebt de eo. Keneuuard tenuit tein regis .E. 7 poterat ire quo uoleb. Ibi .ii. hide. In dnio .e. .i. car. 7 ii. uitti 7 ii. bord cu .i. car 7 dim. Ibi .ii. serui. Val .xl. sol. 7 ualuit.

Isd Rog ten WICHE. Ibi una hida geld. IN BISELEGE HUND. Ernesi tenuit. In dnio .e. .i. car. 7 xxxv. uitti 7 xvi. bord 7 pbr 7 iii. Radchen. Int oms hnt .lii. car. Ibi .xi. serui 7 iiii. molini de .xxiiii. sol. Silua .v. leuu lg. 7 ii. lat. Valuit .xx. lib. m .xxiiii. lib. Ipse tein poterat ire quo uoleb.

In hac tra ten S MARIA de Cirecestre .i. uittm. 7 parte siluę. hoc cessit ei .W. rex. Val .x. sol.

Isd Rog ten EGESWORDE. Ibi .i. hida 7 dim. geld. Eluuin tenuit. In dnio sunt .iiii. car. 7 iiii. uitti 7 ii. bord. cu .ii. car. Ibi .ii. libi hoes cu .ii. car. Ibi .xv. serui 7 molin de .xxx. den. 7 ii. ac pti. Silua .i. leuua lg 7 dimid lat. Val 7 ualuit .vi. lib.

Isd Rog ten dimid hida cu .i. piscaria in Waie. 7 ibi .i. uitts cu una car. H tra uocat MODIETE. Val 7 ualuit .xx. sol. Brictric tenuit.

Isd Rog ten dim hida in TEDEHĀ. Stigand archieps tenuit. Ibi .i. uitts cu .i. car. 7 iiii. piscarię 7 dimid. Val 7 ualuit .xx. sol.

Isd Rog ten QUENINTONE. Ibi .viii. hide. IN BRICTWOLDESBERG HD. Tres libi hoes tenuer. Dodo 7 alt Dodo 7 Aluuold. p .iii. m. 7 poterant ire quo uoleb. 7 geld. In dnio sunt .iii. car. 7 xx. uitti 7 vii. bord 7 pbr 7 pposit. Int oms hnt .xii. car. 7 ii. radchen cu .i. car. Ibi .xii. serui. 7 ii. molini de .xx. sol. 7 x. ac pti. In Glouuec .i. burgsis redd .iiii. soccos. 7 fab .i. redd .ii. sol. Valuit .viii. lib. modo .x. lib.

Isd Rog ten LECCE. 7 Wills de eo. Ibi .v. hide. Alduin tenuit .T.R.E. In dnio sunt .ii. car. 7 xii. uitti 7 i. bord cu .v. car. Ibi .v. serui. 7 viii. ac pti. Val 7 ualuit .vi. lib.

Isd Rog ten HETROPE. 7 Wills de eo. Ibi .ii. hide. Duning tenuit .T.R.E. In dnio sunt .ii. car. 7 iii. uitti 7 iii. bord cu .i. car. Ibi .vi. serui. Val 7 ualuit .c. sol. IN BERNINTONE HD.

Isd Rog ten WENRIC. 7 Radulf de eo. Ibi .ii. hide. Wluric tenuit .T.R.E. In dnio .e. .i. car. 7 iii. uitti 7 ii. bord cu .i. car. Ibi .v. serui. 7 molin de .v. sol. 7 x. ac pti. Valuit .c. sol. modo .iiii. lib.

Ist Rog ten ibid una hid 7 una v. 7 hugo de eo. Godric tenuit tein R.E. In dnio .e. i. car. 7 ii. bord 7 un seru. 7 molin de .iii. solid. 7 viii. ac pti. Val 7 ualuit .xxiiii. sol. In Grecestre hd.

Ist Rog ten Stratone. Ibi .v. hide. geld. pr ter dominii firm. Edmund tenuit T.R.E. In dnio sunt .iii. car. 7 xvi. uitti 7 vii. bord cu pbro hntes .ix. car. Ibi .v. serui 7 ii. molini de .xx. solid. Valuit .viii. lib. m .vi. lib.

Ist Rog ten Svintone 7 mat ei ten de sua dote. Ibi .vi. hide. Godric 7 Leuuin tenuer p .ii. co. In dnio sunt .iii. car. 7 ix. uitti 7 vi. bord 7 pbr cu .vii. car. Ibi .ii. serui 7 molinu de .x. sol. Valuit .viii. lib. modo .x. lib.

Ist Rog ten Achelie. Ibi .i. hida 7 dimid. Leuuin tenuit. Modo ten Girard de Rog. In dnio sunt .ii. car. 7 ii. uitti cu pbro hntes .ii. car 7 dimid. Ibi .ix. serui. Valuit .iiii. lib. m

Ist Rog 7 mat ei ten Selostre. In Salemanesberie hund. .iii. lib. Ibi .iii. hide. Offa 7 Leuuin tenuer p .ii. co. 7 poterant ire quo uoleb. In dnio sunt .iiii. car. 7 iiii. bord 7 viii. serui. 7 molin de .xii. solid. Val 7 ualuit .vi. lib. De his .iii. hid geldab .i. hida singul annis p .x. solid ad opus regis.

Ist Rog ten Wenrintone. Walt f. erold de eo. In Bretelsloe hd. Ibi .v. hide geld. Eduui tenuit. In dnio sunt .ii. car. 7 vi. uitti cu .ii. car. Ibi .ii. serui. 7 molin de .viii. solid. 7 x. ac pti. Valuit .c. sol. m .iiii. lib.

.xl. TERRA ROGERII DE BELMONT. In Ceolflede hund.

Rogerius de Belmont ten Dorsintune. 7 Robt de eo. Ibi .x. hide. Saxi tenuit. In dnio .iii. car. 7 viii. uitti cu .v. car. 7 vi. serui. Valuit .viii. lib. modo .c. solid.

.xli. TERRA ROGERII DE IVERI. In Bradelege hd.

Rogerius de Iuri ten Hantone. Ibi .x. hide. Eldred arch tenuit. Rex .E. ded ei .ii. hid qetas ex his .x. ut dicunt. In dnio sunt .iii. car. 7 x. uitti cu pbro 7 i. bord cu .v. car. Ibi .xi. serui. 7 In Wincelcube .x. burgses reddt .lxv. denar. Valuit .viii. lib. modo .vi. lib. In Langetrewes hd.

Ist Rog ten Teteberie. Ibi .xxiii. hide geld. Siuuard tenuit T.R.E. In dnio sunt .viii. car. 7 xxii. uitti 7 ii. bord 7 ii. radchen cu pbro. int oms hntes .xiiii. car. Ibi .xix. serui. 7 molin de .xv. den. 7 pastura de .x. solid. 7 x. ac pti.

Ist Rog ten Vptone. Ibi .ii. hide 7 una v geld. Aluricus tenuit de rege .E. In dnio sunt .ii. car. 7 v. uitti 7 iii. bord cu .iii. car. Ibi .viii. serui.

Hec duo m T.R.E. ualb .xxiii. lib. Modo sunt ad firma p .l. lib.

Ist Rog ten Culcortorne. Aluric tenuit. 7 Anschitil de eo. Ibi .i. hida 7 dim. In dnio .ii. car. 7 iii. serui. Valuit .xx. sol. modo .xxx. solid.

Ist Rog ten Hasedene. Ibi .iii. hide 7 iii. virg geld. Elnoc tenuit T.R.E. In dnio sunt .iii. car. 7 vii. dimidii uitti 7 i. bord cu .iii. car. 7 xvii. serui. 7 dimid molin de .xxx. denar. 7 xv. ac pti. hoc m tenuit qda ho Rog de epo baiocsi. p .xvi. lib. postea ded eps eide Rogerio cu firma.

.xlii. TERRA ROGERII DE BERCHELAI. In Respigete hund.

Rogerius de Berchelai ten Coberleie. Ibi .x. hide. Dena tenuit tein regis .E. In dnio sunt .ii. car. 7 xix. uitti 7 iiii. bord cu .v. car. Ibi .iiii. serui. 7 v. ac pti. Silua .iii. qx lg 7 ii. lat. Valuit .vii. lib. modo .viii. lib. In Hedredestan hd.

Ist Rog ten Dodintone. Ibi .iii. hide 7 ii. partes dimid hide. Aluuin tenuit T.R.E. In dnio .e. i. car. 7 vii. uitti 7 iii. bord cu .iiii. car. Ibi .iiii. serui. 7 x. ac pti. Val 7 ualuit .iii. lib.

Ist Rog ten Sistone. Anne tenuit. In Polcrecerce hd. Ibi .v. hide geld. In dnio sunt .ii. car. 7 viii. uitti 7 x. bord cu .iiii. car. Ibi .iiii. serui. 7 viii. ac pti. Val 7 ualuit .c. solid.

.xliii. TERRA RADULFI DE BERCHELAI. In Folchecerce hd.

Radulfus fr ipsius Rogerii ten de rege Wapelie. Ibi .i. hida. Godric tenuit. In dnio .e. una car. 7 iiii. serui. Val 7 ualuit .xx. solid. In Blacelew hd.

Ist Rad ten Stanlege. Ibi .iiii. hide 7 dim. Godric 7 Wisnod tenuer p .ii. co. In dnio sunt .ii. car. 7 vi. uitti 7 xiiii. bord cu .xii. car. Ibi .v. serui. 7 x. ac pti. Valuit 7 ual .c. solid.

.xliiii. TERRA RADULFI PAGENEL. In Grecestre hd.

Radulfus pagenel ten Torentune. 7 Radulf de eo. Ibi .iiii. hide 7 dimid geld. Merlesuen tenuit. In dnio sunt .iii. car. 7 x. uitti 7 i. bord cu .iii. car. Ibi .x. serui. Valuit .x. lib. modo .c. solid. In Langetrewes hd. Teneb Rog de Iuri una v tre 7 dimid de Rad pagen qua utriq dereliqrunt.

.xlv. TERRA RADULFI DE TODENI. In Wetelai hund.

Radulfus de Todeni ten Cheuringaurde. 7 Rogeri de eo. Ibi .x. hide. Brismar tenuit. In dnio .iii. car. 7 xiii. uitti 7 un radchen cu .vi. car. 7 ix. int seruos 7 ancillas. Valuit .viii. lib. modo .vi. lib. In Salemanesberie hund.

Ist Radulf ten Lecbe. 7 Rog de eo. Ibi .x. hide. In dnio .iii. car. 7 xii. uitti 7 ii. bord cu .vii. car. Ibi .viii. serui. Val 7 ualuit .vi. lib. In Botelau hd.

Ist Rad ten Brungareberge. Ibi .v. hide. com Herald tenuit. In dnio .e. i. car. 7 xi. uitti 7 viii. bord cu .xiiii. car. Ibi un seruus. Silua .ii. leuu lg 7 una lat. Valuit .viii. lib. Modo .c. solid. In Gersdones hd.

Ist Radulf ten Harehille. 7 Roger de eo. Ibi .v. hide. Elric 7 Aluuin 7 Vluric tenuer p .iii. co.

Ist Radulf ten Dodehie 7 Cernei. 7 Roger de eo. Ibi .iiii. hide. Quattuor teini tenuer p .iiii. co. 7 poterant ire quo uoleb. In dnio .x. car. 7 i. uitts 7 i. bord. Ibi .xxi. seru. 7 molin de .v. sol. 7 xxx. ac pti. Valeb .x. lib. modo .vi. lib. In Salemanesberie hd.

Ist Rad ten Svelle. 7 Drogo de eo. Ernesi tenuit. Ibi .vii. hide geld. In dnio sunt .iiii. car. 7 x. uitti cu .vi. car. 7 molin de .vii. sol 7 vi. den. Valuit .viii. lib. modo .vii. lib.

.xlvi. TERRA ROBERTI DE TODENI. In Salemanesberie hd.

Rotbert de Todeni ten Risendone. Vlf tenuit. Ibi .xiii. hide geld. In dnio sunt .iii. car. 7 xxiii. uitti 7 vi. bord cu .x. car. Ibi .viii. int seruos 7 ancillas. 7 molin de .x. sol. 7 un burgsis in Glouuecest de .iii. den. Valuit .xii. lib. m .x. lib. In Gretboldestou hd.

Ist Robt ten Horedone. Ibi .x. hide geld. Vlf tenuit. In dnio sunt .iii. car. 7 xi. uitti 7 viii. bord. cu .viii. car. Ibi .vii. serui. 7 molin de .vi. solid. 7 xx. ac pti. Silua .ii. leuu lg 7 una lat. Valuit .xii. lib. modo .vii. lib. In Biselege hd.

Ist Robt ten Sapletorne 7 Frantone. In uno .v. hide 7 in alio .v. hide. Vlf tenuit. In dnio sunt .vii. car. 7 xvii. uitti 7 ix. bord cu .x. car. Ibi .xiii. serui. 7 ii. molini de .vi. solid. Silua dimid leuua lg 7 ii. qx lat. h .ii. m T.R.E. ualb .xiiii. lib. simul. modo .xvi. lib.

.xlvii. TERRA ROBERTI DISPENSAT. In Gretestane hd.

Rotbert dispensator ten Wicvene. Ibi .x. hide geld. Balduin tenuit. In dnio sunt .iii. car. 7 xxii. uitti 7 x. bord cu .xii. car. Ibi .i. seru. 7 ii. molini de .x. sol. 7 x. ac pti. In Wincelcube .i. burgsis de .xvi. den. Valuit .xii. lib. m .xvi. lib.

GLOWEC'SCIRE.

·XLVIII· TERRA ROBERTI DE OILGI. In Salemanesberie Hd.

Rotbert' de olgi ten' Risendune. Ibi·x·hidæ geld. Siuuard tenuit. In dnio·iii·car. 7 xii·uitti 7 ii·bord cu·v·car. Ibi·viii·serui·7 ii·molini de·xx·solid. Valuit·x·lib. modo·viii·lib. In Bradeles Hd.

Ist& Rotbt' ten' Turchedene. Ibi·v·hidæ·7 ii·uirg 7 dimid geld. Siuuard tenuit. In dnio sunt·iiii·car·7 xii·uitti cu·vi·car. Ibi·viii·int' seruos 7 ancill. Valuit·vi·lib. m· c·sol.

Roger' de olgi ten' Niwetone. In Salemanesberie Hd. de osbno·f·Ricardi. Ibi·v·hidæ geld. Turstan tenuit. In dnio·ii·car·7 viii·uitti cu·iii·car 7 dimid. Val·iii·lib.

·XLIX· TERRA RICARDI LEGATI. In Bedredestan Hd.

Ricard' Legat' ten' de rege Toroentone. Ibi·viii· hidæ. Alric' tenuit de rege·E· In dnio sunt·vi·car. 7 xx·uitti 7 iiii·bord 7 pbr 7 un' radchen. Int' oms·xii· car hnt. Ibi·xii·serui. Valuit·xii·lib. m·xv·lib.

·L· TERRA OSBERNI GIFARD. In Langelei Hd.

Osbern' Gifard ten' de rege Rochemtune. Ibi·iii·hidæ geld. Dunne tenuit T·R·E· In dnio sunt·ii·car·7 vi·uitti 7 vii·bord cu·iii·car. Ibi·v·serui·7 xx·ac pti·7 salina ad Wich·de·iii·sumis salis. Silua·i·leuua lg·7 dim lat. Val·vi·lib.

Ist& Osbn' ten' Stoche. Ibi·v·hidæ geld. In Letberg Hd. Dunne tenuit. In dnio sunt·iii·car·7 viii·uitti 7 iii·bord 7 pbr cu·viii·car. Ibi·iiii·serui. Valuit·vi·lib. m·viii·lib.

Ist& Osbn' ten' Brimesfelde. Ibi·ix·hidæ geld. In Respiget Hd. Duns tenuit de com Heraldo. In dnio sunt·iii·car·7 xvi·uitti 7 vi·bord 7 pbr·cu·xii·car. Ibi·viii·serui·7 iii·ancillæ·7 ii·molini de·lxiiii·den. In Glouuec·v·burgses de·ii·sol. Val 7 ualuit·xii·lib.

Ist& Osbn' ten' Aldeberie sed n' ptinuit ad Duns hd tra qua osbn' ten' ut scira dicit. Eilricus tenuit 7 potuit ire quo uoluit. Ibi·i·hida 7 i·car. Val 7 ualuit·x·sol.

TERRA GOISFRIDI ORLETEILE

·LI· Goisfrid' orleteile ten' de rege in Baudintune·ii·hid 7 una v· geld. Bolli tenuit. Non·e in dnio qd. Ibi·ii·uitti 7 viii·bord·cu·iii·car. Val 7 ualuit·xl·sol. Ibi·viii·ac pti.

·LII· TERRA GISLEBTI FILII TUROLD In Circecestre Hd.

Gislebertus fili' Turoldi ten' in Achelie·i·hid de rege. 7 Osulf' de eo. Keneuuard tenuit T·R·E. In dnio sunt·ii·car·7 iii·bord 7 vi·serui. Valuit·xl·solid. m·xxx·solid.

Ist& Gislebt' ten' in Turberie dim' hida 7 Osuuard de eo. Aluuard' tenuit. In dnio·e·i·car. Valuit·x·sol. m·xv·sol.

Ist& Gislebt' ten' Cernei. Ibi·vii·hidæ. In Respiget Hd. Duo teini tenuer' (Edlaf 7 fr ei') p·ii·m·7 poterant ire quo uoleb. In dnio sunt·iiii·car·7 vii·uitti 7 vi·bord·cu·v·car. Ibi vi·seru·7 molin de·viii·solid·7 vi·ac pti. Silua·ii·qx lg·7 una lat. Ibi·iiii·milites Gislebti hnt cu suis hoib vii·car·7 molin de·viii·sol.

Tot T·R·E·ualb·xiiii·lib. modo·xii·lib.

Ist& Gisl· ten' Rindecome. Ibi·v·hidæ geld. Aluric' tenuit. In dnio·e·i·car·7 iii·uitti 7 vii·bord cu·iii·car. Ibi·vii·serui·7 un' francig' ten' tra duoz uittoz 7 molin de·viii·solid·7 iiii·ac pti. Valuit·vii·lib. m·c·solid.

Ist& Gisl· ten' Rindecube·7 Walter' de eo. Ibi·iii·hidæ geld. In dnio sunt·ii·car·7 iiii·uitti 7 iii·bord cu·ii·car. Ibi·vi·serui·7 molin de·v·solid·7 iii·ac pti. Val 7 ualuit·vi·lib.

In Salemanesberie Hd. Ist& Gisl· ten' Elewrde·7 Walter' de eo. Aluuin' tenuit. Ibi·iiii·hidæ geld. In dnio·ii·car·7 iii·uitti cu·ii·car·7 vi·int' seruos 7 ancillas. Val 7 ualuit·xl·sol.

Ist& Gisl· ten' Bureford. Alfer tenuit. Ibi·i·hida geld. In dnio·ii·car·7 iiii·uitti 7 i·bord cu·ii·car·7 ii·serui·7 molin de·v·sol. Val 7 ualuit·xl·solid.

·LIII· TERRA DURANDI DE GLOWEC'. In Westberie Hd.

Durand' uicecom ten' unu m de iii hid. Aluuold tenuit 7 geldab. In dnio·e·i·car·7 iiii·uitti 7 iii·bord cu·iiii·car. Ibi·ii·serui. Valuit·lx·sol. m·xl·sol.

Ist& Durand' ten' in Esbroc·i·hid 7 miles ei' qda de eo. In dnio·i·car·7 i·bord 7 i·seru. In Bernintreu Hd. Val 7 ualuit·x·solid.

Ist& Durand' ten' ii·hid in Duntesborne. In Circecestre Hd. 7 Radulf' de eo. Wiuuard' tenuit p m de rege·E· In dnio sunt·ii·car·7 iii·uitti 7 un' bord cu·i·car. Ibi·iiii·serui·7 ii ac pti. Val 7 ualuit·xl·sol. In Langetreu Hd.

Ist& Durand' ten' Culcortone·7 Roger' de eo. Ibi·ii·hidæ 7·ii·v·7 dimid. Grim tenuit. In dnio sunt·ii·car·7 vi·uitti cu·iii·car. Val 7 ualuit·iiii·lib. In Griboldestou Hd.

Ist& Durand' ten' Dedmertone·7 Anschitil de eo. Ibi·iii·hidæ geld. Leuuin' tenuit de com Heraldo. In dnio sunt·iii·car·7 viii·bord cu·i·car·7 iiii·serui·7 vi·ac pti. Valuit·xxx·sol. m·xl·sol.

Ist& Durand' ten' Wadune. Ibi·v·hidæ. In Dunestane Hd. Quinq; frs tenuer' p·v·m·7 poterant ire quo uoleb·7 pares erant. In dnio sunt·v·car·7 un' uitts 7 vii·bord·cu·v·car. T·R·E·ualb·viii·lib·modo·c·solid. In Celfledetorne Hd.

Ist& Durand' ten' Chiesnecote·7 Walter' de eo. Ibi·ii·hidæ 7 dim. Leuuin 7 Leuui tenuer' p·ii·m. In dnio sunt·ii·car·7 iiii·bord. Valb·xl·sol·modo·lx·solid. In Salemanesberie Hd.

Ist& Durand' ten' Iccube·7 Walter' de eo. Ibi·ii·hidæ geld. Turstan tenuit. In dnio·ii·car·7 ii·uitti 7 ii·bord·cu·i·car·7 vi·int' seruos 7 ancillas. Valuit·xxx·sol·modo·xl·sol.

Ist& Durand' ten' Sciptune·7 Radulf' de eo. In Wacrescube Hd. Eduui tenuit. Ibi·iii·hidæ 7 dimid geld. In dnio sunt ii·car·7 iii·uitti cu·ii·car·7 iiii·serui·7 x·ac pti. Valuit·iiii·lib·m·xl·sol.

Ist& Durand' ten' in Hersefeld·vii·hid geld. In Witestan Hd. Godric 7 Edric·ii·frs tenuer' p·ii·m·7 poterant ire quo uoleb. In dnio sunt·iii·car·7 ix·uitti 7 xi·bord cu·ix·car. Ibi iiii·serui·7 v·figuli reddt·xl·iiii·den. Silua dimid leuua lg 7 iii·qx lat. Val 7 ualuit·vi·lib.

Ist& Durand' ten' Mortune. Ibi·iii·hidæ geld. Aitt tenuit. In dnio·e una car·7 iiii·uitti 7 vi·bord cu·iii·car 7 dimid. Ibi·iiii·serui·7 xx·ac pti. Valuit·iiii·lib·modo·xl·sol.

Ist& Durand' ten' Liteltune·7 Radulf' de eo. In Gretestan Hd. Ibi dimid hida geld. Leuenot tenuit p uno m. Ibi·e una car. Val 7 ualuit·x·solid. In Witelai Hd.

In Caudicote ten' Osbn' de Durando·i·hid 7 dim. Val 7 ualuit·xx·sol.

·LIIII· TERRA DROGONIS FILII PONZ. In Blacheleu Hd.

Drogo fili' Ponz· ten' de rege Frantone. Ibi·x·hidæ geld. Ernesi tenuit. In dnio sunt·iii·car·7 x·uitti 7 viii·bord cu·vi·car. Ibi·ix·serui·7 molin de·x·solid·7 x·ac pti. Silua·i·leuua lg·7 iii·qx lat. In Glouuec·i·burgsis de·vi·den. Val 7 ualuit·c·solid. De hoc m ten Rog' de Laci·i·hid iniuste.

Ist& Drogo ten' Lece. Ibi·x·hidæ geld. In Briestuoldes Hd. Cola tenuit. In dnio sunt·iiii·car·7 xv·uitti 7 iiii·bord cu·ix·car. Ibi·ix·serui·7 molin de·x·solid·7 x·ac pti. Valuit·viii·lib·modo·x·lib.

·LV· TERRA WALTERII FILII PONZ. In Briestuoldes Hd.

Walterius fili' Ponz ten' de rege Lece. Ibi·x·hidæ geld. Tosti com tenuit. In dnio sunt·iiii·car·7 xvi·uitti 7 vi·bord 7 pbr cu·viii·car. Ibi·xii·serui·7 molin de·x·solid·7 xx·ac pti. Valuit·xii·lib·modo·xv·lib.

.LVI. TERRA WALTERII FILII ROGERI. ~~In BERNINTON hd.~~
~~WALTERIUS~~ fili Rogerii ten de rege ~~BERNINTONE~~.
Ibi .viii. hidæ. Turstan 7 Eduuin tenuer p .ii. M.
In dnio sunt .iiii. car. 7 xiiii. uitti 7 pbr 7 v. bord cu .x.
car. Ibi .xiiii. serui. 7 molin de .x. sol. 7 xx. ac pti.
Val 7 ualuit .viii. lib. ~~In GERSDONES hd.~~
Isd. Walter ten ~~CERNEI~~. Ibi .xiiii. hidæ 7 una v.
Stigand arch tenuit. In dnio sunt .ii. car. 7 xxv. uitti 7 pbr
7 x. bord cu .x. car. Ibi .iiii. serui. 7 c. ac pti. 7 iii. mo
lini fuer de .xx. solid. Valb .xvi. lib. modo .xii. lib.
Hoc M calūniatū est ad ecclam ~~S MARIE~~ de abendone. sed omis
comitat testificat est Stigand arch .x. annis tenuisse uiuente .E. rege.
hoc M dedit .W. com Rogerio uicecomiti patri Walterii.

.LVII. TERRA WALTERII DIACONI. ~~In WITELAI hd.~~
~~WALTERIUS~~ diacon ten de rege ~~CHESNECOTE~~. Ibi .iii. hidæ 7 dimid.
Goduin tenuit 7 potuit ire quo uoluit. In dnio .ii. car. 7 viii.
uitti cu .vi. car. 7 x. serui. Val 7 ualuit .iii. lib.
.LVIII. TERRA WALTERII BALISTAR. ~~In WESTBERIE hd.~~
~~WALTERIUS~~ balistari ten de rege ~~BULELEGE~~. Ibi .iii. hidæ
geld. Toui tenuit de rege .E. In dnio sunt .ii. car. 7 iiii. uitti
7 vi. bord cu .iiii. car. Ibi .iiii. serui. 7 x. ac pti. In Glouuec
un burgsis redd .xviii. den. Valuit .lx. sol. modo .xl. sol.
Isd Walt ten ~~RODELE~~. Ibi .i. hida geld. Toui tenuit. In dnio
e una car. 7 ii. uitti 7 iiii. bord cu .ii. car. Valuit .xl. sol. m .x. sol.
Isd Walt ten dimid hida que n geldat. ~~In BLIDESLAU hund.~~
Palli tenuit. Ibi e molin. Val .xix. solid. ~~In LANGELEI hund.~~
Isd Walt ten ~~FRANTONE~~. Ibi .v. hidæ geld. Alestan de boscobe tenuit.
In dnio .e. i. car. 7 x. uitti 7 xi. bord cu .v. car. Ibi .v. serui.
7 ii. molini de .v. solid. Ibi 7 eccta q n fuit. Valuit .viii. lib. m .iii. lib.

.LIX. TERRA HENRICI DE FERIERES. ~~In BRICTUOLDESBERG hd.~~
~~HENRICUS~~ de ferreres ten ~~LECELADE~~. Siuuard bar tenuit.
Ibi .xv. hidæ T.R.E. geldant. Sed ipse rex excessit .vi. hid quietas
a geldo. hoc testat omis comitat. 7 ipse q sigillū regis detulit.
In dnio sunt .iiii. car. 7 xx ix. uitti 7 x. bord 7 un francig
ten tra uni uitti. Int oms hnt .xvi. car. Ibi .xiii. serui.
7 iii. molini de .xxx. sol. 7 piscaria de .cc. anguitt. xxv. min.
De pratis .vii. lib 7 vii. sol. pter fenū boum. In Wicelcube
.ii. burgses redd .xvi. den. 7 un In Glouuec sine censu.
Tot M T.R.E. ualb .xx. lib. 7 m similit.

.LX. TERRA ERNULFI DE HESDING. ~~In BRICTUOLDESBERG hd.~~
~~HERNULFUS~~ de hesding ten ~~CHENEMERESFORDE~~.
Ibi .xxi. hida geld. Osgod tenuit de com heraldo. In dnio sunt
vi. car. 7 xxx viii. uitti 7 x. bord 7 i. radchen cu .xviii. car.
Ibi .xiiii. serui. 7 iiii. molini de .xl. sol. 7 xl. den. 7 de pratis
x. lib pt pastura bou. 7 de ouib .c.xx. pensas caseor.
In Glouuec .vii. burgses. redd .ii. solid.
Tot T.R.E. ualb .xxx. lib. Modo .lxvi. lib. 7 vi. sol. 7 viii. den.
Isd hernulf ten ~~ETHEROPE~~. Ibi .vii. hidæ. Vluuard uuito tenuit.
In dnio sunt .vi. car. 7 xxiii. uitti cu .x. car. Ibi .xii. serui.
7 molin de .xv. solid. Valuit .viii. lib. modo .xii. lib.
Isd hernulf ten in ~~DANTESIE~~ .iiii. hid. ~~In GERSDONES hd.~~
7 ii. uirg 7 dim. Elric 7 Godric tenuer p .ii. M.
In dnio sunt .iii. car. 7 vii. uitti 7 ii. bord. cu .ii. car. Ibi .iiii. serui.
Tot ualuit 7 ual .vi. lib.

Isd hernulf ten ~~ALDEBERIE~~. Ibi .v. hidæ geld. ~~In BRUMBOLDESTOU hund.~~
Edric tenuit. In dnio sunt .iii. car. 7 iiii. uitti cu .iiii. car.
7 ibi .x. serui. 7 un francig hns .i. car. Ibi .vi. ac pti.
Val 7 ualuit .x. lib.
Isd hernulf ten ~~MADMINTUNE~~. Ibi .iiii. hidæ geld. Edric
tenuit. In dnio sunt .ii. car. 7 vi. uitti 7 viii. bord cu pbro
hnt .xiii. car. Ibi .x. serui. 7 viii. ac pti. Val 7 ualuit .x. lib.
Isd hernulf ten ~~ACHETONE~~. Ibi .v. hidæ geld. Edric tenuit.
In dnio sunt .iii. car. 7 iiii. uitti 7 iii. bord cu .iiii. car.
Ibi .xv. ac pti. Val 7 ualuit .c. sol. ~~In SINESHOVEDES hd.~~
Isd hernulf ten ~~HANUN~~. 7 hubald de eo. Edric tenuit.
Ibi dimid hida. In dnio sunt .ii. car. cu .viii. bord.
7 iiii. seruis. Val 7 ualuit .xl. solid.

.LXI. TERRA HERALDI FILII RAD. COMITIS.
~~HERALDUS~~ fili com Radulfi ten de rege ~~SUDLEGE~~. Radulf pat eius tenuit.
Ibi .x. hidæ geld. In dnio sunt .iiii. car. 7 xviii. uitti 7 viii.
bord cu .xiii. car. Ibi .xiiii. int seruos 7 ancitt. 7 vi. molini
de .lii. sol. Silua .iii. leuu lg. 7 ii. lat.
Isd herald ten ~~TODINTUN~~. pat ei tenuit. Ibi .x. hidæ geld.
In dnio sunt .iii. car. 7 xvii. uitti 7 vii. bord 7 ii. libi hoes
int oms hnt .viii. car. Ibi .x. int seruos 7 ancitt. 7 ii. molini
de .xx. solid. De una salina .L. mittas sal.
H duo M ual 7 ualuer .xl. lib.

.LXII. TERRA HUGON DE GRENTEM. ~~In CEOLFLEDE hd.~~
~~HUGO~~ de Grentemaisnil ten ~~PEBEWORDE~~. Ibi .ii. hidæ
7 una v. Duo teini tenuer p .ii. M. Ibi .iii. car. 7 i. uitts
7 un bord 7 vii. serui.
Isd hugo ten ~~MERESTUNE~~. Ibi .ii. hidæ
Isd hugo ten ~~QUENINTUNE~~. Ibi .ii. hidæ. Un tein tenuit.
In dnio .ii. car. 7 v. uitti 7 i. bord cu .iii. car. Ibi .iiii. serui
7 una ancilla. Valuer .vii. lib. m .iiii. lib.
Isd hugo ten ~~QUENINTUNE~~. 7 Roger de eo. Ibi .xii. hidæ.
Balduin tenuit T.R.E. In dnio .iii. car. 7 xvii. uitti 7 ii.
bord. cu .ix. car. Ibi .vi. serui. Valuit .vii. lib. m .vi. lib.
Isd hugo ten ~~WESTONE~~. 7 Roger de eo. Ibi .iiii. hidæ.
Balduin tenuit. In dnio .ii. car. 7 vi. uitti 7 cu .iii. car.
Ibi .iiii. serui. 7 v. ancillæ. 7 molin de .x. sol. Valuit .vii. lib.
Isd hugo ten ~~WILCOTE~~. 7 deric ei de eo. modo .vi. lib.
Ibi .ii. hidæ 7 dimid. In dnio .ii. car. 7 ii. uitti 7 i. bord cu .i.
car. Ibi .iiii. serui 7 una ancilla. Valuit .xl. sol. m .xxx.
Leuric tenuit.

.LXIII. TERRA HUGONIS LASNE. ~~In DUDESTAN hd.~~
~~HUGO~~ Lasne ten de rege ~~BROCOWARDINGE~~. Ibi .v.
hidæ. Turchil tenuit de rege .E. In dnio sunt .ii. car.
7 viii. uitti 7 vi. bord. 7 pbr 7 ii. libi hoes 7 ppositus. Int oms
hnt .xv. car. Ibi .iiii. serui. 7 molin de .ii. solid. Silua
una leuua lg. 7 dim lat. Valuit .vi. lib. m .c. solid.
Isd hugo ten ~~SCIPTUNE~~. Ibi .v. hidæ geld. Wluuard ~~In WACRESCUMBE hd.~~
tenuit. In dnio sunt .ii. car. 7 iiii. uitti 7 i. bord cu .ii.
car. Ibi .v. serui. 7 molin de .x. solid. Valuit .iiii. lib. m .iii. lib.
Isd hugo ten ~~SALPRETUNE~~. Ibi .x. ~~In BRADELEGE hd.~~
hidæ geld. Wluuard tenuit. In dnio sunt .iii. car. 7 x.
uitti 7 pbr cu .vii. car. 7 xi. int seruos 7 ancitt. 7 v. ac
pti. Valuit .x. lib. modo .vii. lib. ~~In RESPIGETE hd.~~
Isd hugo ten ~~BENWEDENE~~. 7 Gislebt de eo. Ibi .iii. hidæ
geld. Wluuard tenuit. In dnio sunt .iii. car. 7 v. uitti cu .iii.
car. 7 vi. serui. 7 molin de .x. sol. 7 viii. ac pti.
Val 7 ualuit .iiii. lib.

.LXI. TERRA MILONIS CRISPIN. In Dudestan hd.
Milo crispin ten in BRVVRNE. iii. uirg terre.
Wigot tenuit. In dnio. i. car. 7 vii. bord cu
ii. car. 7 dimid piscaria. Valuit. xl. sol. modo. xxx. sol.
Isd Milo ten CERNINTONE. 7 Goisfrid de eo. In Langetreu
haminc tenuit de rege. E. Ibi. ii. hide geldant. hd.
In dnio sunt. iii. car. 7 iii. uitti 7 viii. bord cu. iii. car
7 dimid. Ibi. xii. serui. 7 molin de. xx. den. 7 iiii. ac pa.
Vat 7 ualuit. iiii. lib. In Grimboldestou hd.
Isd Milo ten ALRELIE. Wigot tenuit. Ibi una hida.
In dnio sunt. ii. car. 7 vii. uitti 7 v. bord cu. vii. car.
Ibi. iiii. serui. 7 molin de. x. sol. 7 xii. ac pa. Vat 7 ua
luit. c. solid.

.LXII. TERRA VRSONIS DE ABETOT. In Witelai hd.
VRSO de Wirecestre ten in CHEISNECOTE una hid.
Eluuin tenuit p o. 7 geld. In dnio. i. car 7 iiii. serui.
Valuit. xl. sol. modo. x. solid.

.LXIII. TERRA HASCOIT MVSARD. In Witelai hd.
HASCOIT musard ten de rege SVINEBERIE. Che
nuicelle tenuit. Ibi. x. hide. In dnio. iii. car. 7 xviii.
uitti 7 iii. bord cu. ix. car. 7 x. int seruos 7 ancitt.
7 molin de. vi. den. Valuit. xii. lib. m. x. lib.
Isd hascoit ten. i. hida in CHEISNECOTE. 7 geld. Vluuin
tenuit p o. Ibi. i. car 7 i. bord. Vat 7 ualuit. x. sol.
Isd hascoit ten LITORDE. Ibi. v. hide geld. In Salemanes
Ernesi tenuit. In dnio sunt. ii. car. 7 xii berie hd.
uitti 7 i. bord cu. v. car. Ibi. viii. int seruos 7 ancitt.
Vat. iiii. lib. In Bretestan hd.
Isd hasc. ten ESTVNE. Ibi. vi. hide geld. Ernesi te
nuit. In dnio sunt. iii. car. 7 xii. uitti cu. iiii. car.
7 ix. int seruos 7 ancitt. Ibi molin de. viii. solid.
7 xx. ac pa. Vat 7 ualuit. vi. lib. In Cirecestre hd.
Isd hascoit ten SVDINTONE. Ibi x. hide geld. pter
dnium. Ernesi tenuit. In dnio sunt. iii. car. 7 viii. uitti
7 x. bord cu pbro hntes. v. car 7 dimid. Ibi. vii. serui.
7 xx. ac pa. Valuit. x. lib. m. viii. lib.
Isd hascoit ten GRENHASTEDE. Ibi. i. hida In Biselege hd.
geld. Ernesi tenuit. In dnio sunt. iii. car. 7 viii. uitti
7 v. bord 7 pbr 7 un radchen. Int oms hnt. ix. car.
Ibi. x. serui. 7 viii. ac pa. Silua. i. leuua lg. 7 dim lat.
Valuit. c. sol. modo. vii. lib.

.LXIIII. TERRA TVRSTINI FILII ROLF. In Gersdones hd.
TVRSTINVS filius Rolf ten de rege OMENIE.
Ibi. vii. hide. Toui tenuit de rege. E. In dnio sunt. iii.
car. 7 viii. uitti 7 pbr cu. viii. car. Ibi. viii. serui.
De hac tra ten Toui. ii. uittor tra. 7 qda miles tra
iiii. uittor. Ad ecclam ptin dim hida. 7 iiii. ac pa.
Valuit. viii. lib. modo. vi. lib.
Ibid ten ipse Turstin. i. hid. Vluui tenuit p o. 7 po
terat ire quo uoleb. In dnio. ii. car. cu. i. bord. Valuit
Isd Turstin ten in ACHELIE. una hid. In Cirecest hd. xl. sol.
Brictric tenuit p manerio de rege. E. In dnio. e una car. 7 iii. uitti
cu. iii. car. Ibi. vi. serui. 7 iiii. ac pa. Vat 7 ualuit. L. sol.
Girui ten de Turstino. In Grimboldestou hd.
Isd Turst ten HILDESLEI. 7 Bernard de eo. Ibi. i. hida.
Aluric tenuit. In dnio sunt. ii. car. 7 v. dimidii uitti.
7 vii. bord cu. ii. car. Ibi. viii. serui. 7 iii. molini
de xviii. sol. 7 viii. ac pa. Valuit. xl. sol. m. lx. sol.
Isd Turst ten TORTEWORD. Ibi In Bachestanes hd.
una hida. Aluuold tenuit. In dnio sunt. ii. car. 7 vi. uitti
7 vii. bord cu. vii. car. Ibi. vi. serui. 7 iii. molini de. xv. solid.
7 x. ac pa. Silua. i. leuua lg. 7 dimid lat. redd. v. solid.
Valuit. vii. lib. modo. c. solid. In Blachelaue hd.
Isd Turst ten STANTONE. Ibi. v. hide. Toui tenuit de rege. E.
In dnio sunt. ii. car. 7 viii. uitti 7 vi. bord cu. x. car. Ibi. iiii.
serui. 7 ii. molini de. xxv. solid. 7 x. ac pa. Silua. i. leuua
lg. 7 dimid lat. Vat 7 ualuit. c. sol. De hac tra ten
Toui. ii. hid. elemosina regis. W.
Isd Turst ten TRIDORNE. Atta tenuit. Ibi. iii. hide geld.
In dnio. e una car. 7 iii. uitti 7 iii. bord cu. ii. car. 7 un serui.
Valuit. lx. solid. modo. xxx. sol.

.LXV. TERRA ANSFRIDI DE CORMELIIS. In Biselege hd.
ANSFRID de Cormelies ten WINESTANE. Ibi. v. hide
Vluuard tenuit. In dnio sunt. iii. car. 7 x. uitti 7 iii. bord
7 un francig cu viii. car. Ibi. viii. serui. 7 molin de. x. den.
Vat 7 ualuit. vii. lib. In Celfledetorn hd.
Isd Ansfr ten WESTONE. Duo teini tenuer. un ho heraldi com.
alter Leuric. Ibi. x. hide p. ii. o. 7 poterant ire quo uoleb.
In dnio. iiii. car. 7 xviii. uitti 7 i. bord cu. ix. car. 7 xii. serui.
Valuer. c. sol. modo vii. lib.
Isd Ansfr ten in NORTVNE. v. hid. Duo teini tenuer p. ii. o.
7 poterant ire quo uoleb. In dnio. iiii. car. 7 x. uitti 7 ii.
bord cu. iiii. car. 7 x. serui. Valuer. iiii. lib. m. vi. lib.
Isd. A. ten BECESHORE. Brismer tenuit. In Witelai hd.
Ibi. iii. hide. In dnio. iii. car. 7 x. uitti cu. vi. car. 7 xvi. serui
7 un ho redd. vi. sochs. Valuit. viii. lib. modo. vi. lib.
Isd. A. ten POTESLEPE. Godric tenuit. Ibi. iii. In Bretestan hd.
hide geld. In dnio sunt. ii. car. 7 iii. uitti 7 v. bord cu. ii. car. Ibi
xi. serui. 7 ii. molini de xv. sol. Silua. i. leuua lg. 7 una lat.
Valuit. c. sol. modo. iiii. lib. In Wacrescumbe hd.
Isd. A. ten in SCIPTVNE. iii. virg tre. Bil tenuit p o. 7 geld.
In dnio. e. i. car. Vat 7 ualuit. x. sol. hic Bil potuit ire q uoluit.
Isdem. A. ten WINESTVNE. Edric 7 Leuric In Bradelege hd.
7 Elric tenuer p. iii. o. 7 poterant ire q uoleb. Ibi. v. hide
geld. In dnio sunt. iii. car. 7 ix. uitti 7 iii. bord cu. v. car.
Ibi. x. int seruos 7 ancitt. 7 molin de. vii. sol 7 vi. den. 7 xv.
acrs pa. Valb. viii. lib. modo. vii. lib. In Cirecestre hd.
Isd. A. ten. i. hid in TANTESBORNE. Elmer tenuit p o. 7 potuit
ire q uoluit. In dnio. e. i. car. 7 un uitts 7 ii. bord. 7 v. ancille.
Valuit. xl. sol. m. xx. sol. In Respigete hd.
Isd. A. ten ELCHESTANE. Duo Leuuini tenuer p. ii. o. Ibi. iii.
hide 7 dimid. 7 In COLESBORNE. i. hid 7 dim. Eluuin tenuit p o.
7 poterant ire q uolebant isti. iii. teini.
In dnio sunt. ii. car. 7 v. uitti 7 ii. bord. cu. iii. car 7 dim. Ibi. iiii.
serui. 7 x. ac pa. Silua dimid leuua lg. 7 ii. qz lat.
Medietate hui o ten. i. miles de Ansfrido. 7 ibi ht. ii. car.
7 v. uitt 7 ii. bord cu. iii. car.
7 Alter miles ten colesburne de eo. 7 ht ibi dimid car. 7 ii. uitti
7 ii. bord cu. i. car. 7 molin de. L. denar.
H ualb. viii. lib. modo. vii. lib 7 x. solid.
Isd. A. ten SIDE. 7 Turstin de eo. Leuuin tenuit de rege. E.
Ibi. iii. hide geld. In dnio sunt. ii. car. 7 i. uitt cu pbro 7 iii.
bord cu. i. car. 7 vi. serui. 7 iiii. ac pa. Valuit. iiii. lib. m. xl. sol.
Isd. A. ten. ii. v 7 dimid in DANTESBORNE. 7 Bernard de eo.
Elmer tenuit p o. 7 poterat ire quo uolb. Ibi. e. i. bord.
Vat 7 ualuit. iiii. solid.

Isd Ansfrid ten̄ ~~Pantelie~~ 7 ~~Chilecot~~ 7 ~~Chitiford~~ 7 ~~Hege~~ .i. hid 7 dim. .i. hid. .i. hida. .i. hida.
Int tot. iiii. hid 7 dimid. Gyfel 7 Eluuard 7 Wiga tenuer
p. iii. m. Vna hida 7 dim lib'a a geldo.
In dnio sunt. ii. car. 7 vii. uilli 7 iii. bord cu. vii. car.
Ibi. ii. serui. 7 molin de. vii. sol 7 vi. den.
Valb. iii. lib 7 x. sol. Modo: iiii. lib. Qui has tras teneb.
poterant ire quo uoleb.
Has tras 7 ~~Quinestan~~ 7 ~~Lintesborne~~. supius scriptas:
habuit Ansfrid de Walterio de Laci cu ei nepte accepit.
Alias u terras: ten de rege.

.LXIX. TERRA HVNFRIDI CAMERARII. ~~In Witelai hund.~~
Hunfrid camerari ten de rege ~~Langeberge~~. Ibi. iiii.
hide geld. Elstan 7 Blacheman 7 Edric 7 Alric tenuer p. iiii. m.
7 poterant ire quo uoleb. In dnio erant. iiii. car. 7 iii. uilli
7 v. bord cu. iii. car. Ibi. ix. serui.
Valeb. xvi. lib. modo. c. solid. ~~In Gersdones hd.~~
Isd Hunfrid ten in ~~Oxenhale~~ .i. hida. Aluui tenuit p m. de
rege. E. In dnio. ii. car. 7 iiii. serui. 7 i. bord. 7 molin de. v. sol.
Vat 7 ualuit. xxv. sol. ~~In Cirecestre hd.~~
Isd. H. ten. i. hid in ~~Presthitone~~. Aluuin tenuit p m.
In dnio. e. i. car. 7 ii. serui. 7 iii. bord cu. i. car. Vat 7 ualuit
xxx. sol. hic q teneb. poterat ire quo uoleb.
Isd. H. ten. i. hid in ~~Norcote~~. Eluuard tenuit p m.
In dnio sunt. ii. car. 7 ii. bord cu dim car. Vat 7 ualuit. xl. sol.
Has. ii. tras ten Witts de Hunfrido. Q teneb. poterant ire quo uolb.
Isd. H. ten. ii. hid in ~~Sudintone~~ 7 Anschitil de eo. Aluuard
tenuit p m. In dnio. e. i. car. 7 ii. bord cu dim car. 7 molin
de. v. solid. Vat 7 ualuit. xl. sol. q teneb. poterat ire quo uoleb.
Isd. H. ten ~~Aetune~~. Herold tenuit ~~In Bachestanes hd.~~
ho Eluui hiles. q poterat ire quo uoleb. Ibi. ii. hide 7 dimidia.
In dnio. e. i. car. 7 iii. uilli 7 iii. bord cu dimid car. Ibi. ii.
serui. 7 molin 7 dimid de. lxiiii. den. 7 v. ac pti.
Vat 7 ualuit. xl. sol.
Isd. H. ten ~~Wichen~~. Ibi. iiii. hide. Tres hoes Brictrici f. Algar
tenuer T.R.E. 7 poterant ire quo uoleb. In dnio erant. iii. car.
7 ix. uilli 7 xiiii. bord. cu. ix. car. Ibi. v. serui. 7 xx. ac
pti. 7 vi. qx de silua. Valb 7 uat. xii. lib.
Has. ii. uillas dedit Regina Hunfrido. Acune 7 Wichen.
Isd. H. ten. i. uirg tre in ~~Estbroce~~. ~~In Gersdones hd.~~
7 Witts de eo. Aluuine tenuit p m. Ibi. e. i. uitts. Vat. ii. sol.
7 ualuit.

.LXX. TERRA HVNFRIDI DE MEDEHAL. ~~In Dunestan hd.~~
Hunfrid de Medehalle ten ~~Vtone~~. Pagen tenuit. Ibi. i.
hida. In dnio. i. car. 7 iii. serui. 7 iiii. bord cu. ii. car. Valuit
xxx. solid. modo. xx. sol. ~~In Witelai hund.~~
Isd Hunf ten. i. hid in ~~Cheisnecot~~. Aluui tenuit p m. 7 geld.
In dnio erant. ii. car. 7 vi. serui. 7 i. bord. 7 ualb. l. solid.
Modo. xii. den tant ppt pta.

.LXXI. HVNFRIDI COCI ~~In Salesmanesberie hd.~~
Hunfrid coqus. ten ~~Lechetone~~. i. hid. 7 ibi ht. i. car. cu. iiii.
bord. 7 uat. xv. sol. 7 geld. Osbn de Keresburg tenuit.
Ordric tenuit p m. T.R.E.

.LXXII. TERRA SIGARI DE CIOCHES. ~~In Holiforde hd.~~
Sigar de Cioches ten de rege ~~Hallinge~~. Goda tenuit
Ibi. x. hide geld. In dnio sunt. iii. car. 7 xx. uitti 7 v. bord
cu. ix. bord. Ibi. vi. serui 7 iii. ancille. Silua. e ibi
Valuit. vii. lib. modo. viii. lib. ~~In Bradelege hd.~~
Isd Sigar ten ~~Hasedene~~. Goda tenuit. Ibi. x. hide.
Witts rex ccessit. iii. hid ex his qetas a geldo. In dnio sunt.
iii. car. 7 xiiii. uitti 7 pbr cu. x. car. Ibi. vi. serui.
Valuit. viii. lib. modo: vii. lib. sic testat comitatus.
Isd Sigar ten ~~Teneurde~~. Goda tenuit. Ibi. v. hide
ex his. iii. fuer qete a geldo p. W. rege. ut dicit ho Sigardi.
In dnio sunt. iii. car. 7 xiiii. uitti 7 ii. bord cu. vii. car.
Ibi. vii. serui. 7 molin de. xl. den. Silua. iii. qx lg.
7 ii. lat. Valuit. vii. lib. modo: vi. lib.

.LXXIII. TERRA MATHIU DE MORETANIE ~~In Langetrewes hd.~~
Maci de Mauritania ten de rege ~~Sciptone~~. Strang danus
tenuit. Ibi. x. hide geld. In dnio sunt. ii. car. 7 iiii. uitti
7 ii. bord cu. iiii. car. Ibi. iiii. serui. 7 molin de. x. solid.
De pastura. ii. sol. Valuit. xv. lib. modo: viii. lib.
Isd Maci ten ~~Sciptone~~. 7 Rubald de eo. Ibi. x. hide
geld. Johs tenuit T.R.E. In dnio sunt. iii. car. 7 iiii. uitti
7 viii. bord cu. iiii. car. Ibi. iiii. serui. 7 molin de. xii. sol.
De pastura. ii. sol. Valuit xv. lib. modo: viii. lib.
Isd Maci ten ibi. i. hid 7 Rubald de eo. Aluuin tenuit.
7 potuit ire quo uoluit. 7 Rainbt flandrensis p'ea habuit.
In dnio. e. i. car. 7 i. uitt 7 i. bord cu dim car. Valuit. xx.
solid. Modo: xiiii. solid.

.LXXIIII. TERRA GOZELINI BRITONIS. ~~In Bachestanes hd.~~
Gozelin brito ten de rege ~~Ciruelde~~. Elfelt tenuit
de rege. E. Ibi. iii. hide. In dnio sunt. ii. car. 7 iiii. uitti
7 vii. bord cu. iiii. car. Ibi. iiii. serui. 7 molin de. x. solid.
7 viii. ac pti. Silua dimid leuua lg 7 lat.
Valuit. iiii. lib. modo. xl. sol.

.LXXV. TERRA ROGERII FILII RAD. ~~Listone~~
Rogerius filius Rad ten un maneriu ~~In Sineshoved hd.~~
qd tenuit Seuuin ppost de Bristou de rege. E. 7 poterat
ire cu hac tra quo uoleb. nec aliqua firma inde dabat.
Ibi. iii. hide. In dnio sunt. iii. car. 7 vi. uitti 7 vi. bord
cu. ii. car. Ibi. iii. serui. 7 viii. ac pti.
Valb. c. solid. modo. lx. solid.
~~In Sineshovedes hd.~~
Rogeri ht. i. maneriu de. i. hida tre. 7 ibi ht. ii. seruos.
hoc appciat. x. solid. Non fuit qui de hac tra responderet.
Walter ht. un m de. i. uirg tre. Valuit. xx. den. m ii. solid.

.LXXVI. TERRA VXORIS GERI. ~~In Holiforde hd.~~
Uxor Geri de Loges ten de rege. iiii. hid ~~In Getinge~~.
Tres taini tenuer p. iii. m 7 geldab. Guluert Loui 7 Turbern.
In dnio. e. i. car. 7 i. uitt cu dim car. Valb. xl. sol. m: xx. solid.

.LXXVII. Balduin ten de rege. iii. uirg tre ~~In Gersdones hd.~~
~~In Oxenhale~~. Aluuin tenuit T.R.E. Ibi. e. i. car cu. ii. bord.
Vat 7 ualuit. x. solid.

.LXXVIII. TERRÆ TAINOR REGIS. IN BERNINTONE HD.

Elsi de Ferendone ten de rege in WENRIC. iii. hid 7 dimid. Wluric 7 Toui 7 Leuuin tenuer p iii. co 7 aner. 7 poterant ire quo uolebt. In dnio sunt. v. car. 7 ii. uitti 7 vii. bord cu. i. car. Ibi. x. serui. 7 molin 7 dimid de xii. solid. 7 vi. den. Valb. iii. lib. Modo: viii. lib.

IN GERSDONES HD.

Chetel ten de rege. i. hid 7 una v in WENRIC. Ipse tenuit T.R.E. Ibi. i. car 7 iii. serui. Val 7 ualuit. xx. sol. IN RESPIGET HD.

Ist Chetel ten. iii. virg 7 dimid in DANTESBORNE. Ipse tenuit. T.R.E. Ibi. i. car 7 ii. bord 7 ii. serui. Valuit. x. sol. m: xv.

OSWARD ten de rege REDMERTONE. IN LANGETREU HD.

Ibi. iii. virg geld. Ipse tenuit T.R.E. Ibi. e. i. car. Valuit. xx. sol. modo. x. sol. IN GRECECESTRE HUND.

Edric. f. Ketel ten BAUDINTONE de rege. Pat ei tenuit T.R.E. Ibi. iii. hide 7 iii. virg geld. In dnio sunt. ii. car. 7 iiii. uitti cu. i. car. 7 iiii. serui. 7 xv. ac pti. Val 7 ualuit. lx. solid.

EDWARD ten de rege dimid hid p co. IN DUHESTAN HD. 7 ibi ht in dnio. i. car. 7 vi. bord cu. ii. car. Val. xx. sol.

EDDIET ten de rege BICHEMERSE. IN CEOLFLEDE HUND. Ipsa tenuit T.R.E. Ibi. i. hida. 7 in dnio. ii. car. 7 i. uitt 7 i. bord 7 iiii. serui. Valet 7 ualuit. xx. solid. IN SALEMANESBERIE HD.

CUENILD monial ten de rege. x. hid in NIWETONE. Ex his iii. hide geldb. Elmer tenuit p co. In dnio sunt. iiii. car. 7 vii. uitti cu. v. car. 7 in habent. i. car. 7 molin de. v. solid. 7 xiii. int seruos 7 ancillas. Valuit. viii. lib. m. v. lib.

BRICTRIC ten de rege. iiii. hid In IN CELFLEDE HD. LECHAMETONE. 7 geld. Ipse. ii. hid. T.R.E. 7 Ordric tenuit alias. ii. Rex W. utranq; ei Brictric ecclie. pgeret in Norman. In dnio ht. i. car. 7 x. bord cu. iii. car. 7 ii. seruos 7 i. ancill. Silua. ii. qx lg. 7 ii. lat. Val. xxx. solid. IN BOLEFORD HD.

ALWOLD ten de rege PIGNOCSIRE. Ipse tenuit T.R.E. Ibi. iiii. hide. Vna ex his n geldb. In dnio sunt. iiii. car. 7 xi. uitti 7 v. bord. cu. iiii. car. Ibi. viii. serui. 7 molin de. xxx. denar. In Wicelcube. i. burgsis redd. viii. denar. Silua dimid leuua lg. 7 una qx lat. Val 7 ualuit. iiii. lib.

ELWARD. f. Reinbaldi ten ALDESWRDE. IN BECHEBERIE HD. Baldri tenuit. Ibi. ii. hide geld. In dnio. e. i. car. 7 iiii. uitti 7 ii. bord cu. ii. car. 7 un seruus. Valuit. xl. solid.

ELSI ten de rege IN WITESTAN HD. / Modo: xxx. sol. LANGENEI. Ibi. v. hide. geld. Ipse tenuit T.R.E. In dnio sunt. ii. car. 7 vi. uitti 7 xii. bord cu. ix. car. Ibi. iiii. serui. 7 x. ac pti. 7 piscaria. Valuit. c. solid. modo. lx. solid. IN SINESHOVEDES HD.

DONS ten de rege BETONE. Ipse tenuit T.R.E. Ibi. ii. hide. Vna ex his geldb. alia ad ecctam ptinebat. In dnio sunt. ii. car. 7 v. uitti 7 ii. bord. cu. v. car. Ibi. iiii. serui. 7 x. ac pti. Valuit. vi. lib. Modo. iii. lib.

BRICTRIC ten de rege WIDECESTRE. IN BLACHELEU HD. Ipse tenuit T.R.E. Ibi. i. hida geld. Ibi sunt. xvi. uitti 7 xii. bord cu. xvi. car. In dnio nichil. In Glouuec. i. burgsis redd. xx. ferra. Ibi molin de. x. sol. Val 7 ualuit. c. solid.

HARDINC ten in uadimonio de Brictric WITENHERT. Ipse Brictric tenuit T.R.E. Ibi. v. hide geld. In dnio. e. i. car. 7 ptr 7 ii. uitti 7 vi. bord cu. v. car. Ibi. iii. serui. 7 molin de. x. sol. 7 x. ac pti. Valuit. c. solid. Modo: xxx. solid.

EDRIC. f. Chetel ten ALCRINTONE. Pat ei tenuit. T.R.E. Ibi. iii. hide 7 dimid geld. In dnio. e. i. car. 7 vi. uitti 7 iii. bord. cu. viii. car. Ibi. iii. serui. 7 molin de. x. solid. 7 x. ac pti.

Silua. i. leuua lg. 7 dim lat. Val 7 ualuit. iii. lib. IN BORSELAU HUND.

MADOCH ten de rege RUDEFORD. Ipse tenuit T.R.E. Ibi. ii. hide. In dnio. ii. car. 7 iii. uitti 7 iii. bord cu. iii. car. 7 molendin redd annona qu potest lucrari. Val 7 ualuit. xl. sol.